Uprooted

Like many of the city's postwar inhabitants, the monument to the Polish playwright Aleksander Fredro was transferred from Lviv to Wrocław after the Second World War. It was erected in the very place on the Rynek where the newly established Polish municipal administration removed the equestrian statue of the Prussian king Friedrich Wilhelm III in 1945 (front cover). Courtesy of Stanisław Klimek and the City Museum of Wrocław (Henryk Makarewicz).

Uprooted

How Breslau Became Wrocław
during the Century of Expulsions

GREGOR THUM

Translated from the German by Tom Lampert and Allison Brown

Translations of Polish sources by
W. Martin and Jasper Tilbury

Princeton University Press   *Princeton and Oxford*

Published by Princeton University Press,
41 William Street, Princeton, New Jersey 08540

In the United Kingdom: Princeton University Press,
6 Oxford Street, Woodstock, Oxfordshire OX20 1TW

press.princeton.edu

Thum, Gregor, 1967–
[Fremde Stadt. English]
Uprooted : how Breslau became Wrocław during the century of expulsions /
Gregor Thum ; translated from the German by Tom Lampert and Allison Brown ;
translation of Polish sources by W. Martin and Jasper Tilbury.
p. cm.
Includes bibliographical references and index.
ISBN 978-0-691-14024-7 (hardcover : alk. paper) – ISBN 978-0-691-15291-2
(pbk. : alk. paper) 1. Wrocław (Poland)—History—20th century. 2. World War, 1939–
1945—Influence. 3. World War, 1939–1945—Deportations from Poland.
4. Forced migration—Poland—Wrocław—History—20th century. 5. Oder-Neisse
Line (Germany and Poland) 6. Wrocław (Poland)—Social conditions—20th century.
7. Social change—Poland—Wrocław—History—20th century. 8. City and town
life—Poland—Wrocław—History—20th century. 9. Collective memory—Poland—
Wrocław—History—20th century. I. Title.
DK4780.3.T4 2011
943.8′52—dc22   2010040001

British Library Cataloging-in-Publication Data is available

The translation of this book is co-funded by the Municipality of
Wrocław and "Geisteswissenschaften International"—Translation
Funding for Humanities and Social Sciences from Germany, a joint
initiative of the Fritz Thyssen Foundation, the German Federal
Foreign Office, and the German Publishers & Booksellers Association.

This book has been composed in Arno Pro

Printed on acid-free paper. ∞

Printed in the United States of America

1 3 5 7 9 10 8 6 4 2

CONTENTS

PART TWO
The Politics of the Past:
The City's Transformation

PART THREE
Prospects

CONTENTS

ACKNOWLEDGMENTS

SCHOLARSHIP IS A COLLABORATIVE ENDEAVOR. THERE ARE MANY PEOPLE who have contributed in one way or another to this book and its English translation. I feel indebted to all of them. Karl Schlögel was the supervisor of my doctoral thesis, which this book is based upon and which I defended at the Europa-Universität Viadrina in Frankfurt (Oder), Germany, in 2002. Schlögel's way of thinking and writing have inspired my scholarly work. It was the lectures of Klaus Zernack that sparked my interest in Polish history, and he is the one who introduced me to the intricacies of German-Polish relations when I was a student at the Freie Universität Berlin.

I have profited a lot from discussing my ideas and research with José Maria Faraldo and Agnieszka Zabłocka-Kos, and I am thankful for the support and constructive criticism this book project received from, among others, Ingmar Ahl, Anna Bungarten, Marek Czapliński, Norman Davies, Christine Hucko, Eva Jaunzems, Elżbieta and Stanisław Klimek, Jerzy Kos, Adam Krzemiński, Norman Naimark, Brigitta van Rheinberg, Gábor Rittersporn, Krzysztof Ruchniewicz, Małgorzata Słabicka, Thomas Sparr, Katarzyna Stokłosa, Jakub Tyszkiewicz, Thomas Urban, Marek Zybura, the anonymous manuscript reviewers at Princeton University Press, and the librarians and archivists in Berlin, Marburg, Frankfurt (Oder), Wrocław, and Warsaw.

The English translation of this book would not have been possible without the generous support of the Municipality of Wrocław and the German initiative "Geisteswissenschaften International," funded by the Fritz Thyssen Foundation, the German Foreign Office, and the German Publishers & Booksellers Association.

GREGOR THUM

A NOTE ON NAMES

EAST CENTRAL EUROPEAN CITIES RARELY HAVE ONLY ONE NAME. THE city of Lviv, for instance, is known not only by its current Ukrainian name, but also as "Lvov" in Russian, "Lwów" in Polish, "Lemberg" in German, and "Lemberik" in Yiddish. Each of these variants is associated with one of the various national groups that have considered the city home and have called it by a name in their own language. Whenever historians write in a language that does not have an established name form for that place, they have to make difficult choices. Which of the variants should they use in order to avoid being accused of favoring one or another of the various national groups that have political or historical claims to the place? Even sticking to the official name does not help, since official names are subject to change. Within the last two centuries, for example, the administrative name of East Galicia's capital changed from "Lemberg" to "Lwów," from "Lwów" to "Lvov," and from "Lvov" to "Lviv." To make matters worse, some of the variations existed in parallel to one another, being used by different levels of the administration.

There are only two names for the city with which this book is concerned: "Breslau" in German and "Wrocław" in Polish. Since the Middle Ages, these two etymologically related names have existed parallel to one another (in various spellings), mirroring the bilingualism of the Polish-German borderland. In 1945, however, when German Breslau was ceded to Poland, resulting in the expulsion of its German population, the city name became a politically sensitive issue. In an effort to legitimize Poland's postwar borders and suppress Wrocław's German past, Poland insisted that "Wrocław" was the only acceptable name for the city. By the same token, the continual use of "Breslau" by Germans not only reflected their familiarity with the German name, but could also express their rejection of the borders drawn in 1945.

As a consequence, one could not use either of these names without making a political statement, however unintended.

This changed in 1990, however. With the definitive recognition of Poland's western border by a reunified Germany and the ensuing German-Polish reconciliation, Wrocław's city name soon ceased to be a political issue. While people no longer question that "Wrocław" is the only official name today, the use of "Breslau" within the German language is fully accepted. Even the Municipality of Wrocław uses "Breslau" in German texts.

When I wrote this book in German, I consistently used "Breslau" for all time periods, thus emphasizing the fact that the city changed its ethnic composition and political affiliation, but always remained the same place. Similarly, "Wrocław" was used throughout the book's Polish translation. When it came to the English edition, "Wrocław" was the obvious choice. I realized, however, that a consistent use of the Polish city name would have sounded awkward and unhistorical in cases where I refer to the city in Germany. I therefore decided to use both name variants—"Breslau" for the period before 1945, and "Wrocław" for the time after. Where I refer to the city in a more general sense, without regard to a specific time period, I use the Polish name. The same approach was taken with respect to all other place names in what was Germany before 1945 and Poland thereafter. For street, square, and neighborhood names, I have used the forms that were common at a given time. Although this strictly historical approach, which necessitates changing place names throughout the book, might challenge the reader, it has the advantage of making tangible the theme of this study: Breslau's transformation into a Polish city.

For all other place names, I use the forms most common in English, thus writing Warsaw instead of Warszawa, or Silesia instead of Śląsk.

PROLOGUE: A DUAL TRAGEDY

WHAT VIENNA WAS AT THE *FIN DE SIÈCLE* AND BERLIN IN THE "GOLDEN Twenties"—that was sixteenth-century Wrocław. The largest city in Silesia and one of the largest in Europe, it was a bustling center of commerce at the crossroads of two major European trade routes: the Amber Road leading from the Baltic Sea through the Danube region and on to the Adriatic; and the Via Regia, a branch of which took the traveler from the mouth of the Rhine at the North Sea to the Black Sea and farther, via the Silk Road, all the way to China. In Wrocław these trade routes crossed the Oder River, a serious barrier that would not become fully navigable until the nineteenth century. From Wrocław, the roads spread out to what are today Toruń, Gdańsk, and Kaliningrad in the north; to Krakow, Lviv, and Kiev in the east; to Prague, Vienna, Nuremberg, Augsburg, Milan, Genoa, and Venice in the south; and to Leipzig, Frankfurt am Main, Cologne, Bruges, and Antwerp in the west. Merchants from all over the Holy Roman Empire, from Poland, Lithuania, and Russia met in Wrocław. At the city's large marketplaces and in the expansive cloth halls, they sold their wares and negotiated new business deals. This hustle and bustle made the city rich and powerful, a splendid Central European metropolis, marked by spacious urban design, magnificent patrician houses, an impressive city hall, and monumental churches, whose steeples proclaimed the city's pride from afar.

But this resplendence would not endure. As the Netherlands and England rose in prominence over the course of the seventeenth century and Europe's economic life shifted northward and westward, Wrocław's star began to wane. The region between Prague and Krakow, Wrocław and Gdańsk, which had been at the heart of Europe in the late Middle Ages, became its periphery, and the Silesian capital gradually lost stature in the hierarchy of

Wrocław's Old Town with its large market squares and monumental churches is one of the most impressive in Central Europe. This aerial view of 1934 shows the main market square, the Ring (Rynek), with the Gothic town hall on the right side and the twin-towered Church of St. Mary Magdalene in the background. In the upper left is the Neumarkt (Nowy Targ). A decade later, the war would turn most of these buildings into ruins. Courtesy of the Library of the University of Wrocław.

European cities. When the metropolises of Vienna and Berlin were enjoying their heyday, each home to a population of several million, Wrocław was a city of just a few hundred thousand inhabitants. To be sure, its population multiplied many times in the course of the demographic explosion of the nineteenth century. The city grew far beyond the former city walls. It became a modern metropolis with respectable industries and a reputation as a trading center and a hub in the expanding European railroad network. Wrocław was also known for its eminent educational and research facilities and sophisticated cultural life. Yet one by one the urban centers in the rising industrial areas of nearby Saxony and, even more, those along the Rhine and Ruhr rivers began to outstrip the Silesian metropolis in population. In the early twentieth century, Wrocław, then known to most as Breslau, was the largest German city east of Berlin, but it was regarded as somewhat provincial and backward, lacking the dynamism of the more progressive cities in Germany. The popular saying of the day, that real Berliners come from Breslau, tells as much about Breslau as about Berlin. It also reflects the notion that Silesia's largest city could no longer retain its ambitious and talented residents. While many famous personalities grew up or spent periods of their lives in Breslau, few of them are buried there.

And yet Wrocław is a city symptomatic of the twentieth century. In this one city, perhaps, more than in any other, it is possible to witness the drama of twentieth-century Europe in full. Wrocław is a looking glass through which Europe's self-destruction becomes manifest: nationalism and provincialization, xenophobia and anti-Semitism, the destructive rage of the Second World War, Nazi fantasies of Germanization and the murder of European Jewry, the total collapse in 1945, the shifting of national borders in Central Europe, the forced resettlements, and, finally, the Cold War division of the continent and the intellectual paralysis inherent in the opposition of East and West. Wrocław was at the center of all these developments. At the same time, the city also became one of the most impressive stages for the resurrection of Europe from the ruins of the war, for the reestablishment of civility, and for the resiliency that ultimately would enable a new vision of an integrated Europe to replace the bloc mentality of the Cold War.

The pivotal point in the history of twentieth-century Wrocław is the cataclysmic year 1945. In the final weeks of the war, the city that had been one of Europe's most beautiful urban centers was turned into a wasteland of ruins. Then, in consequence of an Allied decision to make Breslau Polish, the city was subjected to a complete population exchange. In only three years, all of the remaining German residents were transferred westward and replaced by Polish settlers from the East. In 1949, Friedrich Otto Jerrig attempted to describe the sheer enormity of this event:

> It was as though a landslide had taken place—a landslide that swallowed the ground upon which Breslau had developed over centuries into what it was to its residents, before the inferno erupted "back then." With the force of a natural disaster a political transformation took place,

and six hundred thousand Breslauers lost their homeland. What a landslide! All the more so as it crushed Breslau's German character, shook it to the ground. What was German was driven out by a presence that although it could still somehow be felt, had been slumbering unobtrusively in the background: Breslau's Slavic foundations. That part of the city's rich and eventful past that belonged to the time before "German," "East German–Silesian," became identical with Breslau. At the border to the East, past Hundsfeld to Oels and Namslau, beyond Ohlau and Oppeln where Poland's borders arise, there you could feel yourself stepping out of Central Europe into the East, into the land between Europe and the vastness of Asia [*Vor-Asien*]. This was on the horizon, beyond the city. Within the city, in the background, you could sense this past, but it was buried. It was unthinkable that it might rise up. Such a possibility did not frighten the people, they looked it fearlessly in the eye. Breslau was just as much a city between dream and reality as it was a question addressing its own past and future.

When the ground on which this border metropolis, with all its tensions and affinities, broke open, when a past long believed buried became manifest, it was as if something reluctantly primal were revolting against the negligence and ignorance with which a fast-living metropolis had been built over the centuries. It was as if this happened because no one had paid enough attention in years past to the fact that the city on the Oder River was more a bridge to the countries of the East than a stronghold fortifying a nation against that from which it had itself once risen.[1]

Wrocław could have been one of the few major European cities that survived the Second World War unscathed, at least on the surface. That outcome lay within the power of individual military leaders. The fact that Wrocław is today a city in Poland is likewise the result of decisions made by individual politicians, men who might, under the same circumstances, have made quite different decisions. And yet at the same time the city's fate was in part the result of a development that began after the First World War and led to disaster. One could perhaps claim that it was precisely because of its marginal position, as a declassed city, that Wrocław was particularly susceptible to the pathological nationalism of the twentieth century.

THE DESTRUCTION OF BRESLAU

Wrocław, a city that could not keep pace with the momentum of Western European cities, was less affected by cultural homogenization than the emerging centers of economic activity. Here, at Germany's eastern periphery, the cultural and ethnic ambivalence of premodern Europe endured longer. Wrocław was the urban center of Silesia, a borderland marked by an overlap of cultures with no abrupt breaks between predominantly German-, Czech-, and Polish-speaking regions. Diversity was the outcome of ever-changing state affiliations and a range of cultural influences. Over the course of its history, Wrocław had in turn belonged to Polish, Bohemian, Austrian, and Prussian states. Its appearance was multifaceted: there is within it something of Prague and Krakow, but also something of Berlin and Vienna. Prior to the Second World War, the city was both Protestant and Catholic, but also known for its thriving Jewish community. When the modern University of Breslau was established in 1811, theology departments were created for both Christian denominations. In 1854 a Jewish Theological Seminary was founded, which became one of Europe's most important rabbinical training centers. Nineteenth-century Breslau was characterized by a remarkably peaceful coexistence of these three religious denominations.[2]

Prior to 1945, modern Wrocław was not only a city in Germany known by its German name Breslau, but also a city whose residents largely considered themselves to be German. In the early twentieth century the proportion of Poles, even according to the optimistic estimates of Polish minority organizations, was at most 5 percent of the population. After the First World War, when Poland reemerged as an independent country and center of Polish national life, the figure sank to less than 1 percent due to emigration.[3] Nevertheless, the atmosphere in Breslau continued to be marked by its closeness to Poland and to the ethnically mixed border regions of Silesia. Polish merchants and students, Polish-speaking maids and farmers who brought their produce to Breslau's public markets from the surrounding counties were just as much a part of the city as Jewish immigrants from the East, for whom Breslau was usually a stopover on their way westward. The city's Eastern Europe affinities and the diversity of influences in the German-Polish-Czech borderlands combined to produce a cultural richness that was specific to

Breslau. Champions of German ethic nationalism, however, viewed the city's very diversity as an irritating ambiguity, a sign of economic backwardness and of the incomplete establishment of the nation-state in Germany's eastern provinces.

The struggle over the so-called language frontier, which slowly but surely undermined the foundations of coexistence in the ethnically-mixed regions of Central Europe,[4] affected Silesia as well and turned the German-Polish borderland into a zone of increasingly hostile demarcation between nationalities. Nationalistic tensions, which intensified from the late nineteenth century onwards, peaked during plebiscites held in Upper Silesia in early 1921. The region's inhabitants were asked to vote on the future location of the German-Polish national border in Upper Silesia, and nationalist agitation on both sides erupted into violent rioting and fighting between German and Polish paramilitary units. In the course of these events, Breslau was increasingly portrayed as a "bulwark of the German East."[5] German university students were supposed to complete an "Eastern semester" at Breslau's institutions of higher education. At the "center of the fiercely embattled German East,"[6] at the "front of the German national struggle,"[7] they were supposed to become aware of their patriotic responsibilities toward this region.

This nationalist propaganda, coming on top of Silesia's serious economic problems in the interwar years, contributed to the success of the Nazi party in the city. Breslau was in fact one of the election districts in Germany in which the party achieved its best results. While in 1932 the Nazis received an average of 37.2 percent (July) and 33.1 percent (November) of the vote nationally, they received 43.5 percent and 40.5 percent, respectively, in the Breslau electoral district. In March 1933 the district was one of seven in Germany— of a total of 35—in which the Nazi party achieved an absolute majority.[8] After the Nazis assumed power Breslau's prospects for the future seemed at first to improve. The nonaggression pact between Berlin and Warsaw—concluded surprisingly in 1934—ended the border conflict and reinvigorated trade between Germany and Poland, which was particularly beneficial for Breslau. Also, the government spent significant amounts on modernizing Breslau as a transportation hub and the leading site for trade fairs in eastern Germany.[9] But Breslau's post-1933 boom was short-lived. While the local economy profited from massive state investments, the politics of the Nazis undermined the very existence of this borderland city.

Hitler visited Breslau during the German Sports Festival of 1938. In the last national elections in 1932 and 1933, the city's support for the Nazi party was above the national average. Courtesy of the bpk.

The expulsion of the Germans, which brought to an end Breslau's identity as a German city, was a process that began not in 1945, but in 1933. The first German Breslauers driven out were the Jews. A pillar of the city's middle class, they had been leaders in commerce and founders of the major department stores. They had a substantial influence on the city's intellectual and cultural life as well and helped to establish the outstanding reputation of its universities.[10] Among Breslau's Jewish patrons were the businessman Julius Schottländer, who donated South Park, and the banker Jonas Fraenckel, who made it possible for the Jewish seminary to be established. A number of Breslau's German Jews had in fact attained international renown: Ferdinand Lassalle, Fritz Haber, Max Born, Edith Stein, Ernst Cassirer, Norbert Elias, Henry Kamm, and Walter Laqueur, to name only a few. After 1933, thousands of the city's Jews were compelled to emigrate, companies and stores were "Aryanized," and Jewish institutions steeped in tradition were liquidated one by one.[11]

November 9, 1938, when mobs plundered and demolished Jewish stores and facilities, as well as synagogues throughout Germany, marked the end of Breslau's imposing New Synagogue. Built by Edwin Oppler in a style that accorded with his maxim "The German Jew in a German state has to build in a German style," the New Synagogue, erected in proximity to the royal palace between 1866 and 1872, had been a defining feature of the city center's silhouette.[12] Walter Tausk, a chronicler of the persecution of Breslau's Jews, wrote in his diary on November 12, 1938:

> It was quarter to ten when I reached Schlossplatz, intending to turn onto Wallstrasse. The so-called "Mauschelhalle"[13] . . . was nothing but a smoking ruin. The upper dome had already started sinking to one side and had to be demolished that afternoon between two to four. . . .
>
> Nearby buildings and trees were sprayed down to keep the fire from spreading, but the synagogue itself was burned to the ground using incendiary bombs and additional kerosene. The elderly Aryan castellan Herr Peters, who lives in the new community center, was awakened at two in the morning to open up the synagogue for the aforementioned "people." He was in a fit of tears as he did it. Nothing was saved. Rabbi Vogelstein was even prevented from entering the burning building at two o'clock in the morning to save the Torah scrolls, as was Cantor Wartenberger at eight the next morning.[14]

Roughly 2,500 of Breslau's Jews were arrested during the November pogroms and sent to concentration camps.[15] Most of the Jews who had not yet left the city now intensified their efforts to arrange for emigration as speedily as possible. The more than seven thousand who did not manage to emigrate were deported between November 1941 and April 1944 and murdered—most of them in Kaunus, Majdanek, Sobibor, Theresienstadt, and Auschwitz.[16] Walter Tausk was assigned to the first railroad transport leaving Breslau on November 25, 1941, bound for Kaunas. He was presumably shot there soon after the train's arrival.[17]

Breslauers who were not persecuted by the Nazis and who did not see the burning of the New Synagogue as portending the demise of their city were fooled into a deceptive sense of security. The Second World War even brought to the city an odd kind of vitality. Due to its geographic location far from the bases of the British and American bomber fleets, Silesia became the destination of the *Kinderlandverschickung* program, an effort to evacuate children from the cities; there were as well thousands of people bombed out of their houses in the West who found shelter there. In addition, a large number of government agencies and arms factories were relocated to Silesia during the war. Breslau's factories were expanded and converted for war production. The most significant enterprise in the city, the Linke-Hofmann works, which before the war had been one of the largest producers of railroad cars and locomotives in Europe, now shifted production to armored trains, tank parts, parts for military utility vehicles, and motors for the V-2 rockets. Breslau's population grew by hundreds of thousands over the course of the war to reach almost one million in 1944. The city became one of the most important logistic centers for supplying the eastern front. Trains transported munitions, tanks, and other supplies from Breslau to the combat zones and returned carrying tens of thousands of wounded soldiers, who were treated in Breslau's huge military hospitals and then sent back to the front.

The war did not become a direct threat to Breslau until the summer of 1944, when the Red Army reached the Vistula, bringing the eastern front less than two hundred miles from the city. At the same time, the Americans and British had advanced so far eastward that Silesia was now within range of Allied air raids. In the fall of 1944, in expectation of the Soviet advance, Hitler declared the unfortified city of Breslau to be a "fortress" that under no circumstances was allowed to surrender. It was to be defended to the last man.[18] A garrison was formed of soldiers who happened to be in the city—scattered troops, those serving in the rearguard, those passing through on leave from the front, convalescing wounded—and supplemented by *Volkssturm* (People's Militia) units. Civilians from the entire region were enlisted to build fortifications all around Breslau, and the city's storehouses were stocked with everything that might be needed for an extended siege.

The long-awaited, large-scale Soviet offensive began on January 12, 1945. Within days the eastern front collapsed along its entire length and the Wehrmacht, already in the process of disbanding, retreated westward. The Red Army's offensive wedges, moving rapidly toward Berlin from their posts along the Vistula, pushed the panicked and fleeing civilian population forward like a bow wave. It was only a few days before bands of refugees appeared in Breslau. Paul Peikert, the pastor at St. Mauritius's and a chronicler of the siege, wrote in his entry for January 22, 1945:

> Now Breslau offers a horrendous picture of flight, day and night. Never-ending columns of peasants' carts with horses or cattle tethered alongside, the handcarts of the female workers, columns of prisoners of war,

foreigners—Russians, French, Serbs, etc.—hauling small sleds loaded with their belongings. . . . To make matters worse, the flight takes place on the harshest of winter days; the temperatures fall to between 5 and 8 degrees F, and lower. Children freeze to death and are laid at the roadside by their families. There are reports that entire truckloads of frozen children are being delivered to the mortuaries here.[19]

On January 19, Karl Hanke, Gauleiter of Lower Silesia and the Reich defense commissioner resident in Breslau, issued orders for the city to be evacuated. Only a few weeks earlier it would have been possible to clear the city in a more or less orderly manner, but Hanke had categorically rejected this as defeatism. Now the streets were clogged with refugees and troops, and the German railroad no longer had the capacity to evacuate a city of one million people. Chaos and panic broke out at Breslau's train stations, children lost their mothers in the melee, some were crushed or trampled by the crowds. Orders were announced through street loudspeakers on January 20 that women and children were to leave the city on foot. In the bone-chilling cold, hundreds of thousands of Wrocławians joined endless refugee treks along the snow-filled roads leading into the Sudeten Mountains. Tens of thousands either froze or died of exhaustion.

The vanguard of the Red Army had crossed the Oder at several locations only ten days after the offensive was launched. By the end of February all of Upper Silesia and most of Lower Silesia had been occupied by Soviet troops. Breslau was surrounded on February 15. There were still between 150,000 and 250,000 civilians in the city, including tens of thousands of forced laborers, prisoners of war, and concentration camp inmates. The fortress troops, with their commander General Hans von Ahlfen, were comprised of 45,000 to 50,000 soldiers and *Volksturm* troops. They faced 150,000 troops of the Soviet 6th Army, under the command of General Vladimir Alekseyevich Gluzdovsky. Gluzdovsky's units attacked from the south, ran down the advance defensive positions in their first attempt, and pressed deep into the affluent residential quarter around Hindenburgplatz (Powstańców Śląskich Square). There the advance stalled and do-or-die house-to-house street fighting between Soviet and German troops began; the front moved towards the city center street by street, building by building, and floor by floor. Breslau became the Stalingrad at the Oder River.

The Soviet attack on "Fortress Breslau." For more than three months, Germans and Soviets fought over the city. The German fortress commander's unwillingness to surrender led to the city's devastation and the loss of tens of thousands of lives. Courtesy of the City Museum of Wrocław (Krystyna Gorazdowska).

"Fortress Breslau" was a battlefield as gruesome as it was grotesque. The encircled city area was small and continually shrank with the advance of the Soviet troops. But distinctions were still made between battle zones and the rear. There was a western and a southern front, and the units were shifted back and forth. While thousands upon thousands lost their lives in bitter fighting in the southern and westerns neighborhoods, only a few miles away the wealthy residential quarters in the north and the garden cities in the east remained largely untouched. German soldiers spent their short leaves from the front at the zoo or enjoyed rowing along the Oława as in peacetime.[20]

The defense of Breslau, which had as yet sustained relatively little visible damage in mid-February 1945, led to the city's devastation. Entire neighborhoods were turned into ash and rubble in house-to-house fighting; Breslau's affluent southern districts were completely destroyed between Hindenburg-platz and the central train station. Because the fortification commander and

German soldiers take up positions in a villa in the affluent neighborhood of southern Breslau, where most of the fighting took place. Here the front moved forward street by street, house by house, floor by floor. From Majewski 2000. Used by permission of the publisher.

the German artillery had entrenched themselves in the Old Town, Soviet artillery kept the historic city center under a barrage of fire. Soviet strafers also circled the city, covering the streets with unremitting cannon fire and bombarding buildings in which they suspected German positions. Even more destructive than the Soviet raids, however, were the defensive measures of the fortress troops.[21] German soldiers set countless buildings on fire and demolished the burned-out ruins in order to install nests of machine guns. They wired buildings with explosives and ignited them as soon as Soviet soldiers took up position inside. In anticipation of possible Soviet advances, fire and demolition squads established "internal battle lines" in the Old Town. Thus orders were issued in late March to burn down all the buildings along Websky-, Tauentzien-, and Freiburger Strasse, Elferplatz, Schwertstrasse, Fischergasse, and Einundfünfzigerstrasse, down to the south bank of the Oder, in order to set up a defensive line.[22] The Museum of Applied Arts on Graupenstrasse was blown up without further ado, so that the small plane of the fortress commander could take off and land at Schlossplatz.

The defenders set up command posts, artillery batteries, watchtowers, and munitions depots, sparing not even the most valuable historic buildings. Artillery positions in the garden of the archbishop's palace attracted Soviet fire, and the palace, the Gothic cathedral, and all of the centuries-old structures on Cathedral Island fell into ruins piece by piece. Observation posts were set up in church towers, which made them the target of Soviet artillery fire. The tower atop Liebichshöhe, where the fortress commander's headquarters had been built, was blown up to disorient enemy artillery. When the headquarters was supposed to be moved in mid-March into the extensive cellars of the State and University Library on Sand Island, a former Augustinian monastery, the library administration received merely a perfunctory message stating that the building would soon be burned down and then demolished. Only after vehement protests was permission granted to move the 550,000 remaining books to St. Anne's Church on the other side of the street.[23] Although the planned demolition did not take place, the Soviets learned of the military conversion of the library building and destroyed the Baroque structure under a hail of artillery fire.

The building of an airstrip in the city center became a symbol of the insanity of Fortress Breslau. In order to maintain air support even after losing the city airport in Gandau, a strip 0.8 miles long and almost 1,000 feet wide was cut through the affluent university district between Kaiserbrücke (most Grunwaldzki) and Fürstenbrücke (most Szczytnicki). All of the buildings and everything they contained were set on fire, including the state archives and two churches. Then the entire area was leveled. Thousands of forced laborers and German residents recruited for the job, including women, adolescents, and children, died at this monstrous construction site, as casualties of Soviet strafer raids. The airstrip was never used. By the time it was completed, shortly before the war's end, German air support had long since collapsed.

Distinctions between Breslau residents, prisoners of war, and forced laborers began to blur. As of March 7, the entire population was required to work—including boys ten and over and girls twelve and older. The fortress leadership recruited civilians to build barricades, clear destroyed buildings, and for all other jobs, regardless of the dangers involved. Anyone who refused to work was shot on the spot. Breslau residents were also driven from one district to another, from areas close to the front to areas farther away, and they were chased out of buildings that were to be demolished or used by the

The city of Breslau escaped destruction until the siege began in February 1945. Three months later, it was one of the most heavily damaged cities in Europe. View from the Town Hall's tower over the Old Town looking toward Cathedral Island. Courtesy of the City Museum of Wrocław (Krystyna Gorazdowska).

troops. It was common to see the dispossessed elderly, children, and women, pushing handcarts through the streets. Fortress Breslau, closed off to the outside world, was like a pressure cooker boiling on the inside.

Caught up in the chaotic and largely senseless fighting, the fortress troops devolved into increasingly reckless bands of soldiers. They threw civilians out of their lodgings in order to settle in themselves; they appropriated the property of their compatriots and engaged in rear-echelon carousing. Paul Peikert commented in his diary:

> Again and again, I hear reports of vandalism by the Wehrmacht and of the destruction of furnishings and household items left behind in the residences that have been evacuated by force. They break open locked apartments and steal whatever they can, especially items of value. They strew left-behind linens and clothes all around the rooms, soiling them. Nothing in the homes is safe from them and their devastation. Orgies of vile depravity take place in the bunkers and cellars. It is peak season

for harlots and whores, since there is alcohol aplenty for their revels. This is the moral demise of a people and of a Wehrmacht ruined by twelve years of Nazi ideology. Domine, dona nobis pacem. Let the days of misery end, O Lord.[24]

Since everyone trapped in Fortress Breslau was on the brink of death anyway, discipline was difficult to maintain even with unremitting drumhead courts martial. Some of the judgments did not even constitute disciplinary actions, but rather served to establish a reign of terror. Even before the city was encircled, Gauleiter Karl Hanke had made it unmistakably clear how he intended to govern the fortress. Under the pretext that Deputy Mayor Wolfgang Spielhagen—with whom Hanke had long been fighting a private war—had left the city without permission, Hanke had Spielhagen arrested and shot in front of the Town Hall in the early morning hours on January 28 by a *Volkssturm* unit. His body was then thrown into the Oder and the execution was publicized by means of posters and in the local press with the warning: "Whoever fears an honorable death will suffer a shameful one!"[25]

Breslau gradually became a graveyard. There were so many corpses that it was impossible to inter all of them in the city's cemeteries—fallen soldiers and civilians, the executed, and the growing number of people who had been driven to suicide out of desperation.[26] At first the old church cemeteries were reactivated, then Benderplatz, a park at the Odertor (Nadodrze) train station, was transformed into a cemetery. But soon people began illegally burying their dead everywhere, in the parks and gardens, at first in simple wooden crates and individual graves; in the end the corpses were just put in sacks and thrown into mass graves.[27] Many bodies, however, simply remained lying in apartments and among the rubble of bombed-out buildings,[28] so that soon armies of rats scurried through the ruins.[29]

The longer the fortress resisted, the heavier the Soviet air raids became. At first planes dropped only explosive bombs, but over time more and more incendiary bombs were used. For a long time, the fire department was nevertheless able to prevent major fires from developing. Until late March Breslau was thus a severely damaged city, but except for the immediate battle zone itself, the extent of the destruction was still limited. Then the Red Army command in Breslau threatened to initiate carpet bombing by the 750 heavy bombers stationed in the area if the fortress did not capitulate immediately. General

On Sand Island, all that remained were the ruins of the Church of the Blessed Virgin Mary and of the adjacent State and University Library, a former Augustinian monastery. The German fortress commander had installed his headquarters in the basement of the library. In the background is the tower of St. Elizabeth's Church, which miraculously survived the war with only minor damage. Courtesy of the Museum of Architecture in Wrocław (Krystyna Gorazdowska).

Hermann Niehoff, who had assumed command of the fortress troops in early March, continued to refuse to surrender. On April 1, the morning of Easter Sunday, the announced bombing of the city center began. The fire department no longer had a chance.

> Easter Monday took care of everything that Easter Sunday had left. . . . The weather was stormy all day on Monday. The storm grew into a downright hurricane towards evening. Suddenly the fire licked through the streets of the city and in different places one building after another ignited. Soon entire streets were in flames, and then entire districts. . . . After much effort we finally made it to Kaiserbrücke. On the bridge the hurricane-like storm almost pulled us into the Oder.
>
> From Kaiserbrücke we had an indescribably sad view of the burning city of Breslau. It was an unforgettable, horrific drama. Districts on both sides of the Oder were ablaze. . . . Flames darted out of the

towers of the Cathedral Church. The entire roof of the cathedral was one single flame of fire. St. Michael's Church was burning, the Church of Our Lady on the Sand, the churches of St. Vincent, St. Adalbert, St. Mauritius, St. Bernardine, St. Christopher, and all the streets between these churches, and especially also the current university library. Breslau ablaze on Easter Monday evening and throughout the night was an unimaginably eerie sight, the demise of the most beautiful part of this most beautiful city.[30]

While the bombers were flying, the Red Army attacked from the west, taking Gandau Airport and advancing by mid-April through the burning working-class districts west of the city center. The outrage of the general population at the senseless protraction of the capitulation became open protest. Many civilians began to loathe the German command and the German soldiers more than they feared the Soviet conquest of their city.

> The sooner the Russians come, the sooner this relentless destruction, which is above all else the work of our own leaders, can come to an end. All of the arson, all the devastation of buildings and furnishings, is being caused by our leaders themselves.... They are sacrificing a city ... without in the least altering the course of the war.[31]

But Niehoff followed the "strategy of self-destruction" that characterized the final days of Nazi Germany.[32] He was not willing to surrender until Hitler had committed suicide, Berlin had fallen on May 2, and news of the Wehrmacht's capitulation talks made it to Breslau. On May 6 Niehoff signed the articles of capitulation at the Villa Colonia in Krietern (Krzyki) and joined the German soldiers on their way to Soviet prisoner of war camps. Hanke, whom Hitler appointed in his will to succeed Himmler as leader of the SS and the German police, had fled to Bohemia the preceding night in the fortress's last remaining airplane.[33] On the night of May 6 the Red Army entered Breslau's city center.

The fanaticism of the Gauleiter and the narrow-mindedness of the last fortress commander, who could not muster the courage to end a battle long after it had become senseless, cost tens of thousands of lives. Entire neighborhoods of Breslau became uninhabitable. Most of the monuments were reduced to ruins and a large part of the city's art treasures, libraries, and archives

With a level of destruction close to 50 percent, the Old Town was less devastated than other parts of the city. The lower half of the photo shows the three historical market squares (from left to right: pl. Solny, Rynek, Nowy Targ), while parts of the still habitable neighborhoods north of the river Oder are visible on the photo's upper half. From Smolak 1995. Used by permission of the publisher.

were irretrievably lost. In early February 1945, Breslau was one of only two German cities with populations over 500,000 that were still intact (the other was Dresden); by the end of the war, it was one of the most severely damaged cities in all of Europe.

POLAND'S SHIFT TO THE WEST

While house-to-house fighting was still going on in Breslau, the future of the city had long been settled. Its fate was tied to a political process that is referred to simply as Poland's "westward shift." The term hardly does justice to the human tragedy it denotes, the extent to which centuries-old structures in East Central Europe were destroyed, or the fact that moving Poland's borders roughly 125 miles westward in an unscrupulous act of political engineering irrevocably changed the country. How this westward shift came about can be explained in the language of classical diplomatic history. The actors were the "Big Three," the heads of state of the Soviet Union, the United States, and Great Britain. In addition, the leadership of the Third Reich played an essential role insofar as Hitler and Stalin had made agreements regarding Poland's territory when in the fall of 1939 they had divvied up spheres of interest between the German Reich and the Soviet Union. What they then established as a Soviet-German demarcation line became the Soviet-Polish border claimed by Stalin and accepted by the Western Allies at the end of the war. The Polish government in exile, although it constituted the legal and legitimate government of Poland during the war, was given little say regarding the territorial shape of postwar Poland.

On September 1, 1939, the German Wehrmacht invaded Poland from the west; on September 17, the Red Army followed suit from the east, maneuvers agreed upon between Berlin and Moscow in the Hitler-Stalin Pact of August 23, 1939. After the Polish army was defeated, Germany and the Soviet Union divided Polish territory between them under the terms of the "Boundary and Friendship Treaty" of September 28, 1939. The western half was ceded to German sovereignty and the eastern half to the Soviets. Their common goal was to eliminate Poland as a country. "One swift blow to Poland," the Soviet foreign minister Vyacheslav M. Molotov is said to have declared before the Supreme Council of the Soviet Union on October 31, 1939, and nothing was left of this "ugly offspring of the Versailles Treaty."[34] Already in October

"It is not true that all ruins are the same. Ruins continue to express the character, the individuality of a living city. The devastated city of Wrocław continues to be a defiant and hostile place—defeated, powerless, and yet it has to be conquered again and again. The suggestion of a kind of heavy paralysis is agonizing in the demolished streets and in the smashed houses, as if the weight of all these shattered walls has collapsed forever, suicidally, desperately" (the Polish settler Maria Jarzyńska-Bukowska, writing about her new hometown in 1946). The image shows the former Kaiser-Wilhelm-Strasse (ul. Powstańcow Śląskich), once a magnificent boulevard passing through the burgher neighborhoods south of the city center. Courtesy of the City Museum of Wrocław (Krystyna Gorazdowska).

1939 eastern Poland was administratively merged with the Soviet Republics of Lithuania, Belorussia, and Ukraine. At the same time, hundreds of thousands of Polish citizens, whom the Soviet government considered potential opponents of the ensuing Sovietization of the region, were deported to Siberia.[35] Approximately 22,000 Polish officers, border guards, and police officers who had become Soviet prisoners-of-war after September 17, 1939, were shot in the spring of 1940 in the forests of Katyń, Kharkov, and Kalinin and their bodies hastily buried. Because most of them had been reserve officers, this mass murder deprived Poland of a large part of its college-educated elite.

The northwestern part of the Polish territories was incorporated into the German Reich, while the rest was assigned to what was termed the "General

During the siege, Breslau's most famous restaurant, the *Schweidnitzer Keller* (Schweid-nitz Cellar), located below the medieval town hall, was turned into a field hospital. Some of the soldiers hospitalized here during the fighting did not leave the cellar until Breslau had become a city in Poland. Courtesy of the Ossolineum (Marian Idziński).

Government" (of the occupied Polish territories). As a "buffer zone" under German control it would serve as a kind of discretionary territory where future resettlement and Germanization policies could be implemented. Like the Soviets, the Germans eliminated all institutions of Polish statehood. Tens of thousands of potential dissidents were immediately shot or put in concentration camps. The rest of the population underwent a process of classification according to "racial criteria": Hundreds of thousands were declared ethnic Germans, which meant that they could rise through the various stages of the so-called German People's List (Deutsche Volksliste) and eventually receive German citizenship. This was a mixed blessing, however, because those fit for military service were recruited for the Wehrmacht and SS and sent to the front. Those who were not registered on the German People's List faced the full brutality of the Nazi occupation in Poland. Hundreds of thousands were deported from the territories incorporated into the German Reich and sent to the General Government. Millions were put to work as forced laborers and almost the entire Jewish population was first crowded into ghettos and later murdered. Between five and six million Polish citizens, including almost three million Jews, were killed by the end of the war as a result of the terror of the German occupation, which extended into eastern Poland when the Soviet Union was invaded in the summer of 1941.[36]

Poland disappeared from the world map in September of 1939 and the Polish people were torn apart in the years of the occupation, but the Polish state did not cease to exist under international law. It continued in the form of the Polish government in exile and in the Polish military units, which fought alongside the Allied forces on all fronts. There were also resistance groups in occupied Poland, in particular the large Home Army (Armia Krajowa), which viewed the government in exile as its legitimate political representative. When Stalin, Churchill, and Roosevelt met in Tehran in late November 1943 to discuss the postwar order of Europe, it soon became clear that Poland would not be restored to its prewar borders. Despite the totally altered political constellation caused by the German-Soviet war, Stalin was not willing to give up the Polish territories annexed by the Soviet Union in 1939. Instead he attempted to have the Soviet expansion confirmed within the framework of the anti-Hitler coalition. Working in Stalin's favor was the fact that Roosevelt and Churchill were open to compromise with Stalin as regards territorial issues, this in contradiction to the terms of the 1941 Atlantic Charter, in which they had demanded that no territorial aggrandizement be sought and no territorial changes made "without the freely expressed wishes of the people concerned."

On the very first day of the Tehran Conference, Churchill explained to Stalin that he personally did not feel committed to any specific border between Poland and the Soviet Union, and that he felt Soviet security considerations regarding this border were the decisive factor. "As far as he was concerned, he would like to see Poland moved westward in the same manner as soldiers at drill execute the drill 'left close.'"[37] Roosevelt, too, gave his approval of the westward shift of the Soviet border. He requested understanding only for the fact that he could not publicly concede to making such an agreement. After all, in the upcoming election he did not want to lose the votes of Americans from Poland and the Baltic states.[38] Stalin sympathized and presumably felt confirmed in his low opinion of western democracy. He had managed to get Churchill and Roosevelt to acknowledge precisely those Soviet annexations that he had arranged with Hitler in the fall of 1939, forcing Poland to give up almost half of its state territory, including the predominantly Polish metropolises of Wilno and Lwów, which were about to become Vilnius and Lviv in the Lithuanian and Ukrainian Soviet Republic, respectively.

The only decision that was publicly stated was that Poland's postwar border to the east would correspond to the Curzon line. This was a border proposed in the 1920s in a very different historical context, and it provided no justification for the transfer of Lwów and Wilno to the Soviet Union.[39] Reference to the Curzon line, however, made it possible to conceal the fact that the origin of the new border lay in the Hitler-Stalin Pact. After speedy agreement on the question of Poland's eastern border, the Allied negotiations turned to the issue of the extent to which Poland should be compensated through territorial gains at Germany's expense. On this matter as well, the Allied negotiators were in general agreement, considering the Oder River as the likely Polish western border. However, the Allies did not agree on the precise course of the future German-Polish border until the summer of 1945 at the Potsdam Conference.[40]

It was clear from the outset of the talks that the shifting of the Polish state borders would involve extensive forced resettlements. The future Poland was to be a homogeneous nation-state without major ethnic minorities. This meant that the entire German population would have to be evacuated from areas ceded to Poland.[41] As the end of the war was approaching, the Western powers became aware that this massive population transfer would also have negative repercussions for them. The government in London was especially concerned, fearing the attendant costs and logistical problems, as the British occupation zone in Germany would have to absorb a large portion of the roughly eight million Germans who would be forced to relocate from Poland (in addition to more than four million Germans expelled from Czechoslovakia, Hungary, Yugoslavia, and Romania). On top of that, mistrust of Stalin was growing among the emerging postwar powers in the West. British and American negotiators tried at the last minute not to go as far in reducing Germany's territory as had originally been proposed in Tehran.

At the very least they did not want to accept Stalin's proposal to have the southern part of Poland's western border run along the (western) Neisse River in the Lusatian region. Instead they favored the (eastern) Neisse River in the Glatz (Kłodzko) region. This would have meant that the economically more significant and more populous portion of Lower Silesia would not have gone to Poland, and Breslau would have been divided into a Polish and a German section—as were later Frankfurt-on-the-Oder, Guben, and Görlitz. But Stalin's insistence on the Lusatian Neisse and, ultimately, the Western Allies' limited interest in the precise location of the German-Polish border led to the Soviets' wishes being fulfilled. In the closing communiqué of the Potsdam Conference of August 2, 1945, the Oder and the Lusatian Neisse were declared Poland's provisional western border. Germany thus lost East Prussia, eastern Pomerania, East Brandenburg, and Silesia, one-fourth of its 1937 territory, along with a number of significant cities, the most important of which was Breslau. Despite the pretense that a final decision would be made at a future peace conference, the Allies envisioned that the new border would be permanent. After all, the communiqué approved of the ongoing expulsion of the German population from all parts of postwar Poland, albeit urging that the transfer be carried out "in an orderly and humane manner."

Polish politicians participated only in a limited capacity in working out the country's new borders. The Polish government in exile, which had not been informed of the basic decisions that had been made in Tehran, continued to demand the reestablishment of Poland's prewar border in the east and a territorial expansion in the north and west, calculated to enhance the economic basis for the reconstruction of Poland and to afford a greater level of military security vis-à-vis Germany in the future. The country's political leadership, both in exile and under German occupation, had been considering the annexation of East Prussia, the Free City of Danzig (Gdańsk), and Upper Silesia, as well as some smaller acquisitions in eastern Pomerania. When at the Moscow Conference in October 1944 the government in exile found out about the Tehran agreements, according to which eastern Poland would be ceded to the Soviet Union, Prime Minister Stanisław Mikołajczyk resigned in protest. His successor Tomasz Arciszewski continued the struggle to regain eastern Poland and, in order not to lose Polish territorial claims in the east, vehemently rejected the compensatory offer by the Allied Powers to set the Oder River as the western border.

At that point in time, however, the government in exile, whose persistent refusal to abandon eastern Poland had increasingly become a thorn in the side of the "Big Three," was no longer the only institution that claimed to represent Poland. As early as the summer of 1944, the Soviet regime had begun installing a counter-government to assume power in the future Poland and operate in agreement with Moscow. To this end the Polish Committee of National Liberation (PKWN) was proclaimed on July 20, 1944. It was officially a multiparty government that included representatives of the Polish Workers' Party (PPR), the Polish Socialist Party (PPS), the People's Party (SL), and the Democratic Party (SD). But the key positions were in the hands of socialists and communists loyal to the Soviets.[42] On January 1, 1945, the committee, which had been located in Lublin and was thus known as the Lublin Committee, moved its seat to Warsaw and renamed itself the Provisional Government of the Republic of Poland.

The Western powers initially continued to support the government in exile as the only legal representative of Poland, but at the foreign ministers' conference in Moscow in June 1945 they agreed to recognize the Provisional Government as soon as personnel changes took place to include some representatives of the government in exile. One of the changes enacted was that the former prime minister of the government in exile, Stanisław Mikołajczyk, who was very popular in Poland at the time, joined the Warsaw government as deputy prime minister and minister of agriculture. On June 28, 1945, the government, which was still dominated by communists and socialists, changed its name to the Provisional Government of National Unity, and received diplomatic recognition in the West.

The Lublin Committee and the governments resulting from it consistently supported the Soviet position on the border issue. On July 27, 1944, only a few days after it was founded, the committee had already signed a secret agreement with the Soviet government, in which it accepted the Curzon line as the future eastern border of Poland. As compensation Poland was to receive the southern part of East Prussia and the region of the Free State of Danzig, as well as the parts of Silesia, Brandenburg, and Pomerania that were east of the Oder-Neisse line, including the port city of Stettin. The loss of the eastern provinces, their 70,000 square miles having constituted almost half the former territory of Poland, came as a shock to Polish society. Although the *Kresy*, as the Polish territories in the East were referred to by Poles, were economically far less developed than the rest of the country, they had profound significance for Polish national culture. Here was the birthplace of national poets Adam Mickiewicz and Juliusz Słowacki and of countless other figures in Polish intellectual life, the home of Józef Piłsudski, who founded the Second

Republic of Poland in 1918, and the land of the wealthy Polish aristocracy, where Poland's most magnificent estates and castles could be found. This territory also included the metropolises of Wilno and Lwów, which apart from Warsaw and Krakow were the leading centers of Polish urban culture, famous for their distinguished universities, libraries, archives, and art collections.

Eastern Poland was heterogeneous in ethnic terms. Poles comprised only a relative majority. Together with the Jews their influence was predominant in the cities and their immediate vicinity. Ukrainians, Belorussians, and Lithuanians comprised the majority in most of the rural regions. The ceding of eastern Poland to the Soviet Union was followed by a massive population exchange, the goal of which was to transfer the Polish population in what was now Soviet territory to Poland and to deport the Ukrainians and Belorussians remaining in Poland to the Soviet Union's Ukrainian and Belorussian Republics. Within the scope of this operation, which was officially based on voluntary resettlement but de facto bore traits of ethnic cleansing, millions of people were forced to leave behind their homes, their land, and the graves of their ancestors and to depart to an uncertain fate in an unfamiliar environment.

Through the definitive loss of the *Kresy*, a territorial gain in the West assumed central political significance for the Lublin Committee and the subsequent Polish governments. They could only hope to reconcile Polish society to this enormous war loss—the more glaring as Poland was supposedly in the camp of the victors—if the gains in the west were substantial. They had to be far greater than what the government in exile and the bourgeois political forces had been demanding all along, even without the loss of eastern Poland. For Polish communists it was also a matter of defending themselves against the accusation of lacking patriotism. They were compelled to legitimize their assumption of power, which they in fact owed to the Red Army, by presenting themselves as committed champions of Polish national interests.[43] They therefore began to assert particularly far-reaching territorial claims against Germany. A western border at the Oder and the Lusatian Neisse was likely the maximum they believed they could attain internationally.

It is hard to know how much the Polish communists pushed the radicalization of discourse on the western border on their own accord and how much their demands reflected the general radicalization of the border issue within Polish society once the extent of territorial losses in the East became clear.[44] In December 1944 the prime minister of the government in exile, Tomasz

Arciszewski, was likely expressing the opinion of a majority of Poles when he told the London *Sunday Times*:

> We have put forward our claims against Germany and demanded the incorporation into Poland of East Prussia, Upper Silesia, and parts of Pomerania. . . . But we do not want to expand our frontier in the west to include eight million Germans. We do not want, that is, either Breslau or Stettin. We are claiming just our ethnical and historical Polish territories, which are under German domination.[45]

A few months later, on May 26, 1945, Władysław Gomułka, First Secretary of the Polish Workers' Party and one of the leading Polish politicians in the postwar period, underscored the extraordinary significance of the Oder-Neisse line for the communists in their attempt to gain broad support among the Polish people:

> One reason why the government enjoys popular support is the question of the western territories. It neutralizes various elements. The expansion of the country to the west and the land reform tie the nation to the system. Any concessions would weaken our position in the country.[46]

Gaining Danzig in 1945 symbolized the fulfillment of Poland's traditional territorial demands against Germany. Raising the Polish flag over Breslau and Stettin, however, which up to 1944 had not been in the catalog of serious Polish territorial demands, became a symbol of the fact that Poland had not simply relinquished its territories in the east, but that considerable gains in the west compensated for the loss of Wilno and Lwów.[47] This notion found expression in the term "Recovered Territories" (Ziemie Odzyskane), whereby the German territories ceded to Poland in 1945 were introduced into Polish political language, implying that Poland had merely regained provinces it had lost in the Middle Ages. Alternatively, and less ideologically, the region was referred to as Poland's "western and northern territories" (ziemie zachodnie i północne), often abridged as "western territories."

For Breslau, Poland's western shift meant that the city once again changed its national affiliation. But in contrast to all previous transfers of power, this one involved a complete population exchange. Breslau was not merely to become a city in Poland, it was to be a city inhabited exclusively by Poles. Three days after "Fortress Breslau" capitulated, the vanguard of the new, Polish administration appeared in the devastated city. The population exchange began immediately. Polish settlers who arrived over the course of the coming months, including many who had been expelled from the *Kresy*, entered a city that was completely foreign to them. The Germans, on the other hand, had to leave a city that was becoming more foreign every day. Writer Hugo Hartung, who had come to Breslau in 1940 as the chief dramaturge at the Municipal Theaters and had served as a soldier during the siege, wrote in his diary in early July 1945:

> Dirty piles of bricks, sites of fire in which undefinable things are still smoldering, apartments torn open, façades missing like in doll houses, offering a private world of good fortune to curious and dulled gazes. Here, family photographs still hanging on the walls; there, pretty kitchen furnishings. Further up, out of reach, a black polished piano has suffered the pouring rain and cold nights, falling first out of tune and then silent. . . .
>
> A column of people pushes past ours, pushing carts and baby carriages, tired, plodding, miserable, never-ending: Poles from the Lemberg [Lwów] district. They don't yet feel at home in this city in which we no longer feel at home. Like marionettes of an incomprehensible fate the silent columns move past one another.[48]

Uprooted

INTRODUCTION

TODAY WROCŁAW IS A CITY THAT AT FIRST GLANCE REVEALS LITTLE OF the dramatic rupture of 1945. It appears no different than any other major city in Poland. It is the seat of a voivodeship administration, a university town with important cultural institutions, a transportation hub, an industrial city, and also, increasingly, a magnet for tourists. The central squares and streets in the Old Town look as if they had survived the war without significant damage. Visitors familiar with photographs of the ruins of 1945 stare in amazement at the Baroque façades of the patrician houses and of the university. They hardly believe their own eyes as they stroll along the seemingly old walls on Cathedral Island beneath the towers of the apparently untouched Gothic cathedral. If one recalls the tragedy of 1945, when much of Wrocław was reduced to rubble and an entire country shifted westward, displacing millions of people, this normal and prosperous city strikes the viewer as somewhat disturbing, nothing short of surreal.

Even in an incomparably less complex entity such as a village, we would expect the expulsion of its entire population to lead inevitably to its ruin, for how could any place survive the loss of local knowledge accumulated over generations, of traditions expunged from one day to the next. And in fact the postwar era in many places in Poland's western and northern regions, which had once been the eastern regions of Germany, was marked by such decline. In his fascinating study *Niechciane miasta* (Unwanted Towns), Zdzisław Mach examined the consequences of the population exchange for the town of Lubomierz (formerly Liebenthal) in Lower Silesia.[1] Here, the expulsion of the German population led to the desolation and deterioration of a small town that had been completely intact at the end of the war. This was in part due to the consequences of Soviet-style state socialism, which crushed any form of local autonomy and strangled economic diversity in the town. However, a comparison of Lubomierz with towns in central Poland—that is, in those regions that had not been part of Germany prior to the Second World War—highlights the role played by the forced migration in the town's deterioration. The expulsion of the German inhabitants and their replacement with Polish settlers, who had no ties of any kind to Lubomierz and knew nothing of local traditions, was in fact a fundamental cause of the decline. Only Lubomierz's third-generation Poles, the today forty-something grandchildren of the settlers, have felt sufficiently at home in the town to become interested in revitalizing it. Taking advantage of opportunities arising from the political and economic transformation of Poland following the fall of communism in 1989, they have begun to turn the town back into an attractive place to live. Although Lubomierz might be an extreme case, it is nonetheless symptomatic of conditions in Poland's new western territories.

For decades the economic decline of the regions Germany had to cede was one of the central arguments employed by Germans who refused to acknowledge the permanence of the 1945 territorial losses and who called for a revision of the decisions made at the Potsdam Conference. This line of argumentation combined an accurate economic analysis with erroneous political conclusions. Not only had a revision of the postwar German-Polish border soon become politically illusory; following the population exchange completed in 1948, the "right to a homeland" in a territorial and legal sense, as claimed by the German expellee organizations, increasingly worked in favor of the Poles who had been settled in previously German territories, and favored less and less the Germans who had been expelled from them. The Polish side understandably rejected the demanded territorial revisions, although usually on the basis of arguments that grossly distorted the historical facts. Up to the fundamental political changes of 1989, the Polish government and Polish society invoked historical rights to "age-old Polish land" and referred to the Germans who had once lived there as former "occupiers," as if the seven-hundred-year tradition of German-speaking settlements east of the Oder-Neisse line were merely a chimera. They also denied, at least in public, any negative impact of the border and population shifts on the western territories.

Not until after the definitive recognition of postwar borders in the German-Polish Border Treaty of 1990 did a truly unbiased, scholarly examination of the background and repercussions of Poland's westward shift and the ensuing population movements become possible. Scholars no longer had to serve political interests and supply ammunition for turf battles over the justice or injustice of the Oder-Neisse line and the expulsion of the Germans. Joint German-Polish research projects and publications, even on these sensitive topics, became possible and are today in fact a matter of course. Where it was no longer a matter of politics but of history alone, common ground could be found relatively quickly. Among historians of the two countries, nationally-based standpoints have disappeared. In this regard, German-Polish research projects on the history of forced migrations are playing a pioneering role in contemporary European scholarship.[2]

Nevertheless, the history of forced migrations in twentieth-century Central and Eastern Europe remains a difficult subject and one that can easily fall prey to political instrumentalization.[3] It is not surprising that even sixty years after the fact the issue still gives rise to emotional responses. Unbiased, scholarly examinations and the cross-border public debate about the mutually inflicted suffering began in earnest only *after* the Cold War, though there were a few notable early attempts to analyze these processes from an impartial perspective.[4] The "ethnic cleansing" in the Yugoslavian civil war in the 1990s functioned as a catalyst for international public interest in the history of forced population shifts in Europe and elsewhere. The Yugoslavian case suddenly shed light on how little unbiased research had been done on these violent processes, despite the fact that they have shaped large parts of Europe and continue to shape other parts of the world. Although significant progress in research on the history of forced migrations has been made since the mid-1990s, we are just starting to move forward into this long neglected—and deliberately avoided—field.

One cannot expect that examinations of forced migrations will lead to particularly pleasant findings, as they deal with violent and utterly destructive events. In documenting these processes, scholars confront a dilemma that Karl Schlögel described several years ago: After the expulsions have been instrumentalized politically for decades, it is not easy to find a language that facilitates discussion, avoids becoming politically charged, and at the same time calls things by their real names.[5] In order to achieve this, it is critical to conceive of these forced migrations within their larger historical contexts. In the case of the expulsion of Germans from Poland, this context is first and foremost the Second World War and the German occupation of Poland, the Nazis' monstrous resettlement, "re-ethnicizing" (*Umvolkung*) and extermination policies, and the mass murder of Jews, Roma and Sinti, and Slavs. No simple causal relation exists between these processes, and we have to bear in mind that the history of forced migrations in twentieth-century Europe began already in the nineteenth century.[6] Nevertheless it is clear that the dissolution of Prussia, the eradication of eastern Germany, and the expulsion of millions of Germans from the East would not have been possible without the war of conquest and extermination waged by Nazi Germany in Central and Eastern Europe.

The present study is concerned with both the short- and the long-term consequences of forced migrations for those regions where the established inhabitants were expelled and replaced by new settlers from elsewhere. My approach is to use a case study. The book studies the consequences of forced migration through the lens of a single location: that of Wrocław, the largest city in the German territories ceded to Poland after the war and the largest city ever to experience a total population exchange of this kind. Prior to the original publication of this book in German in 2003, to the best of my knowledge there had been no comprehensive local study of forced migration and its long-term effects on Wrocław or any other place.[7]

I chose to look at the city of Wrocław for a number of reasons. As a large city, it is particularly well suited for an investigation of the complex consequences of such a population exchange. A large city generates a sufficient amount of the sources necessary for historical research. Compared to other large Polish cities with a similar history, such as Szczecin and Gdańsk, Wrocław offered decisive advantages. In 1945, Szczecin became a border city, having lost a significant portion of its hinterland as well as its economically crucial connection to Berlin. In an examination of postwar Szczecin, it would have been difficult to determine which aspects in the development of this city were tied to the population exchange and which to its economically unfavorable peripheral location at a hermetically sealed border. In Wrocław, by contrast, established regional relations were preserved because almost all of Silesia became Polish in 1945. Although Wrocław did lose Berlin as an economic reference point, this could be compensated for—better than in the case of Szczecin—by strengthening economic ties to Krakow and Poznań.

Wrocław was also better suited than Gdańsk because I wanted to investigate the radical rupture of 1945, the sense of foreignness that the Polish newcomers experienced, and the cultural strategies through which they attempted to overcome this foreignness. Although Gdańsk experienced a complete population exchange as well, the break was less pronounced there. Despite its largely German-speaking population prior to 1945, the port city on the Vistula had had traditionally strong economic, political, and cultural connections to Poland. Even before the war, it thus occupied an important place in the Polish collective memory. Gdańsk's incorporation into Poland, a political demand that had been raised repeatedly between the world wars, did not come as a surprise to Poles in 1945. The situation regarding Wrocław was quite different. Although the city had once belonged to Poland (in the Middle Ages), it had gradually grafted onto the Holy Roman Empire beginning in the thirteenth century. Wrocław had thus become a German city over the course of the centuries. While its ties to neighboring Poland had always been an important factor in the history of this trading city, modern Wrocław's ties to Poland were such that, prior to 1945, no one in Poland would have doubted its German character or its affiliation with Germany. Polish society was as unprepared to take over Wrocław as it was to give up Lwów.

The present study is based on three simple questions: How could Wrocław, which was devastated in the Second World War and lost its entire established population, become a thriving city again? How did the Polish settlers and their descendants not only overcome their feeling of foreignness and establish roots in the formerly German city, but also develop a sense of civic pride unsurpassed anywhere else in Poland? And how was it possible to make of Wrocław not merely a city in Poland but also a truly Polish city, if only in the course of an extended process that is still ongoing today?

The search for answers to these questions led to five different fields of research, to which this book hopes to contribute. First, it sheds light on an epoch of Wrocław's history that has long been neglected.[8] Although the present study examines the entire period from 1945 to the present, it does not claim to be a comprehensive investigation of Wrocław's history. The analysis is always centered on the consequences of the forced population exchange. This requires a temporal focus on the years immediately after the war, but also takes into consideration the fundamental changes caused by the great political upheaval of 1989. Many important aspects of the local history not directly related to the border and population shift in 1945 could not be treated here. In the course of my investigation of Wrocław, however, I have become convinced that the "demographic revolution" of 1945, through which a German city was made Polish overnight, has remained the central element in Wrocław's city history ever since. Whether explicitly addressed or tacitly avoided, the rupture of 1945, the new inhabitants' lack of roots in the city, and the psychological problem of moving into the homes and taking over the workplaces of those expelled from the city all had a sustained impact on Wrocław's postwar development.[9]

Second, the book is intended as a contribution to the history of German-Polish relations in the tradition established long ago by Klaus Zernack, whose *Beziehungsgeschichte* methodologically anticipated much of what is known today as *histoire croisée*.[10] Polish settlers did not encounter the German legacies in Wrocław with indifference, but rather within the context of conflict-laden German-Polish relations, which experienced its darkest phase during the Second World War. Many Poles in Wrocław moved into the apartments of their tormentors or suddenly had an opportunity to leaf through the private libraries and papers of political opponents from Germany. Nevertheless, it is important to bear in mind that the relationship was also marked by a great intimacy. The first Polish mayor of Wrocław after the war had earned a doctoral degree at a German university, and many of the professors who built up the Polish university in Wrocław had studied and taught in Germany. One example is the famous Polish physician and microbiologist Ludwik Hirszfeld (1884–54), who established the ABO blood type nomenclature. After graduating from secondary school in the multiethnic Polish-German-Jewish city of Łódź in 1902, Hirszfeld studied medicine in Würzburg and Berlin, earning a doctoral degree at the University of Berlin in 1907. He subsequently worked in Heidelberg and Zurich, where he completed his postdoctoral dissertation in 1914. In 1921, he continued his scientific career in Warsaw. After the German invasion of Poland, Hirszfeld, who had published much of his scholarly work in German, lost his professorship at the University of Warsaw and, because he was Jewish, was deported to the Warsaw Ghetto. However, he was able to flee the ghetto and survived in occupied Poland. After the war Hirszfeld was appointed dean of the medical school at the University of Wrocław. On November 15, 1945, he gave the keynote lecture in the Aula Leopoldina inaugurating the first Polish academic year in Wrocław.[11] As this biography illustrates, the destruction of Polish-German relations—and in the case of Hirszfeld also German-Jewish relations—occurred against the backdrop of a particularly dense web of mutual interaction.

The lives of very few Polish settlers in Wrocław were as tightly intertwined with the Germans as was that of Ludwik Hirszfeld's, but the German past of the city nonetheless had meaning for most of them. The fact that Wrocław did not suffer the same fate as Lubomierz was due not least to the symbolic significance of the largest city in the former German territories of postwar Poland. This was the proving ground where Polish society could demonstrate its ability to reconstruct and revive a city whose destruction had been caused by the Germans. For this reason, Wrocław could not help but communicate with Breslau. The size of the city prior to 1945, the number of its inhabitants, its architecture, and its technical and cultural institutions—all of these became benchmarks for Wrocław after 1945. If the city had been merely a social space, then Breslau would have been extinguished with the expulsion of its inhabitants and a completely new and different city would have arisen after the war. Breslau and Wrocław would have confronted each other like the unrelated texts of a palimpsest. This, however, was not the case. In the background of the postwar city, the prewar city was always present. At first the relation between the two was marked by Wrocław's desire to negate and occasionally to outstrip Breslau. However, with increasing distance from the Second World War and diminishing political tensions between Germany and Poland, an initially interested and ultimately respectful encounter developed between the Polish city and the German one, as I will illustrate in the present study.

The third field of research forming the basis of this book is the history of forced migrations in twentieth-century Europe. As a result of growing research and publications since the late 1990s, our knowledge has expanded significantly. Works such as Norman M. Naimark's comparative study *Fires of Hatred: Ethnic Cleansing in Twentieth-Century Europe* have helped to overcome national perspectives on the history of forced migrations and to sharpen our understanding of the recurring mechanisms of ethnic cleansing.[12] Timothy Snyder's *Bloodlands* and Kate Brown's *History of No Place* remind us of the extent to which the world of Central and Eastern Europe has been shaped and misshaped through the forced removal or destruction of entire populations and the eradication of their traces.[13] Systematic research on the long-term consequences of forced migrations has just gotten started.[14] Wrocław is a particularly fascinating case in investigating the century of expulsions because it was the site of several forced resettlements: the expulsion of Germans, the settlement of Poles expelled from the territories Poland lost to the Soviet Union, the settlement of Ukrainians deported from southeastern Poland in 1947, and the arrival of tens of thousands of Polish Jews, most of whom had survived the Holocaust in the Soviet Union and subsequently fled the rampant anti-Semitism in postwar Poland to the country's western territories. The present study, however, is concerned not with these forced resettlements per se but rather with their repercussions for a city such as Wrocław. One of the central issues here is how the population relocated to Wrocław dealt with the psychologically difficult situation of taking over a place that had previously "belonged" to others. For many this meant a material improvement. Nevertheless, precisely those people who had been expelled from eastern Poland did not regard this as real compensation for the loss of their homeland. No matter how modern and luxurious the new residences in the western territories might have been, many settlers missed their former homes in East Galicia or Volhynia, to which they were tied through personal memories and a sense of tradition going back generations. This sense of uprootedness among the new inhabitants in territories from which the former population was expelled is a dimension of the history of forced migrations that has not yet been adequately investigated. Forced resettlements and ethnic cleansings are political actions that can be carried out in a single historical moment. The negative material and psychological repercussions they have on the societies and regions involved, in contrast, can be overcome, if at all, only in the course of a decades-long cultural process.[15]

The fourth field is research on the rebuilding of European cities destroyed in the Second World War. Even without the expulsion of the German population, the scope of war damages in Wrocław would have resulted in a profound caesura in the city's history. As in other European cities devastated by the war, the loss of cultural assets in Wrocław was enormous and, in general, irreplaceable. Postwar European societies were confronted with a mammoth rebuilding task, which unleashed both creative and destructive potentials.[16] In many places, future-oriented visions of a modern society guided new construction to such an extent that anything regarded as old-fashioned was ruthlessly eliminated. The emphatic dawn of an ostensibly better future heralded by architects and urban planners ultimately caused as much damage to the historic building stock of many European cities as had the air raids. Elsewhere,

8

emphasis focused instead on returning to historic traditions in order to create at least the illusion of stability and familiarity in a world marked by destruction and the loss of tradition. The historical reconstruction of Warsaw's Old Town has become symbolic of the refusal to accept the loss of historic buildings in the war. However, even the reconstruction of Warsaw involved both demolition and historic reconstruction, as was typical for most European cities rebuilt after the war. In examining the reconstruction of war-ravaged cities, Wrocław offers a particularly fascinating case: Here the residents attempted to historically reconstruct "their" devastated city, which they had never known in its intact state. They first had to actively search out the architectural traditions they wished to revive in the reconstruction process.[17]

Related to this is the fifth and final field of research that is of central importance to the present study: cultural memory[18] and the politics of the past.[19] In postwar Wrocław, the gradual transformation of a heterogeneous migration society into a unified citizenry had much in common with a nation-building process. One of the main tasks was the "invention of tradition."[20] The formation of a common cultural memory capable of creating community and a sense of belonging, which in turn could make of a foreign place a home, was crucial for the successful revitalization and Polonization of Wrocław after war, border shift, and forced migration. This cultural memory, of course, did not simply develop on its own. In large part, it was a product of the politics of the past, whose agents were the city's political and cultural elite. The people who came to live in Wrocław after the war had to be convinced and to convince themselves that Wrocław would become a Polish city, no different from Krakow, Poznań, or Łódź. This required inventing, popularizing, and internalizing a tradition that justified the Polish presence, one that moved the beginning of the city's Polish history back from 1945 to the Middle Ages, thereby tying Wrocław's new inhabitants to each other and to the city itself.

Wrocław's postwar history is particularly fruitful ground for examining cultural memory, because the wealth of documentary material, the manageable time frame, and the concreteness of location make it possible to trace quite precisely the construction of a new tradition and its impact on the city and its society. We will observe local historians, philologists, archeologists, and art historians who designed, on the drawing board as it were, a purely Polish city history, thus becoming the engineers of a cultural memory. We will witness a process that expunged traces of the German past from public spaces because they obstructed the popularization of the new, Polish version of local history. We will see how the Wrocław Old Town was not only reconstructed but also simultaneously reshaped into a Polish landscape of memory. However, we will also learn that the invention of tradition had limitations, that the repression and condemnation of Wrocław's German past—which was at first necessary in order to set in motion a process of cultural appropriation—ultimately became an obstacle to this very process of appropriation. In order to complete this process, Polish Wrocławians have since 1989 sought ways to integrate the German past into the collective memory of the city. This development has been accompanied also by a democratization of the politics of the past, which within a pluralist society is determined not only "from above," but is also subject to powerful impulses from "below." In this way collective memory is continually reshaped and revised.

A variety of different sources were examined in order to answer the aforementioned questions. Archival materials provided information above all about official measures and governmental policies, but also about processes such as the deliberate Polonization, which were not discussed publicly. In search of directives issued by the Polish government, I reviewed the central collections at the Archive of New Records (AAN) in Warsaw, especially the files of the Council of Ministers (URM) and those of relevant ministries. The files of the Society for the Development of the Western Territories (TRZZ), which do not appear to have been evaluated prior to this study, also contained important information about cultural policies concerning the western territories after 1956 and about specific difficulties facing the region. The State Archives in Wrocław (AP Wr) proved a rich source of information; many of the archive's files relating to cultural issues and the Polonization of the city had hardly been evaluated prior to the present study. The files of the municipal administration and the voivodeship office in Wrocław provided information not only about the general mood, but also some specifics of the Polonization policies. Interesting files about later years were occasionally found in the collections of the County National Council of Wrocław (PRN), as well as in those of the Voivodeship Committee of the Polish United Workers' Party (PZPR)—noteworthy in the latter particularly were documents regarding the planning and implementation of the major anniversary celebrations of the end of the war. Finally, the files of the Wrocław Directorate for Reconstruction (WDO) and the Miastoprojekt Design Center were illuminating in regard to construction policies, although these contain primarily technical and logistical material and reveal little about the political objectives of the reconstruction. With respect to archival materials in general, I share historian Andreas Hofmann's suspicion that potentially explosive materials were removed from the most interesting collections before they were turned over to the archives.[21] Therefore, however important archival research is for the present study, we must bear in mind that the extant files cannot provide comprehensive information even about administrative and political procedures.

Published recollections and memoirs by settlers have thus proved extremely valuable, despite the caution required in using them due to state censorship of sources of this kind. Collecting *pamiętniki*—recollections by contemporary witnesses—had enormous significance in the People's Republic of Poland and was repeatedly encouraged through elaborate competitions. The versions that were ultimately published, however, often differed significantly from what the authors had actually written.[22] Information about problems with the Soviet military forces stationed in Poland or the labile national identity of the population that settled in the western territories was especially apt to be suppressed or falsified. Nevertheless, the *pamiętniki* are an important source that can be read in a dual manner: On the one hand, they contain a plethora of information that is otherwise virtually impossible to obtain, and provide a lively impression of the atmosphere of the period. On the other hand, precisely because of state censorship they also constitute a central source in understanding the official conception of how the "pioneer era" in the western territories was depicted within the People's Republic.[23] The diaries of Joanna Konopińska, who moved to Wrocław in 1945 as a university student and became an incisive and reflective observer of the situation in the city and the mood of its inhabitants, offer recollections of a completely different kind. Their publication in 1987 and 1991 was no longer subject to state censorship, so they can be regarded as a highly authentic primary source.[24]

Great attention was also paid to those texts that served to create and popularize a Polish cultural memory in Wrocław. This category includes city guidebooks, popular historiographies, local or regional history periodicals and similar materials. These publications contained propaganda far into the 1980s, which has meant that authors of more recent works have not always considered them serious sources. However, apart from the fact that even propagandistic writings include unadulterated facts and information, these texts are an indispensable source in identifying strategies of cultural appropriation and in examining the changes such strategies were subject to over the course of time. The most recent books on local history, Wrocław encyclopedias and other reference works, popular histories, new city guidebooks, and recent editions of the aforementioned local and regional historical journals, which were all published after the abolition of state censorship, have also been evaluated here in this dual sense; that is, both as reference works and as documents reflective of the changing ways of seeing local history. The daily press was utilized sporadically as a source in this study. However, because local Wrocław historians have examined newspapers intensively in recent years, it was possible to a great extent to draw from their findings.

Finally, Wrocław's physical appearance was treated as an important source of local history; that is, as a revealing document that the author, inspired by Italo Calvino, Spiro Kostof, and Karl Schlögel, attempted to read.[25] There is today hardly anything random in Wrocław's appearance. Indeed as a result of rebuilding after the devastation of the war, its cityscape—first and foremost the face of the historically reconstructed and thereby reshaped Old Town—has become a kind of public text. The reconstruction of the city center was, in broad stretches, historiography by means of architecture. Through the interplay of reconstructed and reconfigured historic buildings, monuments, and commemorative plaques, as well as the names of streets and squares, a *Gesamtkunstwerk* laden with meaning has emerged, which—to borrow Jan Assmann's term—might be called a "mnemotope."[26] The Polish inhabitants of Wrocław were able to decode this meaning because it had arisen within their own cultural sphere and was elucidated in published city guidebooks and repeatedly internalized through the rituals of commemorative celebrations. For external observers, however, who are not part of this society, the meaning of all this is anything but obvious.

Meanings fade over time and are eclipsed by new meanings. As a result, even the present-day residents of Wrocław are often no longer able to interpret the symbols inscribed in the postwar cityscape. In addition, a process was set in motion beginning in 1989 that has rapidly and profoundly altered the notions that Wrocław's residents have about their city. Elements of the cityscape that were once central have lost "significance" both in terms of their importance and their ability to signify meaning. In contrast, other elements, which previously played no role, have suddenly moved into the center of attention and become charged with meanings relating to the new era. For this reason, elucidations in the sense of Clifford Geertz's "thick description"[27] are necessary in order to make the cityscape readable as a "cultural system" for observers from different cultural contexts.

PART ONE

THE POSTWAR ERA: RUPTURE AND SURVIVAL

Polish Wrocław emerged out of the ruins of the destroyed German city. The sign on top of the kiosk points to an academic bookstore located around the corner. Courtesy of the Museum of Architecture in Wrocław (Krystyna Gorazdowska).

CHAPTER ONE

Takeover

On August 2, 1945, the final communiqué of the Potsdam Conference announced to the world the Allies' decision to remove from the German Reich all territories east of the Oder and Lusatian Neisse rivers and place them under Polish administration, with the exception of northern East Prussia, which was to be ceded to the Soviet Union. By this point in time a Polish mayor was already in office in Breslau and the population exchange was in full swing. Before the Allies had reached an agreement about the precise location of the new German-Polish border, and while experts in the London Foreign Office and the Washington State Department were still reviewing the economic and logistical consequences of the various border proposals, the Soviet government and the Soviet-installed Polish regime had resolved the border issue on their own.

A Fait Accompli

As early as February 20, 1945, the State Defense Committee (GOKO) of the Soviet Union stipulated in top secret decree no. 7558 that—subject to a definitive decision at a peace conference—the Oder and the Lusatian Neisse rivers were to be regarded as the western Polish border and that the Red Army was to turn over civil administration to Polish authorities in the German territories east of this border. Only a strip of land between forty and sixty-two miles wide behind the front, as well as railway lines, important bridges, and other resources needed to supply the Soviet forces were to be exempt from this transfer.[1] In order to install a Polish administration in German territories east of the Oder-Neisse line prior to the Potsdam Conference, Poland's provisional government was eager to obtain power as quickly as possible—despite the fact that its hands were more than full with rebuilding from scratch the completely devastated Polish state. Every single institution had to be reestablished and innumerable posts filled.

Completing these tasks proved all the more difficult, as the allocation of leadership positions in the country had already set a course toward a Soviet-style socialist regime. In order to maintain the appearance of democratic government, administrative posts were assigned according to proportional representation of all the leading political parties. Behind the scenes, however, the communists and socialists sought to divvy up the key positions among themselves. Until the communists had established themselves as the sole power in Poland, and the Polish Socialist Party (PPS) was merged with the Polish Workers' Party (PPR) to form the Polish United Workers' Party (PZPR) in late 1948, there were bitter power struggles in Poland that further obstructed the already difficult process of rebuilding the country. Appointments according to party affiliation rather than professional qualifications, the sudden dismissal of people who had fallen out of grace overnight, and the continual restructuring of agencies as political spheres of influence shifted—all of this contributed to an atmosphere of instability in the first years after the war and exacerbated the administrative chaos.[2]

The impending Polish takeover of the German territories was listed as a separate agenda item for the first time on March 12, 1945, in the minutes of a session of the provisional government's Council of Ministers.[3] On that day the Red Army was already at the Oder River, preparing for its final major offensive against Berlin. Speed was of the essence if the Polish government was to assume control of the eastern German territories from the Red Army and establish a comprehensive Polish administration, at least symbolically, before the Allies assembled as victors and determined Germany's new borders. On March 14, the Council of Ministers divided the future Polish western territories into four provisional administrative districts: East Prussia (Prusy Wschodnie; renamed Warmia and Masuria shortly thereafter), West Pomerania (Pomorze Zachodnie), Lower Silesia (Dolny Śląsk), and Opole Silesia (Śląsk Opolski).[4] In administrative terms the territory of the Free City of Danzig was not part of the western territories, but instead was merged with the former province Pomerelia and several bordering districts to create the Gdańsk voivodeship, as the provinces of Poland are traditionally called. It was not until May of 1946 that the government harmonized administrative structures in the old and the new provinces by transforming the districts of the western territories into the regular voivodeships of Olsztyn, Szczecin, Wrocław, and Silesia—the latter through a consolidation of the Opole Silesia and Katowice voivodeships. Prior to this, the administration of the western territories differed from that of the rest of Poland owing to the special tasks that had to be addressed there.[5]

Already on March 14, 1945, the Council of Ministers appointed government plenipotentiaries for each of the four districts. In contrast to the regular voivodes in central Poland, these plenipotentiaries were in charge not only of the civil administration in their districts, but also of the railways, the postal service, the citizens' militia (police), and the various "operative groups" (*grupy operacyjne*), as the representatives of the Warsaw ministries operating in the western territories were called.[6] General Aleksander Zawadzki (PPR), who was already voivode of Katowice, was appointed government plenipotentiary in Opole Silesia. The posts of government plenipotentiary in West Pomerania and in Warmia and Masuria were assumed by the previous liaison officers of the Polish government to the Soviet fronts, First Lieutenant Leonard Borkowicz (PRR) and Colonel Jakub Prawin (PRR), respectively. Former Kielce deputy voivode Stanisław Piaskowski (PPS) was appointed head of the civil administration in Lower Silesia, the only civilian and socialist amid high-ranking communist military officers. The government also decided to assign a representative from the Ministry of Public Security (MBP) as a deputy to each of the district plenipotentiaries. Because of uncertainty about how the German population would react to the appearance of Polish officials, ensuring public safety was regarded as one of the most important tasks in the new territories. Thus the establishment of the Polish administration there bore the traits of a military operation.

Reflecting the political significance of the largest city in the new territories, the government also selected on March 14 the future mayor of Polish Breslau. It chose Bolesław Drobner (1883–68), who up to then had directed the department for labor, social welfare, and public health within the Polish Committee of National Liberation. Drobner, who had been born in Krakow, was an experienced socialist politician and functionary of the PPS. During the war he had lived in the Soviet Union and been part of the leadership of the Union of Polish Patriots (ZPP) there. Helpful for this new post in Breslau, Drobner was fluent in both Russian and German. Before the First World War he had studied chemistry in Berlin, Zurich, and in Freiburg, where he later earned his doctoral degree.[7] However, he had never been to Breslau and thus became mayor of a major city he had never seen.

During the transition period the western territories were given not only a special administrative structure but also their own central administration in Warsaw. Most of the responsibilities were initially held by the Ministry of Public Administration (MAP). The Office of the General Plenipotentiary of the Recovered Territories (Generalny Pełnomocnik do Spraw Ziem Odzyskanych) had been located there since April 1945, under the direction of the minister himself—initially Edward Ochab (PPR) and, after the formation of the Provisional Government of National Unity on June 28, Władysław Kiernik from the Polish Peasant Party (PSL). Authority in the western territories was not really centralized, however, until the Ministry of the Recovered Territories (MZO) was created in November 1945. This ministry assumed sole responsibility for establishing a Polish administration in the western territories, for the entire resettlement process, the economic revival, and the distribution of previously German property. It was dissolved in 1948, along with the special administration of the western territories. Władysław Gomułka, who as the First Secretary of the PPR was one of the country's most influential figures, headed this powerful ministry. The communists used the post to secure a key position in the new Poland. Through Gomułka, they controlled one-third of Polish state territory, a significant portion of Poland's industrial potential, and the enormous value of all the former German property in the western territories that had to be redistributed among the populace.[8]

THE MISSION OF THE GOVERNMENT PLENIPOTENTIARIES

The government plenipotentiaries sent to the western territories were confronted with enormous challenges. They had to create a Polish administrative apparatus that could take over responsibility for the occupied territories from the Red Army as soon as possible. All existing assets, in particular industrial facilities, warehouses, and food storehouses, had to be protected from plundering, vandalism, and deterioration. In addition, a minimum of public safety and order had to be ensured—a difficult undertaking in a society brutalized by war and occupation. Authorities also had to allocate apartments and distribute food in order to create somewhat tolerable living conditions for the expanding number of Polish settlers in the territories, especially for the employees of the Polish administration. They had to reconstruct the infrastructure immediately, beginning with water, gas, and electrical service, public transportation, and hospitals. Finally, a groundwork had to be laid on which Polish cultural life could develop: schools and universities were needed, as were libraries, bookstores, theaters, cinemas, newspapers, and radio stations. For help in fulfilling these tasks, the Polish authorities could draw upon the local German population only to a limited extent, since the latter was supposed to be used solely for subordinate activities until its evacuation. Management positions were to be given in principle only to Poles. This proved difficult because the educated Polish elite had suffered the greatest casualties during the war and the occupation. In addition, only supporters of a socialist Poland were considered for key positions. Thus, despite their professional qualifications, people regarded as bourgeois or conservative were from the start excluded or entrusted only with responsibilities devoid of influence or prestige.

In mid-April, authorities began setting up the Polish administration in Lower Silesia. Government Plenipotentiary Stanisław Piaskowski reached an agreement with the staff of the Soviet forces' First Ukrainian Front that he would establish the provisional seat of the district administration in the small city of Trzebnica (Trebnitz), located north of Wrocław. However, after Marshal Konstantin Rokossovsky transferred the staff quarters of his Second Belarusian Front to Trzebnica, Piaskowski moved his administration to the larger city of Legnica (Liegnitz) in June 1945.[9] Legnica, a former Prussian district capital, was well situated in terms of transportation lines and had suffered little war damage. However, this city soon became too crowded as well. After the dissolution of the Soviet fronts in late May 1945, all units of the Red Army stationed in Poland were assembled in the northern army group of the Soviet forces under the leadership of Marshal Rokossovsky, who relocated his headquarters—an enormous complex that not only directed Soviet troops in Poland but also played a central role in supplying the units stationed in the Soviet occupation zone in Germany—to Legnica. In November 1945 Piaskowski again moved his district administration, this time to Wrocław. By then, the government in Warsaw had decided that the city of Wrocław would constitute not an independent province but only an independent municipal district within the voivodeship of Wrocław, which encompassed all of Lower Silesia.[10]

The arrival of the Polish administrative cadre in what had been German territory marked an epochal caesura. Given the prevailing circumstances, however, this was not accompanied by any sort of triumphal demonstration. The first roughly four hundred employees of the Lower Silesian provincial administration who left Kielce on April 20, the advance guard of a significant authority, had to travel the final twenty miles from Trzebnica to Wrocław on foot due to damaged railroad tracks and a shortage of motor vehicles.[11] In May 1945 the authorities commanded only eleven functioning vehicles in the entire province, which much complicated the task of establishing area-wide Polish administration.[12] Plenipotentiaries at the county and municipal level traveled in groups of five to ten to their posts in the countryside, not infrequently on bicycles or even on foot. A few lightly armed militiamen were all they had for their protection.[13] Once in place the plenipotentiaries served for the time being as the sole representatives of the new Polish order and had to stand their ground in an environment where Germans still predominated. This was made all the more difficult by the fact that they usually were not familiar with the area. Since communication networks were down, they were left largely to their own resources during this initial phase. They had to make do with what they had been able to take with them—provisions for the first days, handguns, a Polish flag, and the necessary forms to issue announcements and decrees. Everything else had to be organized locally.[14] Whether it was possible under these conditions to establish both a functioning Polish administration and the prerequisites for Polish settlement was largely dependent on the improvisational skills and engagement of these representatives and their staffs.

"Noah's Ark" in Krakow

Immediately following his appointment as mayor of Wrocław, Bolesław Drobner began to look for a cadre for the future municipal administration. With this in mind he opened an office called the Wrocław Municipal Administration–Krakow Branch (Zarząd miasta Wrocławia–filia w Krakowie) in the city of Krakow.[15] People could volunteer for the "operative group" that was supposed to function as the advance guard of the Polish administration as soon as the siege of Breslau had ended. Civil servants, engineers, craftsmen, as well as militiamen, cooks, and drivers were sought. Parallel to Drobner's staff, Professor Stanisław Kulczyński, delegate of the Ministry of Education, assembled the Science and Culture Group, which was supposed to tend to Breslau's valuable university institutions, the libraries, archives, and museums, and to initiate getting a Polish university established in Breslau.[16] Like Drobner, Kulczyński (1895–1975) came from Krakow. He had studied botany there and had been appointed professor at the Jan-Kazimierz University in Lwów in 1924, serving as its president in 1936 and 1937. Kulczyński began his political career in 1945. He joined the Democratic Party (SD) and subsequently advanced to become a leading figure in the party. Over the course of his life he was appointed to numerous important political posts in the People's Republic of Poland. As first president of the Polish university he also became one of the most prominent figures in Wrocław.[17]

Assembling the two cadre groups, which Drobner described as "a Noah's Ark on the Ararat of Wrocław,"[18] proved extremely difficult. Throughout Poland skilled workers in all professions were in desperately short supply. Krakow had already been combed through repeatedly. The western territories were not attractive to most people, as there had previously been no Polish political life in the region at all, and its political future was uncertain. What is more, fighting was still going on in Fortress Breslau, and it was unclear when the besieged city would fall or what condition it would be in when it did. It was not even clear whether it would be inhabitable given the extensive war damage.[19] While most government plenipotentiaries had already begun their work in the western territories, Drobner and Kulcyzński could do little more than wait in Krakow for Breslau to surrender, and busy themselves with recruiting their advance guards. In mid-April, a three-day inspection in the direction of Breslau became possible—in Drobner's words, a trip "into the jungle of an unknown land."[20] Due to the continued fighting, Drobner's motorcade could advance only as far as the Hindenburgplatz in one of Breslau's southern neighborhoods. After introducing themselves to the future Soviet city commander, Lieutenant Colonel Lyapunov, in Kanth (Kąty Wrocławskie) south of Breslau, the members of the entourage returned to Krakow.[21]

When news reached Krakow that the siege had at last ended, a small advance division with a truck bearing the Polish flag and loaded with provisions

"We have come here as landlords for the first time in centuries. One does not need a historian to appreciate this moment" (Zofia Gostomska-Zarzycka, librarian and member of the Science and Culture Group). The cadre of Wrocław's Polish administration poses for a group portrait in April of 1945. In the first row, third from the left, is the first Polish mayor, Bolesław Drobner. Like the others, he wears a brassard in the Polish national colors, white and red, to indicate his membership in the Polish administration. Courtesy of the Ossolineum.

for the first days was sent immediately to Breslau in the morning hours of May 9. Division Commander Kazimierz Kuligowski reported on the group's arrival in the still burning city:

> We caught sight of enormous clouds of black smoke about twelve miles to the south. The closer we got, the larger the clouds grew, until we could see fires. The whole of Wrocław seemed to be on fire. We became increasingly anxious. At last, the suburbs!
>
> Winding our way between the barricades, we tried to stick to the beaten path since Soviet soldiers had warned that the roads still weren't completely cleared of mines. We took ul. Opolska and ul. Kościuszki into the city. Wrocław was in flames, the streets covered with debris from the burning buildings. We could hear the crack and bang of ammunition detonating in the fire. We lost our way in the burning streets and meandered until we could go no farther. We turned back. Not a soul to be seen. After an hour's journey through the smoke and flames,

we landed at the Soviets' primary command post for the city, at number 1 Nankiera Square, opposite the Ursuline church.[22]

On the advice of the Soviet city commander, the Polish advance division looked for quarters around Waterlooplatz, a district northwest of Cathedral Island that had suffered comparatively little damage. Three large apartment buildings were confiscated at Blücherstrasse 23–27. The German residents were given twenty minutes to vacate the premises. Only the owner of the building at number 27 was allowed to stay. He ran a bakery on the ground floor and agreed to provide the Polish officials with fresh bread in the future. At around 6:00 pm, after guards had secured the occupied buildings, a small ceremony was held, during which the Polish coat of arms was affixed to Blücherstrasse 27, the first provisional residence of the Polish municipal administration, and the red-and-white Polish flag was raised.[23] It was a symbol that marked the end of Breslau and the beginning of Wrocław.

In the following days Drobner and Kulczyński arrived with the rest of the two operative groups.[24] Kulczyński recalled a trip that was adventurous given the demolished roads and the fact that no one was familiar with the place:

> It was eleven o'clock in the morning when we drove to the city via Herdain (Gaj). Our first task was to seek out Dr. Knot's group. Our choice of entry points turned out to be less than fortunate. The road was blocked by barricades, ruins that had collapsed onto the roadway, and fires.
>
> We got out of the car and dispatched scouts in three directions to find a way through, while we ourselves had a look about the empty streets. The day's amazing spring weather stood in odd contrast to the view surrounding us. Everywhere destruction, deathly silence, a void. Except for, here and there, small groups of plunderers wandering about. After a bit, our reconnaissance scouts returned and reported that entering the city by car was out of the question. Except for one of the patrols, which kept us waiting a while. He showed up only around 3 pm with the news that Dr. Knot's group was on the other side of the city. There was a way through, but we would have to hurry because any minute the fires and collapsing buildings might block the road. . . .
>
> Our driver, however, who was guided by pilots running ahead, took the impediments cheerfully and emerged in the area around the central train station, where it was easier to move about freely. We crossed the

narrow streets of the Old Town one after the other, passed by the bridge across the Oder, and ended up on place Świętego Mateusza, where we found our friends, who had been waiting for us since the day before.[25]

Blücherstrasse and the adjacent streets became the nucleus of Polish Wrocław, an island of Poles amid a city otherwise still predominantly German. In order to accommodate the growing administrative staff, additional buildings were gradually confiscated. A schoolhouse on Rosenstrasse at the corner of Matthiasstrasse served as the first provisional municipal office building. The first citizens' militia was established at the intersection of Blücherstrasse and Matthiasstrasse; the operative group of the Polish Workers' Party sent from Warsaw took up its residence nearby. On May 16, the first Polish post office opened at Matthiasstrasse 47;[26] the regional telephone and telegraph office was located at number 49. The first Polish stores also opened in this district and, before the legendary black market arose on the former Kaiserstrasse, on grounds that had been cleared for a runway, trade in everything imaginable blossomed on Matthiasstrasse. Even Germans came to trade their valuables for foodstuffs, thereby providing an important stimulus to trade in the Polish district.[27]

Soon the core of the Polish settlement was served by the nearby Nadodrze train station (Odertorbahnhof), the first station in Wrocław reopened after the war. Numerous railroad trains bringing Polish settlers to the western territories terminated at Nadodrze station; for many thousands of Poles, the station's brick reception building served as the entrance to the city. Many of the new arrivals settled in the immediate vicinity of the station, an area where large numbers of other Poles lived and a variety of Polish institutions had been established. St. Boniface, the first church to hold Catholic Mass in Polish after the war, was a stone's throw away from the station. Curiously the Nadodrze district, which by happenstance became the first Polish neighborhood in postwar Wrocław, had been called the "Polish side" in the Middle Ages due to its primarily Polish-speaking inhabitants.[28] At that time something of a Polish refuge, it now served as a bridgehead for taking hold of the entire city. Apartments in the Nadodrze district soon became scarce, and the growing number of Polish settlers began to take control of other parts of the city. The administrative center shifted to the Old Town, where Polish authorities gradually repaired and occupied the public buildings in which the German municipal administration had once resided. In this way Polish authorities demonstrated their claim to represent all inhabitants of Wrocław, not merely its Polish residents.

The first session of the city's Polish municipal government took place in Drobner's private apartment at Blücherstrasse 27 on the evening of May 10, 1945. At the meeting, members of the new city government identified the most urgent tasks for the coming days and divided up responsibilities among themselves. The first order of business was to explore the city, since most of the staff was unfamiliar with Wrocław, and no one knew the full extent of the war damage. Food warehouses and all other valuables necessary for reconstruction and the establishment of the municipal administration had to be located and then protected from plunderers. Particularly pressing was setting up a fire department to combat the fires that raged throughout the city, threatening an ever-growing number of buildings.[29]

Before Drobner's people could begin organizing Wrocław's urban life, they would have to ensure their own survival amid the ruins. Indeed it took some time before the new administration was able to administer much of anything beyond its own needs. It had to feed and house its growing staff. As buses and streetcars were still not operating, it had to find vehicles ranging from bicycles to trucks so that its representatives could move about the city. Finally, city employees had to locate usable office space and equip it with furniture, typewriters, telephones, paper, and office supplies drawn from what stores remained in the war-ravaged city.

During these initial weeks, improvisation and informal solutions characterized the work of the municipal administration. Not surprisingly, these activities were rarely recorded in official documents such as assembly minutes or decrees.[30] Information about the beginnings of the Polish administration is more readily found in the memoirs of the "pioneers"—as the Polish activists of the first hour were soon called, as if they had colonized stretches of uncivilized land. The first regular, recorded plenary session of the administration took place on June 16, almost six weeks after the arrival of the advance guard.[31] This meeting represented a turning point: Numerous leading positions in the city were reassigned. Most significantly, Drobner stepped down as mayor. Presumably he was dismissed, despite his indisputable service in establishing the Polish administration in Wrocław, because he had acted too independently to suit the government in Warsaw. He may also have been replaced simply to balance power between the PPS and the PPR, as the PPS had up to now occupied the two most important posts in Lower Silesia: the mayor of Wrocław and the district plenipotentiary and future voivode.[32] In any case, Aleksander Wachniewski, a member of the PPR, succeeded Drobner. Commensurate with the prevailing state of affairs, the municipal administration honored the services of its first mayor through a donation in kind—five liters of vodka, 220 pounds of white sugar, 220 pounds of flour, 30 tins of canned goods and compote, cocoa, coffee, three yards of fabric, a piano, two divans, crystal glasses, porcelain, panes of glass, cooking utensils, an electric iron, a blanket, a radio, a sewing machine, towels, and linens.[33]

Municipal authorities and Kulczyński's science and cultural group were not the only representatives of the Polish state in Wrocław at the time. Immediately after the end of the siege, a plethora of officials connected to other institutions, as well as delegations from a number of ministries and large industrial works, appeared in Wrocław and opened branch offices in an attempt to secure influence and at least some of their assets in the city. Because there was initially no clear-cut demarcation of authority, representatives of the different institutions repeatedly clashed over areas of responsibility, especially when larger assets were at stake.[34] Particularly heated were the disputes between the municipal administration and the Economic Committee of the Council of Ministers (KERM), whose operative group of more than twenty people had also arrived in Wrocław on May 9 and had moved into the building formerly housing the Chamber of Commerce and Industry at Graupenstrasse 15 as well as the nearby Ballestrem Palace on Wallstrasse. The government in Warsaw had granted extensive authority to this operative group by making it responsible for securing and appropriating all the industrial facilities in Wrocław. Warsaw's move, however, did not sit well with Dobner, at that time still mayor of the city. He wanted to place the entire industrial potential of Wrocław under the supervision of the municipal government and had berated the delegates of the economic committee who thwarted this plan as "partisans" and "usurpers."[35] The dispute proved to be moot, at least in part. By the time it was settled, the Red Army had long since dismantled many of the factories and shipped them to the Soviet Union.[36] The actual rulers of Wrocław were not the representatives of the Polish state but the commanders of the Red Army.

Poles and Russians—A Secret Hostility

When they assumed control of the eastern German territories, Polish authorities were concerned about how the German population would react to the appearance of Polish officials and settlers. In light of Polish resistance to German occupation, they probably assumed that the Germans would also oppose a foreign power. They expected that scattered soldiers would engage in sabotage operations, that underground "werewolf" groups would fight against the establishment of a Polish state in the western territories, or that there would be at least general recalcitrance on the part of Germans toward Polish decrees. They were surprised to find that the remaining German population met Poles with indifference, apathy, and, in many cases, submissiveness. Situation reports repeatedly mentioned the existence of a German underground. Bolesław Drobner, for example, claimed in May 1945 that thousands of armed German soldiers were holding out in the cellars of the Wrocław central train station.[37] Interestingly enough, despite the many rumors there are hardly any documented cases of acts of German resistance after the war.[38] In this respect the new Polish western territories were no different than other occupied German territories in 1945. After subjecting the world to six years of war, after fighting to the bitter end even when it was clear they could no longer win, the Germans in the end laid down their arms and bowed to the will of the occupying powers. Contrary to expectations, there was hardly any open resistance to the occupying powers on the territory of the former German Reich.[39]

In contrast, serious problems developed between the Polish civil administration and the Soviet armed forces in the western territories—problems that were either trivialized or ignored in Polish accounts prior to 1989, but which have since drawn the attention of Polish historians.[40] Although Poles and Soviets had officially been allies and comrades-in-arms in the war against Germany, their relations at the end of the war were marked by mistrust, contempt, and hostility. Most Poles regarded Russia—which they equated with the Soviet Union—as the state power that had oppressed the Polish people for more than a century during the partition of Poland and from which Poles had been freed only a generation earlier. Fresh in their minds also was the association of the Red Army with the Soviet invasion of eastern Poland in September 1939, the terror of the Soviet occupation of the annexed Polish territories, the mass deportations to Siberia, the execution of thousands of Polish officers who had become Soviet prisoners of war in 1939, and finally the absence of any assistance during the Warsaw uprising in the fall of 1944, when the Red Army had looked on from across the Vistula while German occupation forces brutally crushed the uprising and razed Warsaw to the ground. And now here again were Soviet soldiers acting essentially as an occupying force, installing a Soviet-type communist regime in Poland and supporting Polish communists in their battle against all potentially anti-communist forces in the country.

To make matters worse, many Russians also had negative recollections and stereotypes about Poles. In the nineteenth century, Russians regarded those Poles who were Russian citizens as rebellious and ungrateful. In their view, the Poles had repeatedly risen up against Russian rule despite the autonomy rights the czar had generously granted to his kingdom of Poland in 1815. Unforgotten also was Piłsudski's attack on Soviet Russia in the 1920s, which Soviet elites perceived as an act of counterrevolution against the still fragile Bolshevik government. In fact, the only point of agreement between Poles and Russians was the conviction of each that their respective side was vastly superior culturally.[41] With their mutual relations burdened by such memories and preconceptions, Poles and Soviets began to encounter each other on a daily basis in Poland's western territories.

The provisional Polish government was a Soviet creation that served to implement the objectives of Soviet policies in Poland and to bring about a socialist state allied with the Soviet Union. There was also agreement between Warsaw and Moscow about the necessity to swiftly establish a Polish administration in the western territories and to push forward the integration of the former German territories within Poland. The political objectives shared by the leaders of the communist parties in the Soviet Union and Poland did not mean, however, that the Soviet military administration and the Polish civil administration worked in concert. While the actions of Soviet and Polish representatives at regional and local levels in the western territories did not always correspond to the wishes of their respective governments, conflicts on the national level about how socialist Poland should be established further complicated Polish-Soviet relations. Despite the fact that the communist-dominated Polish government was dependent on Moscow, there was the circle around Władysław Gomułka, whose members, unlike head of state Bolesław Bierut, were communists but not necessarily loyal to the Soviet Union. Until 1948, when total compliance with the Soviet line was enforced and the years of Polish Stalinism began, Gomułka and his supporters called for a certain amount of Polish independence from Moscow.

The asymmetry of power, however, left the Poles little maneuvering room. Especially when it came to the western territories, the Polish administration could do little more than hope for the benevolence of Soviet military commanders. On April 17, 1945, Piaskowski gave the county plenipotentiaries of his region the following instructions:

> Immediately after arriving in their jurisdictions, all district plenipotentiaries are to report to local [Soviet] military commanders, present them with proof of their power of authority, and, invoking the order of Lt. Col. Repin, Director of the Military Command Post of the First Ukrainian Front, of April 10, 1945 to: 1) inform them of the adoption of civil authority; 2) request the swiftest possible transfer of: a) all facilities for the production of foodstuffs . . . , b) all foodstuff storage facilities that are not needed by the Soviet army, c) storage facilities for textiles and accessories.
>
> At the same time, the commanders are to be solicited for the allotment of: a) typewriters, b) the largest possible number of small arms.
>
> I emphasize that the manner in which the plenipotentiaries' approach all of these tasks and their ability to generate good relations with the military commanders are crucial to obtaining the desired results in these tasks as well as a number of others to be undertaken by the plenipotentiaries, who will very often have to avail themselves of the kindness and assistance of the military commanders.[42]

The great emphasis Piaskowski placed on relations with Soviet commanders reflected the actual situation the plenipotentiaries faced. During this initial phase they were representatives of a Polish state whose authorities existed solely on paper. As long as the administrative staffs were small and the Polish police forces insignificant, the local Red Army commanders alone constituted the backbone of the plenipotentiaries' authority. Only they had at their disposal security forces sufficient to command respect.

In addition, they possessed motorized vehicles and means of communication and had already assumed control of a significant portion of buildings, food storehouses, large farms, and industrial complexes even before the Poles arrived. It was up to the plenipotentiaries to persuade local Soviet authorities to allow Polish officials to share control of these resources. They had no legal recourse since executive power and thus supreme decision-making authority lay solely with the Soviet commanders as representatives of the occupation forces. The Soviet State Defense Committee (GOKO) resolution of February 20, 1945, did instruct Soviet commanders to turn administration over to the Polish authorities as quickly as possible. Since no date was mentioned in the resolution, however, it was largely up to the commanders to determine when the transfer would actually occur and how much they would support the Polish civil administration prior to it.

Disputes about former German property, especially valuable industrial facilities and infrastructure, became a key point of conflict between Polish authorities and the Red Army. Lack of discipline within the Red Army was also a serious problem in the western territories. Although Soviet forces were not solely responsible for the precarious security conditions in the territories after the war, they do appear to have made a significant contribution to the lawlessness and daily violence.[43] In December 1945, Piaskowski reported to Warsaw:

> Incessant assault and robbery by marauding Soviet soldiers on streets, in trains, and in people's homes—often with the use of weapons— sometimes involving murder, burglary, forcible appropriation or theft of cattle from their stalls, of horses and cattle from pastures, arbitrary requisitions, and evacuation of residents from their homes, etc. The general feeling is that everyone is waiting impatiently for the army to leave. . . .
>
> It is characteristic that wherever Soviet troops withdraw from an area, conditions improve immediately; and wherever they take control of an area, the level of security immediately declines.[44]

The districts of Wrocław in which Soviet units were stationed were considered the most dangerous in the city and in many cases were totally unsuitable for Polish settlement. Members of the Red Army occasionally robbed even railway transports carrying Polish settlers to Wrocław. These incidents were not always the work of marauding soldiers as the Soviet side apologetically liked to argue, but were often carried out by regular units led by their officers.[45] To the dismay of the Poles, the Polish militia's hands were tied in such cases because soldiers of the Red Army were subject solely to Soviet jurisdiction. Thus the Polish side had no option but to complain to Soviet commanders and hope that they would take action against lack of discipline within their ranks.

It was particularly bitter for Polish officials that the Soviet military, "who often consider themselves the sole masters in the area and hinder the execution of orders issued by the provincial command of the citizens' militia or other authorities,"[46] continually undermined the authority of the Polish state. Even senior dignitaries were not immune to such abuse. Friedrich Jerrig reported on Wrocław in 1949:

> The newly created office of the mayor of the second capital city of Poland is tied to a symbolic tragedy that says more about the new Poland than all the political tracts. Drobner, a tried and true socialist from the PPS camp . . . was beaten by the general of the Russian occupation forces when he tried to object to the continuous plundering by Russian soldiers in the city recovered for Poland. A symbol or an aberration? In any case, a misjudgment of the situation after the war.[47]

The establishment of a Polish civil administration was not tantamount to an actual assumption of power. Also, in Wrocław, the highest authority continued to lie with the Soviet city commander, who only gradually transferred responsibilities to the Polish municipal government. This weakness of Polish officials in their dealings with the Soviets was a problem, not least because the Polish administration had to be able to exercise its authority vis-à-vis the German population of the city. Many Germans in Wrocław initially viewed the existence of a Polish city government as a curiosity that had emerged from the chaos of the collapse and did not believe that it would last long. They had to be convinced that the Polish mayor and his agencies represented Wrocław's future. This was made all the more difficult by the manifest weakness of a Polish administration that lacked a sufficiently large and qualified staff, was unfamiliar with the city, and was unable to provide its representatives with the necessary equipment. In the first weeks and months even senior officials were dispatched through the city by bicycle or on foot, and civil servants were dressed in makeshift retailored German uniforms, so that the Polish administration had to struggle to be taken at all seriously.[48]

When attempts are made to assert authority in the absence of any real power, theatrical shows of strength often play a crucial role. Units of the Second Polish Army under General Karol Świerczewski had participated in storming the fortified city during the siege, only to be withdrawn in early March 1945 by the Soviet supreme command and redeployed beyond the Oder-Neisse line in the offensives against Dresden and Berlin. Thus it was exclusively Soviet troops who took control of Wrocław on May 7. But just three weeks after the capitulation of the city, Polish municipal leaders restaged the taking of Wrocław, this time by Polish soldiers. A victory parade with units of the Second Polish Army was held in the city on May 26, 1945. The mayor proudly narrated:

> Poles!
> Following its victorious march to Berlin and the destruction of the Hitlerist hydra, the victorious Polish Army returns to peacetime quarters in our city and takes up guard over the Oder. . . .
> Poles!
> Do your national duty by coming out in large numbers to the site of the festivities, so that you can pay tribute to the army as it returns bearing victory banners from Berlin, Dresden, and other German cities.[49]

The Polish units marched down Schweidnitzer Strasse through Wrocław's Old Town before arriving at the former Schlossplatz—which had been renamed pl. Wolności (Liberty Square) shortly before this—where the celebrations reached their brilliant culmination. The municipal government and its honorary guests assembled on a festively decorated dais erected before the ruins of the Hohenzollern Palace. As the troops marched past the dais, saluting soldiers and the horses of the Ulans trampled on swastika flags that had been found in the Wrocław town hall and that Drobner had saved specifically for this occasion.[50]

This victory parade, however, did little to alter power relations in Wrocław. Although the offices of most local Soviet commanders in the western territories were dissolved by July 1945, they remained in place along the main transportation routes and in the larger cities, including Wrocław.[51] The municipal government thus had to accept an extended Soviet presence in the city. Soviet military authorities caused resentment not only through their mere presence, but also through their treatment of Polish officials. They often made no effort

Polish units took part in the assault on "Fortress Breslau." By order of the Soviet Supreme command, however, they were reassigned before the fortress surrendered and thus deprived of the triumph of marching into the conquered city. On May 26, 1945, a Polish victory parade staged this symbolically important but unhistorical event. The photograph shows soldiers of the Polish 2nd Army passing the honorary tribune on pl. Wolności. Courtesy of the City Museum of Wrocław.

to provide even a semblance of support for the Polish municipal government in its struggle for authority and for acceptance as the sole representative of future political power in Wrocław. This was evident even in minor issues of merely symbolic importance. While Polish authorities were extremely careful to use only the official Polish name of the city, the Soviet military administration continued to speak of "Breslau" and even had new Soviet seals made with the old German city name; alternately they used ludicrous variations of the city's Polish name, such as "Wraclaw" and "Wroclau."

Particularly irritating for Polish authorities was the fact that the Germans had little difficulty eluding them, so long as they managed to get their names onto the long lists of people who worked for the Red Army. Once Germans were listed as employees of the Soviet forces, Polish officials could no longer touch them, could not commission them to perform any kind of labor, and could not, for the time being, evacuate them; in fact they had to be issued food ration coupons.[52] A telling testimony of the relations between the Polish civil administration and the Soviet military authorities are the certificates through which Germans proved to Polish authorities that they worked for the Soviets. Often these certificates were rather informal documents, sometimes no more than a scrap of paper scribbled in barely legible Cyrillic letters. It was only the Soviet stamp that made them official, and even this was occasionally missing, so that at times a Russian signature was sufficient to demonstrate to the Polish municipal government the narrow confines of its own authority.[53]

In recent works, Polish historians have judged harshly the actions of the Red Army in the western territories, which is understandable given that the subject was taboo for many years. Nevertheless, we should bear in mind that at a time when Polish security forces were still being established, it was the Soviet presence that gave Polish state institutions the authority they needed, in particular vis-à-vis the German population. One must therefore ask whether the task of establishing a bare minimum of public order during this initial phase would not have been even more difficult without the Soviet presence.

RUSSIANS AND GERMANS—AN UNSETTLING FRIENDSHIP

Soviet military forces and German civilians eventually came to a better understanding than what could have been expected in light of the behavior of Soviet soldiers immediately after the siege.[54] When Soviet soldiers entered Breslau, the Germans who were still there became the object of their rage, revenge, and brutalization, a consequence in part of the long years of German warfare and occupation in the East, in which large parts of the Soviet Union had been razed to the ground and several million civilians and soldiers killed. Historian Norman Naimark has described in detail the atrocities that occurred in the Soviet occupation zones in Germany, including mass rape, executions, robbery, and plundering by triumphant soldiers, arbitrary internment in labor camps, and deportation of those deemed fit to work to the Soviet Union.[55] Such acts of violence also set the tone in Breslau in the first weeks after the Soviets took the city.

> The Russians entered on the night of May 6. . . . Masses of carriages pulled by small horses, the noise of the loudspeakers playing waltzes by Strauss, hooting and shrieking, and the marching troops made the city seem frightfully turbulent. It was given over to plundering, which began

immediately in the worst way and lasted for weeks with fires, rapes, and multiple murders. . . . The terrified people fled through breaks in the walls between houses that had been made as escape routes in anticipation of bombings and tried to hide. Especially at night horrible rapes occurred, often in the most perverse forms.[56]

The German population faced the Soviet soldiers from a position of helplessness and with no legal recourse. Complaints were initially of little use. When Joachim Konrad, the dean of Breslau, went to Soviet city commander Lyapunov and requested that measures be taken against rape, the latter is reported to have said, "Soldiers are soldiers! But can you name a case where children have been hurt? . . . I can name many cases where the SS beat children to death in Russia."[57]

The behavior of Soviet soldiers was not solely a consequence of the brutality with which the Wehrmacht and the Red Army had fought against each other (and the enemy's civilian population) over the previous years. It was also a result of Soviet propaganda, which had intentionally incited hatred of the enemy to motivate Soviet troops in their struggle against the German invaders and fueled their desire for revenge—insofar as German troops did not ensure this themselves. Notorious are Ilya Ehrenburg's articles in Soviet front newspapers. One of the most important writers in the Soviet Union and greatly respected in the West, Ehrenburg called for reprisals and violence, using slogans such as "Death to the Germans," "Nothing makes us happier than German corpses," and "We will beat back the attack of the handkerchiefs behind which the wounded beast will seek protection."[58]

When German capitulation was imminent, however, Soviet propaganda took a sharp turn. If hatred previously had to be inflamed to fortify the will to fight, this same hatred now impeded attempts by Soviet leaders in German territories occupied by the Red Army to maintain discipline among the troops, to prevent the destruction of material assets, and to establish a functioning occupation regime. An article published in *Pravda* on April 14, 1945, publicly accused Ehrenburg of simplification. Suddenly the need to distinguish between fascists and the rest of the German population was crucial. Stalin was repeatedly quoted as saying, "The Hitlers come and go; the German people, the German state, remain." Ehrenburg's articles ceased to appear in the military press.[59]

But spirits long aroused could not be quickly laid to rest by altered propaganda. A change in actual behavior would depend on the speed and decisiveness with which local Soviet military commanders acted against their own soldiers to protect the German civilian population. In Wrocław the violent excesses of marauding Soviet soldiers abated after several weeks. Nonetheless, the situation continued to be precarious for the city's inhabitants:

> One should not imagine that after the greatest horror had been overcome things had by any means normalized in the summer of 1945 and the winter of 1945–46. . . . German passersby could expect to be rounded up and deported in trucks to perform clearance work for days and weeks. Or there was a banging on the door and you were ordered, along with terrible insults about Hitler swine, to relinquish your apartment within an hour and to leave almost everything behind. Blackmail was practiced with the coarsest of lies and accusations. Criminal elements as well as marauding militiamen beat terrified people with rubber truncheons, placed them up against the wall and executed them or threatened to do so, confiscated their property, and disappeared again into the darkness. Complaints to authorities were almost always in vain. Especially on the outskirts of the city, entire robber gangs camped out in basements.[60]

Relations between the German civilian population and Soviet soldiers, however, improved rapidly—to the surprise and even dismay of the Poles. Despite the suffering that Germans and Soviets had inflicted on each other during the war, mutual hatred gave way to the respect that had characterized German-Russian relations before the Nazis—with their rabid anti-Bolshevism—came to power.[61] Nothing affected the prestige of the Polish municipal government more acutely than the fact that the Soviet city commander allowed, parallel to the Polish administration, the establishment of a German administration headed by German mayors. This coexistence of two administrations was by no means unique to Wrocław. During the first months after the war, German local administrations existed alongside Polish authorities throughout the western territories. Especially in areas where Germans continued to constitute the majority of the population for an extended time, Soviet commanders were happy to fall back on their support for pragmatic reasons. They permitted German administrations, without worrying too much about Polish sensitivities.[62]

The German postwar administration in Wrocław had no connections with the prewar municipal government. The latter was destroyed during the siege of the city, its end symbolically culminating in the public execution of the city's deputy mayor. After that, only the apparatus of the Nazi Gauleiter and the city's military commander had ruled over the collapsing city. When these were also dissolved with the signing of the capitulation, power was transferred to the Soviet military administration, which was interested primarily in supplying the Soviet forces as well as dismantling German facilities and recruiting German labor. Beyond this, Soviet military commanders had little interest in the daily affairs of the city. In establishing a civil administration the Soviets thus found it useful to draw on the assistance of local Germans, so long as they appeared to be politically reliable.

The search for trustworthy German personnel was facilitated by the fact that antifascist opposition groups had already opposed National Socialist rule during the siege in Wrocław, even engaging in sporadic acts of sabotage. Among the various groups, two were particularly active after the capitulation: the Antifascist Freedom Movement headed by Hermann Hartmann and the German Union of Antifascists led by Paul Marzoll.[63] Both organizations were comprised largely of former members of the German Communist Party (KPD) and the Social Democratic Party (SPD); they were happy to provide support for both Soviet and Polish authorities, not only by assuming administrative tasks but also by searching for war criminals and representatives of the Nazi state. Many of these once-persecuted socialists and communists appear to have taken the search for Nazis quite seriously, which made it all the more bitter when it was later discovered that numerous Nazis had gone into hiding in antifascist organizations.

The Soviet city commander limited the authority of the German administration strictly to the German population. The German administration was responsible for registration and records, civil affairs, locating and allocating housing and food, tending to social welfare, commissioning citizens for work deployment, supervising clearance work, and maintaining order and cleanliness in those city districts populated primarily by Germans.[64] For the latter responsibilities, even the establishment of a kind of police organization was permitted, which, as in the Third Reich, was called the Order Police (Ordnungspolizei).[65] While isolated problems did arise—for example, when the Antifascist Freedom Movement in Wrocław-Sępolno called for "all Jews, half-Jews, Poles, and citizens of any nationality" to report to the German employment office[66]—the German administrations generally acted responsibly and did not exceed their authority, vis-à-vis the Polish civil administration as well as the Soviet. In the initial weeks and months after the war, the Polish administration in Wrocław was hardly in a position to govern the city as a whole anyway. In this respect it could only have welcomed support from German agencies, to the extent that these acted loyally and restricted their activities to German inhabitants.

The problem lay not at a practical but on a symbolic level. The mere existence of German authorities pointed to the fact that the political future of Wrocław had not yet been definitively resolved. As long as the Soviet commander supported the coexistence of two administrative apparatuses, the rule of the Polish mayor was hardly less provisional than that of the German mayor. The German administration was a visible reminder of the possibility that Wrocław might remain German, and thus it challenged the authority of the Polish mayor. The fact that the Soviet commander in Wrocław also held this view is evident in his reaction to the outcome of the Potsdam Conference. Immediately after the conference that decided Wrocław's future, Lyapunov paid an official visit to the Polish municipal government and ceremoniously presented it with a parchment document declaring the transfer of administrative authority to the Polish mayor.[67] The German administration was dissolved without delay, as were the antifascist organizations, by a decree of the Polish government on August 16, 1945.[68] In recognition of their services, the members and the staff of the German postwar administration of Wrocław were treated much better than other Germans during their evacuation. Most of them could leave by the end of 1945. They were informed of the precise evacuation date earlier than usual, were permitted to take significantly more luggage with them, and were taken to the West in a special transport, for which the Soviet commander's office made its own vehicles available.[69]

The three-month intermezzo of parallel Polish and German administrations in Wrocław thus came to an end, and the Polish municipal government officially became the sole governing body in the city. This did not, however, prevent the German population from continuing to regard Soviet soldiers as the actual rulers. A large number of Germans worked for the Soviet armed forces stationed in Wrocław, and many as a result enjoyed the esteem and even patronage of Soviet officers, who occasionally protected them from orders issued by Polish authorities. As early as May 1945, Drobner complained about the pro-German attitude of the Soviet military administration:

> [O]ne notices on the part of Soviet authorities a willingness to adopt a significantly more liberal position in relation to the Germans, which in some cases leads to a two-pronged policy and precipitates undesirable incidents, such as when an industrial plant is assigned to German management and the hitherto Polish managers are forced to leave immediately.[70]

A report of March 1946 by the Wrocław provincial administration struck a similar tone:

> 1. Germans view the Red Army as the principal cause of their misfortune, and their feelings in this regard need no further commentary. 2. An effect of the pliability of the German character, their toadying to the powers-that-be, and their eagerness to provide various services (e.g., prostitution) is that Germans pretend that they had nothing to do with Hitlerism and that their attitude toward the USSR and its citizens is more than congenial. This leads some leaders of the Red Army as well as lower-ranking soldiers to defend the supposed interests of certain Germans, which in turn provokes bitterness among the Polish population.[71]

Germans regularly filed complaints with Soviet authorities regarding measures taken by the Polish civil administration. To the annoyance of the Polish side, these were frequently successful and led to Soviet intervention. In this way the Soviet military became a kind of protective power for the Germans, often demonstrating greater understanding for German requests than for the interests of the Polish municipal government.[72] Soviet military patrols repeatedly caused difficulties for Polish authorities when Germans were supposed to evacuate their apartments or be transferred to the west. Occasionally they even ordered that entire operations be halted and that Germans be allowed to remain in their homes. According to a report about an evacuation operation in mid-1946:

> The Soviet soldiers did not permit the Germans to be removed from their apartments, claiming that they were their friends and worked for

them. As a result, there were incidents with the Soviets, who went so far as to assault Polish soldiers and officers. Shots were even fired, and one member of the evacuation commission was injured. As the train was standing in the station, there was another round of clashes, during which a commanding officer escorting the convoy was injured. The protected and locked apartments were broken into and plundered by Soviet soldiers. . . . It must be emphasized that these acts of violence were committed not by marauders but by soldiers quartered in Leśnica.[73]

Reports of this kind were submitted from all over the western territories to the government in Warsaw. In response Władysław Gomułka complained in a letter dated January 10, 1946, to the Soviet marshals Georgy Zhukov and Konstantin Rokossovsky, as well as to the Soviet ambassador in Warsaw, Victor Lebedev. Gomułka wrote that the coexistence of Poles and Soviets in the western territories was not proceeding "harmoniously," that the attitude of the Red Army toward the Polish population was "frequently hostile," whereas several of the Soviet military commanders had implemented "pro-German policies." Gomułka proposed a strict barracking of Soviet soldiers and a prohibition on private quarters, "which would prevent fraternizing with the Germans and favoring them over the Polish population; on the one hand, this type of conduct generated understandable resentment within the Polish community, and, on the other, it incited German arrogance and provoked resistance to the orders of the Polish authorities."[74] Complaints of this kind had no resounding success. The problematic three-way relationship between Germans, Soviets, and Poles in the western territories was not resolved to the Poles' satisfaction until the German population was evacuated.

Given their precarious situation, it is not surprising that Germans sought to exploit tensions between Poles and Soviets in order to increase their personal safety through friendly relations with Soviet soldiers. Polish reactions were particularly fierce when it was suspected that Germans had intentionally exploited their contacts with Soviet soldiers in order to evade Polish regulations or to behave condescendingly toward Poles.[75] According to an inspection report for Lower Silesia issued in the summer of 1945, although Germans were also subjected to attacks by Soviet soldiers, "they attempted to win favors through their women. . . . They feel confident in showing an attitude to

Poles that is volatile, even brutal, because they have a Soviet soldier's mistress in their family."[76]

It is hardly astonishing that in the Polish western territories—where the Germans' circumstances were significantly more difficult than in the Allied occupation zones in Germany—the phenomenon of the "Fräulein" developed; that is, that German women entered into relationships with Allied soldiers. The numerous Polish reports about such relationships with Soviet officers, which allowed German women to ignore decrees of the Polish administration, at times go to extremes: "It's not that German women are getting raped by Red Army soldiers, it's the Red Army soldiers who are being hounded by German prostitutes."[77] Such statements cannot be taken at face value, of course, but are instead expressions of the bitterness of Poles at the fact that Germans got along better with Russians after the war than Poles did. From the Polish perspective, the speedy rapprochement between Russians and Germans recalled the ominous historical tradition of Russians and Germans repeatedly coming to terms with each other at the expense of Poland—most recently in the Hitler-Stalin pact. Against the backdrop of these historical experiences, it is understandable that Poles were extremely thin-skinned, at times even panicky about German-Russian fraternizations on Polish territory. This sudden rapprochement made the Polish-Soviet friendship propagated by the communists appear all the more farcical.

The Patriotic Reorganization of the Church

In addition to institutions of the Polish state, the church was also a crucial factor in expanding Poland to the Oder-Neisse line. Drobner's operative group included two Polish clergymen, the Catholic priest Kazimierz Lagosz from the Lwów archbishopric and Wiktor Niemczyk, who had been a Protestant minister in Krakow and a theology professor at the University of Warsaw before the war. Lagosz and Niemczyk assumed responsibility for the pastoral supervision of the Polish parishes emerging in Breslau and took the first steps in establishing Polish ecclesiastic organizations. In May 1945 the city of Breslau, of course, was not a tabula rasa with regard to canonical affairs but rather continued to be anchored in the structures of the German Protestant and Catholic churches. Ernst Hornig assumed the leadership in reorganizing the German Protestant Church in Silesia after the war.[78] He had remained in the city during the siege and headed the Confessing Church, a Protestant organization opposed to the efforts of the "German Christians" who wanted the church to toe the Nazi line. In May 1945, the Soviet city commander officially recognized the church represented by Ernst Hornig as the Church of Upper and Lower Silesia and permitted it to continue its pastoral activities. The Catholic Archbishopric of Breslau, which in addition to the Breslau diocese also included the dioceses of Berlin, Ermland and the Schneidemühl prelature, was still relatively functional. All of the bishoprics were filled, and the Breslau cathedral chapter was able to perform its duties despite reductions in personnel. Only Cardinal Adolf Bertram, the 86-year-old prince-bishop of Breslau, who had left the city for Johannesberg Palace, his summer residence in the Bohemian part of the diocese, did not return to Breslau following the war.

The meeting of Polish and German Protestants in Wrocław was relatively unproblematic. The two groups shared a religion but belonged to different institutions, the Protestant Church in Germany and the Evangelical-Augsburg Church in Poland. When Niemczyk began to set up ecclesiastical organizations in Wrocław, he did not become entangled in conflicts with his fellow German Protestants. He interacted with them—as Joachim Konrad, the last German city dean in Breslau and minister of St. Elizabeth's Church, recalled—with a certain reserve but ultimately with benevolence.[79] The two church organizations began simply to coexist, with each one responsible for the supervision of its respective members. The only issue that had to be addressed was the use of church buildings and parish houses. Because Protestants comprised only a tiny minority of the Polish population and thus had quite limited needs in terms of space, the problem could be readily resolved. Niemczyk established his official residence in St. Elizabeth's, the most prestigious and intact city church, but permitted German parish life to continue. It was thanks to him that German services took place there until the summer of 1946. Konrad delivered the last German sermon in the church on June 30, 1946. A few days later, St. Elizabeth's became the Catholic garrison church.[80] Polish Protestants had to make do with the small Court Church on ul. Kazimierza Wielkiego.

As a result of the mass evacuation of Germans that began in early 1946, however, German Protestant parish life throughout the western territories came to an end. In September 1946, the Polish government officially declared that the German Protestant Church in Silesia no longer existed; German Protestants still living in Poland were assigned to the Evangelical-Augsburg Church in Poland. In agreement with the Protestant Church in Germany, the Polish church assumed the supervision of German Protestants in Poland, since a continuation of the remaining German parishes could be achieved only using Polish ministers.

At the same time the expropriation of church assets for the benefit of the Polish state was formally executed by government decree. Most of the formerly Protestant churches were left for the Catholic Church to use.[81] After the confiscation of its church building, the parish of German Protestants in Wrocław (which still exists today) was initially given only a temporary site. In 1958, however, the parish was granted access to the rebuilt St. Christopher's Church in the city center, where—an irony of history—the Polish Protestant minority used to congregate in the period between the two world wars.

The transition within the Catholic Church, by contrast, was conflict-laden and complicated by the terms of canon law.[82] A peaceful coexistence of German and Polish Catholic Church structures was not possible since German and Polish Catholics were not only members of the same denomination but also of the same religious institution. Thus a Polish ecclesiastical organization could not simply be juxtaposed to the existing Archbishopric of Breslau. The leaders of the Polish church had to find a solution, grounded in canon law and agreeable to the Vatican, that would accommodate in ecclesiastical structures the shift of national borders that had been established de facto but not yet recognized by international law. They could be certain, however, that the existing Breslau curia, comprised of German clergymen, would do everything possible to preserve the canonical status quo.

When Cardinal Bertram died on June 6, 1945, the Breslau cathedral chapter immediately assembled to select a successor. It did not want to give the Polish side time to use the vacancy of the Breslau bishop's seat as an opportunity to intervene. On July 16, the former cathedral dean Prelate Ferdinand Piontek was elected chapter vicar in absentia. The cathedral chapter thus followed neither the wishes of the mayor nor the appeals of Katowice Bishop Stanisław Adamski to appoint a Polish clergyman to head the bishopric.[83] However, the German capitulars did accommodate the Polish side insofar as Piontek, the man they had selected, came from Upper Silesia and spoke fluent Polish. He was thus also able to care for Polish clergy and members of his diocese. The leaders of the Breslau bishopric acted cooperatively in other respects as well. For example, they not only gave Kazimierz Lagosz provisional jurisdiction over the St. Boniface parish so that he could tend to the needs of Poles living in the city, but also invited Lagosz to participate in the weekly meetings of the vicar general. However, the leadership of bishopric was careful not to relinquish any legal title.[84] It was nevertheless unable to prevent the extensive changes in church administration advanced by Cardinal August Hlond, the primate of the Catholic Church in Poland.

Cardinal Hlond had left Poland in 1939 and resided primarily in France during the war. He was liberated from German police custody there on April 1, 1945, by American troops and flown to Rome several days later, where he participated in talks with the Vatican that lasted until early July 1945.[85] The exact content of Hlond's discussions with the Curia and Pope Pius XII about reconstructing the Polish Church are not known. However, the Vatican did present the Polish primate with a written declaration dated July 8, 1945, giving him extraordinary powers to reorganize church life in Poland.[86] Among these powers was the authority to appoint apostolic administrators to vacant bishop's seats at his own discretion if telegraphic communication with the Vatican was impossible, which due to downed communication lines was in fact the case for months.

Hlond returned to his Poznań bishopric in July 1945 and began rebuilding the Polish Church. On August 12, ten days after the conclusion of the Potsdam Conference, he visited Chapter Vicar Piontek in Wrocław. Hlond communicated the pope's alleged desire that Piontek relinquish jurisdiction of those areas of his bishopric east of the Oder-Neisse line so that Hlond could appoint Polish administrators there. On August 16, Hlond requested the same from Maximilian Kaller, bishop of Ermland, although the latter, like Piontek, spoke fluent Polish and would have also been able to head a diocese in which most of the members were Polish. Piontek and Kaller complied with Hlond's request and thus gave up their bishop's seats.[87] Hlond was unable to visit personally with Berlin bishop Konrad Graf von Preysing, who was responsible for East Pomerania and East Brandenburg (Neumark), since it was impossible to travel to Berlin under the prevailing conditions. Finally, Danzig bishop Carl Maria Splett was already in Polish custody at the time and subsequently sentenced to an eight-year prison term in 1946 for anti-Polish policies in the former Polish diocese of Chełmno, which he had taken over in December 1939.[88]

Hlond appointed apostolic administrators and simultaneously revised the territory of the Breslau archbishopric east of the Oder-Neisse line. The part belonging to the province of Lower Silesia became the Wrocław administrature, and Karol Milik was appointed apostolic administrator. The Opole administrature was established in Upper Silesia, headed by Bolesław Kominek. The northern part of the Breslau diocese within the Poznań province, the part of the Berlin bishopric now in Polish territory, and the prelature of Schneidemühl were combined into an administrature headed by apostolic administrator Edmund Nowicki with its seat in Gorzów Wielkopolski. The Ermland bishopric became the Olsztyn administrature under Teodor Bensch; the Gdańsk diocese was combined with the Chełmno diocese under Andrzej Wronka.[89] Hlond presented the future apostolic administrators with their documents of appointment at a meeting in Gniezno on August 14. However, not until September 1, 1945, the symbolically significant anniversary of the German invasion of Poland, did the Polish successors to the German bishops officially assume their offices in Wrocław, Opole, Gorzów Wielkopolski, and Olsztyn.

The Catholic Church in Poland has always emphasized that Hlond, in appointing these administrators and in rapidly establishing a Polish church organization along the Oder and Neisse, carried out the will of the pope. The German side, in contrast, has denied that these measures by the Polish primate truly corresponded to the wishes of the Curia, accusing Hlond of nationalism and claiming that he exploited an ambiguous legal situation and the lack of communication lines to the Holy See in order to create a fait accompli favoring the Polish church.[90] Hlond's critics doubt that his extraordinary powers extended to the eastern German dioceses, since no decisions about the future of eastern Germany had been made when Hlond was in Rome. Given the circumstances, they argue, the Vatican had little reason to redraw the borders of the bishoprics; apart from this, Hlond's powers called for the appointment of apostolic administrators solely in the case of vacant bishop's seats. The vacancies in the Wrocław bishopric, however, arose only through the resignations that Hlond had pressured from the German bishops Piontek and Kaller. From this perspective, the Polish primate himself created the very vacancies that constituted the basis for his authorization to take action.[91]

Continuing to dispute the legality of the process, in which both Polish and German clergy employed nationalist arguments, is, however, fruitless. The two positions are based on different interpretations of the meaning under international law of the intentionally ambiguous formulation of the Potsdam Agreement. In August 1945, the Allies moved the German-Polish border de facto to the Oder and Neisse and made this border shift practically irrevocable through the transfer of the entire German population. At the same time they declared the Oder-Neisse line to be provisional and referred to a future peace conference at which a definitive decision would be made. Due to this legal ambiguity different readings of the Potsdam Agreement were possible. For the one side, the German-Polish border established in 1945 was definitive and required only formal confirmation. For the other side, it was provisional and could be revised. The Polish primate, like the Polish government, based his actions on the former interpretation. To the extent that he regarded the German dioceses east of the Oder-Neisse line as historically dissolved through the Allies' decision, Hlond could claim that in establishing a Polish Catholic ecclesiastical administration he was no longer bound to the selection of bishops by the Wrocław cathedral chapter. This selection process was a canonical peculiarity of the German dioceses; it was otherwise common for the pope to freely appoint bishops. Seen in this light, Hlond's appointment of Polish provisional bishops complied with the usual procedures within the Catholic Church in Poland and was grounded in his authorization from the pope.

The Vatican accepted Hlond's new regulations, but never formally confirmed them. The administrators never became bishops, nor were the revised diocese borders ever officially recognized. The Archbishopric of Wrocław continued to operate in the Vatican books as a German bishopric. This provisional solution based in canon law served as a continual and annoying reminder to the Polish government that no definitive decision under international law had been made about Poland's western border. The Polish government attempted to pressure the Vatican into recognizing both the altered borders and Poland's new government. In a circular of September 17, 1945, signed by Minister of Public Administration Władysław Kiernik to the district plenipotentiaries in the western territories, the procedure to be followed was clear:

> The Ministry of Public Administration clarifies that the apostolic administrators may not appear in an official role before the authorities, nor

may they invoke any special entitlement on account of their position, but are to be treated the same as all other clerics of Polish nationality.

With regard to the last paragraph of the Council of Ministers' resolution,[92] and to the fact that the forthcoming organization of a Polish Catholic hierarchy in this area is also desirable for the state, I call on the citizen plenipotentiaries not to interfere with the activities of the apostolic administrators, but rather to provide them assistance and relief as best they can.[93]

The communist government was well aware that the Catholic Church in Poland—over 97 percent of the Polish population was Catholic—had a crucial role to play in expanding the Polish state into the western territories. Polish clergy and the new Polish church administration of the territories would function as agents of Polonization, and would provide stability to the fragile society of recent settlers. Despite the hostility between communists and the Catholic clergy, the two sides shared a Polish-national orientation, especially on the issue of the western territories. They were equally convinced that the shifting of the border was justified and that a rapid population exchange and integration of the new territories were necessary. Here church and state were prepared to work together for the benefit of the Polish national interest.[94]

Wrocław administrator Karol Milik worked with particular verve to this end. In choosing Milik to occupy the Wrocław bishop's seat, Hlond had appointed not a man favoring a national balance, but a fervent Polish patriot who before the war had organized a print run in the millions of a postcard identifying Wrocław and Szczecin as Polish cities.[95] That Milik regarded his position as both spiritual and patriotic is evident in his correspondence with Władysław Kiernik in the fall of 1945. Their letters reveal that both of them regarded the Polish Catholic Church an essential factor in the political battle for the Oder-Neisse line and the integration of the western territories. With this in mind Milik, on September 28, 1945, requested political and financial support from the minister in establishing the Polish Church within the Wrocław diocese:

Pastoral work in Lower Silesia is undoubtedly a decisive factor in reinforcing the strength of our state in this region. Priests thus play a significant role in the life of the state. The nomination of apostolic administrators was a very humiliating blow for the German church organization, within which the Wrocław diocese played a leading role. Germans refer to this nomination bitterly as "ein furchtbarer Schlag" [a terrible blow].[96]

In his response of October 16, 1945, Kiernik made no mention of large-scale funding, but did promise subsidies for church repairs. He also emphasized that the government regarded the work of Polish clerics in the western territories "as a positive factor in reinforcing our statehood in this territory."[97] Milik, however, was not satisfied with this and, in a letter of October 22, 1945, underlined even more clearly the Church's role in supporting the state in the western territories:

> For six weeks now, I have been looking from close range at the problems of Lower Silesia, and I see that they are so difficult that the Polish reason of state will be able to resolve them only through the close cooperation of state and church. . . . I would like to take this opportunity to report that during the six weeks of my diocesan jurisdiction I have succeeded in permanently settling more than seventy-five priests here. We're sinking our teeth into this Lower Silesian reality, as recalcitrant as it may still be today, and removing its character as a geographic German wedge driven into the Polish organism.[98]

In another letter dated the same day, Milik wrote that the issue was "to Polonize the parish as swiftly as possible," and that financial support was needed for this. "Political interests in Polonizing this region also require this. . . . I would be much obliged for immediate assistance. We're on the front here, the Polish front."[99]

The old German archbishopric did not disappear with Piontek's resignation. Piontek remained active as a pastor in Wrocław until June 1946, when he moved to the German border city of Görlitz, where he assumed his position as bishop in the small, remaining territory of the Wrocław diocese west of the Oder-Neisse line. A portion of the cathedral chapter remained in Wrocław to continue to minister to the remaining Germans and perform the official duties of the Wrocław curia. The capitulars, whose number steadily declined as they died or were evacuated, held chapter meetings on a regular basis in accordance with the statutes, thereby maintaining legal claims to the continued existence of the archdiocese, which had not been officially dissolved.[100] The capitulars were subordinate to Milik, who followed their movements mistrustfully but left them alone for the most part, attempting to ignore the representatives of a bishopric that had for all intents and purposes ceased to exist.

During the fierce dispute between church and state in the years of Polish Stalinism between 1949 and 1956, Franz Niedzballa, the last capitular remaining in Wrocław, was a center figure in one final curious episode. Beginning in 1949 the Polish government continually increased pressure on the Polish episcopate to persuade the Vatican to abandon its anticommunist policies and officially recognize the de facto existing German-Polish border. No progress, however, was made on either of these issues, so the government, in a tactical maneuver, dismissed the five apostolic administrators in January 1951. In Poland even communist functionaries had a remarkable sense for issues of canon law. Officials in Warsaw recalled that the old Wrocław cathedral chapter still existed theoretically in the form of the lone capitular Niedzballa. A government plenipotentiary visited Niedzballa and requested that he use his canonic authority to elect a new vicar capitular—otherwise the government would have to make its own appointment, which could lead to a schism. After discussing the issue with his few remaining German colleagues in the cathedral chapter and reviewing whether canonic law even permitted a single capitular to conduct an election, Niedzballa acceded to Warsaw's request. He "elected" Kazimierz Lagosz, city dean and administrator of St. Boniface's Church, to be Wrocław's vicar capitular on the basis that Lagosz was on friendly terms with the Polish political leadership.

Stefan Wyszyński, Hlond's successor as Polish primate, initially recognized Niedzballa's selection, only to declare it invalid a short time later. Apparently he realized that recognizing this appointment would confirm the existence of the old German cathedral chapter and thus possibly call into question the reorganization of ecclesiastical relations in 1945. On the basis of his authority as primate of the Polish Church and general administrator for the dioceses of the western territories, he nevertheless appointed as general vicars Lagosz and the four other successors to the administrators dismissed by the government in Opole, Gorzów Wielkopolski, Gdańsk, and Olsztyn. Despite serious conflicts with the communist government—for which Wyszyński would be arrested in late 1953 and spend three years in political custody—the interests of state and church continued to coincide on the issue of the western territories.

In personal negotiations Wyszyński was able to move the Vatican to make concessions. Although Pope Pius XII refused to anticipate the results of a future peace conference and the definitive regulation of the German-Polish border, in the spring of 1952 he did accept the new appointments to the cathedral chapters in Wrocław and Olsztyn to replace the absent German capitulars. He was also prepared to give the general vicars the rank of titular bishops, although this did not occur until 1956. Wyszyński, who had in the meantime become a cardinal, was released from political custody and demonstrated the church's independence by dismissing the general vicars appointed by the state in 1951. Bolesław Kominek, the apostolic administrator of Opole who had been removed in 1951, was appointed the head of the Wrocław bishopric; he later became archbishop of Wrocław and cardinal, heading the bishopric until his death in 1974.

The Vatican abandoned its hesitant stance on the issue of the Polish western territories in the early 1970s. After West German Chancellor Willy Brandt recognized the inviolability of the Oder-Neisse line in the 1970 Treaty of Warsaw and the West German parliament ratified the treaty in May of 1972, Rome resolved the provisional canonic solution regarding the Polish western territories. On June 28, 1972, the revision of the bishopric borders that had occurred in 1945 was recognized in the papal bull Episcoporum Poloniae, through which the diocesan borders were brought in line with the national borders. The Polish part of the former Breslau archbishopric was reduced to the dioceses of Wrocław, Opole, and Gorzów Wielkopolski, while the Pomeranian dioceses were assigned to the Gniezno metropolis and the Warmia diocese to the Warsaw metropolis. Pope Paul VI also elevated the titular bishops to the rank of diocesan bishops. After a twenty-seven year hiatus Wrocław was once again the official residence of an archbishop.

CHAPTER TWO

Moving People

THE REMAPPING OF CENTRAL EUROPE AFTER THE SECOND WORLD WAR was radical not so much in terms of changes in national borders, as in the broadscale shifting of settlement boundaries. The borders had already been altered after the First World War and new countries created upon the ruins of the fallen Central and Eastern European empires. Prolonged mass migrations also ensued at that time. Many people did not want to live in the countries they found themselves in after the political map was redrawn, or they fled growing discrimination against ethnic minorities. To be sure, the victorious powers asserted at the Paris Peace Conference in 1919 that all people have the fundamental right to remain in their place of domicile. The governments of the new nation-states were obliged to award citizenship with all its attendant rights to every resident, irrespective of nationality or religion. Furthermore, the minority treaties that they had to sign were supposed to offer protection against discrimination.[1] After the Second World War, however, the Allied powers abandoned the principles to which they committed themselves in 1918. They wanted the territory between Germany and the Soviet Union to be made up of homogeneous nation-states that were no longer "burdened" by the existence of ethnic minorities. According to the widespread view at the time, this was the only way to prevent potential nationality conflicts and the practice of instrumentalizing minorities to justify future border revisions.[2]

People who found themselves outside the borders of "their" nation-state in 1945 were generally faced with a choice between being "transferred" to that country or assimilating into the dominant national culture of their host states. Central and Eastern Europe, which had been haunted by forced migrations since the late nineteenth century and had gone through an especially dramatic period of large-scale expulsions and deportations during the Second World War, remained "on the move" in the years following the war.[3] After hundreds of thousands of people had been resettled as part of Nazi Germanization policies, and the Soviet leadership had deported entire ethnic groups from the western part of the country to Siberia and Central Asia, Allied postwar policies again forced millions of people—mostly Germans but also Poles, Ukrainians, Belorussians, Hungarians, and Italians—to abandon their homes and, if they were lucky enough to survive, to start a new life somewhere in the unknown. There were serious consequences to these "ethnic unmixings," culminating in a decade of forced migration from 1939 to 1949. The ethnic heterogeneity still characteristic of this part of Europe was sacrificed to the ideal of ethnically homogeneous nation-states. This was not only accompanied by a drastic decline of ethnic and religious diversity; the resettlements also involved tremendous violence and destruction. People do not easily abandon their homes. Hence, what political planners referred to in their distanced perspective as a population transfer or population exchange was often an "ethnic cleansing" when viewed close-up. The means employed were terror and murder, the creation of lawlessness, plundering, expropriation, and the deliberate destruction of churches, cemeteries, and other buildings of symbolic value that tied people to the locations they were supposed to leave. The decade of expulsions not only changed the appearance of Central and Eastern Europe beyond recognition, but it also profoundly traumatized the people and societies involved.

The removal of the Germans from East Central Europe after the Second World War was accompanied by extreme violence.[4] It is impossible to determine today exactly how many lives were lost. In the final months of the war or directly afterward, more than two million Germans are estimated to have died, although in most cases the precise circumstances of their deaths remain unknown. The exact number of casualties of the heavy fighting on the eastern front in the spring of 1945 can no longer be determined, nor can the count of those who died during evacuation, escape, and expulsion, nor of those people who died somewhere in camps or through abuse by the occupation forces. The orgiastic violence of Soviet soldiers immediately after the war took an especially large toll, costing countless lives.[5] Amid the chaos and devastation of 1945, however, many German civilians also died as a result of hunger, cold, exhaustion, injuries and illnesses that were beyond treatment, or suicide as a result of despair and fear. The often cited figure of two million deaths connected with the expulsion of the Germans[6] is inflated since it actually reflects

The expulsion of the Germans from Poland was a dramatic and complex historical process. When the eastern front collapsed in January and February 1945, the German authorities launched a chaotic evacuation of eastern Germany. At the same time, millions of Germans fled in panic from the rapidly advancing Red Army. When the guns fell silent, Polish military units drove German civilians, often by brutal force, across the future German-Polish border. In the winter of 1945/46, the organized mass transfer to postwar Germany began under dire but gradually improving conditions. The photo shows German refugees in Silesia fleeing the advancing front in early 1945. Courtesy of the bpk.

the total number of deaths from all of these causes; nevertheless, even reliable estimates assume that about half a million Germans died in the course of flight and expulsion.[7]

In some respects the expulsion of Germans represents a special case in the history of ethnic cleansing. More than twelve million Germans were expelled, making it the largest ethnic cleansing in history. Furthermore, it was not just one regime that was responsible, but a global military alliance that included all of the governments in the anti-Hitler coalition. This fact gave it an ostensible international legitimacy. Whereas ethnic cleansing usually involves the expulsion of individual ethnic groups from ethnically mixed regions, that was true only to a minor extent here. Most of the Germans who were expelled came from areas that had previously been inhabited exclusively or primarily by Germans. The largest group was the roughly eight million German citizens who came from territories ceded to Poland and the Soviet Union. Next were the approximately three million Sudeten Germans who had been living in the largely German border regions of Bohemia and Moravia and, prior to the Munich Agreement of 1938, had been Czechoslovak citizens of German nationality. The only German expellees who had belonged to an ethnic minority in the true sense of the word and thus were subjected to a typical form of ethnic cleansing were the roughly one million who had been Polish citizens in 1939 and the approximately 500,000 who were expelled from Yugoslavia, Hungary, and Romania after the war.

The reasons for the expulsion of the Germans are complex. First of all, the Allied powers wanted to drastically reduce or eliminate German minorities in the countries of East Central Europe. It is an irony of history that the resettlement of Germans continued Hitler's "Heim ins Reich" policy. After Poland was occupied in the fall of 1939, Hitler had spoken of the "untenable splinters of the German people" in Eastern Europe; and over the subsequent years he proceeded to bring approximately 500,000 Germans back "home to the Reich" from the Baltic states, Volhynia, Galicia, Bukovina, Bessarabia, and South Tirol. Within the course of this more or less forced resettlement, regional cultures established over centuries were destroyed overnight. Although the leadership of the Third Reich used these policies to obtain the German-speaking settlers they needed to Germanize annexed Polish territories, these forced migrations also followed the principle of creating ethnically homogeneous territories that had guided the establishment of nation-states in Central and Eastern Europe starting in the early twentieth century and which continued to serve as a point of reference after 1945. However, the Allied powers and their allies in East Central Europe were not merely pursuing an abstract notion of order, but also clear-cut political goals.[8]

No German minorities were to remain, especially in the strategically important countries of Poland and Czechoslovakia. It was believed that this was the only way to avoid new nationality conflicts and a German irredenta in East Central Europe. Another important objective was to irreversibly reduce Germany's territory in the east in order to permanently weaken it both strategically and economically, thereby preventing Germany from ever being able to wage another war. The German-speaking settlements in Eastern Europe and the related wide-ranging economic, political, and cultural connections had inspired German imperial fantasies time and again. Starting in 1848, the elites of the German national movement believed that "Mitteleuropa," a Central Europe united under German leadership, would become the basis for Germany's assuming the role of a world power.[9] With a certain consistency, therefore, the dissolution of Austria after the First World War was followed by the liquidation of Prussia after the Second World War. The German territories ceded to Poland and the Soviet Union in 1945 had been the core regions of the Prussian state, without which a later reestablishment of Prussia was hardly conceivable. The expulsion of the Germans must be seen from this perspective. A vast majority of those expelled had been Prussian citizens who were subsequently scattered throughout the entire territory of postwar Germany. They would never again appear as Prussians. In 1945, the Prussian state lost not only its territory and last remaining institutions, but also its people.[10]

The governments of the East Central European countries emphasized during the talks on the postwar order that a continued coexistence with Germans in one and the same country had become impossible after the war. That was a conceivable motive for the ethnic redistribution. However, material interests also played a role. The evacuation of Germans included the confiscation of their assets without any financial compensation, and this took place in part in affluent territories with a high level of urbanization and industrialization, such as Silesia and Bohemia. By deporting the Germans, the postwar governments between Warsaw and Bucharest gained real estate and moveables of substantial worth, which they subsequently had completely at their disposal. They were able to allocate land to farmers in the course of land reform, thereby securing their political support without having first to expropriate parts of their own population. Furthermore, based on the confiscated German assets, socialist state companies could be founded on a grand scale both in agriculture and industry. Especially in Poland and Czechoslovakia, where about one-third of the respective national territories in their 1945 borders had previously been inhabited by Germans, expelling the Germans made it far easier to restructure both economies along socialist lines.

The Western Allies would hardly have been aware of the connection between the expulsions and the bolstering of communist rule in East Central Europe. Nevertheless, toward the end of the war it was with growing concern that they watched the issue of population transfer become increasingly radicalized and the number of Germans to be resettled continue to rise. All these people would ultimately have to be relocated somewhere. If the settlement of millions of people from the East into the territorially smaller Germany caused supply shortages and long-term economic and political destabilization, it was the future occupying powers that would ultimately be responsible. If necessary they would have to draw on their own resources to provide for the German population. Proposals developed within the British Foreign Office to deport the Germans from the East to Siberia, South America, or to the colonies and dominions of the British Commonwealth were not pursued.[11] The victors in the war instead agreed to transfer all expelled Germans to Germany and in small numbers also to Austria. The feared humanitarian disaster never materialized. Thanks to the rapid economic reconstruction in Germany and the expellees' remarkable ability to cope with their bitter fate, the refugee misery of the early postwar years could be overcome. The Germans from the East were integrated into postwar society relatively quickly, at least economically.[12]

In negotiations on the postwar borders of Poland it was assumed as a matter of course that the incorporation of German territories would be tied to the evacuation of the Germans living there.[13] Władysław Wolski, PPR-member, the Government Plenipotentiary for Repatriation and one of the key figures of Poland's settlement policy,[14] presumably expressed the opinion of the majority of Poles when he declared in the summer of 1945:

> We will not have any ethnic minorities [in Poland]. We have proceeded to the concept of a nation-state, asserting that in the end ethnic minorities would only constitute fifth columns within the country. Thus we will remove the Germans from our territory.[15]

Even though this referred primarily to the Germans, Wolski's statement was also applicable to the remaining Ukrainian, Belorussian, and Jewish minorities, all of whom stood in the way of realizing the ethnically homogeneous Poland of which Polish nationalists had been dreaming.

The resettlements necessitated by the border shifts would thus rid Poland off its ethnic minorities, either through evacuation or assimilation, but Polish settlement experts foresaw another benefit. The resettlements would provide a unique opportunity to carry out corrective population policies on a large scale. They hoped to create quasi-ideal socioeconomic conditions by engineering the settlements of the western territories according to scientific planning principles. An optimal population density and farm size would, it was supposed, enable healthy economic development. Further, the resettlement would benefit central Poland by eliminating rural "overpopulation" through a transfer of population to the western territories. Experts hoped that this major policy coup would create the structural prerequisites for the rapid economic modernization of the country.[16]

In the end, however, the resettlement projects of the population planners came to naught. In the spring of 1945 the Polish government was primarily concerned with creating a demographic fait accompli prior to the Potsdam Conference. The rate of resettlement was given highest priority; structural policy and economic considerations were secondary. In contrast to what planners had hoped, therefore, population movements were carried out in such ways as to serve only the aim of territorial appropriation, with little regard to optimizing settlement patterns. In April 1945 the Ministry of Public Administration advised per decree:

> All activities, regardless of their source, that might result in the obstruction, restriction, or postponement of resettlement action, are not to be permitted, and any instance of such activity must be suppressed once and for all.[17]

The Office of the Western Territories (BZZ), a planning agency installed in February 1945 by the Council of Ministers, had initially estimated that the technical preparations for a controlled settlement of the western territories would take two years. The office's settlement plan of May 1945, however, already acknowledged that the situation made it necessary to proceed with greater haste.

> [T]he territory [must] undergo swift, albeit unorganized, settlement and immediate cultivation, without regard for the shortcomings and mistakes that are inevitable under such conditions, if this territory is not to become a land of hunger and desolation in the very near future.[18]

Warsaw historian Tomasz Szarota correctly declared that in 1945 "everyone was aware that from an economic standpoint the poorer option had been chosen; it was dictated however by reasons of the Polish state, which demanded that within the shortest time possible the Recovered Territories be settled as far as possible with Poles."[19]

According to the terms of an order of the Council of Ministers of June 12, 1945, 2.5 million Polish settlers were to be transferred to the western territories by August 1 and another million by the end of 1945. These figures exceed realistic possibilities. In order to attain this target, roughly 400,000 people would have had to have been settled each week until August 1. The numbers can only be understood as the wishful projections of socialist planners. They served more as a symbol of the desired speed than as a realistic framework for action. At the National Congress of the Polish Workers' Party in late May 1945, Edward Ochab, Minister for Public Administration, said that it would be possible to settle 2.5 million Poles in the western territories by as early as July 1. Due to the limited railroad capability, Władysław Wolski went so far as to propose having young settlers set out on a foot march. Historian Andreas Hofmann accurately characterized the communist leadership's approach to the immense resettlement task as "a mixture of rhetorical pomposity and irresponsible planning."[20]

It soon became apparent that one of the greatest difficulties would be to win over a sufficient number of settlers for the western territories. Bolesław Bierut, leader of the Polish delegation at the Potsdam Conference and later president, spoke of seven million Poles who would need to be settled in the new territories. Four million would come from the regions ceded to the Soviet Union, another three million as repatriates and reemigrants from Germany and Western Europe.[21] Bierut operated with estimates based on demographic data from the prewar period. The war, however, had dramatically decimated Poland's population. If one includes the roughly three million Polish Jews who had been murdered, between five and six million Polish citizens had lost their lives during the war, a number that constitutes approximately 20 percent of the total population and represents the highest population loss ratio of all countries involved in the Second World War.[22]

In addition to the losses brought about by the war and the occupation, the conception of an ethnically homogeneous nation-state led to yet another substantial reduction in the population of Poland, as about one-third of its citizens had previously been of non-Polish nationality. The loss of the eastern Polish regions meant that most of the Ukrainians, Belorussians, and Lithuanians, who had been citizens of the Polish state before the war, were no longer in Poland. A majority (roughly 500,000 people) of the Ukrainian and Belorussian minorities that had remained in Poland were transferred to the Soviet Union between 1944 and 1946 within the scope of a Polish-Soviet population exchange. In turn, about 1.5 million so-called repatriates came to Poland between 1944 and 1948; they had been Polish citizens from the lost eastern territories who identified themselves as ethnic Poles.[23] To be sure, the number of people from regions ceded to the Soviet Union who had to be accommodated in postwar Poland far exceeded the balance of roughly one million that represented Poland's population gain through the population exchange. Nevertheless, their numbers were far fewer than the four million that Bierut had spoken of at the Potsdam Conference.[24]

There were high expectations that Poles who had emigrated to western and southern Europe and overseas in search of work, some of them generations earlier, would return to Poland in large numbers. It was assumed that up to 400,000 Poles would reemigrate from other parts of Europe and another 400,000 from overseas. The census of December 1950, however, registered only 205,000 such returnees.[25] The expectation that between 1.5 and 2 million German citizens of Polish descent in the western territories would declare allegiance to Poland was also optimistic, but not as far from the mark. By the end of 1948, more than one million former German citizens were awarded Polish citizenship as so-called autochthons, after their Polish ethnicity had been determined through an elaborate—and not always entirely voluntary—"verification" procedure.[26]

In the end, Poland's population fell from around 35 million in 1938 to 25 million in 1950.[27] This corresponded to a population loss of almost 30 percent in a territory that had been reduced in area by only 20 percent. However, the newly acquired western territories had had a far higher population density than the lost Polish eastern territories and would have to regain this density in order to take full advantage of the region's economic potential. Yet a regional population of almost nine million people—the number that had lived in Germany east of the Oder-Neisse line before the war—could not be created through settlement alone; it would require several decades of natural population growth.[28]

The Evacuation of the Germans

The evacuation of the Germans proved to be more difficult than initially expected.[29] At the Potsdam Conference Bierut estimated that between one million and 1.5 million Germans were still living east of the Oder-Neisse line.[30] Today we know that the actual figure was 4.5 to 5 million. More than half of the population of Germany's former eastern territories had in fact remained in their hometowns or returned there directly after the fighting ended.[31] This means that apart from those who stayed in Poland as autochthons, roughly 3.5 to 4 million Germans had to be evacuated. There is no evidence supporting claims that Bierut deliberately underestimated the figures to make the evacuations appear less extensive in order to allay reservations of the Western Allies about establishing the border along the Oder-Neisse line. Internal estimates by the Polish government of the number of Germans to be evacuated appear in fact to have been within the range of the 1.5 million mentioned by Bierut.[32] In early summer 1945 no one was in a position to make anything like a reliable estimate of the results of the chaotic population movements between the Vistula and Oder rivers that had been set off by the Soviet January offensive.

The mass exodus of Germans out of the territories east of the Oder-Neisse line alone was an extraordinarily complex procedure, which is only inadequately described with the word "expulsion" (*Vertreibung*) that is commonly used in Germany. The process began with the chaotic evacuation of eastern Germany by German authorities when the eastern front collapsed in January 1945. The operation, which came far too late and cost thousands of lives, overlapped with the dramatic movements of people fleeing the advancing Red Army. Casualties rose as treks of refugees fought their way westward on crowded roads through ice and snow. Soviet raids on the refugee convoys and on navy transports, which evacuated the fleeing population across the Baltic Sea to ports in northern Germany, further increased the death toll. Children, the sick, and the elderly were least able to cope with the tremendous physical and mental burdens of this forced migration.

Between the end of the fighting and the conclusion of the Potsdam Conference on August 2, 1945, the districts along the Oder-Neisse line saw the most brutal expulsions, lacking any form of sanction under international law.

The methods of Polish military units engaged in these "ethnic cleansings" were notorious. The army leadership often incited its soldiers to seek revenge. On June 24, 1945, the command of the Polish forces' Second Army directed its troops as follows:

> [They were] to treat the Germans just as they have treated us. Many of us have already forgotten their conduct toward our children, wives, and the elderly. The Czechs succeeded in getting the Germans to flee their territories of their own accord.
>
> We need to execute our task with such harshness and resoluteness that the German scum will be unable to hide in their houses, but will leave voluntarily and, once they find themselves in their own land, will thank God for sparing their necks.[33]

The violent excesses of these units, who operated in the name of the Polish government, damaged Poland's international reputation. They were one of the reasons that the "Big Three" declared in the closing communiqué of the Potsdam Conference that the transfer of the Germans was to be carried out "in an orderly and humane manner." The Polish government had, by that time, already attempted to take action against the excesses of the units. Edward Ochab, Plenipotentiary for the Recovered Territories, made it absolutely clear in a letter to the regional plenipotentiaries (June 25, 1945) that "unplanned and arbitrary evacuations" were not permissible. After offering detailed instructions regarding the orderly transfer of the Germans, he added: "All acts contrary to both the law and our sense of national dignity, such as thievery, arbitrariness, harassment of evacuated persons, etc., are to be ruthlessly combated, and the guilty parties prosecuted."[34]

Parallel to the "wild expulsions" there was also a more or less voluntary emigration of Germans, such as the members of antifascist organizations in Wrocław who coordinated their departure with the local Polish authorities. While presumably 300,000 to 400,000 Germans left the territories east of the Oder-Neisse line either willingly or by force in the months leading up to the Potsdam Conference,[35] hundreds of thousands of Germans, in turn, went back to their homes in the east, from whence they had previously fled. Only gradually were Polish border patrols able to seal the new border and halt the German return movements. By then, however, entire towns that had already been emptied were filled once again with a sizeable German population.

The organizational conditions necessary for a mass transfer of the German population across the Oder-Neisse line could not be put in place before the end of the year. The Polish leadership hoped that by then a large proportion of the Germans would have left of their own accord. In order to promote such a westward migration, the government issued a circular in June 1945 that explained in no uncertain terms:

> The Republic of Poland is interested in having self-avowed Germans depart from all areas within the boundaries of the republic as quickly as possible. Hence a tactic of "making life difficult" for this part of the population must be pursued, so that the hardened enemies of all things Polish [polskość] will be discouraged from remaining in the R[epublic] of Poland.[36]

The exodus prompted by these means was, however, less than optimal from the Polish government's point of view. It is estimated that only about a half million Germans left Poland in the second half of 1945.[37] This relatively low number reflects the fact that the living conditions of the Germans generally improved compared to the months preceding the Potsdam Conference—local and individual variations notwithstanding. Although tens of thousands had to go through the horror of Polish camps such as Łambinowice, Potulice, or Świętochłowice, where conditions hardly differed from those of the Nazi concentration camps and where inmates died by the thousands of murder, mistreatment, hunger, and disease,[38] the wave of violence gradually subsided after the first postwar weeks, and conditions stabilized somewhat. After the initial thirst for revenge was satisfied, Germans who stayed in Poland were viewed more and more as valuable workers needed for the country's reconstruction and, accordingly, were better treated. Many of the Germans must have recognized that resettlement was not likely to improve their living conditions any time soon, given the widespread material hardships and the chaos of the postwar period. Aware that they would have to leave eventually, it nonetheless made sense to remain where things were at least familiar for the time being, rather than to rush toward the uncertainties of life as an expellee somewhere in the west.

The evacuation of the entire German population from Poland could be achieved only by means of an organized mass transfer. It began in winter 1945–46 and within two years took more than three million people—usually by train—to the British and Soviet occupation zones. In the early period especially, the transfer often took place under disastrous conditions. Due to insufficient transport capacities and demolished transportation lines, the settlers were on the road for days and weeks. The train cars, generally freight and livestock cars, were usually overfilled, with inadequate sanitary facilities and insufficient heating. Evacuees were regularly exposed to the elements; food supplies were meager. To make matters worse, Polish authorities did little to protect the evacuees from assault and robberies. The death rate was high. Many elderly and sick simply could not survive the physical and mental duress of the journey. It was only due to pressure from the Soviet and British authorities that the situation improved over the course of time and the death rate dropped.

The transfer was essentially completed in late 1947. Another roughly 140,000 Germans were evacuated from Poland between 1948 and 1950, for the most part people who had been classified as indispensable workers and not been permitted to leave earlier; and in addition more than 35,000 German prisoners of war and a large number of German children from orphanages. All told, more than 3.5 million Germans were transferred from Poland to postwar Germany between 1945 and 1950. This corresponded approximately to the number who had been evacuated or who had fled the Red Army in 1945 without ever returning.[39] From 1950 on, the resettlement of Germans from Poland was carried out on the basis of treaties between the People's Republic of Poland, on the one hand, and the German Democratic Republic or the Federal Republic of Germany, on the other. This was now a regular emigration, which involved small contingents of Germans who had initially remained in Poland and a growing number of the autochthons. Starting in the 1950s, most of the autochthons reversed the decision they had made after 1945 to acquire Polish citizenship and petitioned for permission to emigrate. Their relocation was therefore no longer a forced evacuation, but rather an emigration that had to be pushed through against the resistance of the Polish state.

THE SETTLEMENT OF THE POLES

The expulsion of the Germans was only one side of a comprehensive population exchange, in which the Germans living east of the Oder-Neisse line were replaced by Polish settlers. Since both processes—the evacuation and the settlement—took place simultaneously, the first Polish settlers entered an

Although millions of people in Central and Eastern Europe were (forcibly) relocated after the war's end, this dramatic process was rarely documented through photographs. In this photo, Polish settlers from the territories ceded to the Soviet Union at the end of World War II arrive at one of Wrocław's train stations. Courtesy of the Ossolineum.

environment that was still largely shaped by Germans.[40] In fact, in many places Germans and Poles coexisted for months or even years, sometimes under one roof. In rural areas it was by no means unusual for German farmers to operate their farms together with the new Polish owners for a time. The hardship of surviving the difficult times often bridged their differences. It was not until mid-1946, when the population exchange was in full swing, that Poles began to comprise the majority of the population in the western territories.

It was necessary, however, for the Polish government to initiate an elaborate recruitment campaign to win a sufficient number of settlers. It appealed to patriotism, calling on Poles to take part in the historic return of the Recovered Territories, but settlers were also wooed with promises of material and professional advantages. In May 1945 the Central Resettlement Committee (Centralny Komitet Przesiedleńcy) announced:

Compatriots!

The power of the Third Reich lies in rubble. Lands plundered by the Teutonic Knights, by the Bismarcks, and by Hitler, are coming back to the motherland (*macierz*). The conqueror has fled in panic across the Oder, leaving behind villages and cities, estates and factories, planted fields, stocked ponds, and cultivated gardens. These empty lands lie waiting for us—their legitimate proprietors (*gospodarz*)!

Farmers!

You no longer have to emigrate overseas. In the new Poland there is land aplenty for you to own, to possess in perpetuity. You want bread? There's bread in the west! You want land? There's land in the west! In the west, city dwellers will find workshops and stores left behind by the Germans, and for educated workers there are office jobs and administrative positions.

Compatriots!

To the west![41]

An advertising brochure of 1945 appealed quite openly to the material ambitions of potential settlers:

Go! And before you know it,
You'll have made a hoard,
Because a farmer in the western lands
Will be as well-off as a lord![42]

The inclination to leave one's home and move to the new territories was strongest among those who hoped for a marked improvement in their living conditions. This applied mostly to farmers who previously had owned no land at all or only very small holdings, and to those whose farms had been burned to the ground in the war. People whose villages and cities had been razed, or who had lost their jobs through the destruction of factories were also persuaded in large numbers. Some reckoned on opportunities for quick upward mobility and high-level career positions. Others had no other alternative save to seek a livelihood for themselves and their families in the west, where they were more likely to find work and housing. The decision to relocate was easier for residents of voivodeships adjacent to the western territories, such as Poznań, Łódź, or Krakow. They often had the option of retaining their previous residence and, for the time being, shuttling between their old and new homes. Also, the cultural differences between neighboring regions were less pronounced. For residents of the region of Greater Poland, which—as the province of Posen—had been part of Prussia for many generations, moving to Silesia or Pomerania was much less of a step into unknown territory than it was for residents of eastern Galicia or Polesia at the easternmost end of Poland.

Whereas settlers from central Poland moved to the western territories more or less voluntarily, the so-called repatriates from the Polish eastern territories ceded to the Soviet Union were expellees. They were not "repatriates" but "expatriates," who either had been chased from their homeland, often under threat of fatal reprisals, or had fled Soviet rule of their own accord. The transfers within the scope of the Polish-Soviet population exchange were based, ostensibly, on the principle of voluntary resettlement. However, most of the residents in the regions ceded to the Soviet Union who considered themselves ethnically Polish had no choice but to relocate to Poland, thus abandoning their homeland and leaving behind most of their property. The transfers from eastern Poland were carried out under essentially the same conditions as those experienced by the German evacuees—people were packed in primitive railway cars that sometimes took weeks to reach their destination. There was insufficient food and water, hygienic conditions were deplorable, and no protection was provided against assault and looters. The authorities usually ordered the repatriate transports to proceed directly to the western territories, often against the will of the passengers, who were then discharged wherever Polish settlers were most desperately needed. Frequently they landed precisely in the less attractive areas and towns that had been rejected by settlers from central Poland. Sometimes where the transported ended up was a matter of pure chance. Andrzej Żak, First Secretary of the PPR in Wrocław, described in his memoirs the situation at the Wrocław-Brochów train station in the summer of 1945:

> Later the same month a delegation from the Brochów PPR Committee and from the PUR came to me.
>
> "Come and help, comrade," is the first thing they said. "A few thousand people are living out in the open between the railway tracks. No one cares about them."
>
> That evening I was at the railway station in Brochów. It happened to be cloudy that day; it was raining. I walked over toward the freight train station. . . . And indeed: A tremendous camp stretched out between the tracks, the smoke of hundreds of fires rising overhead.

"Why did you unload all the repatriates here of all places?" I asked the PUR official.

"One train of repatriates, instead of being discharged in Katowice, got sent to Wrocław," the official explained sheepishly. "Furthermore, we were sent two transports of repatriates unannounced. One was supposed to go to Szczecin, the other to Poznań. But since the army needed the railway cars, they were discharged and that's that."[43]

The treatment of a group of settlers from Wilno was more of an exception:

PUR had a distribution center in Toruń, and from there individual families, or entire railway cars, were sent out to various locations in the Recovered Territories. When we arrived, the repatriates were being sent primarily to little towns in Western Pomerania. A PUR employee would write the name of a destination in chalk on the side of the railway car, and the cars would be uncoupled and shunted down the tracks. They wrote a name on our car, too—a small town near Koszalin. But since no one was particularly excited about it, a bottle of vodka was offered, and the name Białogard was replaced with Wrocław. And that is why and how I ended up in Wrocław.[44]

Since the repatriates generally arrived after the settlers from central Poland, all that remained for them of previously German property was whatever the first settlers had not wanted and roaming looters had not stripped of any value. Moreover, it was more difficult for eastern Poles to settle in the west than for settlers from central Poland for yet another reason. In contrast to the central Poles, eastern Poles were unable to maintain any contact to their former homes, which were now on the Soviet side of the border, distant and inaccessible. Out of political consideration for the Soviet Union, they were not even permitted to publicly lament the loss of their homeland and the inhumane circumstances surrounding their forced evacuation.

This officially imposed taboo distinguished the situation of those expelled from eastern Poland from that of German deportees to West Germany. The latter received state support to establish their various Homeland Societies (*Landsmannschaften*) and were allowed to publicly celebrate their days of commemoration. The situation of the eastern Poles was more similar to that of expellees in East Germany, who out of the same political considerations were compelled to remain silent and were not even permitted to refer to themselves as "expellees," but only as "resettlers."[45] Even directly after the war, Polish and German expellees took note of these similarities. The forced settlers from eastern Poland met Germans in the western territories who were about to face the same process of forced resettlement and expropriation. They often saw themselves as fellow sufferers, related through a shared fate.[46]

The Polish reemigrants were the only settlers in the western territories who came entirely of their own free will. They were actively recruited by the Polish government because of their key vocational qualifications in industry and mining. They came to Poland mostly from the industrial areas of France, Belgium, and Germany, as well as from Yugoslavia, and were settled primarily in the Silesian mining areas, where they represented a small but often influential minority.[47] Most famous among them was Edward Gierek, who returned to Poland from Belgium in 1948 and after a career in the Katowice PZPR assumed national leadership in 1970 as the party's First Secretary.

The situation of the autochthons was complicated. These were the populations, especially in Upper Silesia and southern East Prussia, who could not be neatly classified as to national affiliation, as their identity was a complex blend of Polish and German linguistic and cultural influences, more determined by regional and religious identifications than by a sense of belonging to a certain nation.[48] Their specific cultures were the result of centuries of migration and interaction in the German-Polish border zone and had not yet been homogenized by the national movements. They might have been loyal Prussian or German citizens up to 1945, but they spoke mostly Polish or a Polish dialect interspersed with German. The Polish leadership definitely wanted to keep the autochthons, whom it quickly declared to be Germanized Poles who could potentially be re-Slavicized. They would serve as living proof that an unbroken Polish settlement tradition had been preserved in the western territories despite centuries of Germanization. Moreover, there was a general shortage of settlers, especially in the Silesian industrial and mining regions, which rendered the autochthons virtually irreplaceable as a workforce that was in the main well trained and familiar with the area.

While the propaganda of the People's Republic of Poland flaunted the autochthons as preservers of Polishness, the settlers from central and eastern Poland viewed them with suspicion. Many considered them German on account of their culture and language and thus treated them with contempt.[49]

Nevertheless, in order to obtain Polish citizenship and be allowed to stay, more than one million autochthons were willing to prove their Polish ethnicity in an often humiliating verification process. As a result of continuing discrimination, the repression of the German language or Germanized Polish dialects, and Poland's unfavorable economic and political development, however, most of the autochthons began eventually to regard *themselves* as ethnic Germans, and a large number attempted to emigrate to Germany starting in the 1950s.[50]

The emigration of the autochthons made the population exchange virtually complete. Only about 200,000 of them remained permanently in Poland, concentrated in the region around Opole. Today they emphasize their regional identity and refer to themselves as "Silesians" or "Masurians," and to some extent also as a German minority in Poland. The term "autochthon," which had been introduced by the Polish government in 1945 for propaganda purposes, was regarded by the Germans marked for evacuation as an impertinence. After all, they were no less "autochthon" than their Polish-speaking neighbors who were not evacuated. The term, however, even if its inventors did not have this in mind, was justified in reference to the Polish settlers in the western territories. After the expulsion of the Germans, the small group of autochthons was in fact the only remaining vestige of the area's pre-1945 population.

JEWS AND UKRAINIANS

Between 1945 and 1949 roughly 200,000 Polish Jews settled in the western territories. Survivors of the more than three million who had lived in Poland prior to the Holocaust,[51] they had avoided being murdered either by escaping to the Soviet Union or by hiding in occupied Poland, or they were among the few liberated from the concentration camps at the end of the war by the Red Army. Most Polish Jews did not return to their hometowns, either because the towns were now in the Soviet Union, or because their houses and apartments had been destroyed or occupied by Polish residents who were not willing to give them up. In the period directly after the war there were numerous attacks on Jews in Poland, particularly in cases when the few Holocaust survivors tried to regain possession of their property. The anti-Semitic catchword *Żydokomuna* continued to circulate, which labeled Jews as supporters and agents of Poland's communist leadership. Anti-Semitism erupted in sporadic acts of violence, such as the pogrom in Kielce on July 4, 1946, when forty-two Jews were killed. By the summer of 1947, as many as 1,500 Jews are said to have been killed in anti-Semitic incidents.[52]

Given these circumstances, most surviving Polish Jews—if they did not immediately attempt to leave the country—tried to make a new start in the western territories, where settlers were actively sought and property conflicts far less likely. Jewish settlements arose in Lower Silesia more or less by chance, perhaps tracing their roots back to the approximately 12,000 liberated prisoners of the Gross Rosen concentration camp. When in June of 1945 the Polish government considered giving a Jewish voivodeship committee in Lower Silesia a certain degree of cultural autonomy and offering support for an official Jewish settlement area in Lower Silesia, the number of Jews in the district rose rapidly, reaching a peak of roughly 90,000 in the summer of 1946. Larger Jewish communities with a rich cultural life flourished for a short time, in particular in the cities of Dzierżoniów and Wrocław. In Dzierżoniów, Jews comprised 40 percent of the city's population in 1947. Outside of Lower Silesia a large Jewish community formed in Szczecin.

But thriving Jewish life in the western territories was of short duration. For many Jews the cities along the Oder were from the outset only a temporary stop on their path of emigration. Others were forced to acknowledge that while there had been no dramatic incidents in the western territories like the one in Kielce, anti-Semitism was nonetheless ubiquitous. The Voivodeship Office for Information and Propaganda (WUIP) in Wrocław reported in March 1946 on relations between the Jews and the general population, claiming that the former were "generally hated" and seen as "scroungers" and "profiteers." The majority of shops were said to be in Jewish hands, and since they were profitable, they were the "objects of interest and hostile attitudes."[53]

In 1948, the Polish government revised its policies with respect to the country's remaining ethnic minorities, so that Jewish autonomy was no longer an option. Instead the government confronted the Jews with the alternative of either leaving the country with state support or accepting their assimilation into the Polish majority. The number of Jews in the western territories decreased abruptly. Those determined to stay gradually moved to the major cities. In Wrocław a substantial Jewish community developed with numerous Jewish organizations and businesses. But this too would be short-lived since almost all Jews remaining in Poland left the country in response to the government's anti-Semitic campaign in 1968.

The roughly 150,000 to 200,000 Ukrainians in postwar Poland found themselves in a similarly difficult situation. During Operation Vistula in the spring of 1947, the Polish government deported them from their homes in southeastern Poland to the western territories.[54] This radical measure was the last chapter in the history of ethnic conflicts between Poles und Ukrainians, which had already led to acts of violence and counterviolence in interwar Poland. During the Second World War, massacres in Volhynia and Galicia ensued, which cost tens of thousands of lives on both sides.[55] With the loss of the Polish eastern territories, only a few hundred thousand Ukrainians remained in Poland, but after the war some of these persevered in their armed struggle against the Polish state in the Ukrainian-speaking areas of southeast Poland. The fighting between Polish militia and army units on the one hand, and units of the Ukrainian Insurgent Army (UPA) on the other, reached civil war proportions, particularly in wooded and mountainous Bieszczady, the southeasternmost border region. The assassination of the legendary Polish general Karol Świerczewski in the Bieszczady Mountains in March 1947 provided the government in Warsaw with a welcome pretense for a radical resolution of the "Ukrainian problem." Irrespective of the activities of the Ukrainian rebels, the government regretted not having been able to evacuate the entire Ukrainian population during the Polish-Soviet population exchange at the end of the war. Many Ukrainians had avoided being sent to the Soviet Union by temporarily hiding in the forests or in neighboring Czechoslovakia, or by illegally crossing the border back into Poland after having been deported. Thus, following the population exchange, about 200,000 Ukrainians and members of smaller Ukrainian-speaking ethnic groups were still living on Polish territory.

At the time of the assassination, conflicts had calmed down to the point that the Polish security organs reported to Warsaw that they had the activities of the remaining UPA units under control. Nevertheless, the government took advantage of the incident to launch an operation that had secretly been in the planning for months. Operation Vistula, as it was called, had the goal of annihilating all of the traditional Ukrainian settlements in the country. It was preceded by an anti-Ukrainian propaganda campaign that prepared Polish society for radical measures. Then, in a commando-style operation for which roughly 17,000 soldiers and militiamen were called up, the entire

Ukrainian-speaking population was rounded up in June and July 1947—even in areas where the UPA had never enjoyed any support—and deported to the western territories. Resistance was countered with draconian penalties, often handed down by courts-martial that were convened specifically for this purpose and did not shy away from capital punishment. After the population was deported, material evidence of the Ukrainian settlements in southeastern Poland was eliminated through the destruction of orthodox churches and Ukrainian cemeteries and villages.

In order to prevent the establishment of larger Ukrainian settlements in the western territories and to force the total assimilation of Ukrainians into their Polish environment, the government ordered that the forced settlers be dispersed over a wide area. Settlement conditions for the deportees were poor, not least because the local Polish population often believed the government's propaganda and considered Ukrainians to be "bandits" and inveterate enemies of Poland. The entire operation, however, which bore all the marks of ethnic cleansing, ultimately failed. A large segment of the deportees and their descendants retained their ethnic identification until the existence of a Ukrainian minority was officially conceded in the course of the liberalization of Polish nationality policies. In the national census of 2002, roughly thirty thousand Polish citizens identified themselves as ethnic Ukrainians. They were to be found in both the western territories and the traditional areas of Ukrainian settlement in the southeast, to which many had returned long after their deportation.

The Resettlement Apparatus and the Migration of Peoples

The Polish government built up a vast logistical and technical apparatus to handle the enormous task of large-scale population transfers, in which eight to ten million people were shunted back and forth over hundreds of miles within a period of only four years. As early as October 1944, the Lublin Committee created the State Repatriation Office (Państwowy Urząd Repatriacyjny, PUR), a government agency that was initially responsible only for the organizational aspects of the Polish-Soviet population exchange. In May 1945 its responsibilities expanded to include the relocation of Polish citizens who had been deported to the west as forced laborers during the war, as well as the general settlement of the western territories. PUR was further commissioned to offer organizational support in evacuating the Germans. The repatriation office was in fact the most important authority for the technical and organizational implementation of all population movements in postwar Poland. It built up a network of branch offices to receive new arrivals, provide them with all they initially needed for survival, and to distribute them among cities and villages.

In addition to the central settlement authorities, special departments for settlement affairs were established throughout the civilian administration of the western territories, from the voivodeship level down to local communities. Other institutions such as the various operative groups, parties, individual ministries, and industrial firms intervened in settlement policy, especially as regards the settlement of their own staffs and the necessary allotments of living space. Frequently, the diverse interests in play came into conflict with one another. Areas of authority were not clearly defined, and clear-cut instructions often could not be relayed effectively due to the shortcomings of the communications system. The various consulting and planning bodies, such as the Office of the Western Territories (BZZ) and the Scientific Council for the Recovered Territories (RNdZZO), had by and large become meaningless on account of political orders to expedite the population exchange. The settlers thus suffered not only from general material shortages, limited transport capacities, and poor accommodations, but also from the administrative chaos of the settlement policies.[56]

Given time pressures and the difficult conditions immediately following the war, in which neither the logistics nor the technical means to implement a centralized, large-scale settlement policy operation were available, it became necessary to improvise. The repatriation office and its reception camps, as well as the regional and local settlement departments, were entrusted with the important function of trying to coordinate on the ground the population exchange that had been initiated from above. All in all, however, the apparatus was overwhelmed, able to control matters only to a very limited extent. That the mass migrations were merely chaotic and not utterly disastrous was due largely to the migrants and deportees themselves. They took their survival into their own hands, both during the transports and after being settled in foreign environments.

Only in historical and considerably simplified retrospect can the migratory movements in the Polish western territories be described as a German-Polish population shift from east to west. People on the ground at the time, viewing events from a local perspective, saw a virtually incomprehensible jumble of settlement, resettlement, evacuation, and deportation. What occurred between the Oder and the Vistula between 1944 and 1949 was a multilingual, elemental, baffling storm surge of peoples that moved in all directions simultaneously. In this sense, the end of the war did not represent a real caesura. Fear of the Red Army had already set an exodus in motion in late 1944, not only of Germans but also of many Eastern Europeans who had collaborated with the German occupiers or for other reasons sought distance between themselves and the advancing Soviet forces.

As this flow from east to west gradually ebbed when the fighting stopped, counter movements from west to east swelled. Hundreds of thousands of eastern Germans who had fled or been evacuated returned to their homes via the Sudeten Mountains, even though simultaneously the German population along the demarcation line between the Soviet occupation zone and the Polish administration territory was being forced westward by Polish military units. Poles not only migrated to the western territories from the east, but also from the west, as millions of demobilized Polish soldiers, forced laborers, and prisoners of war returned to Poland from Western Europe. They inevitably passed through the territories, where they stayed for weeks or months and often settled permanently. There were also members of other ethnic groups from Eastern Europe, who had been brought westward as prisoners of war or forced laborers and were now attempting to make their way home via Poland, as well as the survivors of German concentration camps, who were on the road in various directions to return home or in search of a new place to live. The flow of migrants in Central and Eastern Europe did not subside until the late 1940s, after a traumatic decade in which millions of people were killed, uprooted, and displaced.

In the late 40s the demographic situation in the western territories began to stabilize as well. According to the census, the Polish population there comprised 5.526 million people as of December 31, 1948. About 2.5 million were settlers from central Poland (45.2 percent), 1.332 million were repatriates and settlers from the Soviet Union (24.1 percent), 936,000 were autochthons (16.9 percent), and 235,000 were reemigrants (4.2 percent). The remaining 524,000 were children under the age of four (9.5 percent), some of whom had been born in the new territories and thus could not be clearly assigned to any of the aforementioned groups. There were also 96,000 Germans who were still in the western territories as prisoners of war or workers, or whose verification procedure as autochthons had not yet been completed.[57]

Within four years the Polish leadership had managed to either transfer or naturalize 4.5 to 5 million Germans and settle roughly four million Poles in the western territories. By the end of 1948 the population there had returned to more than 60 percent of its prewar level, although regional differences were substantial. The capacity to absorb settlers had been exhausted in some areas, around Opole for example, while settlement progressed only sluggishly in other regions. In Pomerania and the former East Brandenburg population figures remained extremely low for decades, much to the detriment of those regions' economic development. It is important to note that the settlement of an area did not necessarily mean that the settlers identified with their new environment and were willing to put down roots. That would require the efforts of generations. Nonetheless, those who had anticipated the complete failure of the project to resettle the territories were, in the long term, proved wrong.

THE LONG TRANSITION PERIOD IN WROCŁAW: GERMAN-POLISH COEXISTENCE

Recollections of the first Polish settlers in postwar Wrocław often mention that in May 1945 the city looked like a ghost town. Germans were nowhere to be seen. That impression was deceiving, however: for fear of violence or of being deported as forced laborers, the Germans avoided the streets during the first days after the war. They continued to hold out in basement hiding places, as they had during the siege. Not until the wave of violence ebbed did people dare to go outside. When that moment came, the seemingly deserted city appeared to repopulate itself.

There are only vague estimates of how many Germans were still in Wrocław at the end of the war. Of the 150,000 to 200,000 inhabitants who had not escaped the Soviet encirclement of the city, tens of thousands presumably died during the siege. On the other hand, thousands of Wrocławians who had left the city returned once the fighting stopped. There were also Germans from other cities and released prisoners of war who sought temporary refuge in Wrocław. The first somewhat reliable figures are based on the summary census that was carried out in the individual districts of the city in August 1945, a time when a fair number of Germans had already left again or had been deported as workers. Polish authorities then recorded a figure of 189,500 Germans, which corresponded to less than one-third of the city's prewar population. In addition, they counted 16,000 to 17,000 Poles, though the actual number must have been greater. Not all Poles had themselves registered, including a large number of looters and criminals, as well as people who preferred to conceal their identity for political reasons; they all attempted to remain below the radar in the anonymity of the western territories.[58] Since census figures showed Germans outnumbering Poles 10 to 1 in Wrocław three months after the war, it is obvious that the city's appearance continued to be predominated by Germans for some time after the war, while Polish settlers constituted a tiny minority—for them, a rather unpleasant situation.

In early April 1945, while fighting was still going on in Wrocław, the city's first Polish mayor, Bolesław Drobner, suggested establishing a "kind of 'ghetto'" for the Germans:

> In my opinion, they should be resettled in the next few days in the area in the northwest that is surrounded on three sides by the Oder River and easily patrolled train tracks, and on the fourth by ul. Fryd. Wilhelma [now ul. Legnicka], the extension of ul. Frankfurtska [now ul. Legnicka], which leads to Berlin, where the outlets to the side streets should be walled off. . . . This population ought to be relocated as quickly as possible, to clean up Warsaw for instance, while the jobs [in Wrocław] should be taken care of by prisoners of war with no connection to Wrocław.[59]

A German ghetto was never established in Wrocław, and Drobner's plan to deport the German population without delay would have been impossible on both logistical and political grounds. Drobner's ideas, which bear an obvious resemblance to the methods of the Third Reich, were not, however, unusual. Local and regional authorities in many towns called for all Germans to wear white armbands in public marked with an "N" for *Niemiec* (German). However, the government in Warsaw issued a circular in November 1945 that prohibited both ghettoization and identifying marks for Germans in the western territories. Such measures, it was argued, were irreconcilable with the spirit of a democratic state. The decree also pointed out the disastrous impression it would make on the international stage if Polish authorities were to adopt

Do Ludności Dolnego Śląska i południowej części Braniboru!

Prastare Ziemie Słowiańskie oderwane germańskim zapędem imperialistycznym od obszarów polskich, dzięki zbrojnemu wysiłkowi zwycięskiej, sprzymierzonej Armii Czerwonej i Dzielnej Armii Polskiej powróciły do Macierzy.

Na mocy uchwały Rady Ministrów Rzeczypospolitej Polskiej obejmuję administrację państwową na tych rdzennie słowiańskich, odzyskanych terenach.

Wzywam wszystkich mieszkańców do lojalnego i bezwzględnego podporządkowania się zarządzeniom polskich władz administracyjnych oraz ścisłego przestrzegania i wykonywania wydawanych zarządzeń.

Jakikolwiek opór czynny lub bierny będzie z całą surowością łamany siłą, a winni wykroczeń będą pociągnięci do odpowiedzialności według prawa wojennego.

Ludność słowiańską, która siłą i podstępem była niemczona, otoczę pełną opieką oraz umożliwię jej powrót do polskości, za którą przelewali krew najlepsi synowie i córki tej prastarej Ziemi Słowiańskiej.

Pełnomocnik Rządu Rzplitej Polskiej na Okręg Administracyjny Dolnego Śląska

p., w kwietniu 1945.

Mgr. ST. PIASKOWSKI

An die Bevoelkerung Niederschlesiens u. der Brandenburger-Südgebiete!

Die urslavischen von Polen durch den germanischen, imperialistischen Drang abgerissenen Gebiete sind dank dem siegreichen Vordringen der verbündeten Roten Armee sowie der heldenhaften Polnischen Armee für die Heimat zurückgewonnen.

Auf Grund einer Bestimmung des Ministerrats der Republik Polen übernehme ich die Staatsverwaltung auf diesen reinslavischen, zurückeroberten Gebieten.

Ich fordere die Bevölkerung zur loyalen und restlosen Unterordnung allen Verfügungen der polnischen Verwaltung sowie zur strikten Befolgung und Ausführung sämtlicher Anordnungen auf.

Jeder aktive sowie passive Widerstand wird mit Gewalt gebrochen und die Schuldigen werden nach den Bestimmungen des Kriegsrechts bestraft.

Die mit Gewalt u. Hinterlist germanisierte slavische Bevölkerung wird von mir betreut und ihr die Möglichkeit gegeben, zum Polentum zurückzukehren, für das die besten Töchter und Söhne dieser urslavischen Gebiete geblutet haben.

Der Beauftragte der Republik Polen für den Verwaltungsgebiet Niederschlesien

Im April 1945.

Mgr ANISLAW PIASKOWSKI

The experience of German occupation in Poland had an impact on the postwar Polish administration and its approach to the newly acquired territories in the west. The first Polish declarations, like Piaskowski's address to the inhabitants of his Lower Silesian district, employed a language strikingly reminiscent of the Nazis' pronouncements in occupied Poland. Courtesy of the City Museum of Wrocław.

Nazi methods.[60] This did not mean, however, that individual local authorities did not in fact force Germans to wear such armbands. Generally, though, given the overwhelming numerical dominance of the Germans in the first few months after the war, it was rather the few Poles who tended to identify themselves through white and red armbands and to concentrate themselves in certain neighborhoods.[61]

Throughout the western territories the desire of the Polish leadership to get rid of the German population as rapidly as possible collided with economic necessities on the ground. An extreme labor shortage soon emerged, especially of skilled workers and professionals that could not easily, even in the medium term, be supplied by the in-coming Polish settlers. It became clear that German workers would continue to be necessary in the foreseeable future and that the immediate evacuation of all Germans would hamper reconstruction efforts considerably. Needed were not only laborers for

During the first two postwar years, Germans were an important part of the labor force in Wrocław. They were not only conscripted to help clear the rubble and tear down ruins (as seen here on Gartenstrasse), but also served in professional capacities and as skilled workers during the reconstruction of factories and public utilities. Courtesy of the Museum of Architecture in Wrocław (Krystyna Gorazdowska).

rubble removal and other clearance work, for which Germans in work gangs were used from the outset, but also the large number of Germans who were employed in factories, public facilities, the administration, the private sector, crafts, businesses, restaurants, and in sales.

In Wrocław, too, German workers, particularly skilled German workers and specialists, were difficult to replace, despite the growing number of Poles in the city. Not only did they have professional qualifications, for which there was a serious shortage in postwar Poland that could be remedied only in the long term, but they were also familiar with the city. This was of prime importance, especially in public enterprises, at the water, gas, and electricity works, and in the municipal transportation companies. Since maps and diagrams had been burned during the siege or lost in the chaos immediately following the war, the help of former employees was needed to quickly repair damages and put businesses back in operation. The first streetcars that started running

again were operated largely by former German personnel until Polish workers could be trained or the Germans replaced by the former workforce of the
Lwów streetcar company.[62] Familiarity with the place proved a decisive quali-
fication even for less specialized jobs. Most of Wrocław's letter carriers were
German until late 1946. Due to deficient language skills, they of course had
some difficulties reading Polish addresses and communicating with their Polish superiors, but their Polish colleagues had a far more difficult time finding
their way around the devastated city using old German maps, especially as
there were no longer either street signs or house numbers in many places.[63]

It was not easy to reconcile the dilemma posed by the political desire to
quickly evacuate the German population and the economic necessity to retain skilled German workers.[64] Resettlement and economic revitalization
were inextricably linked. The new settlers would need jobs, and there would
be none unless economic life and industrial production were revived. Thus
the Poles had to get used to the continued presence of Germans in the western territories. In turn, the living situation improved for working Germans
and their families. Discrimination decreased as appreciation for their labor
and know-how grew. The practical needs of the postwar period began to
eclipse the bitter experiences of the war.

This marked the beginning of a more than two-year transition period of
coexistence between Germans and Poles in Wrocław. They encountered each
other on the streets and in stores. They met as coworkers. They lived in the
same apartment buildings. Both sides therefore had an opportunity to break
down prejudices and hostilities through personal contacts with neighbors
and colleagues. No doubt many Poles came to see the everyday presence of
Germans as normalcy in what were hardly normal times. Others felt bewil-
dered. While state propaganda persistently spoke of Poland's return to the
traditionally Polish areas at the Oder and Neisse, the presence of Germans
in Wrocław fed doubts as to whether the last word on the future of the city
had in fact been spoken at Potsdam. By the same token, many Germans could
not imagine that Wrocław would really ever become a Polish city. Karol
Maleczyński's recollections of his German neighbor in Wrocław-Różanka are
telling:

> Of course, the resettled Germans could not get it into their heads that
> the Potsdam Conference had fixed Poland's western borders once and

for all, and they kept imploring me not to change anything in the apartment I moved into, above all so that "Frau Molke, when she comes back, will find her old bed where it was."[65]

The atmosphere at the beginning of the Cold War, of course, did nothing to strengthen faith in the finality of the Oder-Neisse line. Up to the late 1940s, especially in the western territories, there were continual rumors that the Third World War was in the offing, that the Germans would reclaim their land, or that the Czechs would be granted the territory up to the Oder River.[66] Belief in the imminence of a new war was in fact so widespread that settlers sometimes chose their place of residence accordingly. Czesław Rajca described the thoughts of a group of repatriates in the Wrocław-Brochów reception camp in summer 1945 while looking for a place to settle down:

> The village of Radwanice, a suburb of Wrocław, wasn't far from our camp, and with its workshops and farms it was a dream come true for our convoy. We gave it up, though, because we were afraid that Wrocław would be bombed during the anticipated war. We took our sweet time and ended up deciding on a large village, practically a small city, two and a half miles east of Brochów. Sure, a few people looked askance at the railway station, which could be a target for bombs, but there wasn't a better place for settlement to be found.[67]

Winston Churchill's famous "Iron Curtain" speech at Westminster College in Fulton, Missouri, on March 5, 1946, and the Stuttgart speech by U.S. Secretary of State James Byrnes on September 6, 1946, both gave rise to great insecurity, since the two politicians questioned the Oder-Neisse border. The responses by the Polish population—which ranged from panic and flight from the western territories all the way to militant identification with the status quo created in Potsdam and demonstrative support for the communists—were also reactions to the revisionist statements of Western politicians and their immediate exploitation by Polish propaganda. In an attempt to discredit pro-Western political circles and make the alliance with the Soviet Union appear absolutely essential, Polish state propaganda stoked fears of capitalist camp imperialism.[68] For the settlement of the western territories, however, this was hardly beneficial, since anyone who lacked faith in the Polish future of the territories would be unwilling to tie his or her personal future to it. As powerful as the current of migration had been in the territories at the Oder and Neisse since the summer of 1945, it did not yet constitute a stable settlement movement. Many of the migrants left the area again as soon as the situation proved more difficult than expected. Others had not settled with any intention of staying permanently in the first place.

Wrocław's mayor Aleksander Wachniewski estimated in August 1945 that only about 60 percent of the settlers had come to Wrocław with the intention to stay.[69] This figure accords with calculations by Jędrzej Chumiński. Of the more than 280,000 Poles who registered a permanent residence in Wrocław between 1946 and 1949, roughly 30 percent changed their registered place of residence during that same period. Of the 140,000-odd people who from the outset had established only a temporary residence, 65 percent later left the city. All told, up to 1949, more than 40 percent of the 420,000 Poles registered in Wrocław stayed only temporarily. The actual fluctuation must have been even greater, since these figures included only those who had been entered on the official residential registration lists.[70] The fluctuation was not only a consequence of the general political uncertainty, but also of Wrocław's economic situation. Living conditions for Polish settlers were relatively favorable only in the first few weeks after the war ended, when sufficient food and housing were still available. Conditions worsened as the number of settlers increased without a corresponding increase in foodstuffs being brought into the city, without the housing stock increasing through renovations and repairs, and without any sustained success in reestablishing the municipal infrastructure. The director of PaFaWag, a large rail-carriage factory that grew out of the ruins of the German Linke-Hofmann Works, described the sluggish progress of reconstruction efforts in his regular reports to the Ministry of Industry. In the summer of 1945, he wrote: "The influx of Polish personnel is slow, and those who do turn up see their visit as an opportunity to check out the situation and conditions in Wrocław; afterwards, they go back."[71] By the fall of 1945 much of the progress that had been made in rebuilding the factory was negated by the steady drain of workers, particularly skilled workers: "The primary reason for [their] leaving is the coming winter and the futility of living among ruins without water, electric light, gas, or public transportation."[72]

PaFaWag reports repeatedly mentioned the shortage of qualified personnel. In October 1945 a report noted that of the forty-seven Polish workers sent from Warsaw, only twenty-three had the necessary qualifications.[73] It also complained that construction work on the factory grounds had slowed considerably. Funds were lacking to pay the construction company, and the construction company was facing difficulties due to the mass evacuation of the Germans, who up to now had made up a majority of the workforce.[74]

Even though local Polish authorities backed off from an overly hasty evacuation of Germans, the government in Warsaw insisted on expediting the operation. An attempt was made, however, to minimize economic damage by selecting the Germans to be evacuated according to their economic usefulness.[75] When asked in an interview published in March 1946 how efforts to "cleanse the Recovered Territories of German elements" were proceeding, Minister for the Recovered Territories Władysław Gomułka answered: "We evacuate the nonproductive elements first. In the last phase, it is the German workers in our employ who go. There is also a possibility of retaining a small number of qualified specialists whom we cannot replace."[76]

It was particularly the elderly, children, and invalids who were considered "nonproductive elements." They were to be evacuated first, followed by replaceable workers with limited qualifications. Specialists were not to be evacuated until the very end. Up to then the time was to be used to train Polish workers, often by their German colleagues, with the two working side-by-side.

In order to administer evacuation according to level of qualifications, a system of identification cards was introduced. Low-skilled German workers, whom employers could quickly replace with Poles, received white "category 1" certificates. Blue "category 2" certificates were issued by the voivodeship offices on request for workers who could be replaced in the foreseeable future and who often had to train their replacements. Red "category 3" certificates were given to specialists for whom no replacements could be found quickly and whose evacuation was put on hold indefinitely. Beginning in June 1946, the Ministry of the Recovered Territories also issued a green certificate for top-qualified German workers, whose skills were critical at the national level. Local authorities had to assure that these people would not be evacuated unless the ministry had granted its express approval.[77] The repercussions of this system for Germans assigned to the higher categories were highly ambivalent. On the one hand they were in a privileged position. Employers and agencies actively sought to protect their interests. The Ministry of the Recovered Territories decreed in June 1946 that holders of certificates in categories 2 and 3 and their families be granted, in addition to personal security, guarantees that they could retain their residences and personal property and an assurance of good working conditions. In addition, action had to be taken against all forms of abuse and arbitrary treatment of Germans with certificates in these categories.[78] Because companies competing with each other for highly qualified German workers tried to woo them by secretly offering salary increases, a number of Germans ultimately received better wages than many Poles.[79] On the other hand, highly qualified German workers could be denied permission to emigrate for years. From the moment that they received their high classification, they became an odd kind of forced laborer: they lacked freedom of movement but enjoyed relatively good pay and treatment.

In accordance with stipulations by the Allied forces, the German population had to offer reparations in the form of labor, in Poland as elsewhere. Immediately after the war the Germans were employed as forced laborers—without pay. When regular payment was gradually introduced a few weeks after the war, Germans received substantially less than the Polish workforce. A decree issued by Piaskowski declared that Germans and Poles in Lower Silesia were to receive equal pay for equal work by December 1, 1945 at the latest. However, Polish employees received a special bonus for working in the Recovered Territories, whereas 15 percent of German wages were deducted for the Voivodeship Fund to Support the Victims of Hitlerism. In addition, Germans were to receive only 75 percent of the standard food ration. On the ground, however, payments were handled inconsistently, varying even from company to company. Companies in Wrocław working under the Industry Ministry paid Germans only 75 percent of the standard wage, and the city administration paid only 50 percent;[80] at PaFaWag Germans and Poles received the same pay in name only, because 50 percent of the Germans' income was deducted for the reconstruction of Warsaw.[81] The terms of private employment were virtually impossible to control. Here employers paid their German employees more or less as they saw fit.

The pay system was intended to underscore who had won the war and who had lost it. This was particularly evident in the various deductions for victims of the German occupation or reconstruction of the country. Of course, reference to German historical guilt could also be used as a pretext to employ Germans—who constituted a substantial portion of the workforce in Poland—at low wages, sometimes far below official standards or even without regulated pay at all.[82] There was a saying that every Pole had his

German.[83] However, this sort of discrimination was ultimately injurious to Polish workers, making it more difficult for them to find employment. Since the Germans—with the exception of the few well-paid specialists—provided cheap labor, employers often did not put much effort into searching for Polish replacements. Instead they sought as high an ID classification as possible for their German employees, even if they did not really have the declared qualifications. Consequently, Polish settlers often had difficulty earning a living in the western territories because jobs were filled by real or alleged German specialists.

In the interest of a rapid population exchange, therefore, the Polish government had to push for equal pay for equal work, and it had to pressure employers to finally release their German workers for evacuation. In March 1946 the Ministry of the Recovered Territories issued a confidential circular on the widespread employment of Germans—even in Polish municipal and local administrations:

> This unhealthy state of affairs demands an immediate and radical change due to the necessity not only of maintaining the dignity of the Polish authorities, but of counteracting the demoralizing influence of this national factor.[84]

In the case of irreplaceable specialists at public utilities, the responsible authorities could allow exceptions, but only on condition that the Germans did not supervise any Polish employees. In the name of the same ministry, Wolski issued another confidential and urgent circular on this matter to his voivodes on May 22:

> Repatriating the German population will cleanse the Recovered Territories of hostile elements, creating the political and economic bases for a complete amalgamation of these territories within the country. . . .
>
> Nevertheless, despite these efforts, the rate of re-Polonization is not yet sufficient. This can be observed in those cities marked by the large number of germans [sic] employed there in various industries, institutions, and public posts.
>
> For these reasons, it is necessary to take the most stringent measures possible to remove . . . workers of German nationality from the aforementioned workplaces. . . . This applies in particular to service-sector

jobs in all manner of restaurants, cafes, bars, and other gastronomical establishments, hotels, shops, hairdressers, theaters, and other institutions open to the public. . . . The employment of germans [sic] in such workplaces is prohibited forthwith.[85]

That the word *Niemcy* (Germans) in this document was not capitalized, contrary to Polish grammar rules, was not a typographical error. It is an example of the linguistic discrimination that was directed against Germans (and Ukrainians) during the first postwar years, even in official texts.

Industry and mining companies continued to employ many Germans— often against their will—even after the mass evacuation in 1946–47. Here, unlike the situation in the service sector and in public utilities, they were out of the public eye. Hence their presence contributed less to the outward impression that German workers still played a role in the economy of the western territories.[86] In Wrocław, however, the number of employed Germans dropped very quickly. In early 1946 organized transfers to the British and Soviet occupation zones commenced. At the same time, the number of Polish settlers in Wrocław, and thus also the pool of available workers, grew rapidly. Whereas only around 30,000 Germans had been evacuated from Wrocław in 1945, in 1946 alone almost 140,000 were evacuated, and another 63,000 in 1947. By October 1947 only 4,228 Germans were still registered in Wrocław, and within a year that figure had dropped to 2,416. By the end of 1947 the German population had been virtually eliminated.[87]

Only a small German minority, several hundred people, continued to live in the city.[88] In contrast to Upper Silesia, where the autochthons comprised a large segment of the population and the government rigidly suppressed all traces of anything German that might obscure the Polish character of the region, policies toward the Germans in Lower Silesia were relatively liberal from the 1950s on. There were so few Germans left in the area that their recognition as a national minority could no longer threaten the Polishness of Lower Silesia. Starting in 1950, German schools were even reestablished. From 1951 to 1958 the German-language newspaper *Arbeiterstimme* (The Workers' Voice) was published in Wrocław, at first weekly and later daily, with a circulation of almost 20,000. In late 1956 the Polish government also permitted the founding of the German Social and Cultural Society (Niemieckie Towarzystwo Społeczno-Kulturalne) in Wrocław. However, most of the remaining Germans emigrated to East and West Germany in the 1950s under the aegis of the family reunification policy. The number of students at German-language schools plummeted so quickly that they were closed in the late 1950s. The *Arbeiterstimme* continued to lose readers. In 1958, when it was discovered that most of the remaining readers were autochthons from Upper Silesia who were officially registered as Poles, the authorities ordered the newspaper to discontinue publication.

The German community in Wrocław never disappeared entirely, although its connection to the city's prewar German population became increasingly tenuous, its survival depending mainly on the steady migration of ethnic Germans from other parts of Silesia. The focal point of the community was German church life. A small congregation of German Protestants was initially accommodated in the community center of the Church of St. Mary Magdalene and the church of Leśnica. Beginning in December 1958, however, the congregation gathered in the reconstructed St. Christopher's Church in the city center.[89] The even smaller community of German Catholics first celebrated Mass in one of the cathedral chapels, later in the small St. Giles's Church and, finally, in the chapel of the Sisters of St. Hedwig on ul. Sępa Szarzyńskiego.[90]

In Wrocław as elsewhere, the evacuation of Germans was closely linked to the settlement of Poles. Districts or blocks where Germans had lived were cleared out primarily when larger transports of Poles were expected to arrive in town. Prior to the mass evacuation, Germans were still generally relocated within the city; beginning in 1946, however, when the population movements reached their peak, most were taken directly to assembly camps and from there to the evacuation transports. On balance, Polish migration that year resulted in an increase in the Polish population of 151,000, which corresponded approximately to the number of Germans evacuated that same year. On average, Wrocław gained 12,500 new Polish residents each month in 1946, so there were already 185,000 Poles in the city by December 1946. After that the rate of settlement decreased significantly. In 1947 only 63,000 Poles were relocated there; in 1948, 47,000; and in 1949, 35,000. All told, roughly 250,000 Poles settled in Wrocław between 1945 and 1949.[91]

In subsequent years, the migration balance (incoming settlers minus the many people leaving the city) was still far greater than 10,000 annually. Starting in 1953, the rate dropped to below 1 percent, thereby assuming the character and scope of normal domestic migration.[92] However, postwar Wrocław experienced an extraordinarily high rate of natural population growth, since the population exchange brought a disproportionately large number of young people to the city. In 1950 Wrocław already had more than 315,000 residents; in 1960 there were more than 438,000; and in 1970, more than 526,000. In 1981 the population reached 622,000, its prewar level, albeit the city limits had expanded considerably through the incorporation of several neighboring communities.[93] In the 1980s, Wrocław's population hardly increased at all, and in the 1990s it even decreased slightly due to a drop in the birthrate. In 1991 the population of the city reached its all-time high with roughly 645,000 inhabitants.[94]

SEARCHING FOR URBAN SETTLERS

Statistics are important, but they give little notion of the drama of the population exchange. Behind every number is an individual experience of uprooting and dislocation, of shock at being torn from familiar surroundings and thrown into what is foreign and unfamiliar. And it was not only individual lives that were disrupted. The population shift brought the histories of whole communities, some centuries old, to an abrupt end. It was a disruption that brought with it the egregious destruction of local knowledge and traditions that had developed over generations. In rural areas, the monstrosity of the forced population movements was apparent in the desperate and often unavailing efforts of relocated Polish farmers to get along in regions where they neither knew the soil nor the climate. Wherever the Germans who had previously cultivated the land were already gone, or where the Germans and the Poles could not communicate with each other, or the Germans simply did not want to share their knowledge, there was no one who could explain local conditions to the Polish settlers. The farmers from eastern Galicia, for example, discovered that the seeds they had brought with them and their familiar cultivation methods that resulted in high yields in the fertile eastern Galician soil were of little use in the soil of Pomerania or Silesia. Only the Oder lowlands around Wrocław were as fertile as the black earth of Galicia. Not only had these farmers lost their homes and homeland, but their agricultural know-how, accumulated over generations, was now largely worthless. Unlike the people themselves, it could not simply be picked up and moved to a new location.[95]

Polish flags indicated that an apartment was occupied by Polish settlers. Germans had to move out whenever called upon to do so by Polish authorities. In many cases, however, the city's old and new inhabitants, Germans and Poles, lived next door to each other for months and years. Courtesy of the City Museum of Wrocław (Henryk Makarewicz).

If the break in tradition proved so profound in the countryside, then what might be expected in a major city such as Wrocław? How would a social organism as complex as a city cope with the total exchange of its population and the loss of local knowledge and urban tradition? How could the city, once a cohesive community, avoid being reduced to a mere accumulation of settlements? Answers would have to be found, because the Polish leadership was determined to maintain Wrocław as a major city—and even make of it a model for the successful integration of the western territories. In addition to Polonizing the city, reattaining Wrocław's prewar urbanity and its economic and cultural vitality were goals of utmost political significance. And of course the new Wrocławians shared these goals. It was a matter of honor. Their Polish city should be in no way inferior to its German predecessor.

Publicists Stanisław Sokolewski and Edmund Osmańczyk, who traveled throughout the western territories in the spring of 1945, proposed that Wrocław's need for people with urban experience be satisfied by allowing a large number of its Germans to remain in the city permanently. Even though Osmańczyk and Sokolewski believed that 90 percent of the Germans in Wrocław had been pro-fascist and 100 percent anti-Polish, they nonetheless proposed that roughly 30,000 should be encouraged to adopt Polish citizenship. One Polish ancestor should be sufficient, they felt, for someone to become Polish, even without Polish language competence:

> The operation's success will depend on its immediate implementation once the relocation out of Silesia begins, at which time hopes of being allowed to stay will draw all the Polish grandmothers out of the woodwork, which will in turn provide us with a politically significant number of "Germanized Poles." Singling out these biologically valuable (the resettlement of families with children will only increase Germany's strength) and educated future Poles is an opportunity to show the world how well we're treating the Germans.[96]

They went on to suggest that among the Germans who claimed Polish ancestry in order to stay, a selection should be made on the basis of vocational qualifications and taking the number of children under twelve into account. Those selected would be accommodated in a special district for security reasons until their Polonization process was completed.

Implementing this proposal, which translated into Polish Nazi methods of Germanizing annexed territory, would almost certainly have failed in Wrocław. In contrast to Upper Silesia, Masuria, or the Wałbrzych coal-mining region, very few Wrocław residents could claim a living Polish background in 1945. Their ancestry may have been Polish, but their culture and language was German. The director of a Wrocław city district declared in 1946: "In characterizing the people who are attempting to prove their Polish ethnicity, we must emphasize that there is no autochthonous population that has been living here for two to three generations."[97]

According to official records, there were 2,769 autochthons in Wrocław in 1949, corresponding to about 1 percent of the population. Only a portion of them had lived in Wrocław for an extended period of time prior to 1945.[98] Most had settled there in the first half of the twentieth century, either having found work in Wrocław or after marrying a German. They therefore could hardly be considered autochthons in a true sense.[99] Also among the Wrocław autochthons were a number of "ordinary" Germans who for one reason or another had attempted to stay in the city. The Polish language competence of the autochthons was not always very good. According to official data, of the 2,769 authochthons in 1949, 774 spoke poor Polish, 966 middling Polish, and only 1,029 were fluent—this though they all had already spent years in a primarily Polish environment.[100] Even though the autochthons comprised only a small group within Wrocław's population, their integration proved difficult. The mayor reported in April 1948 that the assimilation of the heterogeneous populace had progressed rather far, but the autochthons remained passive in terms of their political, cultural, and economic life.[101]

Clearly, then, Wrocław's autochthons were not suited to Polonize the city and revitalize its urban culture. They were too few in number and insufficiently rooted in the city. The focus would have to be placed on new urban settlers— yet it was precisely urban citizens wanting to relocate who were in short supply. Poland was a largely agrarian country in which less than 30 percent of the population had lived in cities before the war.[102] War and occupation, the murder of the Jews (who had made up one-third of Poland's city dwellers), and the Nazi annihilation campaign against Polish elites had decimated the urban population. The Bureau of War Losses (Biuro Strat Wojennych) estimated in 1947 that 4.76 million of the 6 million Polish citizens who lost their lives between 1939 and 1945 (78.9 percent) had been urban residents.[103]

In its settlement plan of May 1945, the Office of the Western Territories estimated that there was space in the region's cities for more than four million people. The pool of potential urban settlers comprised roughly 1.8 million people, including 423,000 from eastern Poland, mainly from Wilno and Lwów, and 500,000 from the devastated city of Warsaw.[104] Little attention was paid, however, to the fact that this potential would be distributed across the length and breadth of Poland. Urbanites were in demand everywhere, and in every city of Poland they would find good employment opportunities thanks to their professional qualifications. In view of the uncertain political and economic future of the western territories, people were strongly motivated to remain in central Poland. Moreover, with the exception of the city of Warsaw, where destruction was almost total, central Poland had suffered less devastation than the new territories. And the few urbanites who were nevertheless willing to go west were able to choose from a whole list of destinations. Wrocław, Gdańsk, and Szczecin were three major cities that had to be resettled; there was also the urbanized industrial region of Upper Silesia and a large number of medium-sized and smaller towns between the Baltic coast and the Sudeten Mountains. Compared to demand, the supply of urban settlers was meager in postwar Poland.

The Scientific Council for the Recovered Territories devoted part of its first session of July 30 to August 1, 1945, to the settlement of Wrocław. Many of the experts present argued that Wrocław's urban tradition would be best nurtured if entire urban populations were settled there in groups. It was said that especially settlers from Lwów and Wilno should be relocated to the city in large numbers, if possible, in order to form a kind of urban nucleus that would set the tone and provide orientation for other settlers.[105] The sociologist and historian Paweł Rybicki argued strongly against this idea. He insisted that in quantitative terms the shifting of entire urban populations would contribute only minimally toward settling the cities in the western territories. The successful solution would be a general urbanization of the Polish population. This meant, however, that a large number of people would have to move from villages to the cities and undergo a process of cultural adaptation to urban life. He also argued that settling the people of Lwów or Wilno as a group would promote their isolation and thereby hinder the assimilation of heterogeneous settler groups into a cohesive urban society. Rybicki, who had studied in Lwów, also rejected the idea that that lost city could be restored to life by a wholesale transfer of its population and institutions to Wrocław:

> We won't be making Wrocław into another Lwów; instead, we must create a Polish Wrocław that will not be a copy of a city of the eastern borderlands but instead the great center of the western territories. In order to achieve this, I do not see any other option than to bring together people from various environments according to sober criteria, and to blend them into the new environment. [106]

Rybicki's suggestions were directed at the general goal of homogenizing the Polish nation in ethnic, cultural, and social terms and leveling the differences between citizens from diverse regional backgrounds.

Proposals for settling entire urban populations in Wrocław continued to be considered until the end of 1945. The idea evolved for the city of Krakow, which had assumed patronage of Wrocław,[107] to give up part of its own population to Wrocław. This proved unrealistic. There was little motivation for Krakowians to abandon their venerable city, which had hardly been damaged in the war, and move to Wrocław of all places, which lay in ruins. When in the fall of 1945 it became known that the Municipal National Council in Krakow considered transferring "unemployed persons, profiteers, and parasitical elements that show no interest in rebuilding the country" primarily to the western territories, a storm of outrage broke out in the Wrocław press and among its city leaders. Wrocław was not a "penal colony." It needed people, but people of outstanding character and expertise. The idea of patronage was quickly discredited.[108] Despite the geographic proximity of the two cities, Krakow never played a major role in the settlement of Wrocław.

In the fall of 1945, the Municipal National Council of Warsaw proposed transferring 50,000 of its residents to Wrocław. This idea was enthusiastically received in the city on the Oder. It was hoped that the newcomers would not only be genuine urbanites, but also the trained specialists and college graduates that Wrocław so desperately needed. Authorities in the two cities arranged three weekly transfers of 1,000 people each, and the Polish capital opened a liaison office in Wrocław to coordinate the settlement of its residents there. But this idea, too, soon proved impracticable. Due to organizational difficulties and a lack of enthusiasm among Varsovians for moving to Wrocław, only 1,000–3,000 people had been resettled by late December 1945, including a large number of orphans, invalids, and elderly people.[109]

The settlement of 30,000 people from Lwów in the winter of 1945–46 also ended in failure. Many of them, especially urgently-needed experts in the fields of administration and public utilities, left Wrocław again when the jobs and apartments they had been promised failed to materialize.[110] After this last unsuccessful attempt at a coordinated relocation of a core group of urban residents from major cities to Wrocław, settlement proceeded the same way as elsewhere in the territories: spontaneously and randomly. People came to the former German city from the most diverse regions of former Poland, from large cities and tiny villages. Nevertheless, the widespread belief persists to today that it was mostly eastern Poles, particularly expellees from Lwów, who settled in Wrocław after the war. This is all the more remarkable as Wrocław sociologist Irena Turnau exposed this claim as a myth as early as 1960 in her detailed study on the composition of the city's postwar population.[111]

According to Turnau's analyses, repatriates made up only 20 to 23 percent of the population in late 1947. Of these, the largest group did in fact come from the voivodeship of Lwów, but it comprised only between 6 and 10 percent of

Wrocław's urban population. Furthermore, not all settlers from the voivode-ship of Lwów came from the city of Lwów. Many came from provincial towns and villages in its environs. The majority of settlers in Wrocław, between 70 and 75 percent, had moved there from central Poland. Autochthons and re-emigrants played hardly any role at all, each comprising only between 1 and 2 percent of the total population.[112]

Turnau also demonstrated that the myth of postwar Wrocławians coming from eastern Poland contained a kernel of truth. Among academics and voca-tional groups with above-average education levels, there was a disproportion-ately high number of eastern Poles. Their share among parents of schoolchil-dren who attended college-track secondary schools was 22.3 to 27.5 percent; among candidates for university education the figure jumped to more than 36 percent.[113] More than 60 percent of professors at the university and poly-technic were repatriates in mid-1948, thus comprising the most dominant group.[114] It is therefore not surprising that the Polish expellees from the east played an important role in postwar Wrocław and often set the tone in the city's cultural and academic life, but in fact they comprised only a relatively small segment of the total population. Scholars from Lwów were particularly prominent. Stanisław Kulczyński, one of the last presidents of Lwów Univer-sity before the war, became the first president of the two Polish universities in Wrocław. The office of university vice president was assumed by Edward Sucharda, the last president of the Lwów polytechnic university. Many for-mer Lwów residents played important roles in public life: among them Jerzy Güttler, the first voivodeship conservator in Wrocław, architect Józef Rybicki who headed the Wrocław Directorate for Reconstruction, and writer Anna Kowalska, who became a leading figure in Wrocław literary circles in the 1940s and 1950s. Andrzej Jagielski described the "quasi-Lwówian character" that these elites gave to the cultural climate of postwar Wrocław.[115] In addition there were many Lwów streetcar conductors, like the academics from Lwów recognizable on account of their eastern Polish dialect, who might have added to the impression that lost Lwów had to some extent been resuscitated.

Settlers from the voivodeship of Poznań, on the other hand, are seldom mentioned. But in fact they constituted the largest population group in Wrocław in late 1947, making up 15 percent of the city's inhabitants. If one considers not the birthplace of the settlers but their last place of residence before moving to Wrocław, then their share increases to 19.5 percent. The voivodeship of Poznań was followed closely by the city and voivodeship of Warsaw with 13.6 percent. The voivodeships of Kielce (approx. 8 percent) and Krakow and Rzeszów (7 to 8 percent each) also stand out, while the share from other voivodeships in central Poland was low. A large number of people from the region of Greater Poland, the historic region centered on the city of Poznań, decided to settle in Wrocław primarily because of its geographical and cultural proximity. Many of them had been familiar with Wrocław and environs from the time before 1918, when the province of Posen (Poznań) was part of Prussia and thus the German Empire, or had at least heard accounts of visits to Wrocław from family and friends.[116] Tadeusz Konopiński, the father of the diary writer Joanna Konopińska, is probably typical of this group of settlers. Coming from Poznań, he had been a German citizen until 1918. After his military service in the German Army during the First World War, he studied agriculture in the new Poland and began an academic career, which took him eventually to Lwów. Through his professional contacts he visited Germany regularly, including Wrocław, where he occasionally gave lectures at the university. Konopiński's image of Germany was not determined solely by the terror of the Third Reich. Thus it was by no means an odd idea for him to move to Wrocław after the war and help reestablish a university, whose facilities he already knew and whose revitalization was important to him.[117]

The relatively high proportion of settlers from Warsaw in postwar Wrocław—the figure reached 20 percent in certain industries and educational institutions—was essentially due to the utter destruction of the Polish capital. Many Warsaw residents moved to Wrocław to take advantage of the career opportunities available to urbanites and because they hoped to be able once more to live a metropolitan lifestyle. It is telling, however, that in 1947–48 only 7 percent of Wrocław's college students came from Warsaw, a percentage less than half of Warsaw's overall share in the city's population. This was likely due to the affection that Varsovians continued to feel for their former hometown, which they preferred to Wrocław as a place of study and to which many of them would later return.[118]

The relatively large share of settlers from the southern voivodeships of Krakow, Kielce, and Rzeszów can be explained by the high population density of the area, which induced many to move to the sparsely populated western territories after 1945 in search of housing and work. Large numbers moved to the Wrocław region due to the city's geographic location on the main transportation routes between southern Poland and the western territories. In addition, numerous blue-collar workers from the heavily industrialized Kielce voivodeship moved to Wrocław because their factories had been destroyed. In the early postwar years they comprised up to 20 percent of the workforce in some Wrocław companies.[119]

The coexistence of people with such varied backgrounds was not without conflict. Settlers from central Poland had a very different mentality from those from eastern Poland. In contrast to central Poland, the east was marked by ethnic heterogeneity. Poles lived side by side with people who identified themselves as Belorussians, Ukrainians, Lithuanians, Russians, Jews, Gypsies, Germans, or somewhere in between these categories. In addition, the area was sparsely populated, its rural economy dominated by aristocrats with large estates, and there was virtually no industry and very little mechanized agriculture. Poles from the central region often looked down upon the supposedly backward voivodeships of the east, even though their inhabitants comprised a large segment of Poland's cultural elite, especially residents of the metropolises of Wilno and Lwów. Differences between settlers from central and eastern Poland also stemmed, in part, from their divergent war experiences. Eastern Poles had been victimized not only by the Germans but also by the Soviet occupation. Between 1939 and 1941 they had experienced the ruthless Sovietization of the annexed areas; they lost members of their families through both the NKVD's executions of alleged "class enemies" and the mass deportations of Polish citizens to the Soviet Union. After the war they were expelled from their homes under often traumatic circumstances or transferred against their will to the western territories. These experiences embittered their attitudes toward Polish communists and the Soviet armed forces stationed in Wrocław. The Office for Information and Propaganda in the voivodeship of Wrocław reported in May 1946 that the repatriates were "a destructive element, constantly dissatisfied. They express their hatred for Soviet Russia freely and loudly. They claim they have nothing to lose, because they left everything behind in the east."[120]

Poland's communist government viewed the repatriates as potential political opponents who could never be won over for socialism and who had to be watched more carefully than other population groups.[121] Thus, while they held many of the leading positions in Wrocław's cultural life, they rarely assumed important positions in the state administration.

THE RURALIZATION OF THE CITY

Although the divergent regional backgrounds of Wrocław's population did give rise to some tension, it should be emphasized that coexistence in the city was hindered far more by differences between city dwellers and peasants. It even seems that the friction between settlers from eastern and central Poland was frequently more the result of conflicts between urbanites and country folk than a conflict, as was often claimed, between persons from different geographic regions. Eastern Poles were viewed as symbols of all that was rural and backward, whereas central Poles as a whole were considered more advanced—irrespective of the fact that the percentage of city dwellers among the settlers from eastern Poland was higher than among those from central Poland. The cultural differences between people from Poznań, Warsaw, and Lwów were also far less significant than those between urban and rural dwellers within one and the same voivodeship.

The clash between those who had previously been living in a city and those who were still firmly entrenched in a rural way of life was nothing short of culture shock for both sides. Urbanites found themselves outnumbered by a great mass of settlers unfamiliar with the conventions of city life. In the first few years after the war, the massive influx of village inhabitants subjected Wrocław to a powerful surge of deurbanization—assuming that one could still speak of urbanity in a city so thoroughly destroyed and depopulated. In 1947–48, only 18 percent of the Polish population of Wrocław came from cities with populations over 100,000. More than 40 percent of Polish Wrocławians had resettled from small and medium-sized towns; the remaining 40 percent were former villagers, to a large degree smallholders or landless agricultural workers.[122] The influx of population from the villages continued even after the completion of the population exchange, albeit not to as great an extent. In 1970, 56.6 percent of the 282,000 inhabitants of the city who were older than twenty-five (and thus not native Wrocławians) had been born in a village. One can therefore conclude that in the first half of the 1950s at least two-thirds of Wrocławians had been socialized in a rural-agrarian environment.[123]

In order to gain a sense of the atmosphere in Wrocław during the first years after the war, it is important to keep in mind that almost half the city's inhabitants had come directly from a village, and even among the urbanites many had lived in towns with a semirural character. Rural migration to large cities is not unusual, of course. It had promoted the rapid growth of modern cities throughout Europe. But things were different in Wrocław after 1945. With the expulsion of the Germans, the foundation of urban culture had vanished, leaving the rural immigrants with no role models to follow in learning the ways of city life.[124] Urbanites from Warsaw, Lwów, and Wilno were equipped to be helpful, but they themselves were unfamiliar with Wrocław. Generally better educated, they did assume many of the leadership positions in the administration, industry, and the cultural sector, thereby becoming an influential group within the city. But when it came to maintaining or, better, reestablishing an urban lifestyle in Wrocław, they found themselves overwhelmed by the vast preponderance of rural settlers.

Many of the peasants who moved to Wrocław after the war did not abandon their rural lifestyle. Instead they did their best to maintain it in their new urban environment. A large segment settled on the outskirts of the city, sometimes in the affluent suburbs of the vanished German bourgeoisie, where they could keep livestock in the large backyards and cultivate fruits and vegetables. Others moved to the city center where they felt more secure than in the sparsely populated suburbs, and where the distances to shopping and work were almost as short as in a village. But there were also those who wanted to escape country life and deliberately sought housing in the city center, which in terms of its architecture and traffic density contrasted radically with the environments from which they had come.[125] Even though many of them moved into nineteenth-century tenements that others had rejected in favor of elegant suburbs or modern housing developments, they were nonetheless proud of their new lives:

> We citizens of this great city not only live in apartment buildings, but, more importantly, we travel by streetcar. In those first years after the war, we who used to travel by bicycle or horse-drawn cart were utterly enchanted with this form of locomotion.[126]

Thus former village residents settled not only in the suburbs of Wrocław, but also in the city center, and they inevitably brought their lifestyles and ways of thinking with them. It was not only in the suburbs that veritable farmsteads developed; even in the city center it was commonplace for people to keep cows, pigs, sheep, goats, and fowl.[127] Advertisements such as the following were quite common:

> Goat stolen at ul. Kościuszki 26, flat 10. The finder is requested to please return it to the above address for a reward.[128]

Ul. Kościuszki runs directly through the city center. Here, in the city's most urban district, the sound of a goat bleating embodied this bizarre postwar world in which Wrocław had turned, temporarily, into a huge village. Not all Wrocławians approved:

> A certain segment of the populace in every neighborhood, despite the fact that they have resided in the city for a long time, cannot rid themselves of their rustic habits and influences. Proof of this are those awful sheds they cobble together from sundry old materials, which one finds in courtyards even in the center of town. . . . The sounds of goats, chickens, and even cows can be heard daily in the neighborhoods of Krzyki and Grabiszynek; you can even see cows grazing in the squares and on park lawns. Pigeon-breeding is on the rise throughout the city, especially in the city center and the Old Town.[129]

Unfortunately, Wrocław's apartment buildings and suburban mansions were not well suited for rearing farm animals. In the interests of maintaining the city's urban appearance and preserving its building stock, the municipal government was forced to intervene. In 1947 the Municipal National Council established a commission to deal specifically with the issue of livestock in the city. In April 1947 the Council reported on the situation in one of the formerly well-to-do, middle-class neighborhoods:

> There is a whole series of buildings in the city of Wrocław where cattle and swine can be found: the property at ul. Michałowskiego (Biskupin) 10, for example, where one of the residents keeps cows and horses in the garage and pigs in the cellar. One of the residents at ul. Michałowskiego 4 owns two cows, for which a stable has been constructed. On ul. Pankiewicza, where almost all the residents are officials of the PKP [Polish

State Railway], cows and pigs are kept in unsanitary conditions in the cellars of many of the houses.[130]

Animal husbandry in the city and the agricultural use of municipal parks and green spaces did not result solely from the presence of large numbers of peasants. Food shortages were widespread in postwar Europe, and city dwellers—not in Poland alone—were forced to use their wits and their hands to develop the agricultural potential of urban space in order to make up for the shortfalls in the stores and marketplaces. In Berlin, as in Wrocław, parks and green spaces were converted to fields and vegetable beds, cultivated by city residents acting on their own initiative. The ruralization of urban space was, thus, a postwar phenomenon born of necessity. It did not disappear until supplies became reliable and the need for turnips and potatoes from city parks diminished.

In Wrocław it took far longer for vestiges of the rural way of life and mentality to yield to the hustle and bustle of the metropolis. "At Eastertide, in those first years after the war," said a Wrocławian from the Lwów voivodeship, "people took to the half-barbarian custom of spraying water on one another, so characteristic of the Polish countryside."[131] Those who did not come from eastern Poland, like this settler from the voivodeship of Poznań, held the new arrivals from the east responsible for spreading village customs in Wrocław:

> The inhabitants of Wrocław, who came primarily from the eastern territories of Poland and from beyond the Bug River, held tightly to the habits they brought with them to the Polish western territories. In warm weather and on holidays, they would sit in front of their buildings, on the sidewalk, or on chairs they had brought out of their homes, and chew the fat and drink vodka. The sidewalks in the city center, even around the Rynek, were strewn with potato peelings and crusts of bread, tossed to the pigeons. People would lie about on the greenswards and squares and in the parks, playing cards, drinking vodka, and generally leaving an utter mess behind them. Children would run riot on the lawns and through the flowerbeds, tearing up flowers and destroying blossoming shrubs; and the adults helped them, so long as the police were nowhere in sight. The same thing

happened in the cemeteries, especially on ul. Osobowicka and ul. Grabiszyńska.[132]

Joanna Konopińska wrote a telling report on the ways in which a farmer's family tried to make themselves at home in their new village on the outskirts of Wrocław:

> On our way to Oleśnica, Father, Tolka, and I stopped in the second village past Wrocław, Dlugolece, because the car was overheating, and we needed to add water to the radiator. I went into one of the houses and saw a strange sight there. The inhabitants were building a huge brick oven in the kitchen.
>
> "What do you need such a large oven for?" I asked them, because right next to it was an oven that looked completely new.
>
> "What do you mean, what for?" said a woman, stout as a barrel, in surprise at my question. "What else will we sleep on? Stupid question . . ." she added, picking up a brick from the floor.
>
> I was not particularly interested in pursuing the discussion.
>
> When I went out with the jug of water, I saw people from the house pulling apart the building next door and carrying the pilfered bricks back to their flat.
>
> "Dad," I said, upset about what I had seen. "They're taking apart the barn in order to build an oven to sleep on. That sort of thing should be against the law!" Father was looking through some papers and did not react at all to my oh-so-astute comment.[133]

A former resident of Wilno sneered with unmistakable arrogance at the poor taste of his neighbors from the countryside:

> A large percentage of the people living in Wrocław came from small towns and villages. This was reflected—and continues to be reflected, though to a lesser extent—in their manners, customs, and outward appearance. It is enough to remember how popular the carnivals were in those first years after the war. Today, the people who go tend to have not even five years of "city experience" under their belts. I'm an optimist, and it seems to me that people are less interested now in decorating their apartments with "Rutting Deer." Fewer and fewer people are painting their apartments "with life-like palms and elephants," or so I'm

told by a certain relative of mine, a house painter. The average level of taste seems to be rising. . . . That is better than moving in the opposite direction[134]

When the flow of peasant immigrants gradually dried up in the course of the 1950s, a process of reurbanization began to unfold in Wrocław. "After a few years," according to Włodzimierz Kalicki, "the people and the city adapted to each other. Livestock vanished from the sidewalks and courtyards, as did underwear drying on clotheslines stretched across the streets."[135]

Years and decades passed, however, before Wrocław could again be regarded as a metropolis in a cultural sense. The diverse society that had gathered in the city on the Oder after the war had to undergo a gradual process of acculturation, slowly adapting to urban life so as to develop a consciousness of constituting a whole, that is, of being the new Wrocławians. The settlers at first continued to identify themselves principally as people from Galicia or Mazovia, Lwów or Warsaw, and they maintained close ties to their former homes. It was up to their children and grandchildren, who were born in Wrocław and who quite naturally recognized themselves as Wrocławians, even if they did not yet have a clear idea of what that meant.

Wrocław's reurbanization did not depend only on the rural settlers becoming citified. After all the destruction of the war years, Wrocław also had to be turned back into a city in the physical sense. Everything that makes a major metropolis what it is, the vast expanses of housing, the heavy traffic in the city center and its thoroughfares that connect the city to the world outside, the pulse of the factories and the rhythm of commerce in the shops and department stores, all the vitality and diversity of public life—none of that was left at war's end. Wrocław's urban life was no more. The main settlement areas had already shifted to the north and northeast during the siege. And after the war most people lived north of the Oder, especially in the tenements between Nadodrze train station and pl. Grunwaldzki, and in the affluent suburbs and garden cities of Karłowice, Zacisze, Biskupin, and Sępolno. Many others found shelter in the less damaged parts of the western Old Town and in the densely built-up districts around ul. Traugutta and ul. Kościuszki south and southeast of the historic city center. The districts west of 1st of May Square (now John Paul II Square) and south of the central train station, once the most important residential areas of Wrocław, had been transformed into eerie ruins and remained largely uninhabited long after the war. At first it was the southern and southwestern suburbs of Krzyki and Oporów, far from the city center, that could offer intact houses and apartments and therefore attracted settlers.[136]

There was still no connection between these isolated islands of settlement. Rubble and barricades blocked the streets. Buses and streetcars were no longer running. Areas that had become uninhabitable were scattered across the fabric of the city like dead zones, tearing apart the urban texture. Wrocław had become an agglomeration of loosely connected villages set in an expanse of rubble. Although the architecture was reminiscent of a metropolis, Wrocław had ceased to be one. The municipal transportation network would have to be reestablished, the city center revitalized, and the devastated districts rebuilt before the scattered settlements would regain a context and recover a sense of belonging around a common center. The city would have to become a city for a second time.

CHAPTER THREE

A Loss of Substance

AFTER THE POPULATION EXCHANGE, THE MOST URGENT TASK THAT POL-
ish leaders in the western territories faced was the revitalization of the economy. Władysław Gomułka declared in August 1945:

> The reborn Poland has scored a great political victory at the Potsdam
> Conference. The Polish nation has reason to be happy and triumphant.
> But this victory will only be complete when Poles inhabit all the towns
> and villages in the west and on the Baltic coast, when smoke billows out
> of all the factory chimneys, when all the Recovered Territories begin to
> flourish, and when, along the great Oder river that forms the border of
> our country, ships carrying millions of tons of Polish goods sail to our
> port in Szczecin and from there across the Baltic Sea to wider interna-
> tional markets.[1]

Gomułka's "victory" was still a long way off. The western territories that now
belonged to Poland had been ravaged by the war. The degree of devastation
varied. Along the Sudeten Mountains in Lower Silesia, there were villages
and towns such as Bystrzyca Kłodzka, Kłodzka, Dzierżoniów, Świdnica,
and Jelenia Góra that had survived the war unscathed. The Upper Silesian
industrial region had also sustained relatively little damage, as the Soviets
had deliberately spared it during their advance. But along the Oder and in
Pomerania and East Prussia, where fighting had been heavy, the war damage reached devastating proportions. Countless cities lay in ruin, bridges and
railway facilities had been blown up, farms burned to the ground, seed stock
and agricultural equipment either destroyed or carried away by the Germans
as they fled westward. The livestock, too, had either been killed or chased off,
and the fields and pastureland churned up by tank tracks.

Vandalism and the Great Fires

The end of the fighting did not mark the end of the destruction. In fact, a wave of vandalism followed the conquest of German territory. Whatever fleeing German civilians and troops had left behind became fair game for plundering, demolition, and arson. Poles and Soviet soldiers vented anger that had accumulated over years of war and occupation, and for their part, Germans did not want to leave anything of value for the victors. Much that was urgently needed for reconstruction was destroyed, thereby exacerbating the already dismal circumstances. A witness, one of the first Polish settlers in Legnica, reported in retrospect:

> It was a sprawling town, rich and uninhabited; clean, almost spruce. . . .
> The city lay wide open, exposed. . . . You could take over an apartment, a villa . . . abandoned by a doctor, banker, or general. You could burn down a house. . . .
>
> All those riches, there for the taking like the proverbial diamonds in the desert, were enough to drive some people mad. . . . Even I, who come from a family of doctors, sometimes lost my good sense at the sight of valuables accumulated over the centuries. I can only wonder how those poor people from the shacks and basements must have felt, who had experienced little in life besides hard work and pitiful pay! . . . .
>
> For amusement, they [Soviet soldiers] would hurl luxury items from the top floors of buildings out onto the street: lampshades, crystal vases, stoneware chamber pots, which shattered on the asphalt below. They threw chairs, armchairs, anything they could find. And when they pushed an old harpsichord off a balcony, what a final tone it sounded when it hit the ground![2]

When the vanguard of the Polish administration arrived in Wrocław, much of the city was in flames. The fires reached their peak between May 7 and May 10 and turned the nights to day.[3] The great fire on Sand Island, which probably broke out in the former Institute for Eastern European Studies on May 11, was particularly tragic. It jumped over to the neighboring building and also spread to St. Anne's and to the Church of the Blessed Virgin Mary on the Sand. A large portion of the books from the university library were being stored in St. Anne's Church. Helpers from Kulczyński's Science and Culture Group arrived immediately, but without any equipment they could neither extinguish the fire nor save the books. They had to watch as 300,000 irreplaceable volumes turned to ash.[4]

The fire that broke out on May 17 in the Church of St. Mary Magdalene in the Old Town also led to heavy losses. The opulent furnishings of the impressive Gothic building, which had suffered only minor damage during the siege, fell victim to the flames. The southernmost of the two towers, whose Renaissance spires had long defined the silhouette of the Old Town, collapsed, and St. Mary's five-hundred-year-old bell crashed to the ground and melted in the heat.[5]

These devastating conflagrations are some of the most lasting memories of those who saw Wrocław in the days and weeks after the war.[6] There is no consensus as to the cause of the fires. Joachim Konrad blamed Soviet soldiers:

> They would look into cabinets by candlelight, tear things out, stamp on objects for which they had no use and then burn them. Anyone who did not intervene immediately and courageously would see his house go up in flames. Our fire brigade was held up in Krzyki. They didn't have enough water to put out the fires. . . . For roughly four weeks after the capitulation, every day from the tower [of St. Elizabeth's], I counted twenty or thirty large fires raging in the city.[7]

In contrast, Andrzej Jochelson wrote in his diary:

> Wrocław is in flames and you can hear constant gunfire. Every day there are two, three, or even four fires. The shells of tenement buildings are doused with inflammable liquids and within a few hours they burn to the ground. You can always see at least one plume of smoke on the horizon. The fires are most likely being started by the Germans, the Hitlerites.[8]

It is typical of postwar recollections that people assumed the fires were started by arson. Germans usually suspected Soviet soldiers, whereas Poles, at least in publications prior to 1989, suspected German saboteurs. Since 1989, Polish historians such as Władysław Mochocki tend to seek the guilty parties among

Weeks after the war had ended, fires continued to burn destroying hundreds of buildings and devastating entire quarters. The towers of St. Mary Magdalene, one of Wrocław's most famous landmarks, had survived the war intact. But ten days after the city's capitulation, they went up in flames and partly collapsed (opposite page). Courtesy of the City Museum of Wrocław (above: Henryk Makarewicz; opposite page: Krystyna Gorazdowska).

the Russians.[9] British historians Norman Davies and Roger Moorhouse have even suggested that the Red Army was waiting for the opportunity to set Wrocław on fire once the city had been taken.[10] This assumption, however, for which they offer no evidence, is not very convincing given the strategic significance of Wrocław for the Soviet armed forces.

Marauding Red Army soldiers, German saboteurs, and Polish plunderers who set houses ablaze—out of anger, for fun, or to destroy the traces of their plundering—undoubtedly all did their share in setting countless fires in the

first weeks after the war. However, the fires were also a consequence of the collapse of the previous regime, and nowhere was this collapse more complete than in the western territories. Arson was not even necessary. Entire cities could burn without it. As soon as apartments and houses were abandoned and no one was there to extinguish a fire or when there was no longer any fire department to summon, then even small fires could ignite entire buildings in no time and spread sparks to neighboring buildings. Munitions left lying around and detonating in the heat did their part as well. Then it was only a matter of the weather and the conditions of the buildings whether or not entire districts went up in flames and burned to the ground.

In order to get the blazes in Wrocław under control, the Polish city government reactivated three fire engines from the local fire brigade museum, as no modern equipment was available.[11] But it was not only a lack of vehicles that obstructed the work of the fire fighters. With the city's water system severely damaged, the water supply was insufficient to fight the numerous fires. It took weeks and even months before any semblance of efficient firefighting was possible in Wrocław. During this time the city's residents had to watch helplessly as countless buildings and valuable facilities fell victim to the flames.[12]

SOVIET DISMANTLING

The Red Army engaged in extensive dismantling in Wrocław as elsewhere, which considerably complicated the rebuilding of the city.[13] Material assets that remained were removed from all of Poland, but especially from the western territories, an action that could hardly be reconciled with official proclamations of Polish-Soviet friendship. Poland's communist government was concerned about its reputation among the Polish people, which was compromised not only by the sheer volume of the Soviet dismantling but also by the recklessness with which it was carried out.

On August 9, 1944, the Soviet leadership had stated by order of the State Defense Committee that only militarily relevant goods such as weapons, munitions, motor vehicles, provisions stores, and fuel depots would be sequestered on Polish state territory. Efforts by Polish negotiators to have these limitations on dismantling extended to include the future western territories were unsuccessful. The Soviet Union reserved its right, in compliance with the Allied agreements in Yalta, to seize material assets as reparations throughout all of German state territory, including those regions that would later be ceded to Poland. A resolution passed by the defense committee on February 20, 1945, did stipulate that the Soviet Union would transfer all facilities, factories, and other companies to Poland without delay. However, there was a long list of companies that were excluded, and reference was repeatedly made to clauses that exempted goods directly needed to supply the Soviet armed forces. The Soviet leadership, however, lacked both the reserves and the transport capabilities to adequately provide for their troops at the front, so it had no alternative but to urge the Red Army to take what it needed from the occupied territories.

In the Polish-Soviet intergovernmental agreement of March 26, 1945, in fact, the Polish side had to officially permit the Soviet Union to carry out dismantling operations throughout Polish state territory. The Soviet government laid claim not only to war-relevant goods and all plant facilities and assets that the Germans had transported westward out of the Soviet Union and which were now on Polish territory, but also to some of the "German companies." "German" meant any company on formerly German territory as well as those facilities on Polish soil that had been erected by the Germans during the occupation.[14] The criteria according to which the Soviet Union claimed material assets in Poland were thus very broad and adherence to the rules could hardly be verified on a case-by-case basis. Local Soviet commanders and dismantling commissions could ultimately act as they saw fit, removing anything they considered interesting or valuable.

Soviet units in Poland took particular advantage of the period prior to the Potsdam Conference—which was supposed to make binding decisions on all border and reparations issues—to seize anything they could: stores of provisions, factories, power plants, railroad and port facilities, real estate, motor vehicles, seed stock, and agricultural equipment. The remaining livestock was slaughtered to feed the troops, brought to farms under Soviet control, or gathered into huge herds and driven to the Soviet Union. By the war's end "trophy brigades," specially created by the Red Army, had grown into a massive, centrally organized dismantling apparatus, that could take down entire industrial plants and railroad lines and ship them off to the Soviet Union in hundreds of thousands of freight car loads. The dismantling was often so hasty and carried out with so little care that the dismantled facilities were damaged or totally destroyed, or simply left standing out somewhere at the mercy of the elements. A good proportion of the dismantled facilities never reached its destination in the Soviet Union and was never put back into operation.

Even articles of daily use such as furniture, clothing, linens, household appliances, radios, and musical instruments were seized on a large scale. On top of official requisitioning came massive private looting by Soviet soldiers. Starting in December 1944, Red Army soldiers were allowed to send monthly packages back home—ordinary soldiers up to five kilograms (11 pounds) and officers ten kilograms.[15] Thus soldiers had an enormous incentive to supply their families with goods pilfered from the occupied areas or to collect war trophies.

> Russians passing through [a baggage train] plundered and chased down the last chickens. . . . The Russians left nothing for the Poles. Huge livestock herds, horses, and sheep were driven eastward; all machinery and field equipment was transported off. In Neustettin I saw entire truckloads with pianos or beds and mattresses taken to the train. The Russian commander in Dieck said to me: "The Poles get to keep the soil."[16]

Two reports from Wrocław tell similar stories:

> Russians kept coming, nonstop, usually high-ranking officers, and demanding things to ship out. The mayor dictated through interpreters, for example, "Piano, sewing machine, wardrobe, bedroom, etc." I wrote a report to a highway surveyor who knew where we could still get some items. They mercilessly took the objects from people, without any kind of receipt.[17]

> The main thing the [German] liaisons did was to register all the pianos, bicycles, radios, typewriters, etc. There were serious penalties if they concealed anything. After being entered on the lists, everything was randomly loaded onto trucks, transported off, and then carelessly transferred from the trucks onto freight trains. Ultimately it was all about taking everything before Silesia was transferred to the Poles.[18]

It was only after the Potsdam Conference that the Soviet and Polish governments at last negotiated an agreement that would finalize the terms of reparations and regulate the dismantling. At the talks in Moscow, Poland's deputy prime minister Stanisław Mikołajczyk protested vehemently against the plundering of his country by the Soviet Union.[19] A bilateral agreement was signed on August 16, 1945, in which the Soviet Union agreed to refrain from all further dismantling operations and also promised to pay Poland 15 percent of the reparations from the Soviet Occupation Zone in Germany and 30 percent of those from the western zones. In return Poland had to supply the Soviet Union with Silesian coal for a fixed price far under the world market price for the entire duration of the Soviet occupation in Germany.[20]

Irrespective of this agreement, the dismantling continued. In September 1945 the politburo of the PPR sent a memorandum to the Soviet government demanding an end to it and compliance with the treaties, referring to Poland's economic situation, the increasingly anti-Soviet mood in the country, and the precarious situation in which the dismantling put the pro-Moscow PPR.[21] In view of their dependence on Moscow, however, the Polish communists were unable to exert any serious pressure; again and again they learned the lesson that the Soviet leadership felt little compunction to honor its promises. In particular the local Soviet commanders showed little consideration for Polish rights or interests. Outrageous arguments were often used to justify breaking treaties. With regard to the requisitioning of tiles from Wrocław's Villeroy and Boch plant in Leśnica in July 1946, for example, the headquarters of the North Group of the Soviet armies claimed that the tiles were not even Polish property. Ostensibly they had been ordered in 1938 to build the Moscow Metro, but had not yet been delivered.[22]

A considerable share of the real estate and movables on Polish territory remained in Soviet hands for years. Poland had to permit the Soviet armed forces stationed in the country to use numerous industrial plants, agricultural estates, and building complexes. In the Polish western territories in early 1947, the Soviet army controlled more than 490 industrial facilities and more than 1.8 million acres of land, including 640 farms of more than 250 acres and 3,360 of under 250 acres.[23] Especially around the transportation hubs of Szczecin and Wrocław, large agricultural estates, quite a number of factories, and extensive building complexes long remained in the possession of the Soviet armed forces.[24]

As one of the major industrial locations, Wrocław was of particular interest to the Soviets. Based on the number of industrial and craft enterprises and the number of workers in the city in 1939, Wrocław exceeded the economic potential of the industrial cities Zabrze, Gliwice, Bytom, Wałbrzych, and Olsztyn combined or of the later Polish voivodeships of Olsztyn, Gdańsk, and Koszalin combined.[25] During the Second World War numerous industrial companies from western and central Germany were relocated to Wrocław, and existing facilities, especially in the armaments industry, were expanded. Consequently, Wrocław had a considerably higher industrial capacity at the start of the siege than it had had at the start of the war.[26] Since there are no extant reports detailing the extent of the destruction in individual factories directly after the city was taken over, it can no longer be determined precisely what state Wrocław's industrial facilities were in when the city capitulated. It can therefore only be estimated to what extent the loss of industrial substance was due to each of several possible factors: overuse of the facilities through increased armaments production and lack of renovations during the war; German dismantling and destruction of facilities prior to the end of the war; wartime destruction during the siege; damages due to vandalism, fire, and plundering after the German capitulation; Soviet dismantling; and the removal of facilities by the Polish authorities. Jędrzej Chumiński, who attempted to paint an approximate picture of the condition of industrial facilities, has argued that, based on available data and evidence, the city's economic potential at the time of capitulation was still rather substantial. According to his estimates, 56.3 percent of the facilities of the paper industry, 40 percent of the electrotechnical industry, and 31.1 percent of the chemical industries were in good condition at the end of the war. Only 20.7 percent of the facilities of the metalworking industry, which was traditionally a key industry in Wrocław, survived the war without major damage. About 50 percent of the factories were 30 percent destroyed, 22.4 percent were 70 percent destroyed, and 5.2 percent were completely annihilated.[27]

The Red Army was skillful at exploiting its power and its time advantage vis-à-vis the Polish civilian administration in order to take possession of what was most valuable. More than two hundred of the largest and best-known companies, such as the Linke-Hofmann Works (later PaFaWag), Archimedes, FAMO (later Dolmel), H. Meinecke Works (later Wrocławska Fabryka Wodomierzy), and the Borsig AG (later Państwowe Zakłady Lotnicze no. 3) initially fell into Soviet hands.[28] In addition, the Red Army secured huge provisions storehouses still under municipal control at the end of the siege period, and occupied hundreds of buildings. In late 1946 the Soviet armed forces sequestered more than three hundred residential buildings in Wrocław without paying any rent whatsoever.[29]

The Polish city leaders had no alternative but to politely request that the leadership of the Soviet armed forces transfer the facilities, whereby they were astonishingly successful initially. After Mayor Drobner negotiated with the commanders of the First Ukrainian Front in Żagań on May 12, 1945, the Soviet city commander of Wrocław received orders to transfer all municipal companies to the Polish municipal administration without delay. Furthermore, Drobner was promised in Żagań that Wrocław's academic and research facilities and numerous industrial firms, including some of the most valuable factories, would also be transferred.[30] On June 6, 1945, the municipal administration was promised forty-five major companies; in addition to municipal facilities they also received the large plants: Linke-Hofmann, Archimedes, FAMO, and Adler, as well as a number of consumer goods factories.[31] However, Soviet promises were often of limited value. Even after factories had been transferred to the Polish administration and repairs had already begun, time and again Soviet units would come and unceremoniously kick out the workers and begin dismantling everything, leaving behind only what was impossible to carry off.[32]

The government feared that Wrocław would be totally divested of industry and wanted especially to save the Linke-Hofmann Works, one of Europe's largest producers of railroad cars and locomotives for Poland. Its attempt to intervene in Moscow were, however, rarely successful. The Soviet government did order, on June 29, 1945, that sixteen factories in Lower Silesia be turned over to Poles. Among them was the Linke-Hofmann Works, but only 50 percent of the Archimedes facilities and only 50 percent of the laboratories and libraries of the chemical institute of the Technical University and the laboratories of the University of Wrocław—far less than what Drobner had been promised in Żagań.[33] The dismantling operations were as chaotic in Wrocław as elsewhere. In the case of the Linke-Hofmann Works, Soviets disassembled most of the machinery. Although they later returned some of it, many of the machines came back missing essential and hard to replace parts.[34] Because many factories were plundered after they had officially been transferred to Polish hands and the local Soviet commanders continually made new requisitions for additional machinery,[35] the willingness of the Polish authorities to make larger investments waned and the workforces became dispirited.

It is impossible to determine the exact extent of losses due to Soviet dismantling. Hilary Minc, then industry minister, estimated the losses at 25 percent of all technical facilities in the western territories. Chumiński considers this estimate far too low, at least for Wrocław. In the Wrocław textile industry, for example, of the 2,500 machines in twenty-three factories, only 1,252 were still there when the factories were transferred to Polish hands, according to Chumiński, and most of them had been damaged. In the eighteen factories of the metal industry, he writes, 3,730 machine tools had been dismantled, 1,000 each at Rheinmetall Borsig and FAMO alone. In the Linke-Hofmann Works, 424 machine tools and 694 electric motors had been dismantled and all the tools taken. In the four largest metalworking factories in Wrocław, only 1,352 machines all told remained in place in July 1946, and only 235 of the 809 machines in the possession of PaFaWag were intact. Although the Soviet Union did deliver machinery it had disassembled in the Soviet Occupation Zone in Germany in the second half of the 1940s, this compensated neither quantitatively nor qualitatively for the losses resulting from dismantling on Polish territory.[36] According to Chumiński's estimates, Poland took over only 40 percent of the industrial potential that Wrocław had had in 1939, while the Soviets had removed precisely those pieces of equipment that were most modern and most intact.[37]

The Polish people responded to the Soviet practices with bitterness and anger. Since the Soviet Union had been presented as the triumphant victor of the Second World War and little of what was happening within its borders was known to the outside world, only very few people had any idea of the economic hardships the Soviet Union faced at the end of the war. A large portion of the country had been plundered and ravaged; almost thirty million Soviet citizens had lost their lives. German troops had engaged in scorched earth tactics as they retreated, dismantling or destroying industrial plants and blowing up bridges, roads, and railroad lines. Villages were set on fire and cities razed to the ground. By the end of the war, 1,710 Soviet cities and 70,000 villages had been destroyed.[38] All the while that the Soviet government was preparing to implement its economic and social model throughout Eastern Europe, it proved unable to avert severe famine at home, triggered by a drought in 1946.[39] Even many years after the war, the supply situation in the Soviet Union remained precarious, and agricultural and industrial production was only very gradually restored to its prewar level.

This situation has to be taken into consideration when assessing Soviet dismantling operations in Poland. Poland was of course also a country ravaged by war, but its economic potential had grown considerably as a result of the border shift. It gained possession of the industrial area of Upper Silesia (which had suffered only minor damage), the Silesian mineral deposits, Baltic port cities such as Gdańsk and Szczecin, and the well-developed (as compared with areas in central and eastern Poland) infrastructure of the western territories. The loss of the eastern regions of Poland forced millions of Poles to leave their homes and, with Wilno and Lwów, Poland had lost two of its most significant cultural centers, which could not be compensated for through the gain of German cities. From an economic perspective, however, Poland gained far more in the west than it lost in the east, where there were no appreciable natural resources other than some oil and gas in East Galicia, where industry was only weakly developed and roads and railways were few and far between.[40] Against this background the Soviet dismantling operations in Poland are easier to understand. In essence it was not a matter of collecting war trophies, but a desperate attempt to stimulate the reconstruction of a devastated country. In addition, given the economic hardships in the Soviet Union, the Soviet armed forces were left more or less to their own resources and had little recourse other than to take long-term possession of goods and factories in order to secure the supplies they needed at their bases abroad.

It is difficult to judge how much the dismantling hurt Poland's economic development after the war. Even the reduced industrial potential that was left to Poland could not at first be fully exploited. There was a shortage of workers, especially skilled craftsmen, of funds for necessary investments, and of raw materials. In Wrocław, PaFaWag and the State Machine Tool Factory (Państwowa Fabryka Obrabiarek) were working only at about 75 percent of their capacity in the late 1940s, and Dolmel only at 43 percent.[41] In the phase of Stalinist economic policies between 1949 and 1956, when investments were concentrated entirely in heavy industry and the industrial centers, a large number of consumer goods factories and plants located outside the main industrial centers sat idle. It was only with the political changes of

1956 that the Polish government made an attempt to gradually restore these facilities to operation.

The "Szabrownicy" and the Black Market

It would be difficult to find an eyewitness account of the postwar period in the Polish western territories that did not at some point mention the "szaber." For lack of a better word, *szaber* can be translated as "looting" and, therefore, *szabrownik* as "looter." This translation is not entirely accurate, however, because looting means taking possession of someone else's property by force and is thus a criminal act. *Szaber,* on the other hand, took place in a legal gray zone. Temporarily it was, at least de facto, tolerated. According to a Polish dictionary, *szaber* means "to appropriate objects that have been abandoned by their owners, divested of guardianship (usually in wartime)."[42] In the western territories it became a mass phenomenon, an everyday activity that not only criminals engaged in, but also upstanding people with the best of intentions. Looting was an opportunity for personal gain, but it was also a necessary strategy for survival. People tried to live on what the departing Germans had left behind. Their abandoned apartments and houses were filled with stocks of food, furniture, clothing, linens, dishes, household appliances, radios, and much more. In deserted offices there were typewriters, telephones, office chairs, stores of paper, and writing supplies. Workshops and factories offered all kinds of equipment and raw materials, and in their haste to leave, merchants often left their shops with the shelves and storerooms fully stocked.

The Polish government declared by decree on March 2, 1945, and also in an edict of May 6, 1945, that all the property and possessions left by Germans belonged to the Polish state. All movables and real estate were to be transferred to the control of the Provisional State Administration (TZP), which had the responsibility on behalf of the Ministry of Finance to guard this property and assure orderly distribution.[43] In the first weeks and months after the war hardly anyone was really interested in such matters as legal ownership, however, and the Polish state was not in any position to assert its property claims against an impoverished and hungry population or to preside over any kind of "orderly distribution." People simply took whatever they needed. Poles, Germans, and Soviet citizens; soldiers and civilians; merchants and administrative officers—everyone was forced to loot to ensure their survival. It is unlikely that anyone who lived through those times could honestly claim never to have been a szabrownik. There was in fact hardly anything that *could* be purchased legally in sufficient amounts—neither food nor essential everyday items such as pots and pans, clothing, furniture, linens, candles, or matches. Whatever was needed had to be found somewhere in the abandoned homes. And the principle was "first come, first served."

Wrocław, with its wealth of ownerless property, also attracted a downright plague of professional looters, who roamed the western territories after the war had ended in search of anything valuable.

> As we approached Wrocław, very suspicious-looking people would enter the train. I was astonished at how many repulsive people there were in Poland. Perhaps the dust and their shabby clothes had made them this way. It was unpleasant to travel in such company, but fortunately they were more frightened than I was, since they were looters—*szabrownicy*, as they later came to be known. . . .
>
> Beyond the town of Oleśnica they became increasingly agitated by various rumors. One rumor had it that they would all be arrested before reaching Wrocław, that the city was closed, and that nobody was being let in. Their agitation reached its peak when the train reached its final station before the bridge in Psie Pole. The looters then rushed forward as if in a military assault with us trailing behind.[44]

Until train connections to Wrocław had been reestablished, the szabrownicy made it only as far as Oleśnica and then had to manage the rest of the way on their own. Alfred Górny, an employee of the Wrocław municipal administration, recalled the endless szaber platoons moving between Oleśnica and Wrocław:

> The road to Oleśnica—approximately nineteen miles—was one long line of people; some with carts, some on foot, heading either to Wrocław or to Oleśnica. Gas boilers from bathrooms, bathtubs, kitchen utensils, and God only knows what!—those were the looters' spoils.[45]

The first Polish settlers usually arrived with nothing but the clothes on their backs. They were however generally able to find a job quickly in Polish businesses or in some administrative capacity. At first this work seldom guaranteed a steady salary, but at least they were allowed to go to one of the cafeterias that offered two or three modest meals a day and food packages for family members at home.[46] In this respect, the Germans were worse off. Even those who had a job were sometimes refused entry to the cafeterias, and their food coupons were often for half the rations that Poles received. Even then it was not certain that they could receive the amounts printed on the coupons since distribution in the stores continued only as long as supplies lasted.[47] Germans who could not work—children, the sick, and the elderly—were imperiled as soon as they had used up their own provisions. Unless they had family members to some-how help them keep their heads above water, they were on their own:

> So Mother had no choice but to go out with me, an eleven-year-old girl, to search for something to keep the family going. . . . She did what all [German] Wrocławians who were still in town did. She set out with a small handcart. "No one's going to bring us anything; we have to go out and get it for ourselves," she said. . . . When our reserves started running out, we even dug down under the rubble of collapsed houses, warehouses, and factories to get food that was buried. . . . From the ruins of a destroyed candy factory one day I even pulled out some bonbons and chocolates. Of course we had to clean off the dirt. It was dangerous often to clamber over rubble for a handful of bonbons. Mother reprimanded me, "Stop it! Leave that alone!" She was always afraid for me; she couldn't do it as well as I could though, what with her figure and at her age, or else she probably would have.[48]

For needy people who had no means to care for themselves, the German church congregations served an important function. Joachim Konrad reported that even before the end of the siege he set up hiding places in St. Elizabeth's Church to store the valuables and food of people who had been evacuated. If the owners didn't return, their goods were used to care for the needy. Congregation members who were about to be evacuated often left the church the rest of whatever they had stored.

> Still today, I think of it as a kind of miracle of the loaves and fishes. We were standing with virtually empty hands in our houses and homes, where we had gathered elderly and the sick around us, and no one starved. It's no easy task to improvise a shelter with a hundred or more beds, but to make it through without any provisions at all . . . that often

seemed hopeless. . . . Yet when things looked the worst then suddenly we'd inherit something or someone would discover some foodstuffs under the debris, or someone would send us canned foods that had been hidden, for example, from Schönfelder's, the former gourmet foods store.[49]

Soviet soldiers and Polish settlers were able to assert their claims to movable goods in the city since they represented the new authorities, but Germans had the inestimable advantage of being familiar with the area. It allowed them to ferret out hidden treasures far more successfully than the newcomers, not only for their own use but also in order to trade information about hiding places with the Poles and Russians in exchange for money or food.[50]

The supply situation in the first few weeks after the war was still markedly favorable in Wrocław. During the war, when the city's population had grown to almost a million, a corresponding volume of provisions had been brought to the city and stored there. On top of that, there were large storehouses amply filled with food, clothing, and other items to supply the eastern front. Much had been consumed or destroyed during the siege, but a substantial amount remained after the war, especially given that the population had meanwhile shrunk to roughly 200,000. When the Polish operative groups arrived in Wrocław in May 1945, they found food reserves that far exceeded their expectations. As a result, the municipal administration had hopes of being independent in terms of food supply for many months. Moreover, they initially considered only their own employees and the first Polish settlers, assuming that the Germans would be able to fend for themselves.[51] But these first impressions turned out to be overly optimistic:

> The food situation very soon worsened, however. A constant stream of people from the east and the west—the poor, refugees, prisoners from German camps, and those who had been sent abroad to work, Poles and foreigners alike—changed things in a very short space of time. Wrocław had been well supplied. . . . But this disappeared in at most three weeks, and by the beginning of summer the workforce began to suffer from hunger.[52]

After only a short time the regular food supply—what could be obtained through ration coupons and the legal shops—was unable to fill the needs

Black markets kept Wrocław afloat after the war. In addition to fresh produce brought in from central Poland, the entire inventory of a German metropolis was up for sale. This photo taken in 1961 shows the market bustle on Nowy Targ prior to the square's reconstruction. Courtesy of the City Museum of Wrocław (Tomasz Olszewski).

of the population. With some luck, people could supplement insufficient official rations with such canned goods, flour, and sugar, etc., as they could find in the abandoned homes. But fresh fruits and vegetables, meat, eggs, and dairy products could not be acquired in this way. They could only be obtained illegally. Great demand led to what became a flourishing black market in Wrocław.

Black market prices were of course many times greater than those charged by regular vendors and far higher than what people earning meager postwar wages could afford. But thanks to szaber everyone had a chance to obtain some barter in the form of looted goods to trade for fresh food or other desirables. Szaber, which at first served to ensure basic subsistence, had reached a new level. People no longer pilfered only what they themselves needed; they took anything that would bring a good price on the black market. Szaber and the black market merged and created a lively sphere of commercial activity above and beyond what was available through legal but insufficient channels. It assured survival for many and high profits for some. The main media of exchange were barter goods such as alcohol or meat; but other foodstuffs and clothing coupons were also accepted. A variety of currencies circulated, with the Polish złoty establishing itself only slowly.[53]

Wrocław became the "Mecca of *szabrownicy* and marketeers"[54] and soon was the home of the largest black market in all of Poland. After modest beginnings on Matthiasstrasse (ul. Bolesława Drobnera), where illegal trading went on right in front of the legal stores, wooden booths popped up all over on the expansive pl. Grunwaldzki, as the airfield along the former Kaiserstrasse was called. Some of them were sheds from the allotment gardens on the outskirts of the city that had been taken down and rebuilt on pl. Grunwaldzki.[55]

> Since the beginning of summer, there has appeared on what is now pl. Grunwaldzki, from the intersection with ul. Curie-Skłodowskiej towards Szczytnicki Bridge, something called "Szaber Square" [*szaberplac*], an odd term but one that we understand perfectly. There's certainly lots to see here! People spread out the goods they wish to barter on the ground: porcelain, linens, clothing, shoes, cutlery, paintings, carpets, toys, all manner of objects. The sellers are mainly, but not exclusively, German women. In the evenings the square becomes deserted; all that remains are piles of rubbish, which nobody bothers to clean up. The next day other sellers appear and the trading continues. Barter is king. Money has no value. No police are to be seen among the throng; people jostle, shout, and steal; fights often break out. The surrounding streets are empty and dead; life flourishes only on "Szaber Square."[56]

Hugo Steinhaus mocked these activities in November 1945:

> Pl. Grunwaldzki is now witness to the unending Battle of Grunwald. On the one side, thousands of good-for-nothings in knee-high boots carrying rucksacks, con artists, looters, discharged soldiers, Soviets, Jewish jacks-of-all-trades, humbled ladies, common criminals and, on the other side, Germans with white armbands, German women in trousers

pushing trolleys, carrying bundles of belongings, speaking *Volapük*, haggling, inspecting, handing back, changing their minds, packing, and jostling. The biggest bunch of paupers on the biggest pile of bricks and rubble in Europe.[57]

The bus that ran between the central train station and pl. Grunwaldzki was soon known by locals as the szaber bus,[58] and streetcar conductors had fun announcing the stops of the various black markets—at pl. Grunwaldzki, pl. Nankiera, and many other squares and intersections—using names such as "Szaber Square" or the "College of Commerce."[59]

The Germans gave the black market a powerful boost. Given the fact that their food ration coupons were worth less than those issued to Poles, they had to rely more on trading, exchanging their last belongings and looted wares in order to survive. Wrocławians had already largely lost their sense of ownership during the siege, when they had been forced to move from one district to another, occupying abandoned apartments and making use of whatever furnishings and supplies they found there. After the war only a minority still lived with their own possessions. And even those who did were prepared—as soon as they realized that they would be evacuated sooner or later and would not be able to take any of their possessions with them—to trade anything and everything for fresh groceries. In their desperation the Germans pushed black market prices through the roof, so that within a short time the markets attracted not only traders from the city and its environs, but fresh goods from all parts of Poland.

> Everything was so tempting, spread out on the red brick gravel of the airfield. Lying on cloths, as is often still common today, there were big chunks of exquisite gold-yellow butter. Next to that sat a Polish farmer woman who also tried to sell fresh eggs. It was a fascinating sight as my mother and I walked through the rows of traders. The smell of Polish ham and kielbasa wafted over to us. . . . Little by little my mother gathered up all kinds of things that we could sell at the Polish market. Once there was a vase, another time a coffee pot, and once Mother dug out a tablecloth to sell.[60]

Szaber was primarily an expression of material need. In a time of great privation it also seems to have served many as a kind of substitute for other forms

Wrocław's giant black market on pl. Grunwaldzki became famous throughout the country. "The sellers are mainly, but not exclusively, German women. In the evenings the square becomes deserted; all that remains are piles of rubbish, which nobody bothers to clean up. The next day other sellers appear and the trading continues. Barter is king. Money has no value. No police are to be seen among the throng; people jostle, shout, and steal; fights often break out. The surrounding streets are empty and dead; life flourishes only on "Szaber Square" (Joanna Konopińska in her diary, December 1945). Courtesy of the Ossolineum (Adam Czelny).

of gratification, maybe even a kind of popular sport in which Germans and Poles alike participated. Joanna Konopińska remembered a German woman, Mrs. Weiss, who lived in the same building as she did and devoted her last months in Wrocław almost entirely to szaber:

> If she isn't sitting in an armchair then she's running about town, looting, taking home whatever she finds: bedding, tablecloths, pots. Back home she sorts her booty. The better items she takes up to the attic and packs into bags; those of less quality she takes to *Szaber Square* and trades for food. Mrs. Weiss is unquestionably an expert in her field: she knows where to find any given item. One day I broke the last plate we had. Mrs. Weiss told me exactly in which house one could still find plates, which

house still had pots, and where there were paintings still hanging on the walls. I eagerly took her advice, and from a destroyed cafe located on an embankment by the Oder River I carried home, in a baby carriage, an almost complete set of crockery. Ever since we have been eating off plates that bear the inscription of that cafe. Unfortunately, I couldn't find any more cutlery, so I will have to pay a visit to *Szaber Square* to exchange a bottle of oil for some knives and forks, because we have absolutely nothing to eat with.[61]

During the period of greatest hardship after the war Wrocław had once again become a trading city, with the inventory of an entire metropolis offered for sale on its black markets. But this odd economic boom was short-lived. At first the authorities simply watched the goings-on, aware that it was only the black market that kept people from starving to death. As soon as the situation had settled down though, the communist leadership sounded the call to fight the Battle over Trade (*bitwa o handel*). It began in 1947, and it targeted not only black market trading and speculation, but also any and every act of private trading.[62] When the campaign was successfully concluded, Wrocław had been transformed into a socialist public-supply company as regards the turnover of goods: there was just as little or as much for sale as in every other Polish city.

Polish Dismantling

It was not only residents who went through Wrocław looting and inventing new uses for whatever they found. The employees of all kinds of institutions of the Polish state, from the administration to research facilities and industrial plants, also combed the city for items of value. It was a way of rendering somehow useful whatever was left, of reviving the city through its own potential, however diminished. However, facilities in central Poland also tried to secure their share. In addition to distributing vested rights within the city, the municipal administration in Wrocław was busy trying to satisfy requests from elsewhere. The old voivodeships were constantly asking for food, furniture, industrial goods, books, typewriters, or radios.[63] Pianos from Wrocław were delivered to the conservatory in Krakow, and streetcars were sent to Warsaw. A rotary printing press that had previously been used to print the German newspaper *Breslauer Neueste Nachrichten* was shipped to Warsaw to print the *Express Wieczorny*.[64]

Supplying state offices and Polish companies with goods from the western territories constituted a special form of looting, which people at the time referred to as "official" or "patriotic" szaber.[65] One could also speak of inner-Polish dismantling, since this state looting drained valuable resources from the western territories in order to benefit the central Polish voivodeships. The voivode of Lower Silesia, Stanisław Piaskowski, remembered that more and more delegates from various agencies and institutions in central Poland started flocking to Lower Silesia:

> They concentrated all their efforts on exporting from the region, which they called "milk-giving Silesia" (*dojny Śląsk*),[66] the greatest possible number of objects of varying worth for their superiors, colleagues, and themselves.[67]

The longer the looting and dismantling continued, the more serious the consequences were. For one thing, the fact that even Polish authorities constantly shipped materials and goods to central Poland fed already existing suspicions among the population that the western territories were likely not going to remain Polish. The "official szaber" also threatened to destroy the region's material base, rendering speedy reconstruction impossible. Beginning in May of 1945, Piaskowski did everything possible to stop this ruinous looting of his jurisdiction. In June he warned all county plenipotentiaries that they must no longer tolerate the szabrownicy.[68] On July 31 he issued an ordinance prohibiting the transporting of furniture, motor vehicles, machines, and other objects of value out of Lower Silesia without authorization from his regional or Wrocław's municipal administration.[69] In September he finally sought assistance from Prime Minister Edward Osóbka-Morawski:

> I request that no further ordinances be issued in regard to the export of furniture, equipment, machinery, cars, etc., from our voivodeship. The voivodeship of Lower Silesia has already been largely cleaned out, on the one hand by illegal looting, and on the other by the chaotic export [of goods] to the central voivodeships. . . . I should emphasize that we receive requests every day from all the ministries for the supply of

trainloads of furniture. We are also constantly being visited by "dele-gates" who come to "collect" hundreds of cars that we don't even have.[70]

A government decree issued on November 16, 1945, officially declared sz-aber to be a crime.[71] On November 30, Osóbka-Morawski issued a circular in which he branded any transport of goods out of the western territories as theft at the expense of the settlers. This applied even if the export was carried out with authorization from the central authorities. In the future, according to the letter, only the president himself could issue a special dispensation.[72] Of course the looting could not be stopped from one day to the next, as is obvious from the abundance of new decrees and circulars on the matter; but at least szaber was no longer tolerated by the authorities as a necessary evil, but instead defined as a criminal act.

In Wrocław, even official szaber seems to have continued, although this largely involved only more or less authorized operations. The most extreme form of inner-Polish dismantling in Wrocław was the collection of bricks for the reconstruction of Warsaw in the first half of the 1950s.[73] Given the acute scarcity of building materials throughout the country after the war, the Polish government pushed for full utilization of bricks and other reusable materials found among the ruins and debris. This was supposed to lower the costs of reconstruction and at the same time expedite efforts to clear away the rubble in the cities. The corresponding ordinances, however, especially the notori-ous demolition decree no. 666 of August 20, 1955, which was actually sup-posed to promote the clearance of war damage, ended up having precisely the opposite effect. Particularly in the western territories, the decree led to the demolition of numerous damaged buildings that could have been recon-structed. Moreover, after the removal of the bricks and other building materi-als, the rubble and debris were frequently left and had to be removed later on, often at costs that exceeded the amount saved by recycling the construction materials.[74]

Wrocław, like other cities, was supposed to do its part in reclaiming bricks to support the nationwide campaign: "The entire nation is rebuild-ing its capital." In late August 1953 the headline of the *Gazeta Robotnicza*, "Every Wrocławian is giving 50 bricks to Warsaw—We're helping to build the capital," appealed to all Wrocław citizens to participate. Those who col-lected the most bricks were promised a three-day trip to Warsaw.[75] Tracks

Millions of bricks were recovered from the ruins of Wrocław and shipped eastward to support the reconstruction of Warsaw. Courtesy of the Ossolineum (Adam Czelny).

were laid clear across the Old Town so the gathered bricks could be sent out on trolleys and train cars from the new town past pl. Dzierżyńskiego, ul. Ofiar Oświęmcimskich, pl. Wolności, and an embankment piled up at the city moat, up to the Świebodzki train station.[76] The Municipal Demolition Company was created to coordinate the large-scale operation, which by the early 1950s was collecting up to 165 million bricks annually and shipping them to central Poland. Thousands of workers were involved, including "social volunteers," who were recruited to work free of charge.

A strong incentive for the brick collection operation was the fact that the sale of the building materials promised substantial profits for the companies and traders involved. In February 1949 the municipal administration had already complained that Wrocław's Independent Department of Rubble Clearance (SOO) had not received proper authorization to enter into an agreement with the central authorities in Warsaw to collect 100 million bricks within three months and to deliver 58 million within ten months to Warsaw and other Polish cities.[77] A few years later it was discovered that a number of officials in the Wrocław municipal administration, including Leopold Mondszajn, assistant director of the Municipal Demolition Company, had worked on their own behalf and made enormous profits. The case against the "brick millionaire" was brought before the voivodeship court in Wrocław in 1957, and it resulted in a stiff penalty.[78] The same year Stanisław Wiczak from the voivodeship of Poznań was tried for having sold gullible people stones and bricks from the demolition of the Gothic town hall of Wrocław in exchange for payment up front. The demolition never took place of course and had never even been considered. But Wiczak had evidently been able to gain the trust of his customers by telling them that the town hall was going to be torn down because it was not a Polish landmark.[79]

The brick operation had catastrophic consequences for Wrocław for several reasons. Ninety percent of the bricks went to Warsaw and were therefore no longer available for the reconstruction of Wrocław, where they were just as urgently needed as in the capital. In addition, not only simple bricks were shipped out, but also valuable components of building stock worthy of preservation that was needed for the reconstruction of Warsaw's Old Town—stone door and window frames, façade ornamentation, and treasured Gothic bricks for the reconstruction of medieval buildings. The economic interests of the municipal administration and of the demolition company involved, as well as criminal intrigues by individual officials, led to buildings and entire streets in Wrocław being torn down, especially in the eastern part of the Old Town, which had suffered substantial war damage but could definitely have been rebuilt. Among such unnecessary losses was the impressive main post office at pl. Dominikański (pl. F. Dzierżyńskiego). There were also grotesque cases of buildings being torn down *after* they had been renovated.[80]

The loss of old building stock was irreversible, and the consequences for Wrocław's Old Town remain visible even today. Into the 1990s empty wastelands spread out in many of the areas where extensive brick collecting had taken place. At most a parking lot was built at these sites or, for lack of more creative ideas, uninspired greenery was planted. The brick-collecting operation did not even have the positive effect of clearing the debris and rubble, since everything that could not be sold as building material was left lying where it was. After a considerable portion of the debris had already been cleared

As a consequence of extensive brick collection, large empty spaces marred the face of Wrocław's city center for decades. The photo shows the region around pl. Dominikański in 1984. Courtesy of the Museum of Architecture in Wrocław (Tadeusz Drankowski).

away in preparation for the national Exhibition of the Recovered Territories in Wrocław in the summer of 1948, new mounds of rubble started accumulating in the city center in the early 1950s. By December 1955 the volume had grown to 9.8 million cubic yards, which was only slightly under the estimated 10.5 million that had filled the city in March 1946,[81] and therefore still close to half of the estimated 23.5 million cubic yards of rubble that Wrocław contained directly after the war.[82] The debris attracted vermin, which found such a plentitude of hiding places that they were virtually impossible to combat. Because a substantial part of it was wood, a fungus epidemic began spreading throughout the city.[83] It was not until December of 1960 that a government ordinance was issued setting 1963 as the deadline for completing the clearance of Wrocław's accumulated rubbish and debris.[84]

THE DECAY OF RESIDENTIAL HOUSING

Despite the extensive war damage, there was no shortage of housing in Wrocław in the first few months after the war, due to the fact that the population had dwindled to one-third its prewar level. The arrival of Polish settlers did little to change this at first, since the number of Poles increased at about the same rate as the Germans were evacuated. In comparison with cities in central Poland, the housing situation in the city was downright favorable. The prospect of a ready apartment, larger and of a better standard than what was common elsewhere in the country, provided a great incentive for many Poles to move to Wrocław. The first settlers could virtually take their pick of what best satisfied their needs and taste from among the many abandoned apartments and houses. The relatively well-preserved residential districts around the Nadodrze train station were very sought-after, as were the almost undamaged affluent suburbs of Karłowice and Biskupin. Karłowice was reserved for city employees, and—as if to maintain the tradition of German times—Biskupin was settled predominantly by the city's educated elite, including professors, high-level administrative officials, journalists, and artists. The German population moved to the remaining, still habitable districts in the north and northeast. Sępolno, with its modern and completely undamaged buildings, continued to be considered a German residential district for quite some time. The advantage that the early arrivals had in selecting an apartment was later qualified to some extent, as the value of apartments and houses, including their contents, was appraised and some adjustments made. At least as far as Konopińska remembered, however, these charges were so modest that they did little to diminish the advantages of early relocation.[85]

The housing bonanza did not last long. First apartments in the city center became scarce, forcing people to move to the suburbs and accept long commutes into the city. After a few years the shortage had spread to all of Wrocław. Industrial firms and other institutions began complaining that they risked losing their best specialists if sufficient housing was not soon made available. The scarcity of apartments was caused in part by rapid population growth, beginning in 1946, but the progressive deterioration of housing was also a factor. According to statistics gathered in March 1946 by the municipal administration, there had been 32,000 apartment buildings in Wrocław, of which about 50 percent had been totally destroyed in the war and 25 percent semi-destroyed. The remaining 25 percent required only minor repairs.[86] "Minor repairs" usually meant replacing broken and missing roof tiles and replacing windowpanes, since the windows of almost all the city's buildings had broken during the fighting. Unfortunately, local production could not supply adequate building materials, and transport capacities were inadequate to deliver materials from the factories where they were available to the destinations where they were needed. All kinds of construction materials were in extremely short supply, but windowpane glass was virtually impossible to obtain.[87]

Wrocławians tried to help themselves by combing the length and breadth of the city for reusable materials, or by stripping empty, abandoned buildings.

> The pursuit of glass, sheet metal, lime, cement, roofing, tar, plywood, plaster, and nails was like nothing so much as a foot race. . . . Window glass presented one of the biggest problems for reconstruction. After the siege, there was not a single unbroken pane of glass left in all of Wrocław.[88]

Maleczyński remembers people stealing tarpaper from one another's roofs.[89] Glass, however, could not be pilfered; there was simply none to be had. Many tenants spent months in dark apartments or relied exclusively on artificial lighting, since they had had to cover their windows with boards or rugs for protection from the elements. Until the summer of 1947, even the streetcars traveled through Wrocław without panes in their windows. In the winter passengers had to suffer the torture of icy drafts or sit in the dark behind boarded-up windows, unable to look out.[90] Factories, schools, and universities operated with open windows. The university was so grateful for a gift from the Walbrzych glassworks that it named its reglazed chemistry classroom "Walbrzych Hall" in honor of the benefactor.[91] Even a company as important as PaFaWag, which enjoyed special government support, had to fight for months for a windowpane glass allotment, during which time its sensitive machinery was housed in factory halls with unglazed windows.[92]

The prolonged shortage of windowpanes and tarpaper roofing led to irreparable damage. Buildings whose roofs leaked often remained empty, or tenants took apartments only on the lower floors where the rain did not penetrate. Whatever remained uninhabited soon became uninhabitable. If there were no tenants, windows and roofs were not even provisionally repaired; and within a few months a building that needed only its roof patched and new windowpanes ended up requiring extensive repairs. In many cases, the deterioration progressed so far that there was nothing to be done; the building had to be torn down entirely. Wrocław's building authorities were aware of the dire consequences of these developments, but they lacked the means to save the building stock from falling into disrepair. They were forced to concentrate on repairing at least the buildings used by the Polish administration, for schools and universities, and for cultural facilities such as the opera, theaters, and museums, as well as hospitals and municipal companies. Beyond that, efforts were taken to preserve the city's most significant historic buildings.[93] Industrial firms, banks, and insurance companies were able to finance their own repairs and preserve buildings they used. However, there was hardly any funding available to rehabilitate residential housing. The authorities could only hope that tenants would act in their own interest to maintain their homes.

These hopes proved deceptive for a number of reasons. Financial and material obstacles aside, very few tenants showed any interest in repairing their buildings. The remaining Germans had no incentive to care for apartments that they would sooner or later have to abandon. Even most Polish tenants showed little enthusiasm for maintaining the apartments and houses they had moved into; it was widely believed that they would be living in Wrocław only temporarily, so it made no sense for them to invest in repairs. Thus many watched as rain seeped into buildings through leaky roofs and open windows, gradually destroying the structural fabric. Tenants let stairwells, halls, and basements fall into disrepair; threw their garbage into courtyards; clogged pipes with refuse and sometimes even with plaster and cement. They kept livestock, not only in basements but also on the upper floors. Lacking wood and coal for heating, they burned doors, window and doorframes, parquet flooring, and the floorboards of freestanding dwellings. At times, load-bearing beams were even removed: newspaper reports of collapsing buildings increased in the late 1940s. And then came the szabrownicy, who dismantled bathroom and kitchen installations and even tore pipes out of the walls with no thought to the flooding and damage they were causing. Many water pipes burst in the winter of 1947 due to lack of maintenance. The authorities responded with information campaigns in the media and with threats. But because the problems were so fundamental in nature, based ultimately on a lack of identification with the city, they could not be easily remedied.[94]

In 1955 an internal report on the condition of buildings in Wrocław was prepared for the government in Warsaw. Its conclusions were devastating: The extent of repairs made up to that point were insufficient and qualitatively poor, making it impossible to prevent the further deterioration of the building stock. Mold, which had already been a problem in 1945, had spread to a huge number of buildings, rendering many apartments uninhabitable. Because the population was growing—without a net increase in the number of habitable apartments, despite all the repairs—the housing shortage was worsening. Statistically, there were 1.57 people in each and every room, although the occupancy rate in well-preserved apartments was far higher. According to the report, the overall municipal infrastructure was unsatisfactory because war damage had still not been cleared away and renovations were lacking. Furthermore, large parts of the city were still covered with rubble. The report came to a sad conclusion:

> Because of the lack of planning in the reconstruction, which is particularly evident in the city center, Wrocław gives the impression—to locals and visitors alike—of a sadly neglected city.[95]

Between 1951 and 1955, 28,000 residences were built or renovated in Wrocław, but in the same period 27,000 were lost through deterioration. The authorities estimated that in 1956 the city was short 10,000 apartments. In late 1955, of a total of 202,000 residences maintained by the Municipal

Housing Administration (MZBM)—almost 90 percent of the total housing units available in Wrocław—major renovations were necessary in 85,000; moderate renovations in 83,000; and 100,000 residences were infested with mildew. In early 1957, 3,700 buildings in Wrocław were considered in danger of collapsing.[96]

In the realm of industry, which was the prime focus of investments in Poland's Stalinist period from 1949 to 1956, Wrocław's development continued to falter. Although the city's share of industrial production in Wrocław rose by more than 200 percent from 1950 to 1955, it was still behind the industrial cities of central Poland. In 1950, Wrocław and Warsaw each had a 2.4 percent share of Poland's industrial production, second only to Łódź with 7.4 percent and ahead of Krakow and Poznań, which each had a share of 2.2 percent. In 1955 Łódź still held pride of place with 7.1 percent, but Warsaw was now alone in second place with 3.9 percent, followed by Krakow with 3.0 percent, while Wrocław, still at 2.4 percent, had dropped to fourth place tied with Poznań.[97]

In addition to other factors, Wrocław's difficult situation in the mid-1950s reflected the general economic plight that had befallen the country as a result of the economic errors of Stalinism. In 1956, however, the People's Republic of Poland experienced a political turning point. In his secret speech to the closed session of the 20th Congress of the Communist Party of the Soviet Union (CPSU) in February of 1956, First Secretary of the CPSU Nikita Khrushchev criticized the political wrongdoings of the previous years and denounced Stalin as personally responsible. The process of de-Stalinization began in the USSR, and it would also affect the political establishment of the People's Republic of Poland. The sudden death of Bolesław Bierut, up to then First Secretary of the Central Committee of the PZPR and the most powerful man in the country, shortly after the 20th Party Congress, paved the way for personnel changes in Poland. Władysław Gomułka, once General Secretary of the PPR, Minister for the Recovered Territories, and Deputy Prime Minister—who in 1949 had been stripped of all offices after having been charged with "nationalist deviation" and then disappeared from the political arena for almost seven years—managed a sensational comeback. In October 1956 he was elected First Secretary of the Central Committee and thus Bierut's successor.

Far-reaching reforms, particularly regarding economic policy, were introduced under Gomułka's leadership, first and foremost the end of forced collectivization and the enhanced promotion of branches of production other than heavy industry and the raw materials sector. The reforms had a substantial impact on the western territories, which were particularly dear to the new General Secretary and former Minister for the Recovered Territories. Relatively open public discussion also became possible in the years after 1956, which allowed an airing of the mistakes of the previous years that had particularly affected the western territories. One-sided concentration on heavy industry had caused the economic decline of cities and entire sections of the country where the focus had traditionally been on the trades and small industry. In cities such as Jelenia Góra, which had not been at all damaged in the war, a great many buildings had fallen into disrepair in the postwar years simply because they remained vacant. In October 1957, the Ministry of Communal Economy (MGK) took stock of the sobering situation in a letter to Zenon Nowak, director of the newly established national Commission for the Development of the Western Territories (KRZZ):

> The physical appearance of the vast majority of towns and cities in the western territories has significantly worsened as compared with the prewar era. The local population and authorities are largely indifferent to the matter. Their indifference is the result not only of objective difficulties—the lack of resources—but is also due to simple carelessness and to the fact that they have gotten used to a dirty and neglected environment.[98]

The integration of the new territories and their revitalization, summarily announced in 1949 (along with the dissolution of the Ministry of the Recovered Territories), was never accomplished.[99] As late as the mid-1950s a sense of instability was still widespread and economic development continued to lag behind that of central Poland. Since 1945 there had been too little invested in the western territories and too much living off reserves. In June 1957 Zenon Nowak did not mince words at the founding congress of the Society for the Development of the Western Territories (TRZZ), which was established to foster awareness for the territories' special concerns within Polish society:

> Poland in 1945 was a wheat field ravaged by locusts. When the Polish nation took over the western territories they had been abandoned by

the Germans and hard hit by the maelstrom of war. A mortally wounded nation behaves like a wounded animal. Instead of gaining strength, it draws on all its available reserves to heal its wounds. And so it was in the western territories during the postwar years. Abandoned stocks of food, housing, and other goods saved millions of homeless people from death by starvation and cold. The ruins of houses and factories served to rebuild life not only in the western territories but throughout the whole of our war-ravaged country.[100]

Polish government circles had meanwhile accepted the fact that the western territories needed special support and that reticence toward investments was no longer tenable. Failure to attend to the territories, it was argued, would not only mean that a substantial economic potential would continue to lie idle or risk being irrevocably lost; there was also a danger that ongoing difficulties in the territories would prove grist for the mill of those politicians and lobbyists in the West who were still calling for a revision of the Oder-Neisse line, even if this was often only a means of putting pressure on the socialist camp. In December 1956 the Polish government constituted the Commission for the Development of the Western Territories (KRZZ), which was charged with preparing a plan for the comprehensive economic development of the western territories with the goal of creating there "an atmosphere of stability and a sense of permanence."[101] The Sejm, the Polish parliament, formed another commission in March 1957, the Special Commission for the Western Territories (NKZZ), which was supposed to work out improvements not only as regards economics, but also in all other fields.[102]

In the second half of the 1950s these measures and a stronger awareness on the part of the political leadership of the hardships facing the western territories resulted in palpable improvements. The phase in which losses exceeded investments was over for the time being. This benefited Wrocław as well, though the situation there was already far better prior to the economic turning point in 1956 than it was in the smaller cities of the region. As an important industrial center, Wrocław could always be assured a certain level of investment. With an eye toward the propagandistic value of this capital of the western territories, the national government spent substantial funds on its reconstruction (albeit not at a level that would assure the speedy repair of war damages and a halt to the advancing deterioration of the city's housing). Even before 1956, the reconstruction of Wrocław's city center had commenced. In fact it had advanced beyond both the merely symbolic restorations of a few historical buildings (the cathedral, town hall, and university) and the most urgent practical measures of reestablishing large factories and the city's essential infrastructure.

CHAPTER FOUR

Reconstruction

THE RECONSTRUCTION OF EUROPE'S WAR-DESTROYED CITIES SERVED AN important additional function, one that was not merely practical. It was of course necessary to restore the basic necessities of life. But more than that reconstruction meant the promise of a better future. This was particularly true in Poland, where people tied the rebuilding of devastated cities to the hope of moving beyond the horror of war and occupation and of overcoming the enormous losses the country had suffered.[1] The city of Warsaw, 75 to 80 percent of which had been reduced to rubble by the end of the war, became a symbol of the devastation wrought by the war in Poland; Warsaw's reconstruction in the second half of the 40s was to symbolize the country's resolve to rise like a phoenix from the ashes and erase the humiliation of German occupation. In accord with the slogan, "The entire nation rebuilds its capital," all of the country's human and material resources were mobilized. Leading Polish architects, urban planners, engineers, and craftsmen came to Warsaw, and the government gave the project the highest priority. Any Polish government, regardless of its political orientation, would have acted in the same way. For the Polish Communists, however, reconstruction of the capital razed to the ground by the Germans provided a unique opportunity to present themselves as the leading force of Polish patriotism as well as to make the new Warsaw into the emblem of a new, better, socialist Poland.[2]

WROCŁAW BETWEEN PROVINCIAL CITY AND BUSTLING METROPOLIS

The war damage in Wrocław was only slightly less severe than in Warsaw.[3] However, the preconditions for reconstruction were significantly more difficult there than in the Polish capital. In comparison to Warsaw, Wrocław was merely a large provincial city; and it was located in the western territories, whose political future appeared still uncertain at a time when the reconstruction of Warsaw was already in full swing. Every investment in Wrocław was bedeviled by doubts as to whether it would truly benefit Poland in the long run. A patriotic groundswell of support for rebuilding Wrocław would, therefore, have been unimaginable. Moreover, Wrocław was only one of several provincial capitals in the new territories, all of which had to be rebuilt: 55 percent of Gdańsk and 45 percent of Szczecin had been destroyed. Many mid-sized towns had been severely damaged as well: 95 percent of Głogów lay in ruins, 80 percent of Kołobrzeg, 75 percent of Piła, 70 percent of Stargard, 60 percent of Grudziądz and Racibórz, 55 percent of Nysa and Lubań, and 50 percent of Olsztyn and Gorzów Wielkopolski. Many smaller towns and innumerable villages and farmsteads had also been destroyed, not to mention a large portion of Poland's roads, bridges, railway facilities, and ports.[4]

Given its financial limitations the Polish government was forced to restrict the range of its reconstruction efforts. An obvious place to start was with reconstructing the capital. Rebuilding the western territories, however, was another project of enormous political and economic importance. Unless the devastated cities and towns were restored, it would be impossible either to resettle the region or to tap the enormous economic resources that existed there in the form of industrial plants, raw materials warehouses, buildings, transportation facilities, and agricultural lands. Reconstruction, resettlement, and revival of the economy were inextricably connected.

In late November 1945, Minister of Reconstruction Michał Kaczorowski informed the heads of the reconstruction directorates as well as the provincial reconstruction division chiefs that it had been necessary up to that time to channel the majority of funds to Warsaw in order to ensure a minimal functionality of the capital. Because this had been achieved to some degree, he continued, the government was now turning its attention to the western territories:

> Poland's greatest political and economic task is to take charge of the western territories. Our efforts must be directed toward them. We must demonstrate to the world that we are capable of controlling these outstanding centers and taking responsibility for their future; that is to say, of Gdańsk, Wrocław, Szczecin, and many other smaller towns.[5]

In January 1946 Minister of the Recovered Territories Władysław Gomułka also emphasized the significance of these territories for the reconstruction of the country at large:

> In rebuilding all of Poland, we must make an especial effort to rebuild and redevelop the Recovered Territories. The needs of these territories must be given priority and placed at the top of the state agenda. That is because their reconstruction and redevelopment mean an increase in Poland's security and strength, a magnification of our industrial potential, and the creation of possibilities for development such as this country and its people never before possessed.[6]

Although the reconstruction of the capital did continue to have great significance, rebuilding the western territories was in fact given priority over rebuilding in the central Polish provinces. Nevertheless, the simultaneous reconstruction of all of the devastated cities in the territories exceeded the capacities of the war-ravaged country. Here, too, Poland had to concentrate on those cities, industrial centers, and transportation facilities that had been most severely damaged and that were most important for the nation's overall recovery. While villages and towns were to a large degree left to their own resources, investments were funneled in particular to the Upper Silesian industrial region and to the major cities of Szczecin, Gdańsk, and Wrocław. The latter were supposed to become centers of new economic and cultural life amid the ravaged landscapes that stretched along the banks of the Oder River and the Baltic seashore.[7] From this perspective it might have appeared that prospects for Wrocław, the largest city in the western territories, were good. The Polish government, however, vacillated between two contradictory approaches to the city's future. On the one hand, there were efforts to turn Wrocław into the symbolic capital of the western territories and to use its reconstruction to showcase Poland's determination and ability to incorporate the German territories and to infuse new, Polish life into the devastated region. On the other hand, given that the status of the Oder-Neisse line had not been definitively resolved, the government appears to have long shied away from major investments in Wrocław.

During his first visit to the city on August 28, 1945, Bolesław Bierut, then head of the provisional government, spoke of Wrocław as the second Polish city after Warsaw.[8] Behind the scenes, however, there were those who questioned the wisdom of preserving the city's prewar dimensions and suggested that it should instead be rebuilt as a city of only 200,000 inhabitants.[9] The reports of the Polish spatial planning authorities also proposed a reduction in Wrocław's economic significance relative to its prewar status. They felt that the city should no longer be an industrial center, but instead should play a national role only in the areas of education, culture, and tourism.[10] The goal of diminishing Wrocław's significance was also reflected in plans by the Ministry of Reconstruction during the early postwar years. Although Wrocław played an important role in these plans, the port and border city of Szczecin and other cities near the Oder-Neisse line received greater attention for economic and political reasons.[11]

<h3 align="center">MOMENTUM AND STAGNATION</h3>

Given the Polish government's reservations about large-scale investment in Wrocław, responsibility for reconstruction in the first years after the war fell in particular to local authorities and to the new inhabitants, especially to those well-educated enthusiasts who were prepared to commit their energy and skills to rebuilding the city. The obstacles were enormous. Besides a shortage of building materials, heavy equipment, transportation, fuel, and money to pay workers and construction companies, one of the greatest impediments was the lack of trained personnel. Józef Rybicki, who headed the building department of Wrocław's municipal administration, was an experienced architect and organizer who had previously held the same position in Lwów. His experience was of only limited use, however, given that his Wrocław department, which was supposed to coordinate most of the building operations up to early 1946, was initially unable to find more than two, and later five, Polish technicians. The rest of the staff was composed primarily of Germans who had been recruited more or less at random.[12]

One of the first tasks of the building authorities was damage assessment. For this purpose, the city was divided into seventy-five districts, each of which was assigned two staff members who were supposed to estimate the extent of destruction sustained by individual buildings in their district. In a period of three weeks, data was collected for approximately 27,000 buildings and recorded on a map. The information was not always reliable and it became outdated quickly due to the continued deterioration of buildings. It nevertheless provided an approximate picture of the damage and allowed for a more accurate estimation of what was needed for reconstruction.[13]

The extent of the damage was staggering.[14] Overall 60 percent of the building stock was considered lost. Of the roughly 32,000 buildings in Wrocław, 21,600 had suffered substantial damage. Of the 186,000 apartments, 52,460 had been completely destroyed; 30,290 had been between 70 and 85 percent destroyed; 15,600 between 50 and 70 percent; 42,290 between 10 and 50 percent; and 45,160 had sustained damages of less than 10 percent. The figures for the city's 422 public buildings were a bit less grim: Forty-eight were 85 to 100 percent destroyed; thirty-three 50 to 85 percent destroyed; 128 between 10 and 50 percent; and 160 less than 10 percent destroyed. Of the 179 school buildings, 116 were more than 50 percent destroyed.[15] Seventy of the 104 college and university buildings lay in ruins; laboratories, archives, and libraries were largely or completely destroyed. Sixty percent of the city's industrial facilities had been annihilated; thirty percent had sustained damages between 10 and 50 percent, and only one-tenth were less than 10 percent damaged. Train stations and railway lines had been repeatedly subject to artillery fire during the fighting and had accordingly sustained enormous damage. Three large bridges spanning the Oder River as well as numerous smaller railway bridges had collapsed. The city's public transportation system was wiped out.

The loss of building stock was not evenly distributed throughout the city. The districts west and south of the city center—in which a large portion of the population had lived prior to the siege and where most industrial facilities had been located—were considered 90 percent destroyed and were largely uninhabitable. In contrast, the districts north and northeast of the Old Town had suffered less—the damage was between 10 and 30 percent—and thus contained a significant number of usable, largely intact buildings. The average degree of destruction in the city center including the Old Town was 50 percent. The most severe damage had occurred on the streets around Nowy Targ and pl. Dominikański, where up to 85 percent of the buildings were lost. The damage was markedly less severe in the areas south and west of the Old Town, south of the city moat, and west of the Rynek, where a large proportion of the buildings could be used again following minor repairs.

The Oder islands with their large number of historic landmarks, among them churches and monasteries, had been particularly hard hit. The buildings on Sand and Cathedral Islands were 60 to 70 percent destroyed. The cathedral itself was a ruin. Other historic buildings had also sustained massive damage. Whereas the construction materials used in modern administration buildings and department stores had helped them to withstand artillery and fire, many historic buildings, especially the centuries-old residential houses, had succumbed to flames due to their largely wooden construction and to their narrow, labyrinthine layouts. Most of the great medieval churches and monasteries, too, had been seriously damaged despite their massive brick walls. Church towers that had dominated the silhouette of Wrocław's Old Town for centuries had burned down, been robbed of their spires, and in part collapsed.

St. Elizabeth's, the most impressive Gothic church in the Old Town, was among the few medieval religious buildings in Wrocław that survived the war with only minor damage. The Gothic town hall on the Rynek also survived, miraculously. A single bomb had penetrated its roof and exploded in the interior, but without causing extensive damage. The magnificent patrician houses on the western side of the Rynek had also been fortunate, sustaining only insignificant damage. Many of the other patrician and burgher houses on the Rynek and pl. Solny, however, had suffered greatly from constant artillery fire. Only a few escaped with external damage alone. The buildings on the Nowy Targ were entirely in ruins.

Even in those parts of the city that had not been seriously damaged, window panes had been broken, roofs removed, and attics destroyed. Numerous houses had also burned down completely and collapsed. There were millions of cubic feet of rubble within Wrocław's city limits, and almost half of the city's 430 miles of roads were covered in ash.[16] Large sections of urban infrastructure had collapsed. The sewage and water system had thousands of leaks where bombs had hit. Electric and thermal power plants, waterworks, pumps, and other valuable municipal facilities had been destroyed or dismantled by the Red Army. Telephone lines were down, and there was no electricity, gas, or running water. Street lighting did not function at all, which meant that Wrocław's cityscape of ruins, ghostly enough during the day, sank into obscurity at nightfall.

The destruction percentages given above are of course only approximations. There were not enough experts at the time to compile precise figures for the thousands of damaged or destroyed buildings in the city.[17] Moreover, it is obviously no longer possible today to determine whether specific damage was due directly to war, to vandalism and arson after combat operations ceased, or to subsequent dismantling. Some of the losses that actually occurred long after the war have been incorrectly classified as war damage. Conversely, a 1945 city plan mapping the destruction designates a series of building complexes, especially in the western part of the Old Town—approximately between ul. św. Mikołaja and ul. Włodkowica—as "not destroyed" or only "partially destroyed," where there were in fact large gaps still remaining in the 1960s and 1970s.[18] The selection of photographs published in Polish books after the war has also occasionally contributed to incorrect estimations of the degree of war destruction. In order to demonstrate the accomplishments of the reconstruction efforts, photographs were usually selected of buildings that had been destroyed and then reconstructed. Accordingly, images of buildings and streets that survived the war in relatively good condition are rare, particularly if the buildings were subsequently demolished.

This was true, of course, not only of Wrocław. In Warsaw as well, numerous buildings that survived the war intact, or at least sufficiently intact that they could have been rebuilt at reasonable cost, were sacrificed in the postwar era.[19] In comparison with Western Europe, however, where a virtual demolition rampage followed the Second World War and proved to be the final blow for a number of cities affected by the bombing,[20] the treatment of historic buildings in Poland was cautious. Nevertheless, in Wrocław too reconstruction and demolition went hand in hand. That said, it cannot be denied that, given the enormous scope of the damage in Wrocław, the accomplishments of the People's Republic of Poland in rebuilding the city were impressive.[21]

Reconstruction efforts began immediately after the establishment of the Polish administration in May 1945. Given the difficult conditions that prevailed in these first postwar months, it was inevitable that the earliest attempts were insufficiently coordinated and shortsighted, lacking any long-term urban development perspective, let alone anything like a vision. The initial task of the building authorities was to address the most urgent needs of the Polish administration. These included restoring a minimum of office space and housing for municipal agencies, as well as buildings for a court and prison, two hospitals, schools, printing presses, two hotels, and the city theater. Repairing the bomb damage to the historic town hall also began in this early phase. Parallel to efforts by municipal leaders, the staffs of various government institutions, regional railway authorities, factories, banks, colleges, various cultural institutions, and churches used their own funds—along with szaber and enormous individual engagement—to get resettled in the ruins of the city and provisionally repair the necessary buildings.[22]

Rebuilding the transportation system was crucial in revitalizing Wrocław. Beginning with the principal streets, debris and rubble were removed and damage to street surfaces repaired so that the few still-functioning vehicles were at least able to move within the city and connect distant city districts. At the war's end a public transportation system no longer existed. The streetcars that had been the backbone of Wrocław's public transport were not operational, since 80 percent of the overhead lines, tracks, and streetcars had been destroyed[23]—the latter because many had been used to construct barricades during the siege. Of the 560 streetcars in the city, only a mere seven were functional at the end of the fighting.[24] Because it was impossible to get the streetcars running over the short term, the few buses that were still operational were used to transport at least the city employees residing in Karłowice to their workplaces in the city center.[25] The remaining residents of Wrocław had few options other than tedious foot marches through the far-flung city districts.

The enthusiasm was therefore great when the reopening of the first streetcar line, the Number 1 between Biskupin and pl. Słowiański, was celebrated on August 22, 1945. That same day, the first regularly scheduled buses also began running—the A line between the central train station and pl. Grunwaldzki, which became known as the "szaber bus."[26] Little by little the streetcar network resumed operations, and bus lines were expanded over the following months. On October 6, streetcar line 2 began operating again between Wrocław-Karłowice and Wrocław-Nadodrze station;[27] and on December 21, line 3 began shuttling between the Rynek and pl. Strzegomski.[28] It took several years, however, before the entire public transportation network was back in operation.

Extensive reconstruction was also necessary to reconnect the railway lines around Wrocław. Destroyed tracks and train stations had to be repaired and demolished bridges rebuilt. On June 28, 1945, the first passenger train rolled into Wrocław's central train station from Katowice. Because the Oder bridges had been destroyed, however, train travel to Upper Silesia remained quite irregular, so a bus line operating three times a week between Wrocław, Opole, and Kraków was established in August 1945 as an alternative. On July 19, one track of the railway bridge over the Widawa was opened, enabling regular train connections from the Nadodrze station to Poznań, Łódź, and Warsaw. During this transition period the Nadodrze station became, for all intents and purposes, the central train station in Wrocław. On October 15, commuter and regional transportation in the direction of the Sudeten Mountains was reintroduced via the Świebodzki train station.[29]

In September 1945, seven Polish elementary schools, a secondary school, and a vocational school opened in buildings that for the most part had been reconstructed only provisionally. A number of other schools followed in the next months. An important event, celebrated on November 15, 1945, was the beginning of the first academic year at the two Polish post-secondary institutions in Wrocław—the university and the polytechnic university. Professor Ludwik Hirszfeld, the first dean of the medical school, gave the inaugural lecture in the venerable Aula Leopoldina.[30] The university library reopened at the same time. However, because a large number of its books had burned and the former main building on Sand Island lay in rubble (not to be repaired until the 1950s), the university library was merged with the Wrocław city library, whose collections and library building had survived the war intact. Prior to the beginning of the fall semester in 1945, many of the 3,500 new university students joined instructors and university staff in making temporary repairs to the university buildings.[31] They had to roll up their sleeves and get their hands dirty as bricklayers, carpenters and plumbers before they could turn to the study of anatomy, mathematics, or languages.

During the summer of 1945, numerous cultural institutions took up their work in the ruins of Wrocław. On July 16, the first Polish movie, the documentary film *Majdanek*, was shown in the Schauland Movie Theater on what is now ul. Piłsudskiego, where the Warszawa Cinema (built in 1973) is currently located. German films were shown with Soviet authorization at the Lalka Cinema. The opera house on ul. Świdnicka had sustained only minor damage that could be quickly repaired with the help of its technical and artistic staff, still primarily German at the time. It was reopened as a Polish opera house on September 8, 1945, with the premiere of Stanisław Moniuszko's Polish national opera *Halka*. Initially the building was also used for theater productions, the first of which premiered on December 25, 1945: *I co z takim*

Wrocław's great academic tradition continued despite the historical rupture of 1945. Already in the fall of 1945, the Aula Leopoldina, the university's traditional ceremonial hall, saw the opening of the first Polish academic year. About 3,500 students took up their studies in buildings that, in many cases, were still in serious need of repairs. The majority of instructors came from the former Polish university of Lwów. Courtesy of the City Museum of Wrocław (Krystyna Gorazdowska).

robić, a contemporary comedy by Roman Niewiarowicz, who also played one of the two roles in the production. Thanks to the Soviet city commandant, who actively pushed for a revival of music and theatrical life in Wrocław, there were German vaudeville and cabaret performances at the Liebich Theater as well as regular concerts by the Wrocław Philharmonic, which was at the time composed primarily of German musicians.[32]

The people of Wrocław would have to make do with provisionally restored buildings and makeshift technical facilities for years to come, but some semblance of city life was beginning to make itself felt. Gas, water, and electricity service resumed in parts of the city in the second half of 1945 (it would take years to attain prewar levels). Gas lines for the suburbs could only gradually be reconnected; repair of the water and sewage systems took until 1948.

Even in later years the urban infrastructure was inadequate due both to war damage and to the makeshift repairs carried out in the postwar era. To the dismay of both private households and industry, the electricity supply was particularly unreliable, hampered by insufficient capacity and prone to frequent blackouts.[33]

Despite difficult material circumstances, a good deal more reconstruction work was accomplished in the first postwar years than was needed to fulfill the most pressing practical requirements. Thanks to the support of the state historic preservation agency and the allocation of national funds, it was possible to prevent further deterioration of at least the most valued historic buildings damaged in the war. In 1945 and 1946 roofs were repaired or makeshift coverings installed over ruins, supports were built for walls, and valuable materials needed for the reconstruction were extracted from the rubble. Work began immediately in those cases where the damage was minor. The town hall and the churches of Sts. Elizabeth and Dorothy were essentially repaired by 1946. On Cathedral Island, where most of the buildings required extensive reconstruction extending over decades, the minor damage to St. Giles Church was repaired in 1945, as was the external damage to the palace of the cathedral provost, which then became the residence of the apostolic administrator. Along the former Domstrasse (ul. Katedralna), where various structures belonging to the bishopric had been reduced to ruins, the remains of extant walls were at least partially secured.

The largest rebuilding project of the early period was the restoration of the Wrocław cathedral, which began in 1946. Despite the enormous damage the building had sustained, the first construction phase was completed in 1951, after which the cathedral was reopened. Amid the rubble of Cathedral Island one of Wrocław's most important symbols had thus returned to life. In the course of the 1940s most of the other medieval or Baroque religious buildings that had defined Wrocław's architectural face were at least secured and prepared for reconstruction. The reconstruction of the Baroque main university building on the banks of the Oder River, which took place between 1946 and 1949, was one of these early rebuilding projects. Thus by the late 1940s three mainstays of Wrocław history—the municipal administration, the university, and the Catholic bishopric—were already able to resume their functions in their traditional locations: the medieval town hall, the Baroque edifice of the former Leopoldina, and the Gothic cathedral. Reviewing these first reconstruction projects Józef Zaremba correctly noted in his report to the Ministry of Reconstruction in 1946:

> The immensity of the destruction, which was caused for the most part by the Germans themselves and which approached that of Warsaw in scale, is unparalleled in modern history. If we take into account the extreme difficulties in the areas of public transportation, food supply, and finances, as well as the shortage of specialists and construction materials—above all the catastrophic lack of glass, roof tiles, and lime—then what was achieved is truly impressive, all the more so given that not even historic buildings were neglected in the reconstruction effort. Here, too, the Poles have demonstrated their great understanding for the value of culture.[34]

The establishment of the Wrocław Directorate for Reconstruction (WDO) in January 1946—an institution that had its counterparts in Warsaw, Poznań, Gdańsk, and Szczecin—accelerated the reconstruction work to some extent and improved coordination. Beginning in the summer of 1945 the Ministry of Reconstruction had a delegation in Wrocław, but it did not become a powerful agency until the WDO had been established. Under the leadership of Józef Rybicki, the former chief of the municipal building department, the WDO participated, under commission to the ministry, in larger public-sector reconstruction projects—for the municipal administration, the educational system, and important cultural institutions, as well as in the areas of transportation and historic preservation.

The founding of the WDO coincided with the establishment of construction companies, the monetary reform, the gradual normalization of the economy, and the passing of the Three Year Plan for 1947–49.[35] For the first time construction based on real planning (as opposed to improvisation) and supported by the allocation of loans became possible, though shortages of funds, specialists, and equipment continued to hamper progress. Bottlenecks in the supply of building materials were particularly obstructive. The building minister repeatedly urged the use of extremely economical forms of construction and insisted that as many bricks and other building materials as possible be collected from rubble and from the ruins of demolished buildings.[36]

It was impossible to rebuild rapidly under these conditions, but the WDO nonetheless reported that it had repaired almost 500 buildings between 1945 and 1948. In addition to 276 residential buildings, these included in particular schools and college buildings, municipal administration and public health buildings, several historic structures, as well as buildings on the fair grounds that were needed for the ambitious Exhibition of the Recovered Territories that was to take place in Wrocław in the summer of 1948 and was intended to present to the public the first achievements of the reconstruction efforts.[37] However, since it was necessary to render as many buildings as possible usable in the least amount of time, the directorate initially sought to repair those buildings with minor damage and to limit itself to the most urgent projects, such as the restoration of roofs and interiors. Consequently, progress in the reconstruction efforts was hardly visible even into the early 1950s.[38] This impression was exacerbated by the fact that little reconstruction work was carried out in the city center, as the majority of buildings that could be quickly repaired were located in outlying districts.

Nevertheless, life returned to the city center as well. In the 1940s, a series of institutions had set up offices in the better-preserved buildings of the Old Town. Their presence got things moving once again in Wrocław's historic center of gravity, which had been temporarily displaced to the largely intact districts north of the Oder due to war damage. Municipal leaders began once again to use the prestigious Gothic town hall for official occasions. A number of public institutions such as the directorates of the municipal gas, electricity, and water supply moved into the modern high-rise on the west side of the Rynek. The municipal building department opened offices in the Old Stock Market building on pl. Solny. The WDO, the Regional Directorate for Spatial Planning, and the Wrocław Planning Office were headquartered in Hans Poelzig's office building at ul. Ofiar Oświęcimskich 38–40. University institutes soon reopened in the university district on the relatively intact northern perimeter of the Old Town. The Ossolineum, one of Poland's most important cultural institutions, home to a magnificent collection of historic archival materials and a large and valuable library, was moved from Lviv to Wrocław in 1947, where it was soon ensconced in the former St. Matthew's Gymnasium (secondary school), a splendid Baroque edifice in the old university quarter. Important agencies of the municipal administration, the militia, the Office of Public Security, and the court set up offices in the expansive and largely intact building complex that housed the police headquarters and the courthouse on Podwale. The PPR also had an office on Podwale in the immediate vicinity of the municipal administration and the security apparatus, as well as one in the nearby New Stock Market building on ul. Krupnicza 15, where delegates of the Ministry of Industry and Trade and the Chamber of Industry and Trade had their offices.[39]

The addresses of these important institutions made clear that the Old Town, despite the serious war damage it had sustained, was once again the undisputed center of Wrocław. Many public buildings even retained the functions that they had had prior to 1945, including more than just obvious cases such as the opera house or hospitals. The municipal administration was quickly reestablished in the town hall and in the neighboring civic hall. The university moved into the buildings of the former Silesian Friedrich Wilhelm University, while the polytechnic university took over those of its German predecessor. Police headquarters became the central office of the militia, and the court once again occupied the building next door. There were, however, important changes, most notably in regards to sacred buildings, as the religious makeup of the Polish population was markedly different than that of the German population. Prior to 1945 there had been an almost equal number of Protestants and Catholics within the city's populace, and the number of Protestant and Catholic churches had accordingly been roughly equal. The population of Polish Wrocław was almost exclusively Catholic. Consequently most of the Protestant churches became Catholic after the war. The churches of Sts. Elizabeth and Mary Magdalene no longer served as Protestant counterweights to the cathedral and the other great Catholic churches of the Old Town, but now became Catholic as well. The immigration of Polish Jews, by contrast, created continuity, since many of the buildings that had once served the German-Jewish community—first and foremost the community center on ul. Włodkowica and the White Stork Synagogue between ul. Włodkowica and ul. Antoniego—once again became centers of Jewish life.

Raising the Old Town from Its Ashes

Wrocław's recovery was marked by some encouraging early successes: the public transportation system and the local infrastructure were partly rebuilt, several factories were reopened, administrative buildings were repaired, and work began on the restoration of historic buildings. It was not until the early 1950s, however, that the comprehensive effort of rebuilding the city began. Ruins and rubble continued to dominate the city. Although preparations for the Exhibition of the Recovered Territories in the summer of 1948 provided an important stimulus for accelerating the cleanup and reconstructing key buildings, the speed of such efforts slowed markedly once the exhibition was over. During the political changes of the late 1940s, when Poland's Stalinist period began, many of the earlier accomplishments were undone. People who had been active in the first few years after the war fell out of grace and were abruptly removed from office. In 1949, before reconstruction had really begun, the WDO was dissolved, along with other institutions that had been involved in concrete efforts to plan and carry out the city's reconstruction. From this point on, attention focused on heavy industry. While this may have benefited Wrocław's large factories, the rebuilding of the city as a whole stagnated. The brick collecting operations in the late 1940s and early 1950s had devastating effects: once again piles of rubble and heaps of waste appeared throughout the city. They impeded construction work and made Wrocław look like a bedraggled city in which little had been achieved since the end of the war.

Then, in 1953, the government in Warsaw decided both to accelerate rebuilding efforts in Wrocław and to concentrate on the city center.[40] Priority was to be given to the reconstruction of the most important squares and streets of the Old Town—a policy that did not need to be revised following the political changes in 1956. On the contrary, the new political leadership in Warsaw fully supported these measures, and there was growing support among Wrocław's inhabitants for ridding the city of all signs of war damage, in particular for reviving the historic city center by reconstructing landmarks and beautifying the cityscape.

As a result of the powerful thrust to revitalize Wrocław in the second half of the 1950s, burgher and patrician houses were rebuilt on the Rynek and pl. Solny, as well as on adjacent streets. Most of the churches and monasteries were also restored, as well as the armory, the ramparts in the Old Town, and a number of other medieval buildings. The reconstruction of the city center, which by and large followed Warsaw's example of blending historic and historicist reconstructions, was essentially completed in the course of the 1960s.

Parallel to the historic reconstruction of the central squares and streets, which was the general architectural policy in Poland until the end of the 1950s,

Following the example of work done in Warsaw's Old Town, parts of Wrocław were historically reconstructed. This photo from 1955 shows the Baroque burgher houses on the south side of the Rynek prior to their completion. The buildings had to be rebuilt from scratch. Courtesy of the Ossolineum (Stefan Arczyński).

Wrocław saw as well the rebuilding of entire blocks in the style of Socialist Realism.[41] The official objective of this Soviet-inspired building doctrine as decreed in Poland in 1949 was to oppose cosmopolitanism, constructivism, and formalism—as (Western) architectural Modernism was characterized—"by cleaving to the great architectural legacy of Poland and the world."[42] The classic self-definition of Socialist Realism—a style that was "socialist in substance and national in form"—could indeed be applied to the way in which many historic buildings were reconstructed in Poland in the 1950s. Frequently historical restoration was limited to the façade, behind which modest modern apartments for the working class were built. Wrocław's Old Town was thus externally reconstructed in its historic forms, while it was at the same time transformed into a residential neighborhood for the working class. "Bringing workers into the city center," President Bierut declared programmatically in 1949 (with an eye on the Polish capital), meant building worker's estates in those districts "that previously had been accessible only to the wealthy of Warsaw."[43] In Warsaw the restoration of the Old Town and the erection, along ul. Marszałkowska, of monumental buildings in the Socialist Realist style not only occurred at one and the same time; they were also expressions of one and the same idea—to build housing for the people in the city center and to give those living quarters a face that would recall Poland's great national traditions.

Close ties between historic restoration and Socialist Realism are also evident in Wrocław. In 1955–56, one of the larger construction projects of Socialist Realism was built at the northern end of ul. Świdnicka, directly adjacent to the Rynek with its historically restored Baroque burgher houses. Ul. Świdnicka was widened by significantly setting back the building line on the east side of the street. An elongated row of residential housing with stores on the ground floor was built on the eastern side of the emerging square, which was renamed pl. Młodzieżowy (Youth Square). The new structure was modern in style but was designed to fit into its environs by reason of its height and façade articulation, and through the installation of gables, architectural citations tying the modern structure to the old burgher houses in the neighborhood.

Between 1950 and 1955 two monumental buildings for the polytechnic university were constructed northeast of the Old Town at the southern end of pl. Grunwaldzki, which had been a huge wasteland since the siege. These buildings were initially conceived as the first part of a projected university campus in the style of Socialist Realism that was supposed to extend from the banks of the Oder to both sides of the m. Grunwaldzki in the north. This imposing project clearly drew upon plans dating from the era between the two world wars. After the First World War, Max Berg, the long-time senior building official in Wrocław and designer of Centennial Hall, had suggested uniting the university institutions scattered throughout the city "into a large building complex that would extend along the right bank of the Oder from the Kaiser Bridge to the old Oder."[44] In a draft that was never implemented, Berg and Ludwig Moshamer proposed monumental blocks with buildings up to eight stories high, which would have completely altered the appearance of the northern bank of the Oder. With their rigid axial symmetry and neoclassical forms, the designs from the late 1940s accorded with the principles of Socialist Realism and not those of architectural modernism advocated by Berg and Moshamer. Nevertheless, the two projects shared much more than

The area along the former Kaiserstrasse (pl. Grunwaldzki) was leveled during the siege to make room for an airfield in the city center. Plans of the 1950s to transform the wasteland into a monumental academic quarter in the style of Socialist Realism were not realized, save for the two large edifices visible on the left side. In the 1970s, modern high-rise buildings were erected on the other side of the street. The area in the foreground was rebuilt only recently with a U.S.-style shopping mall. Courtesy of Via Nova (Stefan Arczyński).

their fundamental idea: both foresaw a monumental façade along the Oder and a large square that would open onto the river. The obvious similarities between the two urban designs were never explicitly acknowledged in communist Poland.[45] While Berg's project never got past the draft stage, the project of the 1950s, too, remained unfinished; only the two aforementioned new buildings for the polytechnic university were built. In addition, four student dormitories, which were not directly part of the plan, were erected on the northeastern section of the grounds between 1954 and 1956. They stood lost amid the enormous wasteland of pl. Grunwaldzki until a gradual rebuilding of the grounds began in the 1960s. It was not completed until after the start of the new millennium.

The reconstruction of pl. Kościuszki constituted one of the largest building projects in Wrocław during the fifties. The remaining buildings, such as the former Wertheim department store seen in the background, were integrated into the new ensemble built in the style of Socialist Realism. The ensemble provided ul. Świdnicka with an attractive entrance into the city center and was used for big parades like the one held during the May Day demonstrations in 1961. Courtesy of Via Nova (Stefan Arczyński).

The largest project of Socialist Realism—and one that might be termed a success, if only because it avoided the exaggerated monumentality so often associated with the style—was the rebuilding of the demolished Tauenzien-platz (now pl. Kościuszki) in the south of the Old Town. This, the first signifi-cant investment in residential construction in postwar Wrocław, created new housing for 4,000 people in the city center, along with shops on the ground floor. The Kościuszko Residential Complex, as it was called (Kościuszkowska Dzielnica Mieszkaniowa), was based on the aforementioned residential com-plex along ul. Marszałkowska in Warsaw (Marszałkowska Dzielnica Miesz-kaniowa), although it also took local conditions in Wrocław into account. The project, headed by Roman Tunikowski, reproduced the historic form of the square and integrated a modern building, the former Wertheim department store, as well as two other buildings of eclectic style that, prior to 1945, had housed the Hotel Savoy (there is still a hotel of that name on the square) and the Wrocław branch of the Dresdner Bank. The entire complex extended to ul. Piłsudskiego and served as the new socialist entrance into Wrocław's his-toric city center.

The historic reconstruction of central squares and streets was largely com-pleted by the late 1950s. This amounted to only a fraction of the original plan to reconstruct the basic features of Wrocław's Old Town, but it meant that people were once again able to take scenic walks through the city center from the central train station along ul. Piłsudskiego and ul. Świdnicka across pl. Kościuszki to the north, passing the Rynek and the Town Hall, then along ul. Kuźnicza to the university, and from there to Sand and Cathedral Islands and, finally, to the reconstructed cathedral. A sense was preserved that Wrocław constituted a city with a centuries-long tradition.

1956 AND A CHANGING BUILDING POLICY

Political changes in 1956 brought an abrupt end to building projects in the style of Socialist Realism. With de-Stalinization came markedly different con-struction policies, as well as new ideas regarding architecture and urban plan-ning.[46] Its aggrandized monumentality, its traditionalism, and its detachment from international developments in architecture and urban design rendered Socialist Realism backward, out of touch with the times, an architectural ex-pression of Stalinism. Throughout Poland modernism could now enjoy the breakthrough its many Polish proponents had long desired. In this, economic considerations played a significant role. Issues of aesthetics and historic preservation aside, previous construction projects—both those that aimed at historic reconstruction and those in the style of Socialist Realism—were now considered too expensive and inefficient. The construction of residential housing and the rebuilding of the destroyed city centers needed to proceed at lower cost and with greater urgency.

Because construction in the first fifteen years after the war had been carried out primarily by craftsmen using traditional building methods, "it made hardly any difference from an economic standpoint," according to Poznań art historian and preservationist Konstanty Kalinowski, "whether . . . a Baroque burgher house was reconstructed or a modern residential building erected in its place."[47] However, in light of innovations in construction that were being introduced in Poland in the mid-1950s—such as the use of prefabricated, standardized components and concrete slabs—historic reconstructions became a luxury that was increasingly difficult to justify given the meager funds available and the dire housing shortage. According to Kalinowksi, economics necessitated the abandonment of large-scale programs aimed at recreating the historic appearance of entire city centers.[48] Future historic reconstructions were for the most part limited to truly outstanding historic buildings.

The reconstruction of the Nowy Targ, the youngest of the three large medieval marketplaces in Wrocław, was scheduled to begin in 1957. That project was now canceled and replaced with an architectural design in keeping with the new political guidelines. Between 1961 and 1965 modern residential apartment buildings were erected on the Nowy Targ that were consonant with the market's historic buildings solely in terms of their height and the fact that their building line reproduced the medieval layout of the marketplace. Only two structures from the prewar era were preserved, since they had sustained merely minor war damage. Although the restoration of this large square in the city's center did introduce architectural modernism to Wrocław's Old Town, it did not establish a pattern for the 1960s. The reconstruction of the Nowy Targ was an attempt to devise a contemporary architectural solution that took genuine account of the site's tradition and sought to integrate the extant historical building stock. In subsequent years, however, pressure mounted to erect as many apartments as possible in the shortest amount of time and for the least amount of money. This left little room for ambitious architecture. In

(Above and opposite page) The area around Nowy Targ suffered serious damage during the siege and was one of the focal points for brick collection after the war. Once a thriving center of urban life, it became an eerie wasteland. Courtesy of Via Nova, the Museum of Architecture in Wrocław (Krystyna Gorazdowska), and the Herder Institute in Marburg (Stefan Arczyński).

many cases what passed for "modern" was merely monotonous, highly standardized, mass-produced architecture that satisfied growing housing needs and conformed to rigorous cost guidelines. Large numbers of so-called "fillings" were erected in the Old Town. These were residential blocks built to standard specifications and put up hastily to fill gaps in the rows of buildings. They seriously detracted from the physical appearance of the Old Town as they clashed starkly with the styles of surrounding historical buildings, undoing the efforts of 1940s and 1950s planners to restore a harmonious, intact cityscape. In addition, the poor quality of these buildings often meant that they began to deteriorate prematurely and thus did not provide a satisfactory long-term solution.

The situation improved somewhat in the late 1960s and early 1970s, when the standardization of buildings was relaxed throughout the country, and architects were given greater freedom of design.[49] Creative construction projects that deviated from the monotony of the 1960s thus became possible. One

The revitalization of the area in the 1960s through the reconstruction of Nowy Targ in a modern architectural style was only partly successful. Since most of the new buildings were purely residential, the site did not regain its traditional function as a market square. In the late 1990s, the proposal to restore Nowy Targ to its prewar form triggered intense debate in the city, pitting advocates of an aesthetically pleasing, albeit inauthentic, reinvention of historic buildings against those who defended the authenticity and value of Wrocław's postwar architecture. Courtesy of the Herder Institute in Marburg (Stefan Arczyński).

example of this is the award-winning Wrocław ensemble of six sixteen-story high-rise buildings with three-dimensional façades and large gazebos built on pl. Grunwaldzki. The project was designed by Jadwiga Hawrylak-Grabowska in the late 1960s and built in the early 1970s. A change in construction policy was also evident in Poland's Old Towns. The often ruthless treatment of historic building stock in the 1960s, which can be understood as a reaction to the sacralization of historic architecture and the resulting suppression of the architectural avant-garde in the first decade after the war, gave way to a more gentle treatment of historic buildings in the 1970s. Attempts were made to respect historic preservationists' calls for harmony between the old and the new.[50] In Wrocław's Old Town, architects sought to integrate the remains of historic architecture in contemporary buildings. A fine example is an art gallery built on ul. Wita Stwosza in 1968. Architect Edmund Małachowicz incorporated into the new building the still existing entrance portal of the Hatzfeldt Palace and the hall behind it, including the stairways.

The construction of mass residential housing outside the city center began in 1960. In southern and western Wrocław there were still substantial areas that had been largely destroyed during the siege and had lain idle ever since. Although the houses were destroyed, the land remained extremely valuable. Prewar streets, water and power lines, and sewage canals were still in place, so that major infrastructure investments could be avoided. During the 1960s and 1970s, these neighborhoods were rebuilt with expansive modern residential developments that provided housing for a good deal of the city's population. For practical reasons, extant street layouts were as a rule not altered. (In fact still today it is possible to use a prewar-era map to orient oneself in an area in which all the buildings were erected after 1945). The perimeter block typical of the nineteenth-century European city was, however, abandoned. Instead freestanding buildings were erected, often at right angles to the street in accord with the universal urban planning principle of the day, which insisted on "light, air, and sun."

One of the first industrialized residential construction projects in Wrocław was the Gajowice housing development, which was built in the southwest part of the city between ul. Grabiszyńska, ul. Krucza, and ul. Zaporoska between 1960 and 1968. The development consisted of a combination of ten-story, freestanding high-rise buildings and five-story row buildings. The Południe housing development was erected in the 1960s and 1970s in the large area immediately to the east, between the central train station and pl. Powstańców Śląskich; the Huby housing development was built in the early 1960s between ul. Borowska and ul. Hubska. Beginning in the 1960s there was also construction in city districts west of the Old Town. One of the first projects was to rebuild the area around Rynek Szczepiński with alternating rows of residential housing and smaller high-rise buildings.

From the 1970s on, efforts were also made to mitigate the monotony of the 1960s residential developments. The large Popowice housing development, which was built in the mid-1970s on the grounds of the destroyed Pöpelwitz development, was the first in Wrocław to use prefabricated construction methods on a relatively large scale. The buildings had three-dimensional façades and were not laid out in the rigid perpendicular pattern that was

Beginning in the early 1960s, the growing demand for residential housing was met by building entire neighborhoods out of prefabricated components. What most people today perceive as an aesthetic disaster was in its day (the '60s and '70s) a utopian ideal of urban planning around the globe. The combination of freestanding houses and wide streets stood in proud antithesis to the dense city of the nineteenth century, with its lack of light, air, and sun, and its unsuitability for modern traffic. This photo taken in 1962 shows pl. PKWN prior to its completion. Courtesy of Via Nova (Stefan Arczyński).

conventional in earlier years. Elsewhere architects varied the numbers of stories, employed curved lines and geometrical forms in arranging the individual buildings, and alternated colors. In the 1970s construction began on the large Gaj housing development in the south, and the Kozanów, Kuźniki, Nowy Dwór, and Gandów Mały developments in the west (the latter on the grounds of the former Gandau airport), which began in the late 1970s. This was the first large-scale construction in areas where no residential buildings had existed prior to 1945. The city had grown beyond its prewar limits. The rebuilding of Wrocław was thus essentially a project of the 1950s and 1960s; the construction of new residential developments of the 1960s and 1970s can be counted as part of that process only insofar as they were located in areas that had been developed previously.

Nevertheless, up to the end of the People's Republic of Poland large un-used spaces continued to exist, even in the very city center, as a result of con-struction projects that were never, or only partially, realized. This was espe-cially true of the area around pl. F. Dzierżyńskiego (now pl. Dominikański). Until quite recently there was also a plethora of vacant lots on side streets and on the periphery of the Old Town that had been ignored during the phase of large developments. These gaps disrupted the impression of a city intact for visitors walking along the reconstructed main streets and squares in the historic city center. In the late 1970s, art historian and journalist Tadeusz Chrzanowski wrote:

> In my opinion the rebuilding of the center of Wrocław came to a stand-still about ten years ago and has been unable ever since to find a way out of the impasse. Volumes could be written about the rebuilding of Wrocław, but one fact remains: So many years after the war the city still has not been rebuilt. It is a city of potholes and empty lots, of gaps and abandonments, with urban planning on paper, but not on the ground. [51]

Małgorzata Olechnowicz convincingly argues that the rebuilding of Wrocław did not follow a master urban development strategy.[52] The principles behind planning were altered repeatedly; construction agencies were established and then dissolved; and numerous projects never materialized due to a lack of funding. The work of rebuilding was guided not by a single overarching idea. It was instead subject to abrupt shifts in construction policies and notions of architectural aesthetics. Due to the precarious financial situation in com-munist Poland numerous projects were never, or only partially, implemented, and on-the-spot improvisation was common, with piecemeal solutions dic-tated by cost considerations. This also meant, however, that Wrocław was not fully hit by the modernist euphoria that swept postwar urban planning. While many European cities today bemoan the demolition of historic neigh-borhoods and the dissolution of an irregular street plan in favor of a "mod-ern," "automobile friendly" pattern of streets, damage of this kind is compara-tively limited in Wrocław. Given the enormity of the destruction that the city suffered during the war, the number of its historic buildings that have been preserved is astounding.

PART TWO

The Politics of the Past: The City's Transformation

"As if one were endlessly far away from one's own people, in exile. As if the desires of all those uprooted and transplanted multitudes were emanating from them, saturating the air with excruciating melancholy." —Polish poet Maria Dąbrowska on the atmosphere in postwar Wrocław, 1947. Courtesy of the City Museum of Wrocław.

CHAPTER FIVE

The Impermanence Syndrome

Wrocław, June 12, 1945

I've been in Wrocław for three days already. . . . I'm sitting at a table in someone else's house in a foreign city. I'll do my best to describe in detail our journey and initial impressions.

. . . The train kept stopping; it wasn't until around noon that we made it to the historical Psie Pole. The train came to a stop about half a mile from the station. It was impossible to go any further because the bridge over the river had been demolished.

With some difficulty we got out of the train car. There was a large, marshy field full of hundreds of carts amid puddles that sloshed underfoot—carts of various kinds: baby carriages, wheelbarrows, wooden and metal carts, with wheels and without, even bicycles. While some of the passengers were piling out of the train, others were pushing their way in with their loot: paintings, carpets, linens, everything they could manage to get onto the carts. The train would be going back to Oleśnica any minute.

We'd taken a few provisions with us from Panienka: a jar of canola oil, a large loaf of bread, and a little bag of sugar; I'd stashed a pinch of tea and matches in the bag. We fit all these reserves into a blue baby carriage, one of the ones standing in the field, and started off toward the city. . . .

A heavy cloud of dust and soot hung over the city; the air was saturated with the smell of fire.

Most of the travelers were going straight down Hundsfelder Strasse. We headed left onto Friedewalder Strasse and Kopernikusstrasse, because those streets would take us more quickly to Bischofswalde and the east side of the city, where Father had occupied a villa during his first stay in Wrocław. Somewhere about halfway down Kopernikusstrasse we had to negotiate an enormous crater that spanned the entire width of the street. In one of the deserted gardens, we stopped and ate cherries we plucked straight from the tree. There were quite a lot of them, all red, ripe, and sweet. In many of the yards, roses had begun to bloom, unnecessary somehow in this devastated city. We were dying of thirst; the day was hot and dry, and the water pumps in the street weren't working. Father rested for a bit on a sofa standing—who knows why—in that empty garden. It was sweltering hot, and the air was completely still.

After this brief respite we started off again. On Parkstrasse we came across three overturned army vehicles. I went to get the green blanket lying in the back seat of one of them, but when I inspected it more closely, it turned out to be stained all over with blood, so I threw it down. Parkstrasse was only partially in ruins, but none of the windows had panes in them. The end of the street was littered with the remains of a wrecked streetcar. We took our next break in the shade of tall trees. Under a blossoming chestnut I noticed four graves marked with provisional crosses.

Finally we made it to Horst-Wessel-Strasse. A few of the pillars that had supported the roof in front of the enormous convention hall [*hala widowiskowa*][1] were lying on the street. Across the street there was a zoo. You could see two zebras walking past behind the fence. Someone told Father that the elephants had been eaten during the siege of Wrocław, but I don't know if that's true. Animals were screaming out of view of the street, probably from hunger or thirst. It made for quite an uncanny impression in that desolate place. . . .

In front of the ruin of a round kiosk, a two-car tram was lying on the rails. There were shards of glass, scraps of rubbish, and paper all over the place; in the midst of it all was a woman's purse, lying open, and beside it, photographs of children and a picture of an officer in a German uniform. . . . The tram rails were a bizarre sight; one of them had been ripped out of the ground and it jutted up several meters, rising in a twisted spiral toward the sky. A torn and dirty soldier's shirt was fluttering at the top. That's when we saw our first human being in this terrible city. At the corner of Am Dorffrieden we happened on a heartbreaking, even nightmarish scene. There in the little cemetery a man, no doubt a

German, was standing on a cart harnessed to an emaciated horse and kicking a corpse into a deep pit. There was a horrible stench. The whole thing made me feel sick to my stomach, and at that moment I wanted nothing more than to return to Panienka immediately. ...

In the end we made it to number 7 Heinzelmännchenweg, where Father had earlier moved into one half of a two-family house. I don't know how to describe what I felt when I walked into the house. I was simply so exhausted, I could only think about one thing—going to bed at once. . . . .

Unfortunately the gas hadn't been turned on, and there was no electricity either. The house was entirely dark because Father had nailed boards over the windows and covered them with black paper. Only after we'd opened the windows did we see the utter disarray and neglect of the apartment. The sink in the kitchen was full of dirty dishes, the towels and dishcloths on the hooks were covered with dust, and a blue-and-white striped apron had been tossed over the back of a chair. The plants on the windowsill had dried out; only the cactuses were still thriving—one was even in bloom. . . . .

After supper, which consisted of bread fried in oil, we sat out on the balcony. It was already dark; a gentle breeze was blowing, swaying the branches of the trees, and the garden was fragrant with the scent of roses. It was absolutely quiet and peaceful, and it seemed as if we were completely alone in this dead city.[2]

Joanna Konopińska's account of her arrival in Wrocław reads like the apocalyptic vision of a civilization in complete collapse. Her words illustrate vividly the enormous discrepancy between the actual experiences of Polish settlers and the patriotic appeals of the government, which spoke of the western territories as ancient Polish soil, a land of milk and honey that was to be resettled after centuries and that promised prosperity to all comers.

AN ALIEN PLACE

Polish settlers arriving in the western territories were initially struck by a strong sense of foreignness. The land was foreign, and so were the people they met there, Germans and Poles alike. The settlers had left behind the familiarity of their homes and social surroundings only to find themselves in a kind of no man's land that no longer appeared to belong to Germany but was not yet a part of Poland. It was a bizarre world that had been torn from its foundations; it was anything but welcoming. There were places that had been destroyed and were eerily deserted; others were still inhabited by Germans, with whom—if the settlers decided to stay—they would have to live for an indefinite period of time. Some of the houses and apartments had been completely plundered by the *szabrownicy*, so that even doors, windows, and plumbing were missing. At other locations everything had simply been left in its accustomed place—as if the owners had just stepped out for a moment.

It was a great stroke of luck for settlers, who generally arrived without any belongings at all, to find a furnished apartment—priceless start-up capital for a new future in this time of bitter need. Furniture, dishes, household appliances, sometimes even closets full of clothing and linens, and basements stocked with canned goods and other foodstuffs could be found in the western territories. But there was also a downside to such good fortune. The new occupants had to live with the pots and pans of strangers. It was possible to clear away the pictures on the walls, the unfamiliar family photos on the dresser, and the German books on the shelves. But all the other furnishings had to stay—no one could afford to throw them away. And so the sense of foreignness remained as well. Joanna Konopińska describes the feeling in a diary entry from October 1945:

> I'm sitting now at my desk, writing down my impressions, although I should probably start putting the apartment in order. Cleaning and sweeping the foreignness out, the Germanness that emanates from every corner. Instead of writing, I should be rushing about with a broom and a dust rag. Right now with every step I take I stumble across other people's things, evidence of a life I know nothing about, of the people who built this house and lived here and who may well be dead. How does one start a new life here? Impossible. I can't imagine that I'll ever be able to say that this is my house.[3]

Similar thoughts went through Hugo Steinhaus's mind. The world-renowned Polish-Jewish mathematician had received his doctorate in Germany, made a name for himself in Lwów, and been appointed professor of mathematics in the fall of 1945 at the University of Wrocław. With characteristic acumen he recognized the difficulty of transforming a German city into a Polish one:

> With no show of force whatsoever, ten thousand Poles rule like colonial masters over two hundred thousand Germans, but that does not resolve our German problem. Poles cannot master the Germanness of the villas, the "gardens," the Inselverlag[4] volumes heaped on the floor. What are they to make of the collected works of Hölderlin, Goethe, and Schopenhauer, of apartments where looters have torn out the upholstery, but left behind the *genius loci*?[5]

For most Polish settlers, Wrocław was very different from the villages and towns they had called home. Only the few who came from major cities were familiar with the density of construction and the height of the buildings, the vastness of the urban space that made it necessary to use streetcars and buses, or the peculiarities of urban life in four- or five-story buildings, where views were obstructed by other buildings and one lived under the same roof with families one didn't know. For people from the countryside, moving to Wrocław was a culture shock. Even the city-smart settlers had difficulty orienting themselves in a place where street and traffic signs were in a foreign language, and where they had to adjust to suddenly living among Germans.

> Those first days in a new place. Out the window you could see children walking by with their nanny and singing songs. In German. You could still hear that language everywhere. My parents were in a quandary— should we stay or should we go back to somewhere "in Poland." I witnessed their discussions on this topic. But in the end you have to live on something; and nearby, on what is now Engels Square, the trading that was so much a part of that time was in full swing. So we stayed.
>
> I remember my first timid excursions onto the streets closest to our house. There were signs and advertisements everywhere. And a whole lot of rubble. In many places, crosses had been stuck into the ruins.
>
> Sunday. Where was the church? Following a group of people all walking in the same direction, we discovered the church of St. Boniface.

During the first postwar decade, the reconstruction of Wrocław made only limited progress. Even in the city center, many streets and squares continued to offer a scene of devastation. The photo above, taken in 1955, shows ul. Szewska with the towers of St. Mary Magdalene in the background. On the opposite page, photographed in the same year, are the remains of Rybisch House on ul. Ofiar Oświęcimskich. Courtesy of Via Nova (Stefan Arczyński).

> The sermon was in Polish! And my parents met a few acquaintances from Lwów. With time there would be ever more of them. Slowly, the feeling of being lost faded away.
>
> But the city remained foreign, an alien place. . . . And all the while there was this conviction in the air that this "wouldn't be for long," that "we would go back."[6]

As if the foreignness were not enough, there was also horror, disbelief at the extent of the destruction. How would it ever be possible to build a future in such a landscape of ruins? From the very outset many newcomers lost all faith.

> On the outskirts of Wrocław, in Psie Pole, they ordered us to get off. . . .
> A few people, including Father and myself, made our way on foot to the city. The closer we got, the more fearful we became. All around, charred

remains . . . . Deeper and deeper we ventured into the city, down wind-
ing streets, between heaps of debris and outcrops of rubble hanging
overhead. Dread, growing discouragement. Bewilderment. Why on
earth had we come here?! Maybe we should go somewhere else? This
city is as good as dead! Enormous streets, with German names, alien
. . . The only way to get from place to place was by foot, over broken
glass, through dust, surrounded by the sprawling ruins.[7]

Life in the bombed-out and demolished city was perilous. Buildings and wall
fragments were continually collapsing; mines, unexploded bombshells, and
munitions depots blew up, killing people even months and years after the
war. Apart from danger, there was something so profoundly depressing about
war-ravaged Wrocław, an atmosphere that, according to Karol Maleczyński,
caused "rubble sickness" and the ardent wish, "if even just for a moment, to
breathe a different air, to see no more of charred remains and ruins, to live,
even for a moment, a normal life in a 'civilized' city like Krakow or Łódź."[8]

A Motley Society

Early postwar Wrocław was, in the words of historian Padraic Kenney, "not a city to which one moved and settled, but a camp filled with migrants from all over Poland and Europe."[9] It was not only the presence of so many non-Poles in Wrocław that made Polish settlers feel foreign and lost in the city. The Poles themselves were a collection of persons thrown together completely at random.[10] More than anywhere else in postwar Europe, the Polish resettlers in the western territories formed a "society of the uprooted."[11] They shared little besides their citizenship, their native tongue, and a common feeling of alienation in the unfamiliar environment. Only when contrasted with the Germans might the Polish settlers have seemed like a uniform community. As soon as the Germans disappeared from the city, however, differences between the Polish residents inevitably came to the fore. A pastor in the Wrocław diocese described the conglomerate makeup of his parish:

> [I]n those first postwar years the parishioners were a mix of newcomers from every corner of Poland, and there was no single group that might have outweighed the others or given the congregation a particular direction. A mix of people with diverse habits, customs, and traditions, who had been uprooted from their various milieus and who differed in terms of education, occupation, and trade; an agglomeration of marked regional antagonisms and of distinct, self-segregating groups of people. People from central Poland dubbed all those who came from the east "Ukrainians," whereas the parishioners from the east looked with suspicion and distrust at the so-called "Centralists" [those from central Poland]. When it came to family events such as christenings and weddings, it was common to invite mostly "one's own folk."[12]

Differences were difficult to bridge when city dwellers encountered farmers, and professors lived under the same roof with illiterates. The horizons of experience between the individual settler groups in Wrocław were worlds apart: There were reemigrants from industrial areas in Western Europe or overseas, as well as people returning from a war that had driven them throughout all of Europe, be it as soldiers or forced laborers. They faced settlers from the countryside, who had left their village environment for the first time. They may all have considered themselves Poles, but often they had little in common. They dressed differently, spoke different dialects, thought differently, and behaved differently.

And of course their war experiences varied greatly. There were the autochthons, who had been German citizens up to now. Some of them might have just cast off their Wehrmacht and SS uniforms; others, as members of the Polish minority in Germany, might have survived an odyssey through German concentration camps. There were settlers from central Poland who had suffered six years of German occupation before they were liberated by the Red Army. And then there were people from eastern Poland who had endured not only German occupation but Soviet occupation as well. They had witnessed the Sovietization policies of the years between 1939 and 1941, and after 1944 deportations and executions by the NKVD, the Soviet secret police. As a result of this experience, they viewed Poland under communist rule and the omnipresence of the Red Army in a different light and with different associations than their compatriots who had suffered only under the Germans. Moreover, they were expellees, whose former homes now lay inaccessible, beyond the Soviet border. For them, unlike the settlers from central Poland, there was no way back.

Prejudices held by the different population groups made coexistence all the more difficult. Settlers from central Poland turned up their noses at those "from beyond the Bug" (*zza Buga*). They called them *Zabużanie*, which could be translated as "hillbillies," implying that eastern Poles had been living in the back of beyond and now were lowering the cultural standards of western Poland. In fact, however, the percentage of city dwellers among the settlers from the east was substantially higher than among those from central Poland.[13]

Western Poles also questioned the Polishness of their compatriots from the east, who spoke distinctive dialects, considering them either Ukrainians, Lithuanians, Ruthenians, or Russians. Some had reservations for social reasons. Eastern Poles came from a region that until 1945 was still dominated by the large estates of aristocrats. Thus they were sometimes dismissed as *Pany*, gentlemen from the East, who had lived the high life at the expense of their exploited farmhands.

Eastern Poles in turn distrusted settlers from central Poland. They assumed that the latter had come to the western territories only to loot or for some other shady purpose. Czesław Rajca, who had moved from a village near Lwów to the town of Kattern (now Święta Katarzyna) near Wrocław, remembered the suspicion with which eastern Poles regarded Poles from other parts of the country:

> We were not the only ones from the East; others came from Podolia, Volhynia, even from the area around Wilno. There were small groups of people, one or two families each, from central Poland. Although we lived in the same village, the old regional divisions still prevailed. We from the east considered ourselves more important, and we lumped together all those who came from areas to the west of the regions now occupied by the Soviets and called them "Masurians."[14] We saw them as "deadbeats," who had nothing where they came from and now thought that here they could run their own farms, or else they came just to grab what they could and take it back home with them. We, on the other hand, had been expelled from our homelands; we had nowhere to return to.[15]

The main conflict was between the two largest population groups in Wrocław: settlers from central Poland and those from the eastern territories lost to the Soviets. Autochthons and reemigrants made up only a tiny segment of the population. Of course there were other regional differences as well, such as the cultural distinctions that continue to exist even today between the territories that had been parts of Russia, Prussia, and Austria during Poland's partition, and the rivalry between the residents of Krakow, Warsaw, Wilno, and Lwów, each group claiming to be the country's elite.

Not until the individual groups were suddenly thrown together in the western territories did it become evident that Poland had been a multiethnic state all along. There had never been an ethnically homogeneous Poland. These differences, coupled with the disorienting experience of being uprooted, made people eager to stay with their own kind, to associate only with people who shared their place of origin. According to Wrocław sociologist Irena Turnau, who conducted a survey in 1945 and 1947, the following statements were typical of what the city's Polish residents told her:

> I came here in July 1945, and in a year I have not established any new friendships. The reason for this is that my acquaintances are from different parts of Poland, which makes life enormously difficult.[16]

I socialize only with people I knew in Lwów, who live nearby. My neighbors and I have nothing in common, because they're from the central region and don't even go to church.[17]

Settlers from particular regions sought to preserve their group identity by establishing enclaves in certain streets and neighborhoods. In the long term, however, they could not sustain this degree of separation. Life in a major city necessarily led to encounters and the intermingling of groups. It was impossible to avoid meeting each other in the stairwells of apartment buildings; segregation according to background proved just as difficult to maintain in the home environment as at the workplace. In addition, the state pursued integration policies that aimed to realize the vision of ethnic homogeneity and deliberately discouraged attempts to keep hold of regional and ethnic identities.

Ultimately, the dissolution of the traditional milieus through war and forced migration and the mixing of the different population groups in the course of the nation's westward shift, combined with the homogenization policies of the communist government, led to a leveling of cultural differences. Poland, once so diverse, has become a country virtually without dialects and regional customs. Wrocław was one of the major melting pots in which the ethnic heterogeneity of prewar Poland met its end. It took decades, however, before a more or less homogeneous urban society emerged, a time span marked by major tensions within a highly fragmented populace.[18]

THE CAPITAL OF POLAND'S "WILD WEST"

On July 1, 1946, residents of Leśnica near Wrocław submitted a desperate petition to the Ministry of the Recovered Territories and the provincial governors of Lower Silesia. Although the war had ended more than a year ago, they were not living in peace. Their lives, they said, resembled those of American settlers in the Wild West, and this was due not least to Soviet soldiers who hunted down bicycles, robbed pedestrians, and broke into apartments. No one wanted to live such a life indefinitely, and so they were considering leaving the region if nothing was done quickly to rectify the lawlessness.[19] Such murmurings of discontent and references to the former German territories as

Wrocław became an El Dorado for criminals after the war. Entire neighborhoods consisted of deserted ruins, providing an inexhaustible supply of hiding places. Courtesy of the Ossolineum (Adam Czelny).

Poland's "Wild West" (*Dziki Zachód*) are a recurring theme in personal recollections of the period.

The legal vacuum implied by the Wild West metaphor is typical of transitional periods, times when there is often a temporary absence of a state order. German sovereignty, or the pitiful remnants of it that were left after its self-destruction, vanished completely from the territories east of the Oder-Neisse line when Germany capitulated. It took months before the Polish administration was sufficiently organized to establish even a minimum of public order. In the interim the only real authority was the Soviet military administration, which, however, pursued primarily the interests of the Red Army and the Soviet Union. Its priorities were requisitioning (forced) laborers and dismantling factories. It contributed little to stabilizing conditions in the western territories.

After six years of war marked by extreme violence—whether at the fronts or in the hinterlands, under the terror of the German or the Soviet occupation, whether due to the years of suffering and dying in the camps or to the horrors of ethnic cleansing—the moral standards of civil life had evaporated. This situation was exacerbated by general material hardship, hunger, homelessness, and the political upheaval within Polish society that dashed the hopes many people had had for the future. The precarious situation in the western territories, however, was due in large part to another cause: the mass migrations, which resulted in the loss of established ties and the suspension of social controls that stable communities are otherwise able to exercise, to some degree, even in times of political disorder. The violence of the postwar period grew out of the violence of war.[20] In his diary entry of June 10, 1945, Andrzej Jochelson wrote:

> I can remember the traditional sounds of Wrocław: gunfire, the boom of exploding mines, and in the intervals, the singing of nightingales, the chirping of swallows, the twittering of sparrows. All day Wednesday, a dead man in a German railwayman's uniform lay on the street between the hotel and the office. His head was covered with a curtain. No one removed the body. On that street, people were busy clearing the pavement of artillery shells, which they tossed into the ruined houses. Maybe one of them had exploded? Maybe it was a mine? Or maybe the man was simply shot?[21]

Wrocław was a hub of the great postwar migrations. In addition to the remaining Germans and the Polish settlers there, the city was populated by demobilized and scattered soldiers of various nationalities, prisoners liberated from German concentration and POW camps, returning forced laborers and displaced persons, as well as fugitive criminals and prisoners of war, and war criminals in hiding. The chaos of this huge, demolished city made it a haven for criminals of every kind and nationality. There was hardly any authority that could curb the criminal activities. Weapons and ammunition literally lay in the streets, and the vast fields of rubble, especially the uninhabitable districts in western and southern Wrocław, offered hideouts for entire gangs of thieves.

The regional citizens' militias reported in March 1946 that crime in Lower Silesia was four times higher than in the central Polish provinces.[22] "Wrocław," recalled Zdzisław Żaba, "was the subject of fantastic rumors that circulated throughout Poland. It was called the forbidden city and regarded as a hotbed of bandits and the worst kind of riffraff."[23] In his recollections, Stanisław Kulczyński described Wrocław in the first months after the war as "like . . . a forest, where you were as likely to get shot at from behind a corner as to get a knife in your back. We slept with our rifles next to our beds."[24] Crime was rampant, demanding "constant vigilance and presence of mind."[25] Consequently, city residents avoided the districts on the outskirts of town and moved into the more densely populated neighborhoods, living close enough so that neighbors could assist each other if necessary. According to Zdzisław Żaba, the basic rules of survival in Wrocław were: "Stay on the main roads, do not go out into the city at night, do not conduct business transactions with suspicious persons, and do not venture into the labyrinths of ruins."[26]

The activities of the looters, who often roamed from town to town and house to house in gangs, certainly contributed to the Wild West atmosphere; corruption within the state apparatus was another component. A number of extremely dubious figures had been hired to set up the Polish militia. They ultimately did more to obstruct public safety than to establish it. It was commonplace in the first years after the war for militiamen to report for duty intoxicated, to accept bribes, and to conspire with looters and criminals.[27] A large number of people working for the authorities not only performed their functions poorly, but also undermined the reputation of the state administration by lining their own pockets. Wrocław's mayor Aleksander Wachniewski issued a circular in December 1945 calling for efforts to combat the abuse, stating that *szaber*, speculation, and corruption were making it impossible for the state apparatus to function properly.[28]

Regular inspections conducted on behalf of the Warsaw government to review the civil administration in the western territories revealed flagrant abuse in Wrocław. A report of November 9, 1945, on the office of the Lower Silesian voivodeship based in Wrocław, described the situation as follows:

> On the basis of extended observations of conditions in Lower Silesia, I would venture to state with absolute certainty that 80 percent of administrative officials in the region are corrupt, regardless of their function and position. These people dedicate their time and energy primarily to acquiring material possessions or to conducting their private lives on a very high level. . . .

Ministerial directives are undertaken without regard for accuracy or punctuality. . . . I did not encounter a single administrative office in the entire region of Lower Silesia in which all the employees were present during working hours. . . .

The state of the railroad industry in all of Lower Silesia is shocking. It is impossible to get a freight car without paying a bribe, and a second bribe is needed in order to get it to move; as soon as the train starts moving, the guard in charge needs to pay more [bribes] at each station, otherwise it would not reach its destination in one piece. . . .

Among the 80 percent of employees who are corrupt in each administrative office, there are many who are capable and professional, but they do not apply these qualifications to the reconstruction of the state, and I have my doubts as to whether they will ever work honestly in the future. The remaining 20 percent of administrative workers are absolutely honest and have not been and will not be beaten down by the corrupt atmosphere. However, half of this 20 percent are unsuited for administrative work; the remaining 10 percent are industrious, honest, and nothing short of superhuman workers, but they are largely ineffective as they face insurmountable obstacles. . . .

From the beginning our administration in Lower Silesia has suffered from two fundamental maladies: bigwiggery on the one hand, and on the other a dearth of individuals who are free of worries about putting food on their families' tables. This second circumstance has led in large measure to the high level of corruption in the administrative system. . . . Today the majority of public officials, especially those holding managerial positions, own shops and other industries that are registered under the names of close relatives.[29]

This situation clearly was more serious than the initial labor pains of an administration in the midst of complete reorganization. Complaints of abuse in the Wrocław administration persisted.[30] In the spring of 1949, an inspection of the municipal housing office uncovered scandalous abuses, disorganization, a lack of basic knowledge, deficient performance of duties, corruption, and crass injustices in the allocation of apartments:

It is not surprising that the housing office is on its nineteenth director, not counting those who ran it for only a few days or weeks. In a single year, five directors on average pass through, which indicates that they only remain in the position long enough to obtain suitable apartments for themselves and their friends.[31]

In the beginning, the authorities were forced to go to great lengths to find people willing to work in the western territories. Consequently, it was at times necessary to hire anyone who was prepared to take on a position, even if there were doubts about that person's qualifications or motivation.[32] When, in the second half of the 1950s, the government made a serious effort to improve conditions in the western territories, the shortage of qualified workers continued to be one of the most pressing problems. In 1959 Deputy Minister for Labor and Social Welfare Tadeusz Kochanowicz proposed the introduction of material incentives to persuade qualified workers to move to the territories. In this way he hoped to redress the imbalance that saw a disproportionately high percentage of industrial, administrative, and construction specialists working in central Poland. The crux of the matter, however, was not of a material nature, and it could not therefore be resolved through financial means. As with most difficulties in the western territories, the critical factor was a lack of confidence about the permanence of the postwar German-Polish border. The aforementioned inspection report of fall 1945 already addressed this problem:

> Here again I would venture to state . . . that we have enough of everything we need to jump-start the commercial and cultural life of these [Recovered] Territories. All we lack is a deep understanding on the part of society, a profound belief that these territories actually belong to us, so that, as a result, we can learn to cherish them and to give our all to their development.[33]

Sitting on Packed Suitcases

There was a widespread tendency among newcomers throughout the western territories to never really settle into their new surroundings. Instead, for years or even decades, they led a provisional existence, as if they were living far from home. Czesław Rajca, who came originally from eastern Poland, remembered that new residents opened stores and workshops in the village of

Święta Katarzyna near Wrocław, and they rebuilt the destroyed church on their own initiative, but that did not mean

> that they felt a sense of true ownership. What stood in their way was the conviction, unabated through the years, that everything was provisional. There was very little faith that these lands called "recovered" would remain Polish forever. The actions of the authorities were not entirely convincing. Words contradicted deeds. There was so much talk about the Polishness of these territories, but instead of rebuilding Wrocław out of the ruins, the bricks of the demolished buildings were carted off to Warsaw. . . .
>
> In general, people believed that one had to do what was needed for today, and not put a lot of effort into tomorrow. Nobody repaired the fences, the peeling plaster did not bother anyone, roofs got fixed only when it started to rain on people's heads. For the settlers, the feeling of owning something lost its earlier meaning. They had lost what they had in the East, and they did not feel like the owners of what they had obtained in the West.[34]

Wrocław suffered in the early postwar years from this pervading sense that life in the city was transitory, that there was no point in establishing a more permanent life here. Many settlers remained only loosely connected to the city for a long time. As Stanisław Gajewski remembered,

> we cannot regard as city residents all those people—and they were not few—who did not take their residency in Wrocław seriously. Many of them lived "out of suitcases." Some would sing under their breath: "A single atom bomb, and we'll go back to Lwów" [Jedna bomba atomowa i wrócimy już do Lwowa]; others had a cousin somewhere in central Poland who was preparing for their return, setting up a sinecure for them there; still others, having finished exploiting whatever "vein of gold" was to be had in Wrocław, went "back to Poland" to enjoy the fruits of their farsightedness in their hometowns.[35]

Refugees from eastern Poland were generally unable to maintain the kind of secondary residence in central Poland that would have allowed them to leave Wrocław if living conditions in the city worsened. But that did not inspire them to work harder than settlers from central Poland to make Wrocław their new home. Instead, they dreamed of being able to return at some point to their lost homes. Rumors continued to circulate about a new war between the Western powers and the Soviet Union. While they might have frightened the settlers in the western territories, these rumors also fanned secret hopes that the borders might again shift and the Soviet Union be forced to leave the annexed eastern Polish territories. Thus both groups—the settlers from central Poland and those from the lost east—were sitting on packed suitcases.

One indication that the residents of Wrocław did not feel at home was the way they spent their holidays. Instead of using their free time for outings in the nearby countryside, for strolls on the promenades along the city moat, or to visit museums or attend concerts, they literally fled to central Poland. Joanna Konopińska described her first Christmas after the war:

> Every living thing in the city got ready to leave. At the Wrocław-Oder station [now Nadodrze station], throngs of people milled about with bundles and suitcases; evidently all the Wrocławians wanted to take home presents from the "Wild West" for their families and friends. . . . Over Christmas, almost the only people remaining in the city were the Germans . . . because we Poles preferred to spend the holidays with our relatives.[36]

According to Stanisław Gajewski these waves of travel, which "literally depopulated" Wrocław several times a year, continued for a long time and remained above the national average even a quarter century after the war.[37] The last Sunday before Advent, when people visited the graves of deceased family members, was always a day of travel. Nothing revealed the uprootedness of Wrocław residents as clearly as the lack of any connectedness between the urban population and local cemeteries. The graves in Wrocław belonged to strangers; the graves of loved ones lay somewhere in central Poland or far away in the Soviet Union. It took many years for Wrocław's cemeteries to become points of reference for the city's new population. Only gradually did Polish tombstones appear in between the German graves in the cemeteries on ul. Osobowica or ul. Bujwida. Even today it is customary in these cemeteries for Polish residents of the city to light candles under a large cross erected for those "who were not able to come here with us."[38]

The renowned Polish writer Maria Dąbrowska often spent time during the early postwar years in Wrocław with her friend Anna Kowalska, though she gave up on the idea of moving to the city. In May 1947 she wrote in her diary:

> One reason I always feel so awful in Wrocław is the inconsolable nostalgia that pervades the atmosphere there. As if one were endlessly far away from one's own people, in exile. As if the desires of all those uprooted and transplanted multitudes were emanating from them, saturating the air with excruciating melancholy.[39]

The "psychosis of impermanence" (*psychoza tymczasowości*) that is repeatedly described in memoirs was of course a problem that diminished over time. It could not be expected that Wrocław's new residents would be bursting with enthusiasm for a city so severely demolished and unfamiliar. But Wrocław could not be rebuilt and revitalized so long as the notion held that everything was temporary and that there was no knowing what the future might bring.

The fact that the city's Polish inhabitants doubted that Wrocław was worth the effort was not just a local problem. It was also a pressing political matter that threatened the future of the entire country. From the perspective of contemporaries, at least, the permanence of the postwar German-Polish border had not been sufficiently secured through political decisions in 1945 to prevent it from being challenged by the settlers' lack of commitment to the western territories and all the negative consequences arising from that lack of commitment. Polish failures in integrating, settling, and managing the former German territories were followed closely and publicized in West Germany, and they were also exploited for Cold War anticommunist propaganda.[40] The continuous influx of emigrants from Poland provided West Germany with first-hand information regarding Poland's difficulties in dealing with the former German territories. In the end, the Polish government was forced to take measures against the impermanence syndrome.

CHAPTER SIX

Propaganda as Necessity

THE INTEGRATION OF THE FORMER GERMAN TERRITORIES INTO THE POL-
ish state was a complex undertaking. Not only did the area have to be settled
to a sufficient density, but the administrative structures of the old territories
also had to be expanded to serve the needs of the new territories. Efficient
transportation connections had to be created between regions that had previously been separated by a national border, a uniform economic area had to be
developed, and Polish cultural and educational institutions had to be established throughout the western territories. The task of merging two entirely
different parts of a country into a single, homogeneous nation soon revealed
the limits of what political power could accomplish. The authorities could
dispatch civil servants and create new institutions, build a new railroad line,
and found a Polish university in a formerly German city; but the success of
their efforts ultimately depended on whether Poland's populace would come
to regard Silesia, Pomerania, and Masuria as parts of their own country and
become willing to engage in the work of reconstruction and in establishing
Polish life in the new voivodeships.

Among the legends propagated by Polish postwar propaganda was the
claim that Poles had long been yearning for the annexation of the regions
along the Oder and the Neisse. It is true that Polish politicians were dissatisfied with the course of the German-Polish border established after the
First World War and that claims to East Prussia and Upper Silesia had been
continually asserted. Nevertheless, the extent of the territory gained in the
west and north came as a surprise to most Poles—no less a surprise, in fact,
than the loss of major areas in the east that had up to then been considered an integral part of the country. Small wonder that the impermanence
syndrome was most pronounced precisely in Pomerania and Lower Silesia,
which even from a Polish perspective had been considered incontestable

German territory. The farther west one penetrated into the new territories, the harder it was for people to become accustomed to the notion that the territory they were in was Polish, just as Polish as Mazovia or Western Galicia.

The Tradition of Polish Western Thought (Myśl Zachodnia)

As surprising as the new borders in the west and north might have been for most people, Polish society was not entirely unprepared for the idea of incorporating German territories. Already at the time of the partition prior to World War I, Polish national activists were conceiving of ways to maintain the Polish character of Prussia's eastern provinces and to counteract the Germanization policy of the Prussian government. As the reestablishment of an independent Poland became increasingly likely over the course of the First World War, leaders of the Polish national movement discussed the course of the future German-Polish border and considered strategies to reverse the Germanization of what they considered to be Poland's western borderlands. At the center of these deliberations was a school of thought—as well as a network of intellectuals and political activists—within the Polish national movement that came to be known in Polish as myśl zachodnia, literally "Western Thought."[1]

The geographical center of Western Thought was the province and city of Poznań. It was here that German national ambitions to Germanize Prussia's eastern provinces clashed with Polish national ambitions to maintain and strengthen the region's Polish character.[2] The Poznań region became the arena in which the struggle between two national movements was waged, movements that in their mentality and strategies were mirror images of one another. The Polish movement was backed primarily by the Catholic people's associations as well as the important Society for Educational Assistance for the Youth in the Grand Duchy of Poznań (Towarzystwo Naukowej Pomocy dla Młodzieży Wielkiego Księstwa Poznańskiego), founded by physician Karol Marcinkowski in 1841. Marcinkowski's organization took on as its crucial mission promoting the development of an academically educated Polish middle class. In 1894, German nationalists founded the German Society of the Eastern Marches (Deutscher Ostmarkenverein) in Poznań in order to pressure the Prussian-German government to maintain and intensify its

Germanization policies in the east. In 1905, Polish citizens established in Poznań The Guard (Straż), an organization that saw itself as the direct counterpart of the Society of the Eastern Marches.[3]

Poznań was also the stronghold of the Polish National Democratic Party (ND) headed by Roman Dmowski. Founded in 1897, this right-wing nationalist party adopted the concepts of Western Thought and attempted to implement them through concrete policies. Like the proponents of Western Thought, the National Democrats viewed Germany as the most dangerous enemy of the Polish state. Thus, when the reestablishment of an independent Poland became imminent at the end of the First World War, they campaigned at home and abroad for a Poland extending far into the west. The Polish-German border that was laid down in the Versailles Treaty in 1919 and the plebiscites of 1920 and 1921 fulfilled most Polish territorial goals but left German society deeply dissatisfied at having lost major territories in the east. After this, Western Thought took on a different purpose. Now the political goal of its activists was to reverse the Germanization of those Prussian territories that had become part of Poland after the war, to strengthen the region's Polish ethnic majority vis-à-vis the economically powerful German minority, and to stave off German demands to revise the border determined at Versailles. Great significance was also attached to exploring and popularizing the region's Polish past in order to justify, on historical grounds, the incorporation of those partially Germanized territories into a Polish state. One of the leading political organizations behind Western Thought after 1918 was the Committee for the Defense of Upper Silesia (Komitet Obrony Górnego Śląska), which was founded in 1919 to campaign for a Polish victory in the 1921 plebiscite on Upper Silesia. After the plebiscite, its name was changed to the Association for the Defense of the Western Marches (Związek Obrony Kresów Zachodnich); in 1934 it was renamed the Polish Western Union (Polski Związek Zachodni—PZZ).[4]

Scholars, especially historians but also archaeologists, philologists, art historians, and geographers, played a key role in developing and propagating Western Thought. Prior to 1918, its most important intellectual centers were the universities of Krakow and Lwów, the Polish Academy of Sciences in Krakow, the Toruń Scientific Society, and the Poznań Society of Friends of Arts and Sciences. The University of Poznań, founded in 1919, became the flagship institution during the interwar period, especially the university's West Slavic Institute directed by Professor Mikołaj Rudnicki. In addition, regional research institutions were established, such as the Baltic Institute founded in Toruń in 1925 and the Silesian Institute established in Katowice in 1934.

The activities of German and Polish nationalists in the German-Polish borderlands continued to bear an uncanny mirror resemblance. What came to be known after 1919 as "research on the East" (*Ostforschung*) in Germany was, in terms of both goals and methods, the mirror image of Western Thought in Poland.[5] Activists in the respective movements pursued clearcut political goals, provided scholarly arguments supporting the territorial claims of their respective governments, and sought to popularize their findings through public lectures and publications aimed at a broad audience. *Ostforschung* and "Western Thought" constituted two highly politicized branches of area studies. The one was as Germanocentric as the other was Polonocentric, and both developed their respective theses in direct confrontation with each other.

Poland's interwar governments generally sympathized with Western Thought and its agents, although Józef Piłsudski, the leading political figure of the Second Republic, regarded (Soviet) Russia rather than Germany as the main threat to Polish independence. Integration of the country's heterogeneous regions and rejection of German demands for revisions of the border of 1919/1921 were aims shared by Polish political leaders and the promoters of Western Thought. Nevertheless, despite these common interests, institutions promoting Western Thought received only limited state funding. The Baltic Institute and the Silesian Institute remained modest establishments, and larger-scale research on Poland's western regions was possible only at the University of Poznań. The intrinsically anti-German stance of Western Thought also meant that the organizations supporting it were vulnerable to sudden shifts in the political winds. When the government in Warsaw signed the German-Polish nonaggression pact in 1934, anti-German propaganda had to disappear in Poland. Funding for the institutions linked to Western Thought became even scarcer. The Association for the Defense of the Western Marches had to change its name to the more neutral Polish Western Union, and its headquarters were moved from Poznań, the cradle of the Western Thought, to Warsaw.

Nationalism and Communism in the People's Republic

During the Second World War, especially when the defeat of the Third Reich was imminent, Western Thought regained its political relevance. A political situation similar to that at the end of the First World War developed, in which Polish political activists had to campaign for a favorable German-Polish border and prepare for the possible transfer of German territory to a reestablished Poland. Already during the German occupation, activists of Western Thought in the Polish underground had begun to work out strategies for Poland's territorial expansion to the north and west and to train squads for the takeover of German territory. They realized, however, that given the Soviet Union's growing military and political strength the radical Left—and not the National Democrats—would play a key role in postwar Poland. Only by working together with the Left could the policies of Western Thought, which traditionally had been linked to the National Democrats, be pursued.

The Polish communists, who thanks to Soviet support were preparing to assume power in postwar Poland, did not have a policy in place regarding the western border and the takeover of German territories. After all, they had been the most vehement opponents of the National Democratic camp and in the interwar period had branded the annexation of West Prussia and eastern Upper Silesia an act of Polish imperialism. The loss of Poland's eastern territories to the Soviet Union, however, made westward territorial expansion an issue of great political significance for the communists as well. Lacking any expertise of their own on these issues, they had no choice but to draw on that of the National Democratic camp. In the end, therefore, the ideological adversaries began to work together and even to share some basic political convictions: Both viewed territorial expansion to the north and west as critical to the survival of the Polish nation. They foresaw enmity with Germany as a long-term political reality, mistrusted the Western powers, and considered good relations with the Soviet Union imperative for Polish reasons of state.[6]

Political cooperation between the communists and National Democrats led to a merging of their two ideologies that subsequently shaped the political culture of the People's Republic of Poland.[7] This coalescence of nationalism and communism was a consequence of the political situation in Poland at the end of the war, but it also occurred in the other People's Republics of East Central Europe. The course taken by the influential historian Zygmunt Wojciechowski is emblematic of developments in Poland. Although Wojciechowski continued to align himself openly with the tradition of Roman Dmowski after 1945, overarching national considerations nevertheless led him to seek proximity to the communist leadership.[8] The communist leaders for their part were interested in working with Wojciechowski, and they made every possible effort to support his plan to found, in Poznań, the West Institute (Instytut Zachodni), which would advocate the ethnic nationalism communists used to fight against.[9] Despite their willingness to cooperate with the nationalist camp, the communists nevertheless did not leave any politically influential positions to the nationalists and ensured that all leadership positions in the institutions connected with Western Thought were filled by communists who toed the regime's line.

Although no detailed program for taking over German territories existed in 1945, the long tradition of Polish Western Thought did provide a strong base of personnel and ideas for state leaders to build upon. To some extent they could directly draw on Poland's experiences with the integration of Prussian territories after World War I, but there were considerable differences between the situations following the two wars. Above all, there had been no forced population exchange in the Prussian regions ceded to Poland after 1918, although there was a fairly high rate of emigration by Germans, as well as a considerable influx of Poles, during the interwar years. Wartime destruction was also insignificant, especially as compared with the situation after 1945. The reestablishment of Poland after the First World War and the creation of its sovereign territory out of land that had belonged to Russian, Austria, and Prussia since the late eighteenth century was nothing short of a political revolution. Nonetheless, demographic, economic, and cultural continuities in the Polish western territories in 1918 were far stronger than they were in the western territories in 1945. The situations in 1918 and 1945 were, however, very similar to the extent that in both cases Poland had to use historical and political arguments to justify the incorporation and integration of former German territory, both to the Polish people and to the rest of the world.

The Polish Western Union was reestablished in November 1944—tellingly at the seat of the Polish Committee of National Liberation (PKWN) in Lublin. In August 1945 it moved its headquarters back to Poznań and from there began to assume an important political role in Poland. The Silesian Institute in

Katowice and the Baltic Institute, initially in Bydgoszcz and later in Gdańsk, were also reestablished. Both opened field offices—the Silesian Institute in Wrocław and the Baltic Institute in Szczecin. The Masurian Institute was founded in Olsztyn in 1945. In addition, the Western Press Agency (Zachodnia Agencja Prasowa) was created to spread the ideas of Western Thought after 1945. Beginning in 1946, its Western Publishing House (Wydawnictwo Zachodnie) issued a large number of publications on the western territories and on German-Polish relations.[10]

The West Institute founded in Poznań in 1945 became the flagship of Western research.[11] Quickly developing into a major interdisciplinary research institution with field offices in Warsaw, Krakow, and Toruń, it took on all issues concerning the western territories and German studies. The main fields of research were the history and culture of the western territories, Western Slavic studies, and Polish-Czech relations, as well as the history of the German occupation of Poland and German-Polish relations in general. In the first decade of its existence, the research projects of the institute were driven by the notion of an eternal German-Polish antagonism, which had already been developed in the interwar period by the institute's first director, Zygmunt Wojciechowski, whose rapprochement with the communists after 1945 has already been described. In 1945 he presented this idea in one of the first books published in Poland after the war, *Polska—Niemcy. Dziesięć wieków zmagania* [Poland—Germany: Ten Centuries of Struggle].[12]

After the war, Western Thought had as its central theme the idea that the western territories were "recovered territories," which after centuries of separation from Poland had been restored in an act of historical rectification. Because the Polish state around the year 1000 had, coincidentally, roughly the same borders as the Poland of 1945, its territory was portrayed as Poland's natural geographical form. The eastern territories gained in later centuries were downplayed in their significance for the Polish state, whereas territorial losses in the west were presented as a theft of Polish land, behind which the same immutable German "drive to the East" (*Drang nach Osten*) was identified.

This interpretation reduced a millennium of complex historical relations in Central Europe to simple formulas. The Second World War and the German occupation were conceived as the dramatic climax to "ten centuries of struggle" between Germans and Poles, an interpretation that was calculated to put the trauma of recent years into a neat historical framework. The radical westward shift of the Polish state in 1945, which destroyed long-established regional structures and deprived millions of people of their homes, was presented as the rebirth of a Polish territorial tradition established by the dynasty of the Piasts a thousand years earlier. This view became the official history of the Polish nation after 1945. Accordingly, Władysław Gomułka, first secretary of the Central Committee of the Polish Workers' Party and minister for the Recovered Territories, announced in his proclamation of June 10, 1946, in Psie Pole, that

> these ancient Piast lands, which until recently were ruled by the German *Bauer* [peasant], have once again found their rightful owner in the Polish peasant.
>
> Great historical events have enabled our generation to return to the land of our ancestors, to the patrimony of our forefathers. Whether you have arrived here from the Ukraine or Belorussia, or from the overpopulated and fragmented farms of central Poland, you have come not as people searching for a place in the sun. You have returned to your own country—as the rightful owners of these territories. You have taken over this land as your patrimony. The Germans may have Germanized these territories by violence and oppression, by a centuries-long policy of colonization and destruction of national identity, but history cannot be Germanized. Nothing and no one can change the fact that centuries ago these territories were inhabited by the Polish Piasts, a Slavic tribe. Nothing and no one can change the fact that our forefathers, the proprietors of these lands, defended them against German invaders at Głogów and Wrocław. After many centuries of bondage, they have finally been liberated.[13]

This decidedly nationalistic image of the past, largely free of socialist references, reflected the efforts of the communist party after the war to present itself as an advocate for the national cause. Socialist rhetoric could be integrated as needed, however, as demonstrated by a speech by Stanisław Kulczyński at the Congress of the Recovered Territories in Wrocław on September 21, 1952, at the height of Stalinism:

> The victory of the world's first socialist and international army has restored to the Western Territories a political and legal state of affairs that

had been undermined by a centuries-long policy of partition and robbery perpetrated in Polish lands first by German feudal lords and later by German international capitalists. The Western Territories are the property of the Polish nation. They have been inhabited, tended, and administered by the Polish people as far back as our history reaches. The western territories are our property, not only by virtue of our ancient rights to them, our centuries-long presence here, and our will, but also due to the recognition of our claim granted by all socialist and democratic nations. . . .

The Western Territories constitute one third of Poland's ancient territory inhabited by the Silesian, Kashubian, Masurian, and Lubusz peoples, who have fought for their national, social, and political rights for 600 years. . . . The People's Republic of Poland is honored to have helped eliminate the consequences not only of the eighteenth-century partitions, but also of the partitions and robbery inflicted on the organism of Piast Poland six centuries ago. . . .

We are the first fortunate generation since Piast times to be given the opportunity to govern the entire national territory and to decide Polish affairs within the bosom of the entire nation—Wielkopolanians, Silesians, Kashubians, and inhabitants of the Lubusz and Masurian lands. For the first time in history, the Polish People's Republic is the Fatherland, the mother of the Polish people.[14]

THE ADVOCATES OF WESTERN THOUGHT

The task of working out the details of this historical model and furnishing it with solid underpinnings belonged to the field of Polish Western Thought, and it was historians teaching at Polish universities who assumed the lead role in the project. Their colleagues from other disciplines—archaeology, historical linguistics, art history, ethnology, and geography—contributed as well, so that the result was an interdisciplinary "science of legitimation"[15] that sought to justify the western shift of Poland's borders, both to the Polish populace and internationally. Researchers paid particular attention to the medieval Piast history of the western territories and—in later centuries, when the territories were part of the Holy Roman Empire—to their lasting political, economic, and cultural ties to Poland. Areas of interest included the history of the Polish-speaking population in Prussia, Prussian policies of Germanization, and, finally, the German "drive to the East," which was portrayed as a historical constant from the Middle Ages to the present.

One of the most elaborate book projects inspired by Western Thought was the popular history series *Ziemie Staropolskie* (Old Polish Lands), published between 1948 and 1957 by the West Institute and subsidized by the government.[16] In the foreword, Zygmunt Wojciechowski wrote that the series aimed to tie Polish society in spirit to the Recovered Territories and to provide convincing evidence that the Polish-German border established at the Potsdam Conference was historically justified.

> Our publication . . . is biased; in fact, it is consciously biased. . . . We have not gone out of our way to write so-called objective history. Our task was to present the Polish history of those territories and to place the modern Polish reality of those territories within this historical context. Such an approach was dictated not only by the demands of the day, but also by the belief that the Polish history of those territories was their principal history.[17]

Each of the volumes was devoted to the history of a different region: Lower and Upper Silesia, Ermland and Masuria, Pomerania and Lubusz Land, as the former East Brandenburg was called. The work encompassed history from prehistoric times to the present day, examining as well the fine arts, architecture, and literature, and including information on geography, climate, and soil conditions. From all perspectives, the same conclusion emerged: that Poland had not been ceded foreign land in 1945, but instead had regained Polish territories. The language and argumentation were simple and manipulative, and supported by a wealth of illustrations: graphs and maps, facsimiles of old certificates, pictures of art objects and historic buildings, photographs that depicted the beauty of the landscape and captured events of recent history, and, finally, collages that presented the main themes in a suggestive visual language.

The theses of Western Thought would hardly have become such a firm part of collective memory in Poland had they not been popularized after 1945 in a vast number of periodicals and monographs, in textbooks, travel guides, radio reports, and exhibitions. Annual celebrations and commemoration days, as well as elaborate festivities on major anniversaries of Poland's "return to the

Oder," continued to remind Poles of the significance of the western territories. These events were opportunities for the pioneers of the reconstruction and integration of the territories to be awarded medals, as well as occasions for political speeches, posters, banners, and commemorative postage stamps, all repeating the same slogans again and again throughout the country.

All cultural institutions in the People's Republic of Poland—schools and universities, museums, libraries, theater groups, journals, literary circles, and archives—had to serve Western Thought.[18] "Uniting the Recovered Territories with the Motherland," as Gomułka put it in June 1946 during the "Days of Polish Culture" in Wrocław, "means above all reviving Polish culture there."[19] The very existence of Polish cultural organizations was a contribution to Western Thought, and many attempted beyond this to establish Polish life and integrate society in the new territories through special programs. The Lower Silesian Opera, for example, turned its inaugural performance in Polish Wrocław on September 8, 1945, into an act of patriotism: The premiere of the Polish national opera *Halka*, whose composer Stanisław Moniuszko is regarded as the founder of the Polish national style of music, was preceded by festive patriotic addresses and by the singing of the national anthem. Polish compositions were given high priority in the repertoire of the Opera, which in the fall of 1946 referred to itself in a letter to Gomułka as a "factor significant not only for culture, but most importantly, for political propaganda directed abroad."[20] A special attraction was the "resettler opera," which is how audiences perceived the ballet *Z krakowiakiem do Wrocławia* [With a Cracovienne to Wrocław]. It was produced specifically for the western territories by Stanisław Drabik, director of the Lower Silesian Opera, and premiered in May 1946 in Wrocław. This lighthearted composition presented folk dances and folk songs from the various regions of Poland, with the performers wearing their respective traditional costumes. At the conclusion of the ballet, the dancers gathered for a Polonaise led by the voivode, with Wrocław's Rynek as the backdrop.[21]

Eugeniusz Geppert, the first postwar director of Wrocław's State College of Fine Arts, wrote a letter in February 1947 to Gomułka, requesting permission to use the building of the former German Academy of Fine Arts. He argued that "the fact that this building was being renovated would be the best propaganda and proof of the cultural expansion in the Recovered Territories. Geppert went on to say that the planned exhibitions of contemporary works would serve the people's need "to create permanent monuments to Polish culture here, which would function as proof of the Polishness of the region, just as those made hundreds of years ago continue to demonstrate its Polishness today."[22] From a present-day perspective it is of course not always possible to determine if statements such as these were expressions of genuine convictions or merely a calculated use of propaganda boilerplate to win state subsidies. But even the latter case makes apparent the extent to which intellectuals and creative artists could be corrupted by propaganda, if only in their public utterances.

Museums played a major role in propagating Western Thought. According to the responsible Ministry of Art and Culture, their main task was to "reinforce Polishness in the region." While this required the gathering of "relics of material and spiritual culture whose Polish character attests to the struggle for Polish culture,"[23] a large portion of the museum inventories and art treasures found in the western territories was in fact brought to central Poland. We will not be able to determine the extent to which this occurred until the Warsaw Ministry of Art and Culture opens its archives. Isolated documents that have surfaced already reveal that trainloads of cultural assets were shipped to Warsaw in the first few years after the war.[24] The official justification for this action was that the capital had better facilities for conservation and restoration. But some years later, when adequate storage could also have been guaranteed in the western territories and requests were made for the return of the cultural artifacts, these were generally denied. Other considerations were evidently also at play. A memorandum of the Supreme Directorate of Museums and the Preservation of Cultural Monuments in the Ministry of Arts and Culture from August 1947 reveals something of the nature of these considerations:

> As part of the campaign to protect historic artifacts in the Recovered Territories . . . a large volume of cultural assets was collected. It was stored in specially designed warehouses, from which it was gradually transferred to Warsaw in cooperation with the Ministry of the Recovered Territories. . . .
>
> The Ministry of Arts and Culture will not allow the Recovered Territories to be deprived of their historic artifacts. . . . Under the planned reorganization [of the museums], however, not all historic artifacts in

the Recovered Territories will be transferred to newly established museums there. This pertains to artifacts collected tendentiously by the Germans in an effort to demonstrate the presence of German culture in Silesia, Pomerania, and Masuria. . . .

In return for the aforementioned works that are not suited for display in the Recovered Territories, the museums will receive special collections of Polish art from central Poland that emphasize the vital link between the cultures of Silesia or Pomerania on the one hand and Polish national culture on the other.[25]

Clearly, the actual goal of the operation was to reduce the inventory of obviously "German cultural assets" in the western territories and in return to stock museums there with more "Polish" objects. A large part of the art treasures originally removed from the western territories therefore remained permanently in Warsaw or elsewhere in central Poland, where they were either put on exhibition or stored in warehouses. Artifacts that were allowed to remain were those that either could somehow be tied to Polish history or those that could not be ascribed any particular national history. An effort was made, however, to obscure the provenance of certain objects. The museum in Szklarska Poręba, for example, continued to display the natural history collections of writer and naturalist Wilhelm Bölsche, who died there in 1939; but the authorities issued strict instruction that the German labels written by Bölsche were to be removed from the exhibited objects.[26] Numerous precious sculptures and altars from churches and monasteries in Wrocław were transported to Warsaw, as were museum artifacts such as the medieval shields of the town watches, which bore German inscriptions. Even the relic of St. Dorothy, the patron saint of Wrocław's burghers, was removed from the old chapel in the town hall. It took half a century before people protested openly in the western territories against this kind of plundering for the purposes of de-Germanization.

In addition to state institutions, Poland's Catholic Church played a major role in expanding the state westward to the Oder-Neisse line. A functioning Polish church administration—and especially the Polish church congregations—became the centers of Polish life throughout the western territories, representing the first and, for many settlers, the most important reference point in these unfamiliar surroundings. For those who had been forced to leave their homes in eastern Poland, Catholic church life and the Mass in Polish were particularly important, offering a kind of substitute home. In many cases, clerics accompanied their congregation members westward from eastern Poland, so the congregation was able to assemble around its former priest.[27] However, the Catholic Church served an important function not only for those expelled from the east, since congregational life was often the very first bond that developed between settlers who otherwise had little in common.[28]

However, despite its lack of sympathy with the communist government, the clergy, in addition to its role in integrating the population, also actively served both the Polish national interest and Western Thought. The patriotism of the Polish Catholic Church, which seemed to contradict to some degree the universal claims of Catholicism, had its origins in the role Polish clerics had played since the nineteenth century. During the period when Prussia, Russia, and Austria—the powers who had divvied up old Poland among themselves in the late eighteenth century—prevented the reestablishment of an independent Polish state, the Polish Catholic Church and its clergy began to serve as a substitute for the nonexistent state. In particular during Bismarck's *Kulturkampf* in the 1870s and 1880s, when the suppression of the Catholic Church and Germanization policies appeared to merge in the eastern provinces of the German Empire, it became increasingly difficult to distinguish between the struggle for the freedom of the Catholic Church and the Polish national movement. In Polish-speaking regions the Catholic Church acted like an institution of the Polish nation. It was this national character, which the Polish church had assumed during the partition of Poland and which was intensified during the Second World War, that continued to define the relationship of the church to the state and nation after 1945.[29]

On August 15, 1965, during the commemoration of the twentieth anniversary of the Polish Church in the western territories, a solemn Pontifical Mass was held in the cathedral of Wrocław. Poland's bishops gathered in vestments bearing the eagle of the Polish coat of arms. In his sermon, Primate Cardinal Stefan Wyszyński spoke the following often-cited words:

> In the cathedrals, Beloved, we read relics of stone, the signs of the millennium;[30] and these stones, splendid heralds from the past, say to us, "We were here! Yes! We were here! And we are here again! We have

returned to our paternal home [*Dom Ojczysty*]." The message is clear to us, we understand it. We understand this language! It is our language! The stones call to us from the walls! The bones in the crypts, covered in earth, speak to us in our mother tongue [*ojczysty język*]. Just as the sough of Mazovian willows spoke to Chopin, so the relics unearthed from the catacombs of the millennium cathedrals speak to us in our mother tongue.

Nothing is simpler and more effective than to establish connections with church buildings. When we see these Piast churches, when we hear their language, then we know: this is definitely not a German artifact, this is the Polish soul! These churches are not and never were German artifacts. These are our own traces of the royal tribe of the Piasts! They speak to the Polish people in words that need no explanation. We do not require an interpreter, we understand very well what they are saying.[31]

At this point in time, however, the relationship between church and state in the People's Republic of Poland was characterized more by tensions than by cooperation in the fulfilling of patriotic duties. This became especially clear in 1966, when church and government leaders commemorated Poland's millennium in fierce rivalry, each holding their own celebration. While the former celebrated the thousand-year anniversary of the Polish Church, the latter commemorated that of the Polish state.[32] Nevertheless, the Wrocław archbishop Bolesław Kominek did use the opportunity of the twenty-fifth anniversary of the "return to the Oder" in May 1970 to commemorate the common purpose of church and state in integrating the new territories during the early postwar period. "As the place of our path to God, the western territories were more of a unifying force than a dividing one." The older generation of both clergy and lay Catholics, Kominek said, "had fulfilled our Christian and national mandate vis-à-vis the western territories twenty-five years ago." He stressed that the Polish Church, in order to improve understanding between church and state, should now strive to eliminate "any appearance of impermanence"—by which he meant that the Vatican should recognize as permanent the changes in canon law necessitated by the border shift of 1945.[33]

Especially in terms of the Polonization of the western territories and political efforts to defend Poland's western border as drawn in Potsdam, the

Polish Catholic Church and the Polish state acted in concert, regardless of how fierce the conflicts between Catholics and communists in Poland might have otherwise been.[34] During the major celebrations in the postwar period, in which the establishment of church and state institutions in the western territories were commemorated as one and the same historic event and dressed in the same propagandistic slogans, affairs of church and state became inextricably interwoven. The Polish eagle became virtually a religious symbol, often even finding its way into the chancel. Gothic church spires were not only symbols of Christian faith, but also of the Piast cult and thus of Poland's territorial claims to the Oder-Neisse line as the country's western boundary.

Aside from state and church activities, social initiatives were also very important in popularizing Western Thought. The work of the Polish Western Union was key in this regard, even though it was basically a parastatal organization as there were high government officials on its executive committees.[35] Next to the Maritime League (Liga Morska), it was the most influential advocacy organization promoting Western Thought. The primary significance of the Union was that it offered a framework in which supporters of Western Thought (who traditionally sympathized with the National Democrats) and Poland's communist elite could find common ground in their joint efforts on behalf of the western territories. In addition to these larger organizations, a range of local history groups was formed, such as the Society of Friends of Wrocław (Towarzystwo Miłośników Wrocławia) or the Wrocław Society of Friends of History (Wrocławskie Towarzystwo Miłośników Historii), which had influential professional historians among its members. Many of these organizations published their own periodicals, such as the *Śląsk* (Silesia) in Jelenia Góra, which appeared until 1946, the cultural journal *Odra* (The Oder), the historical journal *Sobótka*, the Pomeranian cultural journal *Ziemia i Morze* (Land and Sea), and *Warmia i Mazury* (Warmia and Masuria). These publications, like the organizations themselves, sought to contribute to the creation of a local Polish identity in the western territories. They reported in easy-to-understand language on the cultural life and history of their respective regions, cleaving always to nationalistic Polish interpretations of local history in implicit response to the opposing German nationalist point of view. It is difficult to identify any differences between the history spread within the framework of this social, non-governmental activity and official government history, at least not until the final phase of communist Poland in the 1980s.

Just as with church and state, there seems to have been remarkable unanimity between state and society on the issue of the western territories.

There are unmistakable parallels between the rhetoric and historiographic methods used in the propaganda of the People's Republic to defend its claims to the western territories and those employed by the Third Reich both in its *Ostforschung* and in propaganda respecting the "German East." In their attempt to merge the occupied Polish territories with the Reich, the Nazis too insisted that their claims to the land were based on a firmer foundation than the mere rights of the conqueror. Nazi propaganda, supported by *Ostforschung*, attempted to prove that the occupied parts of Poland were in fact ancient Germanic land. They denied the Polish state and people any independent cultural achievements, and therefore rejected their territorial rights as well. At the same time they declared the Germans and their allegedly Germanic ancestors to be the only builders of culture in Eastern Europe. Parallel to this glorification of German culture in the East, all evidence of Polish culture that could not be recast as a product of German culture was systematically destroyed during the wartime occupation of Poland or stored in archives and libraries out of the public eye. Town names were "re-Germanized," and in large Polish cities such as Krakow, Warsaw, Rzeszów, and Lublin, which were supposed to become German cities, Polish traces were removed from public space.[36]

The propaganda of the People's Republic declared the western territories to be old Slavic settlement land. Accordingly, it referred to Polonization measures as re-Polonization, and attempted to eliminate all traces of a German presence as far as possible. It was a veritable Polish mirror image of Nazi Germanization politics in the occupied Polish territories. And in fact, the propaganda of both sides drew from the same source: the aggressive ethnic nationalism of the late nineteenth and early twentieth centuries. Of course, Nazi propaganda was additionally charged with pseudo-biological racism, which for that matter was not entirely missing from the population policies of communist Poland either.[37]

Nevertheless, there was a fundamental difference. Nazi propaganda attempted to justify the policies of conquest and extermination. In addition to the fact that millions of Poles were killed under German occupation, scores of Polish archives and libraries went up in flames and the destruction of the Polish capital was planned and largely carried out. Polish propaganda, in contrast, attempted to justify in retrospect the westward shift of the Polish state brought about by the victorious "Big Three" after the Second World War. The central aim of propaganda in postwar Poland was to help overcome the immense psychological problems caused by the uprooting of millions of Poles and the foreignness of the new territories. The consequences of Polish propaganda were, however, by no means harmless. In the eyes of many, it seemed to justify acts of violence against the German population in the western territories and vandalism of the material legacy of Prussian and German culture. However, German archives and libraries were not set on fire by Polish authorities and cities were not destroyed, but rebuilt. Until the Germans were resettled outside of Poland, they were subject to severe repression, violence, and inadequate care, which contributed to the death of tens or even hundreds of thousands of civilians. Nevertheless, while the policies of the Warsaw government aimed to expel the German population from Poland, the German occupation policies in wartime Poland aimed to destroy a nation.

THE PHASES OF PROPAGANDA

Western Thought went through various phases after the Second World War, marked by more or less distinct turning points in 1949, 1956, 1970, and finally 1989. In the first years after the war there was a particularly intense phase of propaganda concerning the western territories. It reached a temporary climax in the summer of 1948 with the Exhibition of the Recovered Territories (Wystawa Ziem Odzyskanych) at the Wrocław fairgrounds.[38] This, the largest and most elaborate propaganda show in postwar Poland, was based on an idea put forth by the group around Zygmunt Wojciechowski. Their initial idea had been to put on a large exhibition in Poznań in 1945 entitled "Ten Centuries of German-Polish Conflict."[39] The government adopted this idea but decided to organize the exhibition in Wrocław. It was to be a mixture of propaganda and carnival. The historical conflict between Germans and Poles was a focus, in particular defense of the legitimacy of Poland's western border on historical, economic, and political grounds. Also showcased were Poland's achievements thus far in reconstructing the western territories. Roughly 1.5 million people saw the exhibition. By the time it closed, the political changes brought about by Stalinism had already left their mark on western territories propaganda.[40]

More than 1.5 million people, Poles and foreigners alike, saw the "Exhibition of the Recovered Territories" on the Wrocław fairgrounds in the summer of 1948. The exhibition was a mixture of festival and propaganda, designed to entertain and to educate visitors about Poland's achievements in reconstructing, revitalizing, and integrating the new territories. Courtesy of the City Museum of Wrocław (Adam Czelny).

In the late 1940s and early 1950s, almost all institutions advocating Western Thought vanished. This was due in part to the centralization of the entire political system and the enforced conformity of all research. Against this background the decentralized structure of the institutions and organizations of Western Thought no longer seemed appropriate. Another factor was the establishment of historical materialism, which saw many of the country's historians being accused of bourgeois sentiments and of not paying due attention to class struggle as the central force in historical development. All research on the western territories was branded as a "nationalist-clerical deviation." In addition, the government summarily declared that the integration of the western territories had been accomplished and that it was no longer necessary for the region to enjoy special status within Poland. In early 1949 the Ministry of the Recovered Territories was dissolved. In 1950 the Polish Western Union was integrated into the Maritime League, which was subsequently disbanded in 1953. In 1948 the Silesian and Masurian Institutes were closed down, followed in 1950 by the Baltic Institute. Only the West Institute in Poznań remained, thanks to the reputation and political finesse of its director Zygmunt Wojciechowski, though the facility did have to accept drastic financial cutbacks. When Wojciechowski died in 1955, the government intended to close this institution as well. However, its action was preempted by the political upheaval of 1956, which marked the beginning of de-Stalinization in Poland.[41]

In the debates that took place after 1956 on the failures of Stalinism, the problems of the western territories received great attention. The new government recognized the necessity of reviving institutions devoted to Western Thought. In 1957 the Silesian Institute was refounded in Opole and the Silesian Science Institute (Śląski Instytut Naukowy) was created in Katowice. A Baltic Institute was refounded in 1959, now located in Gdańsk. The Poznań West Institute received considerably more funding and was also given a new focus. No longer tied to the idea propagated by Wojciechowski of a thousand-year history of German-Polish conflict, it would now address current issues to a far greater extent. Sociological research, which in Poland at that time was methodologically more innovative and far less ideological than historiography, grew in status within the institute. Polish sociologists produced important studies on issues of integration and identity-building in the territories that retain their relevance even today. The West Institute also dedicated a larger share of its research to the history of East and West Germany.

The Society for the Development of the Western Territories (TRZZ) was founded as the successor organization to the Polish Western Union in Warsaw in June 1957. It was a mass organization that continued the tradition of the Polish Western Union, but attempted to imbue its national program with socialist content. In this regard the TRZZ was characteristic of the People's Republic of Poland, as it was both a socialist and a nationalist institution. Its aim was to encourage greater public involvement in all issues pertaining to the western territories, to support stronger identification with the territories among its inhabitants, and to promote interest in the western voivodeships in other parts of Poland as well. The semi-governmental and semi-social character of the TRZZ made it a multifaceted entity. On the one hand its state-controlled organizational platform was centrally organized and, like the party, structured according to voivodeships and counties. On the other hand, the individual branches did maintain a degree of autonomy. The TRZZ addressed the practical concerns of the western territories and convened special commissions charged with such matters as, for example, promoting shipping on the Oder or tourism. At the same time, however, it was also a propaganda institution that was supposed to popularize a new version of Western Thought enhanced with socialist slogans.[42]

The centralized character of this organization charged with imparting a uniform view of history is apparent in the "Instructions for the Commemoration of Persons and Events Attesting to the Historic Polishness of the Western and Northern Territories," which was published by the Supreme Council of the TRZZ in 1959. It laid down in detail how remembrances were to be anchored in the "national memory" (*pamięć narodu*) and included an appendix with a list suggesting people who were particularly suited to be commemorated with a memorial plaque or a street named after them.[43] In the late 1960s plans were even made to compile a "Lexicon of the Struggle for Polishness in the Western and Northern Territories," with entries for all the "deserving persons, organizations, and events that had played a decisive role in the preservation of Polishness and in the struggle for the return of the western territories to the Polish state."[44] In its heyday in the mid-1960s the TRZZ had almost 130,000 members. The organization was represented in all eighteen voivodeships, with the regional branches in the western territories having the most members. The voivodeship of Katowice held pride of place, followed with some distance by Opole, Poznań, and Wrocław. Thus the traditional strongholds of Western Thought—Upper Silesia and Greater Poland—were strongly represented.[45]

In the western territories after 1956 there was, in addition to the work of the TRZZ, a wealth of other initiatives to found local and regional societies for the purpose of supporting cultural developments in the various regions and promoting the integration of the Polish population in its new home. Many of the societies published their own periodicals so that in the second half of the 1950s new regional journals began to mushroom everywhere. Since the western territories remained delicate political terrain, the party kept a constant eye on these publications. Political pressure and state censorship, which influenced research and publications in communist Poland in general, could be especially felt when it came to the western territories.[46] After a period of relative freedom in the second half of the 1950s, when even the problems of the new territories could be debated rather openly, in the 1960s the reins were tightened. Symptomatic of this is that the TRZZ—whose founding charter was modeled on the democratic structures of the Western Union and which, despite its closeness to the state, was not strictly a party affair—was placed under the control of the leadership of the PZPR in 1965.

Another important turning point came in 1970. West German chancellor Willy Brandt signed the Treaty of Warsaw in December 1970 during his visit to Warsaw, thereby officially recognizing the inviolability of the postwar German-Polish border. His kneeling before the Warsaw Ghetto memorial became a symbol of Bonn's new *Ostpolitik* (Eastern policy), which became an integral component in international rapprochement efforts aimed at overcoming the East-West conflict. Western Thought lost much of its relevance after 1970. The TRZZ was disbanded on January 1, 1971, and no successor organization was ever formed.[47] The West Institute, which had demonstrated remarkable flexibility in the face of all the political upheavals in postwar Poland, increasingly developed in subsequent years into a center for research on Germany, its propagandistic activities assuming less and less of a role.

The state leadership, however, never changed its fundamental stance regarding the western territories. Commemorations of the "return of territories" continued to be celebrated with great pomp, and the political rhetoric that marked these events remained unchanged. But the celebrations became more and more a hollow ritual performed by the political establishment and by organizations that specialized in propagating Western Thought. For the people, the issue of the western territories was increasingly eclipsed by everyday problems, in particular by the country's growing economic difficulties. Confidence in the ruling class waned. Many came to reject the political system in principle, and they were supported in this position by the Catholic Church in Poland, which had gained prestige and influence in Polish society, not least owing to the election of Krakow cardinal Karol Wojtyła as Pope John Paul II in 1978. The free, non-party-controlled labor union Solidarność (Solidarity) developed in the early 1980s into a powerful opposition movement with almost ten million members. After a decade of fierce conflict with the government and tenacious resistance, it would bring about the downfall of the communist system. Solidarność enjoyed particularly strong support in the western territories, where the cities of Gdańsk, Szczecin, and Wrocław became the country's leading centers of opposition to communism. Interestingly enough, however, the specific problems of the western territories hardly played any role within Solidarność.

Language Conventions

During the Second World War the future Polish territories of the German Empire were referred to as the "claimed territories" (*ziemie postulowane*), "new territories" (*ziemie nowe*), or "returning territories" (*ziemie wracające*). After 1945, "Recovered Territories" became the preferred name and was made official with the establishment of the Ministry of the Recovered Territories. The term "Recovered Territories" also found its way into everyday jargon in Poland. It was dropped, however, from the official language of the People's Republic after 1949, by which time the former German territories were no longer supposed to be perceived as special territories within the country. The term was then replaced by the more neutral "western and northern territories," but Poles continued to use it, and to some extent they still do today.

"Return to the motherland" (*powrót do macierzy*) also became a standard collocation. It took up the linguistic and notional concept of "motherland" (*macierz*) and the "motherland territories" (*ziemie macierzyste*) that Zygmunt Wojciechowski had coined already in the interwar period to refer to all those regions that in medieval times had once been part of the Polish state.[48] "Motherland" and "motherland territories" filled a linguistic gap after 1945 that was not covered by the word "fatherland" (*ojczyzna*). The concept of "fatherland" is clearly defined in Polish as the country in which one was born, from which one comes, the country of one's citizenship. For that reason the German regions that were ceded to Poland in 1945 could not be spoken of as "fatherland." The Polish settlers had not been born there; and Silesia, Pomerania, and Masuria could at best become the fatherland of their children and grandchildren.

Thus "motherland," both in its nominal and attributive forms, became a substitute concept. The coinage had been rarely used prior to this in the Polish language and its meaning was thus not specified beyond the definition it was given by Wojciechowski. Also, the emotional weight of the word was on a par with that of "fatherland," especially for Poles. Polish society was greatly influenced by the Catholic veneration of the Virgin Mary in particular and the Mother in general, so that "motherland" evoked exceptionally positive, even sacred connotations. To characterize the western territories as "motherland territories" and the intended, natural and original form of Polish national territory as the "motherland" was therefore an ideal linguistic construction. The motherland was the fatherland of the ancestors, which had allegedly been torn away many centuries ago and was restored to its rightful place in 1945.

The concept of "motherland" and the phrase "return to the motherland" can be regarded as the Polish counterpart of the German word *Vertreibung*, or "expulsion." The term "expulsion," like "motherland," is calculated to evoke a normative judgment and an emotional reaction; and, like "motherland," "expulsion" came to be used after the war (at least in its noun form) almost exclusively in this one context. The only other common use of the term in German was to denote the expulsion from Paradise, the biblical Garden of Eden. The psychological significance of this pairing of contexts is ambivalent. On the one hand, it amounts to the sacralization of German suffering. On the other, it hints at an insight that was generally absent from the official statements of the German expellee organizations: in the Bible, the expulsion from Paradise was preceded by the Fall of Man.

According to the official Polish reading of events, the ceding of the German territories represented the return of lands that were originally Polish. Thus the measures that served the cultural integration of the western territories with the rest of Poland were usually referred to as "re-Polonization" (*repolonizacja*). Behind the scenes, in the official correspondence of the authorities, there was no consistent terminology. In addition to "re-Polonization" or the less common "re-Slavization," other fitting, albeit non-propagandistic terms that were used included "Polonization" (*polonizacja*) and "de-Germanization" (*odniemczanie*). The phrase "removal of the traces of Germandom" (*usuwanie śladów niemczyzny*) also continued to crop up. The terminology was not clearly defined and its usage was correspondingly inconsistent. Sometimes the various words were used as synonyms; sometimes they referred to different things. But they always denoted an ethnic, administrative, and cultural reorganization of the former German territories that would facilitate their seamless incorporation into the national territory of Poland.[49]

When the terms were used according to a more narrow definition, "de-Germanization" usually referred to "eliminating the vestiges of Germandom," which meant eliminating German historic monuments, street and town names, and German inscriptions and signs. At times it also referred to the struggle against "German" sentiments among the autochthons, in which case it could cover anything that seemed to stand in the way of this population's complete assimilation or that could be interpreted as resistance to official measures. In contrast, "Polonization" and "re-Polonization" had broader definitions and served to characterize any measures that aimed to eliminate all obvious evidence of the German past and to give the western territories a Polish appearance. This included expanding Polish facilities, especially cultural institutions in the new territories. In most cases, however, "re-Polonization" referred more specifically to measures to assimilate the autochthons. At times it denoted policies toward ethnic minorities in general, including the Polish reemigrants, to the extent that the policies aimed to create a "homogeneous Polish nation" (*jednolity naród polski*).

Tellingly, the terms "de-Germanization" and "elimination of vestiges of Germandom" were not used publicly. In official correspondence they appeared only in documents classified as "confidential" or "secret." This was not the case for the terms "Polonization" and "re-Polonization," especially "re-Polonization," which was incorporated into the colloquial language of postwar Poland and was also employed in academic language, whether consciously or unconsciously. It is understandable that "de-Germanization" and "re-Polonization" were used differently. From an official perspective, the (re-) Polonization of the western territories was a constructive measure aimed at uncovering the originally Polish identity of the western territories that had been buried—whether by making architectural evidence from Polish times visible again, bringing back old Polish names, or granting Poles who had been Germanized by force the opportunity to regain their Polish mother tongue and identity. "De-Germanization," on the other hand, was the destructive flip side, a process that people preferred not to talk about.[50] It created nothing new, but instead "cleansed" (this too was a common term in the officialese of the People's Republic) the western territories of all cultural traces of their German past. Removal of all things German was, it was believed, necessary before the thesis of the Polish character of the western territories could be credible. De-Germanization and Polonization were thus two sides of one and the same process through which the western territories underwent a total national reorganization.

The Success of Propaganda and the Requirements of the Time

Many of these terms and expressions, together with the key propaganda formulas of Western Thought, have become firmly entrenched in the Polish language. This is one indication of the extraordinary success of the western territories propaganda. As ideological as the questions and findings inspired by Western Thought were, it was nonetheless propaganda with an academic imprimatur that lent to it a certain power to persuade. This should not be underestimated, but it was most probably not the scholarly quality of the propaganda that was the decisive factor in its broad acceptance. After all, the notion of Polish-Soviet friendship was promoted after the war as well, but does not appear to have had much of an impact on Polish society.

The success of the western territories propaganda can be explained only by the fact that the historiography propagated within the framework of Western Thought satisfied a real need within Polish society. Speaking of the "Recovered Territories" or the "return to Piast land" was healing, a kind of therapy against the syndrome of impermanence. The fact that it came with considerable side effects and in the long term even hindered the integration of the territories is a topic for the final chapter of this book. But in the first postwar decades this therapy appeared to be the only remedy for Cold War anxieties, and especially for the widespread conviction that influential "revanchist circles" in West Germany were simply waiting for the proper moment to make their move against the Oder-Neisse border. Settlers in the western territories eagerly clung to a vision of the past that offered historical legitimation to their present lives in regions formerly inhabited by Germans. It was a vision that opened up future prospects as well, that let them hope for a speedy rise out of the ruins of the war. In an illustrated book about Wrocław published in Poland in the early 1970s, Ignacy Rutkiewicz expressed this psychological need with great immediacy:

> And this concept—the new Polish presence or, if you will, the return to the former Polish homeland—has an essential moral significance for the Poles, which foreigners do not always appreciate and understand. There is a consciousness that Poland has returned to Wrocław—that it is not just newly-arrived—that this historical reversal represents not only compensation for the recent injustices, but also restitution of the ancient rights of the people, rights not subject to a statute of limitations. This consciousness guided the Poles who in 1945 chose this territory as their homeland, and it has become a critical dimension of the national consciousness of today's Poland. To this consciousness is joined a pride that is fully justified. For this land, which has risen out of the ruins and is growing in prosperity, is testimony of a well-managed Polish economy. It tells of the "Polish miracle on the Oder."[51]

CHAPTER SEVEN

Mythicizing History

THE STUDY OF LOCAL HISTORY AS AN "ACT OF SELF-REASSURANCE" HAS EV-erywhere grown in importance as societies have become mobile and people are less tied to a specific location. "To put it bluntly," historian Helmut Flachenecker writes of modern society, "one is no longer the citizen of a location primarily by birth but rather by history."[1] This is true to an extreme degree of the Polish city of Wrocław, whose society came into being as the result of a complete population exchange. Societies of this kind typically yearn for tradition just as much as they lack it. And so it was in Wrocław. Only by identifying collectively with the history of the city could a coherent citizenry develop out of a random assortment of settlers thrown together by the population shifts of postwar Poland.

In 1945, however, there was no local historiography to which the city's new inhabitants could easily turn. The history of Wrocław, up to this point, had been written by Germans, and they, especially the authors of the more recent works, had a habit of calling attention to the city's ostensible "German essence."[2] It was this Germanocentric perspective that offered no points of reference for Polish settlers. The history of the city had to be written anew.

The Polish local historians who took on the task engaged in what Eric Hobsbawm has called the "invention of tradition."[3] They did not invent historical occurrences, but they constructed a historical continuity that would lead without disruption from the past to the present and thereby provide historical justification for Wrocław's postwar situation. Silesia's early Slavic-Polish history, the founding of the Wrocław bishopric in 1000 CE by Piast Duke Bolesław Chrobry, and the long reign of the Silesian Piasts offered historians manifold points of departure. And they would make good use of them to generate a narrative that extended up to the present day, and depicted Wrocław's incorporation into Poland in 1945 not as an act of political arbitrariness, but rather as the logical consequence of a protracted historical development. They functioned as the engineers of a new collective memory, designing an image of the past that overrode Wrocław's foreignness and made it into an "age-old Polish city," a place to which Poles could "return," where they could find the roots of their own nation and old Polish traditions upon which to build.

One of the fundamental reasons for the success of the historians who became the demiurges of Polish Wrocław was that they helped satisfy the need for rootedness. A yearning for local ties made Wrocław's new Polish inhabitants eager to accept the medieval Piasts as their ancestors. And since they no longer had family graves of their own to visit, pilgrimages to the stone sarcophagi of the Piasts would have to do. As this "founding history" was written—a history that, according to Jan Assmann, served above all to legitimate the present— Wrocław's past was slowly but surely turned to myth. There was in this process little regard to how much the image of Wrocław as an age-old Polish city corresponded to historical fact and how much was mere fiction. The new historiography was less about illumination than transfiguration.

In 1958, Wrocław historians Wacław Długoborski, Józef Gierowski, and Karol Maleczyński published *Dzieje Wrocławia do roku 1807* (The History of Wrocław to 1807),[4] which would remain the standard scholarly work in Polish on the history of the city until 1989. In their preface the authors wrote:

> The return of Silesia and Wrocław to Poland in 1945 imposed on the Polish historians of Silesia the responsibility of revising the often mendacious assertions of German historiography, of submitting their own critique, and of presenting the history of the city in accordance with contemporary scholarly interpretations . . . .
>
> With the needs of Polish historiography in mind, the authors took it upon themselves to pay special attention to the role of the Polish component in the city's historical development. . . . They fully acknowledge the influence of the German component, which grew stronger over time, eventually becoming dominant within the patrician class and even among common workers. Often depending on indirect sources, the authors have attempted to collect as much information as possible about the population of the Polish city.[5]

This objective appears at first glance to correspond neatly to the demands of scholarship formulated by Zygmunt Wojciechowski in his preface to the series *Ziemie Staropolskie* (Old Polish Lands). However, the three authors also mention that prior to the publication of their book, the sum of Polish historiography was "exceedingly meager" measured against the number of German-language publications on Wrocław city history.[6] This statement indicates an important distinction between their book and the *Old Polish Lands* series, which certainly would not have included such an observation as it contradicts one of the central theses of the Polish Western Thought, according to which the Polish nation never accepted the loss of Silesia and always remained tied to the land.

The Wrocław historians' remark that in their efforts to portray the city's Polish dimension they "often" had to use indirect sources—which, if one reads between the lines, means simply that there was little direct evidence about Wrocław's Polish inhabitants—was also a statement that would hardly have been included in the *Old Polish Lands* series. The latter pursued the unequivocally propagandistic goal of persuading as broad a reading public as possible that "the line drawn in Potsdam was not the mechanical delineation of a border, but the expression of a profound insight into historical processes."[7] This required that numerous facts be omitted and that others be presented in distorted form—in other words, there was more manipulation than information. *The History of Wrocław to 1807*, by contrast, was intended for an audience of specialists, a limited readership that, however, included scholars outside of Poland, not least in Germany. Its authors were thus obliged to adhere to scholarly standards if they wanted to be taken seriously and if their book was to stand up to critical examination by German specialists in the city's history. However polemically they dealt with the work of their German colleagues, they nonetheless conducted these disputes according to established scholarly practices. They identified the theses of their opponents before they contrasted them to their own, and their claims were verifiable on the basis of documentary evidence.

The possibilities of presenting radically different versions of Wrocław history within this framework were limited. Scholars could shift emphases and investigate areas of study that had been previously neglected or ignored by historians. They could counter one-sided German interpretations with convincing arguments and analyses of the city's history that focused on Wrocław's ties to Poland and the life of its Polish-speaking inhabitants. In broad stretches, however, accounts by Polish historians were not unlike those of their German colleagues. Their works did not portray Wrocław as a city that was always Polish, in which Germans played only a marginal and primarily negative role. Instead the history of the city was depicted as that of a complex relationship in the Slavic-Germanic border region that precluded one-sided nationalistic interpretations.

However, the lengthy and complex presentation of Wrocław's city history by Długoborski, Gierowski, and Maleczyński probably contributed only marginally to how Wrocław's postwar inhabitants came to perceive the local past. Since the present chapter is concerned primarily with the interpretation of history presented to a broader public, the primary focus here will be on popular historical publications. They usually consisted of relatively short texts that were written and argued in simple language. As a rule these publications contained neither footnotes nor a bibliography, but were often richly illustrated and attractively designed. This chapter will examine a representative selection of such texts that were published in postwar Poland, including the two volumes on Lower Silesia in the *Old Polish Lands* series[8] (which were groundbreaking in developing a new image of regional history), as well as a number of Wrocław guidebooks and, insofar as they contained chapters on local history, illustrated books about Wrocław.[9]

It is, of course, impossible to draw a sharp line between such popular historical works and the results of professional historiography. The latter provided information and material from which the authors of the former drew, and the same authors often wrote for both an expert and a lay audience. Medievalist Karol Maleczyński, who became chair of Silesian and Western Slavic History at the University of Wrocław in 1945, was one such scholar. Maleczyński composed numerous scholarly articles and monographs, but he wrote many popular historical publications as well. A comparison of these two types of texts written by one and the same author demonstrates that there can be worlds of difference between popular and scholarly historiography. The texts that Maleczyński wrote for a broader public are not merely simplified and abridged versions of his scholarly works, but often deviate from these in content, at times significantly. While as a scholar Maleczyński avoided omitting and distorting facts despite his desire to emphasize the Polish dimensions of regional history, his popular writings—for instance, the articles and lectures published posthumously in the small volume *Proste*

Słowa o Śląsku (Plain Words about Silesia)—are in long stretches pure propaganda.[10]

This astounding inconsistency derives from the different functions of the two genres. While Maleczyński's scholarly writings were part of international academic discourse, his popular historical texts were aimed at a readership limited to Poland. We can safely assume that the latter were subject to state censorship to a much greater degree, as the authorities of communist Poland kept a watchful eye on the popular press. The authorities could be less vigilant when it came to Maleczyński's scholarly works, which reached a far smaller audience; indeed they had to be more generous if Polish historians were not to embarrass themselves internationally with untenable assertions.

The effects of censorship on authors writing within the strictures of an authoritarian regime, however, should not be overestimated. In fact, John Connelly has shown that Polish universities were able to uphold a remarkable degree of academic freedom vis-à-vis the communist regime.[11] Therefore, we must take into account that the readers' need for a "founding history" often coincided with the authors' own understanding that this was precisely what the situation called for in the western territories. The writers of such works were usually themselves inhabitants of the region and presumably felt the same need as their readers to justify their presence in a formerly German place. In many cases, the selective Polonocentric portrayal of the local past corresponded to their own perceptions and political convictions.

These popular presentations of local history were effective with readers because readers were prepared to believe them. They had no interest in critically examining the version of the city's history presented in such works, though that would have been quite possible, even for laypeople. The scholarly literature on the subject, including alternative interpretations and additional information, was accessible, and it would have required no great effort to uncover inconsistencies in the popular historical texts. Moreover, the physical presence of the city itself also told stories that were frequently irreconcilable with what had been written in local guidebooks. But the population of Wrocław demanded the myth of the "always Polish city." And as long as they were prepared to overlook evidence to the contrary, distorted historiographical interpretations and the authentic testimony of the actual city they encountered on a daily basis could safely coexist.

The Land of the Piasts

It is hard to find a place in Poland today that does not have prominent streets named after Mieszko I, Bolesław Chrobry (the Brave), Bolesław III (the Wrymouth), or Kazimierz III (the Great)—the best-known figures of the Piast dynasty who became the first dukes and kings of medieval Poland. The Piasts are omnipresent, especially in the western territories. Not only streets and monuments commemorate them; the names of numerous hotels, residential buildings and restaurants, newspapers, associations, and cinemas, as well as businesses, factories, and mines refer to the rule of the Piasts over six hundred years ago. Wrocław's largest brewery—prior to 1945 named Schultheiss-Patzendorfer—was rechristened Piast in 1946, as was the former Hotel Kronprinz at the central train station. A recently dissolved Wrocław residential cooperative and a weekly newspaper that started publication in 1995 also bear this name. It has even been inscribed above one of the entrances to the Korona Center, a shopping mall that opened in Wrocław a few years ago.

According to legend, Mieszko I (ca. 922–992), the first historically documented ruler of the Polish state that emerged in the tenth century, was the descendent of a poor peasant named Piast, whose son Siemowit advanced to become duke of Poland and the founder of the dynasty. For four hundred years Poland's rulers came from the house of Mieszko, until King Kazimierz III the Great died issueless in 1370. The house of Anjou ruled Poland for the next fifteen years, then the Jagiellonian dynasty assumed the throne (1386) and reigned for the next two centuries. The Mieszko line did continue in peripheral branches of the ruling family for several hundred more years. The branch of the Masovian Piasts died out in 1526; and the last representative of the Silesian line, Jerzy Wilhelm, Duke of Legnica and Brzeg, died in 1675, bringing the dynasty to a definitive end.

The earliest mention of Poland's oldest dynasty as that of the Piasts, named after its legendary ancestor, is from the sixteenth century.[12] In the era of the electoral monarchy after the end of Jagiellonian rule in 1572, the Piast name already possessed enough symbolic power that aspirants to the Polish throne tended to designate themselves Piasts to legitimate their rule. The Piasts, however, did not attain popularity until the nineteenth and twentieth centuries. It was only through the emergence of the Polish national movement that their name came to symbolize authentic Polishness and the unity of the Polish nation, despite the fact that the Piasts had split into feuding branches, thus contributing considerably to the fragmentation of medieval Poland. In the Second Republic—the Polish state reestablished after the First World War—a new dimension of Piast mythology saw modern political concepts ascribed to the Piasts. The National Democratic camp led by Roman Dmowski was especially eager to identify itself with them, repeatedly invoking the "Piast idea," the "Piast heritage," and Poland's "Piast traditions" to distinguish itself from the allegedly antithetical "Jagiellonian idea" pursued by the republic's first leader Józef Piłsudski and his political followers.[13]

Piłsudski and Dmowski themselves always invoked the legacy of both the Piasts and the Jagiellons. But most people at the time understood the opposition between the two defining political figures of the Second Republic as an opposition between Dmowski's Piast and Piłsudski's Jagiellonian conceptions of the state. The Piasts stood for the idea of an ethnically homogeneous Polish nation-state oriented geographically toward the West, which sought to expand territorially into Upper Silesia and East Prussia and was presumed therefore to be in perpetual enmity with Germany. The Jagiellons, on the other hand, stood for the dream of a federal empire under Polish leadership that would extend far into the East and include Lithuanian, Belorussian, and Ukrainian territories. The concept of "Jagiellonian Poland," which could only be realized in conflict with Russia, was based upon the premise that Poland had to seek a settlement with the Germans and thus must be prepared to compromise on territorial issues in the West.

After the Second World War, the Piast name was no longer used to characterize one political program in contrast to others. The Piasts simply became the state myth of the People's Republic of Poland. Since the territory ruled by the first Piasts in the eleventh century approximated—albeit only for a brief period of time—that of postwar Poland, recourse to the Piasts made the country's westward shift of borders appear to be a return to Poland's traditional geographical configuration. In addition, the stories of Mieszko I, Bolesław Chobry, and Bolesław III the Wrymouth contained several incidents that could be read as emblematic of the historic roots of Polish-German enmity. Every vestige of the Piasts in the western territories was taken as proof of the eternal Polishness of the lands along the Oder and Neisse rivers, every Piast castle a manifestation of Polish national will in the contested German-Polish borderlands, and every conflict between Piasts and princes of the Holy

Roman Empire became a chapter in the "thousand-year struggle" between Poles and Germans.

Needless to say, these nationalistic interpretations in no way corresponded to the actual situation in the Middle Ages, when allegiance was primarily to dynastic and religious powers, and nations in the modern sense were unknown. Territorial conflicts with neighboring states to the west did not prevent the Piasts from establishing dynastic ties with the princes of the Holy Roman Empire. Beginning in the twelfth century, the Silesian Piasts in particular increasingly went their own way, establishing an ever denser web of familial ties to the Empire and opening themselves to cultural influences from the West, especially from Bohemia. From the nineteenth century onward, however, these dimensions of Piast history were ignored in favor of the reinterpretation that saw in the history of medieval dynasties and states a history of nations in battle.[14] Maleczyński, for instance, wrote in a text first published in 1948:

> Since the very first moment of Silesia's political union with the Polish state, we have heard not a single word about Silesian regional separatism. . . . On the contrary, in [Bolesław] Chrobry's first German wars, in his deadly struggles with the forces of the whole German empire, the people of Silesia—knights, townspeople, and peasants—showed that they felt themselves to be Poles, that they thought the same way as their leader, and that they would stand in solidarity with him against the *furor Teutonicus*.[15]

It was advantageous for the Polonocentric interpretation of Wrocław's history after 1945 not only that the city had been one of the pillars of the early Polish state, but also that the oldest recorded event in local history—the founding of the Wrocław bishopric in 1000 CE related in the chronicle of Thietmar von Merseburg—coincided with a significant event in Polish national history.[16] According to tradition, in that year Emperor Otto III made a pilgrimage to the grave of Saint Adalbert in Gniezno, where Piast Duke Bolesław Chrobry received him. As a result of this meeting, the Gniezno archbishopric was established, along with its three suffragan bishoprics of Kołobrzeg, Krakow, and Wrocław. This creation of an independent Polish church organization was intended to document, simultaneously, the independence of Poland and its acceptance into the family of Christian nations.

After 1945 the Polish national master narrative presented the establishment of the Wrocław bishopric as the founding of an autonomous Polish city by Bolesław Chrobry, sometimes with no mention whatsoever of the emperor's involvement. It was frequently omitted that a castle had already existed on what was later called Cathedral Island, which in all probability had been built in the tenth century by the Bohemian Přemyslids, who also gave the city of Wrocław its name.[17] In order to make medieval Silesia appear to be uncontested Polish territory threatened at most by attacks from German princes, the military conflicts between the Piasts and the Přemyslids for possession of the province, which continued into the twelfth century, were usually overlooked or mentioned only in passing. In the first Wrocław city guidebook of 1946, written by a lay historian, not only are the Přemyslids completely absent, but the name of the city is claimed to have been derived from Warcisław, "a Polish name since time immemorial."[18]

Wrocław's elevation to a bishopric underlined the strategic importance of its castle, situated at one of the most important Oder crossings and at the intersection of European trade routes. The town was clearly destined to become the administrative center of Silesia. Initially the residence of a castellan and surrounded by a rapidly growing settlement, the castle became the permanent residence of a Polish prince in 1138. In 1249 Wrocław was elevated to the status of a duchy; beside the Duchy of Legnica it was one of the main residences of the Silesian Piasts. Polish historians have been particularly interested in Wrocław as both a bishop's seat and a Piast residence. These two elements of the city's past could readily be connected to Polish national history as the Piasts were regarded as exemplars of Polishness, and the Wrocław bishopric remained part of the Gniezno archbishopric until 1821, thus in terms of canon law maintaining its ties to Poland at a time when Silesia had long been part of the Bohemian-Habsburg and then Prussian monarchy. This focus on the bishop's seat and ducal residence eclipsed the fact that Wrocław's significance was to a large degree based on its role as a trading center. The city's location on trade routes had drawn merchants and artisans to Wrocław from very early on. At a remove from the bishop's seat and ducal residence on Cathedral Island, an expansive city centered on three large marketplaces was built in the thirteenth century on the left bank of the Oder and granted Magdeburg city rights soon after. The municipal council was able to further expand its rights to self-government at the expense of the dukes, whose role in the development of the city diminished accordingly. Whereas the Wrocław citizenry, led by wealthy patrician families, enjoyed growing prosperity and displayed its wealth in a lavish town hall, the splendor of merchants' houses, and the impressive city churches, the ducal residence remained rather modest. At most the bishopric attempted to match the free city by building magnificent churches. Its authority, however, was restricted essentially to Cathedral Island, which was legally separate from the city.

Polish historiography had difficulty dealing with the rise of the merchant city, as it undermined the power of the local Piast dukes. Unlike the Piasts, Wrocław's burghers were hard to integrate into Polish national history. The merchants and artisans who had come to Wrocław in large numbers beginning in the thirteenth century and played such a large role in the city's development were mostly German-speaking; and the fact that the municipal council always used either German or Latin as its official language rather than Polish was an obvious and added embarrassment. There were clearly good reasons why Polish historians persistently reverted to the history of the Piast court, as if Wrocław had been primarily a royal seat and not a merchant city. But even their portrayals of the Wrocław Piasts were not free of distortions. They sought, for example, to downplay dynastic connections to the Holy Roman Empire as well as the Piasts' growing political and cultural orientation toward the West. The treatment of Silesian duchess Hedwig (Jadwiga) (1178/1180–1243), wife of Henryk I and later patron saint of Silesia, is symptomatic in this regard. The fact that she was the daughter of Berthold Duke of Andechs-Meran of Bavaria and had been educated at the monastery of Kitzingen in Franconia was incongruous with the image of the Piast court as the standard-bearer of Polishness. Hedwig's ancestry was therefore regularly overlooked, and when it was noted at all, her special loyalty to Poland was always immediately emphasized. Historian Ewa Maleczyńska did mention that Henryk I married a "German," but identified the woman only as "Jadwiga of Meran" and asserted that, "in any case, she was brought to Poland as a child and was thoroughly Polonized."[19]

Polish historians sought to qualify the Silesian Piasts' growing orientation toward the Holy Roman Empire by insisting that they always remained Poles in the national sense. Karol Maleczyński wrote in 1970: "German scholarship

. . . is mistaken in its assumption that the swift Germanization of the dynasty and the country were a primary effect of those relations. The court and the people remained Polish."[20] And Henryk IV, who "was partly viewed in German literature, albeit incorrectly, as a knightly Minnesinger, soon proved to think, feel, and act like a true Pole."[21] The more historians insisted on the Polish identity of the Piasts, however, the more difficult it was to explain why one after another, the Silesian dukes of the thirteenth and early fourteenth centuries had subjected themselves to the Bohemian king—a national tragedy as it meant that a Polish province was lost to the Holy Roman Empire. Since Piast dukes could not simply be labeled as traitors without undermining the credibility of the entire historical conceit, political exigencies had to be created and guilty parties identified. Under the revealing heading "On the Marketplace of Dynasties," Ewa Maleczyńska argued in the *Old Polish Lands* series that ignoble haggling by European princely houses had been responsible for the loss of Silesia.[22] Kaczmarczyk and Maleczyński blamed the German inhabitants of Wrocław: "Intrigues of the Germanized portion of the patriciate," which were not explained in greater detail, led to "that fateful resolution" of Henryk VI to place his duchy under the suzerainty of Bohemian King John of Luxembourg in 1327 and thus to put an end to the independence of the Polish dukes.[23] In his overview of Wrocław city history, Kazimierz Ślązak placed the blame on cooperation between a disloyal German citizenry and aggressive German powers abroad, the Crusaders in the north, and Bohemia's German dynasty.[24]

WROCŁAW'S ETERNAL TIES TO POLAND

Polish accounts of the dynastic history of Wrocław devoted significant attention to the era of Piast rule. After Wrocław fell to Bohemia and a non-Polish dynasty came to power, however, interest in the city's dynastic history waned. The focus shifted to the enduring economic and cultural ties between Silesia and Poland, which, it was argued, had not been broken by an artificial separation brought about solely through political maneuvers. Moreover, according to this thesis, Polish rulers had never accepted the loss of Silesia, even though they had to officially abandon their claims in the fourteenth century. In Maleczyńska's opinion, Silesia "never fully bonded with the crown of Saint

Wenceslas, despite its incorporation into Bohemia."[25] For its inhabitants, Silesia continued to be Polish land.

> In the twelfth and thirteenth centuries Silesia was linguistically and nationally Polish in every respect, throughout all social strata, even the highest. Not only did it become the core and anchor of the Polish economy and Polish culture, but at the same time it was one of those regions in which a Polish national consciousness may have first and most fully developed.[26]

The arbitrariness of dynastic politics, Maleczyńska argued, had ridden roughshod over immutable facts, and the establishment of infelicitous borders had wrought serious economic damage to Silesia as "an ever organic part of the Polish sector of the economy."[27] It is indisputable that Wrocław's trade relations with Poland were always important. The city was vulnerable to any disruption in the flow of goods, whether through high tariffs, border closings, or unfavorable economic developments in Poland. Polish postwar historians, however, turned this into complete dependence on the Polish market. And they neglected to mention that Wrocław's incorporation into Bohemia had positive effects as well; it gave the city entrée to the enormous economic arena of the Holy Roman Empire, which had been undergoing extraordinarily dynamic development since the late Middle Ages. Bohemian Wrocław now had access to leading Central European trade centers such as Prague, Nuremberg, Augsburg, Leipzig, and Amsterdam.[28]

Occasionally, this downplaying of Wrocław's economic connections within the Empire led to glaring omissions. When an illustrated volume published in the 1970s stated that "Wrocław's merchants grew wealthy through trading with partners from cities in Flanders, Italy, Scandinavia, Russia, and even England and Scotland,"[29] the Holy Roman Empire, its primary trading partner, was not even mentioned. Every encyclopedia article on Wrocław contained the information that the city was founded at the intersection of two major trade routes: the Amber Road from the mouth of the Vistula River to the Danube area, from Gdańsk and Toruń to Prague and Nuremberg or Vienna and Venice; and the Via Regia, probably the most important East-West land route in Europe during the Middle Ages. The Via Regia led from the middle Rhine to the Black Sea or farther along the Silk Road all the way to China, connecting Wrocław with Krakow, Lviv, and Kiev in one direction, and with Leipzig, Erfurt, Frankfurt am Main, and Cologne in the other. Ślązak, however, simply omitted the Via Regia in his description of Wrocław's geographic location as a commercial center.[30] Andrzej Jochelson did mention the intersection of two trade routes in Wrocław, but he stated that one ran "from Pomerania to the south" through Polish and Czech cities, thereby reducing the Amber Road to a route of merely regional significance; the other trade route, according to Jochelson, was not the Via Regia but the Oder—a blatantly erroneous assertion, as the Oder River had little significance as a trade route well into the nineteenth century due to its limited navigability.[31]

Depictions of Wrocław's cultural relations were similarly selective. The city's unbreakable ties to Poland were emphasized, along with occasional references to cultural relations with Italy, France, Flanders, and Holland. The links to German-speaking regions of the Holy Roman Empire, however, were hardly mentioned. The city was portrayed above all as a center of Polish culture, even under Habsburg rule. To this end, lists were compiled with the names of famous Wrocław citizens of Polish heritage and local scholars who had studied at the Jagiellonian University in Krakow. Polish publishing houses and their most important works were enumerated; the first successful publication of a Polish book in Wrocław in 1475 was mentioned; and all of the churches in which Polish masses were held were named, as were Wrocław's Polish associations and societies. It was possible in this way to fill countless pages with proof of Wrocław's status as a Polish cultural metropolis, but this was done at the cost of leaving untold the full story of the city's cultural life. That story would hardly have supported the thesis of Wrocław's unsullied Polishness.

Prussia's Conquest and Wrocław's Decline

In December 1740, only a few months after becoming King of Prussia, Friedrich II (the Great) began his invasion of Habsburg Silesia. Wrocław's inhabitants, a majority of whom were Protestant, did not take up arms against the forces of Protestant Prussia. In January 1741 Friedrich advanced without a struggle into the city, where he would set up his winter quarters in many of the following years. After three long wars, Empress Maria Theresa was forced to relinquish Silesia once and for all in the Treaty of Hubertusburg (1763). Until very recently Polish historians have tended to portray Prussia as the epitome of imperialism and an unrelenting source of anti-Polish policies, and Friedrich II as an especially despicable figure.[32] Accordingly the Prussian conquest marked for Polish historians the beginning of one of the bleakest chapters in Wrocław's history:

> The flourishing city, the largest in Silesia and one of the wealthiest in the Habsburg Monarchy, tempted Friedrich II, the "noble son of the Piasts" (he considered himself their descendant and circulated this information intentionally). Taking advantage of circumstances, he wrested Silesia from the young Maria Theresa in 1741, violating Wrocław's long and deftly-defended independence, and annexed it to the absolutist state of Prussia, thus securing for himself a fine source of revenue and destroying by whatever means—force, cunning, bureaucracy, corruption, taxes, forgery—all that had come together over the centuries.[33]

Prussian leaders, according to the People's Republic's official version of history, instituted a "robber economy"[34] in Silesia and treated "the land and the city like a semicolonial territory, from which Prussia would draw great profits without giving anything in exchange."[35] The result, so the official history alleged, was Silesia's economic decline: As a Prussian city Wrocław no longer played the brilliant role it had during the period of Bohemian rule, to say nothing of its grandeur in the days of the Piast court. Prussian policies, it was claimed, reduced the great metropolis on the Oder to a dreary provincial city.

> It is well known that all the famous travelers who visited Wrocław, beginning with Pope Aeneas Silvius Piccolomini [Pius II] in ca. 1460 and ending with the grandfather of Goethe in 1716, expressed the highest admiration for its beauty and cleanliness. But only half a century after the Prussian army annexed the Silesian capital, Goethe himself (in 1790) found only squalor and stench there, nothing else. Until the mid-nineteenth century Goethe's judgment was shared by other German travelers, who regarded the city with indifference and even as downright foreign.[36]

There is indeed abundant evidence documenting the drastic economic deterioration that Wrocław and all of Silesia experienced due to the Silesian wars. Like other provinces, Silesia had to finance the Prussian war machine and was in addition ravaged by troops passing through. In response to the Prussian conquest Austria closed its borders with Silesia, thereby cutting the region off from its traditional trade routes and economic contacts. The Silesian economy, however, had already begun to decline long before 1740. The Thirty Years War between 1618 and 1648 had devastated the entire region and brought about a precipitous drop in population, the economic consequences of which were felt for an entire century. In addition, the economic and political decline of the Polish-Lithuanian Commonwealth significantly affected Wrocław as a trading center by decreasing the flow of goods between East and West.

After a further deterioration as a result of the Silesian Wars, however, the economic situation improved perceptibly. Prussian reforms—in response to Prussia's loss to Napoleon in 1807—laid the groundwork for a sustained recovery. Over the course of the nineteenth century Silesia was to become one of the most important industrial regions in Europe, a development that also benefited its largest city. Thanks to the demolition of Wrocław's fortress complex (ordered by Napoleon), the rapidly growing city could finally expand beyond its old borders. The Prussian Municipal Ordinance of 1808 restored a portion of the city's self-government; and the abolition of mandatory guild membership and the introduction of freedom of trade (*Gewerbefreiheit*) in 1811 allowed it to regain economic power. Wrocław became a railroad hub and an important center of the flourishing textile and metal industries. Moreover, the Berlin government decided in 1811 to move the protestant university Viadrina from Frankfurt an der Oder to Wrocław and to merge it with the Leopoldina, a Jesuit Academy, to form a large and modern university. This made Wrocław the most important academic center in Prussia, after Berlin. The university was complemented by the emergence of a rich landscape of museums and libraries, in part because the valuable collections in Silesian monasteries had been consolidated in Wrocław in the course of secularizing church assets in the early nineteenth century.

One does not have to be a Prussophile to recognize that the faded merchants' city of the Middle Ages was enjoying a second heyday as a flourishing nineteenth-century metropolis. Precisely for this reason Polish historiography had more difficulty with this epoch of Wrocław's past than with any previous or subsequent period. Given the negative judgment they had passed on Prussia, how were Polish historians to depict the period in which Wrocław overcame the consequences of the Silesian Wars and again became a vibrant Prussian city? Some outrageous solutions to this quandary can be found in the literature, for example, in the *Old Polish Lands* series, where Józef Kokot ribed the Prussian period between 1741 and 1945 as a phase of progressive economic exploitation and underdevelopment culminating in the intentional destruction of the entire province through the scorched earth policies of 1945.[37] The predominant approach of popular historiography, however, was to provide at best limited information about population growth, industrialization, and the modernization of infrastructure and to focus instead on isolated aspects of local history, such as the life of the Polish minority,[38] the economic and social problems of capitalism, the "flight from the East" (*Ostflucht*) caused by the economic backwardness of the eastern provinces, Wrocław as the center of *Ostforschung*,[39] the Nazi regime, and the city's destruction by German troops during the siege in 1945.[40]

It is worth examining as well the approach taken by Polish historians in their academic writings. Not surprisingly, they too were focusing on the negative dimensions of Prussian policies, but they avoided making claims that would not stand up to scholarly scrutiny. Against this background, it is understandable why the major study of Wrocław's history, which was published in 1958 and remained unsurpassed in communist Poland, concluded with the year 1807, precisely the moment in history when Wrocław's resurgence began. There was no explanation in the book's preface as to why the period after 1807 was not addressed, nor was there any mention that a sequel was planned.[41] Prior to the collapse of communism in 1989–90, Polish historiography in fact did not produce a single work of any stature that did justice to Wrocław's development into a modern Prussian metropolis, although this was one of the most fascinating periods in the city's millennial history.[42]

A BASTION OF POLISHNESS

The popular histories not only assumed as a matter of course that Wrocław's population was Polish when the city was founded in the tenth century, but also that the people who had settled the region in prehistoric times were the direct ancestors of the Polish people. In 1948, for example, Maleczyński claimed: "Although the earliest history of Silesia leaves many questions un-answered, one thing is certain: The Silesian tribes spoke Polish."[43] In view of the absence of written documents from the prehistoric period, there is no evidence for such an assertion. That aside, we know that Slavs were not the first settlers in the region. Diverse cultures including Celts, Scythians, Huns, and Germanic tribes preceded them. The question as to the "original" settlers is in any case historically moot, as the lack of evidence precludes any defini-tive conclusion. At best we can search for the first verifiable cultures in the region. The fact that this question was nevertheless raised in Polish popular historiography reflects a desire to legitimate the postwar political order on the grounds of prehistorical precedent.[44] Most surveys of the history of Sile-sia and Wrocław thus omitted any and all mention of the existence of non-Slavic cultures in early history, but emphasized the presence of Slavic tribes from the moment of Wrocław's founding.[45]

The thesis that Wrocław had always been a Polish city forced Polish his-torians to marginalize as far as possible the massive immigration of German-speaking settlers during the Middle Ages. While this eastward migration (*Ostsiedlung*), a crucial factor in the shaping of Europe,[46] could hardly be concealed completely, it was possible to omit precise information about the settlers' geographic origins or to limit mention primarily to the Walloons, the French, and the Flemish. Ewa Maleczyńska, for example, wrote of the ethnic composition of Wrocław's population in the mid-thirteenth century:

> It must be remembered that the entire extended settlement was built by Polish hands and governed by Poles. The number of foreigners was still negligible; there was a group of Walloons, which we know about, and there were Jews, who had their own cemetery. As for Germans: if we discount the merchants who passed through the city only briefly, we find that only a few isolated individuals had actually settled in the city.[47]

In her remarks on rebuilding and resettling Wrocław after its destruction during the Mongol invasion of 1241, Maleczyńska stated only that the Pol-ish population returned from nearby forests. She failed to mention the in-flux of Germans and—incorrectly—tied the emergence of a larger German-speaking population in Wrocław to Bohemian rule.[48] In a lecture to a group of

Canadian Poles in 1963, Karol Maleczyński painted this picture of Wrocław's medieval settlement history:

> With time, more and more craftsmen and merchants flowed into the city from the west; they were not, as one might expect, Germans, but rather Frenchmen from Artois and Wallonia, who towards the end of the twelfth century established a settlement of Walloon weavers that quickly prospered and played a dominant role in the city.[49]

This statement is technically correct, because it refers to the end of the twelfth century, when German-speaking immigration did not yet play a significant role. The historical distortion arose only in the perception of Maleczyński's listeners, who were unable to evaluate the actual significance of the date, mentioned in passing, and did not notice Maleczyński's failure to cite the massive immigration of German speakers that began in the thirteenth century. Only in his discussion of class conflict in Wrocław did he, surprisingly, bring German patricians into play. Their origins, however, remained unexplained. As these examples indicate, it was possible to create a misleading picture of the medieval migrations without resorting to prevarications. The trick was to guide the audience in the desired direction through omissions, ambiguities, and intentionally imprecise information, while avoiding blatantly false statements.[50]

The background of German settlement in the east was normally suppressed, above all the fact that in the thirteenth century Piast dukes themselves had recruited settlers from the Holy Roman Empire, caring little about what language these people spoke, as was typical in the pre-national era. In popular postwar Polish historiography, however, the appearance of German-speaking settlers and the Germanization of Silesia, a gradual process of acculturation that stretched over centuries, were presented as acts of foreign intervention perpetrated on Polish soil by illegitimate German rulers. All of the German dynasties that ruled in Silesia, whether Luxembourg, Habsburg, or Hollenzollern, were presumed to have engaged in concerted Germanization policies. While it was conceded that these had been successful to a degree, it was also emphasized that the territory remained basically Polish. A German dimension had at most been applied like a "thin varnish" over Silesia, its effects limited to the affluent classes and the influential urban patricians.[51]

It is difficult to estimate the relative proportions of ethnic groups over the course of the German settlement in Silesia, because there is little reliable evidence regarding the ethnic makeup of the population prior to the nineteenth century. In general, however, it is safe to assume that the share of German speakers grew more rapidly among the urban upper classes than among the lower classes, and that—irrespective of regional differences—it tended to increase more rapidly in cities than in villages. Polish popular historiography went further, asserting that even into the Prussian period Germanization did not go beyond the upper classes, whereas the broader population remained predominantly Polish. In this way, not only was the German portion of the population marginalized, but the relationship between Germans and Poles in Wrocław could be depicted as one of oppressor and oppressed, as a class conflict between German urban patricians on the one hand, and a Polish proletariat fed by steady peasant immigration from purely Polish villages in the surroundings of Wrocław on the other.

Popular presentations attributed the Germanization of parts of Wrocław's population—although it can be traced back to the thirteenth century—primarily to a deliberate policy of the Prussian rulers. Immediately after 1741, it was claimed, Wrocław had been subjected to a "calculated, systematic program of Germanization,"[52] which sought to make the Polish element disappear as quickly as possible.[53] Only then, the argument continued, did Germandom begin to spread through all of Wrocław, although the Prussian Germanization policies ultimately failed:

> For many Germans from the central and western regions of Prussia, Wrocław, though ostensibly Germanized, remained a foreign, quasi-Polish city, surrounded on all sides by an ocean of Slavs, a city where it was impossible to get by without knowing Polish. This center of Prussian aggressiveness was deeply embedded in Polish reality, in its history and past, in the economy, culture, and consciousness of the Polish nation, which was divided between three powers. For many decades of the nineteenth century, the city retained even external hallmarks of the Polish presence there and manifold connections with Polish lands. In the middle of the nineteenth century, ethnic Poles were numerically quite strong in Wrocław, and Polish was the everyday language of Wrocław's streets.[54]

Estimates of the Polish portion of the population in the nineteenth and twentieth centuries were generally not included in such accounts, because even generous interpretations of existing documents would show the Poles to have been reduced to a small minority.[55] Instead the thesis that Wrocław remained basically a Polish city was usually supported by more or less unverifiable statements along the lines of: "Even in the first and second halves of the nineteenth century Poles traveling through Wrocław observed that a great deal of Polish was heard on the street."[56] Popular historians repeatedly cited Polish writer Wincenty Pol as their principal witness. He had noted on a trip passing through Wrocław in 1841 "that excellent Polish is spoken in all the shops, the signs on the displays are bilingual, Polish and German. The droshky drivers and salespeople speak Polish."[57]

The fact that Polish books were published in Wrocław, in addition to the majority of German titles, was not interpreted as an expression of the cultural proximity and interaction in the German-Polish borderlands, but instead as "the best evidence that in the late eighteenth and in the nineteenth centuries the people still used the Polish language."[58] The university in Wrocław, which employed professors of Polish descent and attracted a fair number of Polish students from the eastern provinces of Prussia, was styled a center of Polish spirit and the Polish national movement.[59] Thus it was argued that Polish scholars—Slavic specialists Wojciech Cybulski and Władysław Nehring as well as surgeon Jan Mikulicz-Radecki were always mentioned in this context—had established a Polish academic tradition in Wrocław in the nineteenth century. A nationality-conscious generation of Polish university students, who organized in groups and participated in the Polish uprisings of 1830, 1848, and 1863, as well as in the battles for independence at the end of the First World War, were also credited with making the Prussian university into a stronghold of Polishness.[60]

The tenor of all these accounts suggested that, until its collapse in 1945, Prussian-German rule had been unable to break the continuity of Polish settlement in Wrocław, despite the unscrupulousness of its Germanization policies. Viewed from this perspective, the evacuation of Germans from Wrocław after the Second World War no longer looked like a rupture in the city's demographic history, but rather like a corrective to the artificial inflation of the German population that had occurred especially during the Prussian period.

FROM FRIEDRICH II TO HITLER: GERMAN CONTINUITIES

Popular histories have repeatedly implied that Hitler's attack on Poland was merely the continuation of a process that Friedrich II had begun with the partitions of the Polish-Lithuanian Commonwealth. Maleczyńska, for example, declared:

> The "great" Fritz, the moral author of this act [of partitioning Poland], was quite aware from the outset that capturing a territory did not yet mean ruling it fully. Hence, in order to truly seize control of the newly annexed territory from a national perspective, he strove not only to remove and destroy the Polish element, but to engorge on the blood of the conquered nation, to thrive on its strengths. This was not something learned from French or any other brand of politics—it was the Prussian state's own particular way of thinking.
>
> Each time Prussian policies of denationalization and expropriation are instituted, the scale of the planning and the careful calculation devoted to the process freezes the blood in one's veins. This is not something that started during the last world war; it was in place already in the eighteenth century.[61]

Given the trauma of war and occupation, remarks such as these likely had the desired effect in Poland. In the language of everyday political life after 1945 the Germans were "occupiers," and no distinction was made between the German-speakers living in Silesia and the Nazi occupation forces in Poland. The Germanization of the region in reality had been a protracted and complex process, in which manifold phases and factors must be discerned: the immigration of German speakers in the Middle Ages and the attendant reciprocal acculturation processes; the peopling policies of absolutist rulers; the cultural and linguistic homogenizing effects of the bureaucracies, schools, and armies of the modern state; the concerted Germanization policies of the German Empire after 1871; and finally Nazi Germany's genocidal policies in the East. In popular accounts these were all conflated and traced back to one and the same Germanization drive, forced on Poland by ruthless German rulers over the centuries.

The greater the alleged confluence between Prussian policies of the eighteenth and nineteenth centuries and those of the Third Reich, and the more convincingly the thesis of the continuity of Prussian-German imperialism in Eastern Europe from Friedrich the Great's attack on Silesia in 1740 to Hitler's invasion of Poland in 1939 was championed, the more illegitimate Silesia's affiliation with Prussia and Germany had to appear. For this reason Polish

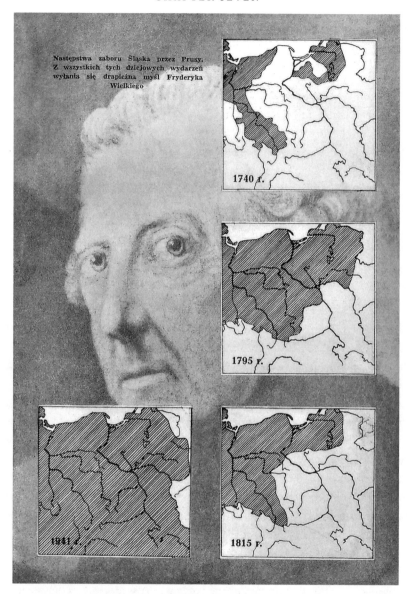

As demonstrated by this suggestive illustration from the book *Lower Silesia* (published by the West Institute in Poznań in 1950), the propaganda of postwar Poland presented the Prussian king Friedrich the Great as the precursor of Adolf Hitler. From K. Sosnowski and M. Suchocki, eds., *Dolny Śląsk*, vol. 2 (Poznań: Instytut Zachodni, 1950). Used by permission of the publisher.

historians sought to blur the differences between Prussian policies of the eighteenth century, imperial German policies of the late nineteenth and early twentieth centuries, and the practices of the Nazis. This they did both through argument and insinuation, which often started with the books' chapter titles and the way periods were defined. In the Lower Silesia volume of the *Old Polish Lands* series, early history, the Piast era, the Bohemian-Habsburg era, and the period after 1945 were each examined in separate chapters, whereas the over-two-hundred-year period from 1740 to 1945 was covered in a single chapter titled "In Prussian Talons."[62]

The historiographies of Wrocław treated the Third Reich in a less uniform manner than any of the preceding epochs. Occasionally this phase of the city's history was omitted entirely[63] or addressed only briefly.[64] As a rule, however, they devoted significant space to the siege of the city in 1945,[65] since this period was attributed great importance in the Polish interpretation of Wrocław's history. The actions of the German leaders during the siege confirmed the notion that the "German element" had been primarily a negative factor in the local history because the Germans had never particularly valued Wrocław as a "semi-colonial" city. In contrast to previous epochs, it was possible here at last to portray the time of the siege objectively and still obtain the desired effect. And there was even a German witness available, Father Paul Peikert, whose diary of the siege days had been published in Polish translation in 1964. Peikert's angry accusations of ruthlessness against German military leaders were cited again and again. One reason why Peikert became such a highly valued source is that the published version of his diary is incomplete, the entries ending with the end of the siege. Peikert, however, was not evacuated immediately but continued to live in Wrocław for some time after the Soviet-Polish takeover of the city. Thus he also witnessed postwar Wrocław and, as his letters demonstrate, his descriptions of this period were no less harsh than those of the siege.[66]

Histories of the city presented the inferno of the besieged "Fortress"—a once splendid metropolis being reduced to rubble and ash—as the dark final chord of a long historical aberration in which Polish Wrocław had become a German city, and ultimately paid for this with its destruction by the Germans. Implicit here is the notion that the Germans had forfeited any rights they might have had in Wrocław through their own actions, leaving behind a tabula rasa in 1945, upon which the reconstruction of Wrocław as a Polish city could begin.

> The Germans themselves destroyed Wrocław in the winter and spring of 1945, and they evacuated the largest part of its residents. It is hard to ignore the historic symbolism of these facts. The city was suddenly rendered a blank slate. It was the German hand that wiped out the age-old achievements of German material culture; a German order expelled the German civilian population. It was left to the Poles to write anew on this blank slate.[67]

THE PIONEERS OF 1945

Early postwar publications concluded their overviews of the city history with sentences that read something like the following examples:

> After the last destruction of the city in 1945 . . . Wrocław, the capital of Silesia, returned to the bosom of the Motherland (łono Macierzy).[68]
>
> Today the great transformations have brought about a correction of historical errors and injustices; Wrocław has again become a completely Polish city.[69]
>
> On May 6, 1945, the time of German rule in Piast Wrocław came to an end forever.[70]

Over the course of time, the period after 1945 became yet another subject of popular historiographies. These focused on the achievements of the city's reconstruction. The postwar period was depicted as, above all, an era in which Polish pioneers encountered nothing but a pile of rubble in Wrocław and set a magnificent reconstruction effort in motion. A technique frequently used in Polish city guidebooks and illustrated books was to present contrasting photographs of the same buildings, first as war-decimated ruins and then after their reconstruction—juxtaposing an apocalyptic "yesterday" and an optimistic "today." Published memoirs of the first settlers, the "pioneers," particularly those who had held important posts, developed into a separate literary genre, which sought to inculcate the general population with the idea that the postwar epoch was an especially heroic, dedicated, and patriotic era.[71]

These memoirs comprise reminiscences from all strata of society, from senior functionaries, mayors, party chairs, factory leaders, and library directors to minor functionaries at branch post offices and fire departments, all the way down to ordinary citizens who occupied low-level positions during the rebuilding of the city. Their accounts are full of pathos as well as information—even regarding the difficult aspects of the postwar period. This contrasts with the popular historiographies, which restricted themselves to the heroic achievements of the pioneers, rarely mentioning the problems and setbacks that beset the reconstruction, be it the shortage of funding and workers, looting, corrupt officials, criminality in the streets, the deterioration of residential housing, doubts about the future of the western territories, or conflicts between Poles and Soviets.

MIGRATIONS

Most accounts did not even mention the forced population exchange, the central occurrence in the twentieth-century history of Wrocław.[72] When the issue was addressed at all, it was most often covered by a brief reference to the settlement of Poles after 1945 and the demographic developments in the 1950s and 1960s, as if the disappearance of the Germans had been the result of a normal migration.[73] A small book on Wrocław edited by Bolesław Siwon took a slightly different approach, stating:

> Gradually the face of Wrocław's population changed. The first organized transports of Germans left Wrocław as early as July 1945; the next followed in October. By the end of 1945, approximately 28,000 Germans had left Wrocław. By the summer of 1946, the German population was no longer a problem for the city. Wrocław had become a purely Polish city.[74]

The evacuation of the Germans is mentioned, however in a way that does more to obfuscate the process than to clarify it. No light is shed on the compulsory nature of the operation, nor is there any indication of the number of Germans living in Wrocław at the end of the war. The figure of 28,000

Germans evacuated by the end of 1945 is misleading because readers, given the absence of other figures, will remember this one and suppose that it represents the total number of Germans evacuated. These 28,000 evacuees, however, constituted only a fraction of the prewar German population, which was significantly more than 600,000, and also only a small portion of the approximately 200,000 Germans who were forcibly evacuated from Wrocław after the end of the war.[75]

An exception is the chapter "Wracamy . . ." (We Return) in the Lower Silesia volume of the *Old Polish Lands* series, which was published when the population exchange was still on going. The text openly addressed the evacuation of Germans in an attempt to justify it.[76] According to author Kiryl Sosnowski, the German "drive to the East" had been a fiction. The population density in the eastern territories of the German Reich prior to 1945 had been quite low, significantly lower than that of the adjacent regions in Poland.

> The *Drang nach Osten* was a political theory, the *Osthilfe* [Eastern Aid] a government program; our drive to the west, on the other hand, was spontaneous, elemental, and organic. That is why a Polish researcher dealing with these issues was able to establish that there had been in the border regions "a continuous biological phenomenon of the German population being supplanted by Poles. This phenomenon had all the characteristics of an organic and irreversible historical process and necessarily led to the shifting of the Polish-German border westward. The present war only accelerated this development."[77]

Sosnowski also wrote about the characteristic psyche of the Germans from the East:

> The German population of Eastern Europe, east of the Oder and Neisse rivers to be precise, never felt completely . . . "at home" in the region. A German here considered himself, who knows why, as a colonizer, a *Kulturträger* [bearer of culture], as the executor of a great mission, etc., but not as an autochthon inextricably bound to the land. . . .
>
> In the awareness that he was serving his state, he went east; and heeding a call from that state, he returned from the east; as a member of a minority in a foreign state he automatically became an irredentist. But as soon as the German state was demolished, he suddenly lost the

foundation on which his intellectual posture depended and was over-come by fear of living in a society alien to him; he lost his composure and "took to his heels."[78]

Coming generations, according to Sosnowski, might at some time generously extend their hands to the Germans, just as the visionless Yurand in Henryk Sienkiewicz's novel *Krzyżacy* (*The Knights of the Cross*) pardoned his Ger-man hangman following his horrible blinding. After September 1, 1939, Sos-nowski wrote, Poland had no choice but to evacuate the Germans.[79] While German propaganda railed against the ostensibly poor treatment of Germans by Polish authorities and omitted any mention of how poorly German evacu-ees were treated by their own compatriots in Germany, the Polish state, the author insisted, had sought to ensure the most humane conditions possible for the evacuation. Two contrasting photographs were presented as evidence of this. The first depicted Germans peacefully strolling down a shady street with luggage in hand, the older men even with walking sticks; the second pre-sented a column of Polish refugees in tattered clothing being driven through the ruins of Warsaw with meager bundles under their arms. The caption be-neath the photos read: "The Germans left Poland with their suitcases . . . and this is how they drove us out of the capital."[80]

Attempted justifications of this kind remained the exception in popular portrayals. They had the distinct disadvantage of reminding a broad reader-ship about the population exchange, about the fact that Germans had been forced to leave in great numbers, that it was a process that required a good deal of legitimating, and that complaints had been raised in the West about the inhumane treatment of the German population. In the following decades in Poland the evacuation was a subject for scholars only. The rule for popular historiographies was that the population exchange in general and the evacu-ation of the Germans in particular was to be broached as little as possible. Popular city histories cast a veil over the demographic revolution that was the pivotal point in the modern history of Wrocław and that continues to preoc-cupy the city and its inhabitants to this day.

CHAPTER EIGHT

Cleansing Memory

INCORPORATING THE GERMAN TERRITORIES INTO POLAND ENTAILED A large-scale renaming operation.[1] More than 30,000 place names, tens of thousands of natural features such as rivers, streams, lakes, forests, meadows, and mountains, as well as hundreds of thousands of streets and squares were to be given Polish names. And time was of the essence. In order for state authorities, the railways and the postal service, the military, and other institutions that had to rely on fixed place names not to descend into chaos, the renaming procedures had to be carried out as quickly as possible. It also had to be implemented systematically and competently in order to avoid the duplication of names and to assure that the assigned names would be permanent.

POLONIZATION: PLACES, STREETS, AND PEOPLE

Despite these demands, the Polonization of place names began chaotically. In the early days there were no clear instructions or standard procedures for renaming, and even the general principle of restoring former Polish names wherever possible was of little help as long as the archival materials that would supply these historical names were not accessible. The Polish Railways, local authorities, and even settlers frequently assigned Polish names as they saw fit, without the approval of the central authorities. Often German names were simply adapted to the Polish language phonetically or translated directly into Polish. Some towns were named after a random personage, sometimes the village elder; other places were assigned names reminiscent of the regions whence the settlers came.[2] Widespread confusion was the quick result. In the western territories the postal service, railways, and other state agencies came dangerously close to the brink of losing their bearings. Places suddenly had multiple names, railroad stations had names that differed from the names of the corresponding towns, and similar or homophonous names accumulated, sometimes in close proximity to each other. Furthermore, signs and guide-posts with the new names were often missing. The Council of Ministers is-sued a circular in mid-June 1945 advising all responsible ministries not to remove German signs without first replacing them with Polish ones,[3] but comprehensive Polish signposting was a long time coming. People had two alternatives: They could continue to orient themselves according to the exist-ing German signs, or they could follow the ones mounted by the Red Army in Cyrillic script.[4]

As there were no systematic guidelines to standardize renaming, it is not surprising that the process turned into a general nuisance. The Ministry of Education wrote in September 1945 to the Ministry of Public Administra-tion, which was responsible for the undertaking:

> One already notices a kind of uncertainty, or even chaos, in this area. Even in official documents, various names are used to describe the newly recovered voivodeships, not to mention the individual counties within those voivodeships.[5]

The Foreign Ministry urged in October 1945 that a system be quickly worked out to codify the new names: Some towns had already changed their names several times so that place names differed on the various maps that were in circulation, and of course permanent place names and uniform maps would be essential for the upcoming talks to resolve the border issue. For politi-cal reasons as well, the ministry stressed, it was necessary to put up Polish signs in the western territories without delay: "Currently most road signs are exclusively in Russian. A foreigner entering these territories would not get the impression that he was entering Poland."[6] The government plenipoten-tiary of the Lower Silesian town of Środa Śląska pointed to the foreign policy consequences of the naming chaos in a complaint about unauthorized name changes by the railway administration:

> Aside from the fact that it creates confusion, I should emphasize that the Germans know all about this. They call it "polnische Wirtschaft" ["Polish (mis)management"]. Such ill-conceived orders on the part

of the railway authorities and their completely unfounded stubbornness could also be taken advantage of by the hostile foreign propaganda machine.[7]

In January 1946 the Ministry of Public Administration reactivated the Commission for the Determination of Place Names (Komisja Ustalania Nazw Miejscowości), which had already existed in the interwar period. It was supposed to put an end to the chaos and create a systematic renaming process. The appointments to the commission show that the assignment of Polish place names in the western territories was more than simply a pragmatic measure. In addition to representatives from the ministries for postal and telegraph services, transportation, and defense, leading scholars of Polish Western Thought were named. They were supposed to assure that the new place names were suitable for propaganda purposes. Geography professor Stanisław Srokowski, chairman of the commission, had been one of the protagonists and first director of the Baltic Institute in Toruń before the war. Other members of the commission were professors Kazimierz Nitsch, a philologist and, from 1946, president of the Krakow Academy of Sciences; Mikołaj Rudnicki, a Slavicist and director of the West Slavic Institute in Poznań during the interwar period; and Polonist Witold Taszycki.

The main tasks of the commission, however, were carried out by its three regional branches, each of which was affiliated with research institutions working in the spirit of Western Thought. These branches submitted their proposed names to the main commission, which convened several times a year. The proposals were generally approved and the new names published in the official gazette *Monitor Polski* as a form of public notice.[8]

As historian Anna Magierska noted, "the Polish sound of the place names, aside from its political significance, was important from an educational and social perspective. It affected the consciousness of the newly arriving settles. It gave them evidence of Polish life."[9] Accordingly, the renaming was based on the principle that Polish place names should reflect the ancient Slavic-Polish settlement history of the new regions. As early as September 1945, Mikołaj Rudnicki spoke at the First Onomastic Congress in Szczecin on the historiographical significance of the renaming process:

> We are not newcomers to this land; we are returning to it. We are resurrecting that which has remained and retrieving the old names, chiefly

from documents: if a name was deliberately distorted or changed by chance, we will restore its proper form.[10]

The topographical names that were current in the western territories in 1945 were in large part of Slavic origin. Over the course of centuries, however, they had gradually been adapted to the German language in terms of both pronunciation and spelling. At some point they became official designations, such as Breslau, Liegnitz, or Pommern. Whereas only a few towns founded in the Middle Ages had always had German names (Marienburg, Landeshut, and Hirschberg, for example), the names of all the colonist villages established through the settlement policies of Friedrich the Great during the eighteenth century had been German from the beginning. The latter were often named in honor of their royal or noble founders, such as Friedrichswalde (Friedrich's woods), Sophiental (Sophie's valley), and Königswille (king's will). Others had simply been given names like Sommerfeld (summer field) or Neuendorf (new village).

After the founding of the German nation-state in 1871, parts of German society began to take offense at "non-German" place names. Caught up in the national ardor, the authorities soon began renaming towns, often on the initiative of their patriotic residents. Exotic-sounding Masurian place names such as Dziurdziewo and Krzyonoga disappeared in favor of Thalheim and Krummfuss. The town of Inowraclaw in the province of Posen was renamed Hohensalza in 1905, and the Upper Silesian Zabrze became Hindenburg in 1915 in honor of the victor in the Battle of Tannenberg the year before. After the First World War the trend to Germanize place names gained momentum. Once the nation-state principle had been asserted at the Paris Peace Conference and after the new national borders were defined according to the proportions of the respective ethnic groups, foreign names, like foreign-language-speaking ethnic minorities, were seen as a threat to the territorial integrity of a state.[11]

After the Nazis assumed power, a systematic operation was initiated to eliminate all remaining non-Germanic place names, especially those of Slavic origin. Pressured by Nazi authorities and with the support of the League for the German East (BDO), thousands of towns and other topographical features in the eastern part of the Reich were Germanized within only a few years.[12] The arguments used to persuade communities to change their names are plain in this letter that the BDO addressed to the mayor of the village of Brzezin in August 1937:

> It cannot be tolerated that some places within the German Empire have foreign-sounding names that refer to a period of foreign settlement, albeit a relatively brief one. Many of the towns certainly already existed prior to being settled by Slavs in the years from 700 to 1100, but they were simply renamed by the large numbers of Slavs that kept coming . . . and those names, regrettably, have been retained to this day. . . . The name of your community is derived from the Polish word for birch (brzoza). I would like to propose that you change it to Birkenhain [German for birch grove].[13]

The arguments advanced for Germanizing Polish place names in eastern Germany prior to 1945 and for the Polonization of German names in the western territories after 1945 are astonishingly similar.[14] In both cases the governments advocated the complete elimination of foreign language designations, to which end they were supported by organizations such as the League for the German East, on the one hand, and the Polish Western Union, on the other. In both cases university professors offered their services in order to veil the political campaign in ostensibly academic arguments, and in both cases the employment of linguistically "pure" name forms was allegedly intended to re-establish an original state. In reality, however, the motive was solely political: to expunge the traces of multiethnic settlement history in the Slavic-German borderlands that were embedded in the area's place names.

After 1945 the changing of German place names in the western territories was passed off by Polish propaganda as re-Polonization, despite the fact that even those places that only ever had a German name were now given a Polish one. In an appraisal report in 1946, Mikołaj Rudnicki made the case for eliminating the German town name Paradies (Paradise) or its Polish version Paradyż, which could be traced back to the Cistercian monastery that had been founded there under that name in the thirteenth century. Rudnicki's argument:

> The purpose of changing place names is precisely to restore the rightful, purely Polish character of the Recovered Territories. The Germans, in this instance, monks of German descent, tried to obliterate this

character by introducing purely German names or hybrid names such as *Paradies*.[15]

Kazimierz Kolańczyk wrote in *Przegląd Zachodni* in the same year about the purpose of Polonization:

> And hence the task of the historian in returning Polish names to the Recovered Territories is exceedingly important and rewarding. . . . Every Slavic name that can be traced and reconstructed is a new legal title for us.[16]

Wherever place names were no longer permitted as evidence of a changing history, but were instead made to serve as a legal title in the struggle for territory, ethnically hybrid place names were no longer acceptable. Experts in the field of onomatology had to ensure that the new and unambiguous geographical designations were in line with historically verifiable Polish or West Slavic medieval names. As a rule, they went back to the oldest name forms they could find and accepted, at most, minor modifications to adapt them to the modern language. If no original Slavic names could be found, either because sources were lacking or because a place had always had a German name, Polish names were invented that harmonized with verifiable Slavic names from the surrounding area. The new-old geographic names were also supposed to manifest the regional history of Silesia, Pomerania, and southern East Prussia by embodying the distinctive linguistic features of the different West Slavic peoples, such as the Polabs in Pomerania and the Szlonzoks in Silesia. In Masuria also Baltic names were allowed, since they could be traced back to the Old Prussians (Prussen), a Baltic tribe that had vanished after the region was conquered by the Teutonic Order. Unlike the Germans, the Old Prussians could no longer assert any territorial claims.

In Polonizing place names, Polish researchers imagined themselves undergoing a kind of examination in which they had to prove themselves under strict and begrudging eyes from abroad. Only experts of rank seemed able to master the demands of such a situation, as any laymanship in the field of name-giving was met with a cry of outrage. In an attempt to make Minister of the Recovered Territories Władysław Gomułka aware of the allegedly unscientific, absurd decisions of the First Onomastic Congress, Kazimierz Nitsch claimed in December 1945 that the entire congress was "patriotic tomfoolery," and he urged the minister to ensure that name-giving not be left up to "all manner of dilettantes."[17] Bolesław Olszewicz assumed a much more severe tone in a brochure published by the Baltic Institute in 1946, in which he castigated the "toponymic graphomania, which takes no account of anything, neither the history of the territory nor the elementary principles of Polish word formation nor even our grammar."[18]

But even acknowledged experts locked horns on the issue of "proper" place names.[19] For years a debate raged over whether the Lower Silesian town of Neisse should be renamed "Nysa" or "Nisa." The dispute centered on the minor difference in the pronunciation of "y" versus "i," and it would be worth no more than a footnote had it not brought to light the problem of overloading place names with meaning and pursuing an academic purism, for which even the Slavic settlement history of the region did not seem pure enough. "Nisa" was the version of the name that corresponded to ancient sources and was used in Polish literature. "Nysa," on the other hand, was the form used in the Slavic dialect of the (Upper) Silesian autochthons. It should also be noted that prior to 1945 there had not only been a centuries-long process of Germanizing Slavic names, but also a Slavization of originally German names and a re-Slavization of Germanized Slavic names: Through the German-speaking settlers, the West Slavic "Kostrzyn" became "Küstrin," which the local Slavic population then turned into the hybrid form "Kistrzyn"; the same was true of the city "Legnica," which appeared in German sources as "Liegnitz," but was called "Lignica" by the Silesian autochthons.[20]

These hybrid forms attest to the complex history of migrations and mutual assimilation processes in the German-Slavic borderlands. They did not, however, satisfy the desire in postwar Poland for a Polish historical landscape in the western territories purged of all German traces. Nevertheless, the hybrid place names and the wishes of the autochthon population to codify the names in accordance with their everyday linguistic usage could not simply be ignored. The autochthons ultimately served the state propaganda as proof of a continuous history of Polish settlement in the western territories since the Middle Ages. The fact that the dispute over the new name for Neisse was ultimately decided in favor of the autochthon form "Nysa" was an exception to the rule, however, as the renaming commissions generally instated the "pure" Polish forms. Thus, even the Polonization of place names is evidence of the contradictory policies of the Polish state toward the autochthons. Propaganda styled them as valuable champions of the Polish cause, while at the same time the authorities subjected them to a mistrustful policy of re-Polonization.

One motivation for the renaming process was the hope that the Slavic names would make the Polish settlers in the west feel more like the legitimate heirs to a native homeland. According to Kolańczyk, the names were now

> alive and indisputable proof of the eternal Polishness of these lands, since they were passed on by the enemy. They provide a special and direct link between today's victorious generation and those fortunate generations in the past who knew nothing of Germans or bondage, as well as those who suffered and were killed off by violence. The names they once used sound to us like a historical memento, a testimony, a call to arms. Today's peasant living in Boczów, Górzyca, Drzeńsko, or Sułów finds huge moral support in the knowledge that his forefathers used exactly those same names centuries ago![21]

But Kolańczyk was mistaken. Not everyone drew his or her sense of home from a feeling of connectedness to alleged ancestors via the names of their towns and cities. It was not only the autochthons who wanted to retain their familiar place names. The settlers, too, often expressed dissatisfaction with officially decreed designations and could not care less about the opinions of the experts.[22] Some simply wanted pretty names for the places in which they lived. Others wanted names that would remind them of their lost homeland in the East. When the new residents of Miłochów in the county of Świdnica expressed a desire to name their village after the first Polish child born there, the voivode consulted with the Silesian Institute and received a negative response: The town should please use the historically verified name Miłochów Dolny; it should not be called Stefanówka, "just because the first child born to settlers there was given that name."[23]

Cases like this were by no means isolated incidents. The central authorities had their hands full enforcing the consistent use of officially assigned names. In late 1946 the Ministry of the Recovered Territories saw occasion to issue a circular to explain once again the procedure for changing names. If the local population or journalists were not satisfied with the official name, the ministry wrote, the only possible reason for this would be that they did not have enough information about the historical character of the name. If civil servants refused to use the official names, then severe disciplinary measures would be taken.[24] The Lower Silesian voivode Stanisław Piaskowski repeatedly sent circulars to the *starostas* (county executives) in his voivodeship, insisting that they adhere to the assigned names and stop continually introducing local initiatives to rename towns. He ultimately felt compelled in late 1946 to threaten his administrative staff with disciplinary procedures and official consequences if it continued to ignore the official names.[25] Yet even threats of this kind did not seem capable of breaking the recalcitrance on the name issue. In a circular of April 1947, Vice Minister Józef Dubiel of the Ministry of the Recovered Territories stated that while the voivodes in the western territories had demonstrated understanding for the significance of re-Polonization measures, the introduction of official place names was still progressing only very slowly, especially in Silesia:

> Inappropriate names, usually constituting an inept adaptation of German names, are still being used. This is happening in part because of a certain resistance on the part of the local population, but primarily because of the careless way this issue has been tackled. Sometimes the arbitrariness of local officials is to blame, who use names that are inconsistent with the wording announced in the *Monitor Polski*.[26]

Even if the new names did eventually catch on, it is telling that that same year the ministry requested, with a degree of resignation, that all communities in the western territories report their town names for the compilation of a directory of Polish place names—not only the official names of the towns and villages, which were known in Warsaw in any case, but also the names that were used most frequently in everyday parlance.[27]

The procedure for the renaming of city districts in Wrocław was the same as for town names. In cases of Germanized Slavic designations, these were re-Slavicized: Brockau became Brochów, Mochbern Muchobór, Oswitz Osobowice, Scheitnig Szczytnicki, and Krietern Krzyki. Sometimes names that had not been changed until the late 1930s were simply reinstated. Thus Schwoitz, which had become Güntherbrücke, and Oltaschin, which had been changed to Herzogshufen, reverted to their Polish names Swojczyce and Ołtaszyn. In cases where only German names existed, these were directly translated into Polish: Bürgerwerder (Burghers' Island) became Kępa Mieszczańska, and Höfchen (small manor) became Dworek. Sometimes it was necessary to modify a translation due to national considerations, as in the case of Wilhelmsruh. Since Wilhelm, the name of Prussian-German rulers, did not sound good to Polish ears, but the "-ruh" (quiet) ending invoked pleasant associations, the district name was changed to Zacisze (quiet place). In a few rare cases completely new names were invented, such as Wojnów for Drachenbrunn and Partynice for Hartlieb.[28]

The situation was different regarding the names of streets and squares.[29] In the area of the Old Town there was little difficulty, since most of the old street names could be translated without any problem. This was true for geographically determined street names such as Schweidnitzer Strasse (Schweidnitz Street) or Domstrasse (Cathedral Street), and for names such as Rossmarkt (Horse Market), Schmiedebrücke (Blacksmiths' Plank Road), or Gerbergasse (Tanners' Lane), which expressed the former economic function of the respective streets. In any case, some of the street names already had Polish forms prior to 1945. Most of the streets in Wrocław were outside the Old Town, however, and had not been built until the tumultuous urban growth in the nineteenth and early twentieth centuries. Names based on functions or directions and names that had something to do with the history of the street were more the exception than the rule here. Most of the smaller streets had been given meaningless, random names by the German municipal authorities in a kind of assembly line manner: In Kleinburg (Borek) the residential streets were named after trees, in Zimpel (Sępolno) they were named after songbirds, and in Bischofswalde (Biskupin), after fairy tale characters. Starting in the nineteenth century, however, there was a growing trend to name larger streets especially and squares in honor of historical figures and to commemorate significant events of the national past. Such names were political monuments. They served to embed a canon of patriotic commemoration in the very street grid. The rank of a person honored in the street name or the importance of the historical event commemorated could be gauged by the length and width of the street, and by the level of its function in the urban traffic system, from a main thoroughfare to a side street.

Some of the people honored in German street names were outstanding personalities in local history. There were streets named for famous residents such as poet Karl von Holtei, military theorist Carl Clausewitz, politician Arthur Hobrecht, and entrepreneur August Borsig, whereby the city not only paid its respects to these personages, but also claimed a certain right to share their fame. The names of the most significant streets, squares, and bridges reflected mostly the Prussian and German state cults of the nation, which after 1871 were inextricably linked. Emperor Wilhelm I, founder of the empire, was honored several times: the monumental Kaiserbrücke (Emperor's Bridge); the magnificent Kaiserstrasse (Emperor's Street) passing through Alt-Scheitnig (Stare Szczytnicki); and Kaiser Wilhelm Street and Kaiser Wilhelm Square, which served as the main artery and square in the southern middle-class residential neighborhood. King Friedrich Wilhelm III also gave his name to both a square and a street, and many other streets were named after representatives of the Hohenzollern dynasty. There were also streets honoring Prussian military leaders such as Tauentzien, Blücher, and York, Prussian reformers Hardenberg and Stein, and again and again of course Bismarck, who after Wilhelm I was the most important symbol of the founding of the German Empire.

The lifespan of political street names can be short. They are an expression of the Zeitgeist and thus inevitably vulnerable to the effects of time and tide. A Gerbergasse can continue to exist even after the tanner's trade has long since died out and hardly anyone remembers the meaning behind the street name. But since the French Revolution, renaming streets in order to convey a political message has been one of the most important rituals of revolution; and of course the continued existence of a street bearing such a name signifies that the person honored is still esteemed, at least to some degree. When the German Empire collapsed in 1918 and the Weimar Republic attempted to inscribe itself into the street grid, Breslau's Kaiserbrücke became Freiheitsbrücke (Freedom Bridge) and Kaiser-Wilhelm-Platz became Reichspräsidentenplatz (Reich President's Square). Schlossplatz (Castle Square) was renamed Platz der Republik (Square of the Republic). In honor of Walther Rathenau, the murdered first foreign minister of the republic, Gröschel-Brücke and Oswitzer Strasse became Rathenau-Brücke and Rathenaustrasse. Two other representatives of the young democracy were honored when Tiergartenstrasse and Grüneicher Weg, the two main streets of Zimpel and Bischofswalde, were renamed Friedrich-Ebert-Strasse and Gustav-Stresemann-Strasse.

After 1933, the Nazis erased any and every name that might recall the Weimar Republic and set in place their own symbols. The Freiheitsbrücke reverted back to Kaisersbrücke, and Kaiser-Wilhelm-Strasse became Strasse der SA. Reichspräsidentenplatz was renamed Hindenburgplatz. Many of the main thoroughfares were named after Nazi party idols, the fallen fighters in the movement, both great and small, and unabashedly also after Nazi functionaries who were still alive. Friedrich-Ebert-Strasse became Adolf-Hitler-Strasse in 1933 and Gustav-Stresemann-Strasse was changed to Horst-Wessel-Strasse. Rathenau-Brücke was changed back to Gröschel-Brücke and Rathenaustrasse became Schlageterstrasse in commemoration of Albert Leo Schlageter, a member of the Freikorps whom the Nazis considered one of their martyrs. Streets were also renamed to honor Erich Ludendorff, Karl Litzmann, Hermann Göring, Silesian Gauleiter Helmuth Brückner, and SA leader and Wrocław chief of police Edmund Heines, until the last two named fell out of favor and the streets named after them were given new designations.

Of course, the names of socialists such as Karl Marx and Ferdinand Lassalle disappeared from the street scene, as did those of Jews, such as Heinrich Heine and Julius Schottländer. Street names that were tied to Polish-Slavic history had to vanish as well. In 1938, Governor and Gauleiter of Silesia Josef Wagner issued orders for the term "Piast" to inconspicuously disappear in Silesia. After all, he said, there were scholarly doubts as to "whether the Piast dukes could be considered Germans."[30] Piastenstrasse in Wrocław fell victim to this request; it was renamed Memellandstrasse in the summer of 1939, after Hitler forced Lithuania to return the Memel Territory to Germany.[31]

After the Second World War, Mayor Bolesław Drobner personally ordered Wrocław's first street name changes. On his instructions Schlossplatz (Palace Square), where the final rally of the May 26, 1945 victory parade was to take place, was given the name pl. Wolności (Liberty Square). In view of relations with the Soviet allies, it was also deemed imperative to change the name of the important Matthiasstrasse, where the first institutions of the Polish administration were set up in May of 1945, to ul. Marszałka Stalina (Marshal Stalin Street). These are only a very few examples. The Commission for the Renaming of Streets (Komisja do Zmian Nazw Ulic), which was created by the municipal administration in June 1945, was charged with Polonizing all of the roughly 1,500 street names and geographical features in Wrocław. The commission was initially made up of four, then five members: Stefan Podgórski, deputy mayor of the city and head of the commission; Józef Rybicki, director of the municipal building department; the director of the Municipal Office of Information and Propaganda, first Koft and then Szyszkowski; and, as the delegate of the university, director of the university library Antoni Knot. In November 1945 Andrzej Jochelson joined the commission. He was head of the department of culture, art, and schools in the municipal administration and was also an avid city historian who wrote the first Polish guidebook on Wrocław. Polonist professor Witold Taszycki also worked closely with the commission.[32] The names proposed by the commission were at first confirmed by the city administration and then, as of 1946, by the Municipal National Council.[33]

At the beginning Warsaw provided no instructions to guide the renaming of streets. Jochelson's recollection is that the Wrocław commission oriented itself according to only two tenets. First, direct translation of German names into Polish was to be avoided unless there were important historical, toponymic, or geographic reasons for doing so. Second, the existing house numbers were to be retained, which meant that for streets along which different segments had different names, the same number of Polish names had to be found.[34] In March 1947, when most of Wrocław's streets had already been renamed, the Office of the President did finally issue some guidelines. According to a circular decree, main thoroughfares and arteries were to receive (or retain) names that indicated their geographic direction. Historical names that referred to the past of a particular place or street were also to be preserved. In these cases, simple translations were preferred. In all other cases, suitable names would "include those of deceased national heroes, deceased scientists, artists, and writers, as well as deceased persons who had rendered an exceptional service to the given locale." It was prohibited to name streets after persons who were still alive.[35]

In October of the same year, the Ministry of the Recovered Territories proposed a supplement to these instructions, according to which no names could be retained "that have any connection whatsoever with the history of Germandom in this region."[36] Although the circular decree of March 1947 was modified in November, this addition was not included, probably because by that time the instruction was self-evident. The original version was, however, amended to note that names referring to turning points and important events in history, such as those marking moments of victory, liberation, and renaissance were particularly desirable. Also, it was underscored once again that streets could not be named after living persons. Cases in which that had already been done were grandfathered in, however, and did not have to be renamed—probably a pragmatic concession in view of the many streets in the western territories that had been named in honor of Stalin and Zhukov. Their renaming would have been politically inopportune at this time.[37]

The names of streets referring to German cities were retained in Polish translation if, after the shifting of the border in 1945, the city was located in Poland. Thus today there are still streets named after former German towns and cities such as Gdańsk, Szczecin, Katowice, Zielona Góra, Wałbrzych, whereas references to places such as Berlin, Frankfurt, Greifswald, or Wilhelmshaven have all vanished. Notable exceptions to this practice were the streets named after cities in Lusatia, such as Cottbus, Bautzen, and Spremberg. Although this region southeast of Berlin remained part of Germany after the war, the Slavic versions of these names—Chociebuż, Budziszyn, and Grodk—were retained: Lusatia is inhabited by Slavic Sorbs, and the Polish government after 1945 had briefly hoped that the region could be separated from Germany at the future peace conference and perhaps joined with Poland.[38]

In many cases Polish equivalents were sought for German city names. Thus the streets named after the German Baltic Sea cities of Bansin, Warnemünde, and Greifswald were renamed after the Polish Baltic Sea cities of Kamień Pomorski, Słupsk, and Kołobrzeg. Mosel-, Saarbrücker, Mettlacher, and Eupener Strassen, which had referred to areas around Germany's westernmost borderlands, were renamed after places in eastern Poland: Chełm, Lublin, Łuków, and Zamość.[39] One explanation for these odd analogies might be that it simplified the work of the commission not to have to think of completely new names. However, this does not fully explain them, as, in most instances, it was not a simple endeavor to replace nationally coded German names with Polish equivalents. It required commission members to decipher the significance of the German street names and then to search for a Polish analogy. Setting national cult against national cult, general against general, and ruler against ruler required a certain amount of historical research.

The Kaiserbrücke and Kaiserstrasse became the Grunwaldzki Bridge and pl. Grunwaldzki, in commemoration of the Battle of Grunwald in 1410, in which a Polish-Lithuanian army trounced the Teutonic Knights, and which in the nineteenth century became one of the most important sites of memory of Polish national history.[40] Strasse der SA became Aleja Powstańców Śląskich (Boulevard of the Silesian Insurgents) in remembrance of the Polish patriots who had fought for a Polish Upper Silesia after the First World War. Bismarck, who was regarded in Poland primarily as the initiator of Germanization policies, was replaced by Bolesław Chrobry, the symbol of Poland's historical rights to the territories along the Oder and the Baltic Sea. A square and a street that honored the Prussian general Friedrich Bogislaw von Tauentzien was renamed in honor of Tadeusz Kościuszko, the legendary Polish general and contemporary of Tauentzien. Prussian general field marshal and army reformer August von Gneisenau was replaced by the Polish general and military theorist Józef Bem. And Gebhardt L. Blücher was succeeded by Józef A. Poniatowski. Blücher and Poniatowski had fought on opposite sides in the Battle of Nations at Leipzig in 1813, the latter on the side of Napoleon, and the former on that of his adversary. One led the Polish army and the other, the Prussian-Russian "Silesian Army"; and both were promoted to the rank of marshal in 1813 for their military merits.

This list could be extended. Polish analogies were not always sought, and certainly such perfect equivalents were not always found for all nationally coded German names. Nevertheless, the tendency to seek Polish analogies, especially for the main thoroughfares and central squares that carried names in honor of events and famous people of German national history, is unmistakable. This involved a kind of exorcism, an attempt to ward off German national symbols by converting them into Polish national ones. It also demonstrated that the heroes of Polish national history could be a match for Prussian-German princes and generals. It was a form of national inversion, and it unintentionally initiated a kind of dialogue between Polish and German sites of remembrance, enabling the German past and the Polish present to begin communicating with each other, despite the rupture in 1945. It is unclear whether the commission members knew enough about the meaning of German street names to work out adequate Polish counterparts on their own. However, they were in all probability familiar with Hermann Markgraf's book *Die Straßen Breslaus nach ihrer Geschichte und ihren Namen* (The Streets of Wrocław according to Their History and Names).[41] After reading Markgraf's comments on street patrons, all they needed to devise Polish equivalents was knowledge of their own national history.

It was of course out of the question to search for Polish equivalents for streets that had been named after Adolf Hitler, Erich von Ludendorff, and Horst Wessel. This problem was resolved by substituting the political symbolism of these street names with cultural symbols. Adolf Hitler was replaced by the greatest of Polish poets, Adam Mickiewicz; Ludendorff by the Polish philosopher, journalist, and literary critic Edward Dembowski; and Horst Wessel by the scientist and activist of the January Uprising of 1863, Zygmunt Wróblewski. Here the commission contrasted the barbarism of the Third Reich with beacons of Polish intellectual life.

In a few isolated cases, historic street names in the Old Town were deliberately *not* preserved. Herrenstrasse was changed to ul. Kiełbaśnicza, the Polish translation of Wurstgasse (Sausage Lane), the street name that had supposedly been in use at some time prior to 1700. Whether officials no longer wanted to commemorate the German *Ratsherren,* or councilmen, to whom the name most likely referred, or whether the name invoked unpleasant associations because it recalled the Nazi ideology of the *Herrenrasse,* the master race, the decision was made for the translation of Wurstgasse, even though historical evidence for this name was less certain. Junkernstrasse (Junker Street) was also not preserved through translation, although its name could be traced back to the Middle Ages. Instead it was renamed ul. Ofiar Oświęcimskich (Street of the Victims of Auschwitz). The logic behind this name, which was derived neither from the history of the street nor from that of Wrocław, lies in the relationship between the old and the new names. The widespread view not only in postwar Poland was that the Prussian Junkers were particularly responsible for the Third Reich and the crimes it committed. The intent of the name change was not, however, commemoration of the Shoah in today's sense. Auschwitz was at the time a symbol primarily of the suffering of the Polish people and did not yet stand for the murder of European Jewry.

According to Jochelson, the municipal administration approved all proposals made by the renaming commission, except for one. When the commission proposed giving Karlsplatz the Polish version of the name it had had until 1824, pl. Żydowski (Jewish Square), the administration rejected the suggestion and named it instead after the "heroes of the ghetto," pl. Bohaterów Getta.[42] It can be assumed that a "Jewish" square did not fit into the concept of an ethnically homogeneous Poland. Naming the square after the heroes of the ghetto–a reference to the Warsaw Ghetto Uprising of 1943–would invoke the history of Jews, but without identifying them as a specific ethnic group. In addition the name created a correlation with Poland's resistance against the German occupation, through which the Jews were integrated into the postwar Polish national cult.

Only three streets named for German-speaking persons did not fall victim to the purging of everything German but were retained in their Polish translation: Pestalozzistrasse (ul. Pestalozziego), named after the Swiss educational reformer; Röntgenstrasse (ul. Roentgena), named after the inventor of X-ray technology; and Comeniusstrasse (ul. Komeńskiego), named after the seventeenth-century educator and theologian whom Poles considered a Czech. All the others disappeared, even if they were not necessarily symbols of the German national cult, but instead significant representatives of European culture, such as Bach, Mozart, and Beethoven, Dürer, Holbein, and Cranach, Kant and Hegel, Goethe and Schiller. Even a street named after Gutenberg was no longer deemed appropriate after 1945, so the street bearing his name became ul. Drukarska (Printer's Street). Jochelson indicates that there was considerable displeasure expressed at the disappearance of this famous and, also in Poland, highly esteemed personage. The Municipal National Council was in fact compelled to reopen the matter, but in the end did not revise its decision.[43]

By the spring of 1946, almost all of the streets, squares, and bridges in Wrocław had Polish names. But this was not the end of the matter. Political upheavals in 1949, 1956, and 1990 triggered new waves of renaming. Up to 1947, almost all of the designations and names, aside from neutral ones, had been drawn from Polish national history, but hardly any of them honored socialist leaders. Only Stalin, Bolesław Bierut, and the voivode Stanisław Piaskowski had streets named after them in Wrocław—and they were still alive. After 1947 street names began reflecting the establishment of a socialist system patterned after the Soviet model, with streets and squares named after Karl Marx, Friedrich Engels, Rosa Luxemburg, Karl Liebknecht, Klement Gottwald, Sergey Kirov, Feliks Dzierżyński, Vladimir Mayakovsky, and Maxim Gorky. The effects of Stalinism became apparent beginning in 1949: ul. Świdnicka was changed to ul. Stalingradzka (Stalingrad Street) in 1950; and ul. Katowicka (Katowice Street) was changed to ul. Stalingrodzka (Stalinogród Street) in 1953, to accord with the renaming of that city. A square was named in honor of the Moscow-loyal Polish Committee of National Liberation (PKWN), and streets were renamed to honor the State National Council (KRN), the Young Guard, and Polish-Soviet Friendship. When numerous suburban counties were incorporated into the city in 1951, many names had to be changed to eliminate a repetition of street names within the city limits, and the occasion was used to assign "Soviet names." In Muchobór Wielki, streets were named after the peoples of the Soviet Union, and ul. Główna (Main Street) was renamed ul. Radziecka (Soviet Street); the streets in Klecina were given names of major Soviet cities.[44]

The Sovietization of street names in Wrocław differed in one characteristic way from that in, for instance, the cities of East Germany. Although socialist leaders and institutions, and the Soviet Union itself, were honored in Wrocław, the streets and squares named after them were usually situated outside of the city center, and often even at rather unattractive locations. Since a street's importance in the town's grid determined the stature of the name it would be assigned, with prominent streets receiving the names of the most esteemed persons and events, the placement of some socialist leaders seems almost like an insult. The former pl. Braniborski on the western periphery of the Old Town was renamed after Sergey Kirov, Soviet secretary of the Central Committee who was assassinated in 1934. Czech communist Klement Gottwald had to make do with the marketplace in Karłowice. Karl Marx and Friedrich Engels, on the other hand, couldn't be kept out of the city center. Their names were given to pl. Strzelecki and pl. Legnicki, two appealing locations in Wrocław, but neither in the prestigious Old Town nor on a main thoroughfare. Liebknecht and Luxemburg were banished to Muchobór and Ołtaszyn on the outskirts of the city. And side streets in Kuźniki, Karłowice, and Oporów were good enough for Mayakovsky and Gorky. Polish communists were treated far better. Pl. Dominikański (Dominican Square), which was a wasteland after the war but at least located in the Old Town, was renamed in honor of Feliks Dzierżyński, the first head of the Soviet Cheka. Karol Świerczewski, the Soviet-loyal general and commander of the Second Polish Army, was honored after he was assassinated in 1947 by having the main artery running past the central train station named after him.

There was never a street commemorating Zhukov or Rokossovsky in Wrocław, and surprisingly enough, never a Lenin Street. The County National Council (PRN) had approved renaming ul. Nowowiejska in Lenin's honor, but out of consideration for the street's old historical name this decision was reversed and no other was ever found for Lenin.[45] The streets named after Stalin were renamed in the course of de-Stalinization after 1956. Ul. Stalina became ul. Jedności Narodowej (Street of National Unity), ul. Stalingradzka was reverted to ul. Świdnicka and ul. Stalinogrodzka once again became ul.

Katowicka. Other socialist names remained, and over time many more were added, but most served to designate only secondary streets somewhere in the outer districts of the city.

The historiography of street names says a lot about the political culture of a country and a city. In Polish Wrocław it speaks of recalcitrance toward forced Sovietization. While it was impossible to avoid Sovietization, it was possible to avoid toeing the line with great rigor. The city's street names also demonstrate the powerful role that nationalism played in socialist Poland, with national heroes predominating over socialist ones. Finally, the renamings in postwar Wrocław indicate how difficult it was to find Polish personages with a connection to the local history of the city. The historical memory embedded in the street names was essentially a national one. For those street names that did have local significance, such as those referring to Silesian Piast dukes or Wrocław bishops of Polish descent, the connection was most often so distant in time that it could at best veil the Poles' lack of rootedness in Wrocław. It would be decades before the streets and squares of Polish Wrocław would bear the names of deserving local citizens as well as those of out-of-town celebrities.

There are cases where the evolution of a local Polish identity in Wrocław can be read through the changing names of a single street. Typically the sequence begins with a nationalistic renaming in which a Polish analogy to the former German name is chosen, followed by a name prescribed by the communist Zeitgeist, which in the end yields to a name drawn from a new, local culture of remembrance: In 1945 Damaschkestrasse in Oporów was renamed after the great nineteenth-century Polish historian Joachim Lelewel. For a few years after 1956 it was called Brussels Street, before being given the name Patrice Lumumba Street in 1961 in honor of the assassinated Congolese Prime Minister, who was celebrated in the socialist camp as a hero in the struggle against the capitalist colonial powers. After the collapse of communism the street was renamed yet again in 1992, this time for Marcin Bukowski, who as an architect, architectural historian, and historic preservationist had played a major role in the reconstruction of Wrocław's Old Town after 1945.

Not even personal names were safe from the name-changing zeal. The Polish authorities encroached on personal liberties, particularly those of the autochthons, by pressuring if not coercing them to adopt Polonized versions of

German-sounding first and last names.[46] The measures had begun as a move toward the liberalization of naming rights. The government issued a decree on November 10, 1945, that introduced a simplified procedure for changing first and last names. Many citizens had used aliases during the German occupation and now wished to make these names official. The new law, however, introduced an unrelated provision stipulating that a non-Polish-sounding name was in and of itself sufficient grounds for a change. This measure targeted the autochthons in particular, many of whom had German first and last names, or Slavic names that had been adapted to German spelling.

Thus, what began as an opportunity to follow a simplified and less costly procedure to get rid of what might have been a disliked name rapidly became coercion to abandon German names altogether. In March 1946 the Ministry of the Recovered Territories advised the authorities via circular decree to quickly re-Polonize names that had been Germanized during the period of German rule.[47] The intolerant spirit behind this push for Polonization is revealed in a draft of a circular decree of December 1947, written by Aleksander Zawadzki, the energetic voivode of Katowice and plenipotentiary in Opole Silesia, whose harsh measures for dealing with the German population and for re-Polonizing the western territories commonly set the nation-wide standard:

> By Polonizing German first and last names, we should and must sever all ties that might suggest even a superficial link between a given Polish man or woman and the hated invader, at the hands of whom the Polish nation has suffered so much over the centuries. . . . By Polonizing his name, the Polish citizen proves not only to the Polish nation but also to the entire world that he feels fully part of his nation . . . not only for his own benefit, but also for the benefit of his children and for future generations, because Polish surnames will now be passed down through the generations for centuries to come.[48]

Most autochthons, however, preferred to retain their names even if they did sound German and did not follow Polish spelling conventions. After all, the autochthons were not the only Polish citizens with German last names. As a result of centuries of migrations between the Rhine and the Vistula, German names in Poland had become as widespread as Polish names in Germany. The autochthons, who had already refused to obey the Nazi authorities' requests for them to change their names,[49] were highly reluctant to make this concession now to the Polish authorities. The latter intensified the Polonization operation starting in mid-1947 by further reducing the amount of red tape necessary for changing one's name and exempting the autochthons entirely from the usual fees levied on the change.[50] In a confidential circular of May 1948, the Ministry of the Recovered Territories declared that too few people were taking advantage of the right. The voivodes were thus to make it clear to their officials that the matter was urgent and that they were to convene assemblies

> at which town mayors and administrators, as well as Polish officials from all areas of life (social, political, national, religious, etc.), will be obliged to cooperate with the authorities in the struggle against manifestations of Germandom and, in particular, to cooperate in regard to the Polonization of first and last names.[51]

The officers were supposed to make direct contact with people who had German names and persuade them to change them. In addition, they were to impose the following successively severe penalties on anyone who still refused: "reprimand with warning, assignment to an inferior job or inferior apartment, dismissal from the administration, withdrawal of a license, or a fine of up to 30,000 złoty."[52] In another circular dated December 1948, the ministry also declared that there was no reason for Polish citizens to bear a foreign name. The registry offices were thus in principle supposed to enter only the Polish version of names into the register: Piotr instead of Peter or Pierre, and Małgorzata instead of Grete.[53]

In September of 1948 the mayor of Wrocław reported on difficulties encountered in carrying out the measure. Many autochthons had not had ID cards issued to them, and now no one knew where they lived; others were still recorded as Germans in the registry books.[54] According to the head of the county administration (starosta) of Namysłów, only seventeen of ninety-four county residents with German names had filed to change their name; all others refused categorically.[55] The starosta in the community of Bystrzyca Kłodzka reported that by September 30, only two people had filed for a name change, so he had commenced "compulsory Polonization of first and last names."[56] The starosta of Jelenia Góra explained what he presumed were the reasons for the autochthons' attitude:

> Some argue . . . that they had and still have family members in Poland with the same German surnames, who were nevertheless good Polish citizens who did not profess their German nationality during the [wartime] occupation, and that those family members now continue to keep their name. They, on the other hand, are being compelled to change their name despite their being from the same family.[57]

The measure had, clearly, a quality of the absurd about it. Pressure to change one's name was exercised only in the western territories, because it was there that propaganda requirements called for all German traces to disappear. However, since the authorities did not want to discourage anyone from settling in the western territories because of pressure to give up his or her name, they set their sights only on the autochthons.[58] It was thus possible that two Poles with the same name could meet in the western territories, and one would have been forced to give up his name since he came from that region and had once possessed German citizenship, while the other was permitted to retain his German-sounding name unhindered.

Authorities paid little heed to Wrocław linguist Stanisław Rospond when he advised that historically established dialect features should be taken into account when changing a person's name—for example, that spellings should not be altered simply to conform to conventions in central Poland. Consequently, Silesian variants of Polish names disappeared, which Rospond felt were well worth preserving. These included spellings such as Kowol, Kamuzela, and Dambowy instead of their central Polish counterparts Kowal, Kamizela, and Dębowy.[59] After the height of the forced Polonization in 1947 and 1948, a more liberal course was taken in 1949. The authorities were instructed to accept German first names such as Hubert, Albert, Artur, and Robert, which were very popular in Poland. Also, it was again emphasized that Jews, repatriates, and settlers were not subject to the requirement to change German-sounding names, at least so long as they were not officials in the state or local government.[60]

In Upper Silesia, where most autochthons lived, almost 300,000 first and last names had been Polonized by the end of 1949.[61] Wrocław, however, was barely affected by this measure, as there were few autochthons in the city. Nevertheless, even here there is a city administration file from 1949 that bears witness to the elimination of undesirable historical traces by changing personal names. Erika Theresa Margarete Hille, who was born in Glogau at the beginning of the twentieth century, became Teresa Grabowska. Konstanze Müller, daughter of Valentin and Marianne Müller, born in Radtstein in Upper Silesia, became Konstancja Magowska. Her son, who had been raised in Breslau in the 1930s as Rudi Franz had his name changed to Rudolf Franciszek Magowski. Ella Hildegard Helene Tauchen, born prior to the First World War in Posen to Friedrich Karl and Emmy Semmler, became Elżbieta Helena Kochmańska. August Ortmann assumed the birth name of his wife and his name became August Słaby. Otto Max Rinke of Breslau suddenly became Karol Renkowski. About half of the name changes recorded in this file were those of people of Jewish descent who gave up their German- or Jewish-sounding name in favor of a Polish name. Thus Benjamin Breslauer became Bronisław Wrocławski, Bronia Goldring became Bronisława Polesiak, and Szamy Rozenblatt was henceforth to be known as Eustachy Banski.[62]

DE-GERMANIZATION: INSCRIPTIONS, MONUMENTS, CEMETERIES

Early in 1945 Alexander Zawadzki had already begun the de-Germanization process in Upper Silesia. He ordered that German-language inscriptions— that is, any visible evidence of a German presence—be removed from public places, streets and squares, public buildings, and even residential buildings. As early as February 1945 he assigned hundreds of workers in Katowice to the task of erasing German inscriptions, preferentially selecting Polish citizens who had put themselves on the German People's List (Deutsche Volksliste) during the war.[63] This was a way of making them perform penal labor of a symbolically significant nature. Eliminating German relics was the external correlate to the self-cleansing of their German identity, which was also demanded.

In Wrocław as well, traces of the German past were everywhere evident in the form of German inscriptions—on road signs, street signs, shop signs, on the façades of businesses and residences and sometimes even in the mottos and construction dates inscribed under their roof gables. The slogans on out-door advertising placards were in German. German was indoors as well—on walls, in staircases, corridors, and even in apartments, one read "Keller" (basement), "Fluchtweg" (emergency exit), "Ausgang" (exit), "Briefe" (let-ters), "Licht" (light switch), or "Bitte keine Fahrräder abstellen" (Please do not park bicycles here). German inscriptions could also be found in the train stations, on and in railroad cars, in streetcars and buses, on park benches and manhole covers. The German insignia of fire insurance companies and of the water and gas works were everywhere, as were memorial plaques and chis-eled inscriptions on monuments and boundary stones. The scales and cash registers in stores had German writing, as did the machines and tools in workshops and factories, and the typewriters, files, and other supplies in of-fices. The museums, libraries, and archives were full of German inscriptions. Every object was labeled and named and all the catalogs written in German. Churches were filled with German: memorial slabs, epitaphs, Bible quotes on altars, paintings, inscriptions on the walls; and finally there were the cemeter-ies, in which not only the names of the deceased but also the text on grave-stones bore witness to the German past.

The total obliteration of all this German would prove arduous in the ex-treme. It took longer than originally planned, and it was labor-intensive and expensive. Sometimes considerable technical effort was required. Often, for example, it was necessary to set up scaffolding to remove a single façade in-scription, an advertising sign, or a neon light high up on a façade, and then to repaint or replaster part of a house front where the impression of an in-scription was still visible even after the letters had been removed. The state authorities felt that such operations were important enough to justify the at-tendant expenditures of effort and money. The local authorities, however, did not always demonstrate the requisite zeal in removing German relics. Lower Silesia, for example, appeared to be far behind Upper Silesia, at least accord-ing to the report on a mid-August 1945 inspection in Wrocław:

A visitor from the Opole region is immediately struck by the varying level of de-Germanization across Poland. While in neighboring Opole-Silesia external vestiges of the German language have all but disap-peared, in Wrocław one gets the impression that the city's Polonization policy is just getting underway. The streets still bear German names . . .

in places one still finds German road or shop signs, and on the squares there are monuments to the Wilhelms—all of this, not to mention the predominantly German population on the streets, paints a picture that is surprising, to put it mildly, given that the Polish administration has been operating for three months. This state of affairs is not only a matter of curiosity for the visitor; it is also critical from the perspective of Poland's national interest, since it creates an impression of indecisiveness on the part of our authorities and nourishes unreasonable hopes and desires in the German population.[64]

The Lower Silesian voivodeship administration also complained to the local administrations in late July 1945 that the "vestiges of Germandom" (*ślady niemczyzny*) had still not been completely removed three months after they had taken over the region. The campaign was now to be accelerated and progress reports submitted to the voivode within two weeks.[65] In late August another explicit directive followed, ordering the removal of all remaining German inscriptions and signs.[66] A circular dating from the same period reported on the Polonization campaign as follows:

> In cooperation with the administrative authorities, we need to conduct a propaganda campaign whose purpose would be to definitely remove the vestiges of Germandom [*usunięcie śladów niemczyzny*] from towns, villages, and roads. . . . Particular attention should be paid to railroad stations. Railroad stations should, without exception, be decorated with emblems and flags. Where there are portraits of state dignitaries, these should be located inside the station building along with banners bearing slogans such as, "Silesia was and will be Polish."[67]

The total obliteration of German inscriptions at a time when Germans still comprised a majority in the western territories was premature. Not only did the authorities have to reckon with open protest by the Germans in response to the removal of grave inscriptions or even entire gravestones, but many Poles also took offense at de-Germanization measures that did not even make an exception for cemeteries. In addition, the purposes of the campaign were baffling. It occurred at a time when many people were struggling to survive and the administration would have had its hands full simply providing for them, reestablishing the destroyed infrastructure, and fighting crime. It was also obvious that German inscriptions were being painstakingly removed in one place while elsewhere they remained clearly visible.

Since the Polish administration at first had to use German typewriters that did not have Polish letters, even official correspondence and announcements either had to make do with incorrect spellings or the Polish diacritics had to be added by hand. The paper, too, usually came from existing inventories. The reverse sides of forms and files originally belonging to German authorities and companies were used for the purposes of the Polish administration. This led to bizarre palimpsests, unintended collages in which the actions of a Polish bureaucracy in the making were superimposed onto those of the defunct German authorities. The December 1945 Polish circular of the cultural division of the Lower Silesian provincial plenipotentiary that dealt with the registration of German music instruments was written on one side of paper the reverse of which bore, printed in German: "Press Department, Foreign Office/PXII b Special Department for Political News (SPN)/ Confidential! Forwarding to non-authorized persons is strictly prohibited."[68] A letter of November 26, 1947, from the starosta of the Oława county administration regarding the safeguarding of the local Piast castle, was typed on a Wehrmacht form that was meant to be used to report enemy air raids, with blanks left for times and coordinates of the flight movements, and for the numbers, models, altitudes, and routes of enemy planes. The back of the form of the SS "Reich Security Main Office, Press Archive—VII A 2/Secret" that was meant to evaluate reports from the *Chicago Daily News* was used on September 27, 1945 by the plenipotentiary of the community of Góra Śląska near Głogów to report new Polish place names in his county to his superior.[69] Depending on the position within the hierarchy of a particular administrative branch and the importance of a particular official action, it could take months or even years for German print to disappear from the correspondence of the Polish authorities—and this despite continued rebukes by the government.[70]

Although no direct order regarding this matter could be found in the archives, the de-Germanization campaign appears to have been interrupted sometime in the summer of 1945. According to a circular by the Voivodeship Office of Information and Propaganda in Wrocław dating to the spring of 1947, the interruption was called "in consideration of the general mood."[71] Although German street and town signs continued to be removed and inscriptions eliminated, there was no longer talk of a complete removal of all vestiges within a few months. The change in strategy came at the same time as the government's realization that it was temporarily dependent on German labor and that the evacuation of the Germans would take longer than initially expected. Against this backdrop, it might have seemed wiser to avoid unnecessarily snubbing the German population through all too rigorous de-Germanization policies. Further evidence of a direct link between the discontinuation of the operation and the continued presence of Germans in the western territories is the fact that a renewed effort to remove traces of German began in the spring of 1947, when the evacuation of the Germans was all but complete.

In the aforementioned circular of the Office for Information and Propaganda, it was mentioned that due to the interruption of the re-Polonization campaign, German inscriptions, street signs, and monuments could still be found in many places. With an eye toward the opening of the tourist season and the upcoming exhibition in Wrocław on the "Second Anniversary of the Recovered Territories," it was now deemed urgently necessary "to commence the undertaking immediately and bring it to a definitive completion."[72] Visitors from Poland and abroad would be interested in the progress of re-Polonization. Only a few days earlier, on March 7, the leading Lower Silesian newspaper *Słowo Polskie* had organized a competition under the motto, "We are removing the vestiges of Germandom," and offered prizes to participants who eliminated the greatest number of German inscriptions. The first awards were announced in April, but the competition was brought to an end already on May 1, before it could possibly have produced the intended results.[73]

Once again the cleansing effort got underway, and once again it was not carried through to its end, due this time to the fact that the announced exhibition was postponed for a year. When the opening was finally set for the summer of 1948 and millions of visitors were anticipated, the authorities yet again had a powerful incentive to tackle de-Germanization and this time to see it through. On February 14, 1948, voivode for Lower Silesia Stanisław Piaskowski addressed a circular to all the heads of county administrations and mayors with the urgent demand that they finally "remove permanently any and all Germanic traces [*naleciałości germańskie*]." In view of the upcoming celebrations of the third anniversary of taking over the western territories and the opening of the exhibition in Wrocław, he stressed that time was of the essence: "Domestic and foreign guests who come here should under no

circumstances find any signs that might recall the former presence of the occupier." Piaskowski set May 1, 1948, as the deadline for the thorough removal
of all "vestiges of Germandom," informing the addressees that they were to
submit reports at regular intervals to the voivode.[74]

In April 1948 the Ministry of the Recovered Territories also issued a circular pressing for the "intensification of the re-Polonization campaign." This
secret government order is one of the few extant documents confirming the
rigid and methodical nature of the de-Germanization campaign in the western territories, and it is accordingly worth excerpting at some length:

> The campaign to re-Polonize the Recovered Territories has not pro-
> duced satisfactory results everywhere, a fact confirmed during the offi-
> cial visits and inspections by ministry staff. Also, reports in the local and
> national press suggest that the eradication of all *vestiges of Germandom*
> has not been fully and universally implemented.
>
> In light of the above, in order to address this state of affairs I recom-
> mend that controls in this area be strengthened and intensified in the
> nearest future and that a campaign be undertaken that should encom-
> pass, in particular, the following:
>
> 1. Eliminating the German language;
> 2. Removing all remaining German inscriptions;
> 3. Polonizing first and last names;
> 4. Struggling against all forms and remains of Nazi and
>   Germanization ideology.
>
> . . . *re:* 2. Above all, it is unacceptable for public offices to use forms
> with German inscriptions . . . as they have been doing so far. All inscrip-
> tions must be removed, not only from public buildings, where hardly
> any can still be found, but also from private buildings (entrances and
> staircases) as well as restaurants, cafes, shops, etc., especially when they
> appear on pictures of no artistic value (prints) or on various kinds of
> small objects such as *ashtrays or beer coasters. Particular attention should
> be paid to goods with German packaging, etc.* Finally, the campaign to
> eradicate German inscriptions should encompass: *churches, chapels,
> cemeteries, wayside crosses, and other religious objects,* except those of

outstanding historical value, which in case of doubt should be determined by the competent authority.

All public offices and central and local government officials should participate in the re-Polonization campaign, each in his own sphere of responsibility. However, it is recommended that a person responsible for the campaign as a whole be appointed from the staff of each county authority (Social and Political Section) and voivodeship office (Social and Political Department). . . .

The results of the campaign conducted in accordance with the recommendations contained in this circular should be reported in the next situation report.[75]

In Wrocław, the elimination of German traces carried special weight, as it was to coincide with the Exhibition of the Recovered Territories in the summer of 1948 and would confirm that the city was both the vibrant capital of the western territories and an originally Polish place.[76] In mid-March of 1948, the mayor had a team assembled from the technical department of the municipal administration and the fire department for the specific purpose of monitoring and to some degree carrying out the removal of German inscriptions.[77] The municipal rubble clearance division was likewise commissioned to remove all remaining German monuments.[78] In late June the mayor reported:

> The campaign to remove vestiges of Germandom, which has been on-going for several months now, has resulted in the city's walls being cleaned of German inscriptions. The appeal to local inhabitants to remove all remaining inscriptions from the interiors of residential buildings has also met with some success. A conference was even held on the definitive eradication of vestiges of Germandom, attended by political parties, professional associations, and youth organizations and clubs.[79]

The regular reports that the county administrations sent to the voivodeship offices depict the successes and problems of the de-Germanization campaign in the Wrocław voivodeship. The starosta of Góra reported that all German labels in the administrative offices, including those on files and maps, had been covered over,[80] and that the rest of the campaign was also very successful. German inscriptions were said to remain only at some cemeteries and on tombs, the removal of which would involve certain costs.[81] The starosta of Żary, on the other hand, reported that some institutions regarded the elimination of German vestiges to be of secondary importance and that segments of the population regarded the measures as "not entirely positive."[82] It was reported from Jelenia Góra that disciplinary actions were being taken against communities in noncompliance with the deadline to eliminate all German vestiges.[83] The starosta of Strzelin informed the voivodeship administration that he had already initiated sixty disciplinary proceedings for failure to remove German inscriptions.[84] The starosta in Jelenia Góra complained in a circular letter to his communities that his orders to remove German vestiges were evidently not taken seriously, that these vestiges could still be found in public buildings, hotels, restaurants, and churches, and that German forms were still being used in correspondence. He said that joint efforts were now needed in order to finally, three years after taking over the administration, completely eliminate "signs and vestiges that might recall the former presence of the occupier."[85] The starosta in Lubin also reported problems to the voivode, stating that local authorities, workshops, and private persons did not show proper understanding for the operation and displayed a degree of negligence. For that reason, he wrote, there were still "vestiges of the occupation" in the form of advertising inscriptions, German monuments, and here and there German posters could even be seen on advertising columns.[86] The starosta felt it was necessary to inform mayors and heads of the communities about the historical significance of the "cleansing" campaign in no uncertain terms:

> The Recovered Territories, which have been an integral and indigenous part of the Polish state since its inception, have, as a result of historical events, been severed from the Motherland and desecrated by the presence of the eternal enemy—the Germans. Over centuries, the Germans have tried to consolidate their position in those territories, using any available means to this end.
>
> Since these ancient Piast lands have now returned to Poland, we must express our connection with them and emphasize our rights to them. We must stress that what the enemy has been saying about our Western Territories, namely, that they are their rightful owners, is a perfidious lie, as history has confirmed.

Recognizing these facts as proof of the justness of our demands, we must do everything in our power to remove permanently all Germanic traces.[87]

With the flames of anti-German sentiment so vigorously fanned and German writing condemned as "evidence of the occupation," it was inevitable that here and there things would get out of hand. In Wrocław, historic preservationists were horrified to discover that some of the workers delegated to remove German traces had taken hammers and chisels to centuries-old inscriptions, irretrievably destroying valuable epitaphs such as the ones on the wall of the Hospital of the Holy Ghost and the façade of St. Barbara's Church. In these cases, the intervention by the voivodeship conservator telling workers to refrain from removing German inscriptions from old churches, monasteries, and other historic buildings came too late.[88]

The elimination of German inscriptions in Wrocław was complete in late 1948, with the exception of the occasional oversight. Now and again a manhole cover with a German inscription or the lock on the door of a public toilet marked "besetzt" (occupied) and "frei" (vacant) would be overlooked and accidentally put back into use. Sometimes a German inscription that had been painted over resurfaced years later when the paint started peeling. The Soviet armed forces maintained extensive installations in Poland, and these were subjected to de-Germanization efforts to only a limited degree, as Soviet officials cared little about German vestiges and regularly refused to grant the Polish authorities access to their grounds.[89] Nevertheless, with few exceptions, hardly any German inscriptions have remained in Wrocław—an amazing fact considering the enormous number that existed there when Polish authorities took over the city.

Traces of German were obliterated, but the exorcism campaign left traces of its own. On many Wrocław buildings they are visible to this day. There are, for example, numerous "cleansed" gable inscriptions in which only the year of construction remains, but there is a glaring gap where the words "Erbaut" (built) or "im Jahre" (in the year) have been erased. On many public buildings the stone inscriptions were not thoroughly removed, so that the words can still be made out today. Above the entrance to the former Pestalozzi School on ul. Nowowiejska, for instance, a bust of the school's original namesake still exists. Its vaguely female features might have convinced Polish pupils that it depicted

The double-headed eagles on the doors of the Aula Leopoldina (left), which testified to the Habsburg period in local history, remained even after the city came under Prussian rule. After 1945, however, they fell victim to the Polonization process and were replaced by a combination of a Silesian and a Polish eagle (right). Responding to criticism regarding the "falsification" of the historical door, the administration of Wrocław University reconstructed the Habsburg eagles a few years ago. This, however, raises the tricky question of whether the removal of the postwar eagles rectifies a falsification of history or is in itself a new falsification. Courtesy of the Herder Institute in Marburg and the author.

their school's postwar namesake, the poet Maria Dąbrowska. Over the bust, however, the superficially gouged-out stone inscription giving the German name of the school can still be read. The former building trades school, now the polytechnic university's department of architecture, on ul. Prusa used to have ornamentation and the name of the school, as well as various aphorisms, chiseled into its stone frieze. The German words were rendered illegible with a pick and hammer, but the spaces were never filled and have remained as permanent gaps, unsightly evidence of the de-Germanization campaign. Above the entrance to the building, one could still make out the sloppily removed

Polish authorities insisted on the removal of all German inscriptions. In some cases, however, the exorcism campaign left its own traces. Even though the German name of the Dąbrowska School on ul. Nowowejska is not legible anymore, it hardly escapes the observer that the school's original name has been defaced. Courtesy of the author.

German epigram "Ohn' Fleiss kein Preis" (No cross, no crown), even before someone recently painted the words back in.

Eliminating German monuments posed less of a problem than the inscriptions, since there were relatively few of them. But a decision had to be made in each individual case. Should the monument be disposed of as a "relic of Germanness," permitted to remain as it was neutral from a national perspective, or placed under protection as a distinguished work of artistic or historical merit? The city's national monuments were, for the most part, monuments in a narrow sense, commemorating historical persons or events, usually connected with the Prussian or German imperial cult of the state. Among these were the monumental Kaiser Wilhelm memorial on Schweidnitzer Strasse, the Bismarck monument at the western entrance of the Old Town, the Blücher statue on Salzring, the Tauentzien memorial on Tauentzienplatz, as well as the centrally located equestrian statues of Friedrich the Great, King Friedrich Wilhelm III, and Emperor Friedrich III, to name only the most important. The monuments commemorating Friedrich Schiller and Joseph von Eichendorff in what is today Szczytnicki Park were also deemed "national" monuments. Although the two poets are figures in world culture, their monuments were erected in the context of the national movement and their benefactors saw them primarily as landmarks of German national culture, just as the monuments for Alexander Pushkin in Russia or Adam Mickiewicz in Poland were also symbols of national cult.

After the war all of Wrocław's German national memorials were torn down, bronze statues melted, and stone pedestals reused as building material or sometimes as the pedestals for new monuments. Although the statue of Eichendorff was removed, the monument's plinth can still be seen in Szczytnicki Park. The removal of these monuments was generally carried out without much ado, usually in the first few months after the war ended. Only the monumental Kaiser Wilhelm statue on Schweidnizer Strasse, saturated as it was with a full measure of German national pathos, was destroyed as part of a public ceremony on October 21, 1945. "The fall of this little Fritz," wrote *Naprzód Dolnośląski*, the party organ of the Wrocław socialists, "is a symbol for the fall of the whole Nazi and Prussian regime."[90] The sheer dimensions of the monument's setting and the bellicose expression of the emperor on horseback made its toppling a suitable metaphor for the victory over the Third Reich and over Prussianism—this though the German emperor Wilhelm I had had nothing at all to do with the Third Reich and can only to a limited degree be regarded as a symbol of Prussia. Joanna Konopińska, who witnessed the ceremonial destruction of the monument, described the scene in January 1947 in her diary:

> Almost every newspaper reminds us of the need to eradicate German inscriptions from public buildings, shops signs, wherever they appear. This is completely understandable, because if we encounter inscriptions

in a foreign language at every step, it constantly reminds us of the Germanness of a city that we wish to embrace as our own. German monuments are another matter. They should indeed be removed, but not in the way it is being done—not in my view, at any rate. Once, entirely by accident, I witnessed a monument of Wilhelm I being torn down from its plinth. The monument stood by the city moat, next to the department store on ul. Świdnicka. The mayor of Wrocław, Dr. Drobner, arrived from Krakow to attend the ceremony (he was no longer our mayor at the time) and made the requisite speech. Many people had gathered; the streets were decorated with Polish flags; there were all sorts of banners and placards; an orchestra played. But the whole event . . . left a very unpleasant taste in my mouth. The euphoria of the crowd and the applause when the monument to the emperor fell to the ground seemed to me rather base and embarrassing. Of course German monuments should be removed, but would it not be better to do it discreetly, without all the pomp?[91]

The Kaiserbrücke, now Grunwaldzki Bridge, called for special measures. The bridge was dedicated in 1913 by Emperor Wilhelm II himself and was both a triumph of engineering—in its day one of the longest single-span suspension bridges in Europe—and a monument to the cult of the state. Its steel girders ran through two triumphal arch–like portals that with their massive form and coarsely hewn granite blocks symbolized the might of the German Empire, while the structure's Neo-Romanesque design made reference to the medieval dynasty of the Ottonians. The portals were crowned with pyramidal spires reminiscent in their shape of Prussian spiked helmets, and were decorated with political insignia. At their apex the name "Kaiserbrücke" (Emperor's Bridge) was chiseled in the stone with, above it, a relief of the imperial crown, and below, on the sides of the portal, the Silesian eagle and Wrocław's traditional coat of arms. After 1945 the bridge underwent nationalistic recoding; it was renamed most Grunwaldzki, commemorating the Polish victory over the Order of Teutonic Knights in 1410, and all German symbols were removed. The spiked helmet–like towers on the portals vanished, as did the stone inscription, the relief of the imperial crown, and the eagle. Only the coat of arms was allowed to stay. The missing stones were replaced in such a way that once the work was completed the modifications were not recognizable to the untrained eye.

Elsewhere as well, Prussian and German state symbols disappeared. It was not always a simple matter to decide whether ornamental elements on buildings had truly German-national or Prussian significance. In such cases experts had to be called in. When asked by the Justice Ministry in June 1947 what was to be done with the eagles on the district court building in Jelenia Góra, Poland's General Conservator Jan Zachwatowicz responded a month later:

> The Ministry of Arts and Culture is of the general opinion that the symbol of the eagle with such a wing structure is known from the decoration of historic buildings across Europe dating from the second half of the eighteenth and first half of the nineteenth century. On the other hand, the Ministry of Arts and Culture takes the view that the always-hostile Prussian and later Nazi state misused this formerly Roman emblem to such a degree that in the territories of the former Prussian Partition this type of eagle is justly regarded by the Polish population as symbolic of Prussian barbarism and bondage.
>
> Naturally, we take an entirely different position on the state emblem that is the Silesian eagle, regardless of its date or how it is used, but that is not the case with respect to the eagles crowning the District Court building in Jelenia Góra.
>
> Prussian-type eagles, where they appear on public buildings constructed in the second half of the nineteenth and the twentieth centuries, within the territories of the former German Partition, should be removed, but in each case the local voivodeship conservator of historic monuments should be consulted on the matter.[92]

The government clearly felt the need for stricter de-Germanization measures in formerly German areas than in the rest of Poland. It is irrelevant here whether Zachwatowicz was expressing the true feelings of the Polish people or pursuing on his own the patriotic goal of extinguishing all memories of the German and Prussian past. What is most striking is his mention in the same breath of Prussia and the Third Reich, and the suggestion that eliminating symbols of the Prussian state was as urgent as the removal of Nazi emblems.

In comparison with the number of monuments devoted to the Prussian and German-national cult of the state, there were very few local monuments in Wrocław. Three commemorated famous people in the city's history: the bust of Wrocław poet Karl von Holtei (1798–1880) on the Holteihöhe, an elevation named after him; a column in memory of the famous surgeon Johann von Mikulicz-Radecki (1850–1905), who had worked at the university hospital in the late nineteenth century; and the Knorr Fountain, honoring former city building commissioner Johann Friedrich Knorr (1775–1847), who had been an advocate for the building of the Old Town promenade and the park beltway along the city moat. Insofar as these memorials had been dedicated to German notables, they too were generally removed or de-nationalized. The Holtei monument was removed and the Holteihöhe renamed Polish Heights (Wzgórze Polskie). The Knorr Fountain remained standing, but the medallion commemorating Knorr was removed. Because Jan Mikulicz-Radecki had a Polish background—he was born into the Galician aristocracy and, in addition to German universities, had also taught at Krakow's Jagiellonian University—his column was allowed to stand, but its German inscription was covered over by a bronze plaque memorializing Mikulicz-Radecki in Polish. A bust of the Swedish natural scientist Carl Linnaeus (1707–1778), who established the system of binomial nomenclature that is still used by biologists today, is one of the few monuments that survived the radical upheaval of 1945 without any external modifications. Thanks to Linnaeus's non-German ancestry, it still stands in Wrocław's botanical garden where it was erected in 1900.

In addition to monuments to national and local culture, there were also a large number of religious monuments: a statue of the Virgin Mary in front of the cathedral; two St. John of Nepomuk statues, one in front of the Church of the Holy Cross, the other at St. Matthew's Church; and a wealth of funerary monuments, tomb slabs, grave inscriptions, and epitaphs in and around the churches. Many of the tomb slabs and epitaphs were removed if de-Germanization would have resulted in their destruction. Those that were of artistic value were put in storage in museums or the back rooms of churches, where they were out of the public eye.

For officials, the goal of de-Germanization had been achieved as soon as public spaces no longer contained obvious signs of the former presence of the Germans. When it came to artifacts that were not identifiable as German, the question of whether to preserve, restore, or remove was decided on aesthetic grounds or on the basis of their historical significance. The Baroque sandstone sculptures in the parks and gardens were preserved, as was the Fencer Fountain in front of the university, created in 1904 by Hugo Lederer; the bronze sculpture of Amor riding Pegasus erected at the city moat in 1914 was preserved as well. The pillory in front of the Town Hall, which had been completely destroyed in the war, was even historically reconstructed in 1985 and returned to its original location. The Voivodeship National Council had initially pressed in late 1949 to have the Fencer Fountain removed because it believed that the Art Nouveau sculpture represented a "vestige of Germandom" and blemished the appearance of the university building in the background.[93] The Ministry of Art and Culture commissioned the Voivodeship Conservator Jerzy Güttler to appraise the fountain. He determined in December 1949 that the fountain was

> of no . . . major artistic value; on the contrary: the Secessionist forms of the fountain itself and the naturalistic, dull shape of the fencer set against the university's elaborate Baroque façade produce an effect that is decidedly unfortunate. On the other hand, the sculpture contains no elements that could be seen as politically sensitive, and despite its undoubted ugliness it has apparently (in the public view) already become a part of the cityscape.[94]

In the end the voivodeship conservator was undecided and suggested that perhaps, if the fountain were removed from its present location, it might be erected somewhere in a park. It ended up remaining right where it was. At some point the fencer had become so firmly associated with the University of Wrocław that the university press adopted the figure as its logo.

The way in which the monument ensemble on 1st of May Square (as of 2006 "John Paul II Square") was handled is a fascinating example of how monuments, though stripped of the symbolism they were originally intended to convey, nonetheless sometimes retain a measure of their original meaning. The Bismarck monument that was erected there between 1900 and 1905 originally consisted of the statue of the chancellor at the northern end of the square and, at the opposite end, the "Bismarck Fountain," which included two allegorical sculptures of Struggle and Victory. When the Bismarck statue was removed in 1945, the fountain lost its point of reference and thus also its German national connotation. The remaining figures became generic symbols of Struggle and Victory. As such, they could be understood, within the context of the square's new name, as symbolizing the struggle and victory of the working class.[95]

Many of the city's monuments and sculptures were not eliminated entirely but simply de-Germanized. For this purpose, it was generally sufficient to erase the German inscriptions, but the result was not always satisfactory, as for example when the space for an epitaph remained but the text had vanished. An example of this awkward kind of de-Germanization is the three remaining boundary posts of the originally six (once called the "century stones") that had been erected in 1900–1901 on the arterial roads to mark the city limits. All of these granite posts had the same form: a pedestal that could also be used as a seat bearing a column marked with the inscription "Gemarkung [Boundary] Breslau 1900–1901." Atop the column was a cube whose sides were decorated with the four elements of the city's coat of arms.[96] After the war these posts were preserved, including the coat of arms symbols and the date; all that was removed was the German inscription.[97] On one of these columns on ul. Karkonoska the empty space was recently filled by adding the Polish city name "Wrocław" to the existing "1900–1901."[98]

In 1948 the Ministry of the Recovered Territories issued express instructions that cemeteries were to be included in the de-Germanization campaign as long as there were no objections from a historical preservation perspective. Some, such as the starosta in Środa Śląska, welcomed this move. In February of 1948 he explained: "Next to many Roman Catholic churches are cemeteries that are already full. The Polish clergy views such cemeteries with displeasure, since it has nowhere to organize processions, and would happily eliminate them."[99] In general, however, ethical objections seem to have trumped calls to remove German grave inscriptions, or even entire cemeteries, within the standard time limits.[100] Aside from reasons of piety, there were also complex historical, propagandistic objections. Most of the grave inscriptions in Lower Silesian cemeteries were written in German, but many of the deceased buried there had Polish names.[101] The authorities debated whether the connection between Polish names and German inscriptions was to be seen as a valuable document supporting the argument that the western territories had a long Polish past, or whether it was instead evidence of the successful Germanization of the Polish population and should therefore be removed. Wrocław's city center was peppered with cemeteries by the time the war ended, as numerous parks and green spaces had been converted into emergency burying sites during the siege of the city. When efforts were undertaken after the war to eliminate these temporary cemeteries and transfer the mortal remains of those buried there, many of the smaller church cemeteries in the city center were also closed and their old gravestones removed. This same fate befell the cemetery between ul. Braniborska and ul. Legnicka, which had been in use until 1867 and contained the graves of many well-known local residents; it was dismantled in the early 1950s because the land was needed to build factory facilities.[102] Generally, however, the larger cemeteries that had been established outside of the city center in the nineteenth and twentieth centuries and which had been in use until the end of the war were at first preserved. Because the need for cemetery space had declined considerably in the early postwar years as a result of the city's reduced population size and the fact that it was comprised largely of young people, only very few cemeteries continued to be used for funerals.

In the late 1950s, more than 3,000 German cemeteries in the western territories were no longer in use, covering a total area of almost 5,000 acres; this became an increasing source of concern for the authorities. The sites were often in a state of neglect; graves had been plundered or devastated, and in major cities such as Wrocław criminals often sought hiding places in the undergrowth and in the open tombs of abandoned cemeteries.[103] In order to rectify this situation, in 1958 the government instructed local authorities to perform minimal repairs on the German cemeteries, fill bomb craters, remove rubble and undergrowth, seal open graves, reposition displaced gravestones wherever possible, and remove those that could no longer be identified. In response to this order, more than fifty old cemeteries in Wrocław were more or less restored by 1960, not only to improve the appearance of the city, but also to counter the negative impression that neglected cemeteries had on visitors from within Poland and abroad. At that juncture it was also stipulated that German cemeteries would be converted either to parks and other green spaces or to Polish cemeteries forty years after the last burial they presently contained.[104]

In Wrocław the authorities didn't wait that long. Between 1964 and 1968, about twenty years after the last funeral, all of the remaining German cemeteries were dismantled. Some of the memorial slabs and gravestones were stacked into huge piles on the grounds of the former municipal cemetery on ul. Grabiszyńska and offered for sale to stonecutters. Some were used as

Many of Wrocław's cemeteries fell out of use after 1945 and lay idle for decades. In the second half of the sixties, the authorities gave orders to remove the German grave-stones and transform idle cemeteries into public parks. What is Skowronia Park today (opposite page) was once St. Salvator and St. John Cemetery (above). Courtesy of the Herder Institute in Marburg and the author.

building material to fortify the city moat, to repair the stands in the athletic stadium, and in constructing a new outdoor enclosure in the zoo, so that with a bit of luck it is possible to find old gravestone inscriptions in all kinds of surprising places.[105]

Today Władysław Anders Park and Skowronia Park occupy the sites of the former cemeteries of the churches of St. Mary Magdalene, St. Mauritius, St. Salvator, and St. John, as well as the Reformed Church. Municipal cemeteries I and III on ul. Grabiszyńska became Grabiszyński Park; the grounds of the municipal cemetery on ul. Pilczycka became part of West Park; and the cemetery of the Church of the Eleven Thousand Virgins in the Wrocław suburb of Karłowice was converted into Maria Dąbrowska Park. The cemeteries of St. Bernardine at and around ul. Krakowska have become green spaces, whereas a part of the cemetery of the Protestant Lutheran church between ul. Sztabowa and ul. Kamienna has given way to blocks of apartment buildings.

The former military cemetery on ul. Ślężna has disappeared under an industrial site.

Municipal Cemetery II west of ul. Grabiszyńska (Grabiszyński Cemetery), the municipal cemetery on ul. Osobowicka (Osobowicki Cemetery), the cemetery in Sępolno (Holy Family Cemetery), the St. Lawrence Cemetery on ul. Bujwida, as well as St. Heinrich Cemetery on ul. Bardzka (today Holy Ghost Cemetery) all became Polish cemeteries. Graves from the years prior to 1945 were gradually removed, unless they were the burial sites of notable personages such as the famous Breslau Slavicist Władysław Nehring, who died in 1909 and was buried in what became the Osobowicki Cemetery and whose grave was preserved as a monument of Breslau's Polish heritage. It was too late to save the grave of Polonist Wojciech Cybulski, Nehring's predecessor as professor of Slavic studies at the University of Breslau. Polish workers had already removed his gravestone in 1947 for use as building material for the local faience factory. Historic preservation authorities learned of this outrage in 1949 and searched the factory grounds in vain for Cybulski's gravestone, which had meanwhile come to be viewed as "important testimony to the presence of Polish culture in Lower Silesia."[106]

Only three Wrocław cemeteries from the period before 1945 have been preserved. The cemetery for Italian soldiers who died in Breslau as German prisoners of war during the First World War still exists on ul. Grabiszyńska. Once part of Municipal Cemetery III, it is located today in the middle of Grabiszyński Park. There are also two large Jewish cemeteries, one on ul. Lotnicza in the western part of the city and the other, the Old Jewish Cemetery on ul. Ślężna in the south. Only the old Jewish cemetery on ul. Gwarna, close to the central train station, which had not been used since 1856 and was already being dismantled in 1937, was removed in 1945 and its grounds later built over. The cemetery on ul. Lotnicza, which had been opened in 1902, was taken over by Wrocław's new Jewish community after 1945. Some of the graves at the Jewish cemetery on ul. Ślężna, the beginnings of which date back to 1856, were severely damaged during the siege; at first this cemetery suffered the fate of the other abandoned cemeteries and fell into ruin. In 1975, however, the entire site, along with its artfully designed gravesites and impressive family memorials, was designated a historic landmark. This cemetery contained the graves of many famous Wrocławians, foremost among them Ferdinand Lassalle, one of the founders of the German labor movement. In the early 1980s, urgently needed repairs were begun and the site was opened to the public in 1988 as the Museum of Cemetery Art.[107] Today, it is one of the most impressive Jewish cemeteries in Central Europe, bearing witness both to Wrocław's Jewish and its German history.

The dissolution of the cemeteries and the removal of German gravestones were only partially the result of de-Germanization policies; in fact, the government's 1948 instructions to dismantle German gravesites were implemented only sporadically in Wrocław as elsewhere. The dissolution of old cemeteries in the 1960s was not so much a propaganda move as a measure to eliminate empty lots and add to the green space within the city limits, though there is no denying that some people might have welcomed the elimination of the remaining German vestiges that came with it. Today residents of Wrocław generally regret that efforts were not made to preserve at least some individual graves. But the earlier years of the postwar period were not a time for such considerations. Polish Wrocławians did not yet think old German gravestones worth preserving; at best they were regarded as meaningless relics, while some considered them embarrassing evidence of a past they did not wish to acknowledge.

One can only speculate what would have happened if the authorities had adhered to the original plan and waited until the 1980s to remove the German cemeteries. It is difficult to imagine that the Polish society of that period, which had been so radically affected by the Solidarity movement, would have simply acceded to the destruction of old cemeteries. Poland's collective memory had changed, and as a result the image of the German enemy so assiduously cultivated by the communist leadership was beginning to erode. There would likely have been open protests, or perhaps the government, which had other troubles to occupy it, would simply have left the cemeteries in peace. If they had survived into the 1990s, the old German cemeteries would probably today enjoy the esteem of most Polish Wrocławians as impressive documents of the city history, and, like the two Jewish cemeteries, they would be listed in city guidebooks as attractions of special interest.

CHAPTER NINE

The Pillars of an Imagined Tradition

HISTORIANS LIKE KAROL MALECZYŃSKI PROBABLY HAD A GREATER IM-
pact on Wrocław's postwar history than all of the city's mayors prior to 1989
taken together. It was their writings, both popular and scholarly, that shaped
the perception of Wrocław as the "age-old Polish" city. Maleczyński's first
lecture on November 15, 1945, was a significant historical event. The ever-
observant Joanna Konopińska noted in her diary that

> without much ceremony, as if his classes had been interrupted only for
> a few days, Professor Maleczyński began his first history lecture at the
> Polish university in Wrocław. He spoke beautifully about Silesia's rela-
> tions with the Motherland, about its cultural, scholarly, and economic
> ties with Polish lands.[1]

Not least due to Maleczyński's efforts, it was only a few years before studies
of local Wrocław history appeared in a scope that eclipsed everything that
had been produced in the previous centuries. Much in these studies was one-
sided and selective. But the residents of Wrocław were not interested in learning *everything* about their city's past. They wanted to know what was Polish
about it, what justified their presence in Wrocław, what might kindle the hope
within them that one day they would feel at home in this place. To this end
local historians would have to work together with Polonists, art historians,
and archaeologists, and they would have to work at two levels. They would
have to conduct scholarly research and at the same time present their findings
and interpretations of the Polish character of Wrocław to a broad public. And
so they did. They wrote articles for daily newspapers, city guidebooks, popular scientific journals, and illustrated books; they made radio broadcasts and
delivered public addresses; they assisted in designing exhibitions, supported
the reconstruction of historic buildings and the erection of monuments,

actively participated in local history associations, and contributed to patriotic celebrations such as the annual Wrocław Days or the major anniversaries commemorating "Wrocław's return to the Motherland." All of these activities served a single goal: to canonize a new, Polonized view of local history and anchor it in the collective memory of Wrocław's Polish residents. The University of Wrocław became the intellectual center for the creation and cultivation of a new tradition. The foreword to an anniversary volume celebrating its twenty-five years as a Polish university stated the matter quite accurately:

> From the very beginning the University of Wrocław was an integrating force, shaping the national, social, and political consciousness of the inhabitants of these ancient Piast regions. It placed its scholarly and educational resources at the service of truly epochal events, and thanks to these efforts the Polish people have become the proprietors of territories saturated with centuries of Polish blood. . . .
>
> Historians from the University of Wrocław entered the long-neglected terrain of research into Silesian history, and we have their diligent scholarship to thank for the vast panorama we now have of Silesia's Polish past, its culture, and the popular movements for national and social liberation that were at home there. . . .
>
> This fortification of Polishness at such a time in history resulted in an unprecedented phenomenon: as a rule, a university is a late fruit in the development of a city; here, however, it was the city that developed under the influence of the university and other institutions of higher learning.[2]

So many of Wrocław's scholars and intellectuals contributed to the creation of a Polish local tradition that it will be possible in this chapter to consider only a few representative individuals. It is not surprising that the most powerful impetus came from historians and Polonists. The historian couple Ewa Maleczyńska (1900–72) and Karol Maleczyński (1897–1968), who both had studied and initially taught in Lwów, played a leading role after 1945 in medieval studies and Silesian history at the University of Wrocław.[3] Karol Maleczyński had already come to Wrocław in May 1945 with the Science and Culture Group, took part in setting up the university, and, beginning in 1946, served as director of its Historical Institute. He was also director of the Wrocław division of the Silesian Institute from 1945 to 1950 and head of the Wrocław Society of Friends of History from 1946 to 1968. Maleczyński's main area of research was the medieval history of Silesia and Wrocław, about which he published scholarly studies as well as shorter, more propagandistic essays aimed at a broad public. His wife Ewa came to Wrocław in 1946 and worked as a schoolteacher before accepting a chair in Polish and general medieval history at the university in 1950. She was also editor of *Sobótka*, a journal of Silesia's regional history, from 1950 to 1970, and she set up the division of Silesian history at the Polish Academy of Sciences in 1953. Like her husband, Ewa specialized in the medieval history of Silesia, but she was the more active of the two in establishing Marxist historiography.

What the Maleczyńskis were for historiography, Tadeusz Mikulski and Stanisław Rospond were for Polish language and literary studies. Mikulski (1909–58) had studied in Krakow and Paris; before the war he worked in Warsaw and later participated in the Warsaw uprising of 1944. In the fall of 1945, he assumed the chair in Polish literature at the University of Wrocław and set about what he saw as his principal task: to familiarize the inhabitants of Wrocław with the city's Polish literary traditions. This he did primarily through essays such as those contained in his book *Spotkania wrocławskie* (Wrocław Encounters), first published in 1950.[4] Until his early death in 1958, he was one of the defining figures of Wrocław's literary life. Together with writer Anna Kowalska, he founded the literary journal *Zeszyty Wrocławski* (Wrocław Notebooks) and was also a co-founder of the local Circle of Friends of Polish Language and Literature.[5]

Linguist Stanisław Rospond (1906–82), who was born near Krakow, taught at the universities of Krakow and Lwów before the war and, like Mikulski, was active in the Polish underground during the German occupation. In the fall of 1945, he was appointed to the chair in Polish language at the University of Wrocław. As a specialist in onomastics, he also headed the Silesian Regional Commission for the Determination of Place Names and was a leading figure at the Silesian Institute and co-founder of the Circle of Friends of Polish Language and Literature. His most important publications include *Polskość Śląska w świetle języka* (Silesia's Polishness from the Perspective of Language, 1948), *Zabytki języka polskiego na Śląsku* (Relics of the Polish Language in Silesia, 1948), and *Dzieje polszczyzny śląskiej* (The History of Silesian Polish, 1959).[6]

These four scholars willingly placed themselves in the service of Poland's national interest and through their scholarly and propagandistic activities laid the groundwork for the emergence of a local Polish identity in Wrocław. Their research on Wrocław's Polish traditions benefited from the fact that the city, despite its extensive war losses, quickly reacquired significant library collections. Many of the books and manuscripts relocated during the war were subsequently discovered in basements, estates, monasteries, and mining tunnels and returned to Wrocław. In addition, the university library received collections of Silesian literature from monasteries and aristocratic estates for its Silesian-Lusatian Cabinet established in 1946.[7] Even more important, however, was the decision by the government to relocate the Ossolineum (Zakład Narodowy im. Ossolińskich) to Wrocław. The Ossolineum dates back to 1817, when Count Józef Maksymilian Ossoliński founded a collection of manuscripts, archival documents, and books in Lwów, which grew into the largest and most valuable library on Polish history and literature aside from the National Library in Warsaw and the Jagiellonian Library in Krakow. Even today the Ossolineum, affiliated with the publishing house of the same name, continues to be one of the most important cultural institutions in Poland. When the Soviet Union declared in 1946 that it was prepared to relinquish at least a part of the collections located in what was now western Ukraine, Warsaw and Krakow—as the two remaining Polish cultural centers—were obvious candidates as future locations for the Ossolineum. The decision for Wrocław reflected the Polish government's intention to make this once German city into a center of Polish culture on an equal footing with Warsaw and Krakow. In 1946–47, more than 200,000 volumes, thousands of manuscripts, and tens of thousands of old prints were transferred to Wrocław, along with several thousand additional manuscripts, documents, old prints, and graphics that had been plundered in Lwów by the Germans and rediscovered in Silesia by Poles after the war. The Ossolineum was set up in the building of the former St. Matthew's *Gymnasium* (secondary school), a Baroque monastery building in the north of the Old Town.

After being moved to the Oder, the Ossolineum attended especially to the Polish culture of Silesia. In order "to awaken the Polish soul among the autochthons" and "to fuel a feeling of connectedness" between the settlers and the new territories, it was deemed important to demonstrate the "eternal

Polishness of these territories."[8] The Ossolineum publishing house focused on publishing works on Silesian Piasts, Polish kings, and important Silesians, as well as excerpts of old Polish literature from the western territories and from other regions of Poland. In addition, short books illuminating "the true Polishness of Silesia" were to complement its program.[9]

Wrocław's museums also put themselves at the service of the new official history, first and foremost the Historical Museum, which opened in the Town Hall in 1948, and the Silesian Museum, founded by a government resolution in 1947 and housed in the old provincial administration building on pl. Powstańców Warszawy. The Silesian Museum took over museum collections located in Wrocław, as well as parts of collections from German museums that had been moved to Silesia, and Polish collections from Lviv and Kiev. Elevated to the rank of a national museum in 1970, it became a powerful institution that exercised control over all state museums in Silesia until 1975 and was particularly committed to propagating the Polishness of Silesia and its cultural significance within Poland. Unique in Wrocław is the Museum of Architecture located in the rebuilt Bernardine Monastery, which was inaugurated in 1965 (it was then called the Museum of Architecture and Reconstruction) by Municipal Conservator Olgierd Czerner. Until the end of communist Poland, this museum focused primarily on medieval Wrocław and the reconstruction of its historic buildings after the Second World War, but paid little attention to the centuries in between.

Private societies and organizations played an equally important role in cultivating a Polish tradition and propagating the official view of history, so much so that when it comes to western territories propaganda we cannot simply speak of a version of history decreed from the top down, at least for the first postwar decades. Two of the earliest such organizations established in Wrocław were the aforementioned Society of Friends of Polish Language and Literature and the Society of Friends of History. Beginning in 1946, the latter organization published *Sobótka*, the quarterly journal on Silesian history.[10] The foreword to the first issue laid out the journal's program:

> We must defend the territory of Silesia against German designs in all fields of endeavor. Not the least of these is the field of culture; we must defend Silesia by proving that we are capable of ruling it not only demographically and economically, but also culturally . . . [and] that we have

precise knowledge of the history of these territories and are shedding light on the details that the occupiers cravenly suppressed. . . .

The objective is . . . above all: to push back as quickly as possible the flood of German literature that has presented a biased view of the German contribution to Silesia's culture and to assiduously recoup from oblivion the true face of the past.[11]

Despite these political objectives *Sobótka* was a scholarly journal, just as the Wrocław Society of Friends of History was a consortium primarily of professional historians. The Society of Friends of Wrocław (TMW) was, however, a different kind of organization.[12] It was founded during the phase of political change after 1956, when local history associations sprang up like mushrooms throughout the western territories. An appeal published in the Wrocław daily newspaper *Słowo Polskie* called for the establishment of an association "to promote within the Wrocław community an emotional attachment to the city and a love for its beautiful traditions, as well as concern for its appearance and for the intensive development of the city in the future."[13] Within a few days, more than 800 Wrocław residents—allegedly ranging from workers to scholars and from young people to retirees—declared their interest in working with the organization.[14] The society began its work in the summer of 1956. An executive committee was elected, with university president and professor Stanisław Kulczyński as president, and journalist Mieczysław Markowski and engineer Eugeniusz Król as vice presidents. The election of Kulczyński, whom Maria Dąbrowska called a dull conformist in her diary in 1948, ensured the society's ties to the political establishment.[15] In the course of the various political phases through which the People's Republic passed, Kulczyński occupied a variety of prestigious government posts, including vice marshal of the Sejm and deputy chairman of the Council of State. The TMW was thus an association begun as a civil initiative that was at the same time a part of Polish officialdom—a dual identity that was possible so long as the rift had not yet developed between Polish society and the Polish state that was later caused by the opposition movements of the 1970s and especially the 1980s.

Reviewing the first ten years of the TMW's existence, Bolesław Siwon identified its most important areas of work as popularizing the city, issuing publications, beautifying Wrocław, promoting the "culture of the Polish history of the city," research, working with young people, and social welfare.[16] Several divisions were established within the organization to honor particular groups: "Wrocław's Polonia" (the Polish minority in Wrocław prior to 1945); the "Wrocław pioneers" of the postwar era; people with the "P" insignia (Poles who had been interned in German camps during the war); and "builders of Wrocław" (those who had made special contributions to Wrocław's development after the war). The group also set up a number of special commissions, including one for street names, which submitted naming proposals to municipal authorities. The society's most visible work included the installation of numerous commemorative plaques recalling "famous Poles who spent time in Wrocław,"[17] organizing the annual Wrocław Days (Dni Wrocławia) celebration, and the publication of the two journals, *Rocznik Wrocławski* (Wrocław Yearbook) and *Kalendarz Wrocławski* (Wrocław Calendar). The TMW also sponsored numerous special publications on local history.

The TMW is probably the most interesting of the organizations involved in cultivating the Polish tradition in Wrocław, if only because it has continued to exist without interruption up to the present day. Through its annual *Kalendarz Wrocławski* and *Rocznik Wrocławski* we can trace attempts to enhance the ties of the people to the city over the years and can explore as well the means that were used to foster civic pride. From the tone and themes of the articles it is possible to detect subtle political changes in the People's Republic and in Wrocław, though the organization remained politically conformist up to the collapse of the People's Republic. Its view of Wrocław's past, for example, never deviated from the state-sanctioned interpretation of history. Into the 1980s, when the People's Republic began to disintegrate and, with it, the official history, it was probably only a very small number of Poles who regarded the TMW's stance as excessively Polonocentric and objected to reducing the city's history to the story of a struggle for Polishness. To this extent, the publications of the TMW are a quite reliable source for evaluating the views that a majority of Wrocław's Poles held about their city and its past.

A NEW COAT OF ARMS

One of the first official acts of Wrocław's Polish municipal government after the war was to reintroduce the old city coat of arms, which had been conferred on Wrocław in 1530 by Bohemian King Ferdinand I and Emperor Karl

Wrocław's coat of arms, conferred on the city by Bohemian king Ferdinand I and Emperor Karl V in 1530 (left), was abandoned twice in the twentieth century—in 1938 (center) and in 1948 (right).

V. It had remained in use until 1938 when the city council, under Nazi direction, replaced it with a new coat of arms.[18] The original heraldic shield testified to the city's legal status at the time of its conferral. It was parted quarterly with a central inescutcheon. On the four quarters there were—in heraldic rank—the Bohemian lion, symbol of the liege lord; the eagle of the Silesian Piasts, a symbol of the duchy of Wrocław; the initial "W" of the Latin city name Wratislavia (which can be traced back to the legendary Bohemian city founder); and the patron saint of the Town Hall chapel, Saint John the Evangelist, whose facial features appear here so feminine that even today it is unclear whether this image was intended simultaneously to represent Saint Dorothy. However, since Saint Dorothy is also a patron saint of the Town Hall chapel, where her relic was located until 1945, doubts about the identity of the fourth heraldic field are politically insignificant. The head of John the Baptist, patron saint of the city as well as of Wrocław's cathedral, was at the center of the coat of arms.

In the spirit of the Third Reich, the symbols of the Bohemian liege lord, the Slavic city name, the city council, and the bishopric were removed in 1938. Only the Silesian eagle remained. A completely new coat of arms was designed with only two fields: the upper half bore an eagle, the lower half the Iron Cross conferred on the city by the Prussian king in 1813. This new coat of arms was German-national and contained neither religious elements nor, significantly, any reference to the tradition of municipal self-government. The reintroduction of Wrocław's traditional coat of arms in 1945 by the Polish municipal government was, however, only a provisional measure. Just as this traditional coat of arms had not appeared German enough to the city's

German leaders in 1938, Polish municipal authorities did not regard it as Polish enough after 1945. Although the old coat of arms was filled with Christian references and recalled Wrocław's Slavic history, it had nonetheless been conferred by German rulers in 1530 and referred to the city council, which was regarded as an instrument of the ruling German patricians. The Bohemian lion was also anathema to Polish leaders; Czechs were not viewed favorably in Wrocław at the time because they had raised territorial claims to Kłodzko County in Lower Silesia.

Wrocław's Polish municipal government first considered modifying the traditional coat of arms. The Polish eagle would take the position formerly held by the Bohemian lion, and the lion would move to the lower left field, a lesser position in heraldic ranking. Saint John the Evangelist—and thus all reference to the city council—would be removed altogether. However, historians objected to this proposal because it was neither supported by historical sources nor did it comply with the basic rules of heraldry. Karol Maleczyński was commissioned to work out a historically viable proposal. He immediately began searching for heraldic symbols that had been used in Wrocław during the Piast era, long before the city had been officially conferred a coat of arms.[19] In the course of his investigations, Maleczyński found diverse Piast eagles as well as the figure of Saint John the Baptist, which had been used on various seals since the thirteenth century. Here he was compelled to acknowledge nolens volens that the eagle symbolizing ducal power had been gradually pushed aside in favor of John the Baptist, which the city council had preferred. For Maleczyński, this did not demonstrate the growing confidence of the city and the shrinking power of the dukes, but instead stood for the suppression of Polishness in Wrocław. In addition, he doubted that the "W" in the coat of arms of 1530 represented exclusively the initial of the Slavic city name. It might also be connected to Johannes Wittel, a ducal chancellor in the fourteenth century.

Maleczyński's most important discovery, however, was that of the oldest known seal of the city of Wrocław, dating from 1262. This seal bore an eagle, although it could no longer be determined whether the figure was a double-headed eagle or two eagle halves set together. Since a double-headed eagle would have referred to the imperial power of the Holy Roman Empire, the latter alternative was preferred. Opinions diverged, however, as to what eagle could have been depicted aside from that of the Silesian Piasts. Maleczyński did not want to rule out at least the possibility that it could also have been a Polish eagle—the ambiguity of the seal and the absence of other sources proved advantageous for the political purpose of the heraldic investigations. Maleczyński wrote in 1946:

> The most urgent task both for our research and for the administration of the city should now be choosing a new coat of arms for the city; or rather, reestablishing a connection with the noble tradition, dating back to the good, Polish times, that links Silesia and Wrocław to the rest of Poland, interweaving in harmonious unity the past and present, the Polishness of the thirteenth century with that of today.[20]

In a bold interpretation of the iconographic original of 1262, a new coat of arms for Wrocław was designed and approved in 1948.[21] It was composed of two eagle halves: on the right side the Polish white eagle on a red background, on the left the Silesian-Piast black eagle on a yellow background. The parallels between the coats of arms designed in 1938 and in 1948 are striking. Both reduced the number of heraldic fields from five to two and both were devoid of religious elements as well as any references to municipal self-government. Both were expressions of an age that valued unambiguous nationalism above all else and denied the historical complexity of Wrocław's past. The coat of arms of 1948 was used for four decades, until it was replaced yet again in 1990, the third change in the twentieth century, and one that signaled the dawn of a new era.

THE POWER OF OLD MONUMENTS AND THE PLACELESSNESS OF NEW ONES

Yuri M. Lotman and Boris Uspensky have studied the enduring quality of holy sites in old Russia. Following the Christianization of the country new churches were usually built on ground previously occupied by pagan temples. In this way sacred places survived the break in tradition brought on by the introduction of Christianity; the new culture re-codified the site, but it retained its basic function.[22] The longevity of sacred locations is also a feature of the secular religion of nationalism, though here the holy sites are national monuments.[23] In Wrocław, for example, German monuments removed after 1945 were in most cases replaced by Polish monuments. The regime may have

In April 1956, the Aleksander Fredro monument, perhaps the most popular of Wrocław's monuments today, arrived in the city. Dedicated to the famous Polish poet, it had originally been erected in Lwów, when that city was the predominantly Polish-speaking capital of the Austrian province of Galicia. After Lwów became the Soviet-Ukrainian city of Lviv (Russian: Lvov) in 1945, Soviet authorities agreed to transfer the monument to Poland. It found a new home in front of Wrocław's town hall, only a few steps from the spot where the equestrian statue of Prussian king Friedrich Wilhelm III had stood until 1945. Courtesy of the Ossolineum (Adam Czelny).

changed, but the monument site, coded as a place of national commemoration, survived to play the same role for a new audience.[24]

The most famous monument in contemporary Wrocław, the sculpture of poet-dramatist Aleksander Fredro, stood originally in Lwów. In 1956, it was moved to Wrocław and erected at the very site on the Rynek where, until 1945, the equestrian statue of the Prussian king Friedrich Wilhelm III had been located. On pl. Kościuszki, at precisely the site where the sarcophagus of General Field Marshal von Tauentzien once stood, there has since 1946 been a monument to those who fought in Poland's armed struggles for independence in 1791, 1794, 1830–31, 1846, 1863–64, 1905, 1914–18, and 1939–45. The monument to General Field Marshal Helmuth von Moltke on ul. Pretficza, located in front of a German army office building that was taken over by the Polish army after 1945, was simply transformed into the Victory Memorial: The bronze sculpture of Moltke was removed in 1948 and a stone statue

While the monument to Prussian general Helmut von Moltke on ul. B. Pretficza (left) was removed after the war, the pedestal remained. Since 1948, it has supported a statue commemorating the "Victory of the Polish Soldier." The original inscription on the pedestal was covered with a brass plaque, bearing a new dedication (right). Used by permission of the publisher of *Encyklopedia Wrocławia* (Wrocław: Wyd. Dolnośląskie, 2006) and courtesy of the author.

of a Polish soldier holding a flag and treading on a swastika was put in its place on the old granite pedestal. The inscription on the base "Moltke 1800–1891" was covered over with a bronze plaque bearing the new dedication, "To the Soldier of the Reborn Polish Army in Gratitude from the Society of Lower Silesia."

Until 1945 an impressive series of monuments stood in the parks along the eastern perimeter of the Old Town from Podwale north to the Oder promenade vis-à-vis Cathedral Island. They honored, among others, Carl von Clausewitz, the theologian and philosopher Friedrich Schleiermacher, Wrocław botanist Heinrich Göppert, the advocate of national sports Friedrich Roedelius, Johann Friedrich Knorr, and Karl von Holtei; and there was as well a Neo-Gothic memorial on the Oder promenade commemorating the German War of Unification of 1870–71. When these German monuments were taken down after the war, a plethora of new Polish monuments carried on the tradition of the sites.

The cornerstone for the national re-dedication of this terrain was laid in the late 1950s. This occurred not through the erection of a monument per se, but rather with the decision by the government to erect a building on ul. Purkyniego to re-exhibit the Racławice Panorama. The panorama, a grandiose painting 400 feet long and 50 feet high depicted the victorious battle of Polish troops led by national hero Tadeusz Kościuszko over the Russian army at Racławice on April 4, 1794. It was unveiled in Lwów on the centennial of the battle. The painting was moved to Wrocław in 1946 together with the collections of the Ossolineum, an event that marked only the beginning of the panorama's astounding postwar story.[25]

For the People's Republic of Poland the painting was politically explosive for more than one reason. Not only did it come from a once-Polish city now annexed by the Soviet Union, but it also portrayed a Polish uprising against Russian occupation. As if that were not enough, the Polish soldiers in the painting are depicted as noble and courageous fighters prepared to die for Poland's freedom. The Russian units, by contrast, are an undisciplined horde pictured in chaotic retreat. There was no place for such an image in Soviet-dominated Eastern Europe. In the socialist camp, the valiant and victorious Soviet army was ever to be honored and celebrated as a liberator from foreign occupation.

Generous public donations soon provided the means for restoring the panorama, and the construction of a new rotunda began in 1966. The actual re-exhibition of the painting was, however, postponed indefinitely in consideration of Soviet sensibilities and the Polish-Soviet friendship promoted by Poland's communist party. The frame of the rotunda remained empty, which, ironically, transformed it into a veritable memorial to Poland's lost independence. The situation changed with the rise of a powerful opposition movement in Poland and the founding of the Solidarność trade union in 1980. The communist government, under increasing political pressure from its own people, began to play the nationalist card and overcame its reluctance to re-exhibit the Racławice Panorama. Behind-the-scenes wrangling took place over possession of the panorama, as Warsaw and Krakow also asserted claims to this national icon. In 1980, against the backdrop of an impressive public campaign mounted by Wrocław, the government chose the Silesian capital as the painting's permanent location. When the rotunda with the restored panorama opened in 1985, it immediately became a national pilgrimage site of the highest caliber. It is today a symbol of the Polish aspiration for freedom, one of Wrocław's greatest attractions and the pride of its residents.

The power of sites once consecrated is also evident wherever a gap has *not* been filled following the removal of a German monument. As soon as the Kaiser Wilhelm memorial on ul. Świdnicka was taken down in 1945, the idea of erecting a major Polish memorial in its place soon arose. The implementation of this idea proved difficult, however, in part because of the significance of the German monument. Its replacement would have to be a Polish monument as grand in form and profound in meaning as the creator of the German Empire on horseback. In the 1960s the municipal authorities filled the vacancy, provisionally, with a large bed of red and white flowers, the Polish national colors, arranged to depict the city's new coat of arms. But, as the developments described in the final chapter of this book will show, the specter of the German national monument lingered in the space from which it had been banished. The horror vacui aroused by the removal of Kaiser Wilhelm could ultimately be healed only by erecting a monumental Polish national memorial on the site.

Most of the monuments erected in Wrocław during the communist years served to promote the Polish national cult. In 1967 eighteen "monuments to battle and martyrdom" could be identified within the city limits,[26] which— so long as reminders of Soviet occupation and the victims of Stalinism were taboo—were understood to be memorials to soldiers killed in the Second World War and to the victims of the German occupation. These were not always elaborate monuments, but often simple memorial stones or obelisks set up in cemeteries. The only monument in Wrocław dedicated explicitly to the "return of the western territories to the motherland" is an inscribed stone slab that is easily overlooked at the northern end of Pokój Bridge (Bridge of Peace), which was dedicated on the anniversary of the end of the war on May 8, 1966. The more than sixteen-foot-high stone sculpture of Pope John XXIII, however, belongs in the same political context. Ceremoniously unveiled on the grounds of the former Piast castle in 1968, it depicts the Pope in the pose of the priest giving his blessing, but it is not a religious monument. It was

The Emperor Wilhelm I monument on Schweidnitzer Strasse (ul. Świdnicka) was the most imposing of the city's national monuments (top, opposite page). After 1945, Polish authorities held a patriotic ceremony to topple the equestrian statue, followed by the removal of the monument's remaining structure. The memory of the liquidated monument remained, however, and held sway over the place like a ghost. In the 1960s, local authorities tried to combat the *horror vacui* by means of a flowerbed in the shape and colors of the city's Polish coat of arms (bottom, opposite page). In 2007, the massive equestrian statue of Bolesław Chrobry was unveiled, financed by private donations and public funds (above). Chrobry was the Polish king who in the tenth century extended the western border of his country to the Oder (Odra) River and founded a Polish bishopric in Wrocław. Courtesy of Via Nova; the publisher of Tomasz Olszewski's *Moje miasto* (Wrocław: Ossolineum, 1972); and the author.

erected because Pope John XXIII had spoken during an audience with Polish bishops on October 8, 1962, of the city of "Wrocław in the Western territories recovered after centuries."[27] In doing so he not only anticipated the Vatican's official recognition of the Oder-Neisse line, but also simultaneously gave his blessings to western territories propaganda regarding Poland's "return to the Oder."

One certainly might have expected the erection of a monumental memorial in Wrocław commemorating the return of the western territories. Such a project was in fact explored exhaustively during preparations for the millennial celebration of Poland in 1966.[28] In collaboration with the Society of Polish Architects and the Association of Polish Sculptors, the national committee of the Front of National Unity sponsored a competition for a "monument for the return to the motherland," which was held in Wrocław in March 1966. The northern bank of the Oder between Grunwaldzki and Pokój Bridges had been chosen as the location of the future monument. There, it was felt, the monument would appear to greatest advantage and could serve as a potential link between the historic and newer districts of the city—that is, between the historic medieval buildings on Cathedral Island and the modern university district. Moreover, the Oder bank, the "bonding element for the western voivodeships" and a symbolic location in the language of western territories propaganda, seemed tailor-made for a monument commemorating the Recovered Territories.[29]

The jury selected one first-place, one second-place, and two third-place winners from the 189 entries in the competition. First place was awarded to Krakow artists Mirosław Dzikiewicz and Józef Sękowski for their design "The Stakes of Chrobry" (Słupy Chrobrego). In keeping with the legend that Bolesław Chrobry, the first king of Poland, had marked the borders of his territory with stakes, the design called for four monumental upright posts to be erected on the banks of the Oder.[30] The sponsors of the competition, however, decided to commission the second-place winners, Alicia and Hieronim Litowski, to rework this design. Their decision was said to be based primarily on urban development considerations and on the expectation that the chosen monument would create "an excellent setting for celebrations and festivities on the banks of the Oder."[31]

In March 1968 the Litowskis announced that the central focus of their revised design would be a symbolic expression of the "eternal Polishness" of the western territories and the creation of a "stately and austere" site of "monumentality." At the center of the memorial complex, which would include numerous sculptures, they envisioned a massive mound of earth rising over thirty feet above the surface of the bridge roadways, crowned with two stylized border standards bearing white eagles on a red background. The earthen hill was supposed to be accessible from the north via a path that would rise gently to the top of the hill. The steps along this path were to

In 1962, at a time when Poland was fighting for international recognition of its western border, Pope John XXIII spoke during an audience with Polish bishops of "Wrocław in the western territories recovered after centuries." The Polish government considered the Pope's statement important enough that it sponsored a John XXIII monument on the grounds of Wrocław's former Piast castle. This is presumably the only monument a communist regime has ever erected to honor a pope. The picture shows the unveiling ceremony that took place on June 5, 1968. Courtesy of the Ossolineum (Tadeusz Drankowski).

be inscribed with pivotal dates and the names of significant places in the thousand-year-long battle for the Polishness of the western territories, and at the end there was to be an inscription of the well-known propaganda slogan "BYLIŚMY–JESTEŚMY–BĘDZIEMY" (We were here, we are here, we will be here).[32]

After years of discussion, the monument was never built. Following West Germany's recognition of the Oder-Neisse line in 1970, the government in Warsaw was apparently no longer prepared to furnish the necessary funds for the project, which required 1,800 short tons of a special white concrete imported from France. Also, in November 1969, leading Wrocław architects and artists had sharply criticized the design and called for a completely new competition.[33] It is entirely possible that this was an attempt by critics to undermine the entire project. At a time when ambitious projects in the mode of architectural modernism were being designed and implemented and a modern university campus in Wrocław was planned in the immediate vicinity of the terrain earmarked for the monument, a memorial in this form would have seemed like an aesthetic relapse into Stalinism.

It is telling that most of the monuments erected in Wrocław after 1945 were dedicated to historical figures or events that bore no direct relation to the city and could just as well have been built anywhere else in Poland. There were isolated exceptions—the memorial to Wrocław Pioneers on ul. Jedności Narodowej, for example, and the monument for Bolesław Drobner as patron of Elementary School No. 18 on ul. Poznańska. The vast majority of Wrocław's postwar monuments, however, were rootless. This absence of local ties distinguished them from those erected prior to 1945. Although there were monuments with no special local significance even in the prewar era, such as those for Emperor Wilhelm I, Bismarck, or Schiller, these were exceptions, as even the majority of national monuments from this period had some relation to the city. Friedrich the Great, for instance, whose equestrian statue was installed on the Ring (Rynek) in the mid-nineteenth century, not only conquered Breslau in 1741, but also resided in the city on numerous occasions in subsequent years. Friedrich Wilhelm III, and Prussian generals Tauentzien and Blücher represented not only Prussian-German national history, but local history as well, and the sponsors of their monuments wanted to illuminate precisely this connection between the history of the city and the history of the German nation.

After 1945 it proved difficult to find known figures of Polish national history who had ties to Wrocław. Occasionally desperate attempts were made to contrive such a connection. For example, in his guidebook on monuments Zygmunt Antkowiak wrote of the Aleksander Fredro monument that the Galician writer was by no means a stranger to the region: During the Napoleonic Wars he spent several days in Lower Silesia as a Polish captain, although he did not actually visit Wrocław. In 1855 he briefly considered moving from Galicia to Lower Silesia, and in 1856 he almost certainly traveled through Wrocław at some point.[34] That said, it is hardly surprising that Antkowiak styled the poet Juliusz Słowacki, who spent a few weeks of his life in Wrocław, as a virtual resident of the city.[35]

Most of the monuments erected in Wrocław after the war thus became monuments to displacement and uprootedness, albeit unintentionally. As long as the Polish settlers' own relationship with the location was brief and tenuous, their collective memories had to be enriched with "imports" from their former homeland such as might create common points of identification—if not *with* Wrocław then at least *in* Wrocław. Nevertheless, attempts were also made to mitigate the placelessness of the larger monuments by means of a plethora of commemorative plaques that were affixed to local buildings over the years in order to establish relationships of some kind between these locations and Polish history and culture. In late 1959 the board of the Society for the Development of the Western Territories even provided instructions on how to accomplish this:

> External symbols are to be used to commemorate all those great Poles who were born or worked in the Western Territories, as well as all-important events that testify to the Polishness of the region. . . . For example: the founding of a city by this or that Polish or Slavic prince; an edict issued in Polish in past centuries; events in the history of the Polish people's struggle against Germanization, etc.
>
> We should not neglect commemorating other events of local or regional history, which—though they are of no use in documenting the Polishness of the region—may contribute to the deepening of local, regional, and national patriotism.[36]

The instructions also included a list of twenty-five historic figures who might be honored—including Florian Stanisław Ceynowa (1817–1849), who had researched the Kashubians; Władysław Nehring (1830–1909), historian [*sic*] and president of the University of Wrocław; and Martin Opitz (1597–1639), the German poet who was also court historiographer to the Polish King Władysław IV. The Society of Friends of Wrocław regarded the installation of commemorative plaques as one of its most important activities, which it carried out in accord with the aforementioned instructions. A plaque on the Old Stock Exchange building at pl. Solny reads in Polish:

> Wincenty Pol, author of *Song of Our Land,* visited pl. Solny in August 1847.
> The Society of Friends of Wrocław
> April 20, 1957, on the 150th anniversary of Wincenty Pol's birth

At the corner of ul. Fredry and pl. Kościuszki, the former site of the house in which Juliusz Słowacki resided during his tenure in Wrocław, a plaque was mounted with the inscription:

> Wrocław, June 2, 1848: *I'm in Wrocław, wishing that Sally (if only she could) would come here . . .* Juliusz Słowacki
> On the sesquicentennial of the poet
> The Society of Friends of Wrocław, May 9, 1959

The fact that this plaque was not concerned solely with the Polish poet is evident from the date of its unveiling, which occurred not on the day of the author's birth or death, but instead on the anniversary of the Wehrmacht's capitulation to the Red Army in Berlin-Karlshorst, which was also the day the advance guard (grupa operacyjna) of the Polish administration arrived in Wrocław.

A plaque was placed on the city theater stating that Chopin had once performed there; a plaque on the main building of the university commemorates the Polish students who participated in the January Uprising of 1863; and at the Church of the Holy Cross a plaque was mounted in honor of Julian Ursyn Niemcewicz, citing his own words about having heard a Polish sermon during his visit there on June 8, 1821. There were of course also plaques on a number of buildings commemorating the pioneers of the postwar period who had set up their first offices there. It is doubtful that these plaques had any real effect. Presumably some people were appreciative of the references.

To others, however, the fact that a brief visit by a Polish author or composer was worthy of a commemorative plaque must have underscored the shortage of genuine Polish reference points in the history of Wrocław.

Finally it is important to point out the special significance of monuments such as the Fredro monument, the Racławice Panorama, and the Memorial to the Victims of Fascism, unveiled at Pl. Grunwaldzki in 1964, that honored murdered Lwów professors and their families. These are monuments that refer to a specific place—but the history that they implicitly commemorate is not that of Wrocław but of Lwów. This circumstance relates to the widespread view in Poland that Wrocław served as a substitute for Lwów, and that some of the traditions of the lost Polish metropolis, which became the Soviet-Ukrainian city of Lviv in 1945, were transferred to and survived in the Polish city of Wrocław. However, commemorating the loss of eastern Poland, which for many Wrocław residents represented the major trauma of their lives, was politically explosive. It challenged the taboo on discussion of Soviet annexation policies toward Poland and the hostile character of Polish-Soviet relations in the twentieth century. As long as Poland remained a part of the political camp dominated by the Soviet Union, Poland's lost eastern territories and the victims of Soviet deportations and executions in eastern Poland could not be publicly mourned. After the war neither restaurants nor cafes in Wrocław could be named after locations in the former eastern Polish territories, nor was it permitted to name central streets or squares after Lwów or Wilno.[37] In contrast to West Germany, where expellees and their organizations were encouraged and indeed funded to indulge in recollections of their lost homeland, and where streets were named as a matter of course after locations in the lost territories, Polish expellees did not have the option of public commemoration. Their fate was similar to that of deportees in East Germany, who lost not only their homeland but also the right to recall this loss in public.

The Polish government did not go quite this far. It permitted commemoration of the lost territories in the East, if only in the form of a disguised, though nonetheless semi-public ritual. The Fredro monument was not merely a memorial to an author, but also a memorial to the expulsion of the Poles from the East. After all, the monument had followed the same path many Polish deportees had taken from Lwów to Wrocław. It was apparently one of the unwritten rules of this hidden ritual that the memorial inscription identified only the author's name but—as long as the People's Republic of Poland existed—no reference was made to the location whence the monument had come. The large inscription on the memorial for the murdered Lwów professors—"Our Fate Is a Warning"—was also unspecific and did not mention the name of the city. The exhibition of the Racławice Panorama, in contrast, did make the origin of the painting public. However, this monument was reopened only four years before the end of the People's Republic, by which time it belonged within the context of the great political upheaval of 1989.

The Noisy Silence of Local Historiography

Thanks to the work of the Society of Friends of Wrocław (TMW), the Ossolineum, and the university, there was no dearth of publications on the local history of Wrocław. The major anniversary celebrations of the "Return to the Motherland" in 1960, 1965, 1970, and 1985 served as occasions for new books on local history, new city guidebooks, and new editions of pioneer memoirs. The periodicals *Rocznik Wrocławski* and *Kalendarz Wrocławski*, which were published by the TMW and sought to strengthen civic pride in Wrocław, also played an important part in this promotion of all things local. They offered a colorful mix of articles about current urban development projects, the Polish history of the city, local cultural events, and deserving Wrocław residents. They thus provided an informative and kaleidoscopic view of Wrocław as a Polish city and were testimony to its search for tradition and its pride in its postwar accomplishments. *Kalendarz Wrocławski*, which was not only so titled but also actually contained an annual calendar, introduced a novelty in 1973. The calendar section identified significant events of Polish city history on as many days as possible, including the birthdays or death-days of important figures; the opening of significant Wrocław institutions, exhibitions, and celebrations; as well as dates in national history and significant dates in the life of Wrocław's Polish minority prior to 1945. The 1984 edition listed the following events for June:[38]

6/4/1764   Prussian Office for Combating the Polish Language established in Wrocław and Lower Silesia.

6/11/1868   Social Circle of Wrocław University Graduates of Polish
Heritage founded; disbanded by Prussian authorities on June 1,
1886.

6/10/1939   Anti-Polish rally at the main university auditorium; several days later (June 20, 1939) Wrocław's Polish students expelled
from the university.

6/10/1946   Scientific Society of Wrocław established.

6/30/1946   Referendum to incorporate the Recovered Territories
into the Motherland approved by the Polish community.

6/1/1949   Day of the Children celebrated in the People's Republic
for the first time.

6/5/1968   The Monument to Pope John XXIII (1881–1963)—the
"Pope of Peace," who recognized Poland's rights to the Western
Territories as "recovered after centuries"—unveiled on Cathedral
Island in Wrocław.

6/27/1978   The first Pole in outer space. The international team of
the Soyuz 30 spaceship included Soviet flight commander pilot-
cosmonaut Pyotr Klimuk and cosmonaut Mirosław Hermaszewski,
a Pole from Wrocław.

6/27/1979   Ramesh Chandra, chair of the World Peace Council,
named an honorary citizen of Wrocław.

6/21/1983   Pope John Paul II visited Wrocław.

Tourist guidebooks are one of the most effective means of establishing and popularizing the image of a place. They steer the attention of tourists by show-ing them "what ought to be seen" and by excluding what their authors regard as irrelevant.[39] A large number of Wrocław city guides were published soon after the end of the war. They were fundamental for the image that the new Polish inhabitants formed of their city, in which they were initially as foreign as any tourist. The authors of such guidebooks were confronted with a par-ticularly difficult task. Because their subject matter was predetermined in the form of existing buildings, they could not limit themselves to those particular aspects that happened to fit the conception of Wrocław as a Polish city by, for example, skipping over buildings that they would have preferred to leave unmentioned. Readers would have noticed the omission. Thus the authors had to be well versed in the art of inconspicuous silence; they had to direct readers around the city, expounding at great length on its Polish life without touching on its German past. This was equivalent to an obstacle course through the city's history in which any contact with non-Polish facts had to be avoided, especially if these concerned positive or productive aspects of German city history, such as patronage of the arts by German patrician families, the achievements of the Wrocław bourgeoisie, or the rapid urban development of the nineteenth century.

Andrzej Jochelson, an official in the Wrocław municipal administration and a dedicated lay historian, wrote the first Wrocław city guidebook in Polish after the war.[40] Published in 1946, the book is an invaluable source for scholars, for Jochelson was not yet adept at skirting German history, a skill that would be finely honed by later writers. For example, he briefly mentioned the remains of the Emperor Wilhelm Monument on ul. Świdnicka,[41] and he noted that Tauentzien's sarcophagus had previously been located at the site of the current Memorial to the Fighters for Poland's Independence.[42] He even informed readers that St. John the Evangelist pictured on the city's coat of arms should be considered the patron saint of the German population of the city.[43] Such references, which could have induced reflection on Wrocław's German history and the rupture of 1945, were rare in later guidebooks. When these works mentioned Germans at all it was usually in the context of such outrages as attacks on Silesia by armies of "German" knights, the suppression of the city's Polish population by German patricians and later by Prussian authorities, the economic decline of the city under the Hohenzollerns, the wanton destruction of Wrocław by German troops during the siege in 1945, and so on. Otherwise the pages of these city guidebooks were filled with detailed reports about the Piasts and exegeses on Polish dynastic history in the Middle Ages, the lives of Poles in Wrocław, the flourishing Polish culture in the city, and the struggle of the local Polish population against Germanization policies.

Like later guidebooks, however, Jochelson did give heavy play to the city's medieval period. In his sixteen-page overview of Wrocław history, ten pages were dedicated to the years before 1335, four to the Bohemian-Habsburg era, but only two to the period between 1741 and 1945, and those two focused on the Napoleonic Wars and a list of famous Poles who had visited Wrocław since 1741. Jochelson mentioned neither Prussian Germanization policies nor the economic decline under Prussian rule. By treating the growth of the city in the nineteenth century in only a single sentence, however, he employed a technique typical of later Wrocław guidebooks: that of mentioning something and simultaneously obfuscating it: "Wrocław grew significantly in the nineteenth century as a result of industrialization, but not to the same extent as other cities of similar size in western Germany or in Poland."[44] Jochelson's commentary on historic buildings was essentially a guide to the churches, which again and again noted Polish architectural traits and made other references to things Polish. Of buildings other than churches, only the town hall was allotted significant space. The Baroque burgher houses on the Rynek were touched upon only in passing, as was the main building of the university. Buildings of the nineteenth and twentieth centuries were hardly mentioned at all.

Przewodnik po zabytkach Wrocławia (Guidebook to Wrocław's Historic Buildings)[45] was published in 1957. This book presented the city's history and its historic buildings in a manner that would not change fundamentally until the end of the People's Republic. The caption of the first illustration, depicting a motorcade driving through the demolished city, is typical: "1945: We're returning to our land."[46] Many of the photographs in the book contrast the devastation of the city in 1945 with the successes of the subsequent reconstruction. The first section, written by Mieczysław Nowak, chair of the Municipal National Council, also focuses primarily on destruction and rebuilding. While this emphasis on the accomplishments of the reconstruction is in many respects justified, it becomes ideological when 1945 Wrocław is depicted as a completely demolished city, as a tabula rasa devoid of any material value. Kazimierz Ślązak began the second section, which provided an overview of city history, by pointing out that the oldest historical sources tell of several Slavic tribes inhabiting Silesia, and he went on to inform the reader that the region in which the Polish city of Wrocław arose had been Slavic since time immemorial. After centuries of occupation, Ślązak concluded, a "correction of historical errors and injustices" has occurred and Wrocław is now "an entirely Polish city again."[47]

The third section of the book, written by Gwidon Król, was dedicated to historic buildings. The central focus of this chapter was on churches and monasteries, although commentaries were also included on the town hall, the armory, individual medieval residential houses, and the Ossolineum. Regarding the university, Król wrote more about the no longer extant Piast castle than about the existing university building, which had been built on the castle grounds in the eighteenth century. Readers were informed that the completion of the Baroque building had been interrupted by the Prussian invasion and that subsequently Friedrich II, "the Prussian King known for his brutality," placed "barracks, storehouses, and a prison" in the venerable building.[48] Król did not mention the fact that when the Prussian government merged the university Viadrina from Frankfurt (Oder) with the Jesuit Academy in Wrocław in 1811, it created the basis for a modern university and turned Wrocław into one of the leading academic centers of Central Europe. The city's Jewish history was also ignored; in Król's discussion of the religious buildings of the Old Town, the only one omitted is the neoclassical White Stork Synagogue. The book closes with the assertion that Wrocław's historic buildings testify to the high level of Polish culture and confirm that the region belongs to the Polish motherland.[49]

Przewodnik po Wrocławiu (Guidebook to Wrocław),[50] edited by the TMW and published in 1960, was similar in design. It too was divided into three chapters: a political introduction by Bolesław Iwaszkiewicz, who painted an optimistic future for a vibrantly developing city and predicted that Wrocław's population in the 1970s would surpass that of 1939; an outline of Wrocław history by Roman Heck, which reproduced the topoi of the official view of city history; and, finally, a guide to the city. This city guide was more detailed than preceding books and was not limited to medieval and Baroque historic buildings; it included newer buildings, as well as information about the important institutions of the city. Nevertheless, owing to avoidance of any reference to the German past, readers learned little more about Wrocław's history than they had in earlier books of this kind.

To illustrate this point: The only information offered about the central train station in Wrocław was that it had been built in the nineteenth century in English Gothic style. There was neither mention of its architect nor any reference to its significance as a rail hub connecting Berlin and Vienna.[51] Readers were informed of the activities of the Pałacyk (Little Palace) student club on ul. Kościuszki 34 but not about the history of the Schaffgotsch Palace, which housed the club.[52] The guide referred to the many historic buildings on the Rynek but included not a word about the patricians who had built the magnificent residences there.[53] Readers were told only that the Hatzfeldt Palace had been built in the eighteenth century by "Silesian architect" Carl G. Langhans, the architect of the Brandenburg Gate.[54] Information about the building containing the Silesian Museum was limited to the fact that it had been built in the late nineteenth century in sixteenth-century style; there was no mention that the Silesian provincial government had been located there under Prussian rule. The author apparently did not dare to point out that the voivodeship building had been constructed during the Third Reich to provide an imposing headquarters for the provincial administration; instead he stated only that the edifice contained many rooms and that it was easy to get lost in its labyrinthine corridors.[55] The description of the Hala Ludowa (People's Hall), originally called Centennial Hall, omitted any reference to the architect, the building's outstanding significance in architectural and structural terms, or the reason it was built:

> On the left side of the street we see the characteristic silhouette of the Hala Ludowa. The hall long sought its ultimate purpose: athletic and artistic events, congresses, rallies, and meetings all took place in it— but its deficits continued to trouble the city administration. In 1957, Hala Ludowa became the home of Giant Cinema, which, with its 4,800 seats, is the largest movie theater in Poland. By February 1960, it had hosted more than two million moviegoers.[56]

Indeed, Wrocław's city guidebooks seemed to spend more time evading the city's history than actually presenting it. Later guidebooks, such as Wanda Roszkowska's 1970 *Wrocław: Przewodnik po dawnym i współczesnym mieście* (Wrocław: Guidebook to the City Then and Now),[57] differed from their predecessors only in that their authors had become even more adept at navigating the obstacle course. They did divulge more about the city's past, but included nothing that would contradict the official view of Wrocław as the age-old Polish city. Anyone who was aware of such omissions would have picked up with interest a short book published in the 1970s with the promising title *Wrocław, jakiego nie znamy* (The Wrocław We've Never Known).[58] However, the introductory statement alone, which declared that the book was dedicated to "Polish folk culture," immediately shattered hopes of learning anything new; this would be nothing more than a rehearsal of what was already known. And, in fact, the author reported only about Poles in Wrocław and made no attempt to examine any era of the city's history that was less than two hundred years old.

In 1989, the year the People's Republic collapsed, Bogdan Zakrzewski published his book *Przechadzki po dziewiętnastowiecznym Wrocławiu* (Walks through Nineteenth-Century Wrocław).[59] It concerned the epoch in which the modern metropolis emerged and which had been ignored after 1945 because it would have been impossible to cover without referring to Prussia and the German Empire. Nevertheless, anyone who had hoped that this book would finally open the door to the suppressed history of nineteenth-century Wrocław was sorely disappointed, for it provided no more than yet another tour through "the Polish-speaking world of Wrocław." The book's audacity lay rather in focusing on the history of Wrocław's Polishness in an era when Polishness played practically no role in the city. It would seem that the author himself was aware of this as chapter 1 begins with a denial:

> The Polishness of nineteenth-century Wrocław was not a vestigial phenomenon, but something that lived in the natural rhythm of the everyday life of the city, embedded in the very foundations of society; it served merchants, craftsmen, and manufacturers (who were tied to the Polish territories through trade); it was omnipresent in the conversation of Polish students, it reinforced the faith of fathers in churches, and was cultivated in the various Polish organizations.[60]

Over the course of time, city guidebooks probably got better and better at convincing people that Wrocław's history was essentially Polish—in part as a result of the growing number of scholarly studies on Polish Wrocław from which these guidebooks could draw. Broad stretches of the city's history would remain long unknown to its residents and visitors alike.

What is truly astounding about this, however, is that even during communist times a different perspective was possible. This is demonstrated by a history of the city published in 1978 under the editorship of art historian Zygmunt Świechowski.[61] This highly unusual book provided a richly illustrated account of historical and art-historical developments in Wrocław that attempted to do justice to all epochs, even that of Prussian rule. Although the publication was not entirely free of the standard obfuscations, there were worlds separating it from standard depictions in the People's Republic. This book allowed a broader readership to gain a complete picture of local history for the first time and made clear that it was impossible to do justice to the city's past solely from the perspective of Polish national history. Given that such a book was published quite some time before the end of the People's Republic, the question should be posed again as to how much popular local historiography suffered from government censorship and how much self-censorship was at play.

THE RITUAL OF COMMEMORATION

Regular celebrations commemorating the end of the war and the incorporation of the western territories played a prominent role in spreading and strengthening the official view of history.[62] The Weeks of the Recovered Territories (Tygodnie Ziem Odzyskanych) had been celebrated since 1946, as had Grunwald Days (Dni Grunwaldu), Silesia Weeks, and Struggle Against Germandom Weeks (Tygodnie Walki z Niemczyzną).[63] After 1956, celebrations of this kind were significantly vitalized and expanded, until they became elaborate annual rituals of commemoration. Wrocław Days, which always took place around May 9 in commemoration of the end of the war and Wrocław's return to Poland, were particularly important for the city. On the one hand, they were cultural, filled with concerts and readings, film and theater premieres, academic conferences, and athletic competitions; on the other, they were also nationalistic, featuring a wide range of patriotic festivities: marches, military parades, wreath-laying ceremonies, the conferral of orders, and the unveiling of monuments. Accordingly the planning involved not only artists, athletes, and scholars, but also the TMW, the city government, and the military.

According to the program of the thirteenth annual Wrocław Days celebration (May 8–16, 1968), the first two days were organized as follows: On May 8 around 5:00 pm, the festivities opened in the town hall with a gala plenary session of the Wrocław Committee of the Front of National Unity and a patriotic-socialist speech by Bolesław Iwaszkiewicz, then head of the County National Council (PRN) and a member of the Polish Sejm.[64] At 7:30 pm, military taps at pl. Powstańców Śląskich; at 8:00 pm, wreath-laying ceremonies at the three military cemeteries; 8:30 pm, fireworks on the Oder. On the next day at 9:00 am, the opening of the "Patriotic and Scholarly Traditions of Slavonic Studies in Wrocław" conference in the Aula Leopoldina;

Inaugurated in 1913 on the one-hundredth anniversary of the victory over Napoleon, Wrocław's Centennial Hall (renamed People's Hall in 1945), was a venue for patriotic celebrations before and after 1945. Courtesy of bpk and the Herder Institute in Marburg.

10:00 am, the opening of the "Wrocław—My City" photo exhibition in the cultural center on ul. Lotnicza; and at 1:00 pm, a historical lecture on the subject "Wrocław as the Senior Citizen Capital of Poland" at the State College of Sculptural Arts. At 3:00 pm, a choral concert and the conclusion of the track and field competition for elementary schools at Olympic Stadium; 4:00 pm, the opening of the "Wrocław's Monuments" photography exhibition in the Muchobór cultural center and a ceremonial changing of the guards at the garrison at pl. Wolności. There were approximately thirty such events each day until the celebrations officially ended on May 16 with an address by the head of the County National Council (PRN), followed by fireworks.[65]

In addition to local events organized by the city of Wrocław, there were also major national celebrations for which Wrocław served as a stage. The western territories and their "return to the motherland" played a significant role in Poland's millennium celebration in 1966, and Wrocław was the site of diverse activities. During the twentieth, twenty-fifth, and fortieth anniversaries of the end of the war and the incorporation of the territories, which were celebrated throughout the country, Wrocław was the most important venue besides Warsaw. The most elaborate celebration was held in 1970 on the twenty-fifth anniversary of the end of the war.[66] According to the PRN in Wrocław, these celebrations were intended to commemorate: "the inviolability of the Oder-Neisse line as the border of peace and European security"; "the existence of permanent links between Lower Silesia and the motherland, as well as its inhabitants' ties to the territories"; "the accomplishments of the Polish people in the reconstruction"; the importance of Lower Silesia for Poland; "the feelings of gratitude and friendship toward the peoples of the Soviet Union and toward the Soviet Army"; and finally, remembrance of "the history of the Polish people's struggle for the liberation of Lower Silesia from Germanic rule, and the role played by Polish soldiers in the liberation of these territories."[67]

On January 21, 1970, the nationwide celebrations began in Milicz, the first city in the western territories "liberated" by the Red Army on that day in 1945, and the commemoration continued until the end of the year. There were numerous scholarly symposia in Wrocław on questions of the territories, as well as exhibitions such as "Lower Silesia in Documents" at the Silesian Museum, "Twenty-five Years of Lower Silesia in Art Photography" at the

Propaganda slogans celebrating the recovery of the western territories were omnipresent in the cityscape (from left to right): "Wrocław welcomes you in the fifteenth year of its return to the Motherland" (1960); "Come and visit Piast Wrocław" (1967); "The Western and Northern Territories forever united with the Motherland!" (1970); "Wrocław forever Polish" (1985). Courtesy of the City Museum of Wrocław (above, Tomasz Olszewski) and Ossolineum (opposite page, Tadeusz Drankowski).

Ethnographic Museum, and two shows at the Archaeological Museum: "We Wrocławians," an exhibition by lay photographers, and "Silesia in the Prehistory of Poland." Many books were also published in the course of the year—new studies of local history, scholarly works, volumes of photography, and anniversary editions produced by numerous institutions, including the University of Wrocław and the Wrocław Polytechnic University, both founded in 1945. There were also diverse nationwide competitions, and major cultural events, such as the Festival of Polish Music in Wrocław, the 11th Wrocław Theater Festival, and the 26th Polish Recitation Competition in Świdnica. The festivities in Wrocław between May 6 and 10 were the climax. The city was whistle-clean and decked out in finery; its historic buildings, the main venues, and the banks of the Oder around the Old Town were all illuminated; and festive flags were flown on ships in the Oder. One event followed the next. There were concerts, theatrical performances, rallies, a youth parade

in Wrocław's Olympic Stadium, and all manner of festivities, including on May 9 the main commemorative celebration, which took place at the Hala Ludowa and was attended by government leaders.[68]

The last major celebrations of this kind took place in 1985 on the fortieth anniversary of the end of the war. By this time the political leadership in the People's Republic was engaged in a struggle for its survival. Solidarność, which had a particularly strong base of support in Wrocław,[69] had grown into a powerful adversary. Government leaders had long since lost their exclusive right to determine cultural memory in Wrocław and were confronted by a resistance movement that was supported by the Church and claimed to represent the true national memory. The communists' monopoly on organizing major celebrations was challenged, most impressively in Wrocław, where the Orange Alternative (Pomarańczowa Alternatywa) had been causing a good measure of commotion since the mid-1980s. Its illegal street happenings, which grew out of student initiatives, took place on socialist holidays such as the Day of the October Revolution, the Day of the Children, or International Women's Day. Spontaneous and direct, they exposed the absurdity of "real socialism" by celebrating, for example, the Day of the (much hated) Militiaman, without whom order could not be maintained in the alleged paradise of workers and peasants, or by wrapping their activists in much-demanded toilet paper, thus hinting that socialism was not even able to supply a sufficiency of such a humble but critical commodity. Events of this nature began in Wrocław and spread throughout the entire country.[70] They had a strong impact on passersby, many of whom were amused by the activists' carnivalesque parodies of socialist state celebrations, which though planned years in advance always offered the same slogans and stagey performances. With the collapse of the People's Republic in 1989, socialist celebrations disappeared overnight. Wrocław Days did continue, albeit as a purely cultural event without political implications. Its date was also shifted from the anniversary of the end of the war to June 24, the Feast of St. John the Baptist, who was once again revered as the patron saint of the city.

CHAPTER TEN

Old Town, New Contexts

JAN ZACHWATOWICZ, POLAND'S GENERAL CONSERVATOR FROM 1945 TO 1957, was the country's most powerful voice in the field of historic preservation.[1] Not only did he personally direct the rebuilding of the devastated old towns of Warsaw, Gniezno, and Poznań, but in a widely regarded lecture delivered at the first postwar congress of Polish art historians in August 1945, he formulated the program for reconstructing Poland's historic buildings:

> The significance of historic buildings[2] for the nation has been made dramatically clear by the experiences of recent years, when the Germans destroyed the monuments of our past in an attempt to annihilate us as a nation. A nation and its monuments are one. From this political thesis one may draw fundamental conclusions that might not always be in keeping with scientific views.
>
> Unable to accept the pillaging of our cultural monuments, we will reconstruct them. We will rebuild them from their foundations up, in order to show future generations, if not the authentic materials, at least the exact form that these monuments continue to have in our memory and that can be ascertained through documents.[3]

Zachwatowicz was aware that these ideas deviated from the principles of international heritage conservation that were accepted at the time. By the turn of the twentieth century, the policy of nonintervention had replaced that of Romantic reconstruction, which prevailed in the nineteenth century. Historic preservation was supposed to be limited to the conservation of buildings—in their existing state. Most Polish historic preservationists adhered to this position. At the First Congress of the Friends of Our Nation's Historic Buildings in Krakow in 1911, Józef Muczkowski asserted unequivocally that "we should not add to or rebuild something that has been lost. . . . For the connoisseur the restored ruin has no value anyway, while for the common people it is simply an illusion."[4]

When an independent Poland was reestablished after the First World War, however, and this new state had to be anchored in the consciousness of its citizens, exceptions were made to the principle of nonintervention, especially for historic buildings regarded as particularly significant for the Polish national cult. Despite protests from many Polish art historians and preservationists, a series of castles and churches, the town hall of Zamość, and the Warsaw city wall were historically reconstructed. Individual historic buildings were altered, including the town hall in Poznań, where changes that had been made during the Prussian era were reversed, and Staszic Palace in Warsaw, which had been converted into a Russian-Orthodox church under Russian rule in the second half of the nineteenth century and was now restored to its original status as a residence built in a neoclassical style. The reconstruction of the Royal Castle in Krakow increased the building's appearance of monumentality, but did not restore its historic condition.[5] These examples, however, were isolated cases reflecting an increased need for displaying the nation's greatness through the medium of its architecture, a phenomenon typical of young nation-states.[6]

This did not imply a fundamental repudiation of established preservationist ideas in Poland. Such a renunciation would occur only in reaction to the devastating destruction of the Second World War, when Poland's historic buildings and art treasures were not only damaged in combat operations, but deliberately destroyed by German occupation forces seeking to annihilate the Polish nation. This intentional destruction of historic buildings and art treasures, libraries and archives, as well as the largely successful effort to raze the Polish capital to the ground after the Warsaw ghetto uprising in 1943 and the Warsaw uprising of 1944 had consequences for Poland's historic preservationists. Holding to the policy of nonintervention after 1945 would have meant simply accepting the colossal loss of historic buildings. Almost 20 percent of Poland's population had been killed, its territory had been shifted westward, and millions of Poles had been forced to give up their homes. The country was also undergoing profound and highly unsettling changes at the time, as a result of the forced socialist transformation of the state, economy, and society. Under such trying circumstances, a turn towards Poland's great historical traditions was supposed to stabilize a country torn from its moorings and, by conjuring up a glorious past, restore the faith of the people that Poland was "not yet lost."

Zachwatowicz was as much a historic preservationist as a patriot.[7] He evaluated historic buildings according not only to their art-historical value but also to the function they fulfilled for the Polish national consciousness. Consequently he believed it was legitimate and necessary, given the war losses, to recoup emotional power by reconstructing even completely destroyed buildings and entire Old Towns. Knowing that Poland would thereby deviate from accepted preservationist practices, Zachwatowicz anticipated objections by art historians:

> A sense of responsibility toward future generations makes it necessary to rebuild what has been destroyed, rebuild with full awareness of the tragedy of conservatorial forgery. Historic buildings do not exist for connoisseurs alone; instead, they are evocative historical documents in the service of the masses. Even deprived of their status as antiques, they will continue to serve a didactic and emotional-architectural purpose.[8]

Zachwatowicz had to win state support and receive the necessary funding for his reconstruction program. To this end, he was prepared to make far-reaching compromises when it came to residential housing and to employ the most cost-effective construction methods. There were voices, such as that of art historian Ksawery Piwocki, who vehemently objected to Zachwatowicz's approach, convinced it would occur at the expense of historical authenticity.[9] However, there was general agreement in Poland after the Second World War that the most significant buildings should be rebuilt in their historic form, even where total reconstruction was necessary.

WARSAW AS A MODEL

The reconstruction of Warsaw's Old Town, which had been utterly destroyed in the war, became the classic expression of Zachwatowicz's program and the model for other demolished cities in Poland. This philosophy of reconstruction has become known throughout the world as the "Polish school of conservation"[10] and has triggered both admiration and consternation.

Reconstruction of Warsaw's Old Town, especially the historic restoration of the royal palace from scratch, is certainly the most important reference point in contemporary European discussions of the pros and cons of historic reconstruction.[11]

On the basis of old architectural surveys as well as investigations carried out during the clean-up operations, it was possible to reproduce the exterior appearance of the Old Town in Warsaw in its more or less precise historic form. However, behind the façades of burgher houses that were restored in detail to their previous condition, for the most part, modern apartments emerged that were totally out of context in the historic buildings. Even more freedom was taken in reconstructing the historic city district adjacent to the Old Town. Here as well, the exteriors of the most important historical landmarks, such as palaces and churches, were painstakingly restored to their original state. In their proximity, however, where precise documentation was often lacking, mere imitations of old buildings were constructed. The results were at best historicist appearance; buildings went up that incorporated façade decorations as well as window and doorframes drawn not from Warsaw but from the ruins of cities such as Nysa or Wrocław. This gave rise to what Konstanty Kalinowski has called "a quite arbitrary historical pastiche."[12] Although these historicist reproductions may have framed the accurately reconstructed historic buildings in an appropriate style, the result was not authentic either in terms of building materials or architectural form.

All this aside, the reconstruction of Warsaw's Old Town aimed not only to symbolically reverse war losses and create a visible expression of the indestructibility of the Polish nation; it also served to underline the city's role as Poland's capital. Given the severity of the destruction in Warsaw and the relatively brief historical period in which it had been the capital of a sovereign Polish state, the city's selection as the capital in 1945 did not go unchallenged. The time-honored royal city of Krakow, which had suffered little war damage, was a strong candidate, as was the intact and centrally-located working-class city of Łódź, which had already been functioning as the provisional seat for a number of Polish government agencies since the end of the war. In this context, reconstructing the city center of Warsaw to its historic eighteenth-century condition also sent a clear political message. The neoclassical urban residences and burgher houses directly recalled the epoch of Polish national history when Warsaw had been the magnificent capital of the Polish-Lithuanian Commonwealth.

The reconstruction of Warsaw also served as a model for Wrocław, although the reconstruction of the two Old Towns differed in one significant way: Wrocław had not been a Polish city before 1945. In Warsaw, with only a few exceptions, every historic building was considered Polish and its reconstruction was seen as an investment in preserving Polish culture. In Wrocław, by contrast, it was decided on a case-by-case basis whether the reconstruction of a particular building was justified in terms of Polish culture or whether, on the contrary, it ran the risk of keeping alive the memory of its German past.

Architectural reconstruction in Wrocław was inextricably tied to the Polonization of the cityscape—as was also true in Gdańsk and Szczecin, and to a certain extent in Poznań as well. The status of historic buildings in western and northern Poland was determined not least by the extent to which they could be linked to Polish history. Elaborate reconstructions usually occurred only when they served the cultural appropriation of the western territories by the Polish state and its society.

Emil Kaliski, who headed the Old Town Task Force at the Wrocław Planning Office (BPW), published an article in 1946 that furnished a blueprint for the task ahead. Entitled "Wrocław has returned to Poland," it focused on the patriotic duty of architects and urban planners in the destroyed city:

> We are fully aware of the weight of the mission that history has placed in our hands, the hands of Polish urban planners; it is a mission to return to our Fatherland the city that once was perhaps more Polish than Krakow. . . .
>
> In Wrocław's case, [the historic buildings] carry a special, specific significance because they are what I would call the city's Polish birth certificate. This certificate is faded, illegible in some places, and destroyed in others. Hence everything that has miraculously survived to this day must, if it is to continue, be reconstructed with utmost care. And not only must we reconstruct that which has, in spite of the devastation, remained above ground, but also that which the Germans did not preserve and which thus fell into decay over the centuries and now lies hidden below the surface. . . .

Polish Wrocław will become the antithesis of German Wrocław. We will bind it inextricably to Warsaw, Poznań, Łódź, and Krakow. . . .

Old Wrocław will become a center for culture and historic architecture. There will be museums here, scientific associations, libraries, and the solemn tranquility of Gothic churches. We may even rebuild the ancient ramparts, towers, and gates to emphasize even more that this part of the city is of unique value.[13]

Kaliski's ideas were entirely consistent with the widespread view in early postwar Poland that urban planners, architects, and historic preservationists in the former German territories should embrace first and foremost architectural traces of Piast-Polish history. Their reconstruction was supposed to substantiate Poland's historical claims to the western territories and create points of reference for Polish settlers in what was for them still an alien environment.[14] Written in the propagandistic rhetoric of the early postwar period, the following passage expresses the purpose of the reconstruction efforts in Wrocław:

A city ravaged, mutilated, and in pain—with what great sacrifices to its external appearance and economic worth did it gain its return to the Republic [of Poland]. . . . The country has recovered one of its ancient capitals in ruins. The destruction is heavy with symbolism—of barbarism on the one hand, and on the other, of love and devotion growing against this backdrop. The restoration of ancient cultural values will be here a measure of the depth of a country's love for this city, this Silesia in miniature. Our affection shows both in our extensive plans for the future and in our reflections about the past. Even today one notices the motherly concern of our people for these historic buildings, which to us, their legitimate owners, are not merely works of art, but deeply moving tokens of our own history, a history that has known its twists and turns but that is nevertheless entirely native and utterly our own. Hence it is that the distinctive face of the historic buildings still standing in Silesia does not unsettle us but is a source of joy. After all, this face is a testament to the wealth of our national culture and allows us to see in Silesian culture a splendid pendant to the cultures of Krakow, of Mazowia, and of Greater Poland.[15]

THE SACRALIZATION OF THE GOTHIC

The Gothic played the role in the reconstruction of Wrocław that neoclassicism had in the reconstruction of Warsaw. From the beginning, Gothic buildings were regarded as Piast and thus as Polish monuments. It did not matter
how much, or how little, Piast dynasty dukes had actually contributed to their
construction, nor was the extent of their real connectedness to Polish history
of much moment. Insignificant as well was the fact that the Gothic epoch extended far into the Bohemian phase of Wrocław's history and that several of
the large Gothic buildings, in particular the cathedral and the town hall, had
not been completed until long after the Wrocław line of the Piasts had died
out. In postwar Wrocław, Gothic architecture was the symbol of the Polish
origins of the city, and that was that.

Wrocław was indeed known for its excellent examples of Gothic architecture. However, this did not mean that the Gothic style still predominated the
cityscape in the mid-twentieth century. During the Renaissance, many of the
Gothic spires had given way to spires more in keeping with new tastes, as for
example the spires on the town hall, the tower of St. Elizabeth's Church, and
the double towers of the Church of St. Mary Magdalene. Many Gothic burgher houses had been replaced by Renaissance buildings or given new façades,
of which frequently only the stone portals survived into the twentieth century. Renaissance art had altered the interior of many of the Gothic churches.
Grand new altars, epitaphs, and tombs were built, as was the famous Renaissance portal to the cathedral sacristy. The Baroque brought even more lasting changes to Wrocław than the Renaissance. On Cathedral Island and Sand
Island as well as in the Old Town, Baroque monasteries and new churches
were built over the course of the Counter-Reformation, while Gothic houses
of worship, such as the cathedral, the Church of the Blessed Virgin Mary on
the Sand, and the churches of Sts. Vincent, Adalbert, and Dorothy were given
magnificent Baroque interiors and new chapels. Baroque burgher houses
and aristocratic palaces were built throughout the city, and one of the most
impressive Baroque ensembles in Silesia, the Jesuit college—which today
houses the university—including its famous Aula Leopoldina and Oratorium
Marianum, was constructed at the northern edge of the Old Town.

Gothic architecture was perceived as a symbol of Wrocław's Polish Middle Ages and thus of Poland's historical claims to the city. Accordingly, to emphasize Wrocław's Polish origins, Gothic fragments were displayed throughout the Old Town. Courtesy of Stanisław Klimek.

After the Prussian conquest of Silesia, neoclassicism held sway, initially in the design of new barracks such as those on Burghers' Island (Kępa Mieszczańska), but soon appearing also in burgher houses and palaces. Architect Carl Gotthard Langhans' Hatzfeldt Palace is one of the most outstanding examples of the style. The construction boom of the nineteenth century stood architecturally under the sign of historicism. Its eclectic forms shaped the expansive new residential districts on the outskirts of the city, and it altered the face of the historic city center as well. There were numerous renovations of existing buildings in historicist styles and the erection of impressive new buildings, too, such as train stations, the city theater, the city library, government buildings, and schools. Finally, modernism had a profound influence on Wrocław's architectural forms in the mid-twentieth century, lending its distinctive accents not only to the exhibition grounds and the Werkbund housing development of 1929 in the eastern part of the city, but also to new department stores and office buildings in the city's center.

Thus, before its destruction in the Second World War, Wrocław offered a fascinating, multifaceted kaleidoscope of architectural styles from the Gothic to modernism. The war's destruction, however, hit the older epochs with greater severity than the younger ones; newer buildings were far less vulnerable to fire, artillery, and bombing. The majority of the extant medieval residential houses were lost during the siege; the trusses of most medieval churches burned, vaults collapsed, and interiors were destroyed. Frequently only walls and wall fragments survived. Seventy-five percent of the cathedral was destroyed, as was St. Martin's Chapel, the last surviving building of the former Piast castle complex on Cathedral Island. The Church of Sts. Peter and Paul suffered serious damage, as did the Church of the Blessed Virgin Mary on the Sand. Of the medieval religious buildings on Cathedral and Sand Islands, only the Church of the Holy Cross and the small church of St. Giles suffered comparatively minor war damage. In the Old Town, the only large Gothic buildings that were spared major damage were the churches of Sts. Dorothy and Elizabeth and the town hall. The Corpus Christi Church and the armory suffered moderate damage; St. Matthew's Church and the Church of St. Mary Magdalene were seriously damaged, while St. Catherine's Church, the Dominican Monastery, St. Vincent's Church, St. Bernardine's Church including the adjacent monastery grounds, and the churches of St. Adalbert, St. Christopher, and St. Barbara were largely destroyed.

The damage sustained by Baroque buildings was less significant. St. Anthony's Church and the Jesuit church, the Jesuit Convictorium, and the Orphanotropheum were slightly damaged; the main building of the university and St. Matthew's secondary school were moderately damaged. Half of St. Anne's Church and the Augustine Monastery were destroyed; St. Clare's Church suffered serious damage, as did the Augustine and the Premonstratensian Monasteries. Many of the Baroque burgher houses on the Rynek, pl. Solny, and Nowy Targ, as well as the Baroque palace, were severely damaged by artillery and fire. The grandest of the Baroque patrician houses on the western side of the Rynek survived. The only historic buildings representative of neoclassicism that were hit hard were Hatzfeldt Palace and the Hohenzollern residence, which consisted of the former Baroque Spaetgen Palace with neoclassicist additions built in the eighteenth and nineteenth centuries. By contrast, damage to the Old Stock Exchange, the Court Church, Wallenberg-Pachały Palace, and the White Stork Synagogue was relatively minor, and many of the neoclassicist burgher houses also escaped largely unscathed.[16]

Most of the great historicist buildings that defined the city center survived the war with only slight damage: the New Town Hall on the Rynek, the buildings of the provincial administration at Nowy Targ and pl. Powstańców Warszawy, the city theater (now the opera), the city library, the New Stock Exchange on ul. Krupnicza, and the Schaffgotsch Palace. The large eclectic department stores and residential buildings, banks, and offices also suffered only exterior damage. The halls of the train stations survived largely intact. In the city center, buildings of the first half of the twentieth century were only slightly damaged. Police headquarters and the main post office along the city moat were largely intact. Due to their steel-concrete construction, the buildings of classical modernism sustained little structural damage: The famous department stores designed by Erich Mendelsohn (Petersdorff), Hermann Dernburg (Wertheim), and Sepp Kaiser (C&A) as well as the office building by Hans Poelzig on ul. Ofiar Oświęcimskich and the one designed by Heinrich Rump on the Rynek were damaged only on their façades. Because they were located outside the actual battle zones, the exhibition grounds together with Centennial Hall (Hala Ludowa) and the Werkbund housing development of 1929 remained intact. Finally, the few large buildings in Wrocław's city center that date to the Third Reich and were built in the monumentalist, neoclassical style preferred by the Nazis—the new employment office

(Arbeitsamt) on the northern bank of the Oder River, the regional Nazi Welfare building (NSV Gauhaus) on ul. Piłsudskiego, and the large building of the provincial administration (Gauverwaltung) on pl. Powstańców Warszawy—all survived.

The extent of war damage suffered by the different architectural epochs appears to have been inversely proportional to the value attributed to those epochs in post-1945 Poland. Emil Kaliski confirmed with bitterness: "Old Wrocław has been obliterated; what has survived is a modern monster."[17] The remnants of medieval Wrocław had, in fact, been largely shattered; small residential houses in the narrow alleyways of the Old Town had burned to their foundations; most of the Gothic churches and old monastery grounds had been ruined. The massive buildings of the Prussian-Wilhelmine metropolis—the train stations and post offices, the hotels, department stores, and administrative buildings—rose all the more conspicuously above the ashes and the blackened wall fragments of medieval Wrocław. This picture was by no means unique to Wrocław. Most of the war-ravaged cities were affected in much the same way, a fact that became an important determinant in the urban architectural modernization that took place in many major European cities after the Second World War. Ruins were cleared away, streets broadened and plain, functional new buildings sprouted up, even in historic city centers. In Wrocław, however, precisely the opposite path was pursued for political and propagandistic reasons. At considerable technical and financial expense, an attempt was made to give the Old Town an archaic appearance that would recapture, as much as possible, the medieval town of the Piasts.

These efforts focused initially on the Gothic churches or what remained of them. The Catholic Church in Poland had assumed control of most of the houses of worship in Wrocław, but it did not have sufficient funds to finance their rebuilding. Much of the cost burden therefore fell to the Polish state. According to Małachowicz, large and severely damaged church buildings were for the most part restored at state expense, while the Polish Church paid for rebuilding smaller and less severely damaged churches as well as ecclesiastical residences and administrative buildings.[18] The situation was decidedly bizarre: a communist government was battling the influence of the church in the country while at the same time investing significant sums in the reconstruction of sacred buildings. The directors of Wrocław's reconstruction efforts sought to justify the expense as a necessary investment from which the

Seventy percent of Wrocław's cathedral was destroyed in 1945. But given the edifice's symbolic significance in postwar Poland, the historical reconstruction began immediately. Courtesy of the Museum of Architecture in Wrocław (Krystyna Gorazdowska) and Via Nova (Stefan Arczyński).

city would derive architectural and propaganda benefits. They also pointed to practices in the Soviet Union, where notable houses of worship, such as the Pechersk Larva in Kiev or St. Basil's Cathedral in Moscow, had been restored.[19]

The state-financed rebuilding of Gothic churches in the western territories thus became part of the Polish national cult, a component of the strategy to legitimate the new national borders by referring back to the Piast tradition. The measures were not intended as support for the Church as an institution. Seen in this light, it is not surprising that the communist government sought to keep the Catholic Church from obtaining as many of the religious buildings restored with state funds as possible, although 98 percent of the population in postwar Poland was Catholic. In Wrocław, one of the two major city churches, the Church of St. Mary Magdalene, was turned over to the tiny group of Old Catholics, while the other, St. Elizabeth's Church, did indeed become Catholic but was supposed to serve as the garrison church of the Polish Army. Eastern Orthodox Christians, including adherents of the Uniate or Greek-Catholic churches, received three religious buildings in the very center of the historic city center: St. Barbara's Church on the western perimeter of the Old Town, the former St. Jacob's Church on Sand Island, and the lower part of the Church of the Holy Cross. This was not an expression of a minority-friendly stance on the part of the Polish government. After all, the Christian-Orthodox minority emerged in the new western territories only as a consequence of the compulsory resettlement of Ukrainian-speaking Polish citizens during Operation Vistula in 1947.

Cathedral Island was especially important for the reconstruction of Piast Wrocław. It was here that the city began. A Piast castle had been located on the island since the tenth century, as had the seat of the Wrocław bishopric, which had officially belonged to the archbishopric of Gniezno from its founding in 1000 CE until the nineteenth century. Little of this remained in 1945. The Piast castle had already lost its significance in the fourteenth century and had gradually deteriorated; its grounds were eventually built over. After the Second World War, only St. Martin's Church, which had once been a part of the castle precincts and now lay in ruins, was still visible. The buildings of the curate had been reduced to rubble, and the cathedral was but a lamentable ruin: The tower roofs had been destroyed by fire, the ceiling and arches had collapsed, and the interior was largely destroyed. Only the Baroque chapels had miraculously survived the war unscathed.

Cathedral Island—seen from the air in 1985—is considered the cradle of Polish Wrocław. Hence no efforts were spared to reconstruct the partly medieval ensemble. The photo's lower half shows the small St. Martin's Church, framed by reconstructed fragments of the former Piast castle. In the upper half of the picture, the Church of the Holy Cross and the restored cathedral, the towers of which are still without the spires built in 1991. From T. Drankowski and O. Czerner, eds., *Wrocław z lotu ptaka*, 3rd ed. (Wrocław: Ossolineum, 1992). Used by permission of the publisher.

There were doubts as to whether rebuilding the cathedral would be technically possible and would make sense given the extent of the destruction. Proposals to build a new edifice or to conserve the ruins as a memorial were ultimately rejected, however, in favor of a complete historic reconstruction of this symbolically significant building.[20] This became the most important reconstruction project in Wrocław in the second half of the 1940s. Work began in 1946 under the direction of Marcin Bukowski and was pushed forward at a rapid pace. The first reconstruction phase included repair of the exterior walls, the roof and the vaults, elaborate masonry work on the interior columns, arcades, cornices, window frames, traceries, and sculptures, and the installation of new windows. This phase was completed in 1951, and the cathedral was then reopened as the main church of the Wrocław bishopric.[21]

Reconstruction work in the vicinity of the cathedral also began quickly. The minor damage to St. Giles' Church was repaired in 1945. The roof of the Church of the Holy Cross was reconstructed in 1947–48 and the church's interior in 1956–57. The rebuilding of the Church of Sts. Peter and Paul began in the early 1950s. Ul. Katedralna was completely restored over time, starting with buildings that had only minor damage, such as the cathedral deanery, which became the bishop's residence; elaborate total reconstructions followed later on. When final construction work was completed in the 1980s, all the buildings on ul. Katedralna had been historically reconstructed or at least rebuilt in historic style. As a result of these efforts, Cathedral Island today possesses, at least at first glance, such an ostensible intactness that it appears as if the war had never occurred. Wrocław was, in this one location, able to match the perfection with which the Old Town in Warsaw had been reconstructed. The destroyed Gothic churches in Wrocław's Old Town and on Sand Island were also reconstructed. Here, however, the work took longer and the environs of the church were not included in the reconstruction to the degree that had occurred on Cathedral Island. Thus several perfectly reconstructed Gothic houses of worship, such as St. Christopher's Church and St. Adalbert's Church, stand like lost souvenirs of a past era amid architecturally uninspired residential housing blocks of the 1960s, abandoned lots, and new urban thoroughfares.

The unique propagandistic significance of Cathedral Island as a symbol of medieval Poland is also evident in the proposals presented in the early 1950s by architect Emil Kaliski. One of these called for Cathedral Island to be separated from the modern buildings in its immediate vicinity by creating a broad green strip along the former riverbanks. This was supposed to underscore its medieval status as an island. Kaliski recommended tearing down the intact nineteenth-century buildings east of the cathedral. On the basis of old engravings and historical imagination, a medieval ensemble would be built at the site, consisting of small Gothic residential houses with steep gabled roofs and, along the ramparts, fortified towers built of untreated wooden beams.[22] This radical project, which would have done away with every trace of architecture younger than the Middle Ages, was never implemented. It remains, however, an important testament to the tendency among Wrocław architects at the time to re-create Wrocław in its earliest possible state, almost as a kind of theme park, in tribute to the Piast era. In his remarkable essay on the postwar city, journalist Włodzimierz Kalicki wrote the following:

> "After the war we assumed that medieval Wrocław had been ours, that the founders of the churches were Polish," said Wrocław Voivodeship Architect Jerzy Rozpędowski. Hence the unwritten rule of pandering to the Gothic, which was unanimously respected by everyone, including the Church. In reconstructing historic buildings, above all churches, obsessive attention was paid to Gothic interiors while later, often extraordinarily valuable layers were destroyed. Plaster was obsessively hacked off, bare brick walls being viewed as a sign of Polishness. Until the late 1960s, money was allocated primarily for renovating the Gothic.[23]

Kalicki correctly identified the psychological core of this re-Gothicization mania in Polonized Wrocław. However, his polemical exaggeration does not do justice to the complexity of the reconstruction process, which extended over many decades and thus underwent marked changes. The recreation of what was Gothic—and also Romanesque, although given the small number of Romanesque buildings in the city this occurred only in isolated cases such as St. Giles' Church[24]—unquestionably expressed a preservationist ideal that has to be viewed within the context of the city's Polonization and the sacralization of its Piast, that is, Polish, origins.[25] Nevertheless, it was far more the damages sustained during the war than postwar re-Gothicization measures that were responsible for the lost interiors of the Renaissance, Baroque, and nineteenth century. In the cathedral, it was not only the neo-Gothic galleries in the presbytery that had burned, but also the famous Renaissance altar, the

The reconstruction of the Church of the Blessed Virgin Mary on Sand Island was accompanied by the church's re-Gothicization. The rich Baroque interior (next page), destroyed during the siege, was replaced by altars taken from churches, monasteries, and
museums in the western territories (p. 341). Courtesy of the City Museum of Wrocław
(Bronisław Kupiec), the Herder Institute in Marburg , and the author.

choir stalls, and the Baroque choir loft with its organ. Only isolated fixtures in the Church of the Blessed Virgin Mary on the Sand—which was primarily Baroque, and legendary for its opulence—survived a fire in the building. Owing to their timely removal, the choir stalls are all that survived of the precious, early Baroque interior of St. Vincent's Church. The list of Baroque interiors destroyed by fire is long and includes not only the inventories of churches but also of monasteries, burgher houses, and the university.

A historic reconstruction of all the Baroque altars, organs, pews, confessionals, and other objects would have been virtually impossible both financially and technically; it was also questionable from a preservationist standpoint. Given the extent of the destruction, the only viable strategy was to reconstruct Gothic churches in their original, plainer form, as a rule without major alterations to the extant structures. For this reason, Gothic furnishings were installed wherever Baroque interiors had been lost. These could be taken from museum inventories containing Gothic interiors (which had been replaced by Baroque interiors) as well as from churches and monasteries able to spare parts of their existing interiors. The cathedral received its Gothic altar from the Protestant church in Lubin, its Baroque choir stalls from St. Vincent's Church in Wrocław, and a new organ assembled from parts of other organs. The Baroque chapels of the cathedral remained untouched, as did the surviving remains of the Baroque interiors of the aisles, the Baroque pulpit, and the Baroque sculptures on the chancel. After reconstruction, the interior of the cathedral was, however Baroque, significantly more austere than it had been before the destruction. It was indeed more Gothic, but the restoration could not fairly be termed an iconoclastic re-Gothicization. The same is true of the reconstruction of the Church of the Blessed Virgin Mary on the Sand. Here, too, the sparse remnants of the Baroque interior were supplemented with carved altarpieces from the Gothic and Renaissance eras. The Baroque interiors in the churches of St. Dorothy and St. Elizabeth had survived the war intact and were not afterwards removed. The loss of the famous Engler organ and other parts of St. Elizabeth's Baroque interior was the result of a tragic fire in the 1970s.

Cases of dubious historic reconstruction, in which achieving a medieval appearance took priority over authentic architectural structure, were limited to the first postwar decade. One such building was the town hall, which between 1949 and 1952 underwent a fundamental restoration under the direction of Marcin Bukowski that altered its external appearance.[26] The building had already undergone a number of restorations beginning in the late nineteenth century and had lost part of its original structure in the process. During the Third Reich, capstones with Nazi symbols had even been placed on the vaults.[27] Bukowski had the stucco on the eastern and western façades removed, thereby exposing the brick walls. In order to expedite the process, not only the stucco but also half a layer of bricks were taken off; the façade surface was then restored with bricks from nearby ruins. On the southern façade, which was made primarily of stone and was richly decorated with sculptures and ornaments, the stucco was initially removed, only to be replastered subsequently for visual reasons. Here a particularly thick layer of plaster was used because, allegedly, it provided a medieval appearance.

Małachowicz, a sharp critic of this postwar restoration, has argued that when the town hall was originally completed around 1500, the building's exterior walls *were* entirely covered with plaster, but with a layer so thin that it revealed the contours of the underlying bricks. According to Małachowicz, the alterations that Bukowski made to the side gables of the eastern and western façades lacked sufficient iconographic documentation, especially those on the eastern side. These included convex quarter circles on the gables, an allegedly native Silesian Renaissance motif modeled on the patrician House to the Golden Crown and the cupola of St. Elizabeth's Church. All things considered, Małachowicz concluded, the authentic surface of the building was unnecessarily and irrevocably ruined. He wrote with bitterness in 1981: "The current exterior architecture of the town hall is the result of successive restorations and not a reconstruction that reflects any one historical period in the building's development."[28]

When Emil Kaliski took over the restoration work of the Gothic Church of the Holy Cross in 1946, he had the intact choir loft torn down, the extant remains of the Baroque and neo-Gothic interior removed, and parts of the plaster stripped to expose the brick walls. In the historic reconstruction of the Church of Sts. Peter and Paul from 1951 to 1962, which Bukowski directed, the interior wall plaster was removed and renovations were made without adequate documentation of the building's architectural history.[29] According to Małachowicz, the removal of the wall plaster in the nave and the presbytery of the cathedral also lacked sufficient historical justification. Małachowicz argued that the interior walls of the cathedral, like other Gothic churches, had

In postwar Wrocław, showcasing a building's medieval origins was more important than aesthetic considerations. Thus Gothic window arches interrupted the symmetry of the Baroque of the Prince-Electors' House on the Rynek. Courtesy of Via Nova (Stefan Arczyński).

probably already been plastered in the Middle Ages. When the historic reconstruction of the Gothic Church of the Blessed Virgin Mary on the Sand took place in the early 1960s under Małachowicz's supervision, detailed investigations were conducted and only the bricks of the ribbed vaults were exposed and set off against larger surfaces of plastered, whitewashed walls and vaults. This church interior design became a model for the reconstruction of other Gothic churches. The phase in which only bare brick walls were regarded as authentically Gothic had come to an end.

During the nineties, the Baroque façade was reconstructed at the expense of the Gothic arches. A reunited Germany at last, in 1990, recognized the postwar borders, and the Gothic arches lost their political significance. Courtesy of the author.

It is important to note, however, that Małachowicz criticized not re-Gothicization per se, but only inaccurate re-Gothicization. When the second reconstruction phase of the cathedral began under his leadership in 1968, he sought to continue the building's re-Gothicization. On the basis of meager and unconfirmed information—drawn, for example, from old paintings and engravings—he returned the gable of the western façade to what he asserted was its original condition. In doing so, he removed a large clock that had been in place since the sixteenth century. Instead of the flat, provisional tower roofs built after the war, Małachowicz installed two steep Gothic spires, which were not however finished until 1991. Their completion marked the end of the cathedral's exterior re-Gothicization. The spires are not authentic, as the architect himself has acknowledged. Only a northern tower actually existed in the Gothic era; the southern tower had still been a stump. Moreover, there is no documentation regarding the shape of the northern tower, which burned down in 1540. In other words, the two spires overlooking Cathedral Island today are less a product of historic reconstruction than of Gothicizing fantasy.[30]

An urge to recall the city's distant past was also expressed in the restoration and partial reconstruction of a portion of the medieval fortifications, which was carried out at great expense (and without any practical purpose). The severely damaged armory stemmed primarily from the sixteenth century and later eras, but it had been built on older foundations, and its overall appearance suggested the Middle Ages. It was among the first historic buildings restored after the war. Many medieval wall fragments had surfaced in the ruins of the Old Town, and these were now exposed and protected. It was deemed more important to recall the medieval origins of a building than to respect its contemporary aesthetic. For example, to reveal the true age of the Prince-Electors' House on the Rynek to passersby, the outlines of Gothic windows and a piece of brick wall were exposed in the middle of the Baroque façade. The façade of the former Dominican Monastery near St. Catherine's Church and many other buildings in Wrocław were treated in a similar manner.

Ironically, war damage was sometimes credited with accomplishing a sort of purification:

> In the artificial cross-section caused by the war, successive historical formations can be seen, as in a house whose interior has been exposed by shelling; there is life from the bottom up as it were, and we need

to burrow down to its firm roots. That lower stratum associated with Wrocław's Polishness lies deep, covered with a veneer of German culture. It must now be seized. . . .

Historic buildings have been purged of these foreign layers . . . largely by the ravages of war, which in many cases laid bare the original fabric of Piast-era architecture.[31]

The medieval architectural fragments that had surfaced in many places as a result of the destruction could, however, hardly compensate for the widespread loss of historic buildings in the war. The mythical core of this notion that the war had washed away the German city and laid free the Wrocław of the Piasts was seriously at odds with a sober perception of reality.

The idea of a Polish Middle Ages and an unbroken continuity of Polish settlement in Wrocław was most impressively embodied, from an architectural and preservationist standpoint, on the grounds of the former Piast castle on Cathedral Island. Here preservationists acted as demiurges—in the words of Teresa Jakimowicz[32]—to create an architectural *Gesamtkunstwerk* visualizing the official Polish view of history. At the end of the war, the last visible remains of the Piast castle complex were the ruins of St. Martin's Church. Eighty percent of the building had been demolished, and its value in terms of art history had already been compromised prior to its destruction. The once-small Gothic church consisting of an octagonal nave and a narrow choir had been disfigured in the fifteenth century by an asymmetrical architectural addition. But for the Polish city of Wrocław after 1945, the emotional significance of these ruins far surpassed their art-historical value. They were not only the last relics of any size of the Piast castle, but the remains as well of a church that had served Wrocław's Polish minority prior to the Second World War.

Following comprehensive archeological investigations of the castle grounds, which brought to light an abundance of new information about the castle's previous form and its architectural evolution,[33] St. Martin's Church was rebuilt in 1959. The project hardly qualifies as a historic reconstruction. In order to make the building's form at least somewhat appealing, the nave was raised in an act of free invention to a small tower and given a sharply tapered roof. The ruins of more modern buildings in the vicinity were removed, creating an expansive open space around St. Martin's that put the church on center stage, so to speak. Commemorative plaques were installed on the building's exterior walls, recounting the history of the church and citing the four patriotic rules of the Association of Poles in Germany, thereby further elevating the building to a monument of Polishness. Wall fragments of the Piast castle were also rebuilt around the church. The interim reconstruction of the grounds was completed in the spring of 1968 with the installation of a monumental stone sculpture of Pope John XXIII, who had spoken of the Polish western territories as the "territories recovered after centuries." The monument stands at a point that provides visitors with the optimal perspective for taking in the overall statement of the complex. Standing in front of the sculpture, visitors see St. Martin's Church from its most attractive side, as well as the entire grounds of the Piast castle and the impressive panorama of Gothic churches on Cathedral and Sand Islands.

The sacralization of certain architectural epochs associated with the zenith of one's own national history and the resulting tendency to archaic reconstructions is widespread.[34] And yet there is a special irony in the Polish reverence of Gothic architecture in Wrocław, for it was precisely the Gothic that Germans celebrated before the war, as evidence of German cultural achievements during the "German colonization" of Eastern Europe.[35] This was reflected, for example, in the re-Gothicization of Wrocław's town hall and of the cathedral that began in the late nineteenth century. Seen in this light, it was a process that merely continued after 1945, though now with a completely different significance in an altered national context. This appropriation of one and the same architectural style with diametrically opposed propagandistic objectives illustrates once again the baselessness of the concept of a national architecture.

THE TOLERATION OF THE BAROQUE

Baroque buildings in Wrocław were never granted the status of Gothic buildings because they could not be linked to the Polish history of the city. They were testaments of the Habsburg era, when German and Latin were the languages of the ruling dynasty and the imperial administrative apparatus. Nevertheless, the Baroque was at least a pre-Prussian phase of the local history. The extreme anti-Prussian sentiments of the Polish collective consciousness in the mid-twentieth century had no anti-Austrian counterpart, even though the Habsburgs, like the Prussian Hohenzollerns, had participated in the partition of Poland in the eighteenth century. The political culture of the Habsburg Monarchy, however, had been more cosmopolitan than that of Prussia; unlike Prussia under Bismarck, the Austrian state did not function as an agent of German national unification, and like Poland it had been predominantly Catholic. While the Prussian government moved towards concerted Germanization policies in its dealing with its Polish provinces in the second half of the nineteenth century, the Austrian government granted its Polish province of Galicia extensive political autonomy. Last but not least, the Habsburg Monarchy served as the defender of Catholicism, a position with which Polish society could far more easily identify than that of Protestant Prussia. Thus from the Polish perspective, Austria and Prussia were worlds apart. After the Second World War, the architectural legacy of the Habsburg era was consequently dealt with very differently in Wrocław than were the buildings tied to Hohenzollern rule. The Polish stance toward Baroque buildings in the city could be described as one of benevolent neutrality.

The Baroque architecture in Wrocław that had been destroyed in the war was reconstructed, although in contrast to the reconstruction of Gothic buildings this was generally not done as quickly nor at as great an expense and was often limited to the restoration of façades. The serious damage sustained by the exterior of the university's main building was repaired soon after the war. The lavish stucco ornamentation and the paintings in the interior, however, were never completely put right, except in the Aula Leopoldina, which was elaborately restored in the 1950s. The adjacent Jesuit church, whose interior suffered moderate damage during an air raid, was restored over the course of several decades. The reconstruction of the completely destroyed Oratorium Marianum, the concert hall on the ground floor of the main university building, did not even begin before the mid-1980s. When the hall reopened in 1997, however, visitors could admire an almost perfect historical restoration.

The extensive damage to Baroque buildings such as the Orphanotropheum on Cathedral Island, the Augustine Monastery on Sand Island, the Premonstratensian Monastery on pl. Nankiera, or the nearby St. Matthew's secondary school was repaired insofar as it affected either the external appearance of the building or the functionality of its interior. Baroque interiors were reconstructed true to the original in cases where the damage had been slight,

The former Jesuit College, which since 1811 has been used as the main building of the university, is the most splendid Baroque edifice in town. Polish authorities did not hesitate to repair the building's serious war damages. Courtesy of the author and the Museum of Architecture in Wrocław (Jan Bułhak).

In the 1930s, historic preservationist and Breslau building commissioner Rudolf Stein fought for a historical reconstruction of the city's old market squares. To this end, he created a model that shows the Ring (Rynek) as it appeared around 1800. When the reconstruction of the square began in the 1950s, Stein's ideas were an important source of inspiration for Polish architects. Courtesy of the Herder Institute in Marburg.

and in simplified form where it had been more severe.[36] Only the exterior of St. Clare's Church was reconstructed in its Baroque form, although to this day it still lacks its Baroque spire, but Gothic fragments in its interior were brought to light, in keeping with its new function as a Piast mausoleum. The façade of the Baroque St. Anne's Church on Sand Island was restored by the late 1970s, but the Baroque interior, destroyed by fire, was not.

The rebuilding of Wrocław's three great marketplaces—Rynek, pl. Solny, and Nowy Targ—was among the most impressive and at the same time most controversial accomplishments of the Old Town reconstruction.[37] These expansive quadrangles, which had been established at the intersection of trade routes in the thirteenth century and had served ever since as centers of economic life in Wrocław, were among the city's defining urban architectural elements into the twentieth century. The Rynek, the largest of the three, is one of Wrocław's most prominent landmarks and certainly one of the most beautiful urban squares in Europe. Spreading over 8.5 acres, the square is framed by magnificent patrician houses, with the Gothic town hall and a large structure that evolved from the former cloth halls at its center.

The Rynek (Ring), pl. Solny (Salzring), and Nowy Targ (Neumarkt) retained their medieval layout into the twentieth century. But inevitably the vitality of market life led to the buildings around the squares being continually expanded, rebuilt, torn down, and built anew in order to adapt them to ever-changing economic needs and, as prestigious buildings, to the prevailing fashions of the times. In the seventeenth and eighteenth centuries, magnificent Baroque and neoclassical gabled houses with artful stone portals were constructed until, gradually, the market squares lost their Gothic appearance altogether. Sporadic traces of the oldest edifices survived only in walls and cellar vaults and in the form of portals and other fragments.

The Baroque-neoclassical visage of the buildings was not permanent either. In the construction boom of the nineteenth and early twentieth centuries, approximately two-thirds of the Renaissance, Baroque, and neoclassical burgher houses on the Ring were torn down to make room for new buildings in historicist styles.[38] Traditional burgher houses, in which the upper floors served as elegant residences while business was conducted on the ground floor, were replaced by buildings used exclusively for retail and services. Modern steel frame construction optimized the use of space and allowed for large display windows. As market business began to shift indoors, the buildings around the squares gradually evolved into department stores, while the residential apartments disappeared.

The accelerating loss of historic burgher houses triggered growing discomfort. When the House to the Golden Crown, a Renaissance building of great art-historical significance and the oldest patrician house on the Ring, was unceremoniously demolished in 1903 and replaced with a modern department store, at least the stone portal was rescued. It was integrated in 1904 into the plans for a new city archive on Tiergartenstrasse. The archive building was not a copy of the lost Renaissance house, but several of its distinctive formal elements were cited in its façade.[39] In the 1920s, city building commissioner Max Berg proposed removing the burgher houses adjacent to the town hall in order to construct a massive high-rise on the Ring.[40] This proposal, which was never realized, played an important role in gradually changing attitudes toward historic buildings in Breslau, as did the construction in the late 1920s of Heinrich Rump's high-rise building for the Sparkasse savings bank, which

Some of the Baroque burgher houses on the south side of the Rynek were rebuilt from scratch. Their historical appearance, however, was strictly limited to the exteriors. Behind splendid Baroque façades working-class tenants found the modest apartments typical of the fifties (above and opposite page). Courtesy of Via Nova (Stefan Arczyński).

required the demolition of several old buildings between the Ring and the Salzring.

In the 1930s, historic preservationist and city building commissioner Rudolf Stein was increasingly successful in attempts to protect the remaining old houses. He published several books on the Breslau burgher house and advocated restoring the Baroque-neoclassical face of the old marketplaces; he compiled elaborate architectural and historical documentation on the subject and even worked out concrete designs for the projects. In the mid-1930s, historic preservationists began to focus on the Ring, calling for a reduction in façade advertising and its stylistic adaptation to the historical character of the architectural ensemble. Reconstruction and even historic restoration began on several of the older façades. Stein's extensive project could not be realized before the beginning of the Second World War, but Polish architects and historic preservationists saw it to completion after 1945.[41]

In the postwar period it was by no means a given that the three market-places and thus the most bourgeois part of the Old Town would be histori-cally reconstructed. Wrocław's burgher houses were especially threatened because they could by no stretch of the imagination be regarded as monu-ments of Polish history; they were inexorably linked to the German patricians who had wrested political power from the Piast dukes. In the first postwar years state funds for historic preservation were spent elsewhere. Given the crucial functions that the three old marketplaces served in Wrocław's city center, however, reconstruction of the destroyed buildings in some form or another eventually proved unavoidable. When the issue was finally addressed in the early 1950s, the principle of historic restoration again prevailed. In this particular case, however, special effort was required to justify the building project. The rebuilt Rynek, pl. Solny, and Nowy Targ could not look like a re-construction of the former German city. Wrocław had to look like its "Polish antithesis," to borrow one of Kalinski's formulations.

Wrocław art historian Marian Morelowski delivered the necessary justifi-cation in a 1950 newspaper article entitled "The Battle against the Bourgeois,

Venture-Capitalist Defacement of Wrocław." Morelowski argued that the former German bourgeoisie, "in its pursuit of profit and pleasure, had lost its way in matters of good taste and destroyed the most beautiful buildings in the city's historic center." By reconstructing them, he continued, Poland could demonstrate its cultural sophistication and create "new monuments of glory by resurrecting the old." The reconstruction of the Wrocław marketplaces would be "a momentous accomplishment for the People's Republic of Poland, a correction to the grave sins of a spiritless bygone epoch of egotistical demolition men and a venture-capitalist bourgeoisie."[42]

Although the reconstruction of Wrocław's burgher houses took up a German preservationist project of the 1930s and was based largely on plans worked out by Rudolf Stein, it appeared from this perspective to be a Polish rescue operation for an older version of Wrocław destroyed by reckless German capitalists. This interpretation fit perfectly with the anti-German and anti-capitalist propaganda of Poland during the Stalinist years.[43] All differences between the rebuilding of the marketplaces in Wrocław and Warsaw seemed to dissolve: both reconstructions now qualified as a Polish response to German cultural barbarism.

The reconstruction of Wrocław's burgher houses was based on their historical condition around 1800, a date that Stein had suggested for historic preservationist motives. After 1945 this date accorded with the desire to give the Wrocław markets at least a pre-Prussian appearance, if not a medieval one. Although Wrocław was already a Prussian city in 1800, its Prussian affiliation did not become evident architecturally until the economic upswing of the nineteenth century, when new department stores, banks, and offices began to eclipse the Baroque burgher houses and palaces of the Habsburg era. Basing the reconstruction on the 1800 status of the squares was advantageous for yet another reason: The marketplaces of the Warsaw and Poznań Old Towns had also been reconstructed in this style. The Old Towns would thus begin to resemble one another architecturally, underlining the alleged historic cohesion of the various regions of postwar Poland.

Reconstruction of the Rynek and pl. Solny was initiated in the early 1950s and was scheduled for completion by the end of the decade. The main investor was the Administration for the Construction of Workers' Housing Estates (Dyrekcja Budowy Osiedli Robotniczych). Since the investor's primary interest was to create as many apartments as possible at the lowest possible cost, the concerns of historic preservationists were often ignored. Moreover, the strict building codes in effect were rarely compatible with historically authentic construction methods.

Almost all the buildings on the Rynek and pl. Solny were rebuilt as residential housing. In the interior of intact buildings, necessary alterations were made for the creation of apartments. Only the ground floors and, in some cases, also the second floors were designated for stores, restaurants, and offices. Generally, what was "historic" was limited to the exterior faces of the buildings since that would be enough to give the marketplaces the desired historic appearance. Thus numerous façades were restored according to old models or refashioned entirely from scratch. The approach was often pragmatic: The façades of only slightly damaged buildings were left unaltered or at most adapted to the desired historical style through minor modifications. Where buildings had been completely destroyed in the war and new buildings were necessary—as on the southern side of the Rynek and the western side of pl. Solny—historic buildings were recreated anew. In doing so, the last relics of authentic historical buildings, such as existing wall fragments, were often destroyed because the expense of integrating them into the new buildings was deemed excessive.

Those who favored an exacting historic restoration were disappointed. The creation of a large number of tiny apartments in an urban quarter where patricians and the wealthy bourgeoisie had lived necessitated a significant sacrifice of authenticity. Pressures of cost forced further, painful compromises. Many of the extant frames of modern buildings were used as shells in reconstructing the old burgher houses, which meant that historic façades were simply slapped onto a modern core; in such cases the façades could not possibly accord with historical proportions. Elsewhere a single staircase was installed for two adjacent buildings, which meant that many of the buildings' entrances led only to the stores at street level, while the upper floors had to be accessed through the neighboring building. Authentic components that happened to still be in place were sometimes relocated: after the reconstruction, columns, stone portals, and painted beams appeared in new locations. Historic authenticity also suffered as a consequence of entire quarters being transformed into working-class residential districts. This required that city blocks be gutted to provide new apartments with sufficient light and open space. Behind the historical façades ahistorically large courtyards thus emerged, which sharply contrasted with the dense fabric of the city center around 1800.

Nevertheless, the reconstruction at the Rynek and pl. Solny in the end produced a quite homogeneous neoclassical-Baroque panorama. In addition to the work of Rudolf Stein, the architects based their designs on old photographs, engravings, and drawings from the eighteenth and nineteenth centuries. However, according to Olgierd Czerner, Wrocław's architectural historian and municipal conservator from 1955 to 1965, there had not been enough time to track down all the available iconographic documents in the city archives, which were still in disarray. The reconstruction had instead relied too heavily on Rudolf Stein's drafts, which resulted in a number of avoidable historical errors in the design of the façades.[44]

The rebuilding of the Renaissance House to the Golden Crown presents a striking example of the kinds of problems that confronted preservationists. The house (which had been torn down in 1903 to make way for a department store) once stood on the southeastern corner of the Rynek. At the time of its reconstruction (1957–60), it was considered very important to include several Renaissance façade elements that had been stylistically formative in Wrocław and the wider region. The ruins of the department store, which now occupied the site, were not cleared away. Instead of removing them and undertaking a total reconstruction of the historic edifice, the reinforced concrete frame of the department store was used as the new building's core. It obviously did not correspond to the proportions of a Renaissance building, and as a result the reconstructed House was fifteen feet higher than the original. Neither the number nor the precise layout of the windows corresponded to the original; the shape of the roof and the famous attic deviated as well. Finally, instead of reconstructing the building's original portal, a portal from another building was installed.[45]

The problematic reconstruction of the House to the Golden Crown marked the conclusion of a comprehensive reconstruction of Wrocław's Old Town, which was at times more historicizing than historical. Preservationist and, increasingly, economic concerns about the execution of the program escalated to such an extent that in the late 1950s advocates of contemporary architecture were able to score a victory even on the terrain of the Old Town. Preparations for a historic reconstruction of Nowy Targ based on the models of the Rynek and pl. Solny were abandoned; the reconstruction of Nowy Targ would instead proceed along contemporary architectural lines.

By this time the Rynek and pl. Solny had been completely rebuilt—except for a single empty lot at the northeastern corner of the Rynek where the House of the Golden Dog had once stood. Historic buildings or their façades were by and large reconstructed, although numerous buildings of the nineteenth and twentieth centuries were still in place. Olgierd Czerner commented on the historic reconstruction of the Rynek in 1978: "There are few buildings whose façades we can consider accurate reconstructions. . . . The rest are more or less successful fantasies based on a specific model."[46] Notwithstanding Czerner's justified objections, reconstruction in the 1950s restored the Rynek and pl. Solny as attractive urban squares. The ensemble that had been destroyed in the war was restored as an appealing centerpiece for the city. Irrespective of the degree of authenticity achieved, the Rynek and pl. Solny have become vibrant city squares again. The rebuilding of Nowy Targ, where the same results were sought through contemporary architecture, was far less successful. It became a lifeless expanse surrounded by rapidly deteriorating residential buildings. As a result, in the late 1990s an intense debate began over a proposal to rebuild Nowy Targ along the lines of the two other marketplaces. It pitted advocates of aesthetically pleasing, albeit inauthentic, reinventions of historic buildings against those who defended the historic value of 1960s architecture.[47]

Anyone seeking the authentic Wrocław of c. 1800 at the Rynek and pl. Solny will be disappointed. As always, however, such disappointment is based on false expectations. If we accept the reconstructions for what they are—evidence of the rebuilding pathos of the 1950s, of the ingenuity of architects in dealing with the economic constraints of this era, and of the dream of a socialist, egalitarian society—we will not be disappointed. We will recognize here the painstaking efforts of Wrocław's new citizens to overcome the alien feel of this war-torn city by reconstructing it, all the while allowing themselves the freedom to reconfigure its architectural appearance in such a way as to make of the remnants of German Breslau their own Polish city. The Baroque burgher houses rebuilt in the 1950s are as little representative of the Baroque era as a Renaissance building is of antiquity. Proportions deviating from the original models; an Art Nouveau department store transformed into a Renaissance building; splendid portals that lead into a tiny shop; Baroque plaster façades that decorate working-class apartments; and playgrounds in the courtyards of patricians' houses—none of these are true to the realities of eighteenth-century urban life. But, be they successful historic reconstructions or not, these buildings are an authentic testimony to the Polish postwar era. They are the architectural monuments of the People's Republic of Poland. As such they can tell us stories; as such they have a unique historical value.

THE ANTI-PRUSSIAN REFLEX

In the western territories after the war it was generally felt that the architectural legacy of Prussian-German rule would necessarily call into question Polish claims to power, all the more if the buildings in question were works of artistic value. Thus it is not surprising that postwar Polish propaganda presented Silesia's Prussian period as an era void of culture. Art historian Gwido Chmarzyński wrote in 1950:

> On the one hand, we have the Silesia of the Piast dynasty in a fever of cultural creativity, not only adopting the achievements of Western culture, but transforming these in its own unique style; a Silesia developing into a leading region of Poland and exerting far-reaching impact on neighboring territories. This was Silesia in its golden age of artistic creativity, the Silesia of the Piast dynasty Henryks. On the other hand, we have the Silesia of the Hollenzollerns, which squandered its rich artistic traditions and stayed mired in the barrenness of Prussian aesthetic thought, unable to move beyond the limits of a narrow provincialism. This was Silesia after the "Prussian taste," the Silesia of the conquerors: the Friedrichs, the Wilhelms, and their successors.[48]

According to Chmarzyński, Wrocław too was caught in this cultural decline:

> The ministerial bureaucrats in Berlin were neither willing nor able to feel their way into the conquered city's rhythm of sentiments and needs. Thus little of note happened in its artistic life for a very long time. Chaotic suburbs developed with no understanding of the logic of urban planning. For the [German] Empire, Wrocław remained, despite everything, a colonial city.

Only now is this changing radically, when, along with other areas of life, Lower Silesian art is returning to its natural evolutionary path; returning, that is, to the fold of Polish national art.[49]

In February 1947, Reconstruction Minister Michał Kaczorowski told the directors of the state construction divisions that in the western territories reconstruction would have the additional aim of eliminating "the alien remains of German culture."[50] At the conference of Polish preservationists in Łańcut in 1948, Zbigniew Rewski, voivodeship conservator in Olsztyn in former East Prussia, called for the "de-Prussification of architecture in the western territories":

> The second half of the nineteenth century was one of the most unfortunate of architectural periods, when for the first time ever people stopped striving for their own style. . . .
>
> Germany, especially Prussia, of all countries in Europe the most lacking in artistic abilities and authentic culture, carried this style of construction into an unparalleled orgy of ugliness and bad taste. . . .
>
> But this Prussian architecture possesses another feature, or pretension, that is neither aesthetic nor practical: It sought by dint of its massive presence to Prussify the urban and rural terrain of the politically disputed, occupied border region and, by its monotonous uniformity and sheer material weight, to bind it to the Prussian state. Objectively we must admit that this goal was to some extent achieved, albeit in a truly barbaric manner. Enchanted as they may be by the beauty of the landscape and the historic buildings, the Polish population of the Recovered Territories as well as tourists sense the foreignness of these regions. The crux of this alien quality lies in nothing if not the Prussian character of the buildings.[51]

Rewski ruled out the demolition of Prussian buildings for pragmatic reasons, "although theoretically this would be the sole effective solution."[52] He recommended instead a progressive de-Prussification of the skylines of towns and cities by "removing towers and spires on particularly Prussian buildings" and advocated painting Prussian-looking brick façades or obscuring them with greenery because plastering would be too expensive.[53] Another eloquent example of such iconoclastic impetus is a May 1947 memorandum by architecture students at the Wrocław Polytechnic University, in which they request support from the Warsaw government in establishing an independent architecture department with the following arguments:

1. The study of architecture is at the forefront in the battle for the Polishness of Lower Silesian culture;
2. The department is a base for research on early Polish architecture in Silesia, which has been assiduously falsified and effaced by the Germans and their researchers;
3. The department will become a pool of architects organically tied to the region, who will rebuild the destroyed villages and cities of Silesia in a Polish manner. . . .
7. Students' enthusiasm for the effort is evident from their attendance levels, which are unmatched elsewhere, and has led to a continual enhancement of work quality. They are motivated by the knowledge that once they complete their degrees, they will be involved in the task of eliminating all Germanic traces in Silesia.[54]

This memorandum was probably an accurate reflection of the prevailing mood among Wrocław architects of this period. Due to the scarcity of professionals and an insufficient workforce, Polish architecture students of the first postwar generation were still taking classes when they began working in architectural offices and at construction sites, where they took part in safeguarding and preparing inventories of historic buildings. This brought them into close contact with the propagandists of the reconstruction, several of whom—such as Marcin Bukowski—were also their instructors at the polytechnic university. A number of this first student generation went on to become leading urban planners, architects, and historic preservationists in postwar Wrocław, including Olgierd Czerner, Jadwiga Grabowska-Hawrylak, Edmund Małachowicz, Mirosław Przyłęcki, and Roman Tunikowski.[55] Later in their professional lives, however, they did not support the de-Germanization or de-Prussification of Wrocław architecture. The radical iconoclasm of the early postwar years proved a passing phenomenon.

Nevertheless, the classification of particular buildings as typically German or Prussian did in many cases result in their destruction, whether through vandalism, officially ordered demolition, or gradual deterioration due to a lack of investment.[56] But when was a building to be regarded as typically Prussian or German? A strictly chronological classification based on a date within the period of Prussian rule would have been completely unthinkable in the case of Wrocław, where the vast majority of buildings were constructed after 1740. On those terms the entire city would have become a "foreign relic." Putting together a catalogue of typically Prussian or German architectural elements would also be problematic. Architectural styles rarely recognize national boundaries, and what was regarded as typically Prussian or German in the western territories of Poland—for example, brick buildings, neo-Gothicism, or the pomp of Wilhelminism—was more specific to the times than to the country. We should bear in mind that neither a "German historic building" nor a "Polish historic building" existed in and of itself. A building became one or the other in the subjective perception of the society in question, and this perception could change at any time. Thus it is not surprising that while there were calls after the war for the removal of the German or Prussian architectural legacy in the western territories, a binding definition of what should be considered German or Prussian was never provided.[57]

This opened the door to interpretation, which could have either negative or positive consequences for the building in question. On the one hand, most of the buildings in Wrocław were in some way connected to the Prussian state or the history of German settlement, so it would have been easy to justify their demolition. On the other hand, nothing was really Prussian or German in the sense of a specific architectural style that could be found exclusively in Prussia or Germany. It was not too difficult for preservationists to come up with ample grounds for removing a historic building threatened with demolition from its Prussian or German historical context and transferring it to a Polish, Silesian, or broadly European context. Whether a building was declared Polish, or at least of unspecific nationality and as such worthy of protection, was dependent to a great degree on the determination and argumentative imagination of the preservationists.

All the same, they faced an enormous task. The rash and improper demolition of ruins during the first decade after the war threatened historic building stock everywhere. The removal of war ruins not only prepared the ground for reconstruction but also served as a means of recovering bricks and other scarce building materials, which meant that the interests of the historic preservationists frequently ran counter to the economic interests of the demolition agencies. When the issue of rubble clearance in Wrocław's Old Town was decisively addressed in the late 1940s, heated conflicts erupted between the two parties.

Little was done for damaged historical buildings that Polish society associated with the Prussian state. The ruins of the Hohenzollern palace (opposite page, top) and the Silesian Museum of Fine Arts (opposite page, bottom) were torn down in the sixties. Of the Palais Hatzfeld (above), a splendid neoclassical palace that had the bad luck of becoming the residence of the Prussian provincial governor, only the portal and the entrance hall survived. Courtesy of the Herder Institute in Marburg (opposite page) and the City Museum of Wrocław.

As is evident from the minutes of a meeting in February 1948 between representatives of the Independent Department of Rubble Clearance of the Wrocław Municipal Administration (Samodzielny Oddział Odgruzowania, SOO) and the regional historic preservation agency, the SOO repeatedly attempted to push through the demolition of ruins with the argument that these were the remains of a "German historic building." For example, the deputy director of rubble clearance in Wrocław, Walerian Lewaszkiewicz, rejected claims by the representative of the Voivodeship Department for Culture and the Arts, Aleksander Krzywobłocki, that the ground floor of the Renaissance house at ul. Ofiar Oświęcimskich 1–3 with its art-historically significant stone portal should be preserved. It would be a shame, Lewaszkiewicz argued, to invest in rebuilding "such a worthless, foreign souvenir (*pamiątka*)." He also called for the demolition of the gate and wall remnants between ul. Ofiar Oświęcimskich 9 and 11, a designated historical landmark, because he felt money should not be spent on preserving and rebuilding a "souvenir of the greatest enemy of our people." Lewaszkiewicz was even more emphatic in his opposition to conserving the ruins of the Hohenzollern palace. He argued that "Friedrich's Palace" was "a political souvenir of Germany" that should be immediately removed. Polish funds should not be used to "maintain the spirit of revisionism and German claims to our country."[58]

Jerzy Güttler, voivodeship conservator in Wrocław from 1946 to 1951, later opposed SOO's transgressions of authority by smugly pointing out to the institution its own incompetence. This went so far, he wrote, "that the SOO is inclined to regard even thirteenth-century monuments as German monuments. This is a deeply pessimistic thesis that does not square with historical truth and is blatantly harmful in political terms."[59]

When the SOO complained that the historic preservation agency had not properly identified historic buildings and that this impeded demolition work in the city, Güttler replied that identifying plaques would be installed if the necessary funding could be found for this in the future: "We have to do this, if only to prevent the irresponsibly obsessive search for traces of German culture and German art."[60] In his letter, Güttler also attempted to avert the threatened demolition of allegedly German historic buildings with an argumentation strategy typical of many historic preservationists of the era:

> Silesian historic buildings are not as a rule German in character, even if they were built during the German occupation of Silesia, with the exception of some structures of the Lutheran cult. The architecture of buildings from the second half of the nineteenth century and the twentieth century, however, is often authentically German—such as the market hall on pl. Nankiera or the courthouse on pl. Wolności. When searching for monuments of Germandom, the voivodeship conservator recommends that attention be paid to buildings of precisely this type. They can provide a great deal of building material, as long as considerations of utility do not speak against their being demolished. Historic buildings, on the other hand, should be protected; they should be safeguarded and preserved, so that for centuries to come they will remain the city's greatest ornaments and delight the contemporary inhabitants of Polish Wrocław with their beauty.[61]

Although this passage appears to concur with the official position on the removal of German vestiges, it must have caused local authorities some embarrassment. The "buildings of the Lutheran cult" that Güttler referred to as German were in particular the neo-Gothic churches outside the city center that had been undamaged in the war and had long since been put back to use. Demolishing these buildings had been ruled out for economic reasons. The same was true for the modern market hall and the neo-Gothic court and prison complex along the city moat. The latter had been one of the first buildings used by the Polish administration after the war because it had sustained only minor damage. In this way, Güttler cleverly pointed out to city officials that the Polish authorities had had no qualms about using Prussian government buildings for their own purposes and that reference to "German traces" elsewhere was often merely a pretense for the lucrative demolition of ruins.

A year earlier, the voivodeship conservator had gone even further: In an extensive letter to the SOO, he called for the preservation of the Hohenzollern Palace on pl. Wolności. This was not, he argued, a palace of Friedrich II, "the Prussian king so hateful to our memory,"[62] but rather a building from the first half of the nineteenth century. The actual "Friedrich's Palace," Güttler continued, had been built in the mid-eighteenth century by Dutch architect Jan Baumann as an extension to the Baroque Spaetgen Palace, but it had been completely destroyed in 1945 and there were no plans to rebuild it.

> The palace on pl. Wolności can thus hardly be considered a "political souvenir of Germany," the preservation of which could help fuel German revisionist ambitions. In any case, its status as a "souvenir" is no greater than that of many other buildings constructed in Wrocław under German rule for one purpose or another. Our task is not, and cannot be, to demolish such structures; it is instead to make them best serve the reconstruction of our own life.
>
> The palace on pl. Wolności is seriously damaged, but it is of unquestionable historic value and is distinguishable from the other buildings around pl. Wolności, which are decidedly German in their architecture, by its tranquil and "cosmopolitan" profile. Buildings of this style can be found throughout Europe.[63]

Güttler was not alone in his efforts to convince the authorities of the non-German character of the palace and other historic buildings. Mirosław

Przyłęcki, one of his successors as voivodeship conservator in Wrocław, recalled the strategies that imaginative preservationists often had to employ:

> The communist authorities attempted to restrict not only the reconstruction and restoration of religious buildings but also conservation work on buildings connected to the history and culture of Silesia during its affiliation with various embodiments of the German state. . . . Fortunately, the party bureaucrats, who were not particularly well versed in the history of Silesia, frequently accepted the sometimes far-fetched arguments of conservators about the Piast pedigree of numerous historic buildings and their links with Bohemia and Austria. In the end, preoccupied with other problems, they did not bother to enforce their own prohibitions and impediments.[64]

Although many buildings were thus saved from ideologically motivated demolition, efforts to rescue the Hohenzollern Palace in Wrocław were not successful. The ruins were demolished and the square was leveled in 1969. Only the western wing remained standing as a stub. The gap left by the demolition of the palace was never filled. As a result, the site lost its character as a square and became a wasteland amidst an otherwise largely intact urban landscape.

The demolition of Hatzfeldt Palace on ul. Wita Stwosza was an even greater loss for Wrocław's architectural legacy. Following the destruction of the Hatzfeldt family residence in Wrocław during the Seven Year War, Prince Adrian Franz Philipp von Hatzfeldt commissioned Isidore Ganevale, a French architect working in Vienna, to construct a new palace on the old site between ul. Wita Stwosza and Nowy Targ on a lot of roughly 50,000 square feet. The new palace was a deliberate demonstration of Hatzfeldt's sympathies for the Habsburgs and, as such, designed to overshadow the local Hohenzollern residence. Carl Gotthard Langhans revised Ganevale's plans, and the actual construction took place between 1765 and 1773. The result was the largest and most magnificent palace in Wrocław. Its construction marked Silesian architecture's turn to neoclassicism and was also the most significant example of this architectural style in all of Silesia.[65] At the beginning of the nineteenth century, the Prussian state purchased the palace and made it the residence of the Prussian provincial administration. This sealed the building's fate. In 1886, the provincial governor of Silesia moved into the palace, and during the Third Reich the Nazi Gauleiter resided there. After the war, the building was regarded as one of the most blatant symbols of Prussian and Nazi rule in Wrocław.

The palace, which had been severely damaged during the siege of Wrocław, remained standing for more than twenty years and fell even further into disrepair. Several reconstruction plans were developed, but none of them was able to garner the necessary political support. Wrocław art historian Marian Morelowski was one of many who fought to preserve the palace, calling the planned removal of the ruins at the end of the 1950s a political scandal. After all, he argued, the palace was a major project of Carl Gotthard Langhans, architect of the Brandenburg Gate in Berlin, and its demolition would thus be a serious affront to the Germans.[66] At the time, reference to foreign policy problems that might arise if the Polish state destroyed historic buildings in the western territories was a frequent and apparently powerful argument that in fact sufficed to save several buildings. There was great fear in communist Poland that West German "revanchist circles" would carefully note how historic buildings were treated in the western territories and would seek to exploit any scandal politically.[67]

Morelowski also sought to separate the palace from its Prussian connotations and to emphasize its positive associations with Polish and regional history. He pointed out that in the seventeenth century one of the Hatzfeldts, who had been an Austrian marshal, had come to the assistance of the Polish King Jan Kazimierz and that Langhans had actually been a Silesian compatriot, "Długi Jan" (Polish translation of his last name) from Kamienna Góra.[68] But even these arguments could not prevent the demolition. The ruins were at least not completely removed in the late 1960s; the portal and the entry hall behind it along with the staircase were preserved and integrated in 1968 into a modern new building housing an art gallery, a project of Edmund Małachowicz.[69]

Other buildings that had been severely damaged during the war and that after 1945 were strongly identified with Prussia suffered a similar fate. The ruins of the Commandant's Office on ul. Świdnicka, a building erected in the mid-nineteenth century following plans by Carl Ferdinand Langhans in the style of a Florentine Renaissance palace, were torn down soon after the war. Like pl. Wolności behind it, this left an unattractive gap in the line of buildings. In addition, the small guardhouse on the other side of the street, which was left standing, lost its architectural reference point. More precise information about why the Commandant's Office was torn down is not available. However, Marcin Bukowksi did make the remarkable claim that the large structure "obstructed" the view of the late Gothic façade of Corpus Christi Church from the west.[70] The Commandant's Office, however, was only two stories plus a mezzanine in height, thus not oversized by any reasonable measure, and it impeded the view of the church no more than any building on one side of a street "obstructs" buildings on the other side.

The ruins of the Silesian Museum of Fine Arts were also torn down in the 1960s. This neoclassicist building, which clearly borrowed stylistically from Karl Friedrich Schinkel's Altes Museum in Berlin, had been constructed on Museumsplatz between 1875 and 1880 as a project of Berlin architect Otto Rathey. The Prussian connotations of the building were obvious, all the more when an equestrian statue of Emperor Friedrich III was installed in front of its main entrance in 1901. Although no intact building was ever demolished for purely political reasons in Wrocław, it cannot be denied that of the buildings that were not reconstructed and later torn down, a majority were perceived as symbols of the Prussian past. The neoclassical barracks on the old Burgher's Island (Kępa Mieszczańska) should probably be included in this category. They had been erected at the end of the eighteenth century on orders of Friedrich II and were expanded in the nineteenth century. After 1945, the Polish army showed no interest in taking over the mostly intact barracks; consequently, the complex, which was at least in part worthy of preservation, began to deteriorate. Frederician barracks, viewed as tokens of Prussian militarism, did not fit within either political or historical parameters that might have argued for their preservation.[71]

It should be noted in this context, however, that the architecture of the nineteenth century enjoyed little respect at this time, not only in Poland but everywhere. The diverse neo-styles that increasingly predominated in cities beginning in the late nineteenth century came to be regarded as an expression of an entire epoch's lack of creativity. Buildings of this kind were generally regarded as unworthy of preservation and were considered aesthetic gaffes by many. If they survived, it was as a rule due solely to their functionality. Not until the 1970s did a rethinking of this judgment begin internationally. The buildings of historicism began to be regarded as objects of historical value and were increasingly designated as worth protecting. During the first two decades after the war in Wrocław, historic preservationists' already low estimation of nineteenth-century buildings was exacerbated in a fateful way by the anti-Prussian reflex.[72] Whenever a building from the Prussian nineteenth century no longer served a practical purpose—if, for instance, restoration would have required a sizeable investment—the fate of that building was quickly sealed.

From a psychological perspective, given the difficult Prussian-Polish and German-Polish relations and the trauma of the German occupation, it is easy to understand the lack of popular support for the preservation of Prussian buildings. There is nevertheless something grotesque about the fact that historically and architecturally significant buildings disappeared from Wrocław's cityscape because they were regarded as symbols of Prussian rule, while all of the Nazi buildings in Wrocław were preserved. The massive former Gau administration building on the banks of the Oder River, which unmistakably reflects the totalitarian aesthetics of the Third Reich, was even one of the first administrative buildings to be elaborately reconstructed after the war, and it was then used as the headquarters of the Lower Silesian voivodeship administration. The voivodeship committee of the Polish United Workers' Party (PZPR) and the Wrocław branch of the State Archive moved into the extensive building complex of the Employment Office constructed northeast of the Old Town in the 1940s. The National Socialist Welfare building on ul. Piłsudskiego continued to be used after the war. Several façade murals from the Nazi era even survived, including one at Ustronie 11 that depicted a blacksmith's shop, presumably because they closely resembled works in the style of socialist realism.[73]

The willful destruction of symbols of German rule in the western territories, through which Poles and Soviet soldiers unleashed their pent-up hatred after the war, is yet another example of anti-German rancor, but here again it was not Nazi properties that took the brunt of the destruction. Prussian aristocratic residences and countryside manors were hardest hit, although these had little to do with the terror of the Third Reich. The Krieblowitz Manor outside of Wrocław, the family grave of Prussian Field Marshal Gebhardt von Blücher, who had distinguished himself in the Napoleonic Wars, was vandalized,[74] but no one thought of setting the Lower Silesian Nazi Gau administration building on fire.

Poles were not alone in this anti-Prussian reflex. The Allies also regarded Prussia as bearing primary responsibility for the Third Reich.[75] In February

1947, the Allied Control Council announced the legal dissolution of the Prussian state with the historically dubious claim that "from early days [Prussia] has been a bearer of militarism and reaction in Germany."[76] It should be noted in this context that the eastern territories of Germany that were ceded to Poland in 1945 had been exclusively Prussian and that the expulsion of Germans from the East targeted primarily former Prussian citizens. Both measures ruled out a continuation or revival of Prussia after 1945. Polish anti-Prussianism in the postwar era was nourished by Polish experiences and reflected the Polish view of history. It stood nevertheless within a broader European context.

HISTORIC BUILDINGS AND FORCED MIGRATION

The fate of Wrocław's historic buildings after the war was fundamentally dependent on the connotations they had for Polish society. In the eyes of the Polish settlers, everything in Wrocław was initially foreign; everything was Prussian and German. None of the buildings appeared to be related either to the history of Poland or to the personal history of the newcomers. They presumed as a matter of course that "their" historic buildings were located not in Wrocław, but in central and eastern Poland.[77] However, this view changed thanks to the efforts of Polish politicians, historic preservationists, historians and others. They provided many of the historic buildings in the western territories with a Polish context, and this made possible a relationship between the new settlers and the old walls. Occasionally, outrageous ideological constructions were used, but Adam Labuda is correct in regarding this process of cultural appropriation as the necessary prerequisite for the survival of the region's architectural legacy. After the exchange of the entire population within just a few years, this legacy was acutely threatened by the "death of context." Historic buildings are of value primarily to their "own" society, but, following the expulsion of the Germans, Wrocław's architecture was bereft of this very society.[78] The town's treasures could only be saved by re-establishing a sympathetic link with the newcomers. It was irrelevant for the survival of buildings what notions induced the settlers to regard them as "their own" and to support their preservation. The process of cultural appropriation began with medieval objects and gradually expanded to encompass the architectural legacies of other epochs, although the relics of later periods were never so intimately embraced by Polish national history as were Piast monuments. In itself the rebuilding of destroyed historic buildings served to provide them with their own Polish chapter. The past of the burgher houses, the town hall, and the buildings of the university could not at first be connected to Polish national history, but their reconstruction made them into integral parts of the now Polish city of Wrocław. The appropriation of this architectural legacy, however, was a protracted and complex process, the success of which was fundamentally dependent on political developments in communist Poland and on changes in German-Polish relations.[79] The concern of professional historic preservationists was not enough. Until the general population began to intervene on behalf of historic buildings threatened by deterioration or demolition, the loss of valuable architecture was unavoidable. In the 1940s there were already alarming reports about the progressive deterioration of historic buildings,[80] a process that affected all of Poland but was especially severe in the western territories. The Warsaw government tried to put a stop to abuses caused by the scavenging of building materials from ruins. The Ministry of the Recovered Territories issued a circular decree to all voivodes in September 1947 informing them that, contrary to government intentions, the demolition of destroyed buildings was proceeding "chaotically, without a plan, or express permission from authorities" and that "old historic buildings of great significance," such as palaces, bastions, city walls, churches, and town halls, had been torn down. The decree stated that a solution was urgently needed and that the demolition of historic buildings was not permitted, even for purposes of street expansion or the creation of marketplaces.[81]

The years after 1956 saw heated accusations and public debate about dramatic failures in the preservation of historic buildings. In this atmosphere of rancor, the extent of losses became clear for the first time.[82] Through vandalism, economic decline, misguided construction policies, excessive demolition operations to acquire bricks, underfinanced historic preservation agencies, and general indifference and enmity toward "German historic buildings," it was not only manor houses and palaces that deteriorated or were destroyed. Entire Old Towns were irretrievably lost, even those that had been largely intact at the end of the war. The city of Nysa, the so-called Silesian Rome, in 1945 one of the most beautiful towns in the western territories, became the symbol of this disaster. Over the desperate protests of local preservationists, municipal authorities ordered the demolition of over one hundred historic burgher houses, including a number of unique Renaissance buildings. According to an internal document of the national Polish historic preservation agency in 1956:

> The net effect of this matter is nothing less than serious damage to our very culture. The greater part of old Nysa has been torn down and carted off to a rubble heap. The recovery of brick was minimal, the cost of removing the rubble enormous. . . . These historic buildings survived centuries of German governments only to be destroyed by Polish hands.[83]

Extreme developments such as occurred in Nysa would have been inconceivable in Wrocław. Largely because it was in the political spotlight, the city lost less of its historic building stock than other locations. In the first decade after the war, numerous buildings deteriorated due to neglect, and serious damage was caused by "brick-recovery operations," but overall the city made significant efforts to preserve its historic buildings. One auspicious factor may have been the fact that the offices of the voivodeship historic preservation agency conservator had been located in Wrocław since 1946. If, due to insufficient personnel and technical equipment, his administration was not in a position to adequately supervise its expanded responsibilities, its staff could at least follow events in Wrocław and intervene when necessary. Public debate on historic preservation in the mid-1950s led to improved government provisions for historic buildings and increased funding for historic preservation. In 1955 Wrocław was assigned its own municipal conservator, and then in 1956 a Steering Group for Conservation Activities (Grupa Wykonawcza Robót Konserwatorskich) was established, which acted as a kind of rapid deployment force to safeguard and rescue historic buildings.[84] However, because conditions before 1956 had been significantly better in Wrocław than in smaller cities, the upswing in 1956 was less evident there.

The improvement of social conditions, especially in the western territories, was just as important as the expansion of historic preservation efforts by state authorities. In the beginning it was chiefly the preservationists who, in their professional capacity, defended the region's architectural heritage. Then, slowly but surely, a sense of responsibility spread throughout all of society.[85] The public discussion of the mid-1950s in particular led to greater popular awareness of the value of historic buildings and fostered social engagement in this domain. The number of volunteer "social conservators" (*społeczny opiekun*), who were absolutely essential due to the perpetual shortage of funds, rose rapidly: from 54 in 1958 to 685 in 1965 to 1170 in 1970 in Wrocław voivodeship.[86]

The fact that old buildings with no intrinsic value to the first settlers suddenly became a matter of concern for everyone also reflects the process of cultural appropriation. This process, however, did not impact every historic building to the same extent. Polish society's image of itself and of history influenced what it regarded as its own and what it regarded as foreign and, accordingly, which historic buildings were dear to its heart and which were not. Against this background, it is significant that the only religious building in Wrocław's Old Town that fell into disrepair after the war was a synagogue— the White Stork Synagogue on ul. Włodkowica. This neoclassical building designed by Carl Ferdinand Langhans had been spared by arsonists on November 9, 1938, only because it was feared that the flames might jump to neighboring buildings. After the war, the new Polish-Jewish community in Wrocław assumed control of the intact building. Polish Jews gradually left the country, however, many in reaction to the anti-Semitic government campaign of 1967–68, and Wrocław's shrinking Jewish community was ultimately unable to maintain the synagogue.

Over protests by the Jewish community, the University of Wrocław assumed control of the building in 1974 with the intention of setting up a library there. The required renovations were never begun, however, and the synagogue continued to deteriorate. Funds were available for the conservation and reconstruction of Wrocław's medieval city walls, but evidently could not be raised for the synagogue. It was a deplorable ruin in 1994, when it was finally returned to the Jewish community. Restorations, begun at pretty much the last moment, were supported financially by the Foundation for German-Polish Cooperation.[87] The old Jewish cemetery on ul. Ślężna suffered a similar fate. After decades of deterioration, it was declared a historic building in 1975 and converted into the Museum of Cemetery Art. Its reconstruction and conservation, however, have proceeded very slowly since the 1980s and have been largely the work of individual benefactors such as Maciej Łagiewski, who much later became the director of the City Museum of Wrocław. Broad social support for the preservation of this landmark was difficult to find among the city's residents. In fact both public and private interest in the restoration of

The White Stork Synagogue, a neoclassical edifice erected in the first half of the nineteenth century in a courtyard between what is today ul. Włodkowicza and ul. Antoniego, survived both the German November pogrom of 1938 and the war with little exterior damage. With the last wave of Jewish emigration from postwar Poland caused by the anti-Semitic government campaign in 1968, Wrocław's Jewish community shrunk to a few hundred members who were not able to maintain the synagogue. As a consequence, the city's only remaining Jewish temple fell into complete disrepair. It wasn't until the mid-nineties that there was sufficient interest in the building to prevent further dilapidation. Today, the restored White Stork Synagogue (opposite page) is a popular place for cultural events and a focal point for the rediscovery of Wrocław's Jewish history. Courtesy of the author and Stanisław Klimek.

the White Stork Synagogue and the old Jewish cemetery lag far behind their historical significance, as do the funds that Polish historic preservation agencies have been able to raise for these projects.

The greatest resistance that historic preservationists encountered, however, was probably in response to their notion that Prussian buildings, too, could become a valuable part of Wrocław's Polish identity. Efforts to garner public support, which had proved so successful for the conservation of Gothic churches and Baroque burgher houses, were largely ineffective for buildings such as the Hohenzollern Palace. As long as the People's Republic of Poland existed, anti-Prussian sentiment within Polish society could not be overcome. This was due not only to the historical experience prior to 1945, but also to

the communist regime's continued exploitation of that experience for political ends. The party's leadership fanned the flames of the anti-German reflex
for decades, and its ire took aim at the Prussian legacy as well. Contempt for
all things Prussian became a significant obstacle to cultural assimilation in the
western territories; indeed it virtually prevented it because the entire cultural
landscape from Masuria to the Sudeten Mountains was shaped to a large degree by the region's long affiliation with Prussia. It was only after the fall of the
People's Republic that more and more Polish intellectuals dared to challenge
the "dark legend of Prussia." [88]

PART THREE

PROSPECTS

The reconstructed Old Town is the pride of Wrocław's Polish citizens, but it is also the place where they encounter the city's non-Polish past. Courtesy of the author.

CHAPTER ELEVEN

Amputated Memory and the Turning Point of 1989

WROCŁAW WAS NOT LOST IN 1945. THE POLISH STATE AND THE PEOPLE who came to Wrocław after the Second World War managed to rebuild and revive this city. Considering the situation at the end of the war—the devastation, the complete collapse of the previous order, the evacuation of its entire population—this achievement borders on a miracle. And if that were not enough, after overcoming its tremendous postwar challenges Wrocław has gone on to become more than simply a functioning Polish city. The secret capital of the western territories ranks next to Warsaw and Krakow as one of Poland's leading cultural metropolises. The Polish government furnished some of the prerequisites for this outcome. It founded a whole series of Polish institutions of higher education in Wrocław, relocated the Ossolineum to the city, and built up the Wrocław Film Studios, at which internationally renowned directors such as Andrzej Wajda and Roman Polański shot their first movies. But Wrocław's cultural life extends beyond the reach of direct state sponsorship. Although many Polish intellectuals and artists again abandoned the city several years after the war because of poor living conditions and what they perceived as a restrictive intellectual climate, Wrocław experienced an astounding cultural upswing in the second half of the 1950s.

In 1956 Henryk Tomaszewski founded the avant-garde Pantomime Theater, which went on to become one of the best-known theaters in the country and soon toured throughout the world. In the mid-1960s Jerzy Grotowski and Ludwig Flaszen moved their Laboratory Theater, which they had founded in Opole, to Wrocław. It was here that Grotowski composed his programmatic text *Towards a Poor Theatre* in 1968, which earned him the status of one of the world's leading theorists of modern drama. Thanks to these and other important theater companies, such as the Contemporary Theater, the Polish National Theater, and various ambitious student groups—first and foremost

"Kalambur" and "Gest"—Wrocław in the 1960s became *the* city of Polish avant-garde theater, with many of its productions enjoying great success internationally as well. In 1968 Tadeusz Różewicz, one of the most prominent poets and writers in Poland, moved to Wrocław. Różewicz's presence acted as a catalyst for the city's rise as a center of Polish contemporary arts. Over the following decades many of his pieces premiered on the city's stages. Significant music events such as the oratorio and cantata festival Wratislavia Cantans, which is unique in Europe, and the jazz festival Jazz nad Odrą (Jazz at the Oder) were also established in Wrocław. Thus the hopes of the early postwar years—that this ruined city might become a flourishing Polish metropolis, which seemed so audacious at the time—were in fact fulfilled.

THE CITY WITHOUT A MEMORY

The power of Wrocław's cultural life and the presence of so many outstanding intellectuals did not mean, however, that local society managed to fully process the rupture of 1945 and develop a sustainable, healthy relationship to the city's past. Behind the apparent normality of big city life, there was a markedly fragile local identity. And this would remain true until quite recently. In the mid-1990s Wrocław Polonist and writer Andrzej Zawada attempted to put into words his hometown's neurosis. In a remarkable essay entitled "Bresław"—a combination of the German and Polish names for the city—Zawada wrote:

> Wrocław is a city with an amputated memory. I had trouble getting used to this city because with every step I found myself unsettled and irritated by its crippledness. It was impossible to walk down the streets of Wrocław without thinking about it. Which is why it was healthy to get out of the city and go elsewhere, where people remembered their past, where the present day was defined by tradition. . . .
>
> Wrocław's past was hidden the way a so-called "good home" conceals the embarrassing secret of someone's illegitimate birth.[1]

The suppression of the German past may have made it easier for the first settlers to acclimate to Wrocław. In the long term, however, it did more to prevent them from establishing roots in the city. Despite all the efforts to "de-Germanize" the cityscape, at best only the most obvious traits of the suppressed past could be eliminated. Even after the archaizing reconstruction of the Old Town and the demolition of symbolic Prussian buildings, Wrocław's architectural visage had more in common with Berlin than with Krakow or Warsaw. It was the same ideas about urban development (and often even the same architects) that had shaped the tenements and garden cities, the factories and the representative government buildings in Berlin, Szczecin, Leipzig, and Wrocław. According to Wrocław Germanist Marek Zybura: "Everything was foreign: the landscape of these territories, the aesthetic configuration and symbolic features of their buildings, the form and degree of their industrial and agricultural development, the fabric of their culture—even the regional history."[2]

In the end, suppressing this foreignness was a hopeless enterprise. However much the German past was avoided in public and concealed under the propagandistic myth of eternal Polishness, it remained present in the private sphere. Apartments in the city were filled with everyday objects from the German era—clothing and linens, dishes, silverware, furniture, paintings and rugs, tools and household implements. Some of these objects had been in place, just where the Germans left them, when houses and apartments were taken over by their new occupants; others had been acquired through szaber and the black market. They were called *poniemiecki*, which means "previously German"; the word became an established colloquialism in Poland. Because these objects were for the most part quite durable in comparison to socialist products, *poniemiecki* also became synonymous with quality. People did not want to give them up; on the contrary, they were happy in the socialist economy of scarcity to hold onto the objects from the era before 1945, be it a sewing machine, a shovel, or a corkscrew. The purge of a material legacy was in this sense incomplete: it was limited to the public sphere. Private apartments were untouched. Given the continued invocation of the "age-old Polishness" of the western territories, a disjunction arose between the public and private spheres.

The material hardships of the postwar years compelled the Polish settlers to drink their tea from the cups of their German predecessors, to sleep in sheets embroidered with their initials, to read books bearing German bookplates. Unintentionally but inevitably a kind of intimacy developed between the newcomers and the city's former inhabitants. In the 1990s Wrocław writer Stanisław Nowicki (alias Stanisław Beres) dared to address the phenomenon:

> Please keep in mind that I was living in a German house in which whole generations of German children had been born and elderly Germans had died. I slept on a German bed, looked at German pictures on the walls, bathed in a German bathtub, ate from German pots and dishes, played with German swords, wrote with a German pen and German ink, leafed through German books. . . . And every time I took my school shirt off its hook, I would see the inscription "Steuernagel." That was the name of the doctor who had lived in my apartment. He had never done anything to me . . . and yet there I was living with his things. Sometimes I would think to myself: "My God, we're living with stolen goods!" . . . We were raised in hatred and fear of the Germans from childhood on; and at the same time our entire world, the entire cosmos of everyday life, even our tastes were shaped by the realm of these German things, appliances, forms, and by the German spirit. Do you know what this means? Don't you think this will have an impact on a person?[3]

These odd encounters with the absent Germans did indeed have far-reaching consequences. Through the everyday objects they left behind, the Germans appeared to the Polish inhabitants of the western territories not only as the occupiers and revanchists portrayed in state propaganda, but also as private individuals who had lovingly furnished their apartments and had led lives as civil and normal as their own. It is perhaps not too much to suggest that the Poles' rapprochement with the Germans following the traumatic experience of the Second World War began with these everyday household objects of the German era. But for all that, political circumstances prior to 1989 did not allow the contradictions between public suppression of the German past and private, everyday encounters with it to be addressed openly.[4]

The settlers in postwar Wrocław were initially concerned with getting their feet set firmly on the ground. This was easier for them the less they preoccupied themselves with the German history of the area. As long as they stood in the direct shadow of the rupture that had occurred in the city and in their own lives, the time was not ripe to speak publicly about these disruptions and their occasionally grotesque consequences. In this respect Wrocław's new residents were similar to other societies that had been affected by the Second World War; they focused their energies on economic reconstruction and establishing stable conditions but avoided open discussion of the traumas of the 1940s. And they accepted more or less readily the inventions and myths of state propaganda, which sought to conceal the rupture of 1945 and obscure the tragedy of the events.

No stable local identity could emerge on this basis. The longer the truth was avoided—that Wrocław had been a German city and in 1945 was transformed into a Polish one through an act of force— the more a feeling of discomfort grew among the city's new inhabitants. According to Marek Zybura, public silence about the German past became an increasingly unbearable burden on the psyche of the city, and some of its inhabitants born after the war began to perceive the continued taboo as a "moral and intellectual scandal": "The barrier they encountered in their attempt to examine the past prior to 1945 was both painful and the source of identity problems among those unquestionably native Wrocławians who were part of a generation shaped by a sense of inauthenticity."[5] But even in reflecting on the suppressed aspects of the city's history one ran into barriers that could not simply be torn down, barriers that were inextricably linked to the development of political relations between Poles and Germans.

THE REVOLUTION IN GERMAN-POLISH RELATIONS

After the Second World War there was throughout Europe widespread hatred of all things German, especially in those countries that had suffered the most under German occupation and had made the greatest sacrifices in defeating Hitler's armies. While anti-German attitudes generally declined over time, giving way to pragmatic perspectives and even to deliberate efforts to overcome old hostilities, they were kept alive artificially in Poland for decades. At the plenum of the Central Committee of the Polish Workers' Party in February 1945, it was explicitly stated that hatred of Germans created opportunities for unifying Polish society politically, "based on the consciousness of the danger that will or may threaten the Polish nation through Germany's defeat, through the desire for revenge that will continue to live for a long time within the German nation."[6] The German threat was the communist leadership's most powerful argument in convincing the Polish people of their need to remain allied with the Soviet Union and to accept the leading role of the communist party. Reference to the German threat served to nip in the bud any criticism of the political system in Poland and any questioning of the postwar international order. Thus it was in the political interests of the communist party to preserve fear of Germans and to fan it by means of propaganda. The thousand-year German "drive to the East" and the existence of "revanchist circles" in Bonn became idées fixes, which over the years diverged increasingly from the political reality of West Germany. Although Polish propaganda did distinguish between the antifascist Germans of the socialist brother nation—the German Democratic Republic (East Germany)—and the forces of reaction and imperialism in the Federal Republic of Germany, the negative image of Germans in general in political propaganda remained largely intact.[7]

There could be no more subversive act in communist Poland than questioning the reality of the German threat and seeking reconciliation with the neighbors to the west. Only with this in mind is it possible to understand the panic with which the communist leadership reacted to a letter of reconciliation sent by the Polish Catholic bishops to their German colleagues in November of 1965. The central message of the letter, "We forgive and ask for forgiveness," was understood in Warsaw as an attack on the political system of the People's Republic. The workers' protests that had troubled Poland's communist leaders since 1956 were no more politically explosive than this pastoral letter. Warsaw must have been relieved to see that the letter's potential to fundamentally alter German-Polish relations was never realized. Polish society demonstrated little understanding for this call for reconciliation, which implicitly also confessed Polish guilt. In addition, the German response was disappointing for the Polish bishops. Instead of reaching for the hand that their Polish colleagues had extended, the German bishops responded with empty political phrases that had been worked out in concert with the Foreign Office in Bonn.

Nevertheless, the pastoral letter—which accorded with the spirit of the *Ostdenkschrift* (Memorandum on the East) that the Protestant Church in West Germany had approved a month earlier—did point to the path that was actually taken several years later. The trip by West German chancellor Willy Brandt to Warsaw in December 1970 proved a milestone in this direction. With the signing of the Treaty of Warsaw, the Federal Republic of

Wrocław's archbishop Bolesław Kominek drafted the famous letter that the Catholic bishops of Poland sent to their German colleagues in 1965. Since 2005, a monument on Sand Island has commemorated Kominek's contribution to Polish-German reconciliation by quoting the letter's most important line in Polish and German: "We forgive and we ask for forgiveness." Courtesy of the author.

Germany officially recognized the inviolability of Poland's western border. The fact that the German chancellor also kneeled at the monument to the Warsaw ghetto uprising was hardly less significant politically, as this gesture profoundly shook the prevailing Polish image of Germans. Although Brandt's trip to Warsaw did not trigger an immediately obvious improvement in German-Polish relations, the year 1970 did mark the beginning of a gradual and fundamental transformation of these relations. The intensification of commerce between Poland and the Federal Republic as well as international efforts to de-escalate the East-West conflict also spurred movement toward rapprochement.

Stereotypes of Germany as an enemy, which had been so long cultivated in Poland, increasingly lost credibility in the 1970s, in part as a result of numerous initiatives such as the German-Polish Textbook Commission. This scholarly body worked diligently to eliminate ideology and mutual stereotypes from schoolbooks and served as a forum where historians of both countries could exchange views in an increasingly open, cooperative atmosphere.[8] West German support during the Solidarność period in the 1980s also had a great impact on Polish society. Truckloads of food packages, financed by millions of private Germans and sent to Poland after martial law had been declared there in December 1981, more than counterbalanced a stepped-up campaign of anti-German propaganda waged by the struggling communist leadership. Even though fear of West German revisionism never completely disappeared, the alleged German threat was by the 1980s no longer a viable political tool. There is in fact an unmistakable connection between the dissolution of stereotypes of Germany as the enemy and the Polish communists' decline in power.

For reunified Germany, the signing of the German-Polish Border Treaty following the collapse of communism in 1989 was essentially a formality. Despite the protest of some functionaries of the German expellee organizations, no serious political or social group in the Federal Republic considered a return of territories lost in 1945 to be an option or even desirable.[9] For Poland, however, the treaty was extraordinarily significant. For the first time its western border was recognized by Germany as legally binding under international law. Poland finally gained certainty that the territorial order of 1945 was no passing phenomenon. People living in the western territories no longer had to ask themselves whether they could feel really at home there. Though a revision of the postwar Polish-German border had become increasingly unlikely over the years, many Poles nevertheless believed it was possible that they might be forced to relinquish their new homes in the west if political circumstances dramatically changed. Another impediment to full cultural appropriation was the fact that Polish national interest did not permit Polish inhabitants to explore the region's pre-1945 Prussian-German history. As long as the German past of Poland's western territories was used as an argument by Germans opposed to the recognition of the 1945 borders, access to the region's past was blocked to its Polish inhabitants—both politically and psychologically. The consequences were difficult to cope with.

> How can one live in a city full of German treasures and have no more than a passing knowledge of their provenance, their actual creators, and their true history? How can one go into a church like those around Łuck or Sandomierz or even Poznań —sometimes half-timbered, with the remnant of a Protestant interior, bare-walled and with galleries— and pretend that it's yours?[10]

In the 1980s the Polish inhabitants of the western territories began to show a growing interest in the silenced history of their homeland. This development was tied in part to the increasingly powerful opposition movement, since private studies of local history were motivated throughout the Eastern Bloc by the need to rebel against the official, state-approved historiography and thus against the omnipotence of the party and its restrictions on free thought. Only with the collapse of communism in 1989 and the definitive recognition of the German-Polish border, however, was the path cleared in Poland for an unbiased examination of the history of the western territories. Overnight the local history of the region ceased to be a political issue. Its residents were suddenly able to decide for themselves how they wanted to remember the past of their hometowns and what meaning they would attribute to the material legacies of the German period. There was an eagerness to learn something about long-suppressed periods in local history. What had their hometowns looked like before 1945, and what were the lives of the people like?

The work of private associations such as Borussia testifies to the profundity of the changes that have occurred in the historiography of Poland's northern and western voivodeships. The goal of this private organization, founded in Olsztyn in 1990, is to explore the multifaceted history of Warmia

As unwanted evidence of Wrocław's German past, German epitaphs were removed after the war. In some cases, postwar exorcism led to the destruction of historically valuable epitaphs like those on the walls of the vicarage of St. Barbara's Church (opposite page). As a consequence of the upheaval of 1989 and improving Polish-German relations, many were returned to their original places, such as those on the outside walls of St. Elizabeth's Church (above). Wrocławians have come to accept and even to appreciate them as testimony to their city's multicultural past. Courtesy of Stanisław Klimek.

and Masuria—the Polish parts of former East Prussia—and to unearth evidence of this history on the ground. In contrast to the selective commemorative policies of the People's Republic, Borussia promoted remembrance for its own sake and thus has not even shied away from restoring old German or Russian war cemeteries. The Karta Center in Warsaw has pursued a similar goal. Its journal (*Karta*), which was published underground already in the early 1980s, has attempted to fill in the gaps in Poland's historical memory through education and by breaking taboos. Karta has also taken on the issue of the forced migrations of the twentieth century. Rather than focusing on the notion of (collective) guilt, Karta has tried to raise awareness of the suffering of the individuals affected by the compulsory migrations and has juxtaposed in its journal the recollections of German and Polish expellees. These changes of approach to the shared past underscore the fact that a revolution has occurred in German-Polish relations.

Political and economic motives have of course contributed to the improvement in German-Polish relations in Poland after the Cold War. No doubt there were Polish politicians who developed an appreciation of their German neighbors only in light of awaited NATO and EU membership, for which the support of the German government proved crucial. Nor can it be assumed that public recognition of the German heritage in western Poland was free of political and economic calculation. An eagerness to attract foreign tourists and investors certainly played a role. The groundwork essential to the transformation of Poland's relations with Germany, however, was laid prior to 1989 by those figures of the Polish opposition movement who—like the members of Borussia and Karta—kept their distance from the 1980s establishment of the People's Republic and saw in their rejection of state-decreed views of history an act of self-liberation. Among them was intellectual and Solidarity activist Jan Józef Lipski, who called in his writings for rejecting nationalist stereotypes and prejudices long before the political upheaval in 1989, despite any immediate political utility that such attitudes might have for Poland.[11] When Lipski condemned not only the anti-German but also the anti-Russian attitudes of Poles, he did so without regard to on-going realignments in foreign policy, characterized by improving relations with Germany at the expense of relations with Russia. Lipski aimed instead at a change in Polish society and its perception of Poland's neighbors that would be its own reward.[12]

THE FALL OF COMMUNISM AND THE
DISCOVERY OF THE BOURGEOIS CITY

The collapse of communism in 1989 was accompanied in Wrocław as else-where by the time-honored rituals of revolution. As soon as the new, demo-cratically elected city council took office in May of 1990, a new wave of street renaming began.[13] A naming commission was once again established, this time with the task of replacing the street names of the People's Republic with names commemorating Poland's democratic and anticommunist traditions. The main thoroughfare to the central train station, renamed in 1947 for Gen-eral Karol Świerczewski (whose affiliation with the communists dated back to the Spanish Civil War), was now named for Marshal Józef Piłsudski, the first head of the Second Polish Republic and hero of the Polish-Soviet War of 1919–20. The square named after the PKWN (the communist-dominated Polish Committee of National Liberation) was renamed in honor of the Legions, the military organization that had struggled for the establishment of an independent Poland during the First World War. The formerly Polish city Stanisławów, today Ivano-Frankivsk in Ukraine, was remembered with a street name at the expense of Karl Liebknecht, as was Polish general and poli-tician in exile Józef Haller at the expense of the Heroes of Labor. The Street of Polish-Soviet Friendship became simply the Street of Friendship. For the first time, representatives of the German past such as Nobel laureate Max Born and philosopher and Catholic nun Edith Stein (canonized in 1998) were hon-ored. Elsewhere Polish translations of historical German street names were adopted at the expense of references to historical figures who had fallen out of favor, such as Friedrich Engels and Karl Marx.

One of the most conspicuous testimonies to the new era in Wrocław was the repeal of the city's coat of arms introduced in 1948, though this act was preceded by a heated debate. A commission was appointed by the Municipal National Council in the fall of 1989 to consider the matter. Its members sup-ported the abolition of the 1948 coat of arms, which was associated with the communist assumption of power, but were unable to agree on an alternative.[14] A proposal to reintroduce the traditional Wrocław arms of 1530, bestowed during the period of Habsburg rule, was rejected by a sizeable number of opponents who favored a coat of arms commemorating Piast origins. They favored a seal depicting John the Baptist that had been used by the municipal council in 1292. Because the commission could not reach a consensus, the city council constituted in 1990 through free elections addressed the issue again. In the summer of 1990 the council voted 31 to 19 in favor of reintroducing the coat of arms of 1530. Supporters of this position carried the day by pointing especially to the fact that this coat of arms had been a victim of totalitarianism in both 1938 and 1948 and, furthermore, that it would reflect Wrocław's multicultural European traditions.

One might be inclined to interpret this debate over the coat of arms— which is now ubiquitous in the cityscape and has long ceased to be an object of controversy—as a conflict between supporters of the pre-1989 mythicized view of history and advocates of demythicization. In view of references to the "antitotalitarian" and "European" character of the Habsburg coat of arms, however, one must also ask whether old national myths have not simply been replaced here by new European ones. In any case, the coat-of-arms debate clearly demonstrates that the reshaping of local awareness after 1989 was and still is not a process devoid of conflict. Wrocław's society had first to come together in the democratic forums created after 1989 and reach an agreement about how it wanted to deal with the city's past, especially with its non-Polish and German aspects.[15]

It is not surprising that the sudden dissolution of the Polonocentric view of Wrocław's city history has also triggered confusion and uncertainty. After the floodgates ruptured that for decades held so firmly against the commemoration of Wrocław's German past, a surge of images has poured over the city, making this past suddenly omnipresent. Lavishly photographed city guides and illustrated books depicting Wrocław before 1945 fill the bookstores. Restaurants, cafés, and hotels have decorated their walls with photographs of old Breslau. Epitaphs removed in 1945 because of their German texts reappeared in churches. Here and there people have even reconstructed German inscriptions that were erased after 1945. The monument to Friedrich Schiller in Szczytnicki Park has been restored, and on the square in front of St. Elizabeth's Church a memorial commemorates Dietrich Bonhoeffer, the famous German theologian and son of the city, who was executed for his uncompromising resistance to the Nazi regime.

The ceremonial transfer of the mortal remains of Cardinal Bertram from his grave in Javornik to the Wrocław cathedral on November 7, 1991, had great symbolic significance.[16] The willingness of the Polish episcopate to entomb the cardinal in his bishopric church in accordance with Catholic tradition, despite the fact that Bertram had not opposed anti-Polish measures in his diocese during the Nazi period,[17] is firm evidence of the Polish desire for reconciliation. At the same time, however, it is an expression as well of a need for historical continuity beyond 1945. In this regard other institutions of the city continue today to search for points of reference prior to 1945, the magical year for tradition-building in Polish Wrocław, that do not invoke the Piast Middle Ages. The University of Wrocław, which was understood in the People's Republic as having been refounded as a Polish university in 1945, celebrated its three-hundredth anniversary in 2002. In doing so it situated itself unmistakably within Habsburg and Prussian traditions.[18] Numerous guests from Germany, including Federal President Johannes Rau, were invited to the festivities in November 2002. American historian Fritz Stern, a native Breslauer of German-Jewish descent, was asked to deliver the keynote lecture.[19]

The transformation of Wrocław since the end of the People's Republic is so profound that even conceptions of time have changed. Prior to 1989, the word "yesterday" in the titles of books on the city's history usually referred to the period immediately after the Second World War, when Wrocław lay in ruins and reconstruction had not yet begun.[20] "Yesterday" now refers to the time before 1945. The evaluation of "yesterday" and "today" has also been inverted. During the communist era the past was something that had been proudly overcome. Today it is regarded as a kind of "good old days"— for instance in the illustrated volume on Wrocław by Maciej Łagiewski, who presents the idyll of the prosperous burgher city not yet damaged by war or blighted by highways and prefabricated high-rise developments.[21] Karl Schlögel correctly pointed out that Wrocław's flood of images nostalgically invokes "the topography of a bourgeois world."[22] Socialist promises of a "bright future" have given way to a yearning for such a past—a phenomenon that can, of course, be observed everywhere in Europe. Today the European city of the nineteenth century has enormous appeal and serves as a model for urban development projects radically different from the urban utopias of the 1960s. Interest in prewar Wrocław is in line with this general trend, but given this city's particular history there are several unique aspects to its reconciliation with its burgher past.

The first is that today's Polish inhabitants of Wrocław have no local Polish burgher traditions to which they can relate. Thus their search for such traditions has been necessarily accompanied by the need to discover and rehabilitate the city's German past. It is Breslau's burghers, Breslau's "bourgeoisie" who have become models for a post-socialist lifestyle. Fascination with the bourgeois and simultaneously German city is particularly evident in Marek Krajewski's detective novels, the first of which was published in 1999 with the provocative title *Śmierć w Breslau* (Death in Breslau) and made Krajewski a celebrated author throughout Poland.[23] Krajewski, a classicist at the University of Wrocław, set his plot in the 1930s. His protagonist, the inspector Eberhard Mock, is depicted as a stylish bon vivant whose investigation leads readers not only through a Breslau with German street names, restaurants, and night clubs, but also into the richly-imagined world of a German upperclass struggling against the coarseness and pettiness of the Nazis.

Wrocław's new appreciation of its bourgeois past has also altered the cityscape. In communist times, Gothic churches and Baroque monasteries, medieval city walls and burgher houses from around 1800 were the focus of historic preservationists. Pictures of these buildings also filled city guidebooks. In contrast, the city of the nineteenth and early twentieth centuries was largely ignored, with its Art Nouveau department stores and brick school buildings, its tenements decorated with stucco and its elegant garden cities. If these structures survived into the present day despite neglect, this was usually due to their durable modern construction. There were indeed calls prior to 1989 urging better treatment of this architectural heritage, which was increasingly threatened by deterioration. A sensation was caused, for instance, by a 1986 memorandum composed by the Wrocław section of the Society of Art Historians that publicly criticized the catastrophic state of historic buildings in Silesia, not least those of the second half of the nineteenth century, which in socialist Poland were regarded as both "bourgeois" and "German."[24] But not until the revolution of 1989 were the political and economic conditions ripe for a revival of the long-neglected architectural legacies of bourgeois Wrocław.

Meanwhile the rebuilding of the historic city center, which concentrated initially on the oldest, symbolically most important edifices, is approaching completion. The process has followed a number of very different paths since

1989, ranging from minutely accurate historic reconstructions of lost buildings, to postmodern collages combining antique and new forms, to a decisive
turning away from the sacralization of the Old Town by inserting buildings
in an explicitly modern style into the historical ensemble. Two decades of
intense building and restoration have completely transformed the Rynek
and pl. Solny. The façades of the burgher houses and department stores now
shine with bright colors, the squares have been repaved with cobblestones,
and considerable sums of money have been invested in an entire series of further beautification measures. New shops, banks, retail chains, and restaurants
and cafés have brought back the life of a vibrant metropolis. Wrocław's old
marketplaces have once again become the uncontested centers of the city, the
pride of its residents, and an attraction for tourists.

Emanating from these central squares, new life has spread into the adjacent
streets as well. Buildings of the late nineteenth and early twentieth centuries,
which were relegated after the war to a marginal existence behind aging façades, have become desirable addresses and have been elaborately restored.
Vacant lots in the city center have filled with new structures: office spaces,
hotels, shopping centers, and other businesses. City leaders now have major
plans for architectural projects beyond the Old Town; they have begun the
gradual development of the long-forgotten Oder islands, and have beautified
promenades and city parks. It is unmistakable that the lost Wrocław of old
has served as a model in these plans. More and more, the city has begun to
resemble its prewar photographs. These developments go hand in hand with
an intense interest in the architecture of the prewar period, from historicism
to classic modernism.

Part of what had been successfully restored in Wrocław's city center after
1989 was destroyed during the devastating flooding of the Oder in July 1997.
But in the end the flood initiated yet another important and ultimately positive turning point in the city's history. People realized that the city had been
caught unprepared because, as Norman Davies and Roger Moorhouse correctly noted, "the Polish population of Wrocław could draw on no collective
memories prior to 1945."[25] They had no experience of the extreme flooding
that had repeatedly occurred along the Oder and that explained why prior
to 1945 certain areas within the city limits had not been developed. Nothing could better illustrate the importance of local knowledge passed down

through generations. In addition, through their joint efforts to combat the floodwaters and rescue local treasures from destruction, the citizens of Wrocław discovered how dear their city had become to them.[26]

The revolutionary change in the relationship between the inhabitants of Wrocław and their city is also evident in the plethora of new monuments. Whereas before 1989 Wrocław's monuments served above all as propaganda for the western territories, its new monuments reflect diverse paths taken in the search for a new image of the city. Many of the monuments erected after 1990 deal with aspects of Polish national history that were taboo prior to 1990. One sees this especially in the parks around the Racławice Panorama, which are filled with national, patriotic monuments. In 1999 a large memorial for the victims of Katyń was unveiled in the immediate vicinity of the Panorama. A memorial for Polish causalities in the battle against the Ukrainian Insurgent Army (UPA) from 1939 to 1947 has been erected at pl. Polski, which before 1945 was the site of the neo-Gothic Prussian war memorial.

The highly popular bronze dwarves (*krasnale*) commemorating the Orange Alternative can be found in ever-growing numbers throughout the Old Town, each of them engaged in some sort of subversive activity. The dwarves—they now even have their own website![27]—belong to a class of memorials in the city that counter the placelessness of the older monuments by commemorating specific dimensions of local history. The Woman with Books, a bronze sculpture on the University Bridge commemorating the collective efforts of Wrocław residents to save their city's cultural treasures from the Oder flood, and the statue of Bishop Kominek, author of the Polish bishops' 1965 letter of reconciliation, also belong to this category.

A significant portion of these new monuments document a new and positive relationship to Wrocław's German past. One such monument is the memorial to Dietrich Bonhoeffer. The most impressive is perhaps the Monument to Shared Memory (Pomnik Wspólnej Pamięci) that was unveiled at Grabiszyński Cemetery in October 2008. In contrast to the Bonhoeffer memorial, which honors a German Breslauer who became a victim of the Nazi regime, the Monument of Shared Memory deals with the treatment of the city's German heritage by Polish authorities. Numerous tombstones from the German cemeteries that were dismantled in the 1960s have been embedded in a 200-foot-long wall. The inscription, in German and Polish, reads: "To the

Bronze dwarves are populating the Old Town. They celebrate in ever-growing numbers Wrocław's Orange Alternative, a carnivalesque anticommunist movement of the 1980s, the mascot of which was the *krasnal* (dwarf). The popular figures are emblematic of efforts to counter the placelessness of the city's postwar monuments and commemorate the Solidarność years. Courtesy of the author.

memory of the previous inhabitants of our city who were buried in cemeteries that no longer exist today."

The most imposing and at the same time controversial of the new monuments is the equestrian statue of the Polish king Bolesław Chrobry, which was unveiled in 2007 on ul. Świdnicka—at precisely the location where the monumental equestrian statue of Kaiser Wilhelm I once stood. This monument, financed by a private organization as well as by the governments in Wrocław and Warsaw, commemorates the monarch who extended Poland's western borders to the Oder River in 1000 CE and established a Polish bishopric in Wrocław. The monument stands in the tradition of western territories propaganda and so would actually fit better in the era prior to 1989. Its inscription does, however, attempt to situate the medieval prince in a "politically correct" context by declaring Bolesław Chrobry—in Polish, German, and Czech—a forerunner of European unification.

Thus, on the one hand, the new monuments document the continued need for an affirmation of Polish patriotism and the role of Poles as martyrs, albeit now with an anti-Soviet rather than an anti-German slant. On the other hand, they testify to a search for deeper local roots, accompanied by a need for reconciliation with the German history of the city and the desire to make Polish commemorative culture compatible with the commemorative culture of Europe at large, in particular that of the European Union. The homogeneous public commemorative culture of the People's Republic has thus fractured into a lively polyphonic chorus. The competing needs for a national, patriotic identity and an identity that transcends nationality have found a "postmodern" resolution: To each his or her own monument.[28] History has lost some of its gravity. Wrocław's residents have gained the self-confidence to develop their own view of the local past, and at times even to play with the pre-1989 historical myths, as for example Tomasz Broda and Mariusz Urbanek do in their hilarious booklet *Zrób sobie Wrocław* (Create Your Own Wrocław).[29]

One common trait of post-socialist commemorative culture in Wrocław, however, is the attempt to remove blind spots in historical awareness and to make public those memories that were once taboo. Since 1989 this has become the most important enterprise of local historians and journalists. Nonetheless, the number of new studies on the history of pre-1945 Wrocław is not overwhelming. Most of what has appeared could be best described as historical surveys. They include the richly-illustrated city history *Wrocław. Dziedzictwo wieków* (Wrocław: The Legacy of Centuries);[30] a new *Historia Wrocławia* (History of Wrocław) in three volumes from prehistory to the present;[31] and a variety of new city guidebooks.[32] All of these publications provide a more detailed and open-minded description of local history than was previously available, although not always from a very stimulating or innovative point of view. At times it seems as if the curiosity of Wrocław's residents and their desire for fresh insights and inspiring perspectives on local history is always a step ahead of the work of professional historians.

One reason for this disparity between supply and demand is the fact that most Wrocław historians studying the period before 1945 have had to overcome a language barrier. Polish historians of the older generation who came to Wrocław after the war often spoke German as a matter of course. They were able to make use of the German archival material in Wrocław and existing German literature.[33] In the era of the People's Republic, however, historians were no longer required to know German. As a result, many young and eager historians of the early 1990s were not equipped with the language skills needed to investigate pre-1945 local history. On the occasion of the city's millennium in 2000, *Gazeta Dolnośląska,* the regional Lower Silesian edition of *Gazeta Wyborcza,* one of the leading Polish newspapers, included a supplement, the "Old Wrocław Gazette," that made a virtue of a necessity. The supplement was simply a collection of Polish translations of articles that had been published in Breslau newspapers between 1900 and 1945. This gave readers an opportunity to examine historical documents themselves in order to familiarize themselves with Wrocław's German past. "The texts in the 'Old Wrocław Gazette,'" explained journalist Beata Maciejewska, "were written as if we'd seen everything with our own eyes. We may not have a time machine at our disposal, but we can make use of writings by colleagues who once worked for German newspapers, the *Schlesische Zeitung* and the *Breslauer Zeitung.*"[34] In this way all Polish Wrocławians became local historians. Suddenly the professionals lost their monopoly on the past.

Apart from Wrocław's Germanists, who always had a more positive, less biased relationship to the German history of the region and were therefore in a sense pioneers of a different way of treating the prewar past,[35] it is art historians who have, since the 1990s, researched and published most extensively on local history prior to 1945. This is due in part to the special tradition of this discipline, in which the German language was held in higher esteem, even after 1945, than it was in history departments. Furthermore, art historians generally did not allow themselves to become political instruments to the same extent as did historians during the communist era. They began much earlier to take an interest in all aspects of the local past and, if necessary, even to challenge the official view of history. Soon after state censorship ended in 1989, they were thus in a position to publish comprehensive studies on neglected or tabooed themes of local (art) history.[36] A particularly impressive example of this is the series of Wrocław architectural atlases edited by Jan Harasimowicz, which covers the entire kaleidoscope of the city's architecture and leaves no doubt as to the importance of the nineteenth and early twentieth centuries in the city's development.[37]

An early achievement in the belated cultural appropriation of the city's history is the *Encyklopedia Wrocławia* (Encyclopedia of Wrocław), also edited by Jan Harasimowicz and published in 2000.[38] The distinctiveness of this voluminous work—its rich illustrations and elaborate layout push the limits of everyday usability, and its price tag presents a serious challenge to the potential reader's budget—can be understood only in the context of another publication. In 1994 hobby historian Gerhard Scheuermann, a German expelled from the city after the war, published a two-volume *Breslau-Lexikon*, which at the time was the most comprehensive reference work on local history.[39] Even though Scheuermann's German-language encyclopedia addressed only the pre-1945 era and its articles did not always measure up to the standards of professional historiography, the local historical knowledge it contained was striking. Harasimowicz's Polish encyclopedia, published six years later, was clearly driven by a desire to surpass Scheuermann's in both scope and quality. It includes around 7,000 articles by over 600 authors, most of whom were Polish, and is a testament to the fact that Wrocław now possesses both the will and the means to take control of its historiography—and this for *all* phases of the city's history.

Wrocław's Search for a New Local Identity

Before 1989 Wrocław could claim no truly local identity. There were no special characteristics that one could point to and say that this or the other quality was typical of Wrocław. The city had instead a kind of western territories identity, which consisted in a pervading awareness that the region was politically threatened in a special way and in the cultivation, above all, of the Piast myth. In the 1990s this changed. A politically-promoted regionalization process began throughout Poland, in which voivodeships and major cities suddenly found themselves in competition with one another. The political centralism of communist Poland, in which everything was concentrated in the national capital, began to fracture as regional and local identifications asserted themselves.

Wrocław's prospects in this new Poland are excellent. The metropolis on the Oder benefits especially from its location at the crossroads of the invigorated European transportation axis between Berlin and Krakow—and in the future perhaps also between Prague and Warsaw. Wrocław's administrative

Wrocław's new monuments testify to changes in cultural memory triggered by the political revolution of 1989. Monuments have been erected to commemorate long-tabooed tragedies such as the mass murder of Polish POWs by the Soviet NKVD at Katyń in 1940 (above), to recall local heroism during the 1997 floods (bottom left), and to honor German Breslauers such as Dietrich Bonhoeffer, who paid with his life for opposing the Nazis (bottom right). Courtesy of the author.

significance has increased through the reorganization of the regional govern-ments in Poland in 1999, as a result of which voivodeships have decreased in numbers but increased in size. Today Wrocław is once again the administrative center for all of Lower Silesia—a status it relinquished in the administrative reform of 1975. Since 1990, the city has had a particularly dynamic munici-pal leadership under the popular mayors Bogdan Zdrowjewski (1990–2001) and Rafał Dutkiewicz (since 2001). Wrocław lost its application to host the 2010 World Exposition to Shanghai, but the bid alone brought the city world-wide recognition. By hosting the International Eucharist Congress in 1997, celebrating the city's millennium in 2000 with distinguished international guests, applying to be the seat of the European Institute of Technology, and winning the bid to host several games of the European Soccer Championship in 2012, Wrocław's citizens have demonstrated their determination to make their city a European metropolis. The fact that Wrocław has been successful in attracting numerous global corporations since 1990, and is today second only to Warsaw in foreign investments in Poland, will help it along this path from the periphery to the center of economic and cultural life in Europe.

Wrocław's emancipation from the old centralism of the People's Republic cannot proceed without conflicts, as became abundantly clear in the "Give Us What's Ours" (*Oddajcie, co nasze*) campaign. In 1991 the director of the Wrocław Historical Museum, Maciej Łagiewski, requested that the Museum of the Polish Army in Warsaw return the medieval shields that had belonged to the city of Wrocław until 1945, when they were relocated to the Polish capital. The Warsaw museum director refused, arguing that it was not advis-able to return the shields because the German inscriptions on them and the monogram of German Emperor Sigismund of Luxembourg, allegedly an em-bittered enemy of Poland, would recall the sorrowful time when Silesia had been separated from the rest of Poland. Exhibiting such objects in Wrocław, he insisted, would have an unfavorable impact on the local population.

Officials in Wrocław, however, did not relent and continued to demand the immediate return of the shields as well as additional art objects that had been transferred from Wrocław to Warsaw museums after the war. In the course of the dispute, a statement made by the director of the Museum of the Polish Army in Warsaw revealed the hypocrisy of Recovered Territories propaganda: "It is incorrect to say that we have something that belongs to Wrocław. After all, that's just an immigrant population; they're resettlers from the East." The head of the Warsaw National Museum spoke in a similar manner: "According to the law, we are the proprietors of the items that you are claiming. They came to Warsaw legally. They are former German (*poniemieckie*) objects."[40] The conflict, which was no longer only about the relationship between the capital and a provincial city, but also about how to deal with the past of the western territories, attracted broader attention when *Gazeta Dolnośląska* took up the issue and initiated a large-scale campaign. The newspaper publicized the statements of the Warsaw museum directors, triggering outrage among Wrocławians. The resulting brouhaha proved infectious, as other communities in the territories now began searching for their lost art objects in Warsaw museums and elsewhere.

The tone of the now public debate became sharper. Varsovians were accused of harboring stolen cultural assets.[41] Wrocławians in turn were said to be insufficiently patriotic, as evidenced by the fact that they had begun to identify with the German history of their city.[42] In the end Wrocław was able to win the support of the minister of culture, who compelled the Warsaw museums to concede. Since that time, art objects have gradually been returned to Wrocław, including the shields of the city guard and the valuable relic of Saint Dorothy (regarded as the patron saint of the city), which had been housed for centuries in Wrocław's town hall.[43] Another indication of the growing self-confidence of the Wrocławians and their desire to elevate the status of their hometown was the 2006 purchase on the international art market of valuable silver once located in the city. This acquisition was remarkable in the sense that the local government raised considerable sums of money for an art treasure associated with prewar Wrocław and that the city's inhabitants enthusiastically supported the effort.

Wrocław's ambition and success in recovering cultural treasures are evidence that a fundamental transformation has occurred in Poland and that a local and regional patriotism has at last developed in the western territories. If necessary, their inhabitants are willing and able to stand up to what remains of Warsaw's centralism. The virulence of the "Give Us What's Ours" debate and the arguments used to oppose the return of the art objects, however, also reveal that Polish society as a whole has yet to reach a consensus on how to deal with the German past of the western voivodeships. While identifying with this past has become natural for some, others have retained old fears, now manifested as concerns about the western territories being sold out to

The Rynek with its Gothic town hall has once again become the heart of the city, a prime address, the place to meet, a venue for cultural events and celebrations, and the most popular destination for tourists and flâneurs. Courtesy of Stanisław Klimek.

German investors or worries about a creeping re-Germanization in the form of masses of German tourists and vacation-home owners. There are those who even fear that the western voivodeships could gradually orient themselves toward the magnet of Berlin (which is far easier to reach from Wrocław than Warsaw) and thus resume their old economic ties to Germany without the need for any manner of border change.[44]

It would be incorrect to suggest, however, that the local identity established in Wrocław since 1990 rests mainly on the commemoration of a long suppressed, prewar past. In the collective memory of the present-day city, patriotic recollections that were taboo in communist times play a no less significant role. The people of Wrocław commemorate the Polish victims of Stalinism; they emphasize Poland's anticommunist, democratic traditions and celebrate the heroes of the Solidarność era; and they continue to remember the loss of the Polish eastern territories, to which people in Wrocław feel especially connected. The Society of the Friends of Lwów was founded in Wrocław in 1989. Streets have been renamed after the cities in the former Polish East. Wrocław bookstores offer a growing selection of nostalgic literature on the *Kresy*, as the lost eastern territories are called in Poland. Some Wrocław restaurants even serve culinary specialties from the former East. The Lwów myth—the notion that it was predominantly expellees from eastern Poland, especially from Lwów, who settled in Wrocław in 1945—gained momentum after 1989. There appears to be a tendency for Wrocławians today to style themselves collectively as Polish expellees and their descendents, although most of the settlers who arrived in the city after 1945 came more or less voluntarily from central Poland. It may be that this powerful sense of affiliation with eastern Poland is only a temporary reaction to the decades-long suppression of any public commemoration of the *Kresy* and the suffering of the people expelled from that region. However, the appeal of the Lwów myth is perhaps also related to the difficult and now inescapable acknowledgement that the prerequisite for the emergence of Polish Wrocław was the expulsion of the city's former inhabitants. If this is true, then the cultivation of the Lwów myth might be seen as an escapist response to an uncomfortable historical reality.

Some of the recently published local histories point in this direction. They attempt to treat all epochs in a balanced manner and thereby emphasize the continuity of the historical development. They do not, however, fully address the profound rupture that Wrocław experienced in 1945. Popular histories, especially, tend to avoid confronting the trauma of this break, presenting it instead as one more episode in the story of a multicultural city that has experienced many caesuras and changes in national affiliation. Used in this way, the notion of a multicultural Wrocław, basically sound though it is, undergoes a kind of transfiguration. The historical myths of the communist era are not abandoned but instead translated into the language of a new epoch and adapted to altered political circumstances. An example is the monograph on the history of Wrocław commissioned by Mayor Bogdan Zdrojewski in 1996 and written by British historians Norman Davies and Roger Moorhouse: true to the prevailing political attitudes of the times, *Microcosm: A Portrait of a Central European City* turned the city of the Piasts into a European metropolis par excellence.[45]

The coming years will show whether this self-image of Wrocław as "the meeting place" (*miasto spotkań*)—the official motto of the city today—is more than an advertising slogan aimed at tourists and investors. If Wrocław is to be a true "meeting place," then its people will have to embrace the full measure of the city's past and present and the entirety of its cultural and ethnic diversity. They will have to take into their story the Ukrainians, the Polish Jews, the Sinti and Roma, and the Russians, all of whom left their traces in the city after the Second World War. They will have to take in as well the growing number of immigrants from around the world who have come to Wrocław since the 1990s. It may even be necessary for Polish Wrocław, which has learned to deal so constructively with its German past, to make peace with Prussia, the state that has perhaps had a more lasting influence on the city on the Oder than any other. But one thing is already certain. While the Piast Middle Ages were repeatedly invoked during the decades of the People's Republic of Poland without giving rise to anything like a credible tradition, the prosperous, freethinking, and hospitable city of today has already begun to give new life to its genuine medieval legacy—as a colorful and vital marketplace at the crossroads of Europe.

APPENDIX ONE

List of Abbreviations

AAN	Archiwum Akt Nowych	Archive of New Records
AP Wr	Archiwum Państwowe we Wrocławiu	State Archive in Wrocław
BDO	Bund Deutscher Osten	League for the German East
BPW	Biuro Planu Wrocławia	Wrocław Planning Office
BZZ	Biuro Ziem Zachodnich	Office of the Western Territories
CZMiOZ	Centralny Zarząd Muzeów i Ochrony Zabytek	Supreme Administration of Museums and the Preservation of Cultural Monuments
FJN	Front Jedności Narodowej	Front of National Unity
GUPP	Główny Urząd Planowania Przestrzennego	Main Directorate for Spatial Planning
KBUA	Komitet Budownictwa, Urbanistyki i Architektury	Committee for Building, Urban Planning and Architecture
KRN	Krajowa Rada Narodowa	State National Council
KRZZ	Komisja dla Rozwoju Ziem Zachodnich	Commission for the Development of the Western Territories
KW	Komitet Wojewódzki	Voivodeship Committee
MAP	Ministerstwo Administracji Publicznej	Ministry of Public Administration
MBP	Ministerstwo Bezpieczeństwa Publicznego	Ministry of Public Security
MGK	Ministerstwo Gospodarki Komunalnej	Ministry of Communal Economy
MIP	Ministerstwo Informacji i Propagandy	Ministry of Information and Propaganda
MKS	Ministerstwo Kultury i Sztuki	Ministry of Arts and Culture
MO	Milicja Obywatelska	Citizens' Militia (Police)
MOdb	Ministerstwo Odbudowy	Ministry of Reconstruction
MPH	Minsterstwo Przemysłu i Handlu	Ministry of Industry and Trade
MRN m. Wr.	Miejska Rada Narodowa miasta Wrocławia	Municipal National Council of the city of Wrocław
MSW	Ministerstwo Spraw Wewnętrznych	Ministry of Internal Affairs
MUO	Miejski Urząd Okręgowy	Municipal District Office
MZO	Ministerstwo Ziem Odzyskanych	Ministry of the Recovered Territories

NDMiOZ	Naczelna Dyrekcja Muzeów i Ochrony Zabytków	Supreme Directorate of Museums and the Preservation of Cultural Monuments
NKZZ	Nadzwyczajna Komisja Ziem Zachodnich	Special Commission for the Western Territories
Pafawag	Państwowa Fabryka Wagonów	State Rail Carriage Factory
PKWN	Polski Komitet Wyzwolenia Narodowego	Polish Committee of National Liberation
PPR	Polska Partia Robotnycza	Polish Workers' Party
PPS	Polska Partia Socjalistyczna	Polish Socialist Party
PRN	Powiatowa Rada Narodowa	County National Council
PUR	Polski Urząd Repatriacyjny	State Repatriation Office
PWRN	Prezydium Wojewódzki Rady Narodowej	Presidium of the Voivodeship National County
PZPR	Polska Zjednoczona Partia Robotnicza	Polish United Workers' Party
PZZ	Polski Związek Zachodni	Polish Western Union
RDPP	Regionalna Dyrekcja Planu Przestrzennego	Regional Directorate for Spatial Planning
RNdZZO	Rada Naukowa dla Zagadnień Ziem Odzyskanych	Scientific Council for the Recovered Territories
SD	Stronnictwo Demokratyczny	Democratic Party
SL	Stronnictwo Ludowe	People's Party
SOO	Samodzielny Oddział Odgruzowania	Independent Department of Rubble Clearance
TMW	Towarzystwo Miłośników Wrocławia	Society of the Friends of Wrocław
TRZZ	Towarzystwo Rozwoju Ziem Zachodnich	Society for the Development of the Western Territories
TZP	Tymczasowy Zarząd Państwowe	Provisional State Administration
UBP	Urząd Bezpieczeństwa Publicznego	Office of Public Security
URM	Urząd Rady Ministrów	Office of the Council of Ministers
UWW	Urząd Wojewódzki Wrocławski	Wrocław Voivodeship Office
WDO	Wrocławska Dyrekcja Odbudowy	Wrocław Directorate for Reconstruction
WRN	Wojewódzka Rada Narodowa	Voivodeship National Council
WUIP	Wojewódzki Urząd Informacji i Propagandy	Voivodeship Office of Information and Propaganda
ZM (Wr)	Zarząd Miejski (miasta Wrocławia)	Municipal Administration (of the city of Wrocław)

APPENDIX TWO

Translations of Polish Institutions

Advance Guard	Grupa operacyjna
Baltic Institute	Instytut Bałtycki
Circle of Friends of Polish Language and Literature	Koło Miłośników Literatury i Języka Polskiego
Council of Ministers	Rada Ministrów
Exhibition of the Recovered Territories	Wystawa Ziem Odzyskanych
Front of National Unity	Front Jedności Narodowej
Maritime League	Liga Morska
Ministry of Arts and Culture	Ministerstwo Kultury i Sztuki
Ministry of Public Administration	Ministerstwo Administracji Publicznej
Ministry of Reconstruction	Ministerstwo Odbudowy
Ministry of the Recovered Territories	Ministerstwo Ziem Odzyskanych
Municipal Demolition Company	Miejskie Przedsiębiorstwo Rozbiórkowe
Municipal National Council	Miejska Rada Narodowa
Provisional Government of National Unity	Tymczasowy Rząd Jedności Narodowej
Science and Culture Group	Grupa Naukowa-Kulturalna
Silesian Institute	Instytut Śląski
Society of the Friends of Lwów	Towarzystwo Przyjaciół Lwowa
West Slavic Institute	Instytut Zachodniosłowiański
Institute of Western Affairs	Instytut Zachodni
Wrocław Directorate for Reconstruction	Wrocławska Dyrekcja Odbudowa (WDO)
Wrocław Planning Office	Biuro "Planu Wrocławia"
Wrocław Society of Friends of History	Wrocławskie Towarzystwo Miłośników Historii

APPENDIX THREE

List of Polish and German Street Names

Polish name after 1945	German name in 1945
al. Karkonoska (temporarily al. Armii Radzieckiej)	Sudetenlandstr. (formerly Julius-Schottländer-Str.)
al. Powstańców Śląskich	Straße der SA (formerly Kaiser-Wilhelm-Str.)
most Grunwaldzki	Kaiserbrücke
most Pokoju	Lessingbrücke
most Szczytnicki	Fürstenbrücke
Nowy Targ	Neumarkt
pl. 1 Maja (today pl. Jana Pawła II)	Königsplatz
pl. Bohaterów Getta	Karlsplatz
pl. Braniborski (temporarily pl. Kirova)	Elferplatz
pl. Dominikański (formerly pl. Dzierżyńskiego)	Dominikanerplatz
pl. F. Dzierżyńskiego (today pl. Dominikański)	Dominikanerplatz
pl. Grunwaldzki	Kaiserstr.
pl. Jana Pawła II (formerly pl. 1 Maja)	Königsplatz
pl. T. Kościuszki	Tauenentzienplatz
pl. Młodzieżowy	Schweidnitzer Str. (upper end)
pl. Muzealny	Museumsplatz
pl. bp. Nankiera	Ritterplatz
pl. Polski	Kaiserin-Augusta-Platz
pl. Powstańców Śląskich	Hindenburgplatz (formerly Reichspräsidentenplatz)
pl. Powstańców Warszawy	Lessingplatz
pl. Słowiański	Weißenburger Platz
pl. Solny	Blücherplatz (formerly Salzring)

pl. k. S. Staszica	Benderplatz
pl. Strzegomski	Striegauer Platz
pl. św. Macieja (temporarily pl. F. Engelsa)	Matthiasplatz
pl. Wolności	Schlossplatz
Podwale	Nikolai-, Ohlauer-, Schweidnitzer Stadtgraben
Rynek	Ring
Rynek Szczepiński	Sturmführer-Demming-Platz (formerly Westendplatz and Tschepiner Platz)
Skwer Pionierów Wrocławski	Waterlooplatz
ul. św. Antoniego	Antonienstr.
ul. Bardzka	Strehlener Str.
ul. Bolesława Krzywoustego	Hundsfelder Str.
ul. Borowska	Bohrauer Str. + Am Lerchenberge
ul. Braniborska	Berliner Str.
ul. A. Brücknera	Friedewalder Str.
ul. Bujwida	Auenstr.
ul. Cmentarna	Am Dorffrieden
ul. M. Curie-Skłodowskiej	Tiergartenstr.
ul. Długa	Einundfünfzigerstr.
ul. B. Drobnera (formerly ul. Jedności Narodowej)	Matthiasstr.
ul. Drukarska	Gutenbergstr.
ul. A. Fredry	Neue Schweidnitzer Str.
ul. Grabiszyńska	Gräbschener Str.
ul. Gwarna	Claasenstr.
ul. Hubska	Hubenstr. + Goethestr.
ul. Jedności Narodowej (today ul. B. Drobnera)	Matthiasstr.
ul. Kamienna	Steinstr. + Kräuterweg
ul. Katedralna	Domstr.
ul. Katowicka (temporarily ul. Stalinogrodzka)	Kattowitzer Str.
ul. Kazimierza Wielkiego	Karlstr., Neueweltgasse, Reußenohle, Goldenergasse, Siebenradeohle, Schloßohle, Hummerei, Altbüßerohle
ul. Kiełbaśnicza	Herrenstr.
ul. Komeńskiego	Comeniusstr.

ul. M. Kopernika	Korpenikusstr.
ul. T. Kościuszki	Tauentzienstr.
ul. Krakowska	Ofener Str.
ul. Krucza	Charlottenstr.
ul. Krupnica	Graupenstr.
ul. Kuźnicza	Schmiedebrücke
ul. Legnicka	Friedrich-Wilhelm-Str. + Frankfurter Str.
ul. Lotnicza	Flughafenstr.
ul. Generalissimusa Stalina (today ul. B. Drobnera)	Matthiasstr.
ul. P. Michałowskiego	Gnomenweg
ul. św. Mikołaja	Nikolaistr.
ul. Nabycińska	Schwertstr.
ul. J.U. Niemcewicza	Rosenstr.
ul. Nowowiejska	Michaelisstr.
ul. Ofiar Oświęcimskich	Junkernstr.
ul. Opolska	Oppelner Str.
ul. Osobowicka	Oswitzer Str.
ul. J. Pankiewicza	Drosselbartweg
ul. Parkowa	Parkstr.
ul. Pestalozziego	Pestalozzistr.
ul. Pilczycka	Pilsnitzer Str.
ul. Marszałka J. Piłsudskiego (temporarily ul. Ogrodowa and ul. gen. K. Świerczewskiego)	Gartenstr. + Am Hauptbahnhof
ul. J. Poniatowskiego	Blücherstr.
ul. Poznańska	Posener Str.
ul. B. Pretficza	Hardenbergstr.
ul. B. Prusa	Lehmdamm
ul. J.E. Purkyniego	Breitestr.
ul. H. Rodakowskiego	Heinzelmännchenweg
ul. W. Roentgena	Röntgenstr.
ul. Rybacka	Fischergasse
ul. Sępa Szarzyńskiego	Hirschstr.
ul. Ślężna	Lohestr.
ul. Świdnicka (temporarily ul. Stalingradzka)	Schweidnitzer Str.

ul. Świebodzka	Freiburger Str.
ul. Sztabowa	Menzelstr.
ul. R. Traugutta	Klosterstr.
ul. Wita Stwosza	Albrechtstr. + Dominikanerstr.
ul. P. Włodkowica	Wallstr.
ul. Wróblewskiego	Horst-Wessel-Str. (Grüneicher Weg, Gustav-Stresemann-Str.)
ul. Zaporoska	Hohenzollernstr. (in parts)
ul. Zgodna	Webskystr.
Ustronie	Seitengasse
Wzgórze Partyzantów	Liebichshöhe
Wzgórze Polskie	Holteihöhe

NOTES

PROLOGUE The Dual Tragedy

[1] Jerrig 1949, 8–9.

[2] van Rahden 2008.

[3] Harasimowicz 2006, 493–94.

[4] Judson 2007.

[5] Thum 2001, 227–52.

[6] *Allgemeines Breslauer Hochschultaschenbuch* 15 (1931–32): 3.

[7] *Schlesischer Hochschulführer* 19 (1939): 49.

[8] Bahlcke 1996b, 137.

[9] Kamiński 1997, 81–128.

[10] Łagiewski 1994.

[11] Ascher 2007. See also the following diaries: Cohn 2006, Tausk 2000.

[12] Zabłocka-Kos 2003, 329–30.

[13] *"Mauscheln"* was a derogative term meaning "to speak Yiddish, to speak incomprehensibly, to mumble." *"Mauschelhalle"* was a *Stürmer* (Nazi newspaper) expression for synagogue—Trans.

[14] Tausk 2000, 183 (entry of November 12, 1938).

[15] Ascher 170.

[16] Ascher 238–39; Harasimowicz 2006, 138.

[17] Tausk 2000, 16–17.

[18] On the history of "Fortress Breslau," the standard reference is Jonca and Konieczny 1963. See also Jonca 1961 and the collection of documents: Jonca and Konieczny 1962. For personal recollections: Ahlfen and Niehoff 1960, Grieger 1948, Hornig 1975, Jerzykiewicz-Jagemann 1995, Majewski 2000; Peikert 1996. See also Hugo Hartung's autobiographical novel, *Der Himmel war unten* (1951).

[19] Peikert 1996, 24–25.

[20] Hornig 1975, 141.

[21] Jonca 1961.

[22] Jonca and Konieczny 1962, 161.

[23] Grieger 1948, 21.

[24] Peikert 1996, 169–70 (March 21, 1945). See also Grieger 1948, 18–19; Hornig 1975, 141.

[25] Scheuermann 1994, 1610–11.

[26] Peikert 1996, 134 (March 13, 1945).

[27] Hornig 1975, 73–74; Peikert 1996, 182 (March 24, 1945).

[28] Peikert 1996, 121 (March 9, 1945).

[29] Grieger 1948, 27.

[30] Peikert 1996, 238–39.

[31] Ibid. and 127 (March 11, 1945).

[32] Schwendemann 1999.

[33] Jonca 1995.

[34] General Sikorski Historical Institute 1961–67, vol. 1, doc. 66, 65.

[35] Gross 1988, Häufele 1999, Lebedeva, 2000, Wóznicka 1999.

[36] Hans-Jürgen Bömelburg and Bogdan Musial 2000, 102–103.

[37] Minutes of the conversation between Churchill and Stalin on the evening of November 28, 1945: U.S. Department of State 1961. *Foreign Relations of the United States. Diplomatic Papers. The Conferences at Cairo and Tehran.* Washington, DC, 509–12.

[38] Roosevelt's declaration of December 1, 1945: ibid., 594.

[39] Sworakowski 1944.

[40] Terry 1983.

[41] Brandes 2001, Frank 2008, Persson 1997.

[42] Kersten 1991, 63ff.

[43] For an excellent study, see Zaremba 2001. See also Snyder 2003, 202–14.

[44] Borodziej 2000, 137–48.

[45] London *Sunday Times* (December 17, 1944), cited in Siebel-Achenbach 1994, 54.

[46] Cited in Koneczny 1998, 262–66.

[47] On this see also Wrzesiński 1995a.

[48] Hartung 1982, 347 (Breslau, June 30, 1945).

INTRODUCTION

[1] Mach 1998.

[2] See the groundbreaking annotated collection of documents edited by Włodzimierz Borodziej and Hans Lemberg, which has been published in Polish (2000–2001) and German (2000–2004). See also the documentation of the Polish debate on the expulsion of the Germans: Bachmann and Kranz 1997 and Bömelburg, Stoessinger, and Traba 2000.

[3] Haslinger, Franzen, and Wessel 2008; Kruke 2006; Troebst 2006.

[4] Kulischer 1948; Schechtman 1962.

[5] Schlögel 2001b, 286–96.

[6] Bloxham 2009, 167–207; Brubaker 1996.

[7] For an excellent pioneering study focused on architectural reconstruction, see Hoppe 2000. There are a number of recent local studies that touch on the long-term consequences of forced population movements: Friedrich 2009, Loew 2003, Musekamp 2010.

[8] In their book on Wrocław, Davies and Moorhouse (2002) devote a single chapter to the period after 1945. This chapter, however, does not fully illuminate the sense of foreignness that determined life in postwar Wrocław. Also, the authors pay limited attention to the reconstruction of the Old Town, which represented a kind of founding act for the Polish city (see my review: "Im Höhenflug, ohne Adlerauge," *Literaturen* 2002, no. 7/8: 62–63). A good overview can be found in the third volume of Suleja 2001, although it can only outline the questions investigated here. Kenney (1997a) provides a vivid description of the chaotic situation in Wrocław during the immediate postwar period. The focus of this well-received study, however, is the relation between workers and the communist leadership, for which he used the industrial cities Wrocław and Łódź as case studies. Wrocław's transformation into a Polish city—which was primarily the work of cultural elites and was closely tied to the history of German-Polish relations—is not a subject of his book. On the first postwar years, see also the informative study by Wrocław historian Kaszuba (1997a). I have also learned a great deal from Ordyłowski's (1991) book on everyday life in those years. Very useful were the chronicles by Tyszkiewicz (2000 and 2001), as well as the *Encyklopedia Wrocławia* (Harasimowicz 2006). These publications on postwar Wrocław, however, hardly touch upon the Polonization of the city, which is the focus of the present study.

[9] On this, see the stimulating essays by Dzikowska (1997). See also Kalicki 1995, Zawada 1996, and Zybura 1998, 369–80.

[10] Zernack 1991, Werner and Zimmerman 2006.

[11] Hirszfeld 1957.

[12] Naimark 2001a; see also Várdy and Tooley 2003.

[13] Snyder 2010, Brown 2004.

[14] As a first encyclopedia of forced migrations in twentieth-century Europe: Brandes 2010.

[15] Over the past decade scholars of forced migrations have shifted their focus to the social and cultural consequences of these migrations: Arburg and Schulze Wessel 2010, Curp 2006, Hofmann 2000, Morawska 2000, Ther 1998. On the cultural appropriation of territories cleansed of their former inhabitants, see Labuda 1997a; Loew, Pletzing, and Serrier 2006; Mach 1998; Mazur 1997b and 2000; Musekamp 2010; and Serrier 2006.

Whereas Polish historians before 1989 avoided dealing with the consequences of forced migrations in Poland, Polish sociologists addressed them early on. Due to their openness to innovative methodological approaches and a remarkable distance from official state propaganda, Polish sociologists long produced more interesting works on the history of the western territories than their colleagues in history departments. These include Frątczak and Strzelecki 1996; Misiak 1973 and ed. 1990; Osękowski 1994; and Turnau 1960.

[16] Beyme et al. 1992; Diefendorf 1990, 1993; Durth and Gutschow 1993.

[17] The literature on the architectural rebuilding of Wrocław is extensive, although only few authors address the symbolic and propagandistic significance of the Old Town reconstruction. The main reason for this is that many of the fundamental works on architectural history were written by the architects responsible for the reconstruction at the time, such as Marcin Bukowski and Edmund Małachowicz. For an excellently researched and richly illustrated handbook on Wrocław's architectural history, see Harasimowicz 1997–99.

[18] An important inspiration was Assmann 1997; for an English translation of the introductory chapter, see Assmann 2003. See also the classic study: Halbwachs 1992.

[19] Sapper and Weichsel 2008; Speitkamp 1997.

[20] Hobsbawm and Ranger 1983; Anderson 1983.

[21] Hofmann 2000, 12.

[22] José M. Faraldo 2008b.

[23] In addition to published memoirs and diaries in the narrower sense, the following collections of *pamiętniki* are of key importance in the case of Wrocław: Markowski 1960–64; Jałowiecki 1970; for a kind of sequel to the early pioneer recollections, with a surprisingly unaltered perspective, see Suleja 1995.

[24] Konopińska 1987, 1991.

[25] Italo Calvino 1978; Kostof 1991, 1992; Schlögel 1995, 2005.

[26] Assmann 1997, 59.

[27] Clifford Geertz 1977.

CHAPTER 1   Takeover

[1] Basiński and Nazarewicz 1987, doc. 24, 86–87. See also the critical remarks in Hofmann 2000, 64–65, note 12.

[2] Kersten 1991; Naimark and Gibianskii 1997.

[3] Minutes for March 12, 1945: AAN, URM 5/1097, fols. 142ff.

[4] Minutes for March 14, 1945: AAN, URM 5/1097, fols. 149ff. On the discussions about a Polish equivalent for "East Prussia," see Kraft 2000, vol. 1, 434, 448, note 44; Lawaty 1986, 215–16.

[5] On the establishment of Polish administration in the western territories, see the still fundamental study by Anna Magierska 1978.

[6] Michalska 1966, 620–47; Osękowski 1994, 34–35.

[7] Markowski 1960–64, vol. 1, 460–61; Kuligowski 1969, 189–90.

[8] Borodziej and Lemberg 2000–2004, vol. 1, 60–61; Gluck 1971, 95–124; P. Madajczyk 1997, 24–25; Strauchold 2003b, 146–54.

[9] Hofmann 2000, 67.

[10] Piaskowski 1964. Wrocław then did become a city-province on January 1, 1957, and retained this status until the local government reform of 1975. During this time the administration of the province of Lower Silesia was located in Wrocław.

[11] Michalska 1966, 624–25; Piaskowski 1964, 226.

[12] Magierska 1978, 98.

[13] Piaskowski 1960, 382.

[14] Michalska 1966, 626.

[15] Kuligowski 1960, 136.

[16] Kania 1952; Drobner 1960, 81; Kulczyński 1960.

[17] Markowski 1960–64, vol. 1, 473ff.

[18] Drobner 1960, 85.

[19] Kuligowski 1960, 135.

[20] Drobner 1960, 82.

[21] Ibid., 81–85; Kuligowski 1960, 136–140.

[22] Kuligowski 1960, 142.

[23] Ibid., 143–44.

[24] ZM progress report of October 4, 1946: AP Wr, ZM Wr 64, fol. 1; Tyszkiewicz 2000, 10.

[25] Kulczyński 1960, 111–12.

[26] Knot 1960, 1962.

[27] Sokołowski 1960, 215.

[28] Scheuermann 1994, vol. 2, 1172.

[29] Kuligowski 1960, 145; progress report of the Wrocław fire department 1945–50: AP Wr, ZM 872.

[30] Michalska 1966, 637. The progress report of the ZM of October 4, 1946, provides several clues: AP Wr, ZM Wr 64.

[31] AP Wr, ZM Wr 1, fol. 1.

[32] For more on the still opaque motives behind Drobner's dismissal, see Chumiński 1990a; Kaszuba 1997a, 75–77. On Drobner's political dreams of Wrocław as a model socialist city, see Jochelson 1995, 12ff.

[33] Transcript no. 9 of August 17, 1945: AP Wr, ZM Wr 1, fol. 38.

[34] Chumiński 1990a, 24; see also the recollections in Oryński 1995, 89–99.

[35] Oryński 1995, 90; Chumiński 1990a.

[36] Chumiński 1990a, 42.

[37] Situation report of May 18, 1945, based on Drobner's information: AAN, MAP 2443, fol. 1.

[38] On this, see Kraft 2001, 230ff. On the rumor about werewolf groups in Wrocław, see the report by a settler: Żaba 1994; on the view that the German resistance groups were imaginary, see Kaszuba 1997a, 173–74.

[39] Bessel 2009, 175–76, 203–204.

[40] Łach 2000; Mochocki 1998, 1999.

[41] On the negative perceptions of Russia in Poland, see Jan Józef Lipski's acclaimed essay, "Dwie ojczyzny—dwa patriotyzmy": Lipski. 1996b [1985].

[42] Michalska 1966, 628.

[43] On Soviet criminality, see Kenney 1997a, 155–56; Naimark 1995; Mochocki 1998.

[44] Kaszuba 1997a, 137–38.

[45] Chumiński 1993, 65; Kaszuba 1997a, 138–39. See also Curp 2006, 50–53.

[46] Report of the Katowice voivodeship MO commander of July 11, 1945: Nitschke 1999, 76.

[47] Jerrig 1949, 20. I have been unable to locate any further confirmation of such an encounter between Drobner and the Soviet commander. Nevertheless, the fact that rumors about the Soviet commander slapping the Polish mayor circulated in Wrocław at the time is significant in itself.

[48] Oryński 1995, 94.

[49] Drobner 1960, 96–97.

[50] Ibid. See also illustrations 9–10; Gostomska-Zarzycka 1960, 326.

[51] Osękowski 1994, 38.

[52] Hofmann 2000, 255–56.

[53] A collection of such documents is located in AP Wr, ZM 143.

[54] On German-Soviet relations in Wrocław, see also Chumiński and Kaszuba 1995, 109–10; Kaszuba 1997a, 144–48.

[55] Naimark 1995. See also Bessel 2009, 148–68; Satjukow 2008.

[56] Konrad 1963, 143.

[57] Ibid., 146.

[58] Naimark 1995, 72; Urban 2003, 241–73; Zeidler 1996, 113–24.

[59] Naimark 1995, 76–78; see also Zeidler 1996, 164–65.

[60] Konrad 1963, 149.

[61] Koenen 2005.

[62] Pasierb 1965; J. Misztal 1998, 71–74.

[63] On antifascist groups in Wrocław, see Kraft 2001, 227–30; Pasierb 1965.

[64] On the activities of the German administration, see also the letter of Wrocław antifascists Paul Barnetzky and Alfred Schneider to the Polish MSW on August 18, 1945: AP Wr, ZM Wr 130, fols. 40–41.

[65] Boćkowski 2001, vol. 4, doc. 170, 283.

[66] Ibid., doc.166, 277; see also 227.

[67] Kaszuba 1997 125.

[68] AP Wr, ZM Wr 130, fol. 40.

[69] Pasierb 1965, 213.

[70] MAP inspection report, based on oral information from Drobner of May 18, 1945: AAN, MAP 2443, fol. 2.

[71] Cited in Chumiński and Kaszuba 1995, 209.

[72] See, for example, the pro-Russian report by a former Wrocław district mayor on the hostile relations between Poles and Russians in Wrocław: Schieder 1954–61, vol. I/2, doc. 217, 327–36.

[73] AP Wr, ZM 128, letter from the director of the MUO VII in Leśnica of June 26, 1946, to the ZM, cited in Chumiński 1993, 68; see also the report on the evacuation operation in the city center in the summer of 1945, in which it becomes clear that Soviet patrols tended to intervene on behalf of the Germans: AP Wr, ZM 1, fols. 136ff.

[74] Borodziej and Lemberg 2000–2004, vol. 1, doc. 77, 205. The editors of the document collection point out that it is unclear whether this letter was actually sent.

[75] Hofmann 2000, 73–74, 255–56.

[76] AAN, MAP 2443, fol. 21.

[77] Report by the Central Committee of the PPR on the current problems in Lower Silesia, July 6, 1945: Boćkowski 2001, doc. 173, 288.

[78] On the German Protestant Church after 1945, see Breyer 1967, 385–414; Neß 1994. For a striking eyewitness account that focuses on Wrocław, see Konrad 1963; see also Bunzel 1965.

[79] Konrad 1963, 146.

[80] Ibid., 159.

[81] Breyer 1967, 389.

[82] Kozłowski 1997, 303–23; Marek 1976; Marschall 1999.

[83] Kaps 1952–53, 81.

[84] Marek 1976, 31–32.

[85] Ibid., 20–21.

[86] Neither the Polish Church nor the Vatican has ever published the official text outlining these powers. The wording, however, can be found in German translation in Scholz 1988, 95–98.

[87] Marek 1976, 20; Scholz 1988, 64.

[88] On Splett's controversial role as Catholic administrator in the Chełmno diocese between 1939 and 1945, his trial, and recent attempts in Poland to rehabilitate him, see Samerski 2002.

[89] Marek 1976, 15–16.

[90] Kaps 1989, Köhler 1980, Marschall 1999.

[91] Scholz 1988, 89ff.

[92] That is, the resolution of the ministerial council of September 12, 1945.

[93] Circular letter of September 17, 1945, issued by the MAP Department for Religious Affairs (Dept. Wyznaniowy) and signed by Kiernik: AAN, MAP 961, fol. 3.

[94] See Robert Żurek's detailed study of the role of the church in the German-Polish conflict: Żurek 2005.

[95] Harasimowicz 2006, 539.

[96] Milik's letter of September 28, 1945, to the minister of the MAP: AAN, MAP 1008, fols. 3ff.

[97] AAN, MAP 1008, fol. 9.

[98] Milik's letter of October 22, 1945, to the minister of the MAP: AAN, MAP 1008, fols. 10–11.

[99] Ibid., fols. 12–13.

[100] Sabisch 1965.

CHAPTER 2   Moving People

[1] Fink 1998, 249–74. Regarding the reality of the residents' right to stay in Poland, see Boysen 2009.

[2] Lemberg 1992, Weitz 2008.

[3] From the growing literature on forced migrations in modern Europe, see a selection of more recent publications: Pertti Ahonen et al. 2008; Bloxham 2009; Brandes, Sundhaussen, and Troebst 2010; Cattaruzza 2008; Czerniakiewicz and Czerniakiewicz 2005; Eberhardt 1996; Lieberman 2006; Naimark 2001a; Ther and Siljak 2001; Várdy and Tooley 2003. See also Snyder 2010.

[4] See the many documents in Borodziej and Lemberg 2000–2001; for the most comprehensive collection of German eyewitness accounts, see Schieder 1954–61; on the problematic political background of this documentation see Beer 1998.

[5] Naimark 1995. See also Bessel 2009, 148–68.

[6] See, for example, Nawratil 1999.

[7] Overmans 1994.

[8] Brandes 2001, Frank 2008, Persson 1997.

[9] Wollstein 1977, Meyer 1955, Mazower 2008.

[10] Clark 2006, 670–81, 685–86.

[11] Brandes 2001, 262–63.

[12] Kossert 2006, Ther 1998.

[13] Dmitrów 1995.

[14] Esch 1998, 55–56.

[15] Esch 1998, 369; citing I. Sesja, RNdZZO, no. 1, p. 44.

[16] On the population policy plans and the paradigm of "overpopulation," see Esch 1998.

[17] MAP circular decree of April 27, 1945: Kersten and Szarota 1966, 160.

[18] Plan Osadniczy BZZ, May 1945: Kersten and Szarota 1966, 146.

[19] Szarota 1969, 82.

[20] Hofmann 2000, 97; on the settlement plans, see Szarota 1969, 96–102.

[21] Siebel-Achenbach 1994, 102–5.

[22] There are variations in population loss estimates. Whereas Łuczak reports a loss of 22 percent, Bömbelburg and Musial assume a figure of approximately 15.7–17.1 percent: Łuczak 1993, 684; Bömelburg and Musial 2000, 103. On the politics of numbers, see Snyder 2010, 401–6.

[23] Of 1,517,983 people who were "repatriated" from the Soviet Union between 1944 and 1948 because they had been Polish citizens on January 1, 1939, 1,258,993 came, according to official data, from the Lithuanian (197,156), Belorussian (274,163), and Ukrainian (787,674) Soviet Socialist Republics; 258,990 came from other parts of the Soviet Union, where they had ended up during the war for various reasons—as deportees, prisoners of war, refugees, or soldiers of the Red Army. On the statistics, see Czerniakiewicz 1987, 54. The option of "repatriation" to Poland was available also to Jews who had possessed Polish citizenship on January 1, 1939. Jews comprised about 10 percent of the total population of eastern Poland before the war. Of the repatriates from Lithuania, Belorussia, and Ukraine, 54,594 (4.3 percent) considered themselves Jewish; 15,103 (1.2 percent) were neither Poles nor Jews, but mostly Russians: Czerniakiewicz 1987, tab. 3, 58–59; see also Kochanowski 2001.

[24] On September 1, 1939, there had been about 11.6 million people living in eastern Poland, 36 percent (or 4.2 million) of whom considered themselves to be of Polish nationality (Czerniakiewicz 1987, 50–51). Many of the men had already left the area before 1944 as soldiers of the Polish army or the various Polish units formed in Western Europe or the Soviet Union after Poland was occupied. Many others fled from eastern Poland before the commencement of the Polish-Soviet population exchange. Of the remaining Polish population, some did not take advantage of the opportunity to resettle while others were hindered from doing so. According to the 1959 census, there were still 230,000 ethnic Poles in Lithuania, 539,000 in Belorussia, and 363,000 in Ukraine; see Ther 1998, 86.

[25] Hofmann 2000, 143–44.

[26] Hopes for a large number of autochthons had been based on vague estimates, as the data was unreliable. German population statistics of May 1939 referred to a figure of 45,600 Poles in Germany, but this took only Polish citizens into account and not German citizens of Polish heritage. The Association of Poles in Germany estimated the number of Poles in Germany before the war at roughly 1.8 million; Strauchold 1995, 11, 23. According to MZO data from January 1, 1949, 1,014,500 people had gone through the verification process; Strauchold 1995, 30. According to the census of December 31, 1948, 935,830 of them lived in the Recovered Territories; Hofmann 2000, tab. 20, 446.

[27] Poland's population in 1938: 34,849,000; as of December 31, 1950: 24,997,000; Seraphim, 1953, 16–17. At the Potsdam Conference on July 24, 1945, Bierut spoke of a reduction from 34 million to 26 million; Basiński and Nazarewicz 1987, 127.

[28] The population of the areas of eastern Germany that later belonged to Poland was approximately 8.8 million in May 1939, according to MZO figures; Łach 1996, 118.

[29] The literature on the expulsion of Germans from Poland is extensive and still growing. While in West Germany—the subject was taboo in East Germany—most works prior to 1990 tended to document the hardships surrounding the expulsion,

Polish scholars focused on the organizational side of the resettlement (if the deplorable circumstances were mentioned at all, they were usually traced back to logistical and technical problems during the postwar years). In both Poland and Germany, renewed interest in the history of the expulsion arose after 1990 and the standpoints and research interests began to converge. With the border question ultimately settled between the two countries, scholars no longer felt compelled to implicitly support or oppose the Oder-Neisse line when writing about the expulsion. Particularly among younger historians, nationally determined perspectives on this subject can no longer be identified. It is important to note, however, that the works published after 1990 do not necessarily render obsolete older depictions—often rich in facts and eyewitness testimonies—but instead supplement these with previously inaccessible archival materials. In addition, they situate the expulsion of the Germans within the broader historical context of violent population shifts in twentieth-century Europe. For an annotated survey of Polish literature on the subject, see Borodziej 1997; for a survey of the German literature, Henke 1995. See also the bibliographic comments in Borodziej and Lemberg 2000–2004, vol. 1; Brandes 2001; Esch 1998; Hofmann 2000; Nitschke 1999; Ociepka 2001. The German-Polish debate on the historical assessment of the expulsion is documented in Bachmann and Kranz 1998; Borodziej and Hajnicz 1998; and Troebst 2006. On the broader Central European context: Haslinger, Franzen, and Schulze Wessel 2008; Kruke 2006. On terminology, with a call for differentiated concepts, see Jankowiak 1997 and Roche 1977.

[30] Basiński and Nazarewicz 1987, 127.

[31] Borodziej and Lemberg 2000–2004, vol. 1, 76.

[32] Ibid., 75.

[33] Borodziej and Lemberg 2000–2004, vol. 1, doc. 35, 160–61.

[34] Jonca and Maciejewski 1997, doc. 1, 96.

[35] Borodziej and Lemberg 2000–2004, vol. 1, 72; Hofmann 2000, 189–99.

[36] Draft by the MAP, cited in Borodziej and Lemberg 2000–2004, vol. 1, doc. 30, 157.

[37] Borodziej and Lemberg 2000–2004, vol. 1, 100.

[38] The dark history of these Polish postwar camps has not been written yet. For general information: Borodziej and Lemberg 2000–2004, vol. 1, 85–99; see also Hirsch 1998.

[39] The figures, which vary from source to source and can only be viewed as approximations, were taken from Borodziej and Lemberg 2000–2004, vol. 1, 104–5.

[40] On the settlement of the Poles see especially Stanisław Ciesielski 2000; Czerniakiewicz 1987; Esch 1998; Hofmann 2000; Kersten 1974; Osękowski 1994; Szarota 1969; Ther 1998.

[41] Szarota 1969, fig. 8, 80; see also Kuligowski 1960, 154.

[42] "Jedź tam, Ani się opatrzysz, Juźeś lepszy i bogatszy, Bowiem rolnik na Zachodzie, Będzie równy wojewodzie!"; cited in Ther 1998, 294.

[43] Żak 1960, vol. 1, 182–83. Żak's account of the situation in Brochów agrees with the recollections of Czesław Rajca about his own arrival in Brochów: Rajca 2000a, 120.

[44] Zaborowski 1970, 175.

[45] On similarities and differences between the situations of German and Polish expellees, see Davies and Moorhouse 2002, 482–88; Ther 1998.

[46] Numerous memoirs describe the special bonds of sympathy between German and Polish expellees in the western territories; see, for example, M.Ruchniewicz 1998, 290–96; Bajer 1998, 237–41; Baranowski 1998, 228ff.; Rajca 2000a.

[47] Hofmann 2000, 142–57.

[48] From the wealth of literature on the autochthons, see some of the more recent works: Blanke 2001, Kamusella 2003, Kossert 2001, and Strauchold 2001.

[49] See for example the report of the government plenipotentiary in administrative district (obwód) no. 19 in Wrocław (1946): AP Wr, UWW VI-748, fol. 5.

[50] Osękowski 1994, 133–38.

[51] On the settlement of Jews in Silesia and in Wrocław after 1945, see Hofmann 2000, 332–80; J. Misztal 1992; Szaynok 2000; E. Waszkiewicz 1999; Ziątkowski 2000.

[52] Gross 2006; Hofmann 2000, 335–36; Michlic 2006; Szaynok 2005, 265–83.

[53] AAN, MIP 935, fol. 2.

[54] Hofmann 2000, 381–421; Misiło 1993; Snyder 2003, 179–201.

[55] Torzecki 1993.

[56] Szarota 1969, 103–108.

[57] Hofmann 2000, 445–46.

[58] Kaszuba 1997a, 42; Chumiński 1993, 57.

[59] Report by Mayor Bolesław Drobner of April 1, 1945, cited in Boćkowski 2001, doc. 157, 263. The word "ghetto" was mentioned in an inspection report of May 18, 1945, based on oral information from Drobner: AAN, MAP 2443, fol. 2.

[60] Circular decree of November 22, 1945, issued by the MAP: Borodziej and Lemberg 2000–2004, vol. 1, doc. 68, 197; see also Esch 1998, 382–83; Hofmann 2000, 199–211; Nitschke 1999, 80ff.

[61] Kraft 2001, 220.

[62] Kaszuba 1997a, 59.

[63] Sokołowski 1960, 217.

[64] On the use of German workers in the western territories, both by Poles and by the Soviet armed forces, see Hofmann 2000, 239–64; on the labor situation in Wrocław specifically, see Ordyłowski 1991, 45–64, Kenney 1997a, 153–55. The treatment of German laborers in postwar Czechoslovakia was quite similar: Gerlach 2007.

[65] K. Maleczyński 1965, 219.

[66] On the rumors that regularly surfaced in the Polish western territories, see Hofmann 2000, 118–19; Szarota 1969, 283–84; Ther 1998, 273.

[67] Rajca 2000b, 136–37.

[68] The press in Wrocław initially responded positively to Byrnes's speech, since he allegedly supported the Oder-Neisse line. Not until a few days later did the PPR campaign against the PSL begin, in which the West was accused of imperialist ambitions. See Chumiński and Kaszuba 1995, 212; Kiwerska 1993, 53ff. ; see also P. Madajczyk 1997, 29–30; Szarota 1969, 287–90; for a collection of letters from the Polish populace, especially in the western territories, protesting revisionist statements by Western politicians in 1946–47, see: AAN, URM 5/204.

[69] Kaszuba 1997a, 42.

[70] Chumiński 1993, 56–57.

[71] Letter of August 31, 1945: AAN, MPH 31, fol. 1.

[72] Letter of November 20, 1945: AAN, MPH 31, fol. 34.

[73] Report of October 20, 1945, AAN, MPH 31, fol. 20.

[74] Ibid., fol. 21.

[75] Nitschke 1999, 82–85.

[76] *Czytelnik*, March 8, 1946, cited in Władysław Gomułka 1964, vol. 2, 54.

[77] Hofmann 2000, 244–45, 250.

[78] Circular decree of June 22, 1946, issued by the MZO, Department of Settlement: AAN, MPiH 203, fol. 17.

[79] Hofmann 2000, 243; Nitschke 1999, 84.

[80] Ordyłowski 1991, 60–61.

[81] Ibid., 47.

[82] Ibid., 61.

[83] Kalicki 1995, 8.

[84] Circular decree no. 3 of March 30, 1946: AAN, MZO 43, fol. 24.

[85] Circular decree no. 4 of May 22, 1946, issued by the MZO (urgent and confidential): AAN, MZO 118, fols. 27–28.

[86] Hofmann 2000, 249, 252–53.

[87] Chumiński and Kaszuba 1995, 220–21; Kaszuba 1997a, 48.

[88] Ociepka 1992, 25, 46–47. For the German minority in postwar Poland in general: P. Madajczyk 2000.

[89] Breyer 1967, 396–97.

[90] On the situation of the German minority in Silesia, see Kurcz 1993; Ociepka 1992.

[91] Kaszuba 1997a, 45. All figures, which are in any case only estimates, have been rounded off. Turnau refers to immigration figures that are significantly lower, based on data from the Statistics Department of the Wrocław MRN: 1947: 34,551; 1948: 24,585; 1949: 15,448, 1950 (no data); 1951: 14,273; 1952: 13,459; 1953: 928; 1954: 325 etc.; this means that immigration dramatically declined after 1953: Turnau 1960, tab. 13, 87. Kaszuba's figures might refer to registration totals not corrected by subtracting the number of people who left the city.

[92] Turnau 1960, 87.

[93] In 1945 the city of Wrocław was contained within the prewar city limits, encompassing 67.5 square miles. By 1951 the city limits were expanded to include 86.6

square miles through the incorporation of neighboring districts. The city expanded again in 1970 to 88.3 square miles, and yet again in 1973 to 113 square miles. Its limits have since remained unchanged. Compared with the period prior to 1951, Wrocław's land area has thus increased by almost 70 percent. On this, see Urząd Statystyczny we Wrocławiu 2000, *Statystyka Wrocławia w latach 1945–1999*, 11–12. However, the population grew only insignificantly as a result of the city's territorial expansion. On this, see Jagielski 1993, 173.

[94] Urząd Statystyczny we Wrocławiu 2000, 19–20. For a detailed description, including many interesting observations on Wrocław's demographic developments since the Second World War, see Jagielski 1993.

[95] On this see Mach 1998, 98.

[96] Travelogue by Sokolewski and Osmańczyk, June 1945, cited in Bóckowski ed. 2001, doc. 163, 272.

[97] AP Wr, UWW VI/748, fol. 3.

[98] AP Wr, UWW VI/784, fol. 30.

[99] Report of the plenipotentiary in Wrocław's administrative district (obwód) no. 19 to the representation of the MZO on the re-Polonization action: AP Wr, UWW VI/748, fols. 1–5.

[100] AP Wr, UWW VI/784, fol. 30.

[101] AP Wr, UWW VI-73, fol. 48; see also fol. 83.

[102] Szarota 1969, 77: According to the last Polish census conducted before the war (December 1931), 8.73 million people, or 27.4 percent of Poland's citizens, lived in cities. Of the 3.13 million Jews, 2.38 million lived in cities.

[103] Szarota 1969, 78.

[104] Kaszuba 1997a, 16; Szarota 1969, 78–79.

[105] First session of the RNdZZO, July 30–August 1, 1945: AAN, MZO 1678–1683; see also Kaszuba 1997a, 17ff.

[106] Szarota 1969, 99.

[107] On the idea of having cities and regions in central Poland become patrons for cities and regions in the western territories, see Szarota 1969, 83–88.

[108] Szarota 1969, 140–41; see also Kaszuba 1997a, 20.

[109] Kaszuba 1997a, 20–21; Szarota 1969, 142ff.

[110] Kaszuba 1997a, 21.

[111] Turnau 1960. On the Lwów myth, see Kalicki 1995; Ordyłowski 1991, 26–27.

[112] For a detailed break down of the data, see Turnau 1960, tab. 2, 31, and the findings of Turnau's critical analysis on p. 38.

[113] Turnau 1960, tabs. 3 and 4, 32–33.

[114] Ibid., tab. 60, 191.

[115] Jagielski 1993, 185.

[116] Turnau 1960, 38–50.

[117] Konopińska 1987, 1991; Harasimowicz ed., 2006, 396.

[118] Turnau 1960, 41; Jagielski 1993, 185.

[119] Turnau 1960, 42.

[120] AAN, MIP 935, fol. 2.

[121] Kaszuba 1990; 1997a, 61–65.

[122] Turnau 1960, 50–81.

[123] Jagielski 1993, 185.

[124] Turnau 1960, 300.

[125] Jałowiecki 1970, 19–20; Turnau 1960, 251–52; see also Jagielski 1993, 184.

[126] Piechocka 1970, 212.

[127] Ordyłowski 1991, 28.

[128] *Pioneer*, December 12, 1945, cited in Ordyłowski 1991, 28.

[129] Talaga 1970, 240.

[130] Ordyłowski 1991, 28.

[131] Szmigulan 1970, 188.

[132] Talaga 1970, 240–41.

[133] Konopińska 1987, 98 (diary entry: Wrocław, November 27, 1945).

[134] Zaborowski 1970, 182.

[135] Kalicki 1997, 18.

[136] Ptaszycka 1956a, 201–204. See also Jerrig (1949, 19–20), who wrote—albeit without citing any sources—that as late as 1949, 55 percent of the population lived north of the Oder, 30 percent in the historical city center, the areas around the central train station, and Oława Gate (Bramy Oławskiej), but only 10 percent in the west and southwest, and all of 5 percent in the southern part of the city.

CHAPTER 3   A Loss of Substance

[1] Gomułka 1945, 56.

[2] Kurdwanowski 2000.

[3] Kuligowski 1960, 144ff.

[4] Gostomska-Zarzycka 1960, 288; Kulczyński 1960, 117–18.

[5] Reports vary from different sources regarding the date and whether the destruction was caused by arson or a bomb blast: Konrad 1963, 143; Scheuermann 1994, vol. 2, 1002; Tyszkiewicz 2000, 13.

[6] For some examples see Gostomska-Zarzycka 1960, 284, 286–288; Kuczyński 1946; Maleczyński 1965, 215.

[7] Konrad 1963, 143.

[8] Jochelson 1997, 201 (June 3, 1945).

[9] Mochocki 1998, 289.

[10] Davies and Moorhouse 2002, 408.

[11] Jochelson 1995, 15.

[12] See the progress reports of the Wrocław fire department 1945–50: AP Wr, ZM Wr 872.

[13] On the issue of the Soviet dismantling actions, which was long taboo, see Hofmann 2000, 80–89; Mochocki 1999; Naimark 1995, 166–83; Osękowski 1994, 39–43; Parsadanova 1990; Zeidler 1996.

[14] Hofmann 2000, 81.

[15] Zeidler 1996, 191.

[16] Report of the mayor appointed by the Soviet military headquarters in Dieck (Pomerania): Schieder 1954–61, vol. 2, doc. 200, 235–36.

[17] Schieder 1954–61, vol. 2, doc. 218, 340 (report from Breslau, January 1953).

[18] Schieder 1954–1961, vol. 2, doc. 219, 345 (report from Breslau, May 1951).

[19] Mochocki 1999, 204.

[20] Hofmann 2000, 82–83.

[21] Memorandum of the PPR Central Committee of September 11, 1945, cited in Wrzesiński 1990–91, vol. 4, doc. 18, 47–48.

[22] Hofmann 2000, 84.

[23] Osękowski 1994, 43.

[24] Mochocki 1999, 203.

[25] Chumiński 1990b, 55.

[26] König 1967, 137.

[27] Chumiński 1990b, 59.

[28] Chumiński 1990a, 33.

[29] Kaszuba 1997a, 129.

[30] Kuligowski 1960, 148–49.

[31] Chumiński 1990a, 36.

[32] Kaszuba 1997a, 133; Chumiński 1990a, 40ff.

[33] Chumiński 1990a, 43–44, cited in Magierska 1986, 185n.

[34] Report of the PaFaWag director of October 10, 1945: AAN, MPH 31, fol. 15.

[35] Chumiński 1990a, 44–45.

[36] Ibid., 46ff.

[37] Chumiński 1990b, 71.

[38] Manfred Hildermeier 1998. *Geschichte der Sowjetunion 1917–1991. Entstehung und Niedergang des ersten sozialistischen Staates.* Munich, 688.

[39] Ganson 2009.

[40] Osękowski 1994, 28–32; Seraphim 1953. For a broader analysis, see also Z. A. Kruszewski 1972.

[41] Chumiński 1990b, 74.

[42] Szymczak 1999, vol. 3, 361.

[43] Szarota 1969, 105.

[44] Młotkowski 1995, 150.

[45] Cited in Kaszuba 1997b, 150.

[46] Kuligowski 1960, 154–55.

[47] Kaszuba 1997a, 171; Ordyłowski 1991, 20.

[48] Kante 1999, 60–61.

[49] Konrad 1963, 150.

[50] Winnicki 1960, 249.

[51] Kuligowski 1960, 147–48.

[52] Gostomska-Zarzycka 1960, 290–91.

[53] Ordyłowski 1991, 102–105.

[54] Chumiński 1990a, 28. On szaber in Wrocław, see Kaszuba 1997c, 145–65; Kenney 1997a, 140.

[55] Gleiss, 1986–97, vol. 6, 476.

[56] Konopińska 1987, 102–103 (diary entry for December 1, 1945).

[57] Steinhaus 1992, 338.

[58] Ordyłowski 1991, 123.

[59] Ibid., 87; Winnicki 1960, 255.

[60] Kante 1999, 67.

[61] Konopińska 1987, 63 (diary entry for October 31, 1945).

[62] Kenney 1997a, 192–98; Ordyłowski 1991, 90–91.

[63] See the minutes of the Wrocław municipal administration sessions in 1945 and 1946: AP Wr, ZM 1–2.

[64] Winnicki 1960, 252.

[65] For example, "szaber urzędowy" in Piaskowski 1964, 228, and "patriotyczny szaber" in Maleczyński 1965, 217.

[66] A Polish play on words, creating "Dojny Śląsk" [literally: milk-giving Silesia] out of "Dolny Śląsk" [Lower Silesia].

[67] Piaskowski 1964, 228.

[68] Szarota 1969, 128–29.

[69] Ordinance no. 4 of July 31, 1945: AAN, URM 5/505, 4.

[70] Letter of September 6, 1945: AAN, URM 5/505, 1.

[71] Szarota 1969, 127.

[72] Circular letter no. 67 of the Chairman of the Council of Ministers of November 30, 1945: AAN, URM 5/505, fols. 23–24. This area of responsibility was transferred to the MZO a short time later. See the circular letter by the chairman of January 10, 1946: AAN, URM 5/505, fols. 19, 34.

[73] Jakub Tyszkiewicz was the first to give a detailed report on the fateful consequences that the "brick operation" had on Wrocław: Tyszkiewicz 1999.

[74] On the negative consequences of the demolition operations, see Saski 1956, 117–18; Krzywobłocki 1955.

[75] Gazeta Robotnicza, no. 207, August 29–30, 1953.

[76] Małachowicz 1985, 142.

[77] Minutes no. 4 of the ZM session of February 11, 1949: AP Wr, ZM Wr 9, fols. 71ff.

[78] *Trybuna Ludu*, no. 342, December 11, 1957.

[79] Sprzedawał . . . ratusz wrocławski, *Trybuna Ludu*, no. 117, April 30, 1957; Die Köpenickiade von Breslau, *Frankfurter Allgemeine Zeitung*, no. 132, June 8, 1957.

[80] Tyszkiewicz 1999, 20.

[81] Message of the ZM to the representation of the MZO of March 4, 1946: AP Wr, ZM 64, fol. 36; *Plan etapowy m. Wrocławia 1956–1960* Prezydium MRN Wr, Miejski Zarząd Architektoniczno-Budowlany, and Pracownia Urbanistyczna of December 1955 [internal booklet stamped "secret"]: AAN, KBUA 11/115, fol. 8; on the volume of rubble in 1956, see the data listed in Ciesielski 1999, 22.

[82] Małachowicz 1985, 102.

[83] AAN, KBUA 11/115, fol. 8.

[84] Council of Ministers resolution (uchwała) no. 417/60 of December 8, 1960: AAN, URM 2.2./96, fol. 135.

[85] Konopińska 1991, 96–97. (February 1947).

[86] AP Wr, ZM 64, fol. 36; according to Józef Zaremba, 52,460 of 186,000 apartments were completely destroyed, 30,290 were up to 85 percent destroyed, 15,900 up to 70 percent destroyed, 42,290 up to 50 percent, and 45,160 up to 10 percent destroyed: *Akcja Odbudowa m. Wrocławia maj 1945—czerwiec 1946*, AAN, MObd 374, fols. 33–46, here: 40.

[87] See Józef Zaremba's report on the reconstruction of Wrocław in the summer of 1946: AAN, MOdb 374, fols. 33–46; here: 40.

[88] Gostomska-Zarzycka 1960, 296–97.

[89] Maleczyński 1965, p. 217.

[90] Ordyłowski 1991, 135ff.

[91] Kulczyński 1960, 129; Skrowaczewska 1995, 133.

[92] AAN, MPH 31.

[93] See the WDO progress reports 1945–48: AP Wr, WDO 239, fols. 30ff.

[94] On the WDO warnings issued to prevent the rapid deterioration of the apartment buildings due to tenant irresponsibility and a lack of minor repairs, see WDO 239, fol. 47; on the situation regarding apartments see also Ordyłowski 1991, 68–75.

[95] *Plan etapowy m. Wrocławia 1956–1960*, ed. Prezydium MRN Wr, Miejski Zarząd Architektoniczno-Budowlany, and Pracownia Urbanistyczna of December 1955 [internal booklet stamped "secret"]: AAN, KBUA 11/115, fol. 13. Even two decades later these problems had not been resolved, as follows from an internal document of February 1973 of the voivodeship committee of the PZPR on the problems of the city of Wrocław: *Uzasadnienie do projektu Uchwały Biura Politycznego KC PZPR w sprawie kompleksowego uporządkowania węzłowych problemów społeczno-gospodarczego rozwoju miasta Wrocławia w okresie do roku 1990*, Wrocław 1973: AP Wr, KW PZPR 74/XVII/12.

[96] Ciesielski 1999, 27–30.

[97] Ibid., 30.

[98] Letter of MGK to Zenon Nowak (October 4, 1945): AAN, URM 2.2/71, fol. 36.

[99] For the dissolution of the MZO, see Strauchold 2003b, 327–36.

[100] Address by Z. Nowak at the founding congress of the TRZZ on June 26, 1957: AAN, TRZZ 2, fol. 139.

[101] Progress report of the KRZZ 1957–59: AAN, URM 2.2/13, fol. 1.

[102] Progress report of the NKZZ: AAN, URM 2.2/10, fols. 2–16.

CHAPTER 4   Reconstruction

[1] On the specific meaning and symbolism of reconstruction (*odbudowa*) in postwar Poland, particularly in Poland's west, see Faraldo 2001, Friedrich 2009, Lubocka-Hoffmann 2004, Musekamp 2010, Zabłocka-Kos 2000. On the broader European context, see Bohn 2008; Diefendorf 1993; Durth and Gutschow 1993; Hackmann 2004; Hoppe 2000.

[2] The standard work on the rebuilding of Warsaw is Jan Górski's *Warszawa w latach 1944–1949* (1988). See also Bartetzky 2009, Tomaszewski 2005.

[3] It was calculated that after the war 68 percent of the building stock in Wrocław had been lost, in comparison to 75 to 80 percent in Warsaw. In absolute terms the destruction in Wrocław also approached that in Warsaw. According to a compilation by the MOdb on March 27, 1947, the number of destroyed or damaged buildings in the Warsaw area was 20,408, amounting to 120,000 cubic yards and a loss of 2.9 million złotys; in comparison, 21,620 buildings were damaged or destroyed in Wrocław, totaling 118,000 cubic yards and a loss of 1.5 million złotys: AAN, MObd 192, fol. 2; fol. 19. The significantly greater loss in value in Warsaw was due to the fact that the average destruction of buildings in the city was greater there, a consequence of the German occupation forces' systematic destruction following the suppression of the Warsaw Uprising in the summer of 1944. In terms of the historic building stock, the absolute damage was probably greater in Wrocław. The Warsaw Old Town was 100 percent destroyed, whereas 50 percent of the Wrocław Old Town survived. The size of Wrocław's Old Town, however, was more than ten times that of Warsaw's: The Warsaw Old Town covered an area of 42 acres, the Wrocław Old Town, 450 acres. Even including the neighboring older suburbs as part of the Warsaw Old Town, it remains significantly smaller than the Wrocław Old Town.

[4] Figures for the extent of destruction are from Kalinowski 1978, 81; Herder-Forschungsrat 1955–67.

[5] Conference of November 26–27, 1945: AAN, MOdb 90, fol. 3. Over 50 percent (5,516,788 złotys) of the loans by the MObd (totaling 10,717,602 złotys) were invested in Warsaw in 1945–46; 2,538,578 złotys in all the remaining cities; and only 1,012,935 złotys in the western territories: see AP Wr, UWW XVIII/46, fol. 2.

[6] Władysław Gomułka, "Otwieramy rok nowy kartą pokoju," *Głos Ludu* (January 1, 1946), cited in Gomułka 1964, 7–8.

[7] AAN, MOdb 88, fol. 34; see also A. Andrzejewski, K. Dziewonski, and J. Goryński, "The Basic Principles of the Plan of Reconstruction for 1947–1949" (paper for a conference in Paris in June 1947): AAN, MOdb 255, fol. 4.

[8] *Pioneer*, August 29, 1945.

[9] Marcin Bukowski 1995, 121.

[10] See the RDPP report signed by Józef Zaremba, "The Industry of the City of Wrocław" (undated, ca. 1947): AAN, GUPP 550, fol. 4; see also AAN, GUPP 503, fols. 4–5; AAN, GUPP 449, fol. 20.

[11] See Memorandum No. 2 of July 1947 prepared for the minister of reconstruction, regarding the first stage in managing the western territories, composed under the leadership of A. Andrzejewski, S. Tworkowski, E. Ciborowski, and J. Guranowski: AAN, MOdb 320; MOdb 321, fol. 24. On Wrocław's loss of importance, see also Tyszkiewicz 1995. For a broader perspective on the entire postwar era, see Wrzesiński 1999.

[12] See the progress report by Józef Rybicki (undated, presumably 1947): AP Wr, WDO 239, fols. 27–28.

[13] AP Wr, WDO 239, fol. 27.

[14] For a detailed breakdown of the destruction percentages, see Bukowski 1985, 5–26; Małachowicz 1985, 101–15; 1992, 209–65. Important information is also contained in the internal reports by Józef Zaremba on rebuilding Wrocław 1945–46 (undated): AAN, MOdb 237, fols. 33–46; see also the photographic documentation of the destruction, M. Smolak 1995.

[15] AAN, MOdb 237, fols. 35–36.

[16] Ibid., 102.

[17] Olechnowicz 1997, 15; see also the doubts Anna Ptaszycka has expressed about the alleged total destruction in several city districts: Ptaszycka 1956a, 205.

[18] Ptaszycka 1956a, 207, ill. 119. Very helpful in assessing the war and postwar damage is the recent publication of Polish aerial photographs taken in 1947: Kaczmarek and Tyszkiewicz 2009.

[19] Majewski and Markiewicz 1998.

[20] Durth and Gutschow 1993.

[21] There is no comprehensive account of the rebuilding of Wrocław. For an overview of the reconstruction of central historic buildings during the first postwar years, see Bukowski 1985. Bukowski was one of the most important figures in the reconstruction. A wealth of information as well as outlines, maps, and photographs can be found in the two fundamental monographs about the reconstruction of the Old Town and the Oder islands: Edmund Małachowicz 1985, 1992 (2nd ed.). Małachowicz was another of the leading Wrocław architects and preservationists of the postwar era. An outstanding depiction of the reconstruction of the Old Town, which is rich in material and critical in its judgment of failures in terms of historic preservation and urban design, is contained in the still unpublished dissertation submitted by Małgorzata Olechnowicz to the Wrocław Polytechnic:

Olechnowicz 1997. Substantial architectural and historical information on the reconstruction can also be found in Harasimowicz 1997–99.

[22] See the progress report by Józef Rybicki (undated, probably 1947), AP Wr, WDO 239, fols. 27–29.

[23] Małachowicz 1985, 102.

[24] Jan Wójcik 1995, 50.

[25] Tyszkiewicz 2000, 17.

[26] Ordyłowski 1991, 133–35.

[27] Tyszkiewicz 2000, 30.

[28] Tyszkiewicz 2000, 41.

[29] Ordyłowski 1991, 133–39; Pussak 1995; Tyszkiewicz 2000.

[30] Tyszkiewicz 2000, 36; 31 AAN, MOdb 374, fols. 36–37; Ptaszycka 1956a, 216.

[31] AAN, MOdb 374, fols. 36–37; Ptaszycka 1956a, 216.

[32] Misiak 1973, 126ff.; Ordyłowski 1991, 158–59; Tyszkiewicz 2000, 41.

[33] Ciesielski 1999, 11–57; Ordyłowski 1991, 144–51.

[34] AAN, MOdb 374, fols. 44–45.

[35] WDO progress report (undated): AP Wr, WDO 239, fol. 2.

[36] On this, see the various circular decrees of the MOdb 1946–48, AP Wr, WDO 2, fol. 3, fols. 39ff., fols. 89ff., fol. 92.

[37] Compilation of the WDO of November 22, 1948: AP Wr, WDO 239, fol. 53.

[38] WDO progress report 1945–48 (undated): AP Wr, WDO 239, fols. 30–52. Between 1946 and 1949, 9,920 buildings are said to have been rebuilt and made usable (AAN, KBUA 11/115, fol. 6). Given the total of 32,000 buildings, this figure amounts to approximately 30 percent of the building stock, only slightly more than the 25 percent that were listed as having no or only minor war damage (damaged roofs and windows) and with which the repair operations began (AP Wr, ZM Wr 64, fol. 36).

[39] See the WDO list of the 269 (mostly only slightly damaged) buildings that it rebuilt between 1945 and 1949, as well as their current occupants: AP, WDO 239, fols. 67–73. The discrepancies between these and the WDO figures of November 22, 1948 (AP Wr, WDO 239, fol. 53), which report the repair of 494 buildings in the identical time period, cannot be resolved. The larger figure, however, also included approximately 200 residential buildings, the addresses of which are not included in the detailed compilation. Under the conditions of the immediate postwar period, makeshift arrangements were common; individual institutions often moved repeatedly and seldom had permanent addresses. On this issue, see the first Polish address books and telephone books of the postwar period: Przedsiębiorstwo 1947; Jabłoński 1945.

[40] Małachowicz 1985, 138.

[41] On this, see Åman 1992, which however contains no information specific to Poland. On Poland, see Basista 2001, 19–28.

[42] Latour 1989, 64.

[43] Basista 2001, 23.

[44] Berg 1921, 38.

[45] Anna Ptaszycka discusses the university campus project of the early 1950s without mentioning its precursors: Ptaszycka 1956b, 241, 270–73. In contrast, in his 1985 review of architectural history Małachowicz examines the urban planning ideas from the period between the two world wars and provides several illustrations, but does not consider the degree to which these served as a model after 1945: Małachowicz 1985, 77–82. In the second edition (1992) of his architectural history of the Oder islands in Wrocław—which included an entirely new chapter, "Nowe centrum nad Odrą" [The new center on the Oder]—Małachowicz noted that the project to construct a university district on the right bank of the Oder that had been worked out in the 1950s was the "decisive continuation and further development of the conception of the 1930s": Małachowicz 1992, 278. A similar case is the circuitous street along the city moat in the Old Town. Plans for such a street, which would require the removal of many old buildings, had first been developed by Max Berg and others after the First World War, but were not implemented prior to 1945. Some of the demolition measures taken during the siege fighting were regarded as preparatory steps for its construction after the war. The route of ul. Kazimierza Wielkiego, which was laid out in the 1970s and represented the most elaborate urban planning project in the Wrocław city center, followed the course of Berg's original plans: Kononowicz 1997, 25–26; Ilkosz 1997b, 33, ill. 27.

[46] On this issue, see Latour 1989.

[47] Kalinowski 1978, 82.

[48] Ibid.

[49] Latour 1989, 70ff.

[50] Rymaszewski 1978, 218.

[51] Chrzanowski 1957, 16.

[52] Olechnowicz 1997. On this, see also Małachowicz 1985, Małachowicz 1992.

CHAPTER 5   The Impermanence Syndrome

[1] Konopińska was referring to Max Berg's famous Centennial Hall.

[2] Konopińska 1987, 36–42 (June 12, 1945).

[3] Ibid., 53 (October 2, 1945).

[4] Inselverlag was, and still is, one of the leading German publishing houses, renowned for its specialization in world literature.

[5] Steinhaus 1992, 332.

[6] Budzinśki 1971, 273–74.

[7] Terlecki 1970, 162.

[8] K. Maleczyński 1965, 217.

[9] Kenney 1997a, 157.

[10] For a vivid depiction of the heterogeneous makeup of the population in the western territories, see Burszta 1995 [1966]. On Wrocław in particular, see the pioneering study Turnau 1960. See also Kaszuba 1997a, 49–71; Kenney 1997a, 149–65. The various *pamiętniki* (memoirs) by Wrocław residents are an important primary source, in which conflicts due to background are a recurrent theme: Jałowiecki 1970. On the relationships between the different groups of settlers in the western territories, see also Ther 1998, 258ff.

[11] Richard Bessel rightly applied the term to inhabitants of postwar Germany; whereas in Germany at least parts of the population still lived in their familiar environment, this was not the case in Poland's western territories (with the exception of Upper Silesia and Masuria): Bessel 2009, 246–78.

[12] W. Urban 1965, 65.

[13] Other common names were *Zabugowcy* or the clearly pejorative *Zabugole* or *Chadziaje*; on this, see Burszta 1995, 94.

[14] By calling them "Masurians," they equated the people of central Poland, including the city dwellers of Warsaw, Łódź, Krakow, and Poznań, with the Polish-speaking peasants and fishermen of Masuria in the southern part of former East Prussia. Since the Masurians were Protestant and not Catholic like the vast majority of Polish society, calling the central Poles Masurians might also have expressed the contempt for the more secularized society of central Poland.

[15] Rajca 2000b, 139.

[16] Turnau 1960, 277.

[17] Ibid., 278.

[18] Harasimowicz 1997–99.

[19] Kaszuba 1997a, 143.

[20] On crime in Wrocław, see Chumiński 1993, 64ff.; Kaszuba 1997a, 136–37; Ordyłowski 1991, 114–32.

[21] Jochelson 1997, 209 (June 10, 1945).

[22] Kaszuba 1997a, 136.

[23] Żaba 1994 [1957], 71.

[24] Kulczyński 1960, 125.

[25] Gostomska-Zarzycka 1960, 292.

[26] Żaba 1994, 72.

[27] On the dubious role of the Polish militia in the early postwar period, see Kochanowski 2000. With regard to the western territories in particular, see the confidential report of the MAP on a tour of inspection through Silesia (August 15–25, 1945): AAN, MAP 2443, fol. 41.

[28] Chumiński 1993, 74.

[29] MAP inspection report: AAN, MAP 2338, fols. 31–37.

[30] See for example the angry protests by Wrocław residents against mismanagement in the city administration in an MRN session of January 31, 1947: AP Wr, ZM 65, fols. 15ff.

[31] Report on the inspection of May 16–June 16, 1949: AP Wr, UWW VI– 750, fols. 36–48.

[32] Kaszuba 1997a, 43. On personnel problems in Wrocław resulting from the unattractiveness of local living conditions and insufficient wages, see the inspection report of November 2, 1945: AAN, MAP 2340. See also the Lower Silesian provincial governor's recollections of difficulties finding people with suitable qualifications and ethics to work in the provincial administration: Piaskowski 1964.

[33] Inspection report of November 9, 1945: AAN, MAP, 2338, fol. 35.

[34] Rajca 2000b, 140–41.

[35] S. Gajewski 1970. Miłość zaczęła się budzić przez irytację. In Jałowiecki 1970, 266; see also Zaborowski 1970, 181.

[36] Konopińska 1987, 136 (December 27, 1945).

[37] Gajewski 1970, 267.

[38] Stankiewicz 1970, 158.

[39] Dąbrowska 1996, vol. 1, 123 (May 5, 1947).

[40] See, for example, the documentation by the Johann Gottfried Herder-Forschungsrat 1955–67. Typical were West German travel reports that lamented the disrepair and decline: Wassermann 1957, E. and P. Ruge 1985.

CHAPTER 6   Propaganda as Necessity

[1] On the history of Poland's "Western Thought," see in particular Mroczko 1986, Strauchold 2003b, Tomczak 1993, Zernack and Friedrich 2004. For an informative resource, albeit at times with a slightly nationalist perspective, see Wrzesiński 1988.

[2] On the particular significance of the Poznań region for the Polish national movement, see the excellent study by Thomas Serrier (2005).

[3] Grabowski 1998.

[4] Musielak 1986.

[5] Burleigh 1988. On the interplay between the two hostile movements, see Piskorski, Hackmann, and Jaworski 2002.

[6] Curp 2006, 39–40, 46–47; Hofmann 2000, 52–59; P. Madajczyk 1997; Strauchold 2003b, 52–58.

[7] Fleming 2010; Zaremba 2001; see also Mevius 2009.

[8] Krzoska 2003.

[9] Hackmann 2001, 243; Strauchold 2003b, 73–78.

[10] For detailed information on the establishments of these institutions, see Strauchold 2003b.

[11] Kwilecki 1994.

[12] Wojciechowski 1945.

[13] Gomułka 1964, vol. 2, 135.

[14] Shorthand record of the speech of September 21, 1952: AP Wr, KW PZPR 74/ VII/73, fols. 1ff.

[15] The term has been borrowed from Peter Schöttler's study on the political function of historiography in Germany: Schöttler 1997.

[16] Instytut Zachodni 1948–57. On the background of this series, see Strauchold 2003b, 217–20.

[17] K. and M. Suchocki 1948–50, vol. 1/1, 10–11.

[18] For a good overview, see Neumann, 1966. Also stimulating is Misiak's sociological study on the role of cultural institutions in shaping a new consciousness in Lower Silesia: Misiak 1973.

[19] Gomułka 1946a, cited in Gomułka 1964, 125.

[20] See the letter of October 14, 1946, from the Lower Silesian Opera to Gomułka: AAN, MZO 79, fol. 69.

[21] Misiak 1973, 137; Ordyłowski 1991, 177.

[22] Letter of February 13, 1947: AAN, MZO 79, fols. 106ff.

[23] Letter of May 2, 1957, from Centralny Zarząd Świetlic i Domów Kultury at the MKS to the deputy minister: AAN, URM 2.2/6, fol. 5.

[24] Letter of June 3, 1946, to Gomułka: AAN, MZO 79, fol. 21, inventory list fols. 22ff; cited in Rutkowska 1997, 269ff. Władysław Misiak mentioned the removal of cultural assets as early as the early 1970s. He left no doubt as to the propagandistic purposes of the operation; see Misiak 1973,124ff. On this, see also Zybura 1999a, 24–26.

[25] NDMiOZ memorandum of August 12, 1947: AAN, MZO 79, fols. 112–13; cited in Rutkowska 1997, 293–94.

[26] AP Wr, UWW XVII/117, fols. 82–85. See also Misiak 1973, 125.

[27] Of the 663 Catholic members of the clergy who worked in the western territories between 1945 and 1950, 344 came from the archdioceses in Lwów and Wilno. In the Wrocław administrature, 190 of 346 clerics came from the east. See R. Marek 1976, 304.

[28] Osękowski 1994, 210–34.

[29] Żurek 2005. An analysis of the special role of the Catholic Church in the western territories is still needed.

[30] In this context, "millenium" refers to the grand celebration of the 1000th anniversary of the Polish Catholic Church in 1966. Initiated by Cardinal Stefan Wyszyński, these celebrations spanned the entire decade from 1957 to 1966.

[31] Cited from Marschall 1999, 10.

[32] Rydel 1997, 231–50.

[33] Cited in Kominek 1971, 24. See also the very nationalistic address by Polish Primate Cardinal Stefan Wyszyński on the twenty-fifth anniversary of the Polish Catholic Church in the western territories: Wyszyński 1971.

[34] On this, see also Zybura 1998, 374–75.

[35] See the progress report of the PZZ 1944–47: AAN, MZO 82, fols. 3ff.

[36] Broszat 1961; Kleßmann 1971, 50ff. See also C. Madajczyk 1988.

[37] On the similarities between the national propaganda of Germany and that of Poland, see Schultz 2001b, 9–15; Thum 2001. On racist elements in the policies of the People's Republic of Poland, see Esch 1998; Koneczny 1998, vol. 2, no. 2, 253–74.

[38] On this, the most comprehensive study is Tyszkiewicz 1997.

[39] Ibid., 71–77.

[40] Ibid., 53–56.

[41] On the crisis facing Western Thought from 1949 to 1956, see Strauchold 2003b, 303–99; see also Borodziej 1997a, 411ff.; Hackmann 2001, 248–49.

[42] AAN, TRZZ; the programmatic reports presented at the founding congress on June 26, 1957, are particularly informative: AAN, TRZZ 2; also the progress report of the TRZZ 1957–70: AAN, TRZZ 246. See also Curp 2006, 172–85; Strauchold 2003b, 424–33.

[43] AAN, TRZZ 1041, fols. 8–20.

[44] AAN, TRZZ 1046, fol. 4. The project was never implemented.

[45] The TRZZ progress report for 1957—1970 reported membership figures as follows: 1958: 20,340; 1960: 47,329; 1965: 128,209; 1968: 126,826; 1969: 119,135. In 1964 the voivodeship association in Katowice had 44,550 members; Poznań 12,660; Opole 12,500; Wrocław 11,112; Zielona Góra 7,994; and Koszalin 6,151. In central Poland, in contrast: Kielce 6,120; Lodz 4,500; Warsaw 2,968: AAN, TRZZ 246, fols. 14, 17.

[46] Kowal 1998, 17; Faraldo 2008b.

[47] AAN, TRZZ 246, fol. 1.

[48] Wojciechowski 1955 [1933]. See also Hackmann 2001, 242; Krzoska 2003, 203–16.

[49] On the terminology, see also Linek 1997a, 11–19.

[50] Against the background of a forty-year-old language convention in Poland, Bernard Linek's dissertation on the policies of the Polish authorities in Upper Silesia broke a taboo, not least because of the title "Odniemczanie" (de-Germanization): Linek 1997a.

[51] Rutkiewicz 1973, 34.

CHAPTER 7   Mythicizing History

[1] Flachenecker 1993, 128.

[2] On this, see Thum 2001.

[3] Hobsbawm and Ranger 1983.

[4] Długoborski, Gierowski, and Maleczyński 1958.

[5] Ibid., 9–10.

[6] Ibid., 8.

[7] Sosnowski and Suchocki 1948–50, vol. 1, 10.

[8] Sosnowski and Suchocki 1948–50.

[9] Daleszak 1970; Jochelson 1946; Król 1957b; Kwaśniewski 1972; Markowski 1960; Mierzecka 1967; Roszkowska 1970; Rutkiewicz 1973; Siwon 1971.

[10] On Maleczyński's dual role as both a scholar and a propagandist of the Polish Western Idea, see Cetwiński and Tyszkiewicz 1999.

[11] Connelly 2005.

[12] Serczyk 1996, vol. 3, 245–56; Strelczyk 1996, 113–31.

[13] On the significance of the Piast tradition in Polish political thought, see Orzechowski 1975, 269–85.

[14] On nationalistic interpretations of German-Polish relations in the Middle Ages, see Riemenschneider 1980.

[15] Maleczyński 1970a, 14.

[16] Holtzmann 2007, vol. 4, 45.

[17] The following works make no reference to the Přemyslids in their portrayal of the city's founding phase: Jochelson 1946; Ewa Maleczyńska 1948, vol. 1, 20–43; Maleczyński 1970b, 118–35; Roszkowska 1970; Rutkiewicz 1973; Ślązak 1957, 13–23.

[18] Jochelson 1946, 3.

[19] Maleczyńska 1950a, vol. 1, 74. On such portrayals of Jadwiga/Hedwig, see Gottschalk 1965.

[20] Maleczyński 1970c, 18–19.

[21] Ibid., 25.

[22] Maleczyńska 1950b, vol. 1, 119–41.

[23] Kaczmarczyk and Maleczyński 1950, vol. 1, 400.

[24] Ślązak 1957, 19.

[25] Maleczyńska 1950b, 122.

[26] Maleczyńska 1950a, 74.

[27] Maleczyńska 1950b, 134.

[28] See, for example, Maleczyńska 1950b, 134; Ślązak 1957, 20–21.

[29] Rutkiewicz 1973, 8.

[30] Ślązak 1957, 15.

[31] Jochelson 1946, 3.

[32] On this, see in particular Dmitrów 2002, Lawaty 1986. See also Hackmann 1996.

[33] Roszkowska 1970, 19.

[34] Rutkiewicz 1973, 11.

[35] Maleczyński 1970b, 128.

[36] Chmarzyński 1948, vol. 2, 48–49.

[37] Kokot 1948, vol. 2, 293–309.

[38] Barycz 1946; Orzechowski 1960, 1968; Raszewski 1952; Zduniak 1964.

[39] Kulak 1981, 1989; Szuszkiewicz 1967–68, 1971, 1974.

[40] Fiedor 1967; Jonca 1961; Jonca and Konieczny 1962, 1963; Rutkiewicz 1973, 16–25.

[41] Długoborski, Gierowski, and Maleczyński 1958.

[42] The following works are typical in this respect: Orzechowski 1968, 1971, 1972. A positive exception is Maleczyński and Ptaszycka 1956, 119–86, an overview that, although it repeats the classical myths, nevertheless provides objective information about the expansion of the city. The extent to which this phase of city history was previously neglected becomes clear in an excellent recent work: Zabłocka-Kos 2006.

[43] Maleczyński 1970c, 12.

[44] "Kto był tu pierwszy?" (Who was here first?) is the title of the chapter on early history by Witold Hensel and Ewa Maleczyńska in Sosnowski and Suchocki 1948–50, 41–61. In contrast to the expressly Germanic settlement history that one finds in German historiography before 1945, the authors argue here that the Oder region had been continuously settled since the Stone Age by ancestors of the Slavs and that other ethnic groups, especially Germans, had had no significant presence.

[45] For example, see Roszkowska 1970, 10: "The lands on which Wrocław arose had been settled for centuries by Slavs. . . . In the early Middle Ages the region was inhabited by the Ślęzanie, a Slavic tribe." For similar accounts: Heck 1960, Rutkiewicz 1973, Ślązak 1957.

[46] Zernack 1994.

[47] Maleczyńska 1948, 25.

[48] Ibid., 26.

[49] Maleczyński 1970b, 120.

[50] Similarly abridged and erroneous information on the German-speaking immigration can be found in Heck 1960, 22; Roszkowska 1970, 11–12; Ślązak 1957, 17. For a brief but—by contrast—factual account, see Rutkiewicz 1973, 8–9.

[51] See for example Maleczyńska 1950b, 127–28.

[52] Ślązak 1957, 22.

[53] Maleczyński 1970b, 127. On Prussian Germanization policies, see also Heck 1960, 30; Maleczyńska 1950c, vol. 1, 164; Maleczyński 1970c, 44ff.; Rutkiewicz 1973, 11.

[54] Orzechowski 1971, 46–47.

[55] An exception is Maleczyński 1970b, 134, which includes statistical information about ethnic groups within the population: "According to official Prussian statistics, our city had only 6,413 ethnically Polish inhabitants in 1890. Quasi-officially, however, that number is reckoned to have been about 25,000. Polish data, moreover, estimate about 50,000 Poles in Wrocław (12 percent of the population). The German data are no doubt biased toward underestimation." The author does not identify any sources or explain the credibility of the figures listed.

[56] Ślązak 1957, 22.

[57] Maleczyński 1970b, 133.

[58] Mierzecka 1967, 14; Roszkowska 1970, 33.

[59] Rutkiewicz 1973, 14.

[60] Maleczyński 1970b, 133; Orzechowski 1971, 47–48; Roszkowska 1970, 31.

[61] Maleczyńska 1950c, 162.

[62] Sosnowski and Suchocki 1948–50, vol. 1, 160–78. Even in her recently published city history, which attempts to provide a new perspective on the issue, Teresa Kulak uses a book title in the old style: *From History of Wrocław: From Friedrich's to Hitler's Fortress*: Kulak 2001.

[63] Jochelson 1946, Maleczyńska 1948, Maleczyński 1970c, Mierzecka 1967, Ślązak 1957.

[64] Heck (1960) touches on Nazi policies in Poland and the destruction of the city in 1945; Maleczyński (1970b) mentions only the suppression of the Polish minority after 1933.

[65] Roszkowska (ed., 1970) dedicates an entire chapter to the Second World War and the siege period, as does Rutkiewicz (1973), who examines more precisely the destruction during the fighting and the responsibility of the siege leadership; Orzechowski (1971) places particular emphasis on Polish acts of resistance.

[66] On this, see Siebel-Achenbach 1994, 127. The original diary is kept in the archives of the Wrocław bishopric.

[67] Rutkiewicz 1973, 5.

[68] Jochelson 1946, 16.

[69] Ślazak 1957, 22.

[70] Orzechowski 1971, 69.

[71] Characteristic here are Bolek 1972; Dulczewski and Kwilecki 1963; Markowski 1960–64; Osmańczyk 1985; Suleja 1995. Countless memoirs were also published in newspapers and local history journals.

[72] Jochelson 1946, Heck 1960, Maleczyński 1970a, Ślązak 1957.

[73] For example, Roszkowska 1970, 41.

[74] Orzechowski 1971, 70.

[75] See also the not very illuminating remarks in the chapter on the population developments by D. Górczyńska, J. Gutt, Bolesław Siwon, A. Wasilewska, and J. Wierzbicki in Siwon 1971, 73–120, especially 75–76.

[76] Sosnowski 1948, vol. 2, 311–27.

[77] Sosnowski 1948, 314; the citation is from Rusiński 1947. Gerard Labuda's book on the development of Poland's western border focuses on this thesis: G. Labuda 1971. See also the article by Klaus Zernack, which can be understood as a response: Zernack 1991a.

[78] Sosnowski 1948, 315–16.

[79] Ibid., 317–18. Sosnowski refers to Henryk Sienkiewicz's 1900 novel, *Knights of the Cross* (trans. Jeremiah Curtin, London, 1990).

[80] Ibid., 322–23.

CHAPTER 8 Cleansing Memory

[1] Wagińska-Marzec 1997, 367–416; Strauchold 2003b, 267–76.

[2] Wagińska-Marzec 1997, 374.

[3] Circular decree no. 33 of June 19, 1945, issued by the Presidium of the Council of Ministers: AAN, URM 5/27, fol. 3.

[4] AAN, MZO 496, fol. 25.

[5] Letter of September 24, 1945, to the MAP, AAN, MAP 560, fol. 41.

[6] Letter of October 19, 1945 to the MAP, AAN, MAP 560, fol. 46.

[7] Letter of January 9, 1946, to Voivodeship in Wrocław: AP Wr, UWW I-84, fol. 6.

[8] On this and the appointments to the regional commissions, see Wagińska-Marzec 1997, 390ff.

[9] Magierska 1978, 113.

[10] Cited in Wagińska-Marzec 1997, 380; on the congress generally, see 378ff.

[11] Pletzing 2006, 263–77; Dyroff 2006, 278–97.

[12] Fiedor 1966, 1981; Borek 1986. The authors tend to blur the rupture in 1933, thereby giving the impression that a systematic Germanization of place names in the East had been ongoing since Prussian times. What is also remarkable is that the indignation expressed over the name changes after 1933 suggests that there was no awareness of the similarities between this and the aims and methods of the Polonization of German names in the western territories after 1945.

[13] Cited in Fiedor 1966, 83–84.

[14] Choros and Jarzak 1995, 144–54.

[15] Cited in Wagińska-Marzec 1997, 407.

[16] Kolańczyk 1946.

[17] Letter of December 10, 1945: AAN, MZO 79, fols. 1ff.

[18] Olszewicz 1946, 9: AAN, MAP 580, fols. 145–61.

[19] See for example the prolonged discussion on correct historical names in Wrocław voivodeship: AP Wrocław, UWW I-85; for additional references on the discussion among experts, see Wagińska-Marzec 1997, 397.

[20] On the debate over the autochthon place names, see AAN, MAP 580, fol. 1–18, fols. 162–75.

[21] Kolańczyk 1946, 543.

[22] On this see Wagińska-Marzec 1997, 403ff.

[23] Copy of minutes (not dated) of the local council meeting of November 8, 1945, and the letter of April 25, 1946, from the Instytut Śląski in Katowice: AP Wrocław,

UWW I-84, fols. 54, 62; see also the comments by Jacek Friedrich about Gdańsk, where new settlers wanted to introduce names from the lost Polish eastern regions, but they failed due to resistance from the authorities: Friedrich 2001b, 32–33.

[24] Circular letter no. 128 by the MZO, November 15, 1946: AP Wrocław, UWW I-84, fol. 130.

[25] AP Wrocław, UWW I-84, fols. 88, 127.

[26] Circular decree no. 25 by the MZO, April 1, 1947: AAN, MZO 118, fols. 184ff.

[27] AAN, MZO 129, fol. 12.

[28] See the German-Polish street directory for Wrocław: Kruszewski 1997.

[29] On the history of individual streets and squares in Wrocław, see Antkowiak 1970; Markgraf 1896; Scheuermann 1994. For references to name changes after 1945, see Jancewicz and Smołka 2000; Jochelson 1968. For other name changes, see Kruszewski 1993. The most detailed presentation on the principles of renaming streets in Wrocław, albeit without any explanation of the ideological background, is an unpublished, 140-page text by Andrzej Jochelson (no date [1948]): Nazewnictwo drożni (ulic, placów, mostów), wód, wysp, wzniesień, lasów i innych elementów geografiycznych na terenie miasta Wrocławia w perspektywie historii i wedle stanu aktualnego: AP Wr, UWW XVIII/63, fols. 1–141.

[30] Confidential letter of the governor, June 5, 1938: Fiedor 1966, 90; on the targeted elimination of the term "Piast" in Silesia in the late 1930s, see also Fiedor 1981, 184–85.

[31] Confidential letter of June 5, 1939, to the provincial governor (Oberpräsident) from the mayor of Breslau about the upcoming renaming of streets: Fiedor 1966, 104.

[32] AP Wr, UWW XVIII/63, fol. 64.

[33] Kruszewski 2000.

[34] Andrzej Jochelson. No date [1948]. Nazewnictwo drożni. In AP Wr, UWW XVIII/63, fols. 64–65.

[35] Circular letter of the President of the Republic of Poland, March 17, 1947: AAN, MZO 130, fol. 37.

[36] Correspondence of October, 14, 1947: AAN, MZO 130, fol. 52.

[37] Circular decree no. 226, Rada Państwa Biuro Rad Narodowych, November 7, 1947: AAN, MZO 130, fol. 56.

[38] Borodziej 1990, 314–20; Strauchold 2003b, 102–4.

[39] This analogy was not coincidental; Jochelson, at least, was aware of the connection: AP Wr, UWW XVIII/63, fol. 81.

[40] Radziwiłłowicz 2003.

[41] Markgraf 1896; Jochelson mentioned Markgraf's book several times in his unpublished manuscript of 1948: AP Wr, UWW XVIII/63, fols. 1–141.

[42] Ibid., fol. 65.

[43] Ibid., fol. 67.

[44] See the minutes of sessions of the PRN Renaming Commission, 1951–52: AP Wr, PRN m.Wr 331.

[45] AP Wr, PRN m.Wr 331, fol. 14.

[46] For the region of Upper Silesia, in which the Polonization of personal names had great significance due to the large proportion of autochthons, who often had German names, see Linek 1997a, 50–59, 104–17; 1997b.

[47] MZO, circular decree no. 24, March 5, 1946: AAN, MZO 326, fol. 2.

[48] Cited in Linek 1997a, 111.

[49] On this see the report of the Silesian Institute of May 1946, according to which only very few Upper Silesians or Masurians had their names Germanized; cited in Linek 1997a, 54.

[50] Zawadzki suggested to the MZO in a letter of October 28, 1947, that the procedure, particularly for changing first names, had to be simplified because it had been too complicated up to then and thus brought correspondingly few results. He enclosed a draft for a new version of the decree of November 10, 1945, as well as a justification, in which he declared that people with German first names would have to reckon with negative treatment by the Polish population, which would make coexistence between autochthons and settlers more difficult: AAN, MZO 326, fols. 41–44.

[51] MZO, circular decree no. 22/48, May 8, 1948 (confidential): AP Wr, UWW, V-174, fol. 21.

[52] Ibid., fol. 22.

[53] MZO, circular decree no. 3/48, December 10, 1948: AAN, MZO 326, fols. 53–54.

[54] Letter of September 16, 1948, to the voivodeship administration: AP Wr, UWW, V174, fol. 84.

[55] Letter of September 15, 1948, to the voivodeship administration: Ibid., fol. 56.

[56] Letter of October 7, 1948, to the voivodeship administration: Ibid., fol. 37.

[57] Letter of September 17, 1948, to the voivodeship administration: Ibid., fol. 42.

[58] The circular decree of Wrocław voivodeship administration, October 22, 1948, with reference to MZO circular decree no. 22/48 of May 8, 1948, clearly stated that, regarding the name issue, pressure could be exerted only in dealing with the autochthons, but not the Polish settlers. If the latter still wanted to change their names, this was neither free of charge nor could the principle of public proceedings be dispensed with: ibid., fol. 3.

[59] Linek 1997a, 112.

[60] Linek 1997a, 113–14.

[61] Ibid., 113.

[62] AP Wr, ZM Wr 141.

[63] Linek 1997a, 59.

[64] Report to the MAP of September 2, 1945, of a city inspection that took place from August 13 to 18, 1945: AAN, MAP 2340, fol. 6.

[65] Ordinance no. 8 by the government plenipotentiary for Lower Silesia, July 31, 1945: AP Wr, UWW, I/83, fol. 2.

[66] Instructions for the cities and counties, August 31, 1945: AP Wr, WUIP 2, fol. 17.

[67] Circular decree no. 17, no date or heading [received September 14, 1945, according to a handwritten remark]: AP Wr, WUIP 2, fol. 26.

[68] AP Wr, ZM 260, fol. 9.

[69] AP Wr, UWW I/85, fol. 73.

[70] Not until May 4, 1948, did the MAP firmly urge the voivode and mayor to discontinue using German forms in their offices; on this, see Linek 1997a, 83.

[71] Secret circular decree no. 23 of the WUIP, March 19, 1947: AAN, MIP 58, fol. 141.

[72] Ibid.

[73] Miodek 2008, 396–97.

[74] AP Wr, ZM 689, fol. 5a. Other ordinances by the voivode on this matter, which were usually marked "secret," were issued on April 28, 1948; May 11, 1948; and July 20, 1948. On this, see also the responses from the individual counties on the progress of Polonization: AP Wr, UWW VI/749.

[75] Emphasis in the original. Secret circular letter no. 18 of the MZO, April 26, 1948: AP Wr, UWW VI/750, fols. 9–10; reprinted in Rutkowska 1997, 298–300; see also the secret implementation rules of the Wrocław voivodeship office of June 28, 1948: AP Wr, UWW VI/749, fol. 1.

[76] AP Wr, UWW VI/73, fol. 44.

[77] The mayor's implementary regulations regarding the voivode's circular decree of February 14, 1946, sent on March 15, 1946: AP Wr, ZM Wr 689, fol. 8.

[78] Mayor's report of April 30, 1948: AP Wr, UWW VI/73, fol. 61.

[79] Mayor's report of June 28, 1948: ibid., fol. 65.

[80] Report from the starosta of Góra of April 27, 1948: ibid., fols. 5ff.

[81] Report from the starosta of Góra of April 29, 1948: ibid., fol. 10.

[82] Report from the starosta of Żary of June 14, 1948: ibid., fol. 38.

[83] Report from the starosta of Jelenia Góra of February 26, 1948: ibid., fol. 11.

[84] Report from the starosta of Strzelin of July 24, 1948: ibid., fol. 11.

[85] Circular letter from the starosta of Jelenia Góra, May 8, 1948: ibid., fol. 12.

[86] Report from the starosta of Lubin, May 20, 1948: ibid., fol. 23.

[87] Ibid., fol. 37.

[88] AP Wr, UWW XVII/100, fol. 45.

[89] See for example the report of the starosta of Środa Śląska: AP Wr, UWW VI/749, fol. 51.

[90] A. Górny in Naprzód Dolnośląski, October 24–30, 1945; cited in Tyszkiewicz 2000, 32.

[91] Konopińska 1991, 94 (January 1947).

[92] Letter of the General Conservator to the Ministry of Justice, July 12, 1947: AP Wr, UWW XVII/102, fol. 85.

[93] AP Wr, UWW XVII/109, fol. 153.

[94] Letter of Voivodeship Conservator Jerzy Güttler to the MKS, December 16, 1949: AP Wr, UWW XVII/109, fol. 156.

[95] A guidebook on Wrocław monuments published in 1985 mentions when the monument was erected and who created it, but says nothing about the fountain's original name or the Bismarck monument that once stood opposite it: Antkowiak 1985, 62.

[96] Harasimowicz 1997-1999, vol. 2, 218–19.

[97] Copy of the report of July 28, 1948 (without letterhead or signature): AP Wr, ZM Wr 274, 11; preceding letter of the MUO VI of July 17, 1948: ibid., fol. 10.

[98] Zybura 1998, 376.

[99] Letter of February 26, 1948, AP Wr, UWW VI/749, fol. 51.

[100] AP Wr, UWW VI/749, fols. 10, 20, 23f., 26, 31.

[101] See for example AP Wr, UWW VI/749, fols. 62, 79.

[102] On September 27, 1949, the Central Dairy and Egg Cooperative (Centrala Spółdzielni Mleczarsko-Jajczarskich) in Warsaw petitioned the Wrocław municipal administration for permission to remove the two cemeteries located on this land in order to build their district headquarters. The voivodeship conservator decided on October 6, 1949, that the cemeteries were not worthy of historic preservation and that he had nothing against their removal so long as some of the graves from the late eighteenth to early nineteenth century were moved to the city's lapidarium: AP Wr, ZM 274, fol. 78, 84.

[103] Information on the plans to restore the abandoned cemeteries in the western territories, September 1960: AAN, URM 2.2/47, fol. 2.

[104] AAN, URM 2.2/47.

[105] Kalicki 1997, 21. I would like to thank Halina Okóska for information on the dismantling of the cemeteries.

[106] AP Wr, UWW XVII/131, fols. 47, 67.

[107] Łagiewski 1995b.

CHAPTER 9   The Pillars of an Imagined Tradition

[1] Konopińska 1987, 83 (November 16, 1945).

[2] The author of the foreword was then university president Włodzimierz Berutowicz: Floryan 1970, v–vi. On the leading role of the University of Wrocław in developing the Western Idea, see also the letter by the minister of higher education to the marshal of the Sejm, September 12, 1958: AAN, URM 2.2/12, fols. 53ff.

[3] On Maleczyński, see Turoń 1969, 191ff.; for a critical appraisal of the influence of Karol Maleczyński and Ewa Maleczyńska, see Cetwiński and Tyszkiewicz 1999.

[4] Mikulski 1954.

[5] See the biographical sketch by Bogdan Zakrzewski in Mikulski 1961, 5–23.

[6] Rospond 1948a, 1948b, 1959. On Rospond, see Januszewski 1992, 103ff.

[7] Gostomska-Zarzycka 1960, 309ff.

[8] Undated text (ca. 1946–48): AAN, MZO 79, fol. 134.

[9] Ibid.

[10] Korta 1970; Matwijowski 1971, 1986.

[11] Knot and Maleczyński 1946.

[12] Kuligowski 1967, 110–13; Siwon 1967, 107ff.

[13] *Słowo Polskie*, May 16, 1956, cited in Kuligowski 1967, 110. See also the society's statutes in *Rocznik Wrocławski* 2 (1958): 400ff.

[14] Kuligowski 1967, 110.

[15] Dąbrowska 1996-1997, vol. 1, 245.

[16] Siwon 1967.

[17] Kuligowski 1967, 113.

[18] On the history of Wrocław's coat of arms, see Łagiewski 1992.

[19] Maleczyński 1946.

[20] Ibid., 23.

[21] Łagiewski 1992, 86.

[22] Lotman and Uspenskii 1985, 30–66.

[23] The removal of monuments and the reassignment of monument sites following national border changes have been examined in different historical contexts. See for example Maas 1997, 79–108.

[24] Antkowiak 1985; Harasimowicz 2006, 689–703.

[25] Tyszkowska 1986.

[26] AP Wr, Presidium WRN, IX/123.

[27] Strauchold 2003a, 82–83.

[28] In July 1965 the propaganda division of the voivodeship committee of the PZPR discussed a large complex consisting of a monument and a cultural center: AP Wr, KW PZPR 74/VII/101, fols. 376ff. In a brochure on the planned celebrations published by the central committee of the PZPR in December 1965, the announcement of a competition for the monument by the MKS is listed as a separate program point for the year 1966: AP Wr, KW PZPR 74/VII/110, fol. 2.

[29] Minutes of the meeting of the secretariat of the OK FJN on November 5, 1959: AP Wr, PWRN, IX/213, fol. 25; for the PRN's statement on the positioning of the monument, which also emphasized the educational function of the monument for young people studying there, see ibid., fols. 15–16.

[30] J. H. 1968, 128–29.

[31] Memorandum by the presidium of the OK FJN on the "Return of the Western Territories" commemorative project in Wrocław: AP Wr, PWRN IX/213, fol. 21.

[32] AP Wr, PWRN IX/213, fols. 1–14.

[33] Discussion on November 14, 1969: AP Wr, PWRN IX 213, fol. 31.

[34] Antkowiak 1985, 57.

[35] Ibid., 154.

[36] Rada Naczelna TRZZ, Instrukcja w sprawie upamiętnienia osób i wydarzen, świadczących o historycznej polskości ziem zachodnich i północnych: AAN, TRZZ 1041, fols. 9–10.

[37] Kaszuba 1997a, 64.

[38] *Kalendarz Wrocławski* (1985), 19.

[39] Koshar 1998.

[40] Jochelson 1946.

[41] Ibid., 20.

[42] Ibid.

[43] Ibid., 23.

[44] Ibid., 16.

[45] Król 1957b.

[46] Ibid., 8.

[47] Ślązak 1957, 23.

[48] Król 1957a, 108.

[49] Ibid., 144.

[50] Towarzystwo Miłośników Wrocławia 1960.

[51] Ibid., 41.

[52] Ibid., 47.

[53] Ibid., 54ff.

[54] Ibid., 72–73.

[55] Ibid., 86–87.

[56] Ibid., 118.

[57] Roszkowska 1970.

[58] Kwaśniewski 1972.

[59] Zakrzewski 1989.

[60] Ibid., 9.

[61] Świechowski 1978.

[62] Strauchold 2003a.

[63] Progress report of the PZZ 1944–47: AAN, MZO 82, fol. 7.

[64] For the text of the speech, see *Kalendarz Wrocławski* 1969, 73–77.

[65] See the program outlines: AP Wr, PRN 1554, fols. 15–19, 50ff.

[66] On the program and the preparations, see AP Wr., PRN 1555; KW PZPR 74/VIII/119.

[67] Program of the celebrations, AP Wr., PRN 1555, fol. 4.

[68] For information on the program of the twenty-five-year celebration in Wrocław in May 1970, see AP Wr, KW PRZR 74/VIII/119, fol. 79.

[69] In the absence of a better local study, see Wloch-Ortwein 2000. A great deal of information on events in Wrocław can be found in Kenney 2002 and 2007.

[70] Kenney 2002, 157–64; Misztal 1992.

CHAPTER 10   Old Town, New Contexts

[1] On Zachwatowicz, see Rottermund 2000.

[2] Polish *zabytek* is usually translated as "monument." Zabytek has a broader meaning than the English "monument," however, encompassing all objects worthy of preservation, from art objects to individual historic buildings up to entire Old Towns or cultural landscapes. Another Polish word, *pomnik*, is used to designate monuments or historic objects in the more narrow sense, such as an equestrian statue, as well as those objects covered by the term *zabytki* that have special significance for national culture, for example, the Royal Castle in Krakow. On this subject, see Rymaszewski 1978, 216. When used in connection with architecture in this chapter, both Polish terms have generally been translated as "historic building."

[3] Zachwatowicz 1946, 52.

[4] Muczkowski 1912, 84. Several years later, Muczkowski wrote his monograph on historic preservation, which is regarded as the quintessential presentation of preservationist ideas in Poland at that time: Muczkowski 1914.

[5] Kalinowski 1978, 84–85; Rymaszewski 2000, 81–95.

[6] M. Marek 1997a.

[7] Rymaszewski 1994.

[8] Zachwatowicz 1946, reprinted in Zybura 1999a, 55.

[9] Friedrich 2001a, 73.

[10] Kalinowski 1978, 87. Teresa Jakimowicz disputes the meaningfulness of this term. She points out that Zachwatowicz, who is regarded as the father of this school, always rejected it as such and himself wrote: "We in Poland did not create a doctrine, but faced with tragedy and the fate of our historic buildings we have applied specific methods as necessary for a given situation." The rebuilding of Warsaw's Old Town was not, Jakimowicz contends, based on a definite, previously worked-out preservationist theory that rejected the orthodoxy of the day; it simply resulted from a readiness to reconstruct on a large scale: Jakimowicz 1994, 422–23.

[11] See for instance: Bingen and Hinz 2005.

[12] Kalinowski 1978, 90.

[13] Kaliski 1946.

[14] See for instance the recommendations on this by the RNdZZO in 1948: AAN, MZO 1677, fols. 56–57. In later accounts of the reconstruction in Wrocław, leading historic preservationists and architects such as Marcin Bukowski and Edmund Małachowicz left no doubt about the political objectives of the Old Town reconstruction; on this, see Bukowski 1985, 4; Małachowicz 1985, 117 and 1992, 244.

[15] Chmarzyński 1948, 44ff.

[16] The destruction dates for individual buildings can differ slightly depending on the source used. The dates given here are from Małachowicz 1985, 111 n8. Małachowicz relied for the most part on WDO estimations.

[17] Kaliski 1946, 5.

[18] Małachowicz 1992. This contradicts statements of cost by the NDMiOZ for the reconstruction of churches. According to the latter, at least in 1946–47, the reconstruction of all church buildings in Wrocław's Old Town was subsidized by funds from the state historic preservation agency: AAN, MAP 962, fols. 8ff., 12ff., 25ff.

[19] Progress Report of the WDO for the period 1945–48 (no date, probably late 1948): AP Wr, WDO 239, fol. 49.

[20] Bukowski 1985, 103; Małachowicz 1992, 211.

[21] Bukowski 1974, 210–20.

[22] Harasimowicz 1999, 301f.

[23] Kalicki 1997, 20.

[24] Małachowicz 1992, 220–21.

[25] On re-Gothicization, see also Czerner 2000, 64.

[26] Małachowicz 1985, 182–87.

[27] Czerner 1976, 99.

[28] Małachowicz 1985, 186; see also Walter 1965, 80–84.

[29] Harasimowicz 1997–99, vol. 1, 9, 11; Małachowicz 1992, 221–24. In his architectural history of the cathedral, Bukowski repeatedly defended his exposure of the bricks: Bukowski 1974.

[30] Małachowicz 1992, 210–20.

[31] Jarczyńska-Bukowska, 1983 [1946], 103, 111. A similar account can be found in Bukowski 1985, 57. This version of events was also adopted in many city guidebooks and popular histories.

[32] Jakimowicz 1994, 426.

[33] Małachowicz 1994a.

[34] On this, see Denslagen, 1994.

[35] See for example Stein, 1936. On the mythologization of the Gothic as a German-national architectural style, see Labuda 1992, vol. 2, 31–38. On the simultaneous adoption of the Gothic as the national style in Germany, France, and England, see Döhmer 1976, especially 103–4.

[36] Małachowicz 1985, 187–91.

[37] For the most richly documented and, for its time, unusually critical architectural history of the Rynek and its reconstruction after 1945, see Czerner 1976.

[38] Czerner 1976, 80–86.

[39] Harasimowicz 1997–99, vol. 1, 179.

[40] Ilkosz 1995.

[41] Czerner 1976, 98–99.

[42] Morelowski 1950, cited in Czerner 1976, 107.

[43] Czerner acknowledged these propagandistic motives as early as 1976: Czerner 1976, 107.

[44] Czerner 1976, 110, 124–27.

[45] Olechnowicz 1997, 47; Harasimowicz 1997–99, vol. 2, 43.

[46] Czerner 1976, 131.

[47] On the public debate in Wrocław's leading newspaper, see, for example, Maciejewska 2007a, 2007b.

[48] Chmarzyński 1950, 183–84.

[49] Chmarzyński 1948, 78–79.

[50] AAN, MOdb. 88, fol. 2.

[51] Rewski 1999 [1949], in Zybura 1999a, 57–58.

[52] Ibid., 60.

[53] Ibid., 62.

[54] Memorandum for the MOdb on May 29, 1947: AAN, MOdb 35, fols. 3ff.

[55] Bukowski 1985, 151–59.

[56] Rymaszewski 1995, 36.

[57] On the impossibility of classifying historic buildings in the Polish western territories according to nationality, see A. Labuda 1997a, 1997b, 1997c; M. Marek 1997b; Mazur 1997a, 636–37; Zybura 1999a, 10–13.

[58] Minutes of February 14, 1948: AP Wr, UWW XVII/110, fols. 220–21.

[59] Güttler's letter of August 1949 to the SOO: AP Wr, ZM 274, fol. 74.

[60] Güttler's letter of August 1949 to the SOO: Ibid., fol. 75. See the previous letter of June 1949 by the SOO, with the demand that historic buildings be identified as such: AP Wr, UWW XVII/109, fol. 28.

[61] Güttler's letter of August 1949 to the SOO: AP Wr, ZM 274, fol. 75.

[62] The aversion to Friedrich II expressed here was probably authentic. In a report submitted to the MKS on December 16, 1948, Güttler recommended removing the portrait of Friedrich from the Aula Leopoldina "in consideration of the disgraceful role played by Friedrich II in the partitions of Poland and his vicious and scornful relation to the Polish nation": AP Wr, UWW XVII/109, fol. 156.

[63] Güttler's letter to the SOO (no date, various receipt stamps from mid-November 1948): AP Wr, UWW XVII/110, fols. 218–19.

[64] Przyłęcki 1995, in Kowalczyk 1995, 77.

[65] Harasimowicz 1997–99, vol. 2, 21.

[66] Minutes of the Third Session of the Conservatory Council of Wrocław Voivodeship on May 6, 1959: AP Wr, Prezydium WRN we Wrocławiu IX/114, fol. 21.

[67] Rymaszewski 1995, 39.

[68] Czerner 2000, 60.

[69] Małachowicz 1985, 188. Małachowicz attributed the demolition of the ruins to economic considerations, which is certainly only half the truth. Nevertheless his book contains two photographs of Hatzfeldt Palace taken soon after the war, documenting that the front façade of the building on ul. Wita Stwosza was indeed damaged, but essentially intact. In other depictions published in Poland before 1990, whenever Hatzfeldt Palace is mentioned at all, it is said to have been

completely destroyed in the war, and no photos of the ruins are included. The same is true of the castle, for which there are no photographs even in the richly illustrated account by Małachowicz. The illustrated volume by Marzena Smolak on Wrocław in 1945 also contains no photographs depicting the condition of the two palace buildings later demolished; see Smolak 1995.

[70] On this, see the comments by Małachowicz, who leaves no doubts about the value of the facility from the point of view of architectural history: Małachowicz 1992, 203–204, 244, 264.

[71] Bukowski 1985, 92.

[72] Beate Störtkuhl 2005, 681–71, 709.

[73] Dobesz 1999, 53.

[74] See the confidential report by Anton Wrzosek, director of the RDPP, to the Lower Silesian voivode, with details about the condition of the vandalized Blücher grave, October 1, 1947: AP Wr, UWW XVII/102, fol. 188.

[75] Clark 2006, 670–681.

[76] Cited in Clark 2006, xii.

[77] Rymaszewski 1995, 37.

[78] A. Labuda 1997c, 135.

[79] A. Labuda 1997b, 19.

[80] See the warnings for Wrocław voivodeship from the second half of the 1940s: AP Wr, UWW XVII/102, XVII/110, XVII/117.

[81] Circular decree no. 67 of the MZO on September 25, 1947: AAN, MZO 118, fol. 237.

[82] The debate was conducted openly in the daily press and in professional journals such as *Ochrona Zabytków*. See Centralny Zarząd Muzeów i Ochrony Zabytków 1957; Chrzanowski 1957; Czerner 1956; Gruszecki 1957; Krzyszkowski 1957; Saski 1956; Zlat 1957. See also the important anthologies and articles from later years: Jakimowicz 1994; Kowalczyk 1995; A. Labuda 1997a, 1997b; Rymaszewski 1978, 1992, 1995; Tomaszewski 1994; Tomaszewski and Mockałło 2000.

[83] CZMiOZ: Materials on the condition of historic buildings in Poland, October 1, 1956: KBUA 1/126, fols. 151–52. See also the published report in which the judgment is similarly severe: Centralny Zarząd Muzeów i Ochrony Zabytków 1957.

[84] Przyłęcki 1995, 75.

[85] On the discussion on improving historic preservation in Wrocław Voivodeship, see the sessions of the Conservator Council (Rada Konserwatorska), convening for the first time in March 1957 at the Voivodeship National Council (WRN): AP Wr, PWRN IX/114.

[86] Przyłęcki 1995, 81. On the importance of social engagement for Polish historic preservation after 1945, see Herbst 1949; Krzywobłocki 1955, 57.

[87] Ziątkowski 2000, 123–24.

[88] Dmitrów 2002; Łukasiewicz 2005; Thum 2010.

CHAPTER 11 Amputated Memory and the Turning Point of 1989

[1] Zawada 1996, 52.

[2] Zybura 1999a, 8.

[3] Nowicki 1993; cited in Zybura 1998, 377.

[4] On the impact of these everyday items, see: Bazuń 2006, Chwin 2002.

[5] Zybura 1998, 377–78.

[6] Cited in Pasierb 1980, 120.

[7] On the political uses of enemy stereotypes of Germany/the Germans in the People's Republic of Poland, see the excellent study: Miodek 2008; see also: Borodziej 1990, 255–56; Dmitrów 2000, 235–64; Kiwerska 1993; Koszel 1993, 94–141; Lipski, 1996a [1981]; Pasierb 1980; Tomala 2000; Zybura 1999b, 21–34.

[8] Ruchniewicz 2005.

[9] Ahonen 2004, 260–65.

[10] Mazur 1997a, 633–34.

[11] On this, see the posthumous bilingual publication of seminal essays by Jan Józef Lipski, which were available underground in the 1980s: Lipski 1996c.

[12] On this, see his best-known essay, Lipski 1996b.

[13] Jancewicz and Smolka 2000, 26ff., 93ff.

[14] Łagiewski 1992, 87–90.

[15] Thum 2009.

[16] Sekretariat der Deutschen Bischofskonferenz 1992.

[17] Dola 1996; Köhler 1996.

[18] See the new history of the University of Wrocław published by the university press on this anniversary: Kulak, Pater, and Wrzesiński 2002. For an attempt to claim the tradition of the universities of both Breslau and Lwów, see Wrzesiński 1995b.

[19] Stern 2006, 516–20.

[20] See for example Rutkiewicz 1973.

[21] Łagiewski 1996; see also Binkowska and Smolak 1994.

[22] Schlögel 2001c, 243.

[23] Krajewski 1999.

[24] Memoriał Stowarzyszenia Historyków Sztuki z 1986 r. o stanie zabytków na Dolnym Śląsku. Reprinted in Kowalczyk 1995, 260–66.

[25] Davies and Moorhouse, 496.

[26] Urbanek 1998.

[27] http://www.krasnale.pl.

[28] Thum 2009.

[29] Broda and Urbanek 1997.

[30] Kaczmarek, Goliński, Kulak, and Suleja 1997.

[31] Galos 2001.

[32] Czerwiński 1993, 1997; Kulak 1997; Łagiewski and Arczyński 1995; Maciejewska 2002.

[33] See for instance the first Polish local history, which was based to a large degree on German literature: Maleczyński 1948.

[34] Maciejewska 2000c.

[35] Joachimsthaler 2000.

[36] Exemplary here are Dobesz 1993, Ilkosz 1997a, and Kononowicz 1997. See also the *Architektura Wrocławia* series, Rozpędowski 1995–98.

[37] Harasimowicz 1997–99. See also the pioneering study on Wrocław as a modern Prussian city: Zabłocka-Kos 2006.

[38] Harasimowicz 2006 (first edition 2000).

[39] Scheuermann 1994.

[40] Cited in Polak 2000.

[41] Maciejewska 2000a.

[42] Maciejewska 2000b.

[43] Maciejewska 2000b, 2000e.

[44] Ostrowski 1999.

[45] On this history of the publication, see Davies and Moorhouse 2002, xv–xvi.

SOURCES AND LITERATURE

ARCHIVAL SOURCES

AAN, ARCHIWUM AKT NOWYCH, WARSAW

GUPP	Główny Urząd Planowania Przestrzennego
KBUA	Komitet Budownictwa, Urbanistyki i Architektury
KSZZO	Komitet do Spraw Zagranicznych Ziem Odzyskanych
MAP	Ministerstwo Administracji Publicznej
MIP	Ministerstwo Informacji i Propagandy
MKS	Ministerstwo Kultury i Sztuki
MOdb	Ministerstwo Odbudowy
MPH	Minsterstwo Przemysłu i Handlu
MZO	Ministerstwo Ziem Odzyskanych
TRZZ	Towarszystwo Rozwoju Ziem Zachodnich
URM	Urząd Rady Ministrów

AP WR, ARCHIWUM PAŃSTOWE WE WROCŁAWIU:

–	Kolekcja fotografii z okresu PRL
KW PPR	Komitet Wojewódzki PPR
KW PPS	Komitet Wojewódzki PPS
KW PZPR	Komitet Wojewódzki PZPR
–	Miastoprojekt
–	Miejskie Biuro Projektów we Wrocławiu
PRN Wr	Powiatowa Rada Narodowa m. Wrocławia
PWRN Wr	Prezydium Wojewódzkiej Rady Narodowej we Wrocławiu
–	PZPR – Ikonografia
UWW	Urząd Wojewódzki Wrocławski
WDO	Wrocławska Dyrekcja Odbudowy
WUIP	Wojewódzki Urząd Informacji i Propagandy
ZM Wr	Zarząd Miejski Wrocławia
–	Zbiór plakatów i afiszów

Published Sources and Secondary Literature

Ahlfen, Hans von, and Hermann Niehoff. 1960. *So kämpfte Breslau: Verteidigung und Untergang von Schlesien*. 2nd rev. ed. Munich: Gräfe & Unzer.

Ahonen, Pertti. 2004. *After the Expulsion: West Germany and Eastern Europe: 1945–1990*. Oxford: Oxford University Press.

Ahonen, Pertti, Gustavo Corni, Jerzy Kochanowski, Rainer Schulze, Tamás Stark, and Barbara Stelzl-Marx. 2008. *People on the Move: Forced Population Movements in Europe in the Second World War and Its Aftermath*. Oxford: Berg.

Åman, Anders. 1992. *Architecture and Ideology in Eastern Europe during the Stalin Era: An Aspect of Cold War History*. Cambridge, MA: MIT Press.

Anderson, Benedict. 1983. *Imagined Communities: Reflections on the Origins and Spread of Nationalism*. London: Verso.

Antkowiak, Zygmunt. 1970. *Ulice i place Wrocławia*. Biblioteka Wrocławia, 11. Wrocław: Ossolineum.

———. 1985. *Pomniki Wrocławia*. Wrocław: Ossolineum.

Arburg, Adrian von, and Martin Schulze Wessel. 2010. *Zwangsumsiedlung und neue Gesellschaft in Ostmitteleuropa nach 1945*. Munich: Oldenbourg.

Ascher, Abraham. 2007. *A Community under Siege: The Jews of Breslau under Nazism*. Stanford: Stanford University Press.

Assmann, Jan. 1997. *Das kulturelle Gedächtnis: Schrift, Erinnerung und politische Identität in frühen Hochkulturen*. 2nd ed. Munich: C. H. Beck.

———. 2003. Cultural Memory: Script, Recollection, and Political Identity in Early Civilizations. *Historiography in East and West* 1 (2): 154–77.

Aubin, Hermann. 1962. Antlitz und geschichtliche Individualität Breslaus. In *Bewahren und Gestalten: Festschrift zum 70. Geburtstag für Günther Grundmann*, ed. J. Gerhardt and W. Gramberg, 15–28. Hamburg: Christians.

Bachmann, Klaus, and Jerzy Kranz. 1997. *Przeprosić za wypędzenie? O wysiedleniu niemców po II wojnie światowej*. Kraków: Znak.

———, eds. 1998. *Verlorene Heimat: Die Vertreibungsdebatte in Polen*. Bonn: Bouvier.

Bahlcke, Joachim, ed. 1996a. *Schlesien und die Schlesier*. Munich: Langen Müller.

———. 1996b. Die Geschichte der schlesischen Territorien von den Anfängen bis zum Ausbruch des Zweiten Weltkrieges. In Bahlcke 1996a, 1–154.

Bajer, Magdalena. 1998. Bitte vergleichen Sie . . . . In Bachmann and Kranz 1998, 237–41.

Bamberger, Sabine. 1990. *Die Oder-Neiße-Grenze in der polnischen Presse, 1950–1990*. Marburg: Herder-Institut.

Banasiak, Stefan. 1963. *Działalność osadnicza Państwowego Urzędu Repatriacyjnego na Ziemiach Odzyskanych, 1945–1947*. Poznań: Instytut Zachodni.

———. 1965. Settlement of the Polish Western Territories in 1945–1947. *Polish Western Affairs* 6:121–49.

————. 1968. *Przesiedlenie Niemców z Polski w latach, 1945–1950.* Łódź: Uniwersytet Łódzki.

Baranowski, Jan. 1998. Das gemeinsame Schicksal. In Bachmann and Kranz 1998, 228–30.

Bartetzky, Arnold. 2009. Stadtplanung als Glücksverheißung. Die Propaganda für den Wiederaufbau Warschaus und Ost-Berlins nach dem Zweiten Weltkrieg. In *Imaginationen des Urbanen: Konzeption, Reflexion und Fiktion von Stadt in Mittel- und Osteuropa,* ed. A. Bartetzky, A. Kliems and M. Dmitrieva, 51–70. Berlin: Lukas.

Barycz, Henryk. 1946. *Rola Polaków w Uniwersytecie Wrocławskim.* Wrocław: Komitet Organizacyjny 'Dni Kultury Polskiej na Ziemiach Zachodnich.'

Basiński, Euzebiusz, and Ryszard Nazarewicz, eds. 1987. *Sojusz polsko-radziecki a zachodnia granica Polski.* Warsaw: TPPR Współpraca.

Basista, Andrzej. 2001. *Betonowe dziedictwo: Architektura w Polsce czasów komunizmu.* Warsaw, Kraków: PWN.

Bazuń, Dorota. 2006. Veränderungen in der Beziehung zum Kulturerbe, insbesondere zu Gebrauchsgegenständen, als Ausdruck der 'Aneignung' von Geschichte durch die Bewohner der westlichen Grenzgebiete Polens. In *Wiedergewonnene Geschichte: Zur Aneignung von Vergangenheit in den Zwischenräumen Mitteleuropas,* ed. P. Loew, C. Pletzing, and T. Serrier, 145–63. Wiesbaden: Harrassowitz.

Beer, Mathias. 1998. Das Großforschungsprojekt "Dokumentation der Vertreibung der Deutschen aus Ost-Mitteleuropa" im Spannungsfeld von Politik und Zeitgeschichte. *Vierteljahrshefte für Zeitgeschichte* 46 (3): 345–89.

Berg, Max. 1921. Zukünftige Baukunst in Breslau als Ausdruck zukünftiger Kultur. In *Deutschlands Städtebau—Breslau,* ed. G. Hallama, 28–41. Berlin: DARI.

Bessel, Richard. 2009. *Germany 1945: From War to Peace.* London: Simon & Schuster.

Bessel, Richard, and Claudia B. Haake, eds. 2009. *Removing Peoples: Forced Migration in the Modern World.* Oxford: Oxford University Press.

Beyme, Klaus von, Werner Duth, Niels Gutschow, Winfried Nerdinger, and Thomas Topfstedt, eds. 1992. *Neue Städte aus Ruinen: Deutscher Städtebau der Nachkriegszeit.* Munich: Prestel.

Bingen, Dieter, and Hans-Martin Hinz, eds. 2005. *Die Schleifung. Zerstörung und Wiederaufbau historischer Bauten in Deutschland und Polen.* Wiesbaden: Harrasowitz.

Bińkowska, Iwona, and Marzena Smolak. 1994. *Nieznany portret miasta: Fotografie Wrocławia z 2: polowy XIX i początku XX w: Katalog wystawy.* Wrocław: VIA.

Blanke, Richard. 2001. *Polish-speaking Germans? Language and National Identity among Masurians since 1871.* Cologne: Böhlau.

Bloxham, Donald. 2009. The Great Unweaving: The Removal of Peoples in Europe, 1875–1949. In Bessel and Haake 2009, 167–207.

Boćkowski, Daniel, ed. 2001. *Niemcy w Polsce, 1945–1950: Wybór dokumentów: Tom 4 (Pomorze Gdańskie i Dolny Śląsk).* Warsaw: Neriton.

Bohn, Thomas M. 2008. *Minsk—Musterstadt des Sozialismus: Stadtplanung und Urbanisierung in der Sowjetunion nach 1945.* Cologne: Böhlau.

Bolek, Jerzy, ed. 1972. *Wróciła Polska: Pamiętniki z pierwszych lat powojennych na Ziemiach Odzyskanych, XXX-lecie PRL*. Warsaw: Iskry.

Bömelburg, Hans-Jürgen, and Bogdan Musial. 2000. Die deutsche Besatzungspolitik in Polen 1939–1945. In Borodziej and Ziemer 2000, 43–111.

Bömelburg, Hans-Jürgen, Renate Stoessinger, and Robert Traba, eds. 2000. *Vertreibung aus dem Osten: Deutsche und Polen erinnern sich*. Olsztyn: Borussia.

———. 2001. *Wypędzeni ze wschodu: wspomnienia Polaków i Niemców*. Olsztyn: Borussia.

Borek, Henryk. 1986. O germanizacji nazewnictwa polskiego na Śląsku. *Studia Śląskie* 44:81–92.

Borodziej, Włodzimierz. 1990. *Od Poczdamu do Szklarskiej Poręby: Polska w stosunkach międzynarodowych 1945–1947*. London: Aneks.

———. 1997a. "Ostforschung" aus der Sicht der polnischen Geschichtsschreibung. *Zeitschrift für Ostmitteleuropaforschung* 46:405–26.

———. 1997b. Historiografia polska o "wypędzeniu" Niemców. *Polska 1944/45–1989: Studia i materiały* 2:249–69.

———. 2000. Die polnische Grenzdiskussion im Lande und im Exil (1939–1945). In *Grenzen in Ostmitteleuropa im 19. und 20. Jahrhundert: Aktuelle Forschungsprobleme*, ed. H. Lemberg. Marburg: Herder-Institut.

Borodziej, Włodzimierz, and Artur Hajnicz, eds. 1998. *Kompleks wypędzenia*. Kraków: Znak.

Borodziej, Włodzimierz, and Hans Lemberg, eds. 2000–2001. *"Nasza ojczyzna stała się dla nas obcym państwem ...": Niemcy w Polsce 1945–1950: Wybór dokumentów*, 4 vols. Warsaw: Neriton.

———, eds. 2000–2004. *"Unsere Heimat ist uns ein fremdes Land geworden ... ": Die Deutschen östlich von Oder und Neisse 1945–1950: Dokumente aus polnischen Archiven*, 4 vols. Marburg: Herder-Institut.

Borodziej, Włodzimierz, and Klaus Ziemer, eds. 2000. *Die deutsch-polnischen Beziehungen 1939–1945–1949: Eine Einführung*. Osnabrück: fibre.

Boysen, Jens. 2009. Staatsbürgerliche Optionen in Posen nach 1918. In *Deutschsein als Grenzerfahrung: Minderheitenpolitik in Europa zwischen 1914 und 1950*, ed. M. Beer, D. Beyrau, and C. Rauh, 175–88. Essen: Klartext.

Brandes, Detlef. 2001. *Der Weg zur Vertreibung 1938–1945: Pläne und Entscheidungen zum "Transfer" der Deutschen aus der Tschechoslowakei und aus Polen*. Munich: Oldenbourg.

Brandes, Detlef, Holm Sundhaussen, and Stefan Troebst, eds. 2010. *Lexikon der Vertreibungen. Deportation, Zwangsaussiedlung und ethnische Säuberung im Europa des 20. Jahrhunderts*. Cologne: Böhlau.

Breyer, Richard. 1967. Die kirchlichen Verhältnisse Niederschlesiens seit 1945. In *Niederschlesien unter polnischer Verwaltung*, ed. E. Bahr and K. König. Frankfurt a.M., Berlin: Metzner.

Brix, Emil, and Hannes Stekl, eds. 1997. *Der Kampf um das Gedächtnis: Öffentliche Gedenktage in Mitteleuropa*. Vienna: Böhlau.

Broda, Tomasz, and Mariusz Urbanek. 1997. *Zrób sobie Wrocław czyli ilustrowany kurs historii miasta*. Wrocław: FUNNA.

Broszat, Martin. 1961. *Nationalsozialistische Polenpolitik 1939–1945*. Stuttgart: DVA.

Brown, Kate. 2004. *A Biography of No Place: From Ethnic Borderland to Soviet Heartland*. Cambridge, MA: Harvard University Press.

Brubaker, Rogers. 1996. Aftermaths of Empire and the Unmixing of Peoples. In *Nationalism Reframed: Nationhood and the National Question in the New Europe*, 148–78. Cambridge: Cambridge University Press.

Brzezicki, Sławomir, Stanislaw Klimek, and Dietmar Popp, eds. 2008. *Breslau im Luftbild der Zwischenkriegszeit aus den Sammlungen des Herder-Instituts Marburg*. Wrocław: Via Nova.

Budziński, Tadeusz. 1971. Zażyłość z miastem. In *Kościół na Ziemiach Zachodnich: Cπwierćwiecze polskiej organizacji kóscielnej*, ed. J. Krucina. Wrocław: Wrocławska Księgarnia Archidiecezjalna.

Bukowski, Marcin. 1974. *Der Dom zu Wrocław*. Wrocław: Ossolineum.

———. 1985. *Wrocław z lat 1945–1952: Zniszczenia i dzieło odbudowy*. Warsaw: PWN.

———. 1995. O początkach. In *Architekci Wrocławia 1945–1995*, ed. J. Zasada and A. Zwierzchowski. Wrocław: Zarząd Oddziału Wrocławskiego SARP.

Bunzel, Ulrich. 1965. *Kirche ohne Pastoren: Die schlesische Laienkirche nach dem Zusammenbruch von 1945: Erlebnisse und Berichte: Material für die Geschichtsschreibung über die evangelische Kirche in schwerster Zeit*. Ulm: Unser Weg.

Burleigh, Michael. 1988. *Germany turns Eastwards: A Study of Ostforschung in the Third Reich*. Cambridge: Cambridge University Press.

Burszta, Józef. 1995. Kategorie społeczno-kulturowe ludności ziem zachodnich [1966]. *Przegląd Zachodni* (2): 79–100.

Buśko, Cezary, Mateusz Goliński, Michał Kaczmarek, and Leszek Ziątkowski. 2001. *Historia Wrocławia: Od pradziejów do końca czasów habsburskich*. Wrocław: Wyd. Dolnośląskie.

Całka, Marek. 1993. Exodus: Wysiedlenie ludności niemieckiej z Polski po II wojnie światowej. *Mówią wieki* 1993 (2): 3–10.

Calvino, Italo. 1978. *Invisible Cities*. Trans. W. Weaver. New York: Harcourt Brace Jovanovich.

Cattaruzza, Marina. 2008. Endstation Vertreibung: Minderheitenfrage und Zwangsmigration in Ostmitteleuropa, 1919–1949. *Journal of Modern European History* 6 (1): 5–29.

Caumanns, Ute. 1994. *Technischer Fortschritt und sozialer Wandel in deutschen Ostprovinzen: Ein Vergleich mit ausgewählten Mittel- und Westprovinzen*. Bonn: Kulturstiftung der deutschen Vertriebenen.

Centralny Zarząd Muzeów i Ochrony Zabytków. 1957. W sprawie ochrony zabytków w Polsce. *Ochrona Zabytków* 10 (1): 6–17.

Cetwiński, Marek, and Lech A. Tyszkiewicz. 1999. Prawda historii i racja stanu: Mediewiści Wrocławscy o średniowiecznym Śląsku: Pół wieku badań. *Sobótka* 1999 (2): 147–64.

Chmarzyński, Gwido. 1948. W aureoli gotycki kościołów. In Sosnowski and Suchocki 1948–50, 44–79.

———. 1950. Ugór na piastowskim łanie. In Sosnowski and Suchocki 1948–50, 179–91.

Cholewa, Beata Katarzyna. 1990. The Migration of Germans from Lower Silesia after World War II. *Polish Western Affairs* 31 (1–2): 53–80.

Choros, Monika, and Łucja Jarzak. 1995. Veränderungen von Orts- und Personennamen in Schlesien vor und nach dem Zweiten Weltkrieg. In *'Wach auf, mein Herz, und denke': Zur Geschichte der Beziehung zwischen Schlesien und Berlin-Brandenburg von 1740 bis heute*, ed. Gesellschaft für interregionalen Kulturaustausch e.V., 144–54. Dülmen: Laumann.

Chrzanowski, Tadeusz. 1957. Polska, ruiny. *Zycie literackie* 37:1–2.

Chumiński, Jędrzej. 1990a. Przejmowanie przemysłu Wrocławskiego przez władze polskie (maj–wrzesień 1945). In *Studia nad społeczeństwem Wrocławia 1945–1949*, ed. B. Klimczak and W. Długoborski, 23–50. Wrocław: Wyd. Uczelniane Akademii Ekonomicznej.

———. 1990b. Stan przemysłu Wrocławskiego w 1945 roku: (wybranie zagadnienia). In *Studia nad społeczeństwem Wrocławia 1945–1949*, ed. B. Klimczak and W. Długoborski, 51–75. Wrocław: Wyd. Uczelniane Akademii Ekonomicznej.

———. 1993. Czynniki destabilizujące proces osadnictwa we Wrocławiu (1945–1949). *Socjologia* 10:55–78.

Chumiński, Jędrzej, and Elżbieta Kaszuba. 1995. Niemcy we Wrocławiu w latach 1945–1949. In *Ludność niemiecka na ziemiach polskich w latach 1939–1945 i jej powojenne losy*, ed. W. Jastrzębski, 205–23. Bydgoszcz: WSP.

Chwin, Stefan. 1996. *Hanemann*. Gdańsk: Marabut.

———. 2002. Region als geographische Tatsache und als Werk der Einbildungskraft. In *Literarisches Schreiben aus regionaler Erfahrung: Westfalen—Rheinland—Oberschlesien*, ed. W. Gössmann and K. H. Roth, 417–22. Paderborn: Schöningh.

Ciesielski, Stanisław. 1999. *Wrocław 1956*. Wrocław: Wyd. Uniwersytetu Wrocławskiego.

———, ed. 2000. *Przesiedlenie ludności polskiej z Kresów Wschodnich do Polski 1944–1947*. Warsaw: Neriton.

Clark, Christopher. 2006. *The Iron Kingdom: The Rise and Downfall of Prussia, 1600–1947*. Cambridge, MA: Belknap Press of Harvard University Press.

Cohn, Willy. 2006. *Kein Recht, nirgends: Tagebuch vom Untergang des Breslauer Judentums, 1933–1941*, 2 vols. Cologne: Böhlau.

Connelly, John. 2000. *Captive University: The Sovietization of East German, Czech, and Polish Higher Education, 1945–1956*. Chapel Hill: University of North Carolina Press.

————. 2005. Polish Universities and State Socialism, 1944–1968. In *Universities under Dictatorship*, ed. J. Connelly and M. Grüttner, 185–212. University Park: Pennsylvania State University Press.

Conrads, Norbert, ed. 1994. *Schlesien*. Ed. H. u. a. Boockmann. *Deutsche Geschichte im Osten Europas,* vol. 3. Berlin: Siedler.

Curp, T. David. 2006. *A Clean Sweep? The Politics of Ethnic Cleansing in Western Poland, 1945–1960*. Rochester, NY: University of Rochester Press.

Czaplicka, John. 1997. Geteilte Geschichte, geteilte Erbschaft: Stadtbild und Kulturlandschaft im Baltikum und in Polen. In *Das Denkmal im nördlichen Ostmitteleuropa im 20. Jahrhundert: Politischer Kontext und nationale Funktion*, ed. S. Ekdahl. Lüneburg: Nordostdeutsches Kulturwerk.

Czapliński, Marek, et al. 2007. *Historia Śląska*. 2nd rev. ed. Wrocław: Wyd. Uniwersytetu Wrocławskiego.

Czapliński, Marek, Hans-Joachim Hahn, Tobias Weger, eds. 2005. *Schlesische Erinänerungsorte. Gedächtnis und Identität einer mitteleuropäischen Region*. Görlitz: Neisse.

Czerner, Olgierd. 1956. O los zabytków województwa Wrocławskiego. *Ochrona Zabytków* 9 (1–2): 199–220.

————. 1976. *Rynek Wrocławski*. Wrocław: Ossolineum.

————. 2000. Zabytki Śląska w Polsce dyktatury proletariatu. In *Badania i ochrona zabytków w Polsce w XX wieku: Materiały konferencji naukowej zorganizowanej staraniem Wydziału Architektury Politechniki Warszawskiej, Generalnego Konserwatora Zabytków i towarzystwa Opieki nad Zabytkami w stulecie urodzin Profesora Jana Zachwatowicza w dniu 5 marca 2000 roku*, ed. A. Tomaszewski and E. Mockałło, 59–72. Warsaw: Oficyna Wyd. Tow. Opieki nad Zabytkami.

Czerniakiewicz, Jan. 1987. *Repatriacja ludności polskiej z ZSRR 1944–1948*. Warsaw: PWN.

Czerniakiewicz, Jan, and Monika Czerniakiewicz. 2005. *Przesiedlenia ludności w Europie 1915–1959*. Warsaw: WSP TWP.

Czerwiński, Janusz. 1993. *Wrocław: Przewodnik*. Wrocław: Leopoldinum.

————. 1997. *Wrocław: Przewodnik turystyczny*. Wrocław: Wyd. Dolnośląskie.

Dąbrowska, Maria. 1996–97. *Dzienniki powojenne 1945–1965*, 4 vols. Warsaw: Czytelnik.

Daleszak, Bogdan. 1970. *Bedeker Wrocławski*. Wrocław: Ossolineum.

Davies, Norman. 2005. *God's Playground: A History of Poland*. Rev. ed. 2 vols. New York: Columbia University Press.

Davies, Norman, and Roger Moorhouse. 2002. *Microcosm: A Portrait of a Central European City*. London: Jonathan Cape.

Denslagen, Wim. 1994. *Architectural Restoration in Western Europe: Controversy and Continuity*. Amsterdam: Architektura & Natura Press.

Derlatka, Tadeusz, and Józef Lubojański, eds. 1966. *Western and Northern Territories of Poland: Facts and Figures*. Warsaw: Western Press Agency.

Diefendorf, Jeffrey M., ed. 1990. *Rebuilding Europe's Bombed Cities*. Basingstoke: Macmillan.

—. 1993. *In the Wake of War: The Reconstruction of German Cities after World War II*. New York: Oxford University Press.

Długoborski, Wacław, Józef Gierowski, and Karol Maleczyński. 1958. *Dzieje Wrocławia do roku 1807*. Warsaw: PWN.

Dmitrów, Edmund. 1995. Die Zwangsumsiedlungen der Deutschen und die polnische öffentliche Meinung der Jahre 1944–1948. *Deutsche Studien* 32 (126/127): 226–34.

—. 2000. Vergangenheitspolitik in Polen 1945–1989. In Borodziej and Ziemer 2000.

—. 2002. Czarna legenda Prus. In Kerski 2002.

Dobesz, Janusz L. 1993. *Wrocław: Czas i architektura*. Wrocław: Krajowa Agencja Wydawnicza.

—. 1999. *Wrocławska architektura spod znaku swastyki na tle budownictwa III Rzeszy*. Wrocław: Oficnya Wydawnicza Politechnika Wrocławskiej.

Döhmer, Klaus. 1976. *"In welchem Style sollen wir bauen?" Architekturtheorie zwischen Klassizismus und Jugendstil*. Munich: Prestel.

Dola, Kazimierz. 1996. Bertram aus der Sicht der polnischen Geschichtsschreibung. *Archiv für schlesische Kirchengeschichte* 54:65–69.

Drankowski, Tadeusz, and Olgierd Czerner, eds. 1992. *Wrocław z lotu ptaka*, 3rd rev. ed. Wrocław: Ossolineum.

Drobner, Bolesław. 1960. Zdobiliśmy polskie Złote Runo! In Markowski 1960–64, 1:75–106.

Dulczewski, Zygmunt, and Andrzej Kwilecki, eds. 1963. *Pamiętniki osadników Ziem Odzyskanych*. Poznań: Wyd. Poznańskie.

Durth, Werner, and Niels Gutschow, eds. 1993. *Träume in Trümmern: Stadtplanung 1940–50*. Munich: DTV.

Dymarski, Mirosław. 1996. Zagadnienia demograficzne ziem postulowanych (ziem nowych) w prognozach polskiej konspiracji. In Frątczak and Strzelecki 1996.

—. 1997. *Ziemie postulowane (ziemie nowe) w prognozach i działaniach polskiego ruchu oporu 1939–1945*. Wrocław: Wyd. Universytetu Wrocławskiego.

Dyroff, Stefan. 2006. Ortsnamen im Gebiet der Provinz Posen. Zwischen Tradition, Fremdheitsgefühl und Nationalisierung. In Loew, Pletzing, and Serrier 2006, 287–97.

Dzikowska, Elżbieta. 1997. Terra recognita: Polnische Schriftsteller über deutsche Vergangenheit ihrer schlesischen Heimatorte. In *Die Rezeption der deutschsprachigen Gegenwartsliteratur nach der Wende 1989*, ed. N. Honsza and T. Mechtenberg, 217–33. Wrocław: FRI.

Eberhardt, Piotr. 1996. *Między Rosją a Niemcami: Przemiany narodowościowe w Europie Środkowo-Wschodniej w XX w*. Warsaw: PWN.

Esch, Michael G. 1998. *"Gesunde Verhältnisse": Deutsche und polnische Bevölkerungspolitik in Ostmitteleuropa 1939–1950*. Marburg: Herder-Institut.

Faraldo, José M. 2001. Medieval Socialist Artefacts: Architecture and Discourses of National Identity in Provincial Poland, 1945–1960. *Nationalities Papers* 29 (4): 605–32.

―――. 2002. The Teutonic Knights and the Polish Identity: National Narratives, Self-Image and the Socialist Public Sphere. In *Sphären von Öffentlichkeit in Gesellschaften sowjetischen Typs: Zwischen parteistaatlicher Selbstinszenierung und kirchlichen Gegenwelten*, ed. G. T. Rittersporn, J. C. Behrends, and M. Rolf. Frankfurt a.M.: Peter Lang.

―――. 2008a. *Europe, Nationalism and Commumism: Essays on Poland.* Frankfurt a.M.: Peter Lang.

―――. 2008b. Materials of Memory: Mass Memoirs of the Polish Western Territories. In Faraldo 2008a.

Fiedor, Karol, ed. 1966. *Walka z nazewnictwem polskim na Śląsku w okresie hitlerowskim (1933–1939).* Wrocław: Ossolineum.

―――. 1967. Obóz koncentracyjny we Wrocławiu w 1933. *Sobótka* 22 (1–2).

―――. 1977. *Bund Deutscher Osten w systemie antypolskiej propagandy.* Warsaw:PWN.

―――. 1981. Usuwanie na Śląsku w czasach Trzeciej Rzeszy nazw miejscowości i określeń ze słowem "Piast." *Sobótka* 36 (1): 183–91.

Fink, Carole. 1998. The Minorities Question at the Paris Peace Conference: The Polish Minority Treaty, June 28, 1919. In *The Treaty of Versailles: A Reassessment after 75 years*, ed. M. F. Boemeke, G. D. Feldman, and E. Glaser. Cambridge: Cambridge University Press.

Flachenecker, Helmut. 1993. Stadtgeschichtsforschung als Akt der Selbstvergewisserung. *Historisches Jahrbuch* 113:128–58.

Fleming, Michael. 2010. *Communism. Nationalism, and Ethnicity in Poland 1944-1950.* London: Routledge.

Floryan, Władysław, ed. 1970. *Uniwersytet Wrocławski w latach 1945–1970: Księga Jubileuszowa.* Wrocław: Ossolineum.

Frank, Matthew. 2008. *Expelling the Germans: British Opinion and Post-1945 Population Transfer in Context.* Oxford: Oxford University Press.

Frątczak, Ewa, and Zbigniew Strzelecki, eds. 1996. *Demografia i społeczeństwo Ziem Zachodnich i Północnych 1945–1995: Próba bilansu.* Warsaw: Polskie Towarzystwo Demograficzne / Friedrich Ebert-Stiftung.

Friedrich, Jacek. 2001a. Dwie wizje Gdańska: "historyczna" i "twórcza," na przykładzie dyskusji wokół zabudowy ulicy Szerokiej. In *Gdańsk pomnik historii*, 71–100. Gdańsk: Regionalny Ośrodek Studiów i Ochrony Środowiska Kulturowego w Gdańsku.

―――. 2001b. Gdańsk 1945–1949: Oswajanie miejsca. In *Gdańsk pomnik historii.* Gdańsk: Regionalny Ośrodek Studiów i Ochrony Środowiska Kulturowego w Gdańsku.

―――. 2009. *Neue Stadt in altem Glanz: Der Wiederaufbau Danzigs 1945–1960.* Cologne: Böhlau.

Gajewski, S. 1970. Miłość zaczęła się budzić przez irytację. In Jałowiecki 1970, 259–74.

Galos, Adam. 1995. Wrocław w ostatnim półwieczu. *Rocznik Wrocławski* 2:9–47.

———, ed. 2001. *Historia Wrocławia*, 3 vols. Wrocław: Wyd. Dolnośląskie.

Ganson, Nicholas. 2009. *The Soviet Famine of 1946–47 in Global and Historical Perspective*. New York: Palgrave Macmillan.

Geertz, Clifford. 1977. *The Interpretation of Cultures*. New York: Basic Books.

General Sikorski Historical Institute, ed. 1961–67. *Documents on Polish-Soviet Relations*, 2 vols. London: Heinemann.

Gerlach, David. 2007. Working with the Enemy: Labor Politics in the Czech Borderlands, 1945–1948. *Austrian History Yearbook* 38:179–207.

Gierowski, J. 1999. W powojennym Wrocławiu. In *Pięćdziesiąt lat duszpasterstwa akademickiego we Wrocławiu*, ed. M. Lubienicka. Wrocław: Centralny Ośrodek Duszpasterstwa Akademickiego.

Gleiss, Horst G. W., ed. 1986–97. *Breslauer Apokalypse 1945: Dokumentarchronik vom Todeskampf und Untergang einer deutschen Stadt und Festung am Ende des Zweiten Weltkriegs unter Berücksichtigung der internationalen Presseforschung, persönlichen Erlebnisberichten von Augenzeugen und eigenen Tagebuchaufzeichnungen*, 10 vols. Wedel: Self-published.

Gluck, Leopold. 1971. *Od ziem postulowanych do ziem odzyskanych*. Warsaw: PAX.

Gomułka, Władysław. 1945. Zwycięstwo polskie w Poczdamie. *Głos Ludu*, August 5, 1945, 2.

———. 1946a. Dajcie narodowi kultur, która wyrosła z rzeczywistości polskiej. *Głos Ludu*, June 12, 1946.

———. 1946b. Otwieramy rok nowy kartą pokoju. *Głos Ludu*, January 1, 1946.

———. 1964. *Artykuły i przemówienia*. Warsaw: Książka i Wiedza.

Górski, Jan. 1988. *Warszawa w latach 1944–1949: Odbudowa*. Ed. S. Kieniewicz. Warsaw: PWN.

Gostomska-Zarzycka, Zofia. 1960. Delegatura Ministerstwa Oświaty we Wrocławiu 1945 r. In Markowski 1960–64, 1:281–372.

Gottschalk, Joseph. 1965. St. Hedwig in der neuesten polnischen Geschichtsschreibung. *Archiv für schlesische Kirchengeschichte* 23:1–12.

Grabowski, Sabine. 1998. *Deutscher und polnischer Nationalismus: Der deutsche Ostmarken- Verein und die polnische Straż 1894–1914*. Marburg: Herder-Institut.

Grieger, Friedrich. 1948. *Wie Breslau fiel . . .* Stuttgart-Metzingen: Die Zukunft.

Gross, Jan T. 1988. *Revolution from Abroad: The Soviet Conquest of Poland's Western Ukraine and Western Belorussia*. Princeton, NJ: Princeton University Press.

———. 1997. War as Revolution. In Naimark and Gibianskii 1997, 17–40.

———. 2006. *Fear: Anti-Semitism in Poland after Auschwitz: An Essay in Historical Interpretation*. Princeton, NJ: Princeton University Press.

Gross, Jan T., and Irena Grudzińska. 1990. *W czterdziestym nas matko v Sibir zesłali: Polska a Rosja 1939–1942*. Warsaw: Res Publica.

Gruszecki, Andrzej. 1957. Ratujemy Zabytki. *Ochrona Zabytków* 10 (1): 1–5.

Hackmann, Jörg. 1996. *Ostpreußen und Westpreußen in deutscher und polnischer Sicht: Landesgeschichte als beziehungsgeschichtliches Problem.* Wiesbaden: Harrassowitz.

———. 2001. Strukturen und Institutionen der polnischen Westforschung (1918–1960). *Zeitschrift für Ostmitteleuropaforschung* 50 (2): 230–55.

———. 2004. Zwischen Zerstörung und Rekonstruktion: Beobachtungen zu historischen Altstädten zwischen Lübeck und Narva nach 1945. In *Perceptions of Loss, Decline and Doom in the Baltic Sea Region,* ed. J. Hecker-Stampehl, A. Bannwart, D. Brekenfeld and U. Plath, 371–97. Berlin: Berliner Wissenschaftverlag.

Halbwachs, Maurice. 1992. *On Collective Memory.* Trans. L. A. Closer. Chicago: University of Chicago Press.

Harasimowicz, Jan., ed. 1997–99. *Atlas architektury Wrocławia,* 2 vols. Wrocław: Wyd. Dolnośląskie.

———. 1999. Architektura Wrocławia w rysunku i grafice. In Harasimowicz 1997–99, 221–315.

———, ed. 2006. *Encyklopedia Wrocławia,* 3rd ed. Wrocław: Wyd. Dolnośląskie.

Hartung, Hugo. 1951. *Der Himmel war unten: Roman.* Munich: Bergstadtverlag Wilh. Gottl. Korn.

———. 1982. *Gesamtausgabe in acht Bänden,* vol. 2 (Schlesien 1944/45: Aufzeichnungen und Tagebücher [1976]). Munich: Schneekluth.

Haslinger, Peter, Erik K. Franzen, and Martin Schulze Wessel, eds. 2008. *Diskurse über Zwangsmigrationen in Zentraleuropa: Geschichtspolitik, Fachdebatten, literarisches und lokales Erinnern seit 1989.* Munich: Oldenbourg.

Häufele, Günther. 1999. Zwangsumsiedlungen in Polen 1939–1941: Zum Vergleich sowjetischer und deutscher Besatzungspolitik. In *Lager, Zwangsarbeit, Vertreibung und Deportation: Dimensionen der Massenverbrechen in der Sowjetunion und in Deutschland 1933–1945,* ed. D. Dahlmann and G. Hirschfeld, 535–525. Essen: Klartext.

Heck, Roman. 1960. Zarys dziejów Wrocławia. In Markowski 1960, 19–37.

Henke, Josef. 1995. Flucht und Vertreibung der Deutschen aus dem Osten: Zur Quellenlage und Historiographie. *Deutsche Studien* 32 (126–27): 137–49.

Herbst, Stanisław. 1949. Rola społeczeństwa w opiece nad zabytkami. *Ochrona Zabytków* 2 (3).

Hildermeier, Manfred. 1998. *Geschichte der Sowjetunion 1917–1991: Entstehung und Niedergang des ersten sozialistischen Staates.* Munich: C. H. Beck.

Hirsch, Helga. 1998. *Die Rache der Opfer: Deutsche in polnischen Lagern 1944–1950.* Berlin: Rowohlt.

Hirszfeld, Ludwik. 1957. *Historia jednego życia.* 2nd ed. Warsaw: Pax.

Hirszfeldowa, Hanna, Andrzej Kelus, and Feliks Milgrom. 1956. *Ludwik Hirszfeld.* Wrocław: Państw. Zakład Wyd. Naukowy

Hobsbawm, Eric, and Terence Ranger, eds. 1983. *The Invention of Tradition.* Cambridge: Cambridge University Press.

Hofmann, Andreas R. 2000. *Die Nachkriegszeit in Schlesien: Gesellschafts- und Be-völkerungspolitik in den polnischen Siedlungsgebieten 1945-1948.* Cologne: Böhlau.

Holtzmann, Robert, ed. 2007. *Die Chronik des Thietmar von Merseburg.* Halle: Mit-teldeutscher Verlag.

Holzer, Jerzy. 1992. Uraz, nacjonalizm, manipulacja: Kwestia niemiecka w komu-nistycznej Polsce. *Rocznik Polsko-Niemiecki* 1:7-17.

Hoppe, Bert. 2000. *Auf den Trümmern von Königsberg: Kaliningrad 1946-1970.* Mu-nich: Oldenbourg.

Hornig, Ernst. 1975. *Breslau 1945: Erlebnisse in einer eingeschlossenen Stadt.* Munich: Bergstadtverlag Korn.

Hryciuk, Grzegorz, ed. 2008. *Wysiedlenia, wypędzenia, ucieczki, 1939-1959. Polacy, Żydzi, Niemcy, Ukraińcy. Atlas ziem Polski.* Warsaw: Demart.

Hultsch, Gerhard. 1967. Polnische Geschichtsumdeutung: Zu Karol Kotula: Der urewige polnische Charakter Breslaus. *Jahrbuch für schlesische Kirchengeschichte* 46:152-76.

Ilkosz, Jerzy. 1995. Koncepcje urbanistyczne Maxa Berga na przykładzie projektów przebudowy Berlina w roku 1910 i Wrocławia w latach 1919-1920. In Rozpędowski 1995, 359-98.

———. 1997a. Gesamtkunstwerk Maxa Berga: Hala Stulecia we Wrocławiu. In *Ars sine scientia nihi est: Księga ofiarowana Profesorowi Zygmuntowi Świechowskiemu,* 101-11. Warsaw: ARS.

———. N.d. [1997b]. Das Hochhaus in der Stadtstruktur am Beispiel Breslaus in den Jahren 1919 bis 1928. Die städtebauliche Konzeption Max Bergs. In Ilkosz and Störtkuhl n.d. [1997], 31-60.

Ilkosz, Jerzy, and Beate Störtkuhl, eds. N.d. [1997]. *Hochhäuser für Breslau: 1919-1932: Ausstellung des Bauarchives der Stadt Breslau in Zusammenarbeit mit dem Fachgebiet Baugeschichte der Technischen Universität Braunschweig.* Delmenhorst: Aschenbeck & Holstein.

Instytut Zachodni, ed. 1948-57. *Ziemie Staropolskie,* 6 vols. Poznań: Instytut Zachodni.

J. H. 1968. Słupy Chrobrego. *Kalendarz Wrocławski:* 128-29.

Jabłoński, Jerzy, ed. 1945. *Skorowidz adresowy urzędów instytucji publicznych, gospo-darczych i społecznych oraz wolnych zawodów we Wrocławiu.* Wrocław.

Jacobsen, Hans-Adolf, and Mieczysław Tomala, eds. 1992. *Bonn Warschau 1945-1991: Die deutsch-polnischen Beziehungen: Analyse und Dokumentation.* Cologne: Wissenschaft und Politik.

Jagielski, Andrzej. 1993. Mieszkańcy powojennego Wrocławia: Zarys rozwoju demo-graficznego i zmian w demografii miasta. *Rocznik Wrocławski* (1): 167-218.

Jakimowicz, Teresa. 1994. Polska szkoła konserwatorska—mit i rzeczywistość. *Kwartalnik Architektury i Urbanistyki* 38:421-27.

Jałowiecki, Bohdan, ed. 1970. *Związani z miastem...Opracowanie i fragmenty wypowiedzi nadesłanych na konkurs: "Czym jest dla ciebie miasto Wrocław?"* Wrocław: Ossolineum.

Jancewicz, Bernard, and Leonard Smołka, eds. 2000. *Nazwy ulic Wrocławia*. Wrocław: Towarzystwo Miłośników Wrocławia.

Jankowiak, Stanisław. 1997. Terminologia w stosunkach polsko-niemieckich. *Sprawa Narodowościowe*, n.s. 4, 2 (11): 285–94.

Januszewski, Bernard Woodrow. 1992. Stanisław Rospond. *Kalendarz Wrocławski*: 103–5.

Jarczyńska-Bukowska, Maria. 1983 [1946]. Impresje Wrocławskie. In *Etiudy i kaprysy*, ed. M. Jarczyńska-Bukowska, 103–18. Kraków: Znak.

Jerrig, Friedrich Otto. 1949. *Aus Breslau wurde Wrocław: Ein Streifzug durch die polnisch gewordene Hauptstadt Schlesiens*. Hannover: Wolfgang Kwiecinski.

Jerzykiewicz-Jagemann, F.E.O. 1995. Innenansichten zum Drama um die "Festung Breslau": Eine persönliche Erinnerung. *Historische Mitteilungen* 8:161–201.

Joachimsthaler, Jürgen. 2000. Die Zukunft der Vergangenheit: Die Auseinandersetzung der polnischen Germanistik mit den deutschen Spuren in Polen. *Jahrbuch des Bundesinstituts für Kultur und Geschichte der Deutschen im östlichen Europa: Berichte und Forschungen* 8:7–32.

Jochelson, Andrzej. 1946. *Przewodnik po Wrocławiu*. Kraków: Przełom.

———. 1968. Jak powstały polskie nazwy ulic i dzielnic w odzykanym Wrocławiu. *Kalendarz Wrocławski*:228–32.

———. 1995. Pionierskie dni Zarządu Mieskiej. In Suleja 1995, 10–43.

———. 1997. *Kronika: Semipałatyńsk—Wrocław: Bearbeitet und eingeführt durch Stanisław Bereś*. Wrocław: Towarzystwo Przyjaciół Polonistyki Wrocławskiej.

Johann Gottfried Herder-Forschungsrat, ed. 1955–1967. *Ostdeutschland unter fremder Verwaltung*, 5 vols. Frankfurt a.M.: Metzner.

Jonca, Karol. 1961. Destruction of "Breslau": The Final Struggle of Germans in Wrocław in 1945. *Polish Western Affairs* 2 (2): 309–39.

Jonca, Karol, and Alfred Konieczny, eds. 1962. *"Festung Breslau"–Documenta obsidionis, 16.II–6.V.1945, Annales Silesiae, Supplementum II*. Warsaw: PWN.

———. 1963. *Upadek "Festung Breslau": 15.II–6.V.1945*. Wrocław: Ossolineum.

———. 1995. Ostatni lot Gauleitera. *Odra* 402 (5): 2–7.

Jonca, Karol, and Marek Maciejewski, eds. 1997. *Wysiedlenia Niemców i osadnictwo ludności polskiej na obszarze Kryżowa-Świdnica w latach 1945–1948: Wybór dokumentów*. Wrocław: Leopoldinum.

Judson, Pieter M. 2007. *Guardians of the Nation: Activists on the Language Frontiers of Imperial Austria*. Cambridge, MA: Harvard University Press.

Kaczmarczyk, Zdzisław, and Karol Maleczyński. 1950. Legnickie pole wstaje buntem wiosny ludów. In Sosnowski and Suchocki 1948–50, 398–422.

Kaczmarek, Michał, Mateusz Goliński, Teresa Kulak, and Włodzimierz Suleja. 1997. *Wrocław: Dziedzictwo wieków*. Wrocław: Wyd. Dolnośląskie.

Kaczmarek, Michał, Stanisław Klimek, and Jakub Tyszkiewicz, eds. 2009. *Breslau 1947. Luftaufnahmen*. Wrocław: Via Nova.

Kaemmerer, Magarete, ed. 1988. *Ortsnamenverzeichnis der Ortschaften jenseits von Oder und Neiße.* 3rd rev. ed. Leer: Rautenberg.

Kalicki, Włodzimierz. 1995. Dom Pawła, dom Małgorzaty. *Gazeta Wyborcza,* September 8, 1995, magazine sec., 6–12.

———. 1997. Breslau—das Zuhause von Paweł und Małgorzata. *Transodra: Deutsch-polnisches Informationsbulletin* 17:14–28.

Kalinowski, Konstanty. 1978. Der Wiederaufbau der Altstädte in Polen in den Jahren 1945–1960. *Österreichische Zeitschrift für Kunst und Denkmalpflege* 32:81–93.

Kaliski, Emil. 1946. Wrocław wrócił do Polski. *Skarpa Warszawska* 9:4–5.

Kamiński, Artur. 1997. Targi w nazistowskim Wrocławiu. *Rocznik Wrocławski* 4:81–128.

Kamusella, Tomasz. 1999. Ethnic Cleansing in Silesia 1950–89 and the Ennationalizing Policies of Poland and Germany. *Patterns of Prejudice* 33 (2): 51–74.

———. 2003. *The Szlonzoks and their Language: Between Germany, Poland and Szlonzokian Nationalism.* San Domenico: European University Institute.

Kania, Wojciech. 1952. Pamietnik z lat 1945–1948. *Sobótka* 7:227–49.

Kante, Gerda. 1999. *Das Inferno von Breslau: Erinnerungen.* Duderstadt: Mecke-Druck.

Kaps, Johannes, ed. 1952–53. *Die Tragödie Schlesiens 1945/46 in Dokumenten: Unter besonderer Berücksichtigung des Erzbistums Breslau.* Munich: "Christ unterwegs."

———. 1989. Kardinal Hlond und das schwierige deutsch-polnische Verhältnis. *Zeitschrift für Geschichte und Altertumskunde Ermlands* 45:145–64.

Karp, Hans-Jürgen, ed. 1997. *Deutsche Geschichte und Kultur im heutigen Polen: Fragen der Gegenstandsbestimmung und Methodologie.* Marburg: Herder-Institut.

Kaszuba, Elżbieta. 1990. Postawy i zachowania społeczno-polityczne migrantów ze Związku Radzieckiego w opiniach instytucji administracyjnych i politycznych w latach 1945–1947 na Dolnym Śląsku. In *Studia nad społeczeństwem Wrocławia 1945–1949,* ed. B. Klimczak and W. Długoborski, 9–22. Wrocław: Wyd. Uczelniane Akademii Ekonomicznej.

———. 1997a. *Między propagandą a rzeczywistością: Polska ludność Wrocławia w latach 1945–1947.* Warsaw, Wrocław: PWN.

———. 1997b. Codzienność powojennego Wrocławia—zjawisko szabru 1945–1947. In *Studia z dziejów XX wieku,* ed. T. Kulak, 145–65. Wrocław: Instytut Historyczny Uniwersytetu Wrocławskiego.

———. 1997c. PPR, PPS—rywalizacja o wpływy w powojennym Wrocławia. In Łach 1997, 85–98.

Kenney, Padraic. 1997a. *Rebuilding Poland: Workers and Communists 1945–50.* Ithaca, NY: Cornell University Press.

———. 1997b. Polish Workers and the Stalinist Transformation. In Naimark and Gibianskii 1997, 139–66.

———. 2002. *A Carnival of Revolution: Central Europe 1989.* Princeton, NJ: Princeton University Press.

———. 2007. *Wrocławskie zadymy.* Wrocław: Atut.

Kerski, Basil, ed. 2002. *Prusy: Pamięć i dziedzictwo: Praca zbiorowa.* Szczecin: Institut Niemiec i Europy Północnej.

Kersten, Krystyna. 1974. *Repatriacja ludności polskiej po II wojnie światowej.* Wrocław: Ossolineum.

———. 1991. *The Establishment of Communist Rule in Poland, 1943–1948.* Berkeley: University of California Press.

———, ed. 1993. *Między wyzwoleniem a zniewoleniem: Polska 1944–1956.* London: Aneks.

Kersten, Krystyna, and Tomasz Szarota. 1966. Kształtowanie się pierwszego planu osadnictwa Ziem Zachodnich w 1945 r: wybór dokumentów. *Polska Ludowa: Materiały i Studia* 5:127–89.

Kiwerska, Jadwiga. 1993. W atmosferze wrogości (1945–1970). In *Polacy wobec Niemców: Z dziejów kultury politycznej Polski 1945–1989,* ed. A. Wolff-Powęska. Poznań: Instytut Zachodni.

Kleßmann, Christoph. 1971. *Die Selbstbehauptung einer Nation: Nationalsozialistische Kulturpolitik und polnische Widerstandsbewegung im Generalgouvernement 1939–1945.* Düsseldorf: Bertelsmann Universitätsverlag.

Knot, Antoni. 1960. Początki uniwersyteckiej pionierki. In Markowski 1960–64, 1:158–72.

Knot, Antoni, and Karol Maleczyński. 1946. Słowo wstępne. *Sobótka* 1:1–2.

Kobylińska, Ewa, and Andreas Lawaty, eds. 1998. *Erinnern, Vergessen, Verdrängen: Polnische und deutsche Erfahrungen.* Wiesbaden: Harrassowitz.

Kochanowski, Jerzy. 2000. Do raportu! Trzeźwy milicjant świeci przykładem. *Polityka,* February 12, 2000, 72–74.

———. 2001. Gathering Poles into Poland: Forced Migration from Poland's Former Eastern Territories. In Ther and Siljak 2001, 135–54.

Kochański, Aleksander. 1996. *Polska 1944–1991: Informator historyczny: Tom I: Podział administracyjny–ważniejsze akte prawne–Decyzje i enuncjacje państwowe (1944–1956).* Warsaw: Wyd. Sejmowe.

Kodeniec, Bożena. 2000. *Statystyka Wrocławia w latach 1945–1999.* Wrocław: Urząd Statystyczny we Wrocławiu.

Koenen, Gerd. 2005. *Der Rußland-Komplex: Die Deutschen und der Osten 1900–1945.* München: C.H. Beck.

Köhler, Joachim. 1996. Das Bertram-Bild in der deutschsprachigen Forschung. *Archiv für schlesische Kirchengeschichte* 54:9–50.

Köhler, Joachim, ed. 1980. Die Romberichte des Breslauer Konsistorialrats Dr. Johannes Kaps aus dem Jahre 1945. *Archiv für schlesische Kirchengeschichte* 38:1–91.

Kokot, Józef. 1948. Wystawiamy rachunek. In Sosnowski and Suchocki 1948–50, 293–309.

Kołacki, Jerzy. 1995. Die Vertriebenen in der polnischen Geschichtsschreibung 1945–1979. *Deutsche Studien* 32 (126–27): 150–62.

Kolańczyk, Kazimierz. 1946. O nazwe polskie na Ziemiach Odzyskanych. *Przegląd Zachodni*:540–47.

Kominek, Bolesław. 1971. Kościół między pokoleniami: Relacja na jubileuszowej sesji episkopatu w archikatedrze wrocławskiej 4 maja 1970 r. In Krucina 1971, 21–24.

Koneczny, Jan. 1998. Polen als homogener Nationalstaat in der Politik der Polnischen Arbeiterpartei (PPR). *Forum für osteuropäische Ideen- und Zeitgeschichte* 2 (2): 253–74.

König, Kurt. 1967. Die gewerbliche Wirtschaft Niederschlesiens seit 1945. In *Niederschlesien unter polnischer Verwaltung*, ed. E. Bahr and K. König, 133–273. Frankfurt a.M.: Alfred Metzner.

Kononowicz, Wanda. 1997. *Wrocław: Kierunki rozwoju urbanistycznego w okresie międzywojennym*. Wrocław: Oficyna Wydawnicza Politechniki Wrocławskiej.

Konopińska, Joanna. 1987. *Tamtem Wrocławski rok: 1945–1946: Dziennik*. Wrocław: Wyd. Dolnośląskie.

———. 1991. *We Wrocławiu jest mój dom: Dziennik z lat 1946–1948*. Wrocław: Biblioteczka 'Nowego Życia.'

Konrad, Joachim. 1963. Als letzter Stadtdekan von Breslau: Chronistische Rückschau. *Jahrbuch für Schlesische Kirchengeschichte* 42:129–71.

Korta, W. 1970. Wrocławskie towarzystwo Miłośników Historii w pierwszym 25-leciu. *Sobótka* 25:221–26.

Koshar, Rudy. 1998. "What Ought to Be Seen?": Tourists' Guidebooks and National Identities in Modern Germany and Europe. *Journal of Contemporary History* 33 (1): 323–40.

Kosiński, Leszek. 1963. *Procesy ludnościowe na Ziemiach Odzyskanych w latach 1945–1960*. Warsaw: PWN.

———. 1969. Change in the Ethnic Structure in East Central Europe. *Geographical Review* 59:388–402.

Kossert, Andreas. 2001. *Preußen, Deutsche oder Polen? Die Masuren im Spannungsfeld des ethnischen Nationalismus 1870–1956*. Wiesbaden: Harrassowitz.

———. 2006. *Kalte Heimat: Geschichte der deutschen Vertriebenen nach 1945*. Munich: Siedler.

Kostof, Spiro. 1991. *The City Shaped: Urban Patterns and Meanings Through History*. London: Thames & Hudson.

———. 1992. *The City Assembled: The Elements of Urban Form Through History*. London: Thames & Hudson.

Koszel, Bogdan. 1993. Między dogmatizmem i pragmatizmem (1971–1989). In Wolff-Powęska 1993, 94–141.

Kowal, Stefan. 1998. Das Bild der polnischen Westgebiete in der polnischen wissenschaftlichen Literatur nach dem Zweiten Weltkrieg. In Schultz 1998, 17–30.

Kowalczyk, Jerzy, ed. 1995. *Ochrona dziedzictwa kulturowego zachodnich i północnych ziem Polski*. Warsaw: Stowarzyszenie Konserwatorów Zabytków.

Kozłowski, Ryszard. 1997. Administracja kościelna na ziemiach odzyskanych po drugiej wojnie światowej (1945–1972). In Łach 1997, 303–23.

Kraft, Claudia. 2000. Wojewodschaft Allenstein: Einleitung. In Borodziej and Lemberg 2000–2004, 433–80.

————. 2001. Ucieczka, wypędzenie i przymusowe wysiedlenie Niemców z województwa Wrocławskiego: Rok 1945. In Boćkowski 2001, 205–37.

Krajewski, Marek. 1999. *Śmierć w Breslau*. Wrocław: Wyd. Dolnośląskie.

Król, Gwidon. 1957a. Zwiedzamy zabytki miasta. In Król 1954b, 40–156.

————, ed. 1957b. *Przewodnik po zabytkach Wrocławia*. Wrocław: PTTK Okręgowa Komisja Ochrony Zabytków.

Krucina, Jan, ed. 1971. *Kościół na Ziemiach Zachodnich: Ćwierćwiecze polskiej organizacji kóscielny*. Wrocław: Wrocławska Księgarnia Archidiecezjalna.

Kruke, Anja, ed. 2006. *Zwangsmigrationen und Vertreibungen: Europa im 20. Jahrhundert*. Bonn: Dietz.

Kruszewski, Tomasz. 1997. *Niemiecko-polski spis ulic, placów i mostów Wrocławia 1873–1997*. 2nd rev. ed. Wrocław: Wyd. Uniwersytetu Wrocławskiego.

————. 2000. Prawne aspekty nazewnictwa ulic. In Jancewicz and Smołka 2000.

Kruszewski, Z. Anthony. 1972. *Oder-Neisse Boundary and Poland's Modernization: The Socioeconomic and Political Impact*. New York: Praeger.

Krzoska, Markus. 2003. *Für ein Polen an Oder und Ostsee: Zygmunt Wojciechowski (1900–1955) als Historiker und Publizist*. Osnabrück: fibre.

Krzyszkowski, Adam. 1957. Problem aktywizacji gospodarczej miast zabytkowych. *Ochrona Zabytków* 10:73–87.

Krzywobłocki, Aleksander. 1955. Dziesięć lat pracy konserwartorskiej w wojew: Wrocławskim. *Ochrona Zabytków* 8 (1): 50–57.

Kuczyński, Stefan. 1946. Dzień 10–11 maja we Wrocławiu. *Śląsk* 3–4.

Kühn, Hartmut. 1999. *Das Jahrzehnt der Solidarność: Die politische Geschichte Polens 1980–1990: Mit einem historischen Anhang bis 1997*. Berlin: BasisDruck.

Kulak, Teresa. 1981. Śląsk—ognisko rewizjonizmu niemieckiego w okresie międzywojennym. *Sobótka* (3): 361–78.

————. 1989. Nauka i polityka: Uwagi nad udziałem środowiska naukowego Uniwersytetu Wrocławskiego w kształtowaniu polityki i propagandy niemieckiej w latach 1918–1939. In *Studia nad przeszłością i dniem dzisiejszym Uniwersytetu Wrocławskiego*, 53–81. Warsaw: PWN.

————. 1997. *Wrocław: Przewodnik historyczny*. Wrocław: Wyd. Dolnośląskie.

————. 2001. *Historia Wrocławia*, vol. 2 (Od twierdzy fryderycjańskiej do twierdzy hitlerowskiej). Wrocław: Wyd. Dolnośląskie.

Kulak, Teresa, Mieczysław Pater, and Wojciech Wrzesiński. 2002. *Historia Uniwersytetu Wrocławskiego 1702–2002*. Wrocław: Wyd. Uniwersytetu Wrocławskiego.

Kulczyński, Stanisław. 1955. *Udział Wrocławia w odbudowie nauki polskiej*. Wrocław: PWN.

————. 1960. Grupa naukowa-kulturalna. In Markowski 1960–64, 1:107–33.

Kuligowski, Kazimierz. 1960. W ruinach. In Markowski 1960–64, 1:134–57.

―――. 1967. Taki był początek. *Kalendarz Wrocławski* 1967:110–13.

―――. 1969. Bolesław Drobner. *Kalendarz Wrocławski*:189–90.

Kulischer, Eugene M. 1948. *Europe on the Move: War and Population Changes 1917–47.* New York: Columbia University Press.

Kurcz, Zbigniew. 1993. Towarzystwa mniejszości niemieckiej na Śląsku. *Socjologia* 10:133–58.

Kurdwanowski, Jan. 2000. Odzyskiwanie miasta. *Karta* (1): 116-120.

Kwaśniewski, Krzysztof. 1972. *Wrocław jakiego nie znamy.* Wrocław: Ossolineum.

Kwilecki, Andrzej. 1994. Instytut Zachodni w pięćdziesięcioleciu 1944–1994: Sprawy i ludzie. *Przegląd Zachodni* 50:1–26.

Labuda, Adam S. 1992. Die Ostsiedlung und die gotische Kunst: Begriffe und Realitäten. In *Künstlerischer Austausch: Artistic Exchange: Akten des XXVIII. Internationalen Kongresses für Kunstgeschichte,* ed. T. W. Gaehtgens, 31–38. Berlin: Akademie Verlag.

―――. 1997a. Niemieckie dziedzictwo historyczno-artystyczne w Polsce: Sądy, stereotypy i opinie po II wojnie światowej. *Artium Quaestiones* 8:5–25.

―――. 1997b. Das deutsche Kunsterbe in Polen: Ansichten, Gemeinplätze und Meinungen nach dem Zweiten Weltkrieg. *Deutschland und seine Nachbarn: Forum für Kultur und Politik* 20:5–23.

―――. 1997c. Kunst und Kunsthistoriographie im deutsch-polnischen Spannungsverhältnis—eine vernachlässigte Forschungsaufgabe. In Karp 1997, 119–35.

Labuda, Gerard. 1971. *Polska Granica Zachodnia: Tysiąc lat dziejów politycznych.* Poznań: Wyd. Poznańskie.

Łach, Stanisław. 1996. Zasiedlanie Ziem Zachodnich i Północnych w latach 1945–1950. In Frątczak and Strzelecki 1996, 115–35.

―――, ed. 1997. *Władze komunistyczne wobec Ziem Odzyskanych po II wojnie światowej.* Słupsk: Wyższa Szkoła Pedagogiczna.

―――, ed. 2000. *Ziemie Odzyskane pod wojskową administracją radziecką po II wojnie światowej: Materiały z konferencji.* Słupsk: Wyższa Szkoła Pedagogiczna.

Łagiewski, Maciej. 1992. *Herb Wrocławia w architekturze miasta.* Wrocław: Ossolineum.

―――. 1994. *Wrocławscy Żydzi 1850–1944.* Wrocław: Muzeum Historyczne.

―――. 1995a. Das kulturelle Erbe Schlesiens: Hindernis oder Brücke. In *'Wach auf, mein Herz, und denke': Zur Geschichte der Beziehung zwischen Schlesien und Berlin-Brandenburg von 1740 bis heute,* ed. Gesellschaft für interregionalen Kulturaustausch e.V, 562–68. Dülmen: Laumann.

―――. 1995b. *Stary Cmentarz Żydowski we Wrocławiu.* Wrocław: ZET.

―――. 1996. *Breslau gestern—Wrocław wczoraj.* Gliwice: 'Wokół nas.'

Łagiewski, Maciej, and Stefan Arczyński. 1995. *Wrocław: Przewodnik.* Wrocław.

Latour, Stanisław. 1989. Rozwój architektury i urbanistyki na Ziemiach Zachodnich po II wojnie światowej. In *Architektura i urbanistyka w Polsce w latach 1918–1978*, ed. PAN / Komitet Architektury i Urbanistyki, 61–81. Warsaw: PWN.

Lawaty, Andreas. 1986. *Das Ende Preußens in polnischer Sicht: Zur Kontinuität negativer Wirkungen der preußischen Geschichte auf die deutsch-polnischen Beziehungen.* Berlin, New York: Walter de Gruyter.

Lebedeva, Natalia Sergeevna. 2000. The Deportation of the Polish Population to the USSR, 1939–1941. In Rieber 2000, 28–45.

Lemberg, Hans. 1992. "Ethnische Säuberung": Ein Mittel zur Lösung von Nationalitätenproblemen? *Aus Politik und Zeitgeschichte* 46:27–38.

Lieberman, Benjamin. 2006. *Terrible Fate: Ethnic Cleansing in the Making of Modern Europe.* Chicago: Ivan R. Dee.

Linek, Bernard. 1997a. *"Odniemczanie" województwa śląskiego w latach 1945–1950 w świetle materiałów wojewódzkich.* Opole: Instytut Śląski.

———. 1997b. Polonizacja imion in nazwisk w województwie śląskim (1945–1949) w świetle okólników i rozporządzeń władz wojewódzkich. *Wrocławskie studia z historii najnowszej* 4:143–68.

———. 2000. *Polityka antyniemiecka na Górnym Śląsku w latach 1945-1950.* Opole: Stowarzyszenie Instytut Śląski.

Lipski, Jan Józef. 1996a. Antyniemiecka karta polskiego reżimu [1981]. In Lipski 1996c, 229–37.

———. 1996b. Dwie ojczyzny—dwa patriotyzmy. Uwagi o megalomanii narodowej i ksenofobii Polaków [1985]. In Lipski 1996c.

———. 1996c. *Powiedzieć sobie wszystko . . . : eseje o sąsiedztwie polsko-niemieckim.* Warsaw: Wyd. Polsko-Niemieckie.

Loew, Peter Oliver. 2003. *Danzig und seine Vergangenheit, 1793–1997: Die Geschichtskultur einer Stadt zwischen Deutschland und Polen.* Osnabrück: fibre.

Loew, Peter, Christian Pletzing, and Thomas Serrier, eds. 2006. *Wiedergewonnene Geschichte: Zur Aneignung von Vergangenheit in den Zwischenräumen Mitteleuropas.* Wiesbaden: Harrassowitz.

Lotman, Iurii M., and Boris A. Uspenskii. 1985. Binary Models in the Dynamics of Russian Culture. In *The Semiotics of Russian Cultural History: Essays by Iurii M. Lotman, Lidia I. Ginsburg, Boris A. Uspenskii*, ed. A. D. Nakhimovsky and A. S. Nakhimovsky. Ithaca, NY: Cornell University Press.

Lubocka-Hoffmann, Maria. 2004. *Miasta historyczne zachodniej i północnej Polski: Zniszczenia i programy odbudowy.* Bydgoszcz.

Łuczak, Czesław. 1993. *Polska i Polacy w drugiej wojnie światowej.* In *Polska: Dzieje narodu, państwa i kultury*, vol. 5, ed. Jerzy Topolski. Poznań: Wyd. Naukowe UAM w Poznaniu.

Łukasiewicz, Dariusz. 2005 [2001]. Pruskie egzorcyzmy. In Kerski 2005,75–82.

Luks, Leonid. 1993. *Katholizismus und politische Macht im kommunistischen Polen 1945 bis 1989: Die Anatomie der Befreiung.* Cologne: Böhlau.

Maas, Annette. 1997. Zeitenwende in Elsaß-Lothringen: Denkmalsstürze und Umdeutung der nationalen Erinnerungslandschaft in Metz (November 1918–1922). In Speitkamp 1997, 79–108.

Mach, Zdzisław. 1998. *Niechciane miasta: Migracja i tożsamość społeczna*. Kraków: Universitas.

Maciejewska, Beata. 2000a. Oddajcie, co nasze: Jak Warszawa zagrabiła nam pawęże. *Gazeta Wyborcza*, Wrocław ed., April 21, 2000.

———. 2000b. Ja protestuję: Reakcja Wrocławian na odmowę warszawskich muzealników. *Gazeta Wyborcza*, Wrocław ed., May 20–21, 2000.

———. 2000c. Stary Wrocław. *Gazeta Wyborcza*, Wrocław ed., June 3–4, 2000.

———. 2000d. Mamy Dorotę! *Gazeta Wyborcza*, Wrocław ed., December 15, 2000.

———. 2000e. Wspólny sukces Dolnoślązaków: Rozmowa z ministrem kultury Kazimierzem Ujazdowskim. *Gazeta Wyborcza*, Wrocław ed., December 16–, 2000, 5.

———. 2002. *Wrocław: Dzieje miasta*. Wrocław: Wyd. Dolnośląskie.

———. 2007a. Architektura z czasów PRL jak cenny zabytek. *Gazeta Wyborcza*, Wrocław ed., December 28, 2007.

———. 2007b. Co z Nowym Targiem: zburzyć czy zostawić? *Gazeta Wyborcza*, Wrocław ed., May 7, 2008.

Madajczyk, Czesław. 1988. *Die Okkupationspolitik Nazideutschlands in Polen 1939–1945*. Cologne: Pahl-Rugenstein.

Madajczyk, Piotr. 1995. Die Aus- und Umsiedlung der Deutschen aus Polen nach 1945: Historisch-politische Probleme und Forschungsperspektiven. *Deutsche Studien* 32 (126–27): 235–41.

———. 1996. *Przyłączenie Śląska Opolskiego do Polski 1945–1948*. Warsaw: Instytut Studiów Politycznych PAN.

———. 1997. Polska Myśl Zachodnia w polityce komunistów polskich. *Przegląd Zachodni* (3): 15–36.

Magierska, Anna. 1978. *Ziemie zachodnie i północne w 1945 roku: Kształtowanie się podstaw polityki integracyjnej państwa polskiego*. Warsaw: Książka i Wiedza.

———. 1986. *Przywrócić Polsce: Przemysł na Ziemiach Odzyskanych 1945–1946*. Warsaw: PWN.

Majewski, Jerzy, and Tomasz Markiewicz. 1998. *Warszawa nie odbudowana*. Warsaw: DiG.

Majewski, Ryszard. 2000. *Wrocław—godzina "0."* Wrocław: Krajowa Agencja Wydawnicza.

Małachowicz, Edmund. 1985. *Stare Miasto we Wrocławiu: Rozwój urbanistyczno-architektoniczny, zniszczenia wojenne, odbudowa*. 2nd ed. Warsaw: PWN.

———. 1992. *Wrocław na wyspach: Rozwój urbanistyczny i architektoniczny*. 2nd rev. and expanded ed. Wrocław: Ossolineum.

———. 1994a. *Wrocławski zamek książęcy i kolegiata św: Krzyża na Ostrowie*. Wrocław: Oficyna Wyd. Politechnika Wrocławskiej.

———. 1994b. *Książęce rezydencje fundacje i mauzolea w lewobrzeżnym Wrocławiu.* Wrocław: Oficyna Wydawnicza Politechniki Wrocławskiej.

———. 2000. Architektura odbudowanych ośrodków miast historycznych. In Tomaszewski and Mockałło 2000, 45–58.

Maleczyńska, Ewa. 1948. Sedes regni principalis—projektowaną siedzibą rządu narodowego. In Sosnowski and Suchocki 1948–50.

———. 1950a. Klejnot w koronie. In Sosnowski and Suchocki 1948–50,20–43.

———. 1950b. Na targowisku dynastów. In Sosnowski and Suchocki 1948–50, 119–41.

———. 1950c. W pruskich szponach. In Sosnowski and Suchocki 1948–50, 161–77.

Maleczyński, Karol. 1946. Herb miasta Wrocława. *Sobótka* 1.

———. 1948. *Dzieje Wrocławia: Do roku 1526.* Wrocław: Instytut Śląski.

———. 1965. Wspomnienia z pierwszego okresu pracy we Wrocławiu. *Sobótka* 20 (1a): 214–21.

———. 1970a. *Proste słowa o Śląsku.* Wrocław: Ossolineum.

———. 1970b. Rzut oka na dzieje Wrocławia. In Maleczyński 1970a, 118–35.

———. 1970c. Więż polityczna Śląska z Polską. In Maleczyński 1970a, 12–73.

Maleczyński, Karol, Marian Morelowski, and Anna Ptaszycka. 1956. *Wrocław: Rozwój urbanistyczny.* Warsaw: Budownictwa i Architektura.

Marek, Michaela. 1997a. Bauen für die Nation: Strategien in der Selbstdarstellung junger/kleiner Völker in der urbanen Architektur zwischen Identität und sozialer Ambition. *Bohemia: Zeitschrift für Geschichte und Kultur der böhmischen Länder* 38:181–88.

———. 1997b. Können alte Mauern "deutsch" sein? Zum Problem "deutscher" Baudenkmäler in Polen zwischen Nostalgie, Politik, Wissenschaft und Denkmalpflege. In Karp 1997, 103–17.

Marek, Ryszard. 1976. *Kościół rzymsko-katolicki wobec Ziem Zachodnich i Północnych.* Warsaw: PWN.

Markgraf, Hermann. 1896. *Die Straßen Breslaus nach ihrer Geschichte und ihren Namen.* Breslau: Morgenstern.

———. 1913. *Geschichte Breslaus in kurzer Übersicht.* 2nd rev. ed. Breslau: Kern.

Markowski, Mieczysław, ed. 1960. *Przewodnik po Wrocławiu.* Wrocław: Ossolineum.

———, ed. 1960–64. *Trudne dni: Wrocław 1945 we wspomnieniach pionierów,* 3 vols. Wrocław: Ossolineum.

Marschall, Werner. 1999. *Das Bistum Breslau: Von 1945 bis zur Jahrtausendwende.* Kehl: Echo-Buchverlag.

Matwijowski, Krystyn. 1971. 25 lat śląskiego kwartalnika historycznego Sobótka, organu wrocławskiego Towarzystwa Miłośników Historii. *Sobótka* 26:403–14.

———. 1986. 100-lecie polskiego Towarzystwa Historycznego i 40-lecie wrocławskiego Towarzystwa Miłośników Historii. *Sobótka* 41:295–301.

Mazower, Mark. 2008. *Hitler's Empire: How the Nazis Ruled the World.* New York: Penguin.

Mazur, Zbigniew. 1997a. Das deutsche Kulturerbe in den West- und Nordgebieten Polens. *Osteuropa* 47:633–49.

———, ed. 1997b. *Wokół niemieckiego dziedzictwa kulturowego na Ziemiach Zachodnich i Północnych: Praca zbiorowa.* Poznań: Instytut Zachodni.

———, ed. 2000. *Wspólne dziedzictwo? Ze studiów nad stosunkiem do spuścizny kulturowej na Ziemiach Zachodnich i Północnych.* Poznań: Instytut Zachodni.

———. 2001. *O adaptacji niemieckiego dziedzictwa kulturowego na Ziemiach Zachodnich i Północnych.* Poznań: Instytut Zachodni.

Mevius, Martin. 2009. Reappraising Communism and Nationalism. *Nationalities Papers* 37 (4):377–400.

Meyer, Henry C. 1955. *Mitteleuropa in German Thought and Action 1815–1945.* The Hague: Martinus Nijhoff.

Michalska, Janina. 1966. Obejmowanie władzy na Dolnym Śląsku przez polską administrację w 1945 r. *Sobótka* 21:620–47.

Michlic, Joanna Beata. 2006. *Poland's Threatening Other: The Image of the Jew from 1880 to the Present.* Lincoln: University of Nebraska Press.

Mierzecka, Janina. 1967. *Wrocław stary i nowy.* Wrocław: Ossolineum.

Mikulski, Tadeusz. 1954. *Spotkania Wrocławskie.* 2nd ed. Kraków: Wyd. Literackie.

———. 1961. *Temat Wrocław: Szkice śląskie.* Wrocław: Ossolineum.

Miodek, Marcin. 2008. *Niemcy. Publicystyzcny obraz w "Pionierze" / "Słowie Polskim" 1945–1989.* Wrocław: Atut.

Misiak, Władysław. 1973. *Działalność kulturalna na Dolnym Śląsku w latach 1945–1949.* Wrocław: Ossolineum.

———, ed. 1990. *Zachodnie i północne ziemie Polski z perspektywy badań socjologicznych, Prace Filozoficzne LXIV. Socjologia 5.* Wrocław: Wyd. Uniwersytetu Wrocławskiego.

———. 1993. *Studia nad procesami integracji i dezintegracji społeczności Śląska.* Wrocław: Wyd. Uniwersytetu Wrocławskiego.

Misiło, Eugeniusz, ed. 1993. *Akcja "Wisła": Dokumenty.* Warsaw: Archiwum Ukraińskie.

Misztal, Bronisław. 1992. Between State and Solidarity: One Movement, Two Interpretations—The Orange Alternative Movement in Poland. *British Journal of Sociology* 43 (1): 55–78.

Misztal, Jan. 1992. Osadnictwo Żydów polskich repatriowanych ze Związku Radzieckiego na Ziemiach Zachodnich i Północnych. *Przegląd Zachodni* 48:161–84.

———. 1998. Przesunięcie Polski na zachód. In Borodziej and Hajnicz 1998, 70–112.

Młotkowski, Eugeniusz. 1995. Młodzież we Wrocławiu. In Suleja 1995, 148–57.

Mochocki, Władysław. 1998. Polnisch-sowjetische Freundschaft—"auf Banditentum und Raub reduziert?": Die Rote Armee in Polens Wiedergewonnenen Gebieten (1945–1948). *Osteuropa* 48 (3): 286–99.

————. 1999. Die Sowjetarmee in Polen: Die wirtschaftliche Ausbeutung der Wiedergewonnenen Gebiete durch die sowjetische Armee 1945 bis 1947. *Osteuropa* 49 (2):195–205.

Morawska, Ewa. 2000. Intended and Unintended Consequences of Forced Migrations: A Neglected Aspect of East Europe's Twentieth Century History. *International Migration Review* 34 (4): 1049–87.

Morelowski, Marian. 1950. Walka z burżuazyjno-spekulanckim oszpeceniem Wrocławia. *Słowo Polskie*, December 24–26, 1950.

Mroczko, Marian. 1986. *Polska myśl zachodnia 1918–1939: Kształtowanie i upowszechnianie*. Poznań: Instytut Zachodni.

Muczkowski, Józef. 1912. Stan dzisiejszej nauki o konserwacji zabytków. In *Pamiętnik pierwszego zjazdu miłośników ojczystych zabytków w Krakowie w dniach 3–4 lipca 1911 roku*. Kraków: Grono Konserwatorów Galicyi Zachodniej.

————. 1914. *Ochrona zabytków*. Kraków: Nakł. autora.

Musekamp, Jan. 2010. *Zwischen Stettin und Szczecin: Metamorphosen einer Stadt von 1945 bis 2005*. Wiesbaden: Harrassowitz.

Musielak, Michał. 1986. *Polski Związek Zachodni, 1944–1950*. Warsaw: PWN.

Naimark, Norman M. 1995. *The Russians in Germany: A History of the Soviet Zone of Occupation, 1945–1949*. Cambridge, MA: Belknap Press of Harvard University Press.

————. 2001a. *Fires of Hatred: Ethnic Cleansing in Twentieth Century Europe*. Cambridge, MA: Harvard University Press.

————. 2001b. The Expulsion of Germans from Poland and Czechoslovakia. In Naimark 2001a, 108–38.

Naimark, Norman M., and Leonid Gibianskii, eds. 1997. *The Establishment of Communist Regimes in Eastern Europe, 1944–1949*. Boulder, CO: Westview Press.

Nawratil, Heinz. 1999. *Schwarzbuch der Vertreibung 1945–1948: Das letzte Kapitel unbewältigter Vergangenheit*. Munich: Universitatis Verlag.

Neß, Dietmar. 1994. Evangelisch-kirchliches Leben in Schlesien nach 1945. *Jahrbuch für Schlesische Kirchengeschichte* 73:51–108.

Neumann, Rudolf J. 1966. *Polens Westarbeit: Die polnischen Kultur- und Bildungseinrichtungen in den deutschen Ostgebieten*. Ed. K. H. Gehrmann. Deutsche Studien. Bremen: Carl Schünemann.

Nitschke, Bernadetta. 1999. *Wysiedlenie ludności niemieckiej z Polski w latach 1945–1949*. Zielona Góra: Wyższa Szkoła Pedagogiczna.

Nowicki, Stanisław. 1993. Amarcord Wrocławski: Rozmowa z Sebastianem Lamarck. *Odra* (5):50–54.

Ociepka, Beata. 1992. *Niemcy na Dolnym Śląsku w latach 1945–1970*. Wrocław: Wyd. Uniwersytetu Wrocławskiego.

————. 1995. Die Vertriebenen in der polnischen Geschichtsschreibung von 1980 bis heute. *Deutsche Studien* 32 (126–27): 163–76.

Ociepka, Beata. 2001. *Deportacje, wysiedlenia, przesiedlenia— powojenne migracje z Polski i do Polski.* Poznań: Instytut Zachodni.

Olechnowicz, Małgorzata. 1997. Architektura na obszarze Wrocławskiego starego miasta po 1945 roku, jej uzależnienie od planów zagospodarowania przestrzennego i przemian budownictwa. Ph.d. dissertation, Politechnika Wrocławska, Wydz. Architektura, Sztuka, Technika.

Olszewicz, Bolesław. 1946. *O naprawę nazewnictwa geograficznego Ziem Odzyskanych.* Toruń: Instytut Bałtycki.

Olszewski, Tomasz. 1972. *Moje miasto.* Wrocław: Ossolineum.

Ordyłowski, Marek. 1991. *Życie codzienne we Wrocławiu 1945–1948.* Wrocław: Ossolineum.

Orłowski, Hubert. 1999. Et in Arcadio ego? Heimatverlust in der deutschen und polnischen Literatur. In *Erlebte Nachbarschaft: Aspekte der deutsch-polnischen Beziehungen im 20. Jahrhundert,* ed. J.-P. Barbian and M. Zybura, 209–25. Wiesbaden: Harrassowitz.

Oryński, Tadeusz. 1995. Fundamenty przemysłu. In Suleja 1995, 89–99.

Orzechowski, Marian. 1960. *Szkice o dziejów Polonii Wrocławskiej.* Wrocław: Ossolineum.

———. 1968. Rola i miejsce Wrocławia w dziejach narodu polskiego w XIX i XX w. In *Studia z dziejów kultury i ideologii ofiarowane Ewie Maleczyńskiej w 50 rocznicę pracy dydaktycznej i naukowej,* ed. R. Heck, W. Korta, and J. Leszczycki, 260–71. Wrocław: Ossolineum.

———. 1971. Zarys najnowszych dziejów Wrocławia. In Siwon 1971, 43–72.

———. 1972. Wrocław in the Recent History of the Polish State and Nation. *Polish Western Affairs* 13 (2): 305–33.

———. 1975. Tradycje piastowskie w polskiej myśli politycznej XX wieku. In *Piastowie w dziejach Polski: Zbiór artykułów z okazji trzechsetnej rocznicy wygaśnięcia dynastii Piastów,* ed. R. Heck, 269–85. Wrocław: Ossolineum.

Osękowski, Czesław. 1994. *Społeczeństwo Polski zachodniej i północnej w latach 1945–1956: Procesy integracji i dezintegracji.* Zielona Góra: Wyższa Szkoła Pedagogiczna im. Tadeusza Kotarbińskiego.

Osmańczyk, Edmund Jan. 1970. *Był rok 1945 . . .* Warsaw: PWN.

Ostrowski, Marek. 1999. Kierunek Berlin. *Polityka,* October 16, 1999, 3–5.

Overmans, Rüdiger. 1994. Personelle Verluste der deutschen Bevölkerung durch Flucht und Vertreibung. *Dzieje najnowsze* 26 (2): 51–65.

Państwowe Przedsięborstwo 'Polska Poczta, Telegraf i Telefon,' ed. 1947. *Spis abonnentów telefonicznych sieci telefonicznych dyrekcji okr: poczt i telegr: Wrocław na rok 1947.* Wrocław.

Parsadanova, V.S. 1990. *Sovetsko-pol'skie otnošenia 1945–1949.* Moscow: Nauka.

Pasierb, Bronisław. 1965. Niemieckie ugrupowanie antyfaszystowskie we Wrocławiu (maj– grudzien 1945 r.). *Sobótka* 20 (2): 205–16.

―――. 1972. *Rok Pierwszy: Z problemów życia politycznego Dolnego Śląska w latach 1945–1946.* Wiedza o Ziemi Naszej 20. Wrocław: Ossolineum.

―――. 1980. Funkcje problemu niemieckiego w pierwszym okresie Polski Ludowej. In *Stosunki polsko-niemieckie: Integracja i rozwój ziem zachodnich i północnych*, ed. B. Jałowiecki and J. Przewłocki, 109–23. Katowice: Śląski Instytut Naukowy.

Paul, Barbara Dotts, ed. 1994. *The Polish-German Borderlands: An Annotated Bibliography.* Westport, CT: Greenwood.

Peikert, Paul. 1996. *"Festung Breslau" in den Berichten eines Pfarrers 22: Januar bis 6: Mai 1945*, ed. K. Jonca and A. Konieczny. Wrocław: Ossolineum.

Persson, Hans-Åke. 1997. *Rhetorik und Realpolitik: Großbritannien, die Oder-Neiße-Grenze und die Vertreibung der Deutschen nach dem Zweiten Weltkrieg.* Potsdam: Verlag für Berlin-Brandenburg.

Piaskowski, Stanisław. 1960. Te lata najmilej wspominam. In Markowski 1960–64, 1:380–87.

―――. 1964. Początki władzy ludowej na Dolnym Śląsku. *Z pola walki* 7 (2): 224–32.

Piechocka, Pelagia. 1970. Wszystkie dzieci są moje . . . In Jałowiecki 1970, 203–19.

Piskorski, Jan M. 1996. "Deutsche Ostforschung" und "polnische Westforschung." *Berliner Jahrbuch für osteuropäische Geschichte* 1:378–89.

Piskorski, Jan M., Jörg Hackmann, and Marek Jaworski, eds. 2002. *"Deutsche Ostforschung" und "polnische Westforschung" im Spannungsfeld von Wissenschaft und Politik. Disziplinen im Vergleich.* Osnabrück.

Pletzing, Christian. 2006. Die Politisierung der Toponymie. Ortsnamenänderungen in den preußischen Ostprovinzen während des 19. Jahrhunderts. In Loew, Pletzing, and Serrier 2006, 263–77.

Polak, Cezary. 2000. Czas zakończyć wojnę. *Gazeta Dolnośląska*, October 26, 2000, 12.

Przyłęcki, Mirosław. 1995. Ochrona i konserwacja zabytków na Dolnym Śląsku w latach 1945–1970. In Kowalczyk 1995, 73–100.

Ptaszycka, Anna. 1956a. Zagospodarowanie Wrocławia w latach 1945–1955. In Maleczyński, Morelowski, and Ptaszycka 1956, 187–234.

―――. 1956b. U progu planu pięcioletniego. In Maleczyński, Morelowski, and Ptaszycka 1956, 234–322.

Pussak, Eugeniusz. 1995. Żelazne szlaki. In Suleja 1995, 62–63.

Radziwiłłowicz, Dariusz. 2003. *Tradycja grunwaldzka w świadomości politycznej społeczeństwa polskiego w latach, 1910–1945.* Olsztyn: Wyd. Uniwersytetu Warmińsko-Mazurskiego.

Rahden, Till van. 2008. *Jews and Other Germans: Civil Society, Religious Diversity, and Urban Politics in Breslau, 1860–1925.* Trans. M. Brainard. Madison: University of Wisconsin Press.

Rajca, Czesław. 2000a. Z Burgthalu do Świętej Katarzyna. In Bömelburg, Stößinger, and Traba 2000, 112–24.

———. 2000b. Von Burgthal nach Kattern-Święta Katarzyna. In Bömelburg, Stößinger, and Traba 2000, 127–42.

Raszewski, Zbigniew. 1952. Dzieje polskiego teatru w Wrocławiu do końca XIX wieku. *Zeszyty Wrocławskie 6.*

Rewski, Zbigniew. 1999 [1949]. O odprusaczaniu architektury ziem zachodnich. In *Pomniki niemieckiej przeszłości: Dziedzictwo kultury niemieckiej na Ziemiach Zachodnich i Północnych Polski,* ed. M. Zybura, 56–62. Warszawa: Centrum Stosunków Miedzynarodowych.

Rhode, Gotthold, ed. 1955. *Die Ostgebiete des Deutschen Reiches: Ein Taschenbuch.* Würzburg: Holzner.

Rieber, Alfred J., ed. 2000. *Forced Migration in Central and Eastern Europe, 1939–1950.* London: Frank Class.

Riemenschneider, Rainer, ed. 1980. *Die Rolle Schlesiens und Pommerns in der Geschichte der deutsch-polnischen Beziehungen im Mittelalter: 12. deutsch-polnische Schulbuchkonferenz der Historiker vom 5. bis 19. Juni 1979 in Allenstein/Olsztyn.* Braunschweig: Georg-Eckert-Institut.

Roche, Reinhard. 1977. "Transfer" statt "Vertreibung"? Semantisch-pragmatische Überlegungen zur Lösung einer aktuellen, komplexen Sprachsituation. *Muttersprache* 87:314–20.

Rogall, Joachim. 1996. Krieg, Vertreibung und Neuanfang: Die Entwicklung Schlesiens und das Schicksal seiner Bewohner von 1939–1995. In Bahlcke 1996a, 155–223.

Rospond, Stanisław. 1948a. *Polskość Śląska w świetle języka.* Warsaw.

———. 1948b. *Zabytki języka polskiego na Śląsku.* Katowice: Instytut Śląski.

———. 1959. *Dzieje polszczyzny Śląskiej.* Katowice: "Śląsk".

Roszkowska, Wanda, ed. 1970. *Wrocław: Przewodnik po dawnym i współczesnym mieście.* 2nd ed. Wrocław: "Sport i Turystyka."

Rottermund, Andrzej, ed. 2000. *Jan Zachwatowicz w stulecie urodzin.* Warsaw: Zamek Królewski w Warszawie.

Rozpędowski, Jerzy, ed. 1995. *Architektura Wrocławia: Urbanistyka do 1945 roku.* Wrocław: Oficyna Wydawnictwa Politechniki Wrocławskiej.

———, ed. 1997. *Architektura Wrocławia: Świątynia.* Wrocław: Oficyna Wydawnictwa Politechniki Wrocławskiej.

———, ed. 1998. *Architektura Wrocławia: Gmach.* Wrocław: Oficyna Wydawnictwa Politechniki Wrocławskiej.

Ruchniewicz, Krzysztof. 1999. Problematyka wysiedlenia Niemców w Polsce i w Niemczech w przeszłości i teraźności. In *Studia z historii najnowszej,* ed. K. Ruchniewicz, B. Szaynok, and J. Tyszkiewicz, 134–53. Wrocław: Gajt.

———. 2001. Warum Wrocław nicht Breslau ist: Überlegungen zur Nachkriegsgeschichte der niederschlesischen Hauptstadt. In *Zwischen Heimat und Zuhause:*

Deutsche Flüchtlinge und Vertriebene in (West-)Deutschland nach 1945–2000, ed. by R. Schulze, 256–75. Osnabrück: Secolo.

———. 2005. Der Entstehungsprozess der Gemeinsamen deutsch-polnischen Schulbuchkommission 1937/38–1972. *Archiv für Sozialgeschichte* 45:237–52.

Ruchniewicz, Małgorzata. 1998. Die Deutschen und die polnischen Übersiedler aus den Ostgebieten nach 1945: "Auch sie haben geweint." In Bachmann and Kranz 1998, 290–96.

Ruge, Elisabeth, and Peter Ruge. 1985. *Nicht nur die Steine sprechen deutsch . . . Polens deutsche Ostgebiete.* Munich: Langen Müller.

Rusiński, W. 1947. Ucieczka Niemców ze wschodnich prowincji Rzeszy przed 1939 r. *Przegląd Zachodni* 3 (4): 265–77.

Rutkiewicz, Ignacy. 1967. Podwójny jubileusz Ossolineum. *Kalendarz Wrocławski:* 198–209.

———. 1973. *Wrocław wczoraj i dziś. Informator Turystyczny: Olgierd Czerner.* Warsaw: Interpress.

Rutkowska, Maria. 1997. Kilka dokumentów lat czterdziestych. In Mazur 1997b, 257–300.

Rydel, Jan. 1997. Sacrum Poloniae Millenium: Bemerkungen zur Anatomie eines Konfliktes im "realen Sozialismus." In Brix and Stekl 1997, 231–50.

Rymaszewski, Bohdan. 1978. Kierunek naszej ochrony zabytków. *Ochrona Zabytków* 31 (4): 215–20.

———. 1992. *Klucze ochrony zabytków w Polsce.* Warsaw: Ośrodek Dokumentacji Zabytków.

———. 1994. Motywacje konserwatorskie Jana Zachwatowicza. *Kwartalnik Architektury i Urbanistyki* 38:367–74.

———. 1995. Zespoły staromiejskie na ziemiach zachodnich i północnych Polski po 1945 roku. In Kowalczyk 1995, 35–52.

———. 2000. Motywacje polityczne i narodowe związane z zabytkami. In Tomaszewski and Mockałło 2000, 81–95.

Sabisch, Alfred. 1965. Die Wahl bzw. die Bestellung des Kapitularvikars in Breslau am 26: Januar 1951. *Archiv für schlesische Kirchengeschichte* 23:190–220.

Sakson, Andrzej, ed. 1996. *Pomorze—trudna ojczyzna: Kształtowanie się nowej tożsamości 1945–1995.* Poznań: Instytut Zachodni.

Samerski, Stefan. 2002. Wunderbare Strafe: Üble Nachrede für den guten Hirten: Bischof Carl Maria Splett. *Frankfurter Allgemeine Zeitung*, April 11, 2002, 44.

Sapper, Manfred, and Volker Weichsel. 2008. *Geschichtspolitik und Gegenerinnerung: Krieg, Gewalt und Trauma im Osten Europas, Osteuropa.* Berlin: BWV.

Saski, Kazimierz. 1956. Usuwanie śladów zniszczeń wojennych. *Ochrona Zabytków* 9 (1–2): 117–19.

Satjukow, Silke. 2008. *Besatzer: "Die Russen" in Deutschland 1945–1994.* Göttingen: Vandenhoeck & Ruprecht.

Schechtman, Joseph B. 1962. *Postwar Population Transfers in Europe: 1945–1955*. Philadelphia: University of Pennsylvania Press.

Scheuermann, Gerhard, ed. 1994. *Das Breslau-Lexikon*, 2 vols. Dülmen: Laumann.

Schieder, Theodor, ed. 1954–61. *Dokumentation der Vertreibung der Deutschen aus Ost-Mitteleuropa*, 8 vols. Bonn: Bundesministerium für Vertriebene.

Schlögel, Karl. 1991. *Das Wunder von Nishnij oder die Rückkehr der Städte: Berichte und Essays*. Frankfurt a.M.: Eichborn.

———. 1995. *Go East oder die zweite Entdeckung des Ostens*. Berlin: Siedler.

———. 2001a. *Die Promenade von Jalta und andere Städtebilder*. Munich: Hanser.

———. 2001b. Sprachefinden für zweierlei Untergang. In *Die Promenade von Jalta und andere Städtebilder*, 286–96. Munich: Hanser.

———. 2001c. Breslau oder vom Zauber der Bürgerlichkeit. In *Die Promenade von Jalta und andere Städtebilder*, 240–51. Munich: Hanser

———. 2005. *Moscow*. Trans. H. Atkins. London: Reaktion.

Scholz, Franz. 1988. *Staatsraison und Evangelium: Kardinal Hlond und die Tragödie der ostdeutschen Diözesen: Tatsachen—Hintergründe—Anfragen*. 2nd rev. ed. Frankfurt a.M.: Josef Knecht.

Schöttler, Peter, ed. 1997. *Geschichtschreibung als Legitimationswissenschaft 1918–1945*. Frankfurt a.M.: Suhrkamp.

Schultz, Helga, ed. 1998. *Bevölkerungstransfer und Systemwandel: Ostmitteleuropäische Grenzen nach dem Zweiten Weltkrieg*. Berlin: Berlin Verlag.

———, ed. 2001a. *Preußens Ostens—Polens Westen: Das Zerbrechen einer Nachbarschaft*. Berlin: Berlin Verlag.

———. 2001b. Einleitung: Brüche und Spiegelung. In Schultz 2001a, 9–15.

Sekretariat der Deutschen Bischofskonferenz, ed. 1992. *Veritati i caritati: Dokumentensammlung anläßlich der feierlichen Überführung Kardinal Adolf Bertrams von Jauernig nach Breslau, 7: November 1991*. Bonn: Sekretariat der Deutschen Bischofskonferenz.

Seraphim, Peter-Heinz. 1953. *Ostdeutschland und das heutige Polen: Mit 87 Kartenblättern von Gerhard Fischer*. Braunschweig: Westermann.

Serczyk, Jerzy. 1996. Confabulationes et/sive transformationes: Über Mythen und Legenden in der politischen Geschichtsschreibung. In *Mythos und Nation*, ed. H. Berding. Frankfurt a.M.: Suhrkamp.

Serrier, Thomas. 2005. *Eine Grenzregion zwischen Deutschen und Polen: Provinz Posen, Ostmark, Wielkopolska, 1848–1914*. Marburg: Herder-Institut.

———, ed. 2006. *Die Aneignung fremder Vergangenheiten in Nordosteuropa am Beispiel plurikultureller Städte*. Nordost-Archiv. Zeitschrift für Regionalgeschichte 15. Lüneburg: Nordost-Institut.

Siebel-Achenbach, Sebastian. 1994. *Lower Silesia from Nazi Germany to Communist Poland*. New York: St. Martin's Press.

Siwon, Bolesław. 1967. Dziesięć lat działalności towarzystwa Miłosników Wrocławia. *Kalendarz Wrocławski*:107–9.

————, ed. 1971. *Wrocław: Rozwój miasta w Polsce Ludowej*. Biblioteka Wiedzy o Polsce Ludowej. Warsaw: PWN.

Skrowaczewska, Zofia. 1995. Ze Lwowa przez Kraków nad Odrę. In Suleja 1995, 131–33.

Ślązak, Kazimierz. 1957. Szkic historyczny miasta. In Król 1957b, 13–23.

Smolak, Marzena. 1995. *Zerstörung einer Stadt: Breslau 1945*. Wrocław: VIA.

Smolka, Georg. 1965. Die deutschen Ostgebiete in der polnischen Historiographie der Zwischenkriegszeit. In *Speculum historiale: Geschichte im Spiegel von Geschichtsschreibung und Geschichtsdeutung: Festschrift für J. Spörl*, ed. C. Bauer et al., 703–19. Freiburg, Munich: Alber.

Snyder, Timothy. 2003. *The Reconstruction of Nations: Poland, Ukraine, Lithuania, Belarus, 1569–1999*. New Haven: Yale University Press.

————. 2010. *Bloodlands: Europe Between Hitler and Stalin*. New York: Basic Books.

Sokołowski, Antoni. 1960. Od skrzynek zielonych do czerwonych. In Markowski 1960–64, 1:212–24.

Sosnowski, Kiryl. 1948. Wracamy . . . In Sosnowski and Suchocki 1948–50.

Sosnowski, Kiryl, and Mieczysław Suchocki, eds. 1948–50. *Dolny Śląsk*. Poznań: Instytut Zachodni.

Speitkamp, Winfried, ed. 1997. *Denkmalsturz: Zur Konfliktgeschichte politischer Symbolik*. Göttingen: Vandenhoeck & Ruprecht.

Stankiewicz, Ludomir. 1970. Narasta nowa, pozytywna tradycja . . . In Jałowiecki 1970, 149–60.

Stein, Rudolf. 1936. *Das alte Breslau: Eine gotische Großstadt*. Breslau: Flemming.

Steinhaus, Hugo. 1992. *Wspomnienia i zapiski*. London: Aneks.

Stern, Fritz. 2006. *Five Germanys I Have Known*. New York: Farrar, Straus and Giroux.

Stokłosa, Katarzyna. 2003. *Nachbarschaft an der Grenze*. Berlin: Arno Spitz.

Störtkuhl, Beate. 1995. Die Breslauer Moderne, 1900–1933. In *'Wach auf, mein Herz, und denke': Zur Geschichte der Beziehung zwischen Schlesien und Berlin-Brandenburg von 1740 bis Heute*, ed. Gesellschaft für interregionalen Kulturaustausch e.V., 144–54. Dülmen: Laumann.

————. 2005. Architekturgeschichte. In *Historische Schlesienforschung: Methoden, Themen, Perspektiven zwischen traditioneller Landesgeschichtsschreibung und moderner Kulturwissenschaft*, ed. J. Bahlcke, 681–718. Cologne: Böhlau.

Strauchold, Grzegorz. 1995. *Polska ludność rodzima ziem zachodnich i północnych: Opinie nie tylko publiczne, 1944–1948*. Olsztyn: Ośrodek Badań Naukowych im. Wojciecha Kętrzyńskiego.

————. 2000. Próba stworzenia jednolitego społeczeństwa ziem zachodnich i północnych w powojennej dekadzie. *Borussia* 22:73–80.

————. 2001. *Autochtone polscy, niemieccy, czy . . . Od nacjonalizmu do komunizmu (1945–1949)*. Toruń: Adam Marzalek.

————. 2003a. *Wrocław okazjonalna stolica Polski: Wokół powojennych obchodów rocznic historycznych*. Wrocław: Wyd. Uniwersytetu Wrocławskiego.

Strauchold, Grzegorz. 2003b. *Myśl Zachodnia i jej realizacja w Polsce w latach, 1945–1957*. Toruń: Wydawnictwo Adam Marzałek.

Strelczyk, Jerzy. 1996. Die Piasten: Tradition und Mythos in Polen. In *Mythen in Geschichte und Geschichtsschreibung polnischer und deutscher Sicht*, ed. A. v. Saldern, 113–31. Münster: LIT.

Suleja, Teresa. 1995. *Uniwersytet Wrocławski w okresie centralizmu stalinowskiego, 1950–55*. Wrocław: Wyd. Uniwerstytetu Wrocławskiego.

Suleja, Włodzimierz, ed. 1995. *Wspomnienia wrocławskich pionierów*. Wrocław: Poligraf.

———. 2001. *Historia Wrocławia*, vol. 3 (W Polsce Ludowej, PRL i III Rzeczypospolitej). Wrocław: Wyd. Dolnośląskie.

Świechowski, Zygmunt, ed. 1978. *Wrocław: Jego dzieje i kultura*. Warsaw: Arkady.

Sworakowski, Witold. 1944. An Error Regarding Eastern Galicia in Curzon's Note to the Soviet Government. *Journal of Central European Affairs* 4 (1): 1–26.

Szarota, Tomasz. 1969. *Osadnictwo miejskie na Dolnym Śląsku w 1945–1948*. Wrocław: Ossolineum, PAN.

Szaynok, Bożena. 2000. *Ludność żydowska na Dolnym Śląsku, 1945–1950*. Wrocław: Wyd. Uniwersytetu Wrocławskiego.

———. 2005. The Role of Antisemitism in Postwar Polish-Jewish Relations. In *Antisemitism and Its Opponents in Modern Poland*, ed. R. Blobaum, 265–83. Ithaca, NY: Cornell University Press.

Szmigulan, Mikołaj. 1970. Swoją historię Wrocławiania zaczynali od nowa . . . . In Jałowiecki 1970, 185–92.

Szuszkiewicz, Zygmunt. 1967–68. Struktura organizacyjna Instytutu Wschodniej Europy i jej niejawna działalność. *Rocznik Wrocławski*: 100–114.

———. 1971. Działalność popularysatorska i propagandowa Instytutu Europy Wschodniej we Wrocławiu w latach 1918–1944. *Przegląd Zachodni* 27 (3): 131–54.

———. 1974. Osteuropa-Institut w latach 1933–1939: Niektóry aspekty działalności. *Przegląd Zachodni* 30 (3): 107–30.

Szymczak, Mieczysław, ed. 1999. *Słownik języka polskiego*, 3 vols. Warsaw: PWN.

Talaga, Jan. 1970. Poznałem grupę Wrocławian wiernych Polsce. In Jałowiecki 1970, 235–48.

Tausk, Walter. 2000. *Breslauer Tagebuch 1933–1940*, ed. R. Kincel. Berlin: Aufbau.

Tebarth, Hans Jakob. 1991. *Technischer Fortschritt und sozialer Wandel in deutschen Ostprovinzen: Ostpreußen, Westpreußen und Schlesien im Zeitalter der Industrialisierung*. Berlin: Kulturstiftung der deutschen Vertriebenen.

Terlecki, Kazimierz. 1970. Czekano na wyjazdu grupowe . . . In Jałowiecki 1970, 161–73.

Terry, Sarah M. 1983. *Poland's Place in Europe: General Sikorski and the Origin of the Oder-Neisse Line, 1939–1943*. Princeton, NJ: Princeton University Press.

Ther, Philipp. 1998. *Deutsche und polnische Vertriebene: Gesellschaft und Vertriebenenpolitik in der SBZ/DDR und in Polen 1945–1956*. Göttingen: Vandenhoeck & Ruprecht.

Ther, Philipp, and Ana Siljak, eds. 2001. *Redrawing Nations: Ethnic Cleansing in East-Central Europe, 1944–1948*. Lanham, MD: Rowmann & Littlefield Publishers.

Thum, Gregor. 1998. Breslau und die "Stunde Null": Kontinuität und Diskontinuität einer mitteleuropäischen Stadtgeschichte. In *Dzieje Śląska w XX w: w świetle badań młodych historyków z Polski, Czech i Niemiec*, ed. K. Ruchniewicz, 200–25. Wrocław: Gajt.

———. 2001. Bollwerk Breslau: Vom "Deutschen Osten" zu Polens "Wiedergewonnenen Gebieten." In Schultz 2001a, 227–52.

———. 2003a. Rekonstruktion und Utopie: Breslaus Wiederaufbau als polnische Stadt. In *DDR-Städtebau im internationalen Vergleich*, ed. C. Bernhardt and T. Wolfes, 81–104. Erkner: IRS.

———. 2003b. Cleansed Memory: New Polish Wroclaw and the Expulsion of the Germans after the Second World War. In Várdy and Tooley 2003, 333–57.

———. 2005. Wroclaw and the Myth of the Multicultural Border City. *European Review* 13 (2): 227–35.

———. 2009. Wroclaw's Search for a New Historical Narrative: From Polonocentrism to Postmodernism. In *Cities after the Fall of Communism: Reshaping Cultural Landscapes And European Identity*, ed. J. Czaplicka, N. Gelazis, and B. Ruble, 75–101. Washington, DC: Woodrow Wilson Center Press; Baltimore: Johns Hopkins University Press.

———. 2010. "Preußen—das sind wir!" Zur Entdeckung der preußischen Kulturlandschaft in Deutschland und Polen. *Zeitschrift für Ostmitteleuropaforschung* 59.

Thum, Gregor, and José M. Faraldo. 2000. Las Regiones Occidentales Polacas: Experimento social y arquitectura de las identidades. *Cuadernos de Historia Contemporánea* 22:325–46.

Tomala, Mieczysław. 2000. *Deutschland—von Polen gesehen: Zu den deutsch-polnischen Beziehungen 1945–1990*. Marburg: Schüren.

Tomaszewski, Andrzej, ed. 1994. *Ochrona i konserwacja dóbr kultury w Polsce, 1944–1989: Uwarunkowania polityczne i społeczne*. Warsaw: Stow. Konserwatorów Zabytków.

———. 2005. Legende und Wirklichkeit: Der Wiederaufbau Warschaus. In Bingen and Hinz 2005, 165–72.

Tomaszewski, Andrzej, and Ewa Mockałło, eds. 2000. *Badania i ochrona zabytków w Polsce w XX wieku: Materiały konferencji naukowej zorganizowanej staraniem Wydziału Architektury Politechniki Warszawskiej, Generalnego Konserwatora Zabytków i towarzystwa Opieki nad Zabytkami w stulecie urodzin Profesora Jana Zachwatowicza w dniu 5 marca 2000 roku*. Warsaw: Oficyna Wyd. Towarzystwa Opieki nad Zabytkami.

Tomczak, Maria. 1993. Polska myśl zachodnia. In Wolff-Powęska 1993, 16–193.

Torzecki, Ryszard. 1993. *Polacy i Ukraińcy: Sprawa ukraińska w czasie II wojny światowej na terenie II Rzeczpospolitej.* Warsaw: PWN.

Towarzystwo Miłośników Wrocławia, ed. 1960. *Przewodnik po Wrocławiu.* Wrocław: Ossolineum.

Trierenberg, Heinrich, ed. 1980. *Heimat Breslau: Bild einer deutschen Stadt im Spiegel der Geschichte: Bildband mit 216 Fotos.* Mannheim: Adam Kraft.

———, ed. 1991. *Breslau in alten und neuen Reisebeschreibungen.* Düsseldorf: Droste.

Troebst, Stefan, ed. 2006. *Vertreibungsdiskurs und europäische Erinnerungskultur: Deutsch- polnische Initiativen zur Institutionalisierung: Eine Dokumentation.* Osnabrück: fibre.

Turnau, Irena. 1960. *Studia nad strukturą ludnościową polskiego Wrocławia.* Poznań: Instytut Zachodni.

Turoń, Bronisław. 1969. Prof. dr. Karol Maleczyński. *Kalendarz Wrocławski*:191–93.

Tyszkiewicz, Jakub. 1995. Koncepcje odbudowy Wrocławia ze zniszczeń wojennych w świetle "Naprzodu Dolnośląskiego" w latach 1945–1947. In *Wrocławskie studia z historii najnowszej,* ed. W. Wrzesiński. Wrocław: Wyd. Uniwersytetu Wrocławskiego.

———. 1997. *Sto wielkich dni Wrocławia: Wystawa Ziem Odzyskanych we Wrocławiu a propaganda polityczna ziem zachodnich i północnych w latach, 1945–1948.* Wrocław: Arboretum.

———. 1999. Jak rozbierano Wrocław. *Odra* (9): 17–21.

———. 2000. *Od upadku Festung Breslau do stalinowskiego Wrocławia: Kalendarium 1945–1950.* Warsaw: PWN.

———. 2001. *W stalinowskim Wrocławiu: Kalendarium, 1951–1955.* Warsaw: PWN.

Tyszkowska, Krystyna. 1986. *Panorama Racławicka: 90 lat niezwykłych dziejów.* Wrocław: Krajowa Agencja Wydawnicza.

Urban, Thomas. 2003. Ilja Ehrenburg als Kriegspropagandist. In *Traum und Trauma: Russen und Deutsche im 20. Jahrhundert,* ed. D. Herrmann and A. Volpert, 241–73. Munich: Wilhelm Fink Verlag.

Urban, Wincenty. 1965. Archidiecezja wrocławska w latach, 1945–1965. *Nasza Prezsłość: Studia z dziejów Kościoła i kultury katolickiej w Polsce* 22:11–68.

Urbanek, Mariusz. 1998. *Powódź, Wrocław, lipiec 1997.* Wrocław: Wyd. Dolnośląskie.

U.S. Department of State, ed. 1955–63. *Foreign Relations of the United States: Diplomatic Papers.* Washington, DC: GPO.

Uschakow, Alexander. 1992. Die Oder-Neisse-Linie/Grenze und der Hitler-Stalin-Pakt. In *Die historische Wirkung der östlichen Regionen des Reiches,* ed. H. Rothe, 299–327. Vienna: Böhlau.

Várdy, Steven B., and Hunt Tooley, eds. 2003. *Ethnic Cleansing in 20th-Century Europe.* Boulder: Social Science Monographs.

Wagińska-Marzec, Maria. 1997. Ustalanie nazw miejscowości na Ziemiach Zachodnich i Północnych. In Mazur 1997b, 367–416.

Walter, Ewald. 1965. Zur sakralen Ikonographie des Breslauer Rathauses und zur Umwandlung der beiden kleineren gotischen Ostgiebel dieses Rathauses in Renaissancegiebel. *Archiv für schlesische Kirchengeschichte* 23:49–84.

Wassermann, Charles. 1957. *Unter polnischer Verwaltung: Tagebuch 1957.* Hamburg:Blüchert.

Waszkiewicz, Ewa. 1999. *Kongregacja Wyznania Mojżeszowego na Dolnym Śląsku na tle polityki wyznaniowej Polskiej Rzeczpospolitej Ludowej, 1945–1989.* Wrocław: Wyd. Uniwersytetu Wrocławskiego.

Waszkiewicz, Jan, ed. 1994. *Raport o stanie miasta Wrocław, 1990–94.* Wrocław: Samorząd miasta Wrocławia.

Weczerka, Hugo. 1995. Breslaus Zentralität im ostmitteleuropäischen Raum um 1500. In *Metropolen im Wandel: Zentralität in Ostmitteleuropa an der Wende vom Mittelalter zur Neuzeit,* ed. E. Engel, K. Lamprecht and H. Nogossek, 245–62. Berlin: Akademie Verlag.

Weitz, Eric D. 2008. From the Vienna to the Paris System: International Politics and the Entangled Histories of Human Rights, Forced Deportations, and Civilizing Missions. *American Historical Review* 113 (5): 1313–43.

Werner, Michael, and Bénédicte Zimmerman. 2006. Beyond Comparison: Histoire croisée and the Challenge of Reflexivity. *History and Theory* 45:30–50.

Winnicki, Bronisław. 1960. Polpress—Naprzód Dolnośląski. In Markowski 1960–64, 1:235–56.

Wloch-Ortwein, Beata. 2000. *Die "Solidarnosc" in Breslau: Die Entstehung einer oppositionellen gesellschaftlichen Bewegung in der Systemkrise 1980/1981 und ihre Bedeutung für den Systemwechsel in Polen 1989.* Berlin: Logos.

Wojciechowski, Zygmunt. 1955 [1933]. Rozwój terytorialny Prus w stosunku do ziem macierzystych Polski. In *Studia historyczne,* ed. Zygmunt Wojciechowski, 17–51. Warsaw: PAX.

———. 1945. *Polska— Niemcy: Dziesięć wieków zmagania.* Poznań: Instytut Zachodni.

Wójcik, Jan. 1995. Pierwsze tramwaje były białe . . . In Suleja 1995, 44–60.

Wolff-Powęska, Anna, ed. 1993. *Polacy wobec Niemców: Z dziejów kultury politycznej Polski, 1945–1989.* Poznań: Instytut Zachodni.

———. 1997. Geschichte im Dienste der Politik: Erfahrungen bei der Bewältigung der Vergangenheit im 20. Jahrhundert. *Osteuropa* 47:215–29.

Wollstein, Günter. 1977. *Das "Grossdeutschland" der Paulskirche: Nationale Ziele in der bürgerlichen Revolution von 1848/1849.* Düsseldorf: Droste.

Wóycicki, Kazimierz. 1995. Der Balken und das Auge. *Deutsche Studien* 32:288–98.

Woźniczka, Zygmunt. 1999. Die Deportationen von Polen in die UdSSR in den Jahren 1939–1945. In *Lager, Zwangsarbeit, Vertreibung und Deportation: Dimensionen der Massenverbrechen in der Sowjetunion und in Deutschland, 1933–1945,* ed. D. Dahlmann and G. Hirschfeld, 535–52. Essen: Klartext.

Wrzesiński, Wojciech. 1988. Kresy czy pogranicze? Problem ziem zachodnich i północnych w polskiej myśli politycznej XIX i XX w. In *Między Polską etniczną a historyczną*, 119–65. Wrocław: Wyd. Uniwersytetu Wrocławskiego.

———, ed. 1990–91. *W stronę Odry i Bałtyku: Wybór źródeł, 1795–1950*, 4 vols. Wrocław, Warsaw: Wyd. Uniwersytetu Wrocławskiego.

———. 1995a. Gdańsk 1939–Wrocław 1945: Dwa symbole. *Odra* (9): 16–23.

Wrzesiński, Wojciech. 1995b. Uniwersytet we Wrocławiu: Tradycje Lwowa i Breslau. *Odra* (11): 21–24.

———. 1999. Metropolia czy prowincja? Wrocław po drugiej wojnie światowej. *Sobótka* 3:435–46.

Wyszyński, Stefan Cardinal. 1971. Godzina apelów narodu na ostrowiu wrocławskim podczas uroczystości XXV-lecia organizacji kościelnej na Ziemiach Odzyskanych. In Krucina 1971, 13–19.

Żaba, Zdzisław. 1994 [1957]. Wrocław nasz. *Karta* 14:69–78.

Zabłocka-Kos, Agnieszka. 2000. Von der Zerstörung zu Rekonstruktion und moderner Bebauung: Altstadtsanierung in Polen nach 1945. *Jahrbuch Stadterneuerung*:161–74.

———. 2003. Breslau und Posen im 19. Jahrhundert: zwei Regierungsstädte, zwei Welten. In *Preussen, Deutschland, Europa, 1701-2001*, ed. J. Luh, V. Czech, and B. Becker, 313–37. Groningen: INOS.

———. 2006. *Zrozumieć miasto: Centrum Wrocławia na drodze ku nowoczesnemu city, 1807–1858*. Wrocław: Via Nova.

Zaborowski, Henryk. 1970. Zamiast Białogard—napisano Wrocław. In Jałowiecki 1970, 175–83.

Zachwatowicz, Jan. 1946. Program i zasady konserwacji zabytków. *Biuletyn Historii Sztuki i Kultury* (1–2): 48–52.

Żak, Andrzej. 1960. Pierwsze dni Partii. In Markowski 1960–64.

Zakrzewski, Bogdan. 1989. *Przechadzki po dzwiewiętnastowiecznym Wrocławiu*. Wrocław: Wyd. Dolnośląskie.

Zaremba, Marcin. 2001. *Komunizm, legitymacja, nacjonalizm: Nacjonalistyczna legitymacja władzy komunistycznej w Polsce*. Warsaw: TRIO.

Zawada, Andrzej. 1996. *Bresław: Eseje o miejscach*. Wrocław: Okis.

———. 1996. Bresław. In *Bresław*, 41–63. Wrocław: Okis.

Zduniak, M. 1964. Udział Polaków w życiu muzycznym Wrocławia w czasach nowożytnych. *Sobótka* 3–4.

Zeidler, Manfred. 1996. *Kriegsende im Osten: Die Rote Armee und die Besetzung Deutschlands östlich von Oder und Neiße 1944/45*. Munich: Oldenbourg.

Zernack, Klaus. 1976. Das Jahrtausend deutsch-polnischer Beziehungsgeschichte als geschichtswissenschaftliches Problemfeld und Forschungsaufgabe. In *Grundfragen der geschichtlichen Beziehungen zwischen Deutschen, Polaben und Polen: Referate und Diskussionsbeiträge aus zwei wissenschaftlichen Tagungen*, ed. W. Fritz and K. Zernack, 3–46. Berlin: Colloquium-Verlag.

————. 1990. Deutschlands Ostgrenze. In *Deutschlands Grenzen*, ed. A. Demandt, 135–59. Munich: C. H. Beck.

————. 1991a. Deutschlands Ostgrenze. In *Deutschlands Grenzen*, ed. Alexander Demandt, 140–65. Munich: C. H. Beck.

————. 1991b. *Preußen, Deutschland, Polen: Aufsätze zur Geschichte der deutsch-polnischen Beziehungen.* Berlin: Duncker & Humblot.

————. 1994. "Ostkolonisation" in universalhistorischer Perspektive. In *Universalgeschichte und Nationalgeschichten: Ernst Schulin zum 65. Geburtstag*, ed. G. Hübinger et al. Freiburg i.Br.: Rombach.

Zernack, Klaus, and Karin Friedrich. 2004. Developments in Polish Scholarship on German History, 1945–2000. *German History* 22 (3): 309–22.

Ziątkowski, Leszek. 2000. *Dzieje Żydów we Wrocławiu.* Wrocław: Wyd. Dolnośląskie.

Zin, Wiktor, ed. 1966. *Zabytki urbanistyki i architektury w Polsce—odbudowa i konserwacja.* Warsaw: Arkady.

Zlat, Mieczysław. 1957. Sprawa opieki nad zabytkami na Śląsku. *Przegląd Zachodni* 13 (2): 201–203.

Żurek, Robert. 2005. *Zwischen Nationalismus und Versöhnung: Die Kirchen und die deutsch-polnischen Beziehungen, 1945–1956.* Cologne: Böhlau.

Zybura, Marek. 1998. Breslau und Wrocław. In Kobylińska and Lawaty 1998, 369–80.

————. 1999a. *Pomniki niemieckiej przeszłości: Dziedzictwo kultury niemieckiej na Ziemiach Zachodnich i Północnych Polski.* Warsaw: Centrum Stosunków Międzynarodowych.

————. 1999b. Von der "deutschen Gefahr" zum "deutschen Tor nach Europa": Polnische Deutschland- und Deutschenbilder im Wandel. In *Erlebte Nachbarschaft: Aspekte der deutsch-polnischen Beziehungen im 20. Jahrhundert*, ed. J.-P. Barbian and M. Zybura, 21–34. Wiesbaden: Harrassowitz.

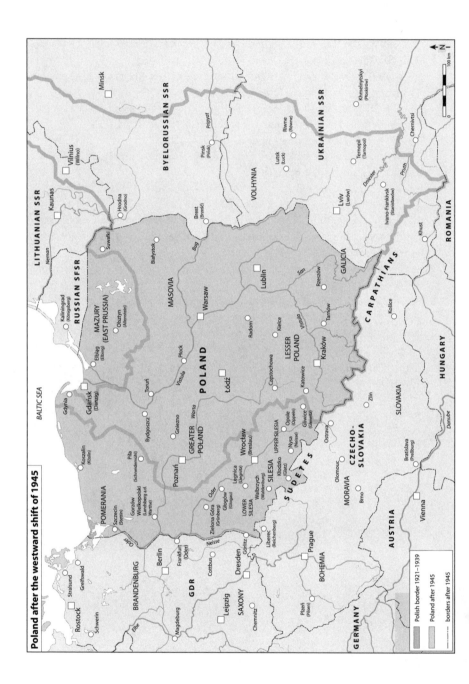

Poland after the westward shift of 1945

Polish border 1921–1939

Poland after 1945

borders after 1945

Simplified map of Wrocław today

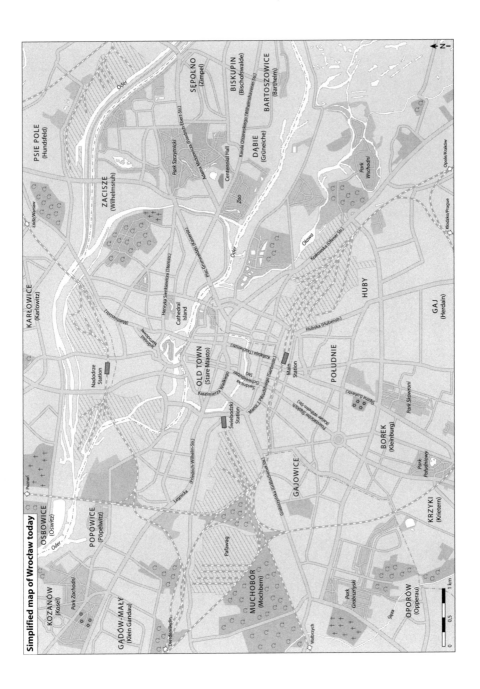

495

INDEX

Page numbers in italics refer to illustrations.